bf

Titles available from boyd & fraser

BASIC Programming
Applesoft BASIC Fundamentals and Style
BASIC Fundamentals and Style
Complete BASIC for the Short Course
Structured BASIC Fundamentals and Style for the IBM® PC and Compatibles
Structured Microsoft BASIC: Essentials for Business
Structuring Programs in Microsoft BASIC

COBOL Programming
Advanced Structured COBOL: Batch and Interactive
COBOL: Structured Programming Techniques for Solving Problems
Comprehensive Structured COBOL
Fundamentals of Structured COBOL

Database
A Guide to SQL
Database Systems: Management and Design

Computer Information Systems
Applications Software Programming with Fourth-Generation Languages
Business Data Communications and Networks
Expert Systems for Business: Concepts and Applications
Fundamentals of Systems Analysis with Application Design
Investment Management: Decision Support and Expert Systems
Learning Computer Programming: Structured Logic Algorithms, and Flowcharting
Office Automation: An Information Systems Approach

Microcomputer Applications
An Introduction to Desktop Publishing
dBASE III PLUS® Programming
DOS: Complete and Simplified
Introduction to Computers and Microcomputer Applications
Macintosh Productivity Tools
Mastering and Using Lotus 1-2-3®, Release 3
Mastering and Using Lotus 1-2-3®, Version 2.2
Mastering and Using WordPerfect® 5.0 and 5.1
Mastering Lotus 1-2-3®
Microcomputer Applications: A Practical Approach
Microcomputer Applications: Using Small Systems Software, Second Edition
Microcomputer Database Management Using dBASE III PLUS®
Microcomputer Database Management Using dBASE IV®
Microcomputer Database Management Using R:BASE System V®
Microcomputer Productivity Tools
Microcomputer Systems Management and Applications
PC-DOS®/MS-DOS® Simplified, Second Edition
Using Enable®: An Introduction to Integrated Software

Shelly and Cashman Titles
Computer Concepts with Microcomputer Applications (Lotus 1-2-3® and VP-Planner Plus® versions)
Computer Concepts
Essential Computer Concepts
Learning to Use WordPerfect®, Lotus 1-2-3®, and dBASE III PLUS®
Learning to Use WordPerfect®, VP-Planner Plus®, and dBASE III PLUS®
Learning to Use WordPerfect®
Learning to Use Lotus 1-2-3®
Learning to Use VP-Planner Plus®
Learning to Use dBASE III PLUS®
Computer Fundamentals with Application Software
Learning to Use SuperCalc®3, dBASE III®, and WordStar® 3.3: An Introduction
Learning to Use SuperCalc®3: An Introduction
Learning to Use dBASE III®: An Introduction
Learning to Use WordStar® 3.3: An Introduction
BASIC Programming for the IBM Personal Computer
Structured COBOL: Pseudocode Edition
Structured COBOL: Flowchart Edition
RPG II, RPG III, & RPG/400

STRUCTURED SYSTEMS DEVELOPMENT

Analysis, Design, Implementation
2d Edition

MICHAEL J. POWERS

Partner
Ernst and Young
Cleveland, Ohio

PAUL H. CHENEY

Professor
Information Systems Department
Texas Tech University
Lubbock, Texas

GALEN CROW

Assistant Professor
Applied Computer Science Department
Illinois State University
Normal, Illinois

boyd & fraser publishing company
20 park plaza
boston ma 02116

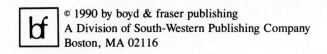
COVER PHOTO: Digital Art/West Light

Library of Congress Cataloging-in-Publication Data

Powers, Michael J.
   Structured systems development : analysis, design, implementation
/ Michael J. Powers, Paul H. Cheney, Galen Crow.
      p.   cm.
   ISBN 0–87835–550–2
   1. System design.   2. Electronic data processing—Structured
techniques.   I. Cheney, Paul Henry.   II. Crow, Galen B.
III. Title.
QA76.9.S88P68   1990
004.2′1—dc20

1 2 3 4 5 6 7 8 D 7 6 5 4 3 2 1 0

Printed in the United States of America

iv

Contents

v

Preface

This text was written to provide a vehicle for students and instructors to work together to create a structured, yet stimulating, environment in which to learn the fundamental concepts of systems development. The stage for systems development is established at the start. This provides the context in which to understand the skills developed later. It provides the basis for a unifying theme. The design of the text is flexible. Depending on the time available and the background and interests of the students, several different course approaches are possible. With each approach a course can be created that captures the enthusiasm and excitement felt by real-life systems developers.

AUDIENCE

This text is designed to support an introductory course in systems development or systems analysis and design. Such a course is normally taught at the sophomore or junior level and follows a sequence of instruction in structured programming. The text also serves as an excellent reference for a subsequent project or major case course.

The text is a replacement for the prior two volume series, *Computer Information Systems Development: Analysis and Design* and *Computer Information Systems Development: Design and Implementation*. It represents a substantial revision and updating of that work. However, the readability, skill orientation, and case illustrations of the earlier books have been retained.

CONTENT FEATURES

Systems analysis and design is a challenge to teach because it is not meant to be taught in a classroom environment. It is practiced in the real worlds of business and government and should be taught in those environments. Many instructors give their students practical experience on a project team actually designing a small real world system. It may be an inventory control system for a hardware store or a circulation system for a library. We believe this work to be essential to the student in an information systems curriculum.

Before this can take place effectively the students must have some knowledge concerning the systems development life cycle and the activities and tasks involved in designing and implementing a computer information system. This book in our opinion provides this basic information. The content of this text includes all of the relevant topics necessary for the students to proceed on their own or as a team to that real world first experience of developing a small system. In an effort to accomplish this we have done the following.

- We have included entire chapters on the following topics:
  - managing the development process
  - data analysis techniques
  - process analysis techniques
  - automating the development process
  - information gathering
  - communication techniques and strategies
  - human/machine interface design
  - software design strategies
  - control and reliability design
  - testing strategies and techniques
  - rapid development techniques
- The book covers all of the tools and techniques used in the development of computer information systems including an introduction to both process analysis and data analysis techniques.
- Structured systems analysis and design techniques are employed throughout the text.
- The text is skills oriented. We emphasize the role of the systems designer and concentrate on the skills that are necessary in each phase of the systems development life cycle.
- The text is designed so that BriefCASE, a student CASE tool, which includes a data dictionary, word processor, report and form design program, screen design program, and a graphics design program may be integrated with the text.
- Part 7 of the text illustrates each of the tools and techniques by using a comprehensive case.
- The text is not only appropriate for classroom use it is an excellent reference source for outside class assignments and that real world systems project.
- Highlighted throughout the text are short discussions that offer insights and examples of systems analysis and design tools and techniques, relevant comments by systems professionals, and discussions of actual systems. This in our opinion makes some of the material more interesting and emphasizes the fact that information systems professionals actually use and view these tools as important in conducting their jobs.

■ The text is written in a conversational manner that undergraduate students can easily comprehend

It is our belief that the content of this text and its writing style will convince you to use it in your next systems analysis and design course.

THE IMPORTANCE OF A PROJECT OR CASE

A key to creating excitement in a systems development course is the opportunity to practice systems development skills. This works best in a project or case study environment. Every effort should be made to provide this opportunity as part of a course or sequence of courses in system development.

USE OF THIS TEXT

The text is divided into seven parts. Part 1, Information Systems: Basic Development Concepts, should be completed first. It establishes the framework and terminology for the remainder of the text. It describes a life cycle for systems development that can be used as a unifying theme for the skills covered in Parts 2 through 6.

It starts with a general discussion of some general systems theory, the various types of computer information systems and the role of the systems analyst in developing information systems. Also covered in this section are some of the techniques that can be used to manage the development process such as PERT and the Gantt chart.

Part 2 discusses the modeling techniques of systems analysis. Both process and data modeling techniques are covered. Part 3 discusses the information gathering and communication skills that the systems analyst must master to be effective. Part 4 discusses the transition from the analysis phase of systems development to the design phase. Topics include data base and file design, physical system architecture, and physical system design. Part 5 discusses human-machine interface design and software design. Part 6 covers control and reliability design and software testing strategies and techniques.

Part 7, The Systems Development Life Cycle: Applying the Tools and Techniques, covers the development process in greater depth, using a substantial case study to illustrate both the flow of a system development project and the techniques presented throughout the text.

Part 7 can be used in two ways. First, it can follow Parts 2 through 6 as an example of the flow and integration of the system development skills on a real project or as a pattern for students to follow on a "live" project or case project. Second, it can be integrated with Parts 2 through 6 as an illustration and reinforcement for the skills as they are covered. Variations are possible depending on the length of the course.

"TOOL KIT"

A "tool kit" software package, *BriefCASE: The Collegiate Systems Development Tool,* is available as an option with this text. *BriefCASE* includes a manual, workbook, and software intended to provide students with Computer Aided Software Engineering (CASE) capabilities using typical university resources. The software contains mostly "Upper CASE" tools and contains the following components:

1. A relatively full featured, but simple *Word Processor* for handling all text related documentation.
2. *Data Dictionary* template files, which are used by the word processor for data and process specification documentation.
3. A *Report and Form Design* program for prototyping input and output hardcopy documents.
4. A *Screen Design* program for prototyping screen displays and creating a "slide show" of screen sequences.
5. A *Graphics Design* program for creating data flow diagrams, structure charts, and virtually any other system representation.

BriefCASE may be used by students to fulfill many potential assignments in this text. Students may be given standalone assignments dealing with an individual component of systems analysis and design or they may develop a continuing "live" or "case" project. The accompanying workbook contains a variety of short assignment which are designed to expose students to actual systems development activities and teach them how to use the *BriefCASE* software. A continuing "case" project system is used as an example throughout the workbook to highlight various systems topics and could be used as a case study throughout the course.

The software is designed to operate on all IBM PC or compatible microcomputers. It requires only a minimum of 256K RAM and a standard graphics card. It does not require a mouse, a hard drive, or any other special hardware or software. The entire *BriefCASE* system resides on one diskette, although a separate work diskette should be used to store student project work.

INSTRUCTOR'S MANUAL

An instructor's manual provides additional support for the text. It includes instructional strategies; answers to all questions, assignments, and cases; a set of transparency masters; and a chapter-by-chapter test bank. Approximately twenty multiple choice questions are included for each chapter in the instructor's manual. In addition, the MicroSWAT II Test Generation System is available at no cost to schools that adopt the text. It allows the user to create and edit questions, to select questions from the test bank to create test files, and to print tests. We have found it to be a very useful product in preparing our course material.

ACKNOWLEDGMENTS

We are most grateful for the constructive criticism and suggestions given by the reviewers of the second edition. Their comments helped to make a better, more accurate text and we thank them for their time and attention to detail. The reviewers for the second edition were

R. John Freese
University of Northern Colorado

Robert I. Mann
Virginia Commonwealth University

Lorrie Steerey
Eastern Montana College

Laurette Poulos Simmons
Loyola College (Maryland)

We also very much appreciate the patience, understanding, and loyalty of the many users of the first edition. Your continued support has been inspiring.

ORDER INFORMATION AND FACULTY SUPPORT INFORMATION

For the quickest service, refer to the map below for the South-Western Regional Office serving your area.

1 ORDER INFORMATION
5101 Madison Road
Cincinnati, OH 45227-1490
General Telephone–513-527-6945
Telephone: 1-800-543-8440
FAX: 513-527-6979
Telex: 214371

FACULTY SUPPORT INFORMATION
5101 Madison Road
Cincinnati, OH 45227-1490
General Telephone–513-527-1490
Telephone: 1-800-543-8444

Alabama	Massachusetts	Pennsylvania
Connecticut	Michigan (Lower)**	Rhode Island
Delaware	Mississippi	South Carolina
Florida	New Hampshire	Tennessee
Georgia	New Jersey	Vermont
Indiana*	New York	Virginia
Kentucky	North Carolina	West Virginia
Maine	Ohio	District of Columbia
Maryland		

*Except for ZIP Code Areas 463, 464. These areas contact Region 2 Office.
**Except for the Upper Peninsula. This area contacts Region 2 Office.

2 ORDER INFORMATION and FACULTY SUPPORT INFORMATION
355 Conde Street
West Chicago, IL 60185
General Telephone–312-231-6000
Telephone: 1-800-543-7972

Illinois	Minnesota	North Dakota
Indiana*	Missouri	South Dakota
Iowa	Nebraska	Wisconsin
Michigan (Upper)**		

*Only for ZIP Code Areas 463, 464. Other areas contact Region 1 office.
**Only for Upper Peninsula. Other areas contact Region 1 office.

3 ORDER INFORMATION
13800 Senlac Drive
Suite 100
Dallas, TX 75234
General Telephone–214-241-8541
Telephone: 1-800-543-7972

FACULTY SUPPORT INFORMATION
5101 Madison Road
Cincinnati, OH 45227-1490
General Telephone–513-527-6950
Telephone: 1-800-543-8444

Arkansas	Louisiana	Texas
Colorado	New Mexico	Wyoming
Kansas	Oklahoma	

4 ORDER INFORMATION and FACULTY SUPPORT INFORMATION
6185 Industrial Way
Livermore, CA 94550
General Telephone–415-449-2280
Telephone: 1-800-543-7972

Alaska	Idaho	Oregon
Arizona	Montana	Utah
California	Nevada	Washington
Hawaii		

Information Systems: Basic Development Concepts

PURPOSE

The three chapters in this initial section of the text are designed to build an understanding that encompasses: (1) the need for a formal approach to systems development, (2) the need for a method of developing computer information systems (CIS), and (3) the need for managing this development in an efficient and effective manner.

Chapter 1 establishes some basic definitions of what systems are and how they are developed. This chapter also describes the environment in which systems development takes place.

Chapter 2 introduces a process for systems development, known as the systems development life cycle. A systems development life cycle provides a tool for managing complex processes by breaking them down into a series of phases and activities with well-defined products or objectives. The five-phase life cycle used in this text is diagrammed in Figure I-1. Also discussed in Chapter 2 are the relationships among the phases of a systems development life cycle and the flow of information within a systems development project. These aspects are represented in the data flow diagram of Figure I-2.

Chapter 3 discusses the need for effectively and efficiently managing the systems development process. Building an information system is much like constructing a highway, airplane, or nuclear power plant. It involves the management of people and other resources in order to accomplish a goal. Project management is a process for defining the goals of a project and describing what is necessary to achieve those goals. Several techniques of project management such as the use of GANTT Charts, project milestones, and PERT are discussed in this chapter.

ACHIEVEMENTS

On completing your work in this part of the book, you should have the background necessary to proceed with the specific study of systems development activities and to build your skills through a series of later chapters designed to help build systems analysis skills. You will also have an overview of the systems development process and how it is managed.

Figure I.1. The systems development life cycle—a control-oriented view.

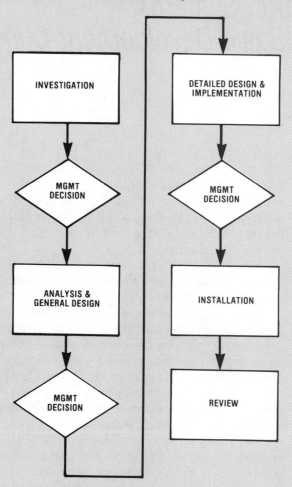

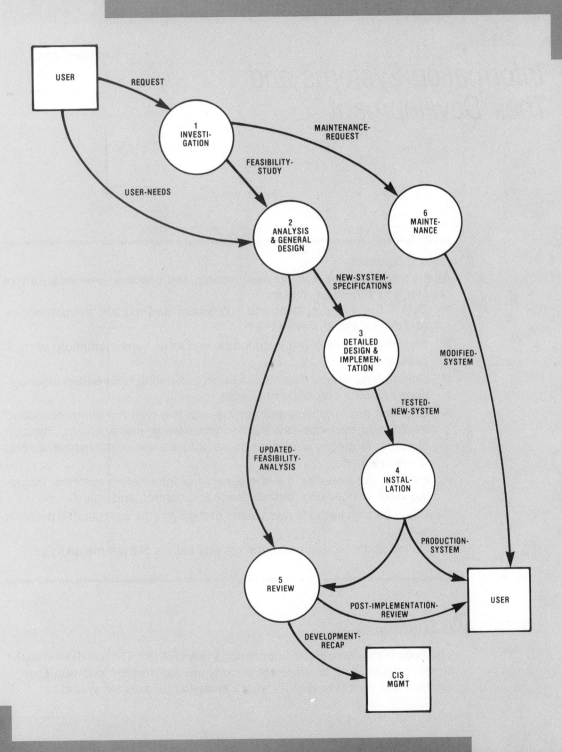

Figure I.2. The systems development life cycle—a process view.

1

Information Systems and Their Development

Learning Objectives
After completing the reading assignments and practice exercises for this chapter, you should be able to:
- Define the terms *system* and *subsystem* and explain the similarities and differences between them.
- Describe the role of organization structures as implementations of business systems.
- Describe the role of information as an integrating force within organizations and as a corporate resource.
- Describe the functions and purposes of five types of computer-based information systems—transaction processing, management, decision support, strategic, and expert—as well as the relationships among these systems.
- Identify and describe the components of information systems, including input, processing, output, feedback, control, and adjustment.
- Describe the methods and values of the systems approach to problem solving.
- Define and describe the purposes and values of systems analysis.

SYSTEMS AND SUBSYSTEMS

This book is about computer information systems (CIS). The text deals with the analysis, design, and development of computer information systems. Thus, a good place to start is to identify what a **computer information system** is.

Definition of a System

As a general definition, a **system** is any set of interrelated, interacting components that function together as an entity to achieve specific results. The components, or elements, that make up a system are closely interdependent; actions or conditions that affect any one element will also affect all others within the system. An effective system will be **synergistic**. This means, simply, that when a system is functioning as it should, it produces results with a value greater than the total value produced by its separate, individual parts.

Identification of Systems

The identification of systems depends upon the viewpoint and the experience of the observer. To illustrate, the earth and the sun can be looked upon as separate entities. However, a person with a systems perspective notes that the earth is dependent on the sun for heat, light, and other characteristics without which the earth could not exist in its present form. Therefore, the earth and the sun can be regarded as elements of a single system. The sun, in turn, has a similar relationship to Mercury, Venus, and other planets. Thus, the earth can be seen as one component, or element, of a solar system. The solar system can be identified, or classified, as a natural physical system. Humanity, a species that is part of the synergism of that system, is in turn part of what can be identified as the biological system of the earth. The biological system, in proper perspective, is related to and dependent upon an ecological system. The point here is that systems are built upon relationships and upon the recognition that complex activities are dependent upon one another. The same is true for other types of systems. For example, in addition to the natural systems like those just cited, there are also many human-made systems. These can be thought of as either abstract or physical. Examples of abstract systems include languages, systems of numbers (mathematics), systems of thought (philosophy, religion), and systems of logic (laws). Physical systems can take many forms. There are mechanical systems, such as automobiles, trains, and aircraft. There are social systems organized around geography or heritage (cities, states, nations). And there are organizational systems, which are commonly broken down according to public and private sectors.

Businesses are organizational systems. A business, as a system, is composed of people, facilities, equipment, materials, and methods of work that function together to provide goods or services.

Definitions of Subsystems

Individual systems can have different degrees, or levels, of complexity. As systems become increasingly complex, a series of smaller systems can be identified within larger ones. These smaller systems are known as **subsystems** of the systems that contain them. A subsystem, in turn, has its own interacting elements that function together to produce identifiable end products. However, these end products are related to and become part of the result produced by the larger system of which the subsystem is a part. Thus, both subsystems and their products become part of more complex, total systems.

Examples of subsystems in a business include:

- **Production Systems:** Collectively, the people, materials, equipment, and procedures that design and produce goods and services.
- **Logistics Systems:** Collectively, the people, equipment, materials, and procedures that together procure the needed materials and/or services used in conducting business activities such as manufacturing, marketing, transportation, or human resources.
- **Information Systems:** Collectively, the hardware, software, people, procedures, and data that transform raw data into useful information.

Relationships of Systems and Subsystems

Subsystems, in effect, are identified by the relationships that exist within larger systems. For example, a family is a social system on its own. But a family is also a subsystem of its local neighborhood. The neighborhood, in turn, is a subsystem of a larger entity called a community. The community is a subsystem of a city, and so on.

The same is true of business organizations. Virtually any large business organization is a complex system made up of a number of subsystems. Subsystems are defined by the way a business organizes itself. Typical designations include production, marketing, accounting, and distribution. Each of the subsystems possesses individual purposes and produces measurable results. The achievements of the subsystems, however, serve primarily to contribute to the goals and to the products or services of the organization as a whole.

Again, recognition of systems and subsystems is a matter of perspective. For example, a large business organization may be regarded as a subsystem of an overall system of free enterprise. The free enterprise system ultimately can be regarded as a subsystem of an economic system that includes elements of governmental and social subsystems as well.

In many instances the outputs from one system are the inputs into another system. This situation is depicted in Figure 1.1 where the outputs from a fabricating area are input into a finishing area and the output from this area is input into a shipping area. In cases where the outputs of one system are the inputs into another system, problems often arise if the subsystems operations are not coordinated. In Figure 1.1, if the fabricating department produces more output than the finishing department can handle, a bottleneck may occur, building up an unwanted inventory of partially completed products. If the fabricating unit isn't producing enough output to keep the finishing department busy, there will be idle resources in the finishing area.

To handle this problem, management has three main options: (1) maintain extra inventories; (2) utilize standards to control outputs; or (3) maintain excess or slack resources for the peak periods of production. The choice of an alternative depends on the individual situation. If the cost of maintaining an inventory is high and the cost of idle resources in the dependent system is low, utilizing

Figure 1.1. Manufacturing system and its subsystems.

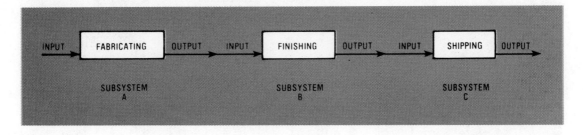

slack resources would be a viable option. In other words, excess capacity would be purposefully maintained in that area to handle increases in production. A good management information system would allow managers to use standards to control outputs rather than excess inventories or slack resources. If management has the necessary information, coordinating the various subsystems to achieve overall system efficiency should be a relatively easy task.

BUSINESS SYSTEMS AND INFORMATION SYSTEMS

Businesses are groups of systems and subsystems that interrelate to accomplish a set of goals and objectives. The subsystems are often functionally designated: marketing, production, inventory, finance, personnel, and logistics, among others. The identification of any system — including a business — lies in the perception of the people who look at it. This perception of a business as a system is implemented through the organization of that business. Thus, the **organizational structure** of a business represents a formal recognition by its management of the subsystems from which it is composed. An **organizational chart** is, in effect, a graphic representation identifying the subsystems of a business and portraying their relationships.

The partial organization chart in Figure 1.2 represents typical departmental designations, lines of authority and responsibility, and reporting for a large organization. From this chart it is obvious that people are departmentalized according to certain criteria. These criteria include such considerations as function performed, the process involved, relationships with customers, geographic territories, products produced, and services rendered. The weighting of such criteria in the building of individual business structures will vary widely both with the type and nature of the organization involved and with the background of its top managers.

In the process of identifying subsystems within an organization and representing them graphically, managers seek to have:

- people grouped according to working relationships and functional subsystems within which they perform their jobs. The subsystems identified are

Figure 1.2. Organization structure chart showing the breakdown of business system into subsystems.

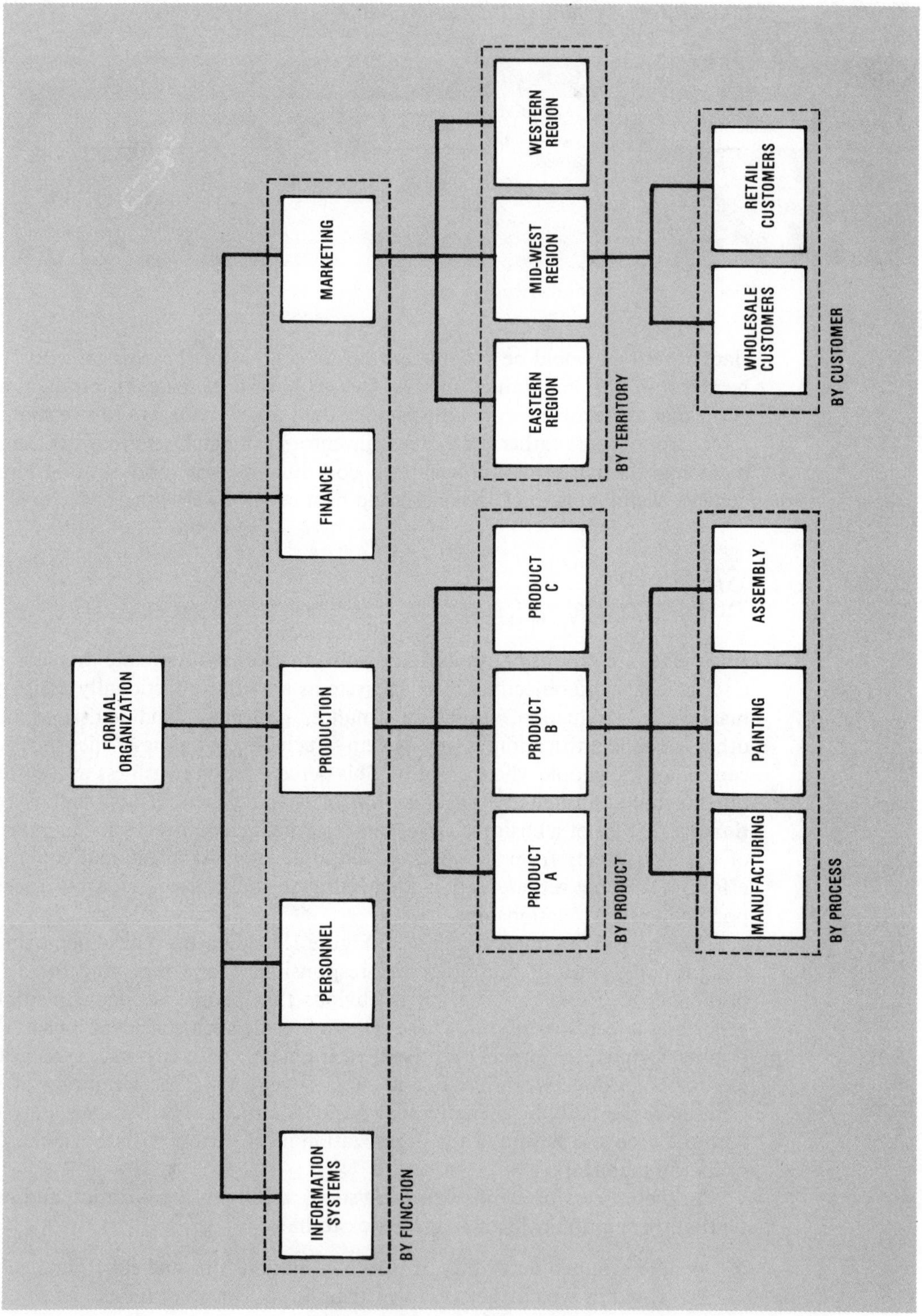

typically called the departments of the organization. Departmentalization of an organization, then, is management's way of establishing subsystems that build the overall system's identity.

- authority and responsibility relationships. In the process of identifying departments or other organizational groupings, management sets up relationships in terms of authority and responsibility not only for performing the tasks within the subsystems but also for delivering the end results of those subsystems.

- authority and responsibility identifications that serve as the basis for establishing work responsibilities and work flows throughout an organization. These work flows and their task definitions serve to determine the methods and procedures through which people, equipment, materials, and other resources are brought together and applied to produce the end-product goods or services of an organization.

Information as an Integrating Force

Any complex system, and any organizational structure that implements a complex system such as a business entity, is made up of interrelated parts that function together. The interrelationships among the parts of the system lie in the sharing of the resources used. One of the resources that must be shared by viable systems is information.

Information is an essential resource for any functional system that delivers planned results. Therefore, any functional system, within any organization, should encompass methods and procedures for developing and delivering information. This is known as an information system.

An **information system** is formed through the coordinated functioning of people, equipment, procedures, data, and other resources to provide uniform, reliable, accurate information. In effect, an organizational system is tied together by its informational elements. Putting it another way, information can be seen as the bonding agent that permits systems to function cohesively. Because information is a universal tool for the operation of any organization, information systems are, typically, not confined within individual departments. Rather, information systems tend to involve persons in multiple parts of an organization, cutting across departmental boundaries.

An inventory control system, for example, receives input in the form of orders from *marketing*, supplies information to *production* about items being depleted so that replacements can be manufactured, and advises *finance* when and to what degree orders are shipped so that the customer can be promptly and accurately billed.

Types of Information Systems

For business organizations, the need for information exists at a number of levels. Informational support is needed in controlling the day-to-day operations of the business, in ongoing management, and also in strategic planning for what the business will look like in the future. Each of these levels of information need has, over the years, evolved its own types of information delivery tools. Five types of closely interrelated information processing systems are implemented to meet specific management needs. These include:

- Operational controls over the day-to-day activities of business organizations are established by **transaction processing systems (TPS)**.
- Managerial control over the ongoing functions of a business is maintained with the aid of **management information systems (MIS)**.
- Strategic planning is supported by the results of **decision support systems (DSS)** and **strategic information systems (SIS)**.
- Specific tasks that require specialized knowledge and expertise are supported by **expert systems (ES)**.

Transaction Processing Systems. A transaction is an event that affects the organization. Typical transactions include paying an employee, updating the status of inventory items, and processing orders. Transactions are usually triggered by an action or a document such as receiving an order from a customer or receiving a bill from a supplier. Once the transaction has been initiated, it begins a transaction-processing cycle that often includes the following steps:

1. transaction recording—the transaction is put into a format so that it can be processed;
2. transaction processing—this includes classifying (i.e., grouping data according to some characteristics such as occupation or age), sorting (i.e., alphabetical or numeric), calculating or selecting (i.e., separating items with a certain set of characteristics from a group of items);
3. transaction updating—permanent history files are often used to support the processing of transactions such as maintaining data on the year-to-date federal income taxes, state income taxes, and social security taxes an employee has paid;
4. transaction outputting—in a typical transaction, one input generates one output (one employee time card generates one paycheck); and
5. transaction reporting—the transaction data are often summarized into transaction listings such as the payroll register report.

Transaction processing is a major part of an MIS, and in fact much of the data eventually used to support decision making are a by-product of this process.

Management Information Systems. The outputs of transaction processing systems, though they stand on their own, are also essential components of an MIS. A management information system, basically, provides procedures for reviewing the results of day-to-day operations and calling attention to situations that require special attention or decisions. In any operating organization, perhaps 90 percent or more of all daily operations function routinely. As long as things are normal, no management actions are necessary.

For example, it is common to establish stock quantity limits for merchandise held in inventory. As long as the inventory quantity for each item remains between established upper and lower limits, a normal condition exists.

Suppose that a large organization has 1,000,000 separate items in inventory and that, at any given moment, some 970,000 are within normal supply limits. It would be extremely time-consuming for the buyers within that organization to review information about the large majority of items for which the status was normal. Instead, it is far more efficient for the buyers to focus their attention on the 3 percent of the items that are not within normal boundaries.

A management information system applies the power of computers to review information records on the basis of their data content. Managers establish the standards, or boundaries, that separate normal conditions from those requiring attention. The system then calls management attention to these **exception** conditions that require human intervention and decision making.

In addition to its capabilities for exception reporting, an MIS provides a resource for responding to management questions about the status of a business. MIS files can be used, for example, to develop responses to information requests about individual segments of a business, such as materials costs, sales of product lines, or other management information requirements. The ability of an MIS to summarize information so that it helps managers derive the meaning they need quickly and accurately adds to the value of this type of system.

Thus, transaction processing systems provide detailed information, whereas management information systems provide selective information through further processing of detailed information. The MIS involves additional processing to add value to the information for the purposes of organizational management.

Decision Support Systems. Transaction processing and management information systems both focus upon the functions of an operational unit as it actually exists. Both of these are important dimensions of management. A third important dimension of management lies in looking ahead to set long-term goals and to envision and plan for the structure and functions of the business entity in the future. This planning dimension of management uses information generated by decision support systems.

Decision support systems utilize the results of TPS and MIS operations. In addition, further data content may be brought in from external sources. For example, a DSS could incorporate, in addition to data on the operations of the sponsoring company, information files on the state of the economy, on market share, on government policies, and on the company's own future capabilities. With such data components, a DSS can, in effect, look ahead and project operating results based upon given conditions supplied by planners. Thus, a DSS becomes a tool for producing a **model** or **simulation** of the future state of the business based upon sets of assumptions or conditions supplied by managers.

Strategic Information Systems. Strategic or competitive information systems are designed and built specifically to give a firm a competitive advantage within an industry. Strategic information systems typically involve transaction processing. Two examples of this type of system are Federal Express's package tracking system and American Hospital Supply's order entry system, which allows customers to enter orders themselves through an on-line terminal.

Michael Porter in *Competitive Advantage* (Free Press, 1985) has identified five ways in which an organization can obtain a competitive advantage:

1. building barriers against potential competitors;
2. enhancing customer loyalty;
3. favorably altering the balance of power with suppliers;
4. changing the basis of competition within an industry; and
5. developing entirely new products.

Information systems have been successfully employed to implement each of these potential approaches for competitive advantage. Any information system can be duplicated, of course; but a firm that develops a successful strategic information system can obtain a tremendous advantage over its competition for several years at the very least, and enhancements may allow it to maintain that competitive edge indefinitely. American Airlines was the first to create a comprehensive on-line reservation system. American followed this innovation with the first frequent-flyer program. Today American's "SABRE" reservations system remains dominant in the airline industry. There are now many others, but American's system remains just as good as or better than these. Most travel agents, who have an established relationship with American, see no need to change.

Expert Systems. An expert system is a computer application that guides the performance of ill-structured tasks that require specialized experience and knowledge. Using an expert system, a nonexpert can achieve performance comparable to that of an expert. Expert systems are often viewed as specialized decision support systems, but in fact they are much more. They contain a "knowledge base" that includes both the data and the decision rules that represent the expertise. Expert systems have been developed to assist in medical diagnosis, oil exploration, and computer configurations. In many instances, expert systems are embedded in a transaction processing system.

VIEWPOINT
by William G. McGowan

THE INFORMATION EDGE

From the day a primitive man struck a stick against a resonant log and warned his tribe of an approaching enemy, advance information has been giving certain groups a competitive edge. Today information technology is leading a revolution in how American businesses compete domestically and internationally. Computers married to telecommunications now bind buyers and sellers together electronically, control inventories and cash flows, and detect new marketing trends. William G. McGowan, chairman of MCI Communications Corporation, is an entrepreneurial pioneer of the information age. MCI recently joined with American Express and others to support a five-year research program by MIT's Sloan School of Management: "Management in the 1990s," which will study the growing impact of the new information technology on business and individuals. The American Express Cardmember newsletter talked with Mr. McGowan about this new force in the marketplace.

IS CORPORATE MANAGEMENT VIEWING INFORMATION IN A DIFFERENT WAY TODAY?

"Yes. Historically, management has looked at information technology—data processing and telecommunications—as just another major expense that had to be monitored and controlled by budget. But now many executives have realized that they can use information not only to manage their company but also as a profit-making tool. As soon as that corporate mind shift takes place, everyone from CEOs to sales people in the field start paying attention. Suddenly the information budgets no longer have to prove themselves in advance to get approval, any more than companies' advertising budgets would have to."

HOW ARE COMPANIES USING THIS "INFORMATION EDGE"?

"There are many examples. American Hospital Supply Corporation, part of Baxter Travenol Laboratories, Inc., established terminals on the premises of their client hospitals, allowing customers to send in orders directly.

"The McKesson Drug Co. also uses information technology to speed orders to customers, and the expertise they've developed in this new discipline has created an entirely new business for them—processing medicaid bills for their customers.

"The Tandy Corporation uses computers and telecommunications to track daily sales at their stores. This helps in their planning and gives them instant information on customer response to their various marketing efforts.

"This kind of finger on the pulse of information can provide a real competitive edge. Companies have less capital tied up in inventory. They improve their marketing efficiency. They've learned that information is money."

HOW IS THIS NEW INFORMATION AGE AFFECTING AMERICAN EXPRESS CARDMEMBERS WHO ARE IN BUSINESS?

"They can use the computer and telecommunications to get just the information they want, when they need it.

"A business person, scientist, or student could tap into any one of the 2,570 public databases in the U.S., and research—for example—everything that's been

been published in the last three months about a competitor's new product, interest-rate trends in home mortgages, California wines, the current price of every stock in a portfolio, or any of thousands of other subjects.

"Many cardmembers then will be able to use information technology to streamline their businesses. Now information can flow directly to the president from sales personnel in the field who are equipped with portable computers. Fewer levels of management will be needed. And the 'paperless office' is already a reality. You can store memos and reports electronically, and access them whenever you need to refer to them. Files stuffed with papers are becoming time-consuming, expensive redundancies.

"All of this is becoming possible because computer power is at least 8,000 times less expensive than it was 30 years ago. If, for example, the automobile industry progressed at that rate, a Cadillac car would cost $2.50 today and get a million miles to the gallon. It would, however, also be very small."

HOW CAN INDIVIDUALS GIVE THEMSELVES AN "INFORMATION EDGE"?

"Fortunately, more people are already starting their first job with information skills. Many colleges now require that students walk in the door with a computer.

"Those already in business should learn to be computer literate. Alternately, those whose primary skills are in data processing should learn more about other facets of business. Individuals who possess both business and information technology skills could become invaluable to their companies and highly prized candidates in the job market.

"Some business executives still shy away from working computer terminals, perhaps because they've never learned to type. But that shouldn't deter them from taking advantage of the efficiency and economies of this new information age. I have three terminals in my office, and I can only type with two fingers. But those two fingers can work wonders." [From *For Members Only: A Newsletter for American Express Card Members,* January, 1986, pp. 1–4.]

Organizational Goals and Information Systems

Organization plans are built for the achievement of the organization's goals and objectives. These plans and their implementing structures may vary widely, depending upon management goals. Thus, some organizational approaches may stress the achievement of targeted profit margins on investments. Others may use market share or sales volumes as their criteria. Still others may adopt societal-based goals as part of their business philosophy and organization plan. In all cases, however, an effective organization must have a clear idea of what is to be accomplished within a particular time frame. These accomplishments represent the measure of success that is to be applied to the company's performance.

Seen in this light, the organizational structure becomes a plan for achieving an organization's goals and objectives. Since the various components of a business organization are integrated and coordinated by means of information, the organization's information system implements the organizational plan. Thus, an information system exists primarily to further the goals of the organization and to meet objectives that contribute to the achievement of these goals.

The technology of information systems makes possible the achievement of organizational goals. At the same time, however, technology can obscure the essential relationship between information resources and company objectives. For persons who do not understand computer technology, computerized methods can generate a fascination — or a degree of complexity — that comes to overshadow the value of the information and the purpose for which it is being developed. This pitfall must be carefully avoided. The purpose of an information system is to help achieve organizational goals and objectives. Technology can either contribute to or detract from this purpose. The overriding concern for business managers or for users of information should be the ability of information systems to meet the goals of the organization.

Components of Information Systems

Information systems, regardless of whether they use computers, all perform certain basic tasks. Systems are assembled by arranging these tasks, or functions, into processing sequences. The basic components of any information system are:

- **Input** consists of the data that serve as the raw material for processing or that trigger processing steps.
- **Processing** includes the activities that transform input data into useful information.
- **Output** is the product, or result, of processing. Outputs are either delivered to specific, authorized persons with a need for the information or are incorporated in files for later reference and use.
- **Feedback** is a specially designed output used for verification, quality control, and evaluation of results.
- **Control** exists in any function that tests system feedback to determine if performance meets expectations.
- **Adjustments** are the products of the control process that bring system input or processing back into line with expectations.

All these system elements work in unison, as shown in Figure 1-3, to transform input data into output information and to maintain system processing at acceptable levels of quality.

As an example of a business information system that includes all of these components, consider a typical utility billing system. Use of electric current in homes or business facilities is recorded on meters. Periodically, say monthly, these meters are read by personnel who record the current figures in a meter book. These data become input to the process of producing monthly bills (output) that are sent to customers as requests for payment. Feedback is provided in listings of delinquent accounts—that is, in reports on customers who have failed to pay their bills. Control processing then produces utility shutoff notices (adjustments) informing customers that service will be discontinued unless payment is received. The purpose of the shutoff notices is to bring system processing back into line with expectations. The flow of processing in the electric billing system is shown in Figure 1-4.

Figure 1.3. Process diagram showing interaction of systems elements.

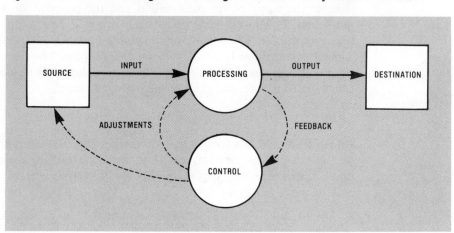

Figure 1.4. Flow of processing for systems that issue bills for electric service.

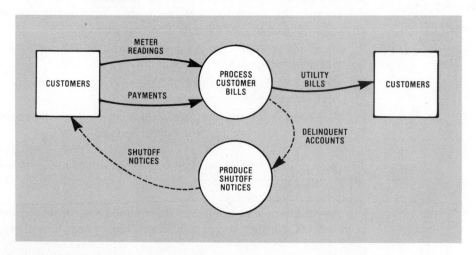

THE SYSTEMS APPROACH

The **systems approach** is a perspective—a way of identifying and viewing complex, interrelated functions as integral elements of systems. Although there is concern for the individual parts of systems, emphasis is on the integration of components to produce the end products of the systems themselves. Because of the way components, or elements, are reviewed as parts of an integrated whole, the systems approach provides an effective method for analyzing and developing solutions to complex problems.

Characteristics of the Systems Approach

The systems approach to problem solving is effective because of the kind of thinking it promotes. With the systems approach, problem solving efforts are first organized and then broken into logical patterns for analysis and solution.

Organization of problem elements under the systems approach is according to their **hierarchical** function. In establishing a hierarchy, the idea is to review the entire problem—one that is normally too complex to be understood as a whole—and to break it down into a series of understandable, workable subproblems with recognizable relationships. The subproblems, in turn, are subdivided successively until elements, or components, of the overall problem are defined in understandable, soluble modules. At each succeeding lower level, the components of the problem can be viewed in relative isolation. However, with the relationships established by a hierarchical structure, the overall problem can be kept clearly in sight.

Figure 1-5 shows the problem-related hierarchy associated with building a successful professional football franchise. The overall goal is straightforward: Each organization sets out to provide an entertainment service and to generate revenue to make the service worthwhile to owners, investors, and employees. Fielding a professional team is a business proposition with many dimensions, all of which must work together to further the goals of the franchise.

The organization (system) itself has several interacting components (subsystems) that have objectives which contribute to the overall goals of the franchise. Thus, there are problem-related functions centered upon the acquisition of personnel (players), team operations (coaching) to produce a winning team, facilities management to make the stadium available and attractive, logistic considerations involved in equipping the team and moving it to its games, marketing and promotion activities necessary to fill the stadium with paying customers, and financial dealings to underwrite the cost of the team. Thus, realization of the overall goals of the franchise depends on the ability of management to recognize and provide for the realization of several contributing objectives of franchise subsystems.

Each of the major subsystems of a professional football franchise has its own realm of problems and its own specific objectives. To illustrate, consider the area of team operations. A football team is a composite of several specialized teams. There is an offensive team, a defensive team, and specialty teams for kickoffs and kick returns. Each of these teams has certain objectives that, when

Figure 1.5. Problem-related hierarchy for a professional football franchise.

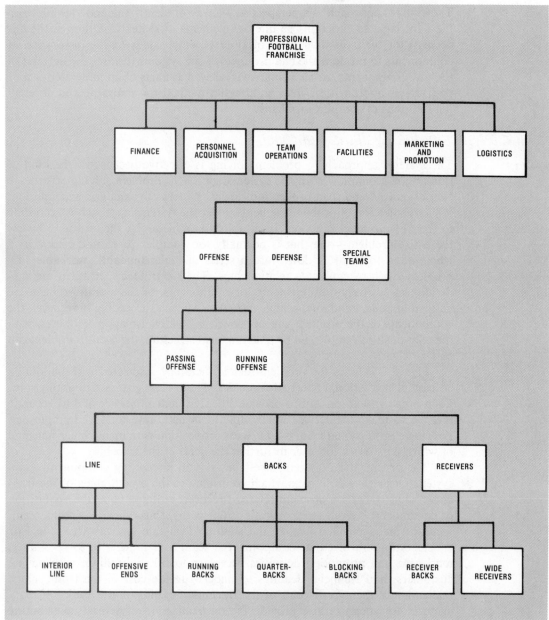

met in combination with the objectives of the other teams, contribute to the larger objective of winning games.

At the next lower level in the functional hierarchy are even more highly specialized teams that are fielded according to specific game conditions, field positions, and strengths and weaknesses of opponents. Within each team are individual positions—such as offensive linemen, backs, and receivers—each of which has specific objectives on every play. Thus, the objective of a player in a particular position contributes to the success or failure in meeting the objectives of the team for the entire game. The performance in each game, of course, contributes to the meeting of or failure to meet objectives for an entire season of games. Overall season performance determines whether the franchise has a winning team. This, in the final analysis, helps to establish the level of success for the entire franchise.

The components of the franchise are organized into a hierarchy in which, at each level, there are functions to be performed that, in combination, further the goals of the organization. The value of the hierarchy rests in this functional **partitioning** of effort. Levels of objectives range from the overall goals of the organization through to specific objectives for individual players.

The value of this hierarchical approach lies in a perspective that forces problem solvers and managers to deal with problems at different levels of **abstraction**. That is, goals and objectives are formulated with increasing levels of detail from the top to the bottom of the hierarchy. At the top of the organization, goals are described functionally in terms of the overall mission. At the bottom level, the objectives are clearly operationalized in terms of specific actions that must be taken or specific results that may occur.

At each level and for each function, the objectives are within the realm of the capability of the person charged with meeting them. Through this abstraction hierarchy, the complexities of running an organization are more easily managed. Although all organizational components are related in some fashion, specialization of function permits somewhat independent consideration of each function.

Thus, in the professional football franchise example, the team owner does not have to be concerned with blocking schemes for the offensive line. Neither does the offensive lineman have to be concerned with ticket sales. Each individual problem area is a concern of the organization as a whole. Yet each can be dealt with in a specific way by specific components of the organization.

Problem Solving with the Systems Approach

The systems approach to structuring an organization is applied to problem solving as well as to the processing of information. Two major problem solving strategies are:

- **Analysis.** With a systems perspective, a problem is partitioned, or factored, into component parts. Subproblems are identified at a level that promotes understanding and makes possible a solution. The partitioning process, in effect, isolates subproblems and their relationships with one another, facilitating individual study and solution.

- **Synthesis.** The systems approach provides a structure for bringing all the parts together into a related, functional whole. As subproblems are solved, the solutions can then be combined into a remodeled system from which problems have been eliminated. A series of subproblems that have been solved go back together again as an altered, improved total system.

The development of information systems is a form of problem solving. Whatever the specifics of the situation, the underlying problem is to provide the right information, to the right person, in the right form, and at the right time. This type of problem is generally too complex to be solved in its entirety, all at once, by a single individual. The solution is likely to entail many different computer programs, processing several streams of input data and producing a number of forms of output and feedback. All these processes must be integrated, along with control and adjustment functions. Clerical, managerial, and training procedures must be established. Given this level of complexity, the systems approach becomes essential to the development of information systems.

The first step is analysis of the problem, partitioning it into smaller, more manageable parts. In this way, a large problem is decomposed into successively detailed levels of subproblems. These subproblems can then be brought into focus and dealt with individually, without the distraction and confusion of trying to juggle all the components of the original problem at the same time. With the hierarchical structure of the problem clearly established, the problem solver can now develop subproblem solutions in relative isolation, without losing overall perspective.

Once solutions have been developed for the identified subproblems, the second step is to synthesize, or integrate, all these solution components into a complete problem solution. At this stage, the hierarchical structure established during problem analysis becomes a point of departure for structuring the solution components as an integrated whole. In this way, the systems approach — with its twin strategies of analysis and synthesis — ensures that the overall solution fits the original problem.

Figure 1-6 illustrates the application of analysis and synthesis in the solution of problems:

1. The problem is analyzed. The problem is partitioned into its component parts, or subproblems.
2. The relationships among the subproblems are identified. The result is a hierarchical structure that isolates the components of the problem and establishes their relationships to one another.
3. Solutions are developed for each of the identified subproblems.
4. These solution components are synthesized, or meshed together, into an overall problem solution. This process of synthesis, in effect, reconstructs the hierarchy of the original problem, so that the structure of the solution matches that of the problem.
5. Finally, the synthesized, structured collection of solution components is now a complete solution to the original problem.

OVERVIEW OF SYSTEMS ANALYSIS AND DESIGN

Systems analysis is the application of the systems approach to the study and solution of problems. Within the information systems (IS) environment, systems analysis is applied to business problems that require the development of computer information systems. Systems analysis makes it possible to understand problems and to shape solutions.

Systems analysis, then, is a mental process—a way of thinking about a problem, analyzing its components, and structuring a solution. It is also a perspective. The systems approach, as applied to business problems, means seeing the business organization itself as a system, analyzing its goals and objectives, and understanding uses for the information that will be the end product of the problem solution. Seeing the problem from the perspective of the user of information is a central dimension of systems analysis.

Systems analysis provides a set of strategies and techniques for dealing with complex problems, based on hierarchical partitioning methods applied through various levels of abstraction to analyze problems and synthesize solutions. Systems analysis is supported by graphic and narrative tools that have been developed to facilitate the process and systematically document its approach. This methodology is discussed in more depth in Chapter 4 and throughout the remainder of the text.

Within the IS field, systems analysis also refers to a certain type of work assignment. Systems analysis is the job of a **systems analyst**. A systems analyst is a problem solving specialist who brings a systematic perspective to the analysis of information processing needs and the design and development of computer-based solutions to these problems. In some organizations one person performs the systems analysis and another does the system design. However, it is common to have the same person (i.e., systems analyst) perform both functions.

Systems analysts are usually assigned to the IS function, department, or group within an organization. In large organizations particularly, computers have become sufficiently important that they are integral components of the organizational structure of their companies. Information systems responsibilities may be at the departmental level, or an IS group may be regarded as a division of a company. The function may be headed by a vice president, an assistant vice president, or a department head. The role and responsibilities of the IS function will vary according to the size of the organization, its goals, and the way in which its resources have been allocated. Figure 1-7 shows a typical organization chart and the placement of the systems analysis function.

Again depending upon company size, goals, and allocation of resources, systems analysts may also be assigned to portions of an organization other than the IS function. Almost any group within an organization—marketing, accounting, production, distribution, and so on—may have its own systems analysts. In all cases, however, the systems analyst is a specialized IS professional who brings technical skills and a systems perspective to the analysis and solution of business problems.

Systems analysis and design are typically done through a team effort. A project team, as it is often called, consists of systems analysts; programmers; experienced users who are usually middle managers from the area of the organization that will ultimately use the new CIS; a project team leader; and in some cases technical specialists, clerical personnel, and administrators. Some project teams may involve over one hundred individuals, but a typical team has six to ten people.

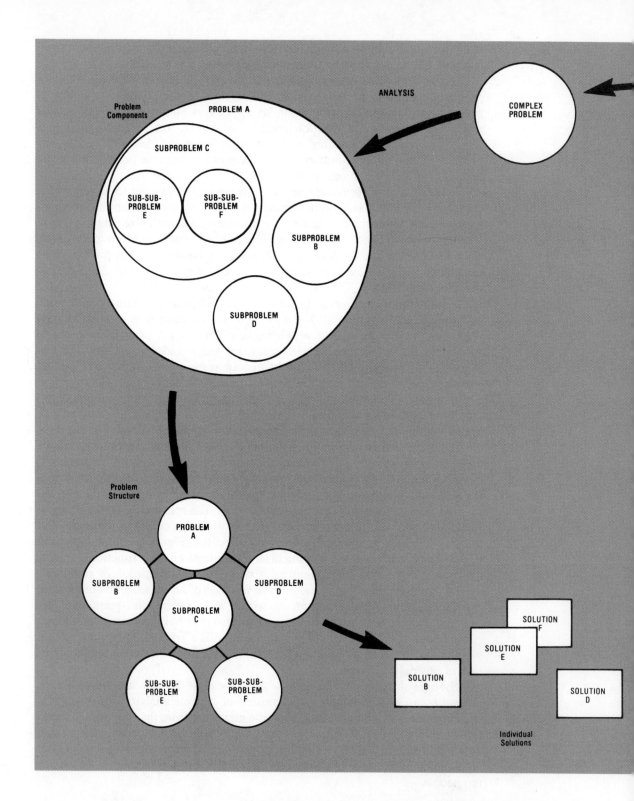

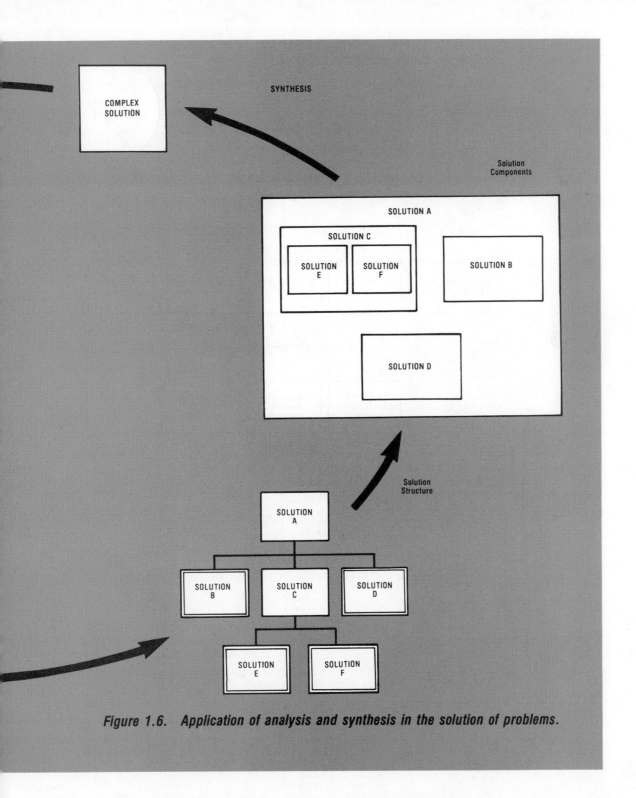

Figure 1.6. *Application of analysis and synthesis in the solution of problems.*

Figure 1.7. *Typical corporate organization chart showing the placement of the IS department.*

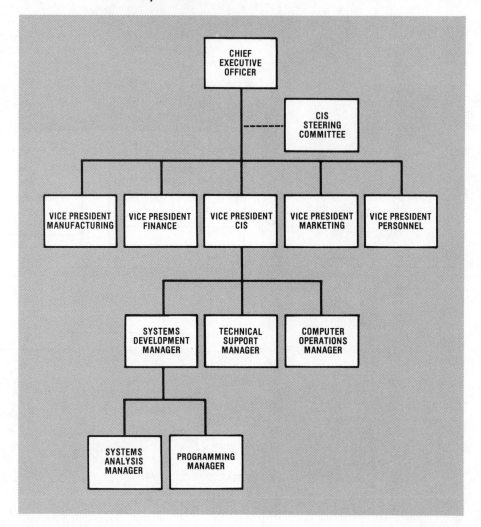

SUMMARY

A system is a set of interrelated, interacting components that function together as an entity to produce a predictable end result.

A business is a system composed of people, facilities, equipment, materials, and methods of work that function together to provide goods or services.

Components of a system can be seen as subsystems. Subsystems, in turn, may have smaller components, or elements, within them. By the same token, any system may be a subsystem of some larger system.

The organizational structure of a business represents a formal recognition by its management of the subsystems from which it is composed. An organizational chart identifies these subsystems (divisions, departments) and shows their relationships (lines of authority and responsibility).

For a system to function effectively, all its components should generate and communicate information. An information system is that subsystem primarily responsible for enabling all other components of the system to develop and deliver information.

Within business organizations, the five major types of information systems include: transaction processing systems (TPS), which control day-to-day operations; management information systems (MIS), which support organizational management; decision support systems (DSS) which facilitate future planning; strategic information systems (SIS), which provide a means to obtain a competitive advantage within a given industry; and expert systems (ES), which allow inexperienced managers to perform tasks and make decisions just like experts in the field.

The basic components of any information system are input, processing, output, feedback, control, and adjustment. These system elements work together to transform input data into output information and to maintain processing at acceptable levels of quality.

The systems approach is a way of identifying and viewing complex, interrelated functions as continuous elements of systems. An organization is seen as a hierarchy, with functions partitioned into subsystems that pursue assigned portions of the organization's goals.

The systems approach provides a valuable tool for problem solving. First, the problem is analyzed, or broken down, into a hierarchy of component subproblems that can then be studied and solved in relative isolation. Then, component solutions are synthesized, or recombined, within a single hierarchical structure. This systems approach is critical to the development of information systems.

The systems approach, as applied to the development of information systems, is known as systems analysis. Systems analysis, in turn, provides a basic perspective on systems-related problems and a specific methodology for analyzing and solving them.

Systems analysis is the job of a systems analyst. A systems analyst is a specialized IS professional who brings a systems perspective to the analysis of information-processing needs and the design and development of computer-based solutions to these problems. Systems analysts are usually assigned to the IS function, department, or group within an organization. In some organizations, systems analysts determine information processing needs and systems designers develop the computer information systems to satisfy those needs.

KEY TERMS

1. system
2. synergistic
3. subsystem
4. organizational structure
5. organizational chart
6. information

7. information system
8. transaction processing system (TPS)
9. management information system (MIS)
10. decision support system (DSS)
11. strategic information systems (SIS)
12. expert systems (ES)
13. exception
14. model
15. simulation
16. input
17. processing
18. output
19. feedback
20. control
21. adjustment
22. systems approach
23. hierarchical
24. partitioning
25. abstraction
26. analysis
27. synthesis
28. systems analysis
29. systems analyst
30. systems designer

REVIEW/DISCUSSION QUESTIONS

1. What is a system? Give two examples of: a natural system; an abstract system; an organizational system. Describe these entities as systems, identifying their subsystems, the individual goals or purposes of the subsystems, and the relationships among the subsystems.
2. What does an organizational chart tell you about a business organization?
3. Describe the role of information in a business organization.
4. Name the five basic types of information systems and explain how they relate to one another.
5. Why does an MIS emphasize the reporting of exception conditions? Describe a business situation in which this type of system would be particularly useful.
6. Computer technology can be a help or a hindrance to a business organization. Give an example both of a help and of a hindrance.
7. Name the six basic elements of an information system. Describe their functions and interrelationships.
8. What is meant by a systems approach? How does this approach make possible the solution of complex problems?
9. Why is the concept of hierarchy, or hierarchical structure, essential to the analysis and solution of problems?
10. What is systems analysis? What is its function in the IS environment?
11. What is a systems analyst? Describe the job function and its place within a business organization.
12. Consider a catalog ordering system for a large merchandiser. Give examples of each of the six elements of a system in this setting.
13. Are strategic information systems different from competitive information systems?
14. Expert systems are different from decision support systems in that they have a knowledge-base. What is a knowledge-base? Give two specific examples that were not presented in the text of areas where expert systems may be used.

The System Development Process

Learning Objectives

On completing the reading and other learning assignments in this chapter, you should be able to:

- Describe the stages in a system life cycle.
- Describe the work that takes place during systems development.
- Explain the need for and value of a step-by-step, process approach to the analysis, design, and implementation of computer information systems.
- Describe the work units or structure of a project, in terms of tasks, activities, and phases, and establish the relationship of these work units to the control of systems development projects.
- Identify and describe the five phases of the systems development life cycle used as the basis for instruction in this book.
- Describe the prototyping process and its relation to the system development life cycle.

THE SYSTEM LIFE CYCLE

This book is about the *development* of information systems. The principles and skills presented here can apply to both large and small systems. But before plunging into the study of how to develop computer information systems, it is best to consider the *context* in which this activity takes place: the **system life cycle**. In many cases the initial work done to create an information system is only a minor part of the total development work done on the system during its useful life.

To oversimplify somewhat, the system life cycle can be thought of in five stages:

1. *Business need*. Changing business conditions motivate a request for new or improved computer systems support. This could be the result of company growth to the point where transaction volumes are swamping current processing capabilities. It could be the result of a desire by management for more sophisticated reporting. It could be the result of a decision to offer a new product line or to cut costs in current lines. The motivations are numerous. The key first step is to recognize the need to change and clearly define what changes are needed.

2. *System development*. A process is followed to analyze the need and to design and implement a system to meet that need. The remainder of this book deals with the skills and methodologies that make up this process.

3. *System installation*. Installation could actually be thought of as the last step in the development process. It is that time period during which the developed and tested system is put into "live" production.

4. *System operation*. This is the longest part of the system life cycle. It is the period of active use — the reason for the development effort.

5. *System obsolescence*. Eventually the business or its environment changes so much that the system no longer supports it properly. The system is obsolete. Replacement or major renovation is necessary. This results in the recognition of a new business need, and the cycle is complete.

The system life cycle is represented in Figure 2-1(a). In reality, the system operation phase is much more intricate and exciting than the one depicted by this figure. Business is dynamic. Conditions change constantly: new market opportunities arise, competitors force adjustments, technology improves, and so on. Yet the installed system is static. It performs in precisely the same way day after day. That is, after all, its strength. Unfortunately, as the business changes the system supports it less well. Users begin to add manual procedures to compensate for the inability of the system to accommodate the business changes. The *need* is recognized for an *enhancement* to the current system. *Development* work is done to implement this enhancement. The enhancement is *installed* and the revised system is placed in *operation*.

In other words, as shown in Figure 2-1(b), the system life cycle described earlier occurs repeatedly as a microcosm within the operation stage. This enhancement activity, often simply referred to as **maintenance** work, is in fact development work. The development time and cost expended for enhancements during the operation stage of the system life cycle can easily be five to ten times the cost expended during the development stage. At some point, the cost for additional enhancements becomes unacceptably large for the benefit received, and the system is obsolete.

More material about maintenance and how to deal with system obsolescence is presented in Part VII. The point to understand now is that enhancement activity is essentially development activity and that the material in this book can be applied to both enhancement and new development work.

Figure 2.1. The system life cycle.

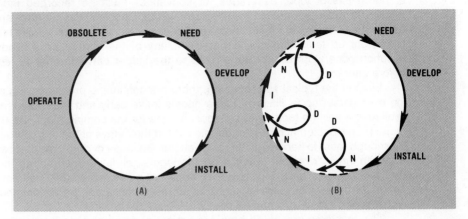

This discussion makes clear the benefit to be gained by producing a *flexible* and *maintainable* system. A major objective during systems development is to produce a system for which enhancements can be made as easily as possible.

■ ■

MINICASE
SLEEP-TYTE INNS

A simplified case study provides a context for discussing the systems development process. Sleep-Tyte Inns is a national hotel chain that franchises a number of local inns. A typical local inn has about 150 rooms and operates its own restaurant, lounge, and banquet facility.

A local inn can gain some important advantages by associating with Sleep-Tyte. One of the most important is an international reservations system. Travel agents everywhere and individuals using an 800 number anywhere in the United States can make reservations through Sleep-Tyte's computerized system. Reservation inquiries to the computerized network create exposure and generate many reservation opportunities for the local inn.

Each morning, the computerized national system delivers information, via teletypewriter, to the front office of every local inn. This information includes the names, addresses, and payment guarantee information for all guests holding reservations that day. The inn acknowledges receipt of this information and also transmits information to the central computer about the availability of its own rooms.

Once the computerized reservation information has been delivered, however, processing is currently manual in the local inns. Individual cards must be created for guests holding reservations. Mangers of the inns must match reservations against available rooms, determining which guests are staying over, which ones are leaving, and so on. As rooms become available, reservation cards are dropped into racks and slots for each room in the inn. When guests arrive, they must fill out registration forms. These forms are then used to create individual ledger cards for each room. The ledger cards, in turn, must be posted manually on bookkeeping machines.

Each transaction between a guest and the inn—whether it be nightly room rent or purchases of food, beverages, or souvenirs—must be recorded individually through keyboard entries on the ledger machine. Opportunities for error are great. Sometimes charges are lost altogether. For example, many guests make telephone calls right up to the time of departure. Many of the charge slips filled out by telephone operators do not get posted to the ledger cards in time for collection before checkout.

Even in the typical 150-room inn, there are continuing problems with overselling or underselling facilities. If some guests leave early and their rooms become available, it may be too late to sell those rooms for the coming night. On the other hand, if unexpected numbers of people extend their stays at the inn, there may not be enough room to handle all the reservations. Because of problems that can occur when an inn is "oversold," most local managers sell fewer rooms than they think they will have available. Typically, they undersell by as much as 10 percent of their available rooms, just to make sure that all reservations can be accommodated. If empty rooms result, this can be costly.

The problems presented here are typical of small and medium-sized hotels. First, opportunities to rent rooms are lost for lack of information about what is available. Second, bookkeeping procedures are cumbersome and costly. Guests often have to wait at checkout time for their bills to be computed. Some charges made by guests are never collected by the hotel.

The general business need is that the corporate office of Sleep-Tyte develop a system to be installed at each local inn to handle its "front office" accounting. This system should tie into the national reservation system. That is, when data on current reservations are transmitted each morning they would go directly into each local inn's own computer. The local computer would then print registration cards that would be ready when the guests arrived. Instead of having to wait in line and fill out registration information, each guest would simply verify existing information and sign his or her name.

The computer at each local inn would show the exact status of rooms at all times. As vacated rooms were cleaned, the housekeeping department, working from its own terminal, would input this information and the master file would be updated immediately. Instead of having to sift through racks full of cards to find available rooms, desk clerks could simply access room status data at a terminal to see what is available, making assignments without having to leave the guests. Throughout a guest's stay, charges could be entered into terminals as they occurred. There would be no need to create batches of charge tickets for postings on machines during off-hours. Instead, when a guest is ready to check out, the computer could simply generate a bill that would be ready in a matter of 10 or 15 seconds.

■ ■ ■ ■ ■ ■ ■ ■ ■ ■ ■ ■ ■ ■ ■ ■ ■ ■ ■ ■

THE SYSTEMS DEVELOPMENT EFFORT—AN OVERVIEW

The development of a computer information system can be a long and complex process. It can involve thousands of interrelated tasks performed by a variety of people, each responsible for different aspects of the development effort. In order to gain an appreciation for the challenges involved in developing an information system, consider the case of Sleep-Tyte Inns.

The computer programming work — designing, coding, and unit testing — will be significant for this project. Its complexity can be easily imagined by anyone with a programming background. But for this project, as for most, the programming-related work represents less than half — perhaps only 30 to 40 percent of the total development effort. In many ways it is the most controllable part. Program design and testing procedures are well-developed. The deliverables are well understood. The people doing the work are skilled professionals.

The program development work is preceded by a significant amount of analysis and system design work. It is followed by integration and acceptance testing, user training, and a lengthy installation process. For all nonprogramming work, deliverables are less understood, procedures are more vague and variable, and the people doing the work are a mix of systems professionals and users unaccustomed to systems work. Project success normally hinges on the quality of the analysis and design work.

Consider some of the analysis and design work required in the Sleep-Tyte Inn project. First, it is necessary to understand the expectations that managers both at the local inn and at the corporate office have for the computer system being considered. These concerns are not expressed in terms of computer programs or hardware. Rather, managers interested in having a computer system developed think and speak in terms such as cash flow, return on investment, rate of occupancy for available rooms, and ratios of payroll to revenue. In short, they think in business terms.

An understanding of the basic business objectives should then lead to a determination of whether the functions involved lend themselves to computer processing and, if so, to what type. In a local inn, for example, the systems analyst must consider the type of computer technology appropriate for the facility, whether its operation could be mastered by the typical employee, and whether the cost would be in line with the revenues expected from its operation. In addition to being able to function at a business level, the systems analyst must also be well grounded in computer technology. In this case, he or she must be able to make relatively quick preliminary judgments about whether and what type of computer technology is appropriate for the application under consideration. Later, if a new system is to be implemented, it will be necessary for the analyst to develop full specifications for the computer and communications equipment that will be needed.

A systems analyst must be (or must become) familiar enough with existing procedures in a business to determine whether and how a computer can do the job better. In the Sleep-Tyte system, for example, the analyst would have to visit one or more local facilities and "walk through" existing systems to understand what is being done physically and how these methods support the overall business objectives of both the local inn and the corporation. To understand the reservation process, the analyst would need to know how cards are processed into racks. The analyst does not need to know how to fill racks, but he or she must understand what information is being created and how it is being used.

Thus, the racks are seen as a means of presenting information on room availability. The analyst then understands that, somehow, the computer system must be able to present better information, on a more timely basis, about the availability of rooms. In effect, the analyst is considering the physical reality of the present system, then deriving a logical or business model that emphasizes the handling of data and their transformation into the information that supports the business objectives of the organization.

Once the logical, or business, purpose of an existing system is understood, a systems analyst can begin to look for opportunities to improve it. These opportunities exist at two levels—logical and physical. At the logical or business level, opportunities are sought either to add useful data for the new system or to make better use of data available in the current system. For example, suppose an inn does a considerable part of its business with tours. Under the existing reservation system, tours are booked as a unit. When reservations are reported to the local inn, however, cards are broken out in the names of individual guests. The fact that these guests are tied to a single tour is lost, creating a gap in information that might be useful to management. For example, suppose an inn in southern Florida learns that a snowstorm has caused cancellation of all flights from Pittsburgh. Suppose further that the hotel has twenty guests in a single tour scheduled to arrive from Pittsburgh. If the cards are already broken out by guest name, it will be difficult to locate the cancellations. However, a computer system could quickly search for and report the names of all guests who will not be arriving. This added dimension of information made available to management represents a system improvement achieved at a logical or business level. Timely information about business problems makes it possible to understand, anticipate, and respond to situations that would not come to light under present methods. On the other hand, the ability to get information into a computer immediately represents a substantial improvement at the physical level. Rooms status is more current, by hours, than was possible under the manual system.

Identified opportunities for improvement can be used to create a model for a new system that will incorporate these improvements. The new system would replace the current manual systems at the local inns. From a logical or business perspective, the model will stress the new information capabilities designed to enhance the basic business objectives of both corporate and local management. From a physical perspective, the model will specify the manner in which this information will be provided.

By this point the emphasis has shifted from analysis to design. The physical model will specify which data are to be stored at the corporate facility, which are to be maintained at the local inn, and which are to be transmitted between the two. It also will specify which processes are to be computerized at the local inn, which of those are to be on-line, and which are to be included in nightly batch processing. Where, for example, should reservation data be maintained, and where should reservation processing occur? In the current system, reservations are accepted at the corporate 800 number until the day before arrival and all reservation data are shipped to the local inn that morning. But this is a bit inflexible. Reservations could be accepted throughout the day at the 800 number. They could also be accepted that day and earlier by the local inn. What design implications does this have? In the process of answering questions of this type, a "general design" is created for the system.

Following general design, detailed design decisions must be made. What hardware will be selected? How will the databases be designed? Are software packages available to address all or part of the desired processing? When these questions have been answered, the overall programming job is known. Global program design decisions are made, including identification of the major program units that will be created. Interactive dialogs, screen designs, and report formats are all specified.

The purpose of this discussion has been to indicate the variety and complexity of the work that takes place in a development effort. Next, the key factors in ensuring the success of this work are considered.

SYSTEM DEVELOPMENT CHALLENGES

Suppose you are given the opportunity to lead the Sleep-Tyte system development project. What key things will cause you to be successful? In other words, what will be your critical success factors? They will be quite similar to the critical success factors associated with all commercial systems efforts.

Critical Success Factors for Systems Development

First and foremost, the resulting system must *effectively meet the stated business need* or solve the business problem. Nothing is more important than this. If the system does not *effectively* meet the business need, the development effort is wasted. This implies the necessity for building a detailed understanding of the business need early in the development process.

The second important factor is to build a *flexible* and *maintainable* system. As was indicated earlier, the amount of effort that is likely to be devoted to enhancing the system during its useful life is great, and a good, flexible design to speed those enhancements is important. Unfortunately, flexibility has a long-term, rather than short-term, payoff. Consequently, it is often shortchanged as project deadlines approach. A highly professional developer will address the flexibility issue, and a well-managed MIS organization will demand it.

A third critical factor is system *integrity* and *reliability*. The system should produce accurate results, and it should do so time after time, without fail. Adequate testing is of key importance in ensuring that these factors are met.

Finally, the development project should be completed *on time* and *within budget*. This implies the need for an estimating process that can predict approximate time and resource requirements early in the development effort and then gradually refine them as the project progresses. The relative importance of this factor varies with the project and with the business organization. For some projects it may be possible to slide the completion date with no harm (other than that to the reputation of the project leader). For others, the date may be crucial—the introducing of a new product or meeting a government deadline. The importance of staying within budget may depend on the extent to which the project was justified on an economic basis.

These critical success factors are easy to state but difficult to achieve in practice. What is a "business need"? How can we be sure that it has been correctly communicated? How do we achieve concurrence between the user and the developer as to what constitutes "meeting" the need. Does it require a fully embellished system, or will a more spartan version suffice? The success factors themselves can be inherently contradictory. For example, pressure to produce the system by a predetermined date at a predetermined price causes the development team to cut corners with respect to flexibility and reliability or accuracy as deadlines approach.

Understanding why systems projects fail can lead to an appreciation for the key items that increase the chances for success.

Why Systems Projects Fail

What is project failure? Quite simply, it is the failure to achieve one or more of the critical success factors discussed in the previous section. But it is easy to be misled about the cause of project failure. Consider what typically happens.

A very large on-line data entry application was being written. The system was intended to accept orders for a wide variety of "made to order" products. In fact, it was to serve as a direct front end to an automated manufacturing process. A large quantity of data was input for each order, and the edits were complex and tight. Half the programming was completed. In reviewing preliminary test results, the users realized that the system was not operating correctly. After considerable discussion and review of the modules being tested, they concluded that although the programs *were* doing what the programmer *thought* they were supposed to do, the programmer's specifications were incorrect in some cases and incomplete in others. The programmer had no way of knowing about the inaccuracies and compounded the problem by making "reasonable assumptions" where things were incomplete. There was no choice but to go back and rework the analysis. When finally completed, the project was, of course, both late and over budget.

But that was not the worst of the problems. Because the changes were fundamental, the entire design approach should have been modified. Because that would make most of the programming work obsolete, however, the programs were simply patched (before ever going into production). When the system was finally installed, not only was it late and over budget, but its poor basic design guaranteed that it would be forever difficult and costly to maintain.

Since problems are usually first recognized during programming or system testing activities, it is easy to conclude that this stage is where the greatest emphasis should be placed during systems development. Nothing could be further from the truth. As the example illustrates, a large percentage of the problems have their roots in the analysis and general system design activities of the development project. What are the most common reasons for system development project failure?

One common cause is *poor communication*. Communication presents a major challenge in a system development effort. At one extreme is the user — expert in a part of the business, but likely to be naive about how systems are constructed. At the other extreme is the programmer — a skilled technician, but unfamiliar with the detailed rules and policies that govern the business. The systems analyst/designer is usually the key link between the two. This can be a difficult, often impossible, job. At the very least, the analyst/designer needs a common language with which to communicate and a standard for what needs to be specified. But this points up other causes of failure.

Many projects suffer from *incomplete analysis*. There are two main reasons for this. First, there is often tremendous pressure on a project team to show results and therefore to begin detailed design and programming as quickly as possible. Second, the proper materials to be produced during analysis and general design are often poorly understood. Analysis is often declared complete because the time allotted for it has been used. In the absence of any objective standard, there is a tendency to take whatever exists and declare it to be the analysis specification or system requirement specification.

Related to incomplete analysis is the *failure to uncover the essence* of the system. The analyst may complete his or her work, document it completely and accurately, but still harbor the feeling that "it shouldn't be this complex." Analysis that concentrates too heavily on the physical aspects of the current processing — the organizational structure, the paper flow, the complex processing steps, and so on — can provide a *logically inconsistent* base on which to build the design. The result of this will be an inflexible, difficult-to-maintain system.

Finally, many projects suffer in their early stages from the *lack of a clearly defined process* to follow. Analysis is often equated with "interviewing people and finding out what they want." System design then becomes "draw a system flow chart that tells the programmer which programs to write." New system specifications become a collection of interview notes, current forms and statistics, and the system flow charts — all tied together with as much narrative as the analyst has time to write.

Ingredients for Success

The problems mentioned here are common but they are by no means inevitable. Tools, techniques, and processes *do* exist that help to greatly minimize these problems. In the following chapters you will learn techniques and processes for modeling systems, for uncovering the logical meaning or essence of systems, for communicating effectively, for designing flexible systems, and for assuring the quality of those systems by providing an effective testing base.

These various techniques and processes must be carried out within a well-defined framework or methodology. A methodology is a framework for project management. It is used to ensure completeness, to verify quality, and to have a base for recovery as the project faces its inevitable problems. Two basic methodologies, the System Development Life Cycle and the Prototyping Life Cycle, are introduced in this chapter.

Before presenting these methodologies, it is helpful to review several basic principles of systems development that should be employed no matter which methodology is followed.

BASIC PRINCIPLES OF SYSTEMS DEVELOPMENT

Successful approaches to systems development incorporate a number of broad, common characteristics. They include iteration; hierarchical decomposition or layering; evolutionary scope and objective; use of graphic tools; use of models; and understanding, imagination, and creativity. The first three are closely inter-related.

Iteration

One important characteristic of the systems development process is **iteration**. No analyst should expect to learn all there is to know about a business or a job with a single review of what is happening. Rather, a process of decomposing the problem into its component parts may be repeated, or iterated, to reach increasing levels of detail and understanding. Systems analysis begins by overviewing the business procedures and policies that comprise a system. Then, following a structured, analytic process that can involve use of models representing the system, a deeper look is taken. As needed, the analyst repeats the process, probing ever deeper until a thorough understanding is built — and there is agreement about purposes, functions, and procedures between the systems analyst and users.

Hierarchical Decomposition or Layering

Hierarchical decomposition or **layering** is the breaking down, or partitioning, of a large problem, or project, into a series of structured, related, manageable parts. This decomposition goes hand in hand with the iterative process. For example, the first iteration in studying a system might identify the major constituent parts or subsystems. Subsequent iterations then take closer looks at the individual system parts that have already been identified. Each part of the system is defined in terms of a series of constituent parts. Decomposition continues until a level is reached at which the functions and requirements of the individual system parts are understood clearly.

Evolutionary Scope and Objective

A clear statement of business **objectives** for the new system is necessary to ensure that the user needs are met. A tightly defined scope will specify what is to be included in the system as well as what is not. This is necessary to establish a budget and calendar for the effort. But it is difficult to write a tight scope and precise objectives before the problem area is well understood. The concepts of iteration and layering permit an **evolutionary** approach. When the project is first proposed, an initial scope and objective should be written. These statements can be made more precise with each iteration as deeper levels of understanding are reached.

Use of Graphic Tools

A range of graphic presentation techniques is available to help the systems analyst. These tools can help build an understanding about what the current system is and what the future system should be. The graphic presentations that result can provide a basis for agreement between systems analysts and users about expectations for systems under development.

One method for achieving this analysis and documentation of a system is the **data flow diagram**. Data flow diagrams are both analytic and communication tools. They provide a means of visualizing how data elements flowing through a system are transformed into information.

A data flow diagram, describing the processing involved in a simplified student registration system, is shown in Figure 2-2. The arrows represent "pipelines" that move the data through the system and the circles represent processes that act on the data. Entities outside the system that supply data to it or receive data from it are represented by squares. Data stores, for the temporary holding of data, are represented by open rectangles.

Figure 2.2. **Data flow diagram for simplified student registration system.**

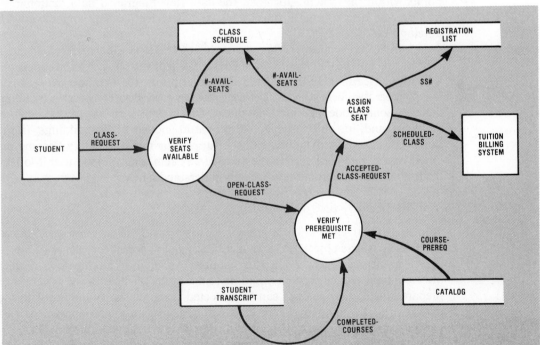

For example, in Figure 2-2, a student submits a class request. The first process to occur is a verification that there are, in fact, open seats in the requested classes. The master class schedule is referenced to determine this. Next, using the course catalog and the student's transcript, prerequisites are verified for each requested class. Finally, seats are assigned. This results in updating the master class schedule and the registration list and in sending a transaction to the tuition billing system. Techniques for building data flow diagrams are discussed in detail in Chapter 4.

Use of Models

Data flow diagrams can provide a clear method for describing systems and for establishing agreement on the basis of these descriptions. It is a well-known phenomenon that a dozen people witnessing an accident will all describe the event differently. Systems cannot be built around vague descriptions or opinions. Rather, a specific understanding must exist about what is to be accomplished and how the work is to be done. To achieve this understanding, data flow diagrams can be used as part of a technique known as modeling.

Models, in this sense, are graphic and written representations of what systems are and how they work. Data flow diagrams can form the basis for a uniform modeling tool. The diagrams themselves are supplemented by **data dictionaries** and *process descriptions*. A data dictionary describes the content of **data items** that flow through a system. Process descriptions are narratives explaining the handling and transformation of data at identified processing points within the system. Together, the data flow diagrams, data dictionaries, and process descriptions form models that describe systems under study or development.

Consider an analogy: When an architect develops a house for a client, a process takes place that begins with a description of the lifestyle to be supported and special features desired. From this description, the architect visualizes a way to meet the client's needs. Before breaking ground to construct a building, however, some modeling must take place. This is done with blueprints, detailed drawings, and, in some cases, actual miniature models of the buildings. In the same way, data flow diagrams and the supporting data dictionary become the model of a system conceived in the mind of a systems analyst for a user. Models, then, are tools for communication and understanding.

Understanding, Imagination, and Creativity

To model effectively, a systems analyst must start with an accurate *understanding* of the business objectives to be met. Once again, consider the case of Sleep-Tyte Inns described earlier in this chapter. An analyst talking to a cashier involved in the present system might be told that the purpose of the system is to prepare bills so that charges can be collected from guests. In talking with the president of the company, however, a different picture might emerge. At this level, the proposed system is seen as a way of providing information that will help management fill its rooms more completely and effectively. Thus, the business objective is to fill hotel rooms, not to generate bills. An analyst who sets out to support the filling of rooms will be more successful than one who concentrates simply on printing bills quickly.

Having understood the objective or the problem to be solved, the analyst must then have the *imagination* to look for the best solution without being inhibited by things as they are. Existing organizational structures and methods should not be accepted as constraints upon analysis and design. They are simply a starting point. The job of the systems analyst is to figure out the best way of meeting the objectives or solving the problem.

Creative thinking is supported by the process of systems analysis. The modeling process begins with the system as it physically exists. From this physical model, a more logical model is derived, one that emphasizes the business objective to be met. Then, as key business objectives for the new system are understood, they are used to create a model for the new system. This modeling process is iterated as understanding gradually increases. Creative thinking is enhanced by being freed from the assumptions that are often automatically made when concentration is on the physical constraints of the current system.

A SYSTEM DEVELOPMENT LIFE CYCLE

In an earlier section the critical success factors for systems development were identified. In considering the problems that are often encountered, the case was made for some type of control structure. A methodology is needed to help organize the literally thousands of different work assignments and end products that must be integrated to produce an information system. A **systems development life cycle (SDLC)** can provide this type of control.

The basic elements of one very effective SDLC are overviewed here. Greater depth is presented in Part VII. An understanding of the basics will provide a framework for learning the various tools and processes of systems analysis and design.

The Basic Building Blocks

Control, in anything as complicated as a systems development project, must be structured at several levels. At the lowest level are the controls over day-to-day work assignments. Many people are involved in systems development. Some of these people may be unfamiliar with the particular business operation, while others may know little about data processing. Therefore, at this lowest level, it is necessary to break down work assignments into relatively small, manageable units. This allows a project leader to review progress with each team member at least once every three or four days. The idea is to make it difficult, if not impossible, for people to go off on tangents and work unproductively.

At a middle level, individual work assignments fit together to produce substantial end products. These end products might include models of current systems, designs for new systems, test plans, or tested programs. Control at this level provides an opportunity to verify the completeness and quality of major portions of work.

The highest level of control is the point at which enough work has been done to present a progress report to management and to go through a full-scale review and decision about whether to proceed with the project.

These three levels of control are the major building blocks for an SDLC. Although individual methodologies may use varying terms, three standard terms have been selected for use throughout this book. These terms are tasks, activities, and phases.

Tasks. A **task** is any unit of work that can be performed by an individual, usually in a maximum of one week. A number of tasks make up an activity. A number of activities, in turn, make up a phase, as diagrammed in Figure 2-3.

A task is the smallest unit of work that can be assigned and controlled through normal project management techniques. Control, as discussed earlier, involves completeness checks, budgeting, scheduling, and quality reviews.

Suppose, for example, in the Sleep-Tyte Inn project, a systems analyst is assigned to study registration procedures under existing systems. This task is budgeted for two working days, with an end product to consist of a model that documents what happens in the course of guest registration. This task is readily and easily budgeted because it is small enough to define and assign. Tasks of

Figure 2.3. *Phases of the systems development life cycle consist of activities, which in turn are made up of tasks.*

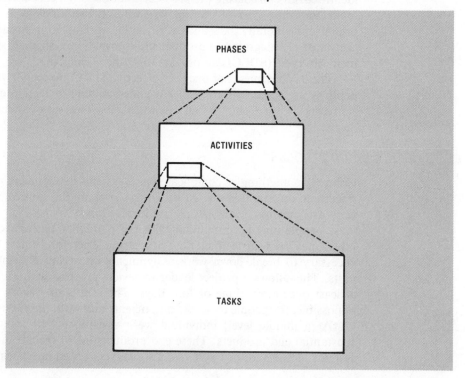

Figure 2.4. Phases and activities of the systems development life cycle.

INVESTIGATION PHASE

1. Initial Investigation
2. Feasibility Study

ANALYSIS AND GENERAL DESIGN PHASE

3. Existing System Review
4. New System Requirements
5. New System Design
6. Implementation and Installation Planning

DETAILED DESIGN AND IMPLEMENTATION PHASE

7. Technical Design
8. Test Specifications and Planning
9. Programming and Testing
10. User Training
11. Acceptance Test

INSTALLATION PHASE

12. File Conversion
13. System Installation

REVIEW PHASE

14. Development Recap
15. Post-Implementation Review

this type are also relatively easy to schedule because the assigned individuals can complete these work units independent of other assignments and of other project team members. Completeness checks and quality reviews are implicit because each task has an end result that can be checked readily by a user or by peer review. If rework is necessary, losses are minimal because tasks are relatively small.

Activities. An **activity** is a group of logically related tasks that, when completed, lead to accomplishment of a specific objective. Activities are defined by the specific end products that are produced. Quality control is applied formally and carefully at the activity level.

Figure 2-4 is a table listing the activities that make up the systems development life cycle used in this book. Note that each activity falls within a specific phase of the systems development process. Activities do not overlap phase boundaries. They all begin and end within the phase of which they are a part. However, the activities themselves can be carried out in parallel. For example, in phase 2 (analysis and general design), tasks that involve modeling the existing system could be going on in parallel with tasks designed to document requirements for the new system. In fact, work could be progressing on Activities 3 through 5 concurrently.

Phases. A **phase** is a set of activities that brings a project to a critical milestone. In most cases the milestone is accompanied by a management review and decision about whether to proceed with the project. Phases exist to assure that, at critical points in the course of the development effort, the project has the necessary management support in terms of personnel, budgets, and business issues that must be resolved in order for the project to proceed.

The systems development life cycle is best understood through a clear understanding of the *objective* and *end-products* of each phase and activity. Figure 2-5 is a data flow diagram that illustrates the relationship among the five phases of the SDLC, showing the end-products of each phase. The discussion that follows will emphasize the objective of each phase and activity.

The Investigation Phase

The **investigation phase** begins with a request for service from a user area. The main objective of the phase is to determine how to handle the request. Is a full system development effort necessary, or will another course of action suffice? Perhaps the request can be satisfied through minor enhancement of an existing system. Or perhaps no action is justified at all.

The investigation phase consists of two activities (see Figure 2-4). The original request for service is likely to be sketchy and imprecise. It may address only one aspect of a multifaceted problem. For example, the Sleep-Tyte Inn request may have originated when several local inn managers complained that the check-out process was too slow. An experienced systems analyst would take this request, try to understand it in its proper context, and establish initial scope and business objective statements. From this it immediately would become clear, without going into any real detail, that this request represented only the tip of an iceberg. There would be no way to significantly improve checkout processing without creating a more complete reservation system. The choice might be between doing this and expanding the scope of the request to include a distributed reservation system linking the various local inns with the corporate office. Assuming there is interest in considering the full reservation system, some initial assessment could be made of potential impact and benefit. But certainly a more in-depth study would be required before management could feel comfortable about committing to a huge system development effort.

This discussion illustrates activity 1 of the SDLC, the **initial investigation**. The objective or purpose of this activity is, first, to construct initial statements of scope and business objectives for the potential project and, second, to recommend a next step. In general, one of four recommendations is possible:

- Refer the request to a maintenance team and treat it as an enhancement to an existing system.
- Satisfy the request by using one or more end-user computing tools available in the organization.

Figure 2.5. ***This diagram illustrates the process flow, information sources, and outputs as related to the phases of the systems development life cycle.***

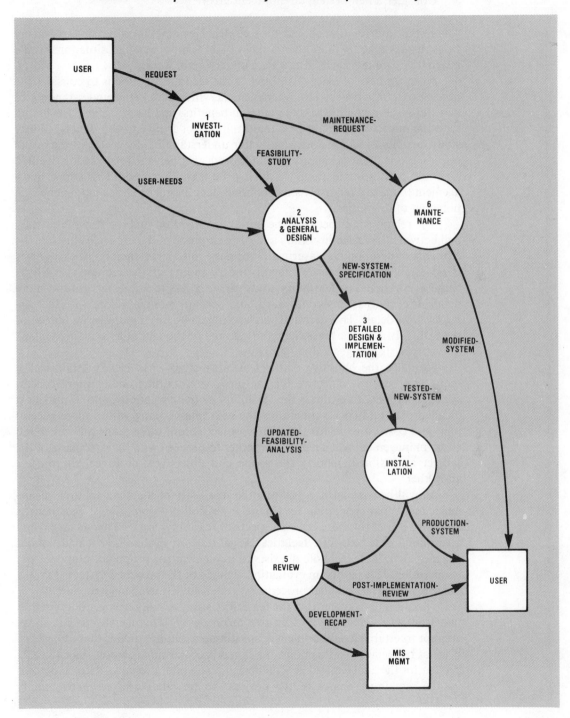

- Take no action at this time.
- Consider a new system development effort.

The initial investigation should be completed as quickly as possible. In many cases, it may take no more than a day or so. In more complex situations where alternatives are less clear, it may take up to several weeks.

As in the case of Sleep-Tyte Inns, if the recommendation is to consider the development of a new system, management will want a better understanding of how the system might work, its potential benefits, and its probable costs before they commit to what might be a multimillion dollar investment. The **feasibility study**, activity 2, will provide that better understanding. Typically, in the initial investigation, these questions are addressed at a general level; and a detailed plan and cost estimate are made during the feasibility study. This allows management to make a relatively small commitment in order to learn more about the potential of the project.

The relationships between the initial investigation and the feasibility study and between the feasibility study and the next phase of the life cycle illustrate the concepts of iteration and layering. During the initial investigation, the emphasis is on establishing a broad, general understanding of the request. Very little detail is covered. The feasibility study, then, covers the same territory in more detail. It encompasses second, third, and perhaps more iterations with increasing levels of detail. This iteration and layering continues into the second phase of the SDLC. In fact, the feasibility study should be thought of as a "baby version" of the analysis and general design phase.

Formally, the objective of the feasibility study is to clearly establish the scope and business objective for the project, to outline one or more general system solutions, to evaluate the feasibility of these solutions, and to provide a detailed plan and cost estimate for the next phase, along with a more general plan and cost estimate for the entire project. From these plans and projected costs, management will determine whether to proceed with the next phase of the project as outlined, modify the scope and objectives, or cancel the project altogether.

As will be seen later, evaluating the feasibility of a system solution means much more than reviewing its **financial feasibility** — preparing a cost benefit analysis. Two of the more critical aspects of feasibility analysis are technical and operational feasibility. In **technical feasibility** an evaluation is made about whether affordable technology exists to implement the proposed solution. And in **operational feasibility** an evaluation is made of the proposed system from the point of view of its manual procedures — the usability of the system.

There is a real danger that the feasibility study activity may get out of hand, that team members may go into too much detail. This usually occurs in an attempt to establish development cost estimates that are tighter than necessary. It is not reasonable, at this point, to expect a cost estimate closer than 15 to 25 percent for the analysis and general design phase and, perhaps, 40 to 50 percent for the remaining phases of the project. To provide closer estimates simply requires unnecessarily detailed work during the feasibility study. Effective application of the layering principle will ensure that excessive detail is avoided.

The time spent on the investigation phase is relatively brief, perhaps 10 to 15 percent of the total project time. Yet the investigation phase is in some ways the most critical phase of the system development life cycle. Here the proper base is established, the scope and business objectives of the project are set, and the basic system approach is determined. The rest of the project adds detail to and implements the basic solution identified here.

The Analysis and General Design Phase

As illustrated in Figure 2-5, the main end-product of the **analysis and general design phase** is the **new system design specification**. It is on the basis of this specification that detailed design and programming tasks are done. The major inputs to the phase are the feasibility study report and a more detailed understanding of user needs and requirements.

The objective of this phase is to establish a general design for the new system, to secure a commitment from the MIS area that the proposed system can be built and installed within the established time and dollar budgets, and to secure a commitment from the user area that the projected benefits can be achieved with the proposed system. A detailed plan for the next phase is also prepared.

On the basis of these results, management will determine whether to authorize continuation of the project. Since, by the end of the analysis and general design phase, 40 to 50 percent or more of the total project time may be expended, project cancellation is rare. However, a rescoping of the project, perhaps to limit development costs or to realize even greater benefit, is not uncommon.

This phase consists of four activities, the first three carried out largely in parallel, as illustrated in Figure 2-6. Successful completion of this phase relies heavily on the principles of iteration and layering. Four general steps are followed:

- Gain an understanding of the existing system.
- Refine the definition of the user requirements that are to be met in the new system.
- Specify the general design of a new system to meet these requirements.
- Evaluate the feasibility of the proposed system.

These steps are repeated or iterated many times, each time going another layer down in terms of increased detail and understanding. These iterations are sometimes formal but more often informal, occurring within the minds of the project leader and analysts.

The analysis and general design phase opens with activity 3: **existing system review**. The primary objective of this activity is to build an understanding of the business goals, objectives, and functions of the application areas that are within the scope of the project. Working from a preliminary review of the existing

Figure 2.6. Gantt chart for analysis and general design phase.

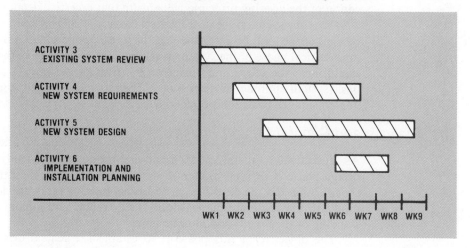

system done during the feasibility study activity, emphasis is first placed on building a model of the existing physical system. This is done by collecting various input forms, reports, and current system documentation. Then, using analysis tools (the subject of Chapter 4), a model is built of the existing system. In addition to the major system inputs and outputs, the model stresses data stored in the system (in computer or, perhaps, manual files) and the various processing steps carried out to transform those data. From this physical model, a more logical business model is derived. This model emphasizes the data and the processes that transform them into intermediate results or final outputs. At this point an attempt is made to thoroughly understand the essence of the business processing independent of the physical means by which that processing is carried out.

As mentioned earlier, the modeling tools used in this book are based on data flow diagrams. Figure 2-7 is a data flow diagram that models the analysis and general design phase itself. Activity 3 corresponds to processes 3a and 3b in this diagram.

Even while the existing system review is in progress, activity 4: **new system requirements** begins. The main objective of this activity is to develop a complete definition of the necessary capabilities of the new system from the user's point of view.

The feasibility study provided a general statement of new system requirements. These requirements are defined in greater detail during activity 4. This definition will include descriptions of changes in processing capabilities (logical or business changes) and also descriptions of new methods of delivery (physical changes). These required logical changes are then used to modify the logical model that is being derived for the existing system and to begin to create a business or logical model of the new system. The physical changes or requirements are then applied to this new logical model in order to package it into a physical model for the new system.

Figure 2.7. *Process view of the analysis and general design phase of the systems development life cycle.*

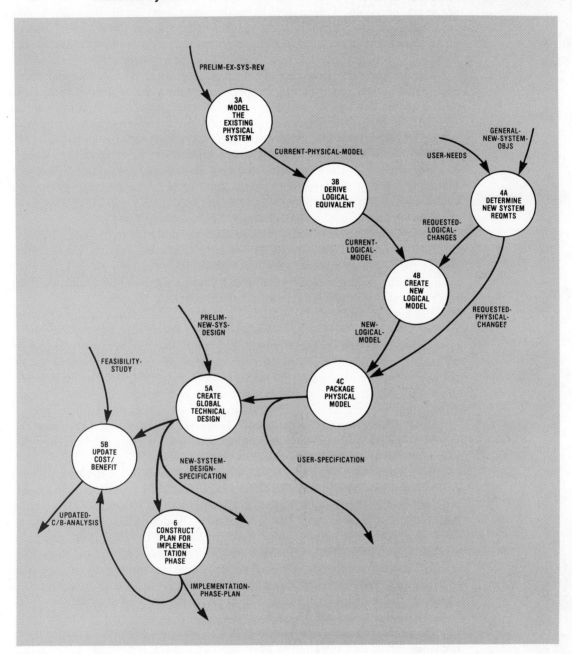

This procedure corresponds to processes 4a, 4b, and 4c in Figure 2-7. Keep in mind that the processes 1 through 5 are not simply completed in order. There are several iterations of these steps in greater and greater detail. Basically, as you gradually build your understanding of the existing system, you are also building an understanding of the user's requirements for the new system. This knowledge is gradually brought together in a model for the new system.

The end-product of the new system requirements activity is a formal document called a **user specification**. It specifies the data and processes to be supported by the new system and the extent to which computer support will be provided. It contains no internal design of the computer portion of the new system. It is a description of the new system from the user's perspective.

During the feasibility study activity, a preliminary new system design was proposed. It is necessary to verify that this preliminary design concept is still feasible in view of the more detailed understanding of the existing system and new system requirements being gained during activities 3 and 4. This requires the creation of a general technical design for the new system.

The main objective of activity 5: **new system design** is to provide sufficient information for management to decide whether to proceed with the implementation of the proposed system. This is achieved by proposing a general technical design for the recommended system and updating the feasibility analysis from this design (this corresponds to processes 5a and 5b in Figure 2-7).

The key end-product of this activity is a formal document known as the **new system design specification**. It includes the user specification as well as sufficient technical design specifications so that remaining development costs can be estimated to within 10 to 20 percent. It includes, for example, specification of the major files or databases, the major on-line programs, and the main batch processing job streams that will be part of the new system. However, it would usually not include detailed file designs, internal program designs, precise screen or printer layouts, and so on. These are not required to update the feasibility analysis or estimate remaining development costs. Hence, they can wait until the next phase of the development life cycle.

In practice the new system design work participates in the iterative process used to complete activities 3 and 4. As the current system and the new system requirements are better understood, this insight is used to gradually evolve the definition of the new system. The new system is not defined in one large burst of work after activities 3 and 4 are completed. Rather, the definition gradually evolves, in parallel with these activities, as options are considered and numerous tradeoff decisions are made. Then, at the end, time is taken to pull all the pieces together and verify the overall quality of the new system design specification. However, the real design process occurs gradually with each iteration of the basic analysis and general design steps.

The remaining activity in the analysis and general design phase is activity 6: **implementation and installation planning**. Before the remaining development costs can be estimated, it is necessary to have a project plan that covers the next two development phases. The objective of activity 6 is to create this plan. This is a relatively small activity, usually the responsibility of the project leader. It occurs toward the end of activity 5, as the new system design becomes formalized. It determines the development costs used to update the feasibility analysis in activity 5.

The Detailed Design and Implementation Phase

The main objective of the **detailed design and implementation** phase is to produce a completely documented and fully tested new system that encompasses computer processing, manual procedures, and interfaces between the two. The phase consists of the five activities shown in the Gantt chart in Figure 2-8. Work is based on the new system design specification prepared during the previous phase. This document serves as a basis for detailed technical design, which includes detailed design of programs, specific design of files, input record designs, and output document or display designs. Next, after test specifications have been prepared, individual program modules are written and tested.

During this same period, user training begins. Once trained, users become involved almost immediately in integration and system testing activities. This testing encompasses both computerized and manual procedures. During the system test, the new system is operated under conditions that are as close as possible to normal production conditions, with the project team observing the procedures and results. Any final fine tuning of the new system takes place during this comprehensive testing activity.

Two strategic decisions can have a great effect on the work that occurs during this phase: the decision to purchase an application software package and the decision about how to install the new system.

Figure 2.8. Gantt chart for detailed design and implementation phase.

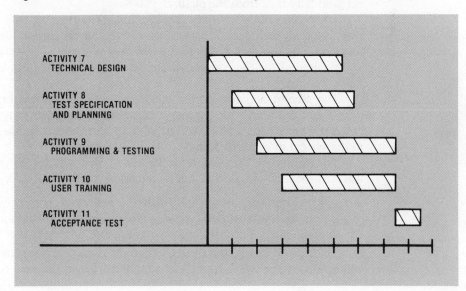

In many cases, 50 percent or more of the development resources of a project are expended in the phase. However, the time and resources required for this phase may be reduced significantly if a decision is made to use an application software package rather than developing the programs internally. This option is becoming increasingly viable as large numbers of software houses bring comprehensive and flexible application systems to market. If purchased application software is used, the programming time may be reduced substantially. Depending on the system, significant programming may still be necessary for converting master files, providing interfaces to other systems, and modifying portions of the software package to meet local needs.

The installation approach can also have a major effect on how this phase progresses. The traditional approach is to design and implement the entire system completely, then to do a massive system test, and finally, to install the system following one of several possible methods. However, in larger systems with reasonably independent components, a far more effective approach can be to implement and install the system in incremental steps, or *versions*. In this way, users can learn to use the system effectively, a step at a time, and developers can produce the system with good control over schedules and budgets.

The identification of the appropriate increments or versions is a complex process, which may begin early in this phase or even toward the end of the previous phase. The net result is an iteration of the detailed design and implementation and the installation phases for each version.

The Installation Phase

Actual development work ends with the installation phase. The main objective is to replace the existing system with the new, tested, documented system. The existing system is removed from daily production, the CIS development personnel gradually fade from the picture.

The phase consists of only two activities. The first, activity 12, **file conversion**, is mainly technical. Programs are run to convert current files, computer or manual, into the files required for the new system. The actual timing and approach used for file conversion are determined by the installation approach that is selected.

The second activity of this phase, activity 13, **system installation**, is a critical transition time for the users. Actual realized benefits, as opposed to the originally projected benefits, will depend on how the user group learns to adapt to the system during this activity.

The method of installation for the new system will depend on its design, its use, and the level of risk that can be tolerated. Options include:

■ The cutover can be abrupt, with the necessary files converted, the old system discontinued, and the new one put into production all at essentially the same time. The installation costs are low, but the risk of failure is great.

■ The old and new systems can be operated in parallel for some time while the results of the two systems are compared. When the new system is clearly operating correctly, a decision can be made to discontinue the old. In this case the risk is low, but installation costs are high.

- There can be a parallel conversion in which the old system is gradually phased out while increasing volume is shifted to the new system. This compromise approach, when appropriate, can minimize both cost and risk.
- **Version installation** can be used. Under this approach, the system would be divided into a series of functional units or incremental steps, called versions, as described in the previous section. Each version can then be installed using any of the three approaches. However, the entire system will not be fully implemented until all of the versions are in place.

The Review Phase

The **review phase** is not formally part of the development effort. Its purpose is to review the development work that has just taken place. The phase consists of two review activities. One is directed internally toward the development effort itself. The other is directed externally toward the new system in its production environment.

Activity 14, **development recap** is done immediately following the installation phase. The project leader and team members review the development project that has just concluded—its successes and its failures. The objective is to help individual team members perform more effectively on future projects. It may also identify modifications in the development procedures, or even the SDLC itself, that could improve future efforts.

Activity 15, **post implementation review** is conducted after the new system has been in production for several months. The objective is to evaluate how well the system is working and the extent to which projected benefits are being achieved. It will typically result in recommendations for better use of the system and a suggested list of maintenance or enhancement efforts that should be undertaken in order to improve the system.

PROTOTYPING

A reliable set of user requirements is a key ingredient in a successful system development effort. The importance of user involvement and the use of modeling tools in completely and rigorously defining these requirements during the Analysis and General Design Phase of the SDLC have been discussed. But in some cases expectations are too high for even the most skilled analyst and the most diligent user. The proposed new system may represent a totally new capability for the user—for example, a real time update and flexible on-line query capability to replace an old nightly cycle processing and batch reporting capability. The user may not be able to accurately identify new system requirements, no matter how much effort is expended simply because it is not possible for that user to visualize how the system would work. This could result in a new system that required fundamental architectural changes very soon after it was installed.

Suppose it were somehow possible to fairly quickly build a working model of the system as initially envisioned by the user. Suppose further that the user could work with this model, suggest changes, and have these changes quickly incorporated into a revised working model. A few iterations of this process would surely result in a much more realistic requirements statement. Since the user had been dealing with a *working* model, there might be some chance that with minor modifications the model could be used in production and the development effort would be complete. But even if the model were not suitable for large-scale production, the resulting user specification would certainly be a more complete and stable document on which to base the design for the new system. This, in a nutshell, is what **prototyping** is all about.

Prototyping can help when the user is unable to visualize how the proposed system will work. This could involve the addition of new capabilities, the automation of currently manual processes, or any situation where the operational impact of the system is unclear.

To illustrate the use of prototyping, consider the case of Sleep-Tyte Inns. The user and the analyst would undoubtedly have noted the need to handle discounted room rates. The user specification might have stated that at check-in time the standard room rate should appear on the screen, but the registration clerk should have the ability to override this and insert a different room rate. This is likely to be the way the system would then be implemented.

But now suppose prototyping is being used. A working model of the system is built according to the initial specifications, and a reservation clerk begins to enter some test transactions. After verifying that the various features seem to work properly, the clerk suggests trying the prototype on last night's "real" data. While entering a transaction for a customer who is entitled to a discount, the clerk hesitates, scribbles something on a pad, then resumes entry. The analyst, realizing that the clerk has just computed the amount of discount, questions and discovers that some discounts are fixed dollar amounts but many are percentages. The prototype is changed to add a discount percentage data element and the ability to calculate the discounted room rate.

Gradually the reservation clerk, through additional work with the revised model, becomes more sophisticated about how on-line registration could work. The clerk realizes it might be possible to extend the discounting functionality. Most of the percentage discounts are standing agreements with local businesses. There are about fifty agreements, all with different percentages subject to change at different times. In most cases the clerk must verify the percentage in a book before entering it. After a discussion of this situation with the analyst, the prototype is revised again to include a table of company codes and current discount percentages. The registration screen allows the clerk to handle discounts in one of three ways: override the standard room rates, enter the discount percentage, or enter the company code. If a code is entered, the system now uses the code to obtain the discount percentage or warns the clerk if the code is invalid.

Two iterations of the prototyping model have resulted in additional data collected by the system, changes in screen content, and additional processing capability. The advantage of knowing all these requirements before beginning to design and build the final production system for all local inns is obvious.

This section provides a brief overview of basic prototyping concepts. Just as with the SDLC, an understanding of the basic concepts will form a base for the study of system development tools and processes presented in this book. The application of this material in live development projects will be clearer. More is said about prototyping in Part VII.

The Prototyping Products

The product of the prototyping effort is referred to as a **prototype** or **working model** of the system. The key word here is *working*. The prototype is not a toy. It is not a mock up series of screen formats for the user to passively review. It is a functioning system or subsystem, doing real processing with which the user can interact. Remember that the main reason for prototyping is to generate a complete set of user requirements for the new system — to uncover those requirements that might have been missed because of the user's lack of sophistication or understanding of how the system could really work in a live setting. This implies a model that actually works. The model, typically, must include functions that handle data entry, file creation and updating, data transformation or processing, queries, and some reporting. The emphasis is normally on the on-line or interactive portions of the system, since this is what the user might have the most difficulty visualizing.

If the prototype must be a true working model, it might appear that building a prototype is essentially equivalent to building the entire system. Certainly, a prototype is not a hastily thrown together, quick and dirty product. Those aspects of the system that are modeled must be realistic, but not all aspects necessarily need to be modeled. Depending on the objective of the prototype, it may not be necessary to spend time on precise screen designs or file structures. Complete editing functions may not be required. Design considerations to ensure efficient high-volume transaction processing are usually not included. In general, things like batch reports, processing controls, recovery procedures, and security are not part of a prototype. The features to be included in a prototype are driven by the objective the prototype is trying to achieve.

The Prototyping Process

Prototyping is an *iterative process*. The starting point is an initial statement of user requirements for whatever part of the system is to be prototyped. From this statement an initial working model is built. At this point a three-step iterative process begins (see Figure 2-9):

- The user works with the prototype.
- Requirements are revised and refined.
- The prototype is revised on the basis of changed requirements.

In some cases, several iterations of this process may result in a working model that can actually be placed in production. It is more likely, however, that the

Figure 2.9. The prototyping process.

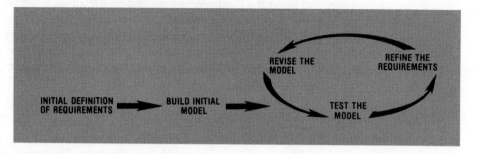

features of the working model will be used to complete the statement of requirements for the new system.

The most important thing that should be understood about the successful use of this process is its *rigor.* Its starting point is the preliminary statement of user requirements from the feasibility study. Its goal is to produce a rigorous user specification document. This is not possible through informal, nondirected "playing" with the model. The model must be realistic, and the user testing must follow a rigorous, well-defined plan to exercise various features of the model in realistic situations. The process may appear spontaneous, and the user insights and ideas may be unexpected. But this spontaneity occurs against a backdrop of careful planning and detailed documentation of evolving requirements.

Prototyping Tools

A prototype is an actual working model of the system, including sufficient functionality to allow the model to be used in a "live" setting. It is also built and revised fairly rapidly—in a matter of days or weeks, not months or years. Models are certainly not built using conventional programming languages and file access techniques. Prototyping requires a set of **interactive software development tools** that allow the designer or even the user to rather quickly define screens, create files and data entry/update routines, generate program modules that handle processing logic, create basic query and reporting functions, and so on. These tools should be integrated around a common data dictionary that maintains the definitions of such things as data elements, edit rules, records, processing modules, screens, reports—in short, all the components of the prototype. A number of good prototyping tools do exist. No tool is perfect. The tradeoff is usually between *flexibility* (and hence the complexity of the processing that can be modeled) and *ease of use* (and hence the speed with which the model can be built and modified).

Prototyping and the SDLC

The goal of prototyping as discussed here is to enhance the quality of the user specification document, the main product of activity 4, new system requirements. It is based on the preliminary statement of new system requirements done during the feasibility study. In reality, it spans and supports the three major activities of the analysis and general design phase. Model building requires an understanding of the existing system (activity 3) and makes some new system design assumptions (activity 5). Depending on the extent of the prototype, it may or may not drastically alter the detailed design and implementation phase. At one extreme, the prototype may be so extensive and the development tools so powerful that it may only be necessary to make minor refinements and additions to the model in order to have a finished system. At the other extreme, the prototype may be totally throw-away with the production system being built using conventional tools.

The definition of prototype used here is admittedly somewhat restrictive. The term is also used, for example, when a model is built during the detailed design and implementation phase to test the feasibility of a design concept. This type of prototype has a different objective and uses different tools. It is beyond the scope of this discussion.

When to Use Prototyping

Prototyping is best used for on-line, interactive systems. It is especially appropriate when the potential capabilities of the system go beyond the user's experience. It is less well suited for batch-oriented subsystems or highly complex or mathematical processes. Prototyping's main purpose is to obtain a more complete and stable definition of requirements for the new system. The process is particularly effective when the user is capable of building and revising the prototype with the intervention of a systems designer.

SUMMARY

The system life cycle consists of five stages: need, development, installation, operation, and obsolescence. The system operation stage is the longest, containing repeated small development efforts in the form of system enhancements. A major objective of the system development process is to produce a system for which these enhancements can be handled as easily as possible.

The key critical success factor for systems development is effectively meeting the stated business need. The second most important factor for most commercial systems is to build a flexible and maintainable system. Other important factors are to build a system that has integrity and reliability and to complete the project on time and within the authorized budget.

Failure to achieve these objectives is usually rooted in the analysis and general system design activities of the development project. Common reasons for failure include poor communication between users and technical people, incomplete analysis, the failure to understand and document the logical or business essence of the system, and the lack of a clearly defined development process.

The general principles on which successful system development is based include iteration; hierarchical decomposition or layering; an evolving scope and objective; use of graphic tools and models; and developer understanding, imagination, and creativity.

The system development life cycle (SDLC) presented in this book contains five phases. These phases, in turn, consist of a number of formal activities. The phases and activities are best understood by gaining a clear understanding of their objectives and end-products.

The investigation phase consists of two activities. Its main objective is to determine how the request for service should be handled—the development of a new system, renovation or enhancement of the existing system, or perhaps no activity at all. The key end-product is a feasibility study report.

The main objective of the analysis and general design phase is to establish a general design for the new system. The key end-products are the statement of user requirements in the user specification and the new system design specification which contains the basis for the technical design work of the next phase. There are four activities in this phase.

The main objective of the detailed design and implementation phase is to produce a complete, documented and fully tested system, including computer processing, manual procedures, and the interfaces between the two. This phase is made up of five activities.

In the installation phase the existing system is replaced with the new, tested, documented system. This is the end of the actual development work. A final review phase provides an opportunity to ensure that the anticipated benefits are actually being achieved with the new system. Each of these phases has two activities.

One of the most difficult aspects of a system development effort is to produce a complete and stable set of user requirements, especially when the user finds it difficult to picture how the system will actually work in production. Prototyping is an iterative process in which a working model of the system is built and then modified on the basis of user experience with the model. After several iterations the working model evolves to the point where a complete set of user requirements can be made.

KEY TERMS

1. systems life cycle
2. iteration
3. hierarchical decomposition
4. layering
5. evolutionary scope and objective
6. data flow diagram
7. models
8. data dictionaries
9. process descriptions
10. data items
11. systems development life cycle
12. task
13. activity
14. phase
15. investigation phase
16. initial investigation
17. feasibility study
18. financial feasibility
19. technical feasibility
20. operational feasibility
21. analysis and general design phase
22. new system design specification
23. existing system review
24. new system requirements
25. user specification
26. new system design
27. new system design specification
28. implementation and installation planning
29. detailed design and implementation
30. versions
31. installation phase
32. file conversion
33. system installation
34. version installation
35. review phase
36. development recap
37. post implementation review
38. prototyping
39. prototype
40. working model
41. interactive software development tools

1. Describe the five stages of the system life cycle. What factors determine the useful life of a system?

2. Discuss the critical success factors for systems development and illustrate each of them in the context of the Sleep-Tyte Inns project.

3. Discuss the overall purpose of a system development life cycle. What are the three major building blocks that make up an SDLC, and how do they relate to one another?

4. List the five phases of the SDLC presented in this chapter. What is the main purpose and key end product of each?

5. Suppose management argues that a given project is mandated. Therefore it is pointless to do a feasibility study. The team should save time and money by skipping the investigation phase and going directly to the analysis and general design phase of the SDLC. Do you agree? Can you think of reasons why this should not be done?

6. Explain the *iteration* concept and illustrate its use in the SDLC.

7. Use the identification, definition, and development of a data entry screen to illustrate the *layering* concept. Explain how the screen would evolve over each of the phases of the SDLC.

8. Explain why it is important to understand the existing system as a part of building a new one. What problems might have occurred in the Sleep-Tyte Inns project had the existing systems been ignored?

9. Describe three methods for installing a new system. Which of these would work best for the Sleep-Tyte Inns project? Why?

10. The type of work done by MIS team members changes during a development project. Based on your understanding of the development process, list several key skills and personal characteristics that would be most important during each phase of the SDLC.

11. What is the main purpose of prototyping? Why might prototyping have been useful in the case of Sleep-Tyte Inns? Explain how it would have worked.

3

Managing the Development Process

Learning Objectives
On completing the reading and other learning assignments in this chapter, you should be able to:
- Describe the role of the system development life cycle in providing a basis for comparison, measurement, and decision making on CIS projects.
- Explain the three functions of project management—planning, scheduling, and control.
- Describe the characteristics of a project that make it definable and manageable.
- Discuss the techniques of PERT and CPM and tell how these techniques differ.
- Show how critical path algorithms are applied to the project management process.
- Demonstrate the use of a Gantt chart.

NATURE OF PROJECT MANAGEMENT

The systems development life cycle is, in effect, a plan, or structure, for conducting the systems development project.

Consider what the lifecycle is and what it does for the development of a computer information system: The life cycle establishes standard phases and activities, creating a series of known tasks, activities, phases, and management checkpoints. This structuring makes it possible to communicate uniformly within an organization about the needs of, and progress within, any systems development project. Further, the standardization of phases and activities makes it possible to compare progress and results among a number of systems development projects. Thus, in addition to providing a work structure, the life cycle provides a basis for comparison, measurement, and, ultimately, investment decision making. The life cycle, then, provides a framework for applying analysis, design, and implementation methodologies. It also establishes a structure for managing the systems development effort.

If the life cycle is, as indicated, a structure that helps make system projects manageable, it is also true that the life cycle by itself falls short of being a project management technique. Putting it another way, the life cycle provides a framework within which each organization must still develop some method for managing individual projects. Also, some means must exist for comparing and reporting to management about plans, schedules, and results. Within this context, the term **project management** refers to a method or combination of techniques to facilitate planning, scheduling, and control—the three components of project management.

Planning

Planning for overall information system support is critically important in any organization. However, the focus of this discussion is on the planning that occurs within the context of a development project. In this setting, planning involves the identification of all of the major segments, or phases, of a project. These phases are then subdivided into specific activities and individual jobs, or tasks. Together, these are the assignments that must be completed in the course of a project. In systems development projects, the standard tasks are fairly well known and established in advance. Thus, while planning and scheduling are critical within the systems development life cycle, planning is done within a fairly structured context. The systems development life cycle itself provides a structure against which an individual project and its goals can be compared to see how well the standard structure matches the specific needs of an individual undertaking. For example, different systems development projects will require varying amounts of technical support, application programming, or user training. In effect, the life cycle provides a matrix against which specific projects can be planned in terms of the end results to be delivered. It also provides interim expectations at managerial checkpoints.

Scheduling

Planning identifies tasks or jobs that must be completed. **Scheduling**, then, relates the tasks in a time sequence. A project scheduling system utilizes resources, as well as time, to establish the sequence of events to be followed. Within the project structure itself, provision is made for the sequence in which jobs are done. Provisions are also made for situations in which activities and tasks should overlap and share findings and results. This basic scheduling is implicit in the project structure, but it can be no more than a skeleton. Time alone is only one dimension of scheduling.

Resources must be identified and allocated as part of the scheduling operation. Within a systems development project, the primary resources are skilled people. Therefore, part of the scheduling work lies in identifying the personnel who must be available for, and involved in, the project. In some instances, the ready availability of people will facilitate task or activity scheduling, causing jobs to be started or completed ahead of normal expectations. In other cases, a shortage of required people may constrain a project, causing delays or overlaps in scheduling. Besides people, other resources may have to be scheduled as well, such as computer time for testing the programs or time on special equipment like digitizers or optical scanners. In the final analysis, then, scheduling is the art of doing the best possible job with the resources available.

Control

Planning and scheduling take place before work is actually done. **Control** involves the monitoring of work to compare plans and schedules with actual performance. Under the control function, results are monitored in terms of time and resources expended; and, as necessary, corrective actions are taken. In extreme cases, the control function includes the responsibility for aborting projects as experience proves that the anticipated results cannot be attained. Ultimately, management decision making resides in the control function.

THE PROCESS OF PROJECT MANAGEMENT

A **project** is an extensive job involving multiple interrelated tasks. But a project has certain other important characteristics that make it manageable — that make it possible to apply project management techniques for planning, scheduling, and control. These characteristics include:

- A project is **finite**. It has a definite beginning and a specific ending point. Before a project is started, its managers should be able to define when it will be concluded. Thus, an ongoing operation, such as management of a computer center or a manufacturing plant, is not a project.

- A project is usually a one-time effort. It is **nonrepetitive**. The system may be completely redesigned at some point in the future; but for the present, it is viewed as a one-time exercise.

- A project consists of a number of segments that can be broken down into separate phases, activities, and tasks. In other words, because a project can be partitioned into identifiable parts, it is said to be **decomposed**.

- Because many tasks are involved that require an assortment of knowledge and skills, projects tend to be **complex**.

- Projects are **predictable**. In this respect, a systems development project would differ, for example, from a research program that sets out to discover some previously unknown phenomenon. In a research program, scientists follow their findings. In a project, a predetermined course of task performance is followed, because the outputs to be achieved are known.

PROJECT MANAGEMENT TECHNIQUES

The tools of project management must assist in the first two management components—planning and scheduling. These tools will also support the reporting of status that serves as a basis for control decisions. Within the CIS project structure, there are two levels of control decisions. The first is the detailed, day-to-day control of the tasks needed to keep the project on track. The second is the decision-making authority vested in an information systems steering committee. The project structure assumes that information will be funneled to the steering committee in an understandable form. Later in this chapter is a discussion of the tools that are available for planning and scheduling, including the feedback of information that will serve as a basis for control.

The challenges in planning and scheduling for projects lie in the interrelationships among activities and tasks. Therefore, the primary tools for supporting the planning and scheduling functions are directed toward dealing with these interrelationships. Two techniques that share many similarities are commonly used for this purpose. These are known as project evaluation and review technique (PERT) and critical path method (CPM).

Project Evaluation and Review Technique (PERT)

The **project evaluation and review technique (PERT)** was developed during the 1950s under the auspices of the United States Navy. PERT represents a project as a network of interrelated tasks (sometimes called activities) that are represented by arrows between nodes. The nodes indicate the beginning and ending points of each activity. The network can be evaluated to determine which activities are on the **critical path**. The critical path is the longest time path through the network. PERT can be used to review the progress of a project once it has begun; and if a project is behind schedule, it can be used to evaluate options for completing the project on time. The Navy was faced with a major project, the development of the Polaris weapon system for firing intermediate range ballistic missiles from submarines. All the characteristic features and problems of project management were present. The computer had also just emerged as a tool capable of rapid completion of all of the calculations necessary to interrelate the thousands of identified activities and tasks.

The project structure was classic in that all of the events and tasks were directed toward a specific single result—putting a weapon into service within a specified time frame. The elements of the project were complex, since multiple components and literally hundreds of manufacturers and other vendors were involved. Special ships had to be designed. Environmental problems had to be overcome in the undersea launching of missiles. Targeting, tracking, warhead, and safety systems all had to be devised and integrated. All these elements could be identified and broken down into manageable components. But there were so many elements that traditional methods of listing, scheduling, and monitoring simply couldn't do the job. PERT provides a method for project managers to:

- Identify the tasks within the project.
- Order the tasks in time sequence.
- Estimate the time required to complete each task, the relationships among tasks, and the time requirement for the entire project.
- Identify the critical tasks that must be performed individually and that, together, account for the total elapsed time of the project.
- Identify noncritical tasks for which some **slack time** could be built into schedules without affecting the duration of the entire project.

Critical Path Method (CPM)

The **Critical Path Method (CPM)** is almost identical to PERT. It was also designed as a planning and scheduling tool for major projects and it again represents a project as a network of activities separated by nodes. In addition, CPM incorporates a capability for identifying relationships between the cost and the completion date of a project, as well as the amount and value of resources that must be applied in alternative situations. On certain types of major projects, it is possible to shorten completion dates by applying greater resources to the effort. In other words, by assigning more people and spending more money, the results can be realized sooner. CPM provides a means of predicting and measuring these tradeoffs. This is accomplished by calculating a normal time estimate and a crash time estimate for each activity. Crash estimates are the amounts of time necessary to complete each activity regardless of costs. Normal estimates have cost constraints. CPM was developed at about the same time as PERT through a joint effort of the Dupont Company and the Univac Division of Remington Rand, which has since been consolidated several times into what is now the UNISYS corporation.

Comparison of Techniques

The methodologies used in PERT and CPM are essentially similar. These methodologies are described in the discussions that follow. The important differences between PERT and CPM center around the assumptions on which the techniques are based. These assumptions, in turn, deal with time allocations for scheduled tasks.

PERT permits broad estimates about the time durations of tasks. Variations in time allocations do not materially affect the use of this technique. On the other hand, CPM assumes that time requirements for the completion of individual tasks are relatively predictable. Within the CPM system also, a relationship is assumed between the time it takes to complete a task and the amount of money an organization is willing to spend by applying resources for its completion.

Because of these basic differences of approach, application areas for PERT and CPM tend to be somewhat different. For the most part, PERT is used for projects involving research and development, situations in which there are apt to be greater variations in the time consumed by individual tasks and in which there are no clear-cut tradeoffs between the application of resources and the production of results. Therefore, systems development projects have proven to be ideal candidates for the application of PERT techniques. In systems development, it is difficult to relate the allocation of resources to the time required to complete any task.

On the other hand, CPM tends to be used on projects for which direct relationships can be established between time and resources. To illustrate, in building a road, completion can be expedited if more earth moving and grading equipment is assigned to a project. The same is true with other types of construction. Therefore, construction projects and some manufacturing projects have been prime application areas for CPM techniques.

There are also some types of systems development projects for which relationships between time and resources can be established. For example, development tools have been introduced recently that can expedite systems analysis and design activities. On the other hand, simply adding more programmers to an application development assignment would not necessarily guarantee earlier completion. In fact, adding people to certain types of assignments could tend to lengthen the schedule because of the need for greater communication. Because of these features, CPM tends to be used only selectively in the systems development area.

PLANNING AND SCHEDULING NETWORKS

Both PERT and CPM use graphic networks as basic tools. Within this context, a **network** is a flow diagram relating the set of individual tasks, or jobs, that must be completed to the sequence in which they must occur. The network of tasks is presented in a graphic format known as a project graph.

To build a visual network, planners begin with a list of tasks, or jobs, as shown in Figure 3-1. This example lists the tasks to be completed during the detailed design and implementation phase of a systems development project. The tasks will lead to the design of a file updating system.

A network constructed from the task list for the file updating system is show in Figure 3-2. In this network, tasks are represented as labeled arrows leading from one circle to another. The circles in scheduling networks are known as **nodes**. The nodes identify the beginning and ending points of tasks. The estimated times for completing the tasks are listed in parentheses next to the job lines. Each node, or milestone event, is assigned a reference number. These numbers are used as alternate identifications in the basic task list in Figure 3-1. The alternate identifications, obviously, consist of the beginning and ending nodes for the task. These numbers are used as basic identification codes and serve as the basis for scheduling when network data are processed using computer programs.

In effect, Figures 3-1 and 3-2 show the same data in table and graphic form. The data in Figure 3-1 could be used directly as computer input for a program

SYSTEM DESIGN PROJECT—FILE UPDATING SYSTEM

Job Identification	Alternate Identification	Immediate Predecessor	Job Description	Time Estimate (days)
a	(1,2)	–	Design overall system structure	30
b	(2,3)	a	Develop program specifications	12
c	(3,4)	b	Design control program	8
d	(3,5)	b	Design update program	15
e	(3,6)	b	Design report program	7
f	(4,7)	c	Code control program	2
g	(4,8)	c	Prepare system user guide	5
h	(7,10)	f	Test control program	2
i	(5,9)	d	Code update program	6
j	(9,10)	i	Test update program	4
k	(10,12)	h,j	Test control/update programs	2
l	(6,11)	e	Code report program	3
m	(11,12)	l	Test report program	1
n	(12,13)	k,m	Integration test	4

that produces a graph like the one shown in Figure 3-2 on a plotter. Using the same data, **network graphs** can also be developed manually.

Finding the Critical Path

Once a network has been established for project tasks, it is possible to pick a path through the network that represents the project completion time for the project. This is done by adding the elapsed-time notations on the task lines to see how long it will take to complete the project. The idea is to form a connecting line, or path, that runs all the way through the project, representing the minimum amount of time for project completion. This minimum requirement for the project will actually represent the **longest path** through the tasks. This is because the set, or sequence, of tasks that will take the longest time to complete represents the minimum amount of time that will be required to get the whole job done. This longest path is called the **critical path**. The critical path is computed when using both PERT and CPM.

Figure 3.2. *Network diagram for file updating system project. Completion times for activities are shown in parentheses. Heavy line represents the critical path.*

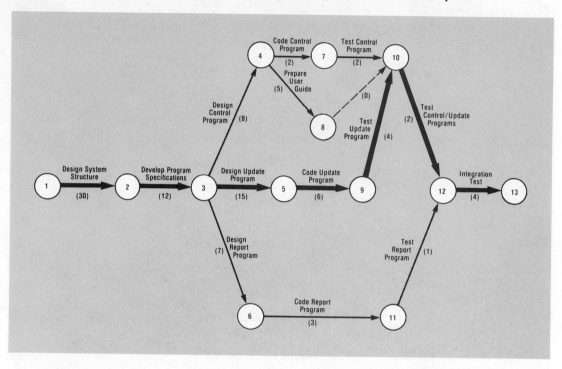

To illustrate, look at the network in Figure 3-2. Four possible paths can be traced for moving through the network from start to finish. Figure 3-3 identifies these four paths. The longest elapsed time traverses the path through nodes 1-2-3-5-9-10-12-13. This path requires a total of 73 working days. The tasks, or jobs, along the critical path are referred to as critical tasks. These tasks are critical because their combined completion time determines the duration of the entire project. Once this critical path has been identified, it is drawn in with darker lines than the other paths, as has been done in Figure 3-2. If the project duration is to be shortened, the tasks along the critical path must be completed in less time. Shortening any other task times will have no impact on the total duration of the project. On projects more complex than the one shown in Figure 3-3, there may be more than one critical path. If this happens, there will be alternate paths, each taking the same longest time span for completion.

Tasks that are not on the critical path are said to have slack. This means that these tasks can slip either in starting times or in durations without affecting the total completion time for the project as a whole. Being able to identify slack tasks can be extremely valuable in project management. Knowing a task is

Figure 3.3. *Identification of alternative paths and the critical path for the file updating system project.*

Paths (Nodes)	Times (in days)	Total Time
1 – 2 – 3 – 4 – 7 – 10 – 12 – 13	30 + 12 + 8 + 2 + 2 + 2 + 4	60
1 – 2 – 3 – 4 – 8 – 10 – 12 – 13	30 + 12 + 8 + 5 + 0 + 2 + 4	61
1 – 2 – 3 – 5 – 9 – 10 – 12 – 13	30 + 12 + 15 + 6 + 4 + 2 + 4	73 (Critical Path)
1 – 2 – 3 – 6 – 11 – 12 – 13	30 + 12 + 7 + 3 + 1 + 4	57

slack, for example, a project manager may divert resources from it to a critical one, helping to keep the entire project on schedule or reducing overall project duration.

Critical Path Algorithm

For a relatively small project like the one shown in Figure 3-3, the critical path can be located relatively easily and quickly through inspection. On major projects, however, this job can become far more tedious. In these situations, a **critical path algorithm** can be used to help identify the longest sequence of tasks. To illustrate, Figure 3-4 presents a redrawn network for the file updating system based on the data presented in Figure 3-1. The numbers within brackets in this illustration represent the task start and finish times used in applying the critical path algorithm. The source of these numbers is explained below.

Early start and finish times. To calculate project completion times, it is necessary to develop projected dates on which tasks will start and on which they will be completed. The start and completion dates are relative to the elapsed time from the very beginning of the project. The **start time** for the project, identified by the symbol S, is always zero. The **finish time** for the entire project is identified with the symbol T. The T time is always the longest time span (critical path).

The **early start** of a task is the earliest possible time at which it can begin. The symbol for early start is ES. The **early finish** time for a task, indicated by the symbol EF, is determined by adding its estimated completion time to its early start time. The symbol for the estimated completion time for a task is t_e. The formula for determining the early finish time, then, is:

$$EF = ES + t_e$$

Assuming that the starting time for a project is zero, the finish time for the first task is derived by adding the estimated time to zero. In Figure 3-4, the first task, *a*, has an early start time of zero and an early finish time of 30. These

Figure 3.4. Network graph for the file updating system project, incorporating start and finish times.

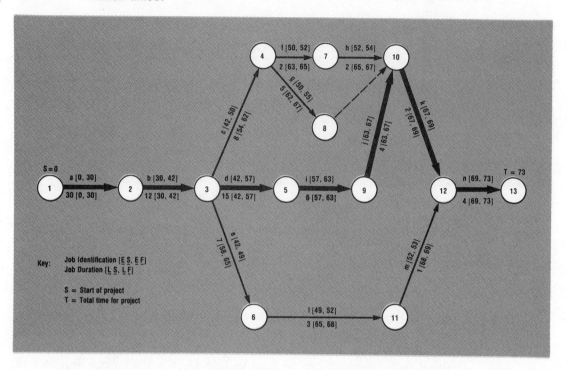

Key:
Job Identification [E S, E F]
Job Duration [L S, L F]

S = Start of project
T = Total time for project

values appear in brackets above the arrow representing this task. Continuing with the example in Figure 3-4, task *b* cannot begin until task *a* is completed. Therefore, its early start time is 30, the same as the early finish time for the previous task. The early finish time for the second task is 42, derived by adding the estimated time to the start time:

$$EF = ES + t_e = 30 + 12 = 42$$

This process is continued for each task on the network. In each instance, the early start time is the latest completion date for the preceding task. This is illustrated in the situation of task *k*. The early start time assigned to this task is 67. This represents the latest of the early finish times for the three jobs that must be completed before task *k* can begin. Task *h* has an early finish time of 54. Task *g* has an early finish time of 55, while task *j* has a finish time of 67. Thus, 67 represents the earliest possible start time for task *k*.

After all tasks along the critical path have been traced in this manner, the early finish time for the last task becomes the total duration time for the project. In the network in Figure 3-4, the early finish time, T, is 73 days. This means that, unless one or more of the critical path tasks can be shortened, the project will require 73 days to complete. Note the line of dashes between node 8 and node 10 in Figure 3-4. This line indicates that task *g* must be completed before task k can start, in other words it expresses a precedence relationship. It is not, however, a task itself because it does not consume resources and takes no time. It is there only to indicate that task g precedes task k.

Late start and late finish times. As noted previously, the tasks not on the critical path offer some slack time. If these tasks are delayed, they will not slow down the entire project unless the delays become so long that they push the task onto the critical path. Thus, it may be possible to shift some people or other resources from slack tasks to critical ones to shorten the entire length of the project. If a project manager wishes to consider these possibilities, it can help to identify slack tasks and calculate the amount of slack that actually exists. This is done by calculating late start and finish times for the slack tasks.

The **late start**, or LS, of a task is the latest time at which it can begin without extending the total project completion time. The **late finish**, or LF, of the task is determined by adding the task duration to its late start time. Thus, to determine the latest possible start time for any task, its elapsed time is deducted from its late finish time:

$$\mathbf{LS = LF - t_e}$$

Calculation of late start and late finish times for a network begin at the end of the network and work backward toward the beginning. In Figure 3-4, this has been done with numbers placed in brackets below the task lines. An example of how slack time can be computed for noncritical tasks is shown in the case of task m. This task must be completed before day 69, when task n must begin. The early dates for this task have been computed as 52 to start, 53 for completion, since the task takes only one day. Working backward, the calculations show that, since this task can conclude as late as day 69; it can also begin as late as day 68. Therefore, the potential slack time for task m — derived by deducting the early start date (52) from the late start date (68) — is 16 days. This same slack time, 16 days, applies to the difference between the late and early finish dates. This time is known as the **total slack** for task m.

Time calculations for the tasks in the file-updating system are shown in Figure 3-5. The data in this table correspond with all the information in the network in Figure 3-4. Separate columns list time estimates for each task: the early start date, the late start date, the early finish date, the late finish date, and the total slack. Thus, tasks with slack time can be identified quickly and easily by reading the figures in the last column. Any tasks on the critical path will have zero slack time. A listing of this type, clearly, becomes a management tool for the possible reassignment or reallocation of resources within the project. The time-estimating examples cited so far are based upon the acceptance of the estimated time for each task as a fixed time for its completion.

In reality, time estimating cannot be done with this precision. The completion time for many tasks cannot be pinpointed this closely. Rather, there will be a range of time estimates for each task. These estimated times will usually be represented by low, medium, and high figures. The PERT method provides a means for dealing with these variations in elapsed time estimates for individual tasks.

Figure 3.5. *Calculations and listings of activity and slack times, including total slack, for the file updating system project.*

Job Identification	Job Description	Time Estimate (t_e)	Early Start (ES)	Late Start (LS)	Early Finish (EF)	Late Finish (LF)	Total Slack (days)
a	Design overall system structure	30	0	0	30	30	0
b	Develop program specifications	12	30	30	42	42	0
c	Design control program	8	42	54	50	62	12
d	Design update program	15	42	42	57	57	0
e	Design report program	7	42	58	49	65	16
f	Code control program	2	50	63	52	65	13
g	Prepare system user guide	5	50	62	55	67	12
h	Test control program	2	52	65	54	67	13
i	Code update program	6	57	57	63	63	0
j	Test update program	4	63	63	67	67	0
k	Test control/update programs	2	67	67	69	69	0
l	Code report program	3	49	65	52	68	16
m	Test report program	1	52	68	53	69	16
n	Integration test	4	69	69	73	73	0

PERT Time Estimates

Under the PERT method, three time estimates are made for each task. These estimates are:

- The **optimistic time estimate** (t_o) represents the best guess of the minimum time required to complete the task. This estimate assumes that all conditions will be ideal.
- The **most probable time estimate** (t_m) represents the best guess of the time that will be required to complete a task, assuming a normal number of problems or delays.
- The **pessimistic time estimate** (t_p) allows for the maximum completion time, assuming that everything that can go wrong will go wrong.

The expected duration of a task is then computed as the weighted average of the three time estimates. That is, it is assumed that the optimistic and pessimistic time estimates are equally likely to occur, while the most probable time estimate

Part 1   Information Systems: Basic Development Concepts

is four times more likely to occur than either of the other two. Applying these relative weights, the formula for calculating the average, or expected, time to complete a task (t_e) is:

$$t_e = \frac{t_o + 4t_m + t_p}{6}$$

To see the application of this formula, refer to Figure 3-1. This table shows that the initial task in the project, *a*, has been allocated 30 days of elapsed time. This figure was derived from application of the formula given above with an optimistic estimate of 18 days, a most probable time estimate of 28 days, and a pessimistic estimate of 50 days. Applying the formula to these estimates produces the following result:

$$t_e = \frac{t_o + 4t_m + t_p}{6} = \frac{18 + 4(28) + 50}{6} = \frac{180}{6} = 30 \text{ days}$$

The expected time for the first task (t_e) is 30 days. This same figure is calculated, in the same manner, for each of the time estimates appearing in the table in Figure 3-1 and in the network diagrams illustrated in this chapter. The total expected time for the entire project is then estimated by adding the time estimates for the critical path tasks. The total estimated time for the file updating system project comes to 73 days.

SUPERPROJECT PLUS: AN AUTOMATED PROJECT MANAGEMENT TOOL

INTRODUCTION

SuperProject Plus combines the classic techniques of project and resource management with the latest in software development to give you an effective tool for managing your projects. SuperProject Plus's graphic display of project information and its use of the latest methods of schedule evaluation allow management of tasks, resources, and money with efficiencies that are not possible by manual methods. SuperProject Plus will run on an IBM PC XT, AT, or any IBM-compatible system with a hard disk using MS/DOS 2.0 or higher.

What Does SuperProject Plus Do?

SuperProject Plus gives you the tools to simplify project control while using the techniques of project management.

Quite simply, SuperProject Plus allows you to define the tasks, the order in which they appear, how long they should take and when they must be completed, and who should complete them. You may then evaluate your schedule and its feasibility, track your project progress, and readjust your project plans.

With a few keystrokes, you can see how changes in resources, time required, start dates, and other data will affect your schedule. SuperProject Plus's features include:

- Multiple task and time relationships (finish-to-finish, start-to-start, finish-to-start, with lead/lag).
- Baseline scheduling for comparison with current schedules.
- Resource pooling, resource dependent scheduling.
- Resolution of conflicts through resource leveling, leveling between projects.
- User-defined subsets for viewing and reporting.
- Fixed and variable costs (planned and actual) by task, resource, and project.
- SuperProject Plus has both a beginner mode which allows you to use a limited set of instructions and selections and an expert mode to gain access to the more complex features in the system.

Why Use SuperProject Plus?

Surprisingly, it can take as much time to develop a schedule using SuperProject Plus as to develop it by hand. What then is the real power of SuperProject Plus?

As discussed earlier, the true power of SuperProject Plus is not planning but replanning. You get to ask "what if" questions that would be prohibitive on a manual system. And, remembering that a plan is as dynamic as the real world, this is a tremendous advantage.

What if the key decision is delayed a week? How will it impact the deadline? What can be done to make up lost time? How will increased labor costs impact the cost of the project? If two projects are in conflict over resources, how will that affect long-term results? If there are several projects in the organization, how can personnel be distributed most efficiently?

Computer Associates, 2195 Fortune Drive, San Jose, CA 95131.

GANTT CHARTS

Networking techniques provide tools for planning and scheduling project tasks. To complete the project management picture, some method for monitoring actual project performance and for reaching decisions about changes in project tasks or structures is necessary. A well-established, commonly used visual tool for displaying time relationships and monitoring progress toward project completion is the **Gantt chart**.

Gantt charts have been standard methods for displaying schedules and work status for production methods since the 1920s. Through the years, they have been adapted to serve the same purposes in multiple-activity projects.

A Gantt chart representing the schedule established in Figure 3-5 is shown in Figure 3-6. This illustration also indicates some of the basic characteristics of Gantt charts, which include:

- Tasks that make up a project are listed vertically, in order of occurrence, starting at the top left of the chart.
- A **time scale** is indicated at either the top or the bottom of the chart. This scale reads from left to right.
- A bar showing the estimated time for each task is drawn in the appropriate time position on the same line as the task listing.
- The current date is indicated on the chart, usually through use of a movable tape or cord.
- An indication of percentage completion is given for each task on which work has begun.

In Figure 3-6, the solid parts of the bars represent the length of time between the early start and early finish dates calculated for each task. (They also represent the time required to complete the task.) To illustrate, task c, *design control*

Figure 3.6.   Gantt chart for the file updating project.

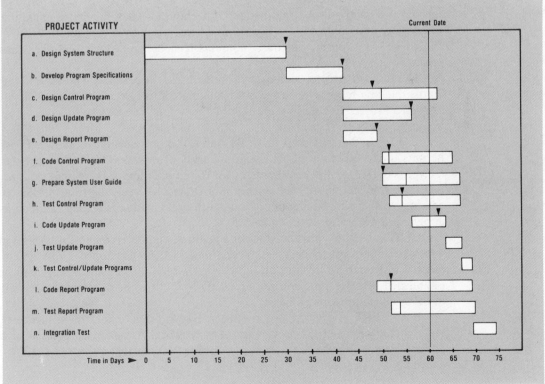

program, had an early start day of 42 and an early finish day of 50. A total of eight days had been estimated for this job. However, since this job was not on the critical path and had 12 slack days, it could be completed as late as day 62 without delaying the project. In Figure 3-6, the available slack days are shown, for tasks on which slack is available, by the white or open areas of the bars.

Figure 3-6 uses an arrowhead to indicate the **percentage of completion** for each task. Task *c*, for example, is approximately 75 percent complete. Although the current date is now past the expected early finish time for this task, the project can still remain on schedule as long as the work is finished before the slack time elapses.

Note, in the entry for task *i*, *Code Update Program*, that work is ahead of schedule. Since this is a critical task, it may be possible to advance the schedule for the entire project — even though some jobs not on the critical path are behind schedule.

Gantt charts can be developed directly from the task list and time estimates. It is not necessary to have a critical path network to prepare a Gantt chart. This technique is also flexible enough to fit into any project management method.

SUMMARY

The systems development life cycle provides a framework for project management — a method or combination of techniques that facilitates planning, scheduling, and control. A project is an extensive job involving multiple, interrelated tasks. A project is finite, nonrepetitive, decomposable, complex, and predictable.

The tools of project management must assist in planning and scheduling. Status must be reported as a basis for making control decisions. Two available tools are Project Evaluation and Review Technique (PERT) and Critical Path Method (CPM).

The methodologies used in PERT and CPM are essentially similar. PERT permits broad estimates about the time durations of tasks. On the other hand, CPM assumes that time requirements for the completion of individual tasks are relatively predictable. A relationship is assumed between the time it takes to complete a task and the amount of money an organization is willing to spend by applying resources for its completion.

PERT is used for projects involving research and development, situations in which there are apt to be greater variations in time consumed by individual tasks. CPM tends to be used on projects for which direct relationships can be established between time and resources. CPM tends to be used only selectively in the systems development area.

Both PERT and CPM use graphic networks, that relate the sequence of tasks to the sequence of occurrence. The network of tasks is presented in a project graph. The chapter describes methods for creating and analyzing these networks.

A visual tool for displaying time relationships and monitoring progress of project completion is the Gantt chart. Gantt charts and their uses are also described.

KEY TERMS

1. project management
2. planning
3. scheduling
4. control
5. project
6. finite
7. nonrepetitive
8. decomposable
9. complex
10. predictable
11. Project Evaluation and Review Technique (PERT)
12. critical task
13. slack time
14. Critical Path Method (CPM)
15. network
16. project graph
17. node
18. longest path
19. critical path
20. critical path algorithm
21. start time (S)
22. finish time (T)
23. early start (ES)
24. early finish (EF)
25. late start (LS)
26. late finish (LF)
27. total slack
28. optimistic time estimate
29. most probable time estimate
30. pessimistic time estimate
31. Gantt chart
32. time scale
33. percentage completion

REVIEW/DISCUSSION QUESTIONS

1. How does the systems development life cycle support the need for project management tools?
2. What are the main functions of project management and what are the characteristics of each?
3. What are the characteristics of a project?
4. What types of projects generally apply PERT techniques?
5. What types of projects generally apply CPM techniques?
6. What are the basic differences between PERT and CPM techniques?
7. What are the relationships among tasks, nodes, and networks?
8. What is the critical path and how are critical path algorithms applied?
9. How can identification of slack time assist in project management control?
10. What relationships are shown in Gantt charts?

PRACTICE ASSIGNMENTS

1. Using the network diagram in Figure 3-7 and the activity table in Figure 3-8, determine the critical path tasks and the total slack for each task in the network. Redraw the diagram to include the same types of information shown in Figure 3-4.

2. Using the information in Figure 3-9, prepare a Gantt chart showing the early start, early finish, and late finish times as illustrated in Figure 3-6. The current date is twelve days past the beginning of the project.

Figure 3.7. Network diagram for use in Practice Assignment 1.

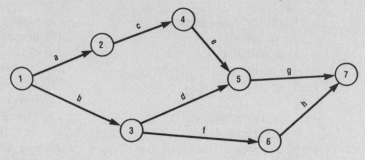

Figure 3.8. Project activity table for use in Practice Assignment 1.

Job Identification	Alternate Identification	Immediate Predecessor	Time Estimate (Days)
a	(1.2)	-	30
b	(1.3)	—	28
c	(2.4)	a	10
d	(3.5)	b	20
e	(4.5)	c	15
f	(3.6)	b	42
g	(5.7)	d,e	17
h	(6.7)	f	22

Figure 3.9. Data for use in preparation of Gantt chart to be completed as Practice Assignment 2.

Project Activity	ES	EF	LS	LF	Duration	Percentage Complete
A	0	5	6	11	5	100
B	0	3	0	3	3	100
C	5	9	11	15	4	75
D	3	10	3	10	7	100
E	9	11	15	17	2	50
F	10	15	10	15	5	60
G	11	14	17	20	3	33
H	15	20	15	20	5	0

Systems Analysis
Modeling Techniques

Systems analysis can be complex and confusing work. The analyst must deal with large amounts of highly detailed and often conflicting information. The analyst needs a way to organize the information, determine where there are gaps in understanding, and identify areas of conflicting or redundant operations. Modeling techniques provide this mechanism.

Two types of models are of interest to the analyst: process and data. Chapter 4, Process Analysis Techniques, presents a modeling technique that focuses on the basic business functions or processes of the business area. It also models the data transformed by these processes and transported between them. Chapter 5, Data Analysis Techniques, provides for an alternate view of the same business area. This view focuses on the key entities of the business—those objects about which data are to be collected.

Analysis is an iterative process. The basic steps of analysis are repeated with increasing levels of detail as the analyst's understanding grows. The modeling techniques must be able to support this iteration, and the data and process models must be coordinated with one another during the process. This is covered in Chapter 6, Using the Techniques: The Modeling Process.

While modeling techniques provide a means of organizing the information and knowledge generated by analysts, the sheer quantity of this information on even moderately large jobs can be overwhelming. It becomes very difficult to maintain the accuracy, completeness, and consistency of the many components. Some type of automation is necessary. This is addressed in the final chapter of this section, Chapter 7, Automating the Development Process: CASE Tools.

4

Process Analysis Techniques

Learning Objectives

On completing the reading and other learning assignments for this chapter, you should be able to:

- Explain the importance of communication in systems analysis.
- Describe the role that modeling, especially with data flow diagrams, can play in effective communication.
- Read and interpret data flow diagrams.
- Evaluate data flow diagrams for mechanical correctness, meaningful names, and correct hierarchical notation and balancing.
- Explain the purpose of a context diagram, diagram 0, and child diagrams and the relationships among them.
- Follow a step by step process for constructing data flow diagrams based on an understanding of key business events.
- Document data structures using three basic constructs—sequence, iteration, and selection.
- Specify processing rules using narratives, decision trees, decision tables, and structured English.
- Use this combination of modeling tools to document an existing system.

MODELING IN SYSTEMS DEVELOPMENT

Systems analysis is the key component of the first two phases of the systems development life cycle. In phase 1, investigation, systems analysis techniques help to build an understanding of existing systems, of the business need that has brought about a request for change, and of the potential solutions to meet that need. In phase 2, analysis and general design, systems analysis is used to further this understanding and to produce specifications for a new system that will meet user needs and requirements. The completion of these new system specifications is the central goal of systems analysis. These specifications, in turn, form the basis for the general design activity that begins in phase 2 and for the detailed design work of phase 3, detailed design and implementation.

Communication: The Need for Models

New system specifications are challenging to produce, in part, because of the critical communications links involved. The specifications for a new system must be understandable to both the user and the designer. The user must be able to verify their accuracy and completeness. The designer must be able to use them as a basis for an accurate, detailed design. The systems analyst, then, is the key communication link between users, who generally have a business outlook, and designers, who have a more technical orientation and outlook.

Communication is the act of imparting information that is understood by its intended receiver. Communication has two parts: *presentation* and *understanding*. If either ingredient is missing, communication fails. Presentation alone is not enough. The real challenge in communication lies in assuring that understanding takes place. A key responsibility of the systems analyst is to facilitate *understanding* between users and systems designers.

The method of presentation has a major impact on the ability of the receiver to understand the information. Historically, a common method of presentation has been the **narrative description**. But this causes problems for analysts. Business requirements, data content, procedures, and so on are all described in words. When a large, complex system is involved, narrative descriptions can become extremely lengthy and difficult to understand. System specification narratives that reach as many as eight or ten volumes would not be uncommon.

The length and complexity of narrative descriptions is due to the high degree of accuracy, precision, and completeness they must convey. Using words alone, this can be extremely difficult. In some situations, it is virtually impossible.

To illustrate, consider the following narrative description of a procedure to be applied in the billing system for the Associated Grocers of America. AGA is a grocery warehouse operation selling to retailers—both AGA members and nonmembers. The following description involves AGA's discount policy:

> A minimum 5 percent discount applies for all purchases. If the retailer maintains an average monthly purchase volume of at least $100,000, a 15 percent discount applies, provided the retailer is an AGA member. When the retailer's purchase volume is under $100,000, the discount rate is 12 percent for AGA members and 7 percent for nonmembers. Retailers who are not AGA members, but who maintain an average $100,000 monthly purchase volume, qualify for a 10 percent discount, unless the individual purchase totals less than $35,000.

Now, imagine yourself as either a user or a system designer reading a few hundred, or even a thousand, pages of this kind of narrative. Even after a thorough reading, would you feel comfortable writing program specifications and coding if this were the only documentation you had to work with? Could you be sure that the explanations and documentation contained in these narratives were accurate and complete? Would you be able to maintain objectivity — an understanding of the major components of the system and their relationships — without becoming lost in the hundreds of pages of details? System models are designed to overcome these problems.

This text stresses a set of graphic modeling techniques and a related analysis process that can help assure understanding — the key component of communication. This chapter and the next cover the models and basic construction techniques. The use of these models to support the analysis process is covered in Chapter 6. First, to set the stage, you should understand which graphic modeling techniques are available and what characteristics you should look for in an effective set of techniques to support analysis.

Modeling Alternatives

A number of different modeling techniques are used in systems development. This chapter discusses in detail a set of modeling techniques based on data flow diagrams. These techniques, because of their simplicity and clarity, are very effective for enhancing communication between users and systems designers. In addition, the resulting models form a good foundation from which to begin design work. Data flow diagrams themselves stress the flow and transformation of data within a system. They tend to hide timing and control features of the system. This is good, since it enhances the ability of the analyst to discover redundancies and inaccuracies in the way data are processed by the current system and eliminate them from the new system. It means, however, that data flow diagrams alone do not constitute a complete model, even for analysis. Supporting documentation — in the form of a data dictionary, processes descriptions, and some narrative — is necessary.

Chapter 5 discusses techniques for modeling data using entity-relationship or E-R models. E-R models stress data — how they are organized and how they are accessed. Data flow diagrams, on the other hand, stress the processes or transformations that are applied to data. They do not emphasize data access paths, nor do they emphasize control and timing of events. In fact, they tend to hide these items.

No graphic modeling technique covers all features of a system equally well. This is not bad. Hiding certain features helps to highlight others. It allows focus to be brought to different aspects of the system separately. The key for the system developer is to know several modeling techniques, apply them at the correct time, and integrate the results of each into a complete picture or model of the system.

Finally, there is a great deal of work being done to automate various parts of the development process. This is giving rise to new graphical modeling techniques—each technique being particularly appropriate for the given approach to automation.

Before turning to a detailed study of data flow diagrams, it is a good idea to briefly review what should be expected from modeling techniques that support the analysis process.

Requirements for Effective Analysis Modeling Tools

As stated earlier, the foremost requirement of an effective modeling technique is to support understanding and, hence, communication among users, analysts, and designers. This implies several very specific, practical things.

The modeling technique must be able to clearly convey the **scope** and **business objective** of the system. A way is needed to specify concisely to both users and developers what data, functions, and procedures are considered to be within (and, hence, not within) the scope of the system under development.

The modeling technique must be able to *deal with complexity* by logically organizing large amounts of information. This organization should enhance the iterative, layered approach to analysis that is a natural part of the system development life cycle. In a hierarchical, top-down fashion the model should support the partitioning of the entire system into its major components or subsystems, the further partitioning each of these components, and so on.

Finally, the modeling technique should be powerful enough to allow us to build a **user specification** document that is at once complete, unambiguous, accurate, and verifiable by the user. It should then support the derivation of a **general design specification** that can be directly related to the user specification and can serve as a base for the detailed system design activity that follows analysis.

DATA FLOW DIAGRAMS

Data flow diagrams are exceedingly easy to read and understand. For this reason, they serve as a strong communication vehicle, especially in dealings with users. Most users, with minimal background knowledge, can readily read, understand, and verify models based on data flow diagrams.

The Power of Data Flow Diagrams to Communicate—An Example

Figures 4-1 and 4-2 are data flow diagrams that constitute a portion of the model of a student registration system. It is presented here not to discuss that system in detail but rather to begin to gain an appreciation for the wealth of information that can be conveyed by a fairly simple picture.

Figure 4-1 is known as a **context diagram.** From this diagram it is clear, for example, that a student submits a registration request to the system and may receive a class schedule, a tuition bill, and an accounts receivable statement from the system. But the real power here is that the *scope* of the entire system can be understood at a glance. A user or analyst knows exactly which other

Figure 4.1. Context diagram for student registration system.

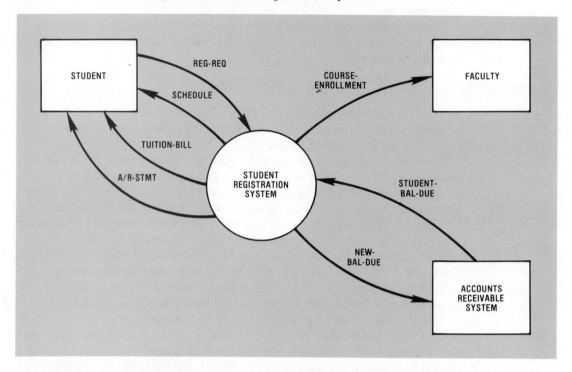

systems or classes of people interact with this registration system and exactly what data are involved in that interaction.

Figure 4-2 is known as a **Diagram 0** for the system. It is the next level of detail under the context diagram. It models the major activities or processes that occur within the student registration system and the data that flow between them. Look, for example, at process 2, add student to class list. Individual class requests for a student, presumably from the student's registration request, enter this process. The outgoing data flows imply that the class list file is checked to see if the class is still open. If it is, the student's ID is added to the list for that class and the student's record in the master file is updated. Then information about this class or notification that the class is closed is sent on to process 3.

The system illustrated by Figure 4-2 is admittedly oversimplified. But notice, nevertheless, the power of this model. In addition to the specific processes and data flows, a glance reveals the overall structure and organization of the system, the relationships between the various parts, and the scope or boundary of each part. It is easy to imagine that the way to add more detail to this model would be to treat each of the five processes in Diagram 0 as a standalone, independent context diagram, then create the corresponding Diagram 0 for each of them. In fact, as is discussed later, this is exactly what happens.

While it is relatively easy to learn to read data flow diagrams, it does require some skill and practice to build them. And it requires even more experi-

Figure 4.2.   Diagram 0 for student registration system.

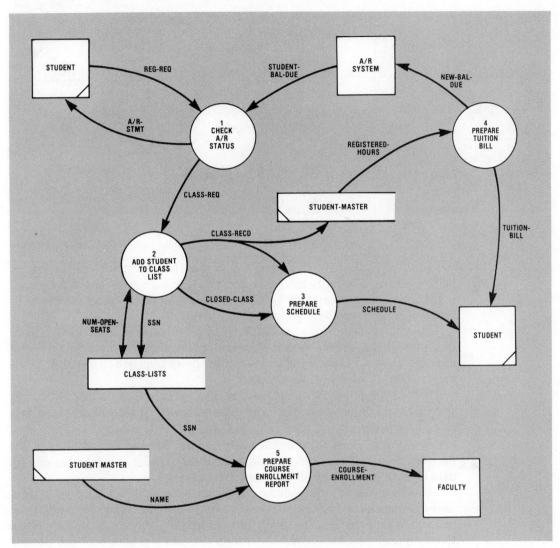

ence to build them well. It is the goal of this section to provide a set of techniques and insights that will spell the difference between a mediocre model and one that communicates crisply and clearly — and at the same time forms a solid foundation for a high quality system design.

Data Flow Diagram Building Blocks

Data flow diagrams are built using a set of four simple, standard symbols (see Figure 4-3). The meaning and use of each symbol is reviewed briefly below.

Chapter 4   Process Analysis Techniques   **83**

Figure 4.3. Data flow diagram symbols.

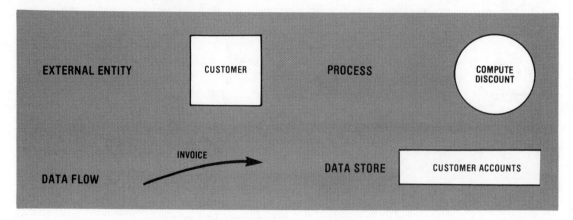

External Entity. A rectangle indicates any entity external to the system being modeled. The entity represented by a rectangle can be a class of people, an organization, or even another system. The function of an external entity is to supply data to or receive data from the system.

Data Flow. Data flows are indicated by arrows marking the movement of data through the system. A data flow can be thought of as a pipeline carrying individual packets of data from an identified point of origin to a specific destination. Data flows denote data in motion.

Process. Bubbles, or circles, are used to indicate those points within the system at which incoming data flows are processed or transformed into outgoing data flows.

Data Store. Open rectangles are used to identify temporary holding points for collections of data. Processes can add data to, retrieve data from, or modify data in these stores. Data stores denote data at rest.

Return to the student registration system illustrated in Figure 4-2 and review that data flow diagram in light of these definitions. What are the external entities? What data elements would likely be held in the two data stores? If data flows represent packets of data, what is the likely structure of the packets labeled REG-REQ and SCHEDULE?

In Figure 4-2 note that both the external entity STUDENT and the data store STUDENT-MASTER appear twice. The reason for this repetition is to avoid crossing data flow lines. A special convention has been established for handling this type of situation. If an external entity must be repeated, each occurrence is marked with a single slash in the lower right corner. If a second external entity is repeated, a double slash is used for each occurrence of that entity, and so on. A similar convention is used when data stores are repeated, with the slashes appearing in the lower left corner. Slashes simply allow the viewer to quickly associate the multiple occurrences of a given symbol with one another.

The Importance of Names

It is clear from the model of the student registration system that the set of names used for the various components greatly influences how well the model communicates. Data flows named "flow 1," "flow 2," or even "registration data" do not communicate nearly as much information as "class request." And a process labeled "Frank processes the registration request" is a nice tribute to Frank; but the label "check A/R status" communicates much more.

The diagram components should be given brief, clear, and meaningful names that support the description of the system. Two simple rules should be kept in mind when assigning names:

■ Data flows and data stores should receive names that describe the *composition of the data* involved.

■ Process bubbles should be named using *strong, active verbs and objects* to stress the basic data transformation or process that is occurring in that bubble.

When trying to sketch the initial draft of a data flow diagram, it is common first to consider several key processes and then to concentrate carefully on the data flowing from one to another. As a result, data flows are often named first. The flows in and out of a process, in effect, define the role of that process. A clear understanding of the role usually suggests an appropriate name for the process.

Beginning early in the construction process, it is a good idea to periodically pause and evaluate the names assigned up to that point using the two rules listed above. Fuzzy names for data flows and stores and weak or mushy verbs for processes usually indicate a lack of understanding about what is happening. Thus a periodic evaluation of the names that have been assigned can serve as a guide to areas where more analysis work needs to be done.

Construction Hints

The next section presents a process for constructing a data flow diagram to model an entire system. First, however, it will be helpful to review several general construction hints. They are simple rules designed to help avoid the common pitfalls people experience when they attempt to construct their first models:

■ *Use bubbles only to show processing or transformation of data.* Avoid thinking of computer program commands as processing steps. For example, look at the two data flow diagrams in Figure 4-4. Figure 4-4 (a) includes a process bubble for the reading of an order from a transaction file. The data themselves have not been processed or transformed in any way. Therefore, this process bubble is not necessary, and the diagram should be revised as shown in Figure 4-4 (b).

■ *Data flows must begin and/or end at a process bubble.* That is, there must be a processing function associated with each data flow. Data flows may not begin and end at data stores or external entities. As an example, com-

Figure 4.4. Drawing (a) contains an incorrect data flow diagram component: READ ORDER is not a process. Drawing (b) is the correct method for presenting the same procedure.

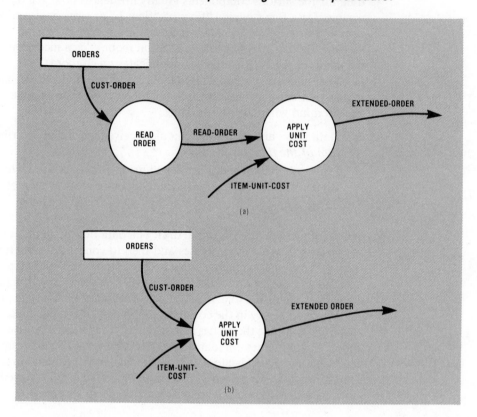

pare the two diagrams in Figure 4-5. This partial system is designed to provide a daily report about inventory status to a purchasing office. Data on parts received update an inventory file. The inventory file then serves as the basis for the purchasing office report content. The data flow diagram in Figure 4-5 (a) is incorrect because it shows data flows beginning and ending at data stores and/or external entities. In effect, this is a processing diagram with no processing shown. The correct way to diagram this procedure is shown in Figure 4-5 (b).

■ *Show only the flow of data, not associated controls.* As an example, compare the two diagrams in Figure 4-6. This partial system processes three types of transactions, identified by numbers 1, 2, and 3. Corresponding processing steps applied to these transactions are identified as A, B, and C. In Figure 4-6 (a), all of the program control logic has been diagrammed. This diagram does not really show the flow of data but instead shows the

Figure 4.5. *Drawing (a) is incorrect because processing bubbles have been omitted. Drawing (b) shows a correct approach.*

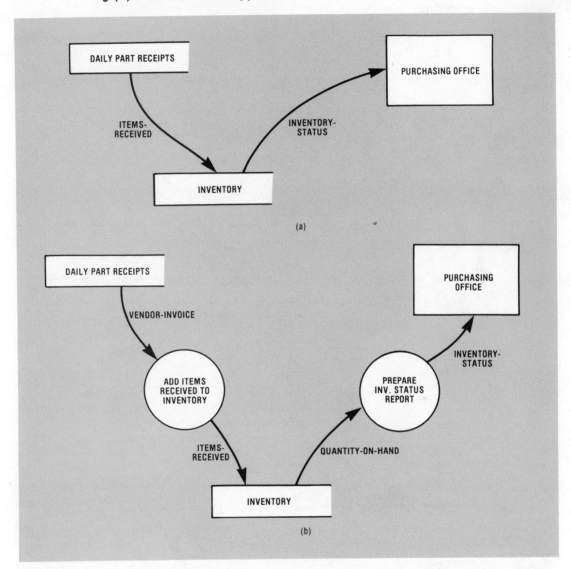

flow of program processing. The correct way to represent this partial system in a data flow diagram is shown in Figure 4-6 (b).

■ *Data flow diagrams can be given a quick visual check to identify obvious errors.* For example, look at the abstraction of a data flow diagram shown in Figure 4-7. Note that the first processing bubble, P1, receives three inputs but does not put out any data. Something is obviously wrong.

Figure 4.6. Drawing (a) is incorrect, providing an extreme example of overemphasis of control in a data flow diagram. Drawing (b) is a correct presentation for this procedure.

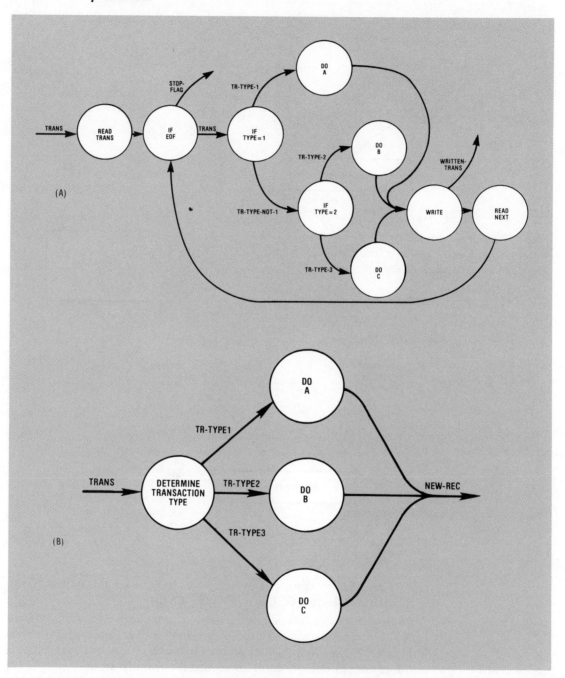

Part 2   Systems Analysis Modeling Techniques

Figure 4.7 Locate the six errors in this abstract data flow diagram.

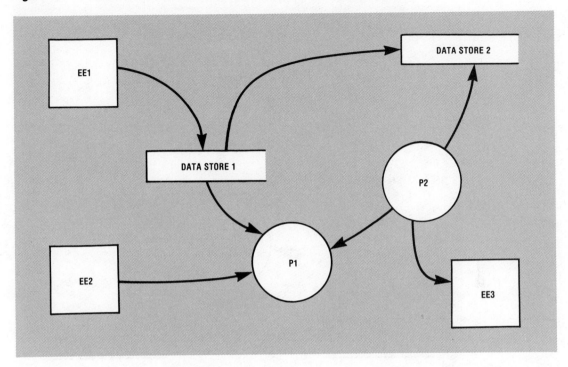

■ PRACTICE EXERCISES

This is a good point to stop and verify your understanding of the basic construction principles. Try the following three practice exercises:

1. The diagram in Figure 4-7 has six errors. One of these errors was identified in the discussion above. What are the remaining errors?
2. Critique the three data flow diagram segments shown in Figure 4-8.
3. Draw a data flow diagram to represent a simplified inventory system whose main processing is described as follows: When parts are received from VENDORS, they are accompanied by an INVOICE. The invoice is first checked against the ORDER file to verify that the parts were actually ordered. (Unordered parts are returned.) If they were ordered, the PART-QUANTITY for those particular parts is updated in the INVENTORY file. For accepted parts, a PAYMENT is sent to the vendor, and the payment transaction is entered in the GENERAL LEDGER file. To check parts out of inventory, people on the shop floor submit a REQUISITION. This requisition form is used to update the inventory file. Each week, the complete inventory file is processed to identify parts whose part-quantity has fallen below the REORDER-POINT. For each such part, a PURCHASE-REQUEST issent to the PURCHASING OFFICE.

Figure 4.8.   Critique the three partial data flow diagrams.

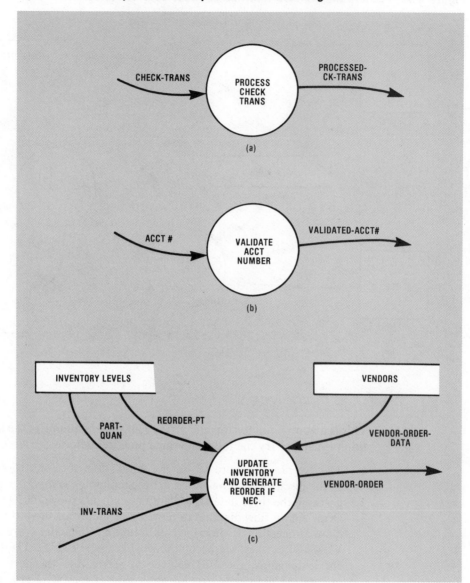

Preparing to Model an Existing System

The focus in the following sections is on using data flow diagrams to model an entire system. Two key skills are essential:

■   First is the ability to partition data flow diagrams into multiple levels in a manner that is consistent with the iterative analysis process. During this process, greater and greater levels of detail are analyzed and documented.

■ Second is the ability to take the bits and pieces of information from a given iteration or level of detail and express them in a single, unified, coherent data flow diagram.

HIERARCHICAL (TOP-DOWN) PARTITIONING OF DATA FLOW DIAGRAMS

The purpose of data flow diagrams is to communicate—to make the relationship among system components clear. One of the basic requirements for effective communication is simplicity. If data flow diagrams become too complex, it becomes difficult to trace data flows and transformations—and their purpose is defeated.

The mechanism used to keep data flow diagrams simple and understandable is a technique known as **hierarchical** or **top-down partitioning**. Partitioning of data flow diagrams means breaking out details associated with individual processing bubbles to create new diagrams that show data flows and transformations in greater detail. (This technique is also referred to as *decomposition*.)

Even a moderate-size computer information system, if it were to be represented in a single data flow diagram, might require as many as 200 separate process bubbles. With this degree of complexity, data flows and transformations would be extremely difficult to follow, and the diagram would be hard to understand. The same amount of information can be presented, instead, using multiple levels of relatively simple data flow diagrams. With a structured system of identification and numbering, increasing levels of detail can be added without creating confusion.

The starting point is the *context diagram,* which, in effect, defines the scope of the system. The context diagram documents the system inputs and sources of those inputs as well as the system outputs an destination of the outputs. These sources and destinations are external entities—departments, other systems, etc. They represent the boundaries of the system.

A *Diagram 0* is used to describe, at a high level, the overall processing in the system. The scope of the system presented in Diagram 0 remains the same as in the context diagram. Consider the abstract context diagram in Figure 4-9. The Diagram 0 shown in Figure 4-10 still contains all of the same inputs and outputs as the context diagram. The only difference is that the single, central bubble in Figure 4-9 has been partitioned or decomposed into a series of components. At the Diagram 0 level, the process bubbles represent major system components, or major subsystems within an overall system.

Now consider the subsystem represented by process P5 in Figure 4-10. It has two inputs (labeled S2 and I2) and two outputs (labeled F5 and F6). The processing that occurs in P5 can be modeled by partitioning P5 into a separate, lower level data flow diagram called Diagram 5. The products of this partitioning process are often referred to as **parent** and **child**. Thus, the process P5 in Figure 4-10 would be considered the parent, and the exploded, lower-level Diagram 5 shown in Figure 4-11 would be the child. Note that the net input and

Figure 4.9. **This is an abstract context diagram.**

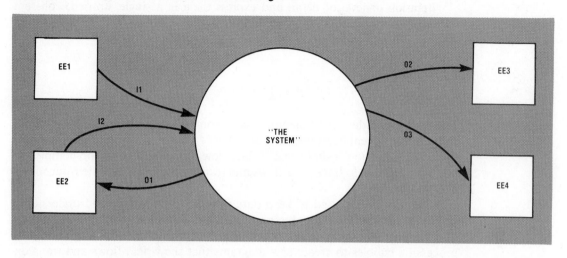

Figure 4.10. **This is an abstract Diagram 0 corresponding with the context diagram in Figure 4.9.**

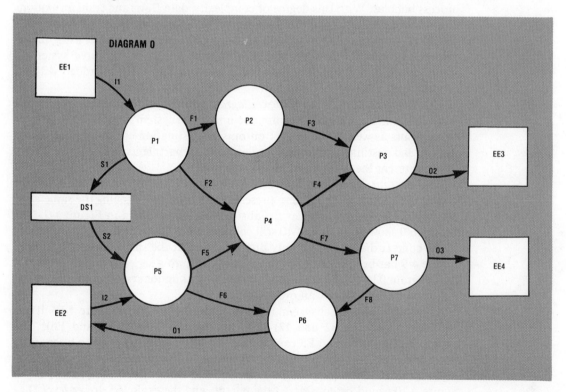

output data flows in the child diagram are S2, I2 and F5, F6 — exactly the same as the input and output flows for the parent process, P5, in Figure 4-10.

At this point the model consists of three levels of diagrams: a context diagram, a Diagram 0, and a set of lower-level child diagrams (Diagram 1, Diagram 2, . . .). Normally there would be one child diagram for each process in Diagram 0.

Some of the processes involved in the child diagrams may be straightforward and easy to understand. At the same time; others might be fairly complex and require further partitioning. For example in Diagram 5 (Figure 4-11), it might be necessary to explode process 5.2. Using process 5.2 as the parent, the child diagram would be called Diagram 5.2 and its processes would be labeled 5.2.1, 5.2.2, and so on. This method of labeling diagrams and processes nicely supports the hierarchical nature of the resulting method. This partitioning can continue to as many levels as necessary in order to define the various processes.

Balancing Parent-Child Diagrams

As succeeding levels of data flow diagrams are developed, it is important to maintain a balance in content. This balance has two dimensions: data and function.

First, the flows in and out of the parent bubble should be the same as the flows in and out of the entire child diagram. This data balancing has already been illustrated using Process 5 in Figure 4-10 and its child, Diagram 5, in Figure 4-11.

Figure 4.11. *This is an abstract Diagram 5 corresponding with process P5 of the Diagram 0 in Figure 4-10.*

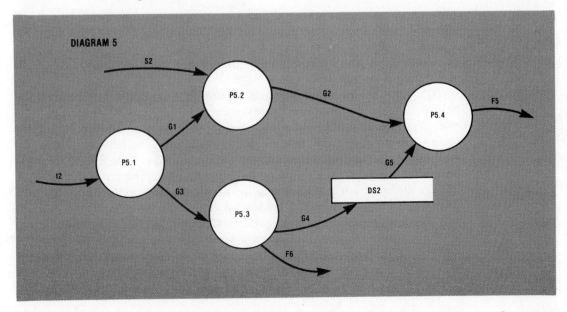

The second balancing requirement is that the functions accomplished by both the parent bubble and child diagram must be the same. The two must be functionally equivalent. Functional balancing is difficult to verify. The lack of functional balancing could be evidenced by a corresponding lack of data balancing, but not always. For example, consider a system to support an automatic teller machine (ATM). The parent process "authorize withdrawal" is shown in Figure 4-12 (a). It has two input and two output flows. The child diagram in Figure 4-12 (b) is data balanced with the parent, but it is not functionally balanced. The diagram in Figure 4-12 (b) completely misses the fact that a daily log is maintained indicating the total ATM withdrawals for that account and that a daily ATM withdrawal limit is imposed no matter how large the customer's balance. The correct diagram is shown in Figure 4-12 (c).

Diagram Depth

A determination of how many levels deep to continue to decompose processes is based on the judgment of the systems analyst. Generally speaking, partitioning is continued as far as necessary to assure understanding of the system. Two rules of thumb may be helpful in this context: First, a process bubble that has either a single input or a single output has probably been partitioned far enough. Second, the lowest-level process bubble diagram should perform a single, well-defined function. A good test is whether the process can be named using a single strong verb and a single object. If these criteria have been met, partitioning has probably been carried far enough. Of course, depth is not uniform. At any given level, it may be appropriate to further partition some processes, but not others.

Diagram Breadth

The question of diagram breadth involves the number of processes in a single diagram. There is an inverse relation between breadth and depth. If all diagrams contain a relatively large number of processes, they each convey more detail and thus fewer levels are required. The optimum breadth depends on the diagram's use.

Diagrams prepared for user presentations and review should generally be limited to between five and ten processes each. While this is not a hard and fast rule, diagrams with many more than ten processes are difficult to follow and those with very few don't convey much information. The same rule of thumb would apply to diagrams maintained using automated or CASE tools, where it becomes difficult to see all aspects of a large diagram on a screen at one time.

On the other hand, when using the diagram as a working document with frequent revisions, it is not uncommon for analysts to fill an entire white-board wall with a diagram of 25 or more processes. Such a diagram is admittedly more complex, but as a working document it provides a more detailed look at major portions of the system. This is often necessary in order to gain a full understanding of the impact of proposed changes or alternative solutions.

Figure 4.12.   An example of functional balancing.

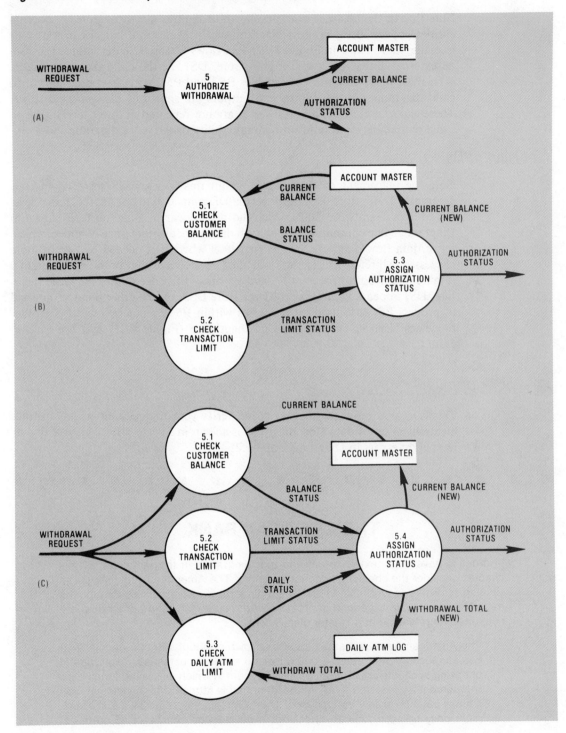

Inclusion of External Entities

Note that in the abstract example shown in Figures 4-9 through 4-11, external entities appear in the context diagram and in Diagram 0 but not in the lower level diagram. Thus, in Figure 4-10, data flows I2 and S2 enter bubble P5 from an external entity, EE2, and a data store, DS1. In the child diagram, Figure 4-11, these flows enter process bubbles P5.1 and P5.2 with no source shown. In child diagrams, the net inputs and outputs are shown as disconnected flows. These external entities and data stores are not repeated at lower levels so as to avoid redundancy and improve maintainability of the set of diagrams.

Inclusion of Data Stores

Note the placement of data stores within this hierarchical set of data flow diagrams. Data store DS1 appears in Diagram 0 but not in the lower level Diagram 5. Data store DS2, which did not appear in Diagram 0, is shown in Diagram 5. The convention is that each data store appears once in a hierarchical set of data flow diagrams, at the first level where it is needed by two or more processes. All references to the store must be shown at that point. In Diagram 0 (Figure 4-10), both processes P1 and P5 must reference data store DS1; therefore, DS1 appears in Diagram 0. Data store DS2, on the other hand, is internal to process P5. It is used by processes within P5 but not by any of the other processes. Hence, DS2 appears in Diagram 5 (Figure 4-11) and not in Diagram 0.

■ PRACTICE EXERCISES

This is a good point to stop again and verify your understanding. An abstract hierarchical set of data flow diagrams is shown in Figure 4-13. Can you find at least eight errors in Diagrams 1 and 1.2?

■　■　■　■　■　■　■　■　■　■　■　■　■　■　■　■　■　■

MINICASE:
THE AMERICAN BANK

In order to have a context for practicing modeling skills in the remainder of this chapter, consider the checking account system of The American Bank (TAB). The existing system is described in the following paragraphs. Read quickly through the narrative now to gain a general impression of the operation. The paragraphs are numbered for reference during later discussions.

1. The American Bank is a small bank in a town of about 100,000 people. TAB has one location and about 8,000 checking account customers. Two types of checking accounts are offered, a NOW account in which deposited funds earn 5¼ percent interest and a regular account that is attractive to a customer with a small balance or few transactions. The NOW account requires a $500 minimum daily balance for free checking. A flat service charge of $5.00 is as-

Figure 4.13. Can you find at least eight errors in Diagrams 1 and 1.2?

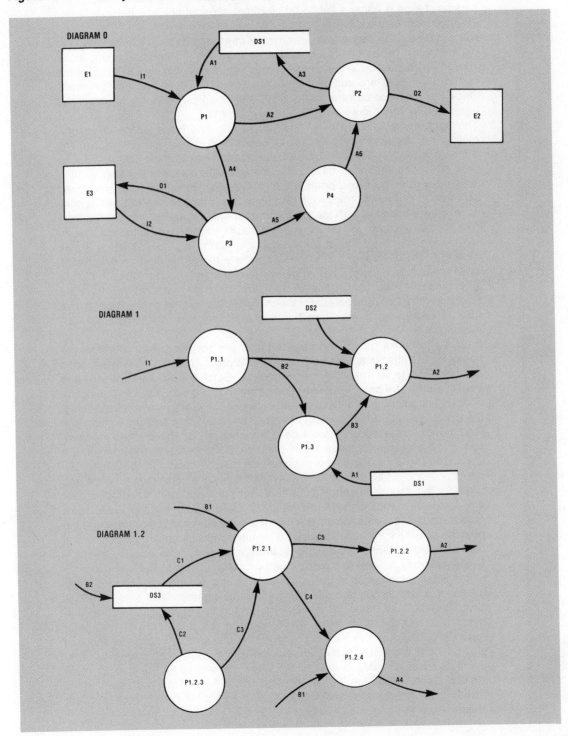

sessed if the balance falls below that minimum. For regular accounts, the service charge is either a flat $3.00 or 20 cents per check whichever is larger. The minimum balance for regular accounts is $100.

2. If a customer also has a loan, such as a mortgage, with the bank, the loan payment can be automatically deducted from the checking account at no charge. A transaction is generated on the fifth, tenth, and fifteenth day of the month until there are sufficient available funds to cover the loan payment. Once the payment can be made, no further loan payment transactions are generated for that month.

3. The bank operations are fairly straightforward. The bank tellers, who know most of the customers by sight, accept deposits to checking accounts, running a machine tape of each deposit. Customers may write their own checks for cash, provided that they have sufficient available funds according to their account status. At several times during the day, teller transactions are picked up to be run through the proof machine. Deposits are verified. All checks received are encoded with the check amount and separated into checks from TAB accounts (known as "on-us" checks) and checks from other banks (known as "foreign" checks). Totals, both batch and daily, are accumulated. Funds from deposits of "foreign bank" checks have a three-day float on availability, while "on-us" have none. (That is, when a foreign check is deposited, the funds are credited to the customer's account, but they are not available for withdrawal for three days.) The total "foreign" funds is encoded on the deposit slip. Checks on "foreign banks" are batched and sent to a clearinghouse each evening.

4. Each day, checks "on-us" and batch totals are received from the clearinghouse. These checks are also run through the proof machine to verify encoded amounts and totals from the clearinghouse. Batch totals are encoded, and these batches are combined with those from the tellers as input to the nightly checking account update. Deposit slips are used to create a credit transaction file while checks, check printing charges, and loan payment drafts from the loan system are used to create a debit transaction file. Batch totals are compared to make sure all totals are in balance. Sorted credits, then debits, are applied to the checking account master file. Each account in the master file has four amount fields—one for the available or collected funds balance and three for the deposited amounts on float. For each account, amounts on float are dumped forward a day and eventually are dumped into the available or collected funds balance. Amounts on float are called uncollected funds and the process is called "bucket dumping." The total balance for an account is the sum of collected funds and uncollected funds.

5. Customers may request to stop payment on certain checks. Each check processed is compared against the "stop pay's," if any, for a given account. If the customer specifies the account number, check number, and amount and a check matches all three, the check is recorded on the stop pay report and rejected. If a check matches on two of the three, it is processed normally and reported on the stop-pay warning report. There is a $5.00 charge for a check stop payment request, and it is processed with the debit transactions. If a loan payment request is paid, a loan transaction is generated for the loan payment system. Each transaction, including overdrafts, is logged into a transaction file that is used for account audits and in preparation of the monthly account statement.

6. A special overdraft protection feature is provided to certain preferred, high quality customers. The standard overdraft policy is to reject any check that cannot be covered in full by the account's available balance and, furthermore, to assess the account a $5.00 overdraft charge. The first time that a particular check is submitted for which there is not adequate funds, the account number, check number, and amount are noted on the overdraft warning report and the check transaction is resubmitted the next day. Failure on the second try results in the penalty described. For preferred customers, noted as such on the account master file, the policy on overdrafts is more lenient. If the amount of the check is more than the funds available but covered by the total balance (= collected + uncollected funds), the check is honored, resulting in a negative balance on funds available. No overdraft charge is assessed. If the check exceeds the total balance, it is noted on the overdraft warning report and resubmitted as above. On a second attempt, if the check still exceeds the total balance, one of two actions is taken. If the amount of the check is within the total balance + 10%, the check is covered, resulting in a negative balance, a $5.00 overdraft charge, and a warning letter. If the amount exceeds this level, the check is rejected and the overdraft charge applied. All rejected checks are sent back to the depositor, the customer is sent a letter with details of the matter, and the reject is recorded on the overdraft-rejects report.
7. An account status report is prepared at the end of the update detailing each account's balances and status.
8. Completely processed deposit slips, checks, overdraft charge slips, and check printing charge slips are sorted by account number and filed in a manual holding file. The signature on each check is compared to that on the signature card to verify authenticity, as a last control. The holding file plus the daily account status report are used to handle customer questions about their accounts.
9. Each month, a statement is sent to each customer with a recap of all activity since the last statement. Service charges, if any, are calculated and applied to the account. For NOW accounts, interest earned is calculated and added to the account balance. All transactions in the holding file are mailed with the computer-printed statement to the customer.
10. Management receives an excessive change in balance report, which identifies accounts with unusual activity. If a deposit is made that exceeds twice the average monthly total deposit or a check is written for one-half the average monthly check total, the account number, transaction, and appropriate messages are printed and further investigation takes place to verify authenticity and correctness. Various other management reports are created to summarize checking account activity and status.
11. Annually, a 1099-interest form is prepared for each NOW account to report the total interest earned during the year. A copy is sent to each customer and a machine-readable copy is sent to Internal Revenue.

In the following section this information on the existing checking account system at TAB will be modeled using a context diagram and a Diagram 0.

Perhaps the single most difficult task in developing data flow diagrams is determining how and where to start. From a diagram-building point of view, the context diagram presents no great difficulties. The entire system is represented by a single process bubble. The external entities and major input and output flows are merely a straightforward documentation of the scope of the system. (Reaching agreement on scope may be difficult, but diagramming the result is not.)

In the case of the checking account system at The American Bank, it is clear that customers, the loan system, and the clearinghouse are major external entities. A closer reading of the case material would also reveal bank management, the IRS, and the check printer as necessary players. Major inputs and outputs would certainly include deposits, checks, monthly statements, foreign and on-us checks, and so on. The context diagram (and, hence, the system scope) used in this chapter and the next is presented in Figure 4-14.

Now the challenge: How can all the collected information be used to construct a Diagram 0 which effectively models the major processes of the TAB checking account system? As with most analyst efforts, there is probably too much information in some areas and not enough in others. If an effort is made to model all that is known in a single diagram, it would be both large and uneven in its detail. Those areas that were well understood would tend to have many process bubbles, while those areas that were not well understood would have few—perhaps none. A step-by-step procedure would help suppress to lower-level diagrams those details that are not appropriate on a Diagram 0. This procedure should also assist in discovering functions or processes that are not well understood or have been overlooked altogether.

A five-step procedure is explained below. While it is described in the context of the TAB system, it is readily apparent that the procedure applies to all settings. The process will focus on major business operations or occurrences rather than on specific, narrow, physical processing functions. A physical processing function, as it presently exists, may be tied to a procedure that is outmoded and will be discarded. However, long after a new system has been developed and installed, the organization will be in the same business, providing the same basic services and conducting the same fundamental business transactions. A procedure that concentrates, from the start, on the key business occurrences or events will establish a good base for a stable model of the system.

Step 1: List the major data stores currently in use. From careful reading of the TAB existing system description, one would find or at least infer the existence of the following data stores. The numbers in parentheses refer to the paragraphs where these data stores are mentioned.

■ The *checking account master file*, with account number and type, name and address, SSN, and certain summary information used for monthly statements. (4)

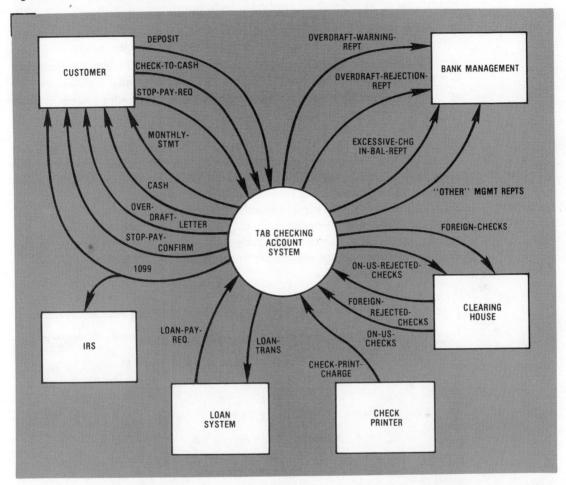

Figure 4.14. *Context diagram for TAB checking account system.*

- The daily *transaction file*, with as many as eight different transaction types: check, deposit, daily-balance, loan payment, interest, service charge, check printing charge, and overdraft. (5)
- A manual *holding file*, where physical checks and signature cards are maintained. (8)
- An *account status file*, detailing each account's balance and status at the end of the nightly update. (3,7)
- A daily *credit transaction file* of deposit transactions, used in the nightly update. (4)
- A daily *debit transaction file* of checks, charges, and loan payment drafts, used in the nightly update. (4)
- A *stop payment file*, noting those accounts and check numbers for which there are stop payment requests. (5)

Step 2: List the major business occurrences or events within the system. To identify these, look for three important indicators:

- *Acceptance of a major input to the system.* In the checking account system, a customer deposit and a check would certainly be major inputs.
- *Production of a major output by the system.* In the checking account system, a monthly statement is certainly a major output.
- *Any function triggered by timing.* In the checking account system, nightly update processing is a major function triggered by timing.

In the checking account application, ten major business occurrences have been identified. These are listed in Figure 4-15. (Again, the numbers in parentheses refer to paragraphs in the minicase narrative.) This list then becomes the basis for the process bubbles to be included in Diagram 0.

The building of this list is, to some extent, judgmental, depending on what the particular analyst considers to be the major business events within the system under study. In fact, each analyst is likely to develop a list that differs slightly from the list that would have been formed by another analyst.

Figure 4.15.   Key business events in the TAB checking account system.

Event tied to the production of major output

    1. Prepare monthly statement (9)

Events tied to receipt of major inputs

    2. Customer cashes check (3)
    3. Customer makes deposit (3)
    4. Clearing house sends "on-us" checks (4)

Additional events tied to minor outputs

    5. Respond to customer questions (8)

Additional events tied to minor inputs

    6. Customer requests stop payment of check (5)
    7. Checks are printed (4,8)
    8. Loan payment is requested (2)

Events triggered by timing

    9. Perform nightly update (4,5,6,7)
   10. Prepare annual tax reports (11)

The events identified in this step will not necessarily all be of the same size or complexity. For example, the processing that occurs during the nightly update is far more complex than the processing to produce a monthly statement. This is not a problem. If Diagram 0 can partition the system into processes that correspond to **key business events,** whatever their size, the additional complexity of some events can be handled by lower-level diagrams.

Step 3: Draw a segment, or fragment, of a data flow diagram for each of the identified events. Each segment will usually contain a single process bubble covering that event. As the data flow diagram is developed, this bubble will become a high-level parent with relatively large numbers of inputs and outputs. A series of fragments corresponding with the list in Figure 4-15 is shown in Figure 4-16.

In developing the diagram fragments, identify the outputs produced as well as the events, or necessary inputs, that cause the processing to take place. In identifying inputs and outputs, be sure to note the source and destination of each. These sources and destinations may be external entities, data stores, or other processes. Specifying inputs and outputs in this way establishes the scope of the process, in effect producing a clear definition of what the process does.

Step 4: Assemble the fragments into a single data flow diagram. Process 9, update accounts, because of its obvious complexity and numerous data flows, is a good starting point. Place it in the center and attempt to build out from there. Even with this start, the first attempt will be rough. It will undoubtedly be necessary to rearrange or reposition some of the components of the diagram to improve its appearance. As explained earlier, it may help to repeat data stores or external entities to avoid having data flows cross one another. Figure 4-17 is the result of several revisions.

Step 5: Evaluate the diagram and reorganize if necessary. As noted above, two different analysts may well come up with two different versions of Diagram 0 for the same system. Following steps 1-4, if they do not agree on the major business occurrences, the Diagram 0 processes will differ. Differences should not be extreme, however, since major business events should be clear.

A technique often employed when an analyst does not feel totally comfortable with the organization of a Diagram 0 is to explode the entire diagram at once. That is, each process bubble in Diagram 0 is replaced by its child diagram, and all the child diagrams are joined into one large diagram. This partitioning process may be repeated, as necessary, incorporating additional levels of detail and forming a very large and complex data flow diagram. Work with this diagram may suggest more natural groupings of processes from which a revised Diagram 0 can be constructed.

Constructing Lower-Level Diagrams

The process of constructing child diagrams is much the same as that involved in constructing a Diagram 0. Simply treat the parent bubble to be partitioned as a context diagram for a small system and proceed with the five-step process just outlined. When constructing data flow diagrams at any level, it is good practice to name the data flows first, then to name the processes. This helps to keep the

Figure 4.16. Data flow diagram fragments corresponding to key business events.

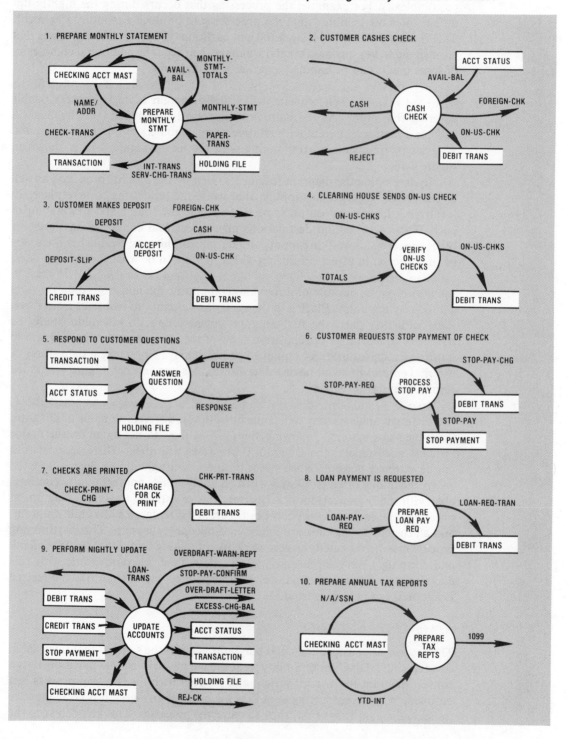

Part 2   Systems Analysis Modeling Techniques

Figure 4.17. ***Diagram 0 for TAB checking account system.***

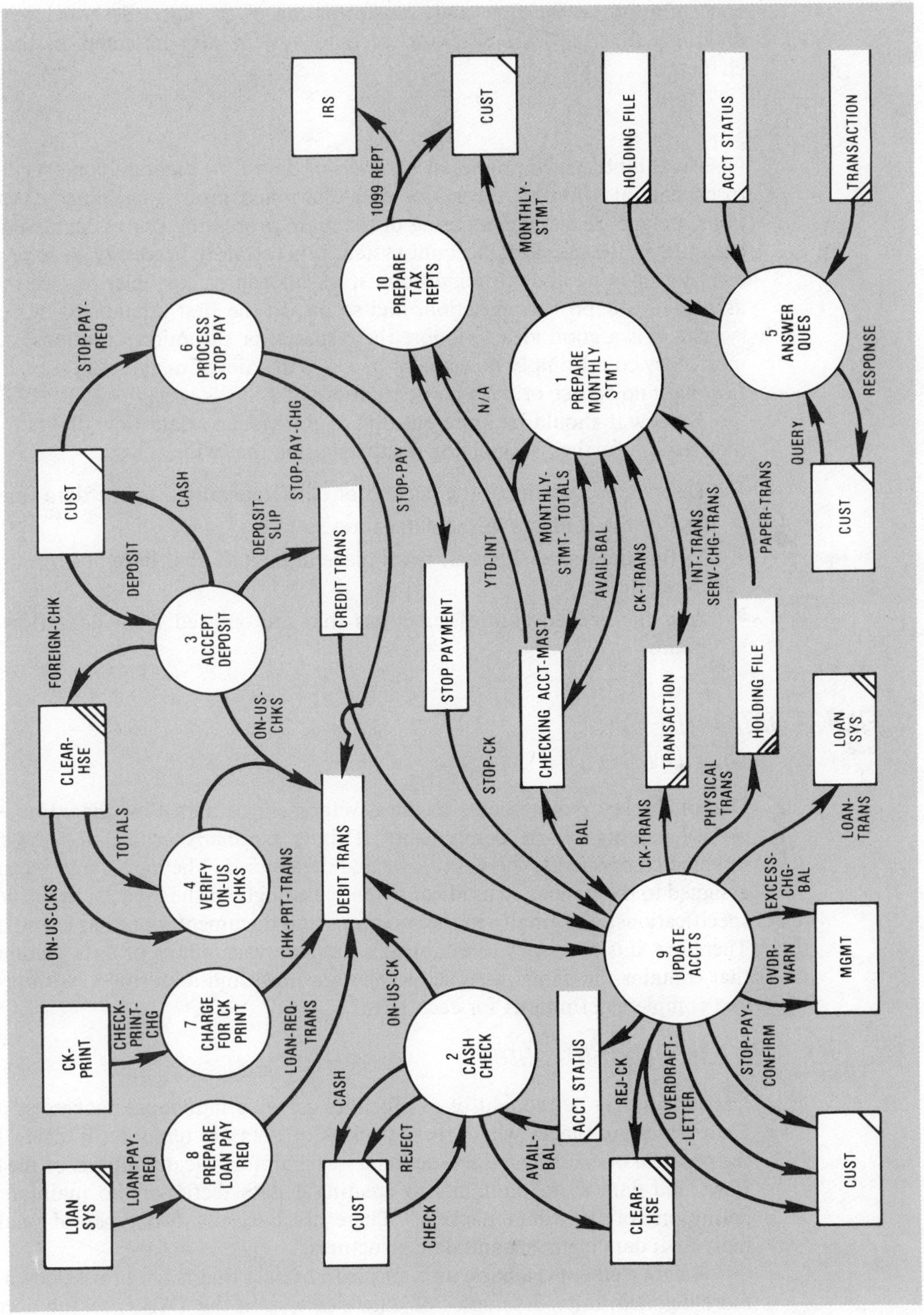

concentration on the flow and transformation of the data. Several lower-level diagrams for the TAB checking account system are presented in the next chapter.

Helpful Hint

One final hint, which applies at all levels of data flow diagram construction, is to concentrate first on the major data flows and processing, ignoring exceptions, until a clear understanding of the main processing steps is achieved. For example, in the checking account system it is certainly necessary to have processes for opening and closing accounts, for allowing a customer to receive cash as part of a deposit transaction, and so on. In the first attempt to model the system, it is a good idea to ignore these special or exception situations. At the most, they could simply be listed or included in a diagram as a **stub** (i.e., a data flow with no source or with no destination).

By now it should be apparent that as powerful as data flow diagrams are, they require further, supporting documentation that will:

- Define the contents of the packets of data transmitted by the data flows.
- Define the contents of the data stores.
- Define the processing that takes place in bubbles that have not been partitioned.
- Add the needed control functions that are omitted from data flow diagrams.

DEFINING DATA—THE DATA DICTIONARY

One of the key requirements in the development of data flow diagrams is the precise naming of the components. This is especially critical for the data-oriented components, the data flows and data stores. The names and meanings assigned to them must be used consistently throughout the models, in the design specifications, and finally in the programs and documentation that are written. Therefore, it is necessary to establish a common vocabulary, or **data dictionary**, that contains the names assigned to all data flows and data stores, with precise and complete definitions for each term.

Data Elements and Data Structures

Data flows may be thought of as pipelines carrying individual packets of data. Data stores are places where these packets of data are temporarily held. Thus the problem of creating a data dictionary to maintain the definitions of the data flows and data stores amounts to creating a data dictionary to maintain the definitions of the "data packets." There are basically two types of packets: individual data elements and data structures.

A **data element** is a basic unit, or piece, of data that is not broken down into more detailed units. Examples of data elements in the TAB checking account system include customer account number, social security number, available balance, service charge, and so on.

A packet of data that can be broken down into more detailed units is known as a **data structure**. Examples of data structures include customer address (consisting of street address, city, and state), deposit amount (consisting of cash amount, on-us check amount, and foreign check amount), deposit transaction (consisting of account number, date, and deposit amount), and so on. Data structures may be composed of individual data elements, of other data structures, or of a combination of the two.

The creation of a precise data dictionary requires a set of rigorous rules for defining data structures and a notation that supports these rules. Data structures can be defined using three basic constructs, or rules of grammar. They are similar in nature to the three basic constructs of structured programming. They are *sequence*, *iteration*, and *selection*. These constructs and their corresponding notation are illustrated in Figure 4-18.

A **sequence** of data elements or structures is denoted by plus signs (+) which have the meaning of "and." The use of a plus sign in this context means a concatenation of parts rather than an arithmetic operation. In Figure 4-18, the data structures CHECK-TRAN and DEPOSIT-TRAN are both constructed as a sequence of data elements.

An **iteration** of data elements or structures within a larger structure is denoted by braces ([. . .]). The data element or structure within the braces is iterated, or repeated, within the larger data structure. As shown in Figure 4-18 subscripts and superscripts can be used to specify the number of iterations if this is an important part of the definition. As a special case, an *optional* element can be considered an iteration used either zero or one times. Alternatively, optional elements are sometimes simply denoted by parentheses. In Figure 4-18, recall that deposits of "foreign" checks must "float" for three days before the money is available to the depositor. The FLOAT-FUNDS structure is an iteration of exactly three amounts. On the monthly statement there will be a DAILY-BAL entry for each business day and an unlimited number of deposit and check transactions. Finally, there is an optional message to preferred customers.

The third construct for building data structures is **selection**. A selection refers to a group of data elements of which one and only one is used in a particular occurrence of a data packet. Selection is indicated by square brackets. In Figure 4-18, an occurrence of ACCT-TRANS could be any one of four different data structures.

These three constructs are sufficient for expressing any data structure. They also provide the rigor necessary to maintain definitions in a data dictionary.

Building and Maintaining the Data Dictionary

There are three major concerns in building and maintaining a data dictionary. First, it is necessary to determine the content. What information must be stored about each entry in order to completely define it? Second, it is necessary to have some organized means of storing and updating entries in the data dictionary.

Figure 4.18. *Data structure notation conventions.*

| SEQUENCE |

EX:
```
CHECK-TRAN = ACCT-NUM    or  DEPOSIT-TRAN = ACCT-NUM
             + TRAN-TYPE                   + TRAN-TYPE
             + DATE                        + DATE
             + AMOUNT                      + CASH-AMOUNT
             + CHECK-NUM                   + ON-US-AMOUNT
                                           + FOREIGN-AMOUNT
                                           + CASH-OUT-AMOUNT
```

| ITERATION |

UNLIMITED ITERATIONS	$\{ \ldots \}$
EXACTLY N ITERATIONS	$^{N}\{ \ldots \}$
ONE TO N ITERATIONS	$^{N}_{1}\{ \ldots \}$ or $\{ \ldots \}_{CONDITION}$
OPTIONAL	$^{1}_{0}\{ \ldots \}$ or $(\ldots)$

EX:
$$\text{FLOAT-FUNDS} = {}_{3}\{\text{FOREIGN AMOUNT}\}$$

```
MONTHLY-STATEMENT = ACCT-NUM
                    + DEMOGRAPHIC-DATA
                    + (PREFERRED-CUST-MSG)
                    + {DAILY-BAL}BUSINESS DAYS
                    + {DEPOSIT-TRANS}
                    + {CHECK-TRANS}
                    + BEGINNING-BALANCE
                    + SERVICE-CHARGE
```

| SELECTION | — EXACTLY ONE OF SEVERAL OPTIONS

```
EX: ACCT-TRANS = ⎡CHECK-TRAN  ⎤
                 ⎢DEPOSIT-TRAN⎥
                 ⎢LOAN-PAYMENT⎥
                 ⎣OVERDRAFT   ⎦
```

Third, it is necessary to have a means of linking data dictionary entries to data flow diagrams and other documents of the development process.

Normally, there are three types of entries in a data dictionary that support the analysis process: data elements, data structures, and data stores. Data elements and data structures are "building block" entries. They are used to build the packets of data that comprise data flows and data stores. A data flow can be fully defined by a corresponding data structure. A data store requires certain information beyond its corresponding data structure to complete its definition. Hence, the need for a separate data store entry in the data dictionary. The usual content associated with each of these is illustrated in the following examples.

Figure 4-19 illustrates a data dictionary entry for the data element ACCT-NUM in the TAB checking account system. In addition to the primary data element name, it is possible to note alternate names or aliases that may be used for the data element. While it would be preferable that each data element and data structure have only one name associated with it, this is often not practical. For example, it could be that for years people in the customer service department at TAB have used the term "overdraft," while people in the accounting

Figure 4.19.   *Example of a data element entry in a data dictionary.*

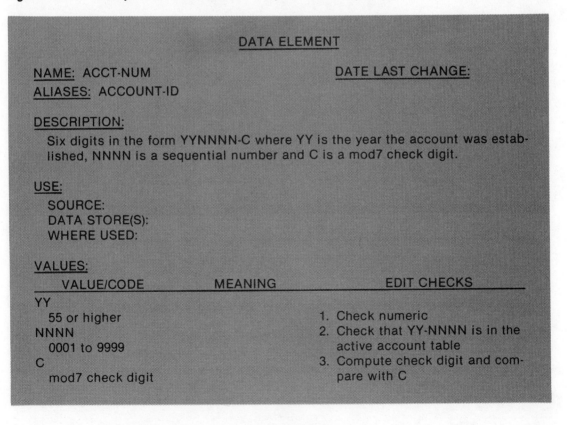

DATA ELEMENT

NAME: ACCT-NUM   DATE LAST CHANGE:
ALIASES: ACCOUNT-ID

DESCRIPTION:
  Six digits in the form YYNNNN-C where YY is the year the account was established, NNNN is a sequential number and C is a mod7 check digit.

USE:
  SOURCE:
  DATA STORE(S):
  WHERE USED:

VALUES:

VALUE/CODE	MEANING	EDIT CHECKS
YY		
55 or higher		1. Check numeric
NNNN		2. Check that YY-NNNN is in the active account table
0001 to 9999		
C		3. Compute check digit and compare with C
mod7 check digit		

department have used "NSF check" to refer to the same thing. It is highly unlikely that either group would be open to change. And there is no need to force it. That is the purpose of an alias.

The "description" area is a freeform area that defines the data element using one or two English phrases. If desired, the "use" area can document where the data element originates, where it is stored within the system, and the processes which use it. The analyst uses the "values" area to document permissible values for the element and edit checks that should be applied during processing. Data elements can assume values that are either continuous or discrete.

Figure 4-20 illustrates a data dictionary entry for the data structure DEPOSIT-TRAN. The composition of the data structure is defined using the three constructs and notation explained earlier.

Finally, Figure 4-21 illustrates a data dictionary entry for the data store STOP-PAYMENT. This format can be used for abstract or logical data stores as well as computer files. The organization section and the length entries in the composition section are physical characteristics that would be used to define computer files when documenting an existing system or presenting design specifications for a new system. These entries would not be used when defining more abstract data stores during the analysis process.

This discussion of the data dictionary has implicitly assumed that a special dictionary was being built specifically for a development project. While this is

Figure 4.20.   *Example of data structure entry in data dictionary.*

DATA STRUCTURE

NAME: DEPOSIT-TRAN   DATE LAST CHANGE:
ALIASES:

DESCRIPTION:
Contains all data associated with a customer deposit
At least one deposit amount must be present

WHERE USED:

COMPOSITION:

                    ACCT-NUM
                    + DATE
                    + TRAN-TYPE (= "DEP")
                    + (FOREIGN-AMOUNT)
                    + (ON-US-AMOUNT)
                    + (CASH-DEP-AMOUNT)
                    + (CASH-OUT-AMOUNT)

Figure 4.21. *Example of data store entry in data dictionary.*

DATA STORE

NAME: STOP PAYMENT   DATE LAST CHANGE:
ALIASES:

ORGANIZATION:
  SEQUENTIAL _X_ INDEXED _X_ DIRECT ___   KEYS:
  NUMBER OF RECORDS _100–500_   PRIMARY ACCT-NUM
  EXPECTED RATE OF GROWTH _stable_   SECONDARY_____
  APPROXIMATE RECORD SIZE _30B_

PRIMARY PURPOSE/USE:
  Used in nightly update to refuse payment

RECORD COMPOSITION   Approx.
  Structure/Element Name   Length

  ACCT-NUM   7
  REQUEST-DATE   6
  CHECK-NUM   4
  CHECK-AMOUNT   10

often the case, many times there will already be a data dictionary in place covering all or a major portion of the organization's data. This can greatly reduce the work of the development team during the initial stages of analysis.

PRACTICE EXERCISES

This is a good place to stop and verify your understanding of the basic data structure notation. Try the following practice exercises:

1. A budget record consists of the fiscal year, division and department numbers, number of line-items budgeted, and, for each line-item budgeted, the line-item number and budget amount. Prepare a data structure notation for this budget record.

2. A checking account master record contains the account number, customer name, home address, and perhaps a business address. It also contains the average daily balance for each month in the current calendar year. Further, it contains the account numbers of any related accounts held by the individ-

ual or members of his or her immediate family. Finally, if the person has opted for a special service—automatic loan on overdraft—there will be an indicator to this effect. Prepare a data structure for the checking account master record.

SPECIFYING PROCESSING RULES—PROCESS DESCRIPTIONS

The previous section presented methods for defining the data flows and data stores. To complete the supporting documentation for a system model based on data flow diagrams, it is necessary to have a means for defining the process bubbles. **Process descriptions** are sets of rules, policies, and procedures that specify the data transformations taking place within the process bubbles.

In a high-level data flow diagram a process bubble is typically defined by exploding it and creating a child data flow diagram. Similarly, process bubbles on the child diagram can be defined by exploding them in turn. Ultimately, however, this exploding stops and it is necessary to use some type of process description to define those process bubbles that will not be further broken down. As mentioned earlier, when the partitioning process reaches the point where a process has one data flow in and multiple flows out or multiple flows in and one flow out, the process would normally not be further broken down. But it is not always necessary to partition even this far. In practice, judgment may indicate that there is no point in partitioning to this level if the process is fairly straightforward and can be described completely in a single page of specifications. Techniques for specifying these lowest-level processes are presented in the sections that follow.

While process descriptions are normally used for lowest-level processes, occasionally it may be necessary to prepare process descriptions for intermediate level bubbles affected by conditions that cannot be shown on data flow diagrams. Typical examples include processes that have critical timing considerations or special procedural relationships within the system. In these cases, even though the intermediate level bubbles are partitioned further, it still may be desirable to prepare brief process descriptions.

The principal techniques used to communicate process descriptions are:

- Brief, explicit narratives.
- Decision trees.
- Decision tables.
- Structured English.
- Combinations of these methods.

Although process descriptions can be prepared in any form or format that provides the needed information, it usually helps to have a standard format. This format serves both to guide the preparation of specifications and also to assure completeness of the results. A typical process description format is shown in Figure 4-22. Process specifications are normally included as entries in a data dictionary or general repository. The particular automated tool, then, may place some restriction on the techniques that can be used for the process definition.

Process Narratives

Process narratives are, basically, verbal descriptions of processes. Words, by their nature, are inexact ways of describing specific events or conditions. Thus narratives should be used only in situations in which other tools are not appropriate. Process narratives should be as brief and as specific as possible. They may be used to describe special timing requirements, system constraints, or relationships among processes. An example of the use of a narrative within the TAB system is given in Figure 4-22. This description covers timing requirements for an upper-level process. The actual calculations are described in specifications for lower-level processes.

Figure 4.22. *Example of process description form.*

PROCESS DESCRIPTION

SYSTEM: TAB Checking Account   DATE PREPARED:
PROCESS ID: 1   PREPARED BY:
PROCESS NAME: Prepare Monthly Statement

PURPOSE: Prepare all checking account statements for a specified cycle

INPUT: CK-TRANS
       MONTHLY-STMT-TOTALS
       NAME/ADDRESS
       AVAIL-BAL

OUTPUTS: MONTHLY-STMT

PROCESS DEFINITION:
In order to balance work loads, monthly statements are prepared in three cycles according to the following schedule:
    Cycle 1 = First business day on or after 1st of month
                All personal accounts with odd sequence number
    Cycle 2 = First business day on or after 10th of month
                All personal accounts with even sequence number
    Cycle 3 = First business day on or after 20th of month
                All commercial accounts

Some process descriptions involve a number of different conditions that may occur in different combinations, with each combination producing a specific outcome. These differing combinations of conditions can be difficult to represent in narrative form. It is difficult to verify that all combinations of conditions have been covered without contradictions. It is even harder to modify this type of narrative specification once it has been written.

Two techniques are available to represent combinations of conditions: decision trees and decision tables.

Decision Trees

A **decision tree** gets its name from the fact that it develops a series of branches representing conditions or processing alternatives. Each condition to be dealt with during processing is represented by a separate set of branches, one for each value associated with the condition. Outcomes are listed, foliage style, at the ends of the branches.

To illustrate the development of decision trees, study carefully the data flow diagram fragment and the narrative description in Figure 4-23. The process determines whether a customer qualifies for an automatic loan when he or she has an overdraft. Note that the process bubble has three input data flows and one output data flow. Thus, the process meets the test of being at the lowest level of decomposition.

From the process description in Figure 4-23, three conditions can be identified. These are listed below, with their possible values:

- CHECKING ACCOUNT BALANCE: values ≥ 1000 or < 1000.
- NUMBER OF OVERDRAFTS: values ≤ 2 or > 2.
- AVERAGE SAVINGS BALANCE: values ≥ 500 or < 500.

Figure 4.23.   Bank policy concerning qualification for automatic loan on overdraft.

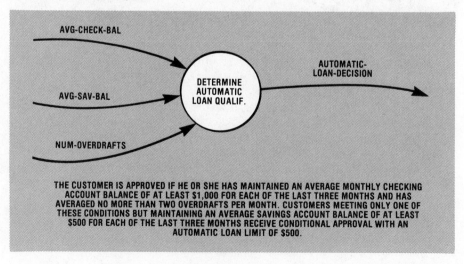

AVG-CHECK-BAL

AVG-SAV-BAL

NUM-OVERDRAFTS

DETERMINE AUTOMATIC LOAN QUALIF.

AUTOMATIC-LOAN-DECISION

THE CUSTOMER IS APPROVED IF HE OR SHE HAS MAINTAINED AN AVERAGE MONTHLY CHECKING ACCOUNT BALANCE OF AT LEAST $1,000 FOR EACH OF THE LAST THREE MONTHS AND HAS AVERAGED NO MORE THAN TWO OVERDRAFTS PER MONTH. CUSTOMERS MEETING ONLY ONE OF THESE CONDITIONS BUT MAINTAINING AN AVERAGE SAVINGS ACCOUNT BALANCE OF AT LEAST $500 FOR EACH OF THE LAST THREE MONTHS RECEIVE CONDITIONAL APPROVAL WITH AN AUTOMATIC LOAN LIMIT OF $500.

The three possible outcomes for this process are:

- Approval (no limit).
- Conditional approval ($500 limit).
- Rejection.

A decision tree representing the processing of these conditions to produce the identified outcomes is shown in Figure 4-24.

Figure 4.24. *Decision tree expressing bank policy concerning qualification for automatic loan on overdraft.*

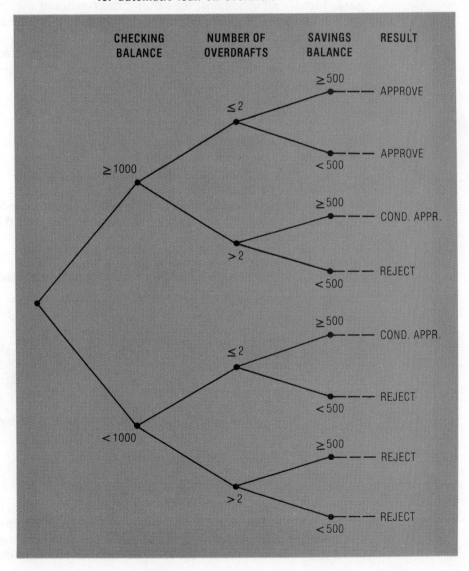

In Figure 4-24, the two values associated with the CHECKING ACCOUNT BALANCE condition are used to determine the two major branches of the tree. Next, the two values associated with the NUMBER OF OVERDRAFTS condition are considered. For each of the two major branches, this condition gives rise to two more intermediate branches (four altogether). For each of these four intermediate branches, the final condition, SAVINGS BALANCE, gives rise to two more branches (eight altogether). Reading the tree, if an account has a balance $\geq$ $1000 and has more than two overdrafts and has a savings balance under $500, then it will not qualify. Note that the order in which the conditions were used to build the tree has no impact on the final number of branches.

The principles for development of decision trees are relatively straightforward. Identify all conditions, the values these conditions may assume, and all possible outcomes. Each condition gives rise to a set of branches—one for each value the condition may assume.

The power of a decision tree is twofold: It is easy to verify that all combinations of conditions and outcomes have been covered, and changes are relatively easy to make (certainly easier than with a narrative).

Decision Tables

Decision tables provide an alternate method of specifying conditions or processing branches. Using the decision table method, conditions and outcomes are listed in a two-dimensional table that shows the outcome that results from each combination of conditions. The decision table shown in Figure 4-25 represents the process for determining qualifications for the automatic loan privilege described in Figure 4-23. This decision table corresponds with the decision tree shown in Figure 4-24.

Figure 4.25. Decision table covering policy for automatic loan qualification.

AVG CK BAL $\geq$ 1000	Y	Y	Y	Y	N	N	N	N
NUM OVERDRAFTS $\leq$ 2	Y	Y	N	N	Y	Y	N	N
AVG SAV BAL $\geq$ 500	Y	N	Y	N	Y	N	Y	N
APPROVE	X	X						
COND. APPROVE			X		X			
REJECT				X		X	X	X

The table is divided into four quadrants. The upper left quadrant has one row for each condition. In this case, the conditions have been stated so that the values will be either yes or no. The lower left quadrant contains one row for each possible outcome. The upper right quadrant contains the values associated with each of the conditions. There is one column for each combination of values. Finally, in the lower right quadrant, an "X" mark is used to designate each outcome that may result from the combination of values in the column above. These quadrants are depicted generically in Figure 4-26.

Figure 4.26. **General format of a decision table.**

THE GENERAL FORM OF A DECISION TABLE IS

LIST OF CONDITIONS	COLUMNS REPRESENTING LOGICAL COMBINATIONS OF CONDITION VALUES
LIST OF OUTCOMES	X'S INDICATING RESULTING OUTCOME(S) FOR EACH SET OF CONDITIONS

■ PRACTICE EXERCISES

This is a good place to stop and verify your understanding of decision trees and decision tables. Try the following practice exercises.

1. The process bubble in Figure 4-27 calculates the discount to be applied to retailer purchases from the Associated Grocers of America (AGA) warehouse operation. The following narrative specifies the processing rules that apply:

    A minimum 5 percent discount applies for all purchases. If the retailer maintains an average monthly purchase volume of at least $100,000, a 15 percent discount applies, provided the retailer is an AGA member. When

Figure 4.27. **Data flow diagram fragment for calculating the AGA discount rate.**

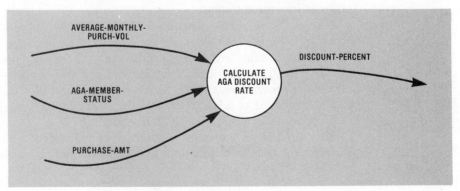

the retailer's purchase volume is under $100,000, the discount rate is 12 percent for AGA members and 7 percent for nonmembers. Retailers who are not AGA members, but who maintain an average $100,000 monthly purchase volume, qualify for a 10 percent discount, unless the individual purchase totals less than $35,000.

Based on this narrative and diagram:

a. List the outcomes.
b. List the conditions.
c. List the values associated with each condition.
d. Develop a decision tree relating these conditions, values, and outcomes.
e. Develop a decision table relating the same conditions, values, and outcomes.

2. The following narrative describes a policy designed to balance demand and availability by specifying the number of CIS classes for which a student may register. Draw a process bubble similar to the one in Figure 4-27 for this situation and follow the steps called for in Practice Assignment 1 above to construct both a decision tree and a decision table that expresses the policy:

CIS majors with below a 2.5 GPA may not register for CIS classes. Those above a 3.5 GPA may register for three CIS classes if they have completed at least 60 hours or two CIS classes if at least 30 hours or one CIS class if under 30 hours. Other CIS majors are limited to one CIS class unless they have more than 60 hours—in which case they may take two. CIS minors below a 3.0 GPA and students who are neither CIS majors nor minors may not register for CIS classes. CIS minors with at least a 3.0 GPA may register for one CIS class.

Structured English

Not all processes involve the consideration of multiple conditions and resulting outcomes like those above. Many processes lend themselves, instead, to a more straightforward sequence of steps or the iteration of smaller processes. In such instances, a series of formal English statements, using a small, strong, selected vocabulary, can be used to communicate processing rules. This technique is known as **structured English**.

One of the values of structured English is that verbal statements are a natural medium of communication between users and programmers. Users are generally comfortable with English statements. At the same time, the format of structured English is sufficiently precise so that it will not be misinterpreted by designers or programmers. To maintain the communication link with the user, however, care must be taken to avoid having structured English statements look like pseudocode, or worse, like COBOL code.

Structured English uses the same three basic constructs used in structured programming: sequence, selection, and iteration. Before reviewing the special characteristics of each construct, several general points can be made that apply to all:

- Structured English statements are brief. Adjectives are not used.
- Statements begin with a strong, action-oriented verb that specifies the action to be taken on a given object. There is no restricted list of verbs that must be used (as there is in a computer language).
- Statements are formatted using multiple levels of indentation. Each level of indentation corresponds with a processing block or group of statements that are processed together.

Sequence. The *sequence* construct simply amounts to stringing structured English statements together, one after the other. The statements can be simple commands or processing blocks arising from one of the other constructs. Each statement in the sequence begins on a new line without indentation.

Selection. The *selection* construct has two possible forms. They are illustrated in Figure 4-28. The IF-THEN-OTHERWISE form is probably easier for

Figure 4.28. *Example of the selection construct in structured English used to document the service charge calculation.*

```
SELECTION (IF-THEN-OTHERWISE):
    If DAILY-BAL is < 300 for any given day
    Then
        Set SERVICE-CHARGE to $5
    Otherwise
        Set SERVICE-CHARGE to 0

SELECTION (CASE CONSTRUCT):
    Select the proper case
    Case 1 (ACCT-TYPE Is NOW)
        If DAILY-BAL is < 300 for any given day
        Then
            Set SERVICE-CHARGE to $5
        Otherwise
            Set SERVICE-CHARGE to 0
    Case 2 (ACCT-TYPE is REGULAR)
        If DAILY-BAL is < 100 for any given day
        Then
            Set SERVICE-CHARGE to greater of
                $3 or 20¢ times NUM-CHECKS
        Otherwise
            Set SERVICE-CHARGE to 0
```

the user to understand when there are only two options possible for the selection. The format of the construct is similar to that used in most programming languages. Note, in Figure 4-28, the use of indenting and the separation of lines.

When three or more options are possible for a selection, the CASE construct usually communicates better than the use of nested IF statements. The two forms can also be used together. Again, note the use of indenting in Figure 4-28.

Iteration. The *iteration* construct also has two possible forms. They are used when there is a sequence of steps that are to be repeated as a group some number of times. The group of statements to be repeated or iterated is indented directly below the iteration statement. The iteration statement specifies the number of times the iteration is to occur. The most common form of the iteration statement is the FOR EACH form, where the number of iterations is based on the "for each" condition (see Figure 4-29). Examples include FOR EACH CUSTOMER IN THE CUSTOMER FILE, FOR EACH MONTH OF THE YEAR, and so on. Occasionally rather than stating a business condition that determines the number of iterations, it may be preferable to state a specific number. In this case the REPEAT N TIMES form of the iteration statement is used.

Figure 4.29.   *Example of the iteration construct in structured English used to document the NOW account interest calculation.*

```
ITERATION:
    For each day of the month
        Set DAILY-INT to DAILY-BAL times DAILY-RATE
        Add to MONTHLY-INT
        Add MONTHLY-INT to YTD-INT
```

Pseudocode and Action Diagrams. There are two other techniques for process definition that are similar to structured English, **pseudocode** and **action diagrams**. As with structured English, they both express the logic flow for a process. Action diagrams follow fairly rigorous construction rules, but those rules are programming language independent. With their more formal structure, action diagrams can serve as input code generator, thereby greatly reducing implementation time. On the other hand, this increased formality may not be as comfortable as structured English for end-user verification. Pseudocode is also more formal than structured English, but it lacks the rigorous construction rules of action diagrams. Thus there is a tendency for pseudocode descriptions to look very much like the target programming language (COBOL, for example). This is not good for the end-user, and it tends to remove options later in the design process.

There are no hard and fast rules concerning which of the process description tools to use. The choice is at the discretion of the analyst. The tools can be used singly or in combination, depending upon the process being described. It would not be uncommon, for example, to use structured English supplemented with a decision tree or decision table.

ACTION DIAGRAMS

Action Diagramming is a diagramming technique based on the use of square brackets ([). A simple bracket encloses a sequence of steps to be performed. A bracket with a double bar at the top ( ) indicates that the sequence of steps is repeated or iterated multiple times. A bracket with multiple lines ( ) indicates groups of exclusive steps to be performed.

Figure 4.30. Action diagram to describe student registration processing.

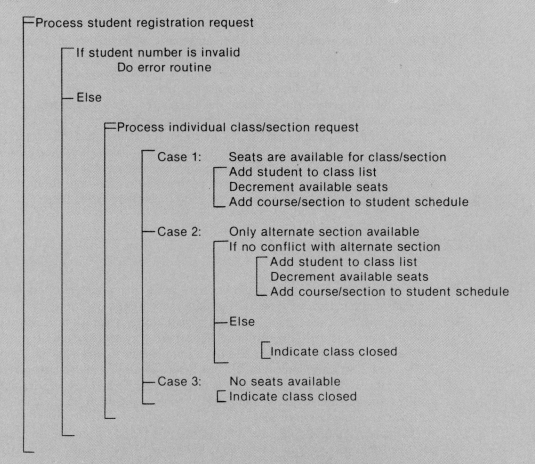

A process specification can be described by using these three basic symbols sequentially and in nested form (see Figure 4-30). The technique is related to structured English or pseudocode, except that control logic can be conveyed graphically rather than with words.

Action diagrams have two significant benefits. First, the same diagramming technique can be used to show high level program structures, as well as individual module specifications. Second, the technique is easily accommodated by many automated tools.

MODELING AN EXISTING SYSTEM

The analysis process begins with documenting the existing system. The techniques presented in this chapter provide an effective means for doing this documentation by building a model of the existing system.

The scope of the system can be expressed using a Context Diagram, and a Diagram 0 can represent the major subsystems. A leveled set of data flow diagrams can be used to model the detailed processing that occurs in the system and to document the use of existing files. A data dictionary and a set of process descriptions can be developed to supplement the collection of data flow diagrams. Taken together, this material documents the essential features of the existing system and forms a solid base for beginning the analysis process.

The ability of these techniques to document a system, while important, is not where their real power lies. The real significance of data flow diagrams is their ability to support a **structured analysis process** that can lead from a model of an existing system to a high-quality model of a new system — one from which detailed design work can be done. This process is covered in Chapter 6.

AUTOMATING THE MODELING PROCESS

In a project of any size, there could easily be more than a hundred data flow diagrams and hundreds or thousands of data elements and data structures. As analysis progresses, the data flow diagrams will evolve. The task of redrawing these diagrams and verifying the balancing between parent and child diagrams can be very large. In addition, the data components must all be uniquely defined and their definitions must be consistently applied by all team members who may be working on the project. It must be easy to add new entries and modify those that already exist. Some level of computer support for these labor-intensive modeling tasks is essential.

Computer Assisted Software Engineering (CASE) tools provide this support. Personal computer based systems, known as "upper-CASE" tools, exist that will automate the construction of all aspects of the models described in this chapter: data flow diagrams, data dictionary components, and process specifications. These tools will also test consistency of various model components. They will ensure, for example, that a data flow used in a data flow diagram has been defined in the data dictionary. They will also enforce data balancing between parent and child diagrams. These tools not only remove some of the labor-intensive aspects of building and maintaining models but also increase the quality of those models through their consistency verification features. CASE tools are described in more detail in Chapter 7.

SUMMARY

The key challenge of analysis is to achieve effective communication among users, analysts, and system designers. Effective communication has two parts: presentation and understanding. Narrative descriptions tend to be long, complex, and ambiguous — not an effective means of ensuring understanding. System developers tend to rely on modeling tools, rather than narrative descriptions, in order to communicate system documentation and specifications.

Models based on data flow diagrams are very effective during the analysis activities of the development process. They emphasize the flow and processing, or transformation, of data within the system. The context diagram defines the scope of the system. Diagram 0 models the system at a major component or subsystem level. A hierarchical set of child diagrams is used to model the more detailed processes.

Data flow diagrams are built using a set of four standard symbols. Skillful naming of the components contributes greatly to the ability of the model to communicate. A number of fairly mechanical steps are available to evaluate the correctness and quality of a set of data flow diagrams. There is a well-defined five-step process to help in the challenging task of constructing a Diagram 0 or lower-level diagram based on the analyst's understanding of key business events.

Data flow diagrams alone are not sufficient to model a system. Additional supporting documentation is necessary. The data dictionary is used to maintain definitions of the data that constitute the data flows and data stores in a data flow diagram. A data dictionary typically has entries for data elements, data structures, and data stores. All data structures can be concisely expressed in terms of data elements and/or other data structures using three basic constructs: sequence, iteration, and selection.

Finally, process descriptions are used to document low-level processes that are not further exploded, as well as some intermediate-level processes where it is necessary to specify timing or control information. Process descriptions are written using one or a combination of several techniques, brief narrative descriptions, decision trees, decision tables, structured English, and action diagrams.

1. communication
2. narrative description
3. scope
4. business objective
5. user specification
6. general design specification
7. context diagram
8. diagram 0
9. hierarchical
10. top-down partitioning
11. parent
12. child
13. key business events
14. stub
15. data dictionary
16. data element
17. data structure
18. sequence
19. iteration
20. selection
21. process descriptions
22. decision tree
23. structured English
24. structured analysis process

REVIEW/DISCUSSION QUESTIONS

1. Why is communication so important in the work of systems analysis? With whom must the analyst communicate?
2. What are some of the advantages of graphic presentations over narrative descriptions in systems analysis work?
3. What are the four major symbols used in data flow diagrams, and what does each represent?
4. Name three types of obvious errors that can be spotted quickly through visual checking of data flow diagrams.
5. What is meant by hierarchical partitioning of data flow diagrams?
6. What does a context diagram tell you about the system under study?
7. Explain the relationships between a context diagram, Diagram 0, Diagram 4, and Diagram 4.3.
8. Assuming that you have a context diagram for an existing system, how would you go about constructing a Diagram 0?
9. In addition to data flow diagrams, what type of documentation does the systems analyst need to prepare? Why?
10. Describe the three basic types of data structures, including the notation generally used for each.
11. What do decision trees and decision tables have in common? How do they differ?
12. Consider the student registration system at your university.
   a. Draw a Context Diagram
   b. Draw a Diagram 0 based on your understanding of the system.
   c. Express your course registration form and your own printed class schedule as data structures.
   d. Write a process description that describes the process for determining whether a student has completed his or her general education requirements.
13. Consider the TAB checking account system in this chapter.
   a. Construct a diagram 1 for preparing the monthly statement.
   b. Construct a diagram 9 for the nightly update processing.

5

Data Analysis Techniques

Learning Objectives

At the conclusion of this chapter you should be able to:

- Understand the evolving role of the value of data and its organizational and CIS implications.
- View data from an enterprise perspective.
- Explain the nature of holistic data modelling.
- Differentiate between data driven and process driven design methodologies.
- Know the purpose and process for developing an Entity-Relationship diagram.
- Define Entity-Relationship diagrams and the three relationship types.
- Develop simple Entity-Relationship diagrams.
- Understand the purpose and advantages of data normalization.
- Know the four steps in the data normalization process.
- Derive third normal form data structures from unnormalized data.

THE VALUE OF DATA

In recent years corporate data have become a critical concern to business management. The changing nature and importance of data have largely paralleled the evolving role of the computer information systems (CIS) within large organizations.

The Past

In the early days of the introduction of computer technology into business applications, CIS functions were fragmented across the existing corporate departments and hierarchy. Figure 5-1 shows a typical organizational structure when data processing was a relatively new concept. The functions of these CIS fragments were subordinate and specialized to the departments which they served. CIS components, programs, and systems sprang up in a laissez-faire manner as individual departments perceived particular needs and secured personnel capable of implementing computing solutions. Often departments within an organization competed for and/or shared available technical expertise.

Likewise the data utilized by these systems were subordinate and highly departmental-specific. For example, the personal information on employees kept in the payroll department had no direct relationship to the data on employees housed in personnel and absolutely no connection to records in purchasing. Under this arrangement, data were "owned" by individual corporate departments. These departments developed and maintained these databases using their internal budgets and thus were reluctant to share either the data or any derived information. CIS functions and data were merely a service to their respective business components.

The Present

Gradually as computing technology progressed and automated solutions became more evident and viable, organizations became swamped in the so called "information explosion." Suddenly computer systems were popping up all over the corporate structure. Individual departments were demanding (and receiving) more computing solutions to their specific needs.

It also became apparent that a great deal of duplication of effort and **redundancy** of data were occurring. For example, both payroll and purchasing were writing separate budgeting programs, neither of which had any relation to a similar program in personnel. Also, when an employee moved, personnel would be informed and change the address on the employee file; but payroll would not be informed, and consequently, important information about taxes would go astray. Thus the problems inherent in CIS function and data redundancy combined with a managerial insistence on taking advantage of economies of scale led to a new organizational structure. Large mainframes were purchased to handle ever increasing quantities of data. With the large mainframes came corporate standards and a centralized CIS function. A CIS authority in the corporate hierarchy was obviously necessary for at least the operation of the computer center.

Figure 5-2 shows a typical corporate structure adjusted to take advantage of shared computing resources. Rather than being subordinate to individual departments, the CIS function became a separate organizational component reporting directly to the CEO. Other departments made requests to CIS for "shared" resources. Typically a steering committee was formed to establish priorities between competing departmental CIS budgets and projects. No one

A typical organizational structure when data processing was in its infancy.

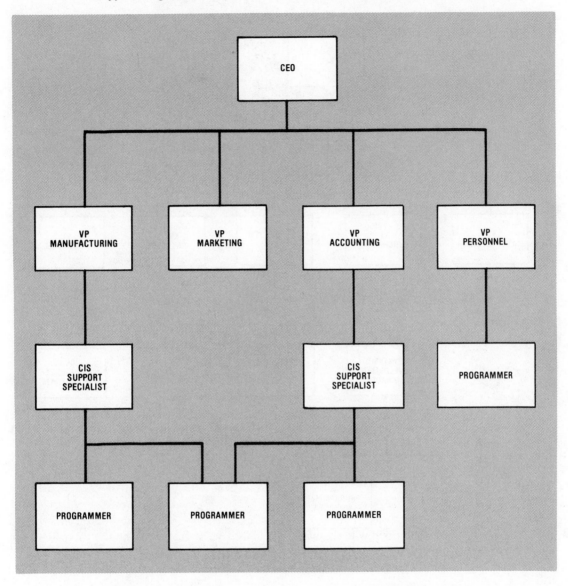

"owned" the computing functions or the data. Under this structure CIS was not merely a service but a full corporate partner in the overall business enterprise. This alignment is now common in organizations.

The nature and value of the data themselves have likewise evolved. Access to vital corporate data proved to be a measure of business success or failure. (It could also be argued that data access became a measure of status and power.) Data became viewed as a corporate capital asset, much like money, to be con-

Figure 5.2 *Organizational structure that takes advantage of shared computing resources.*

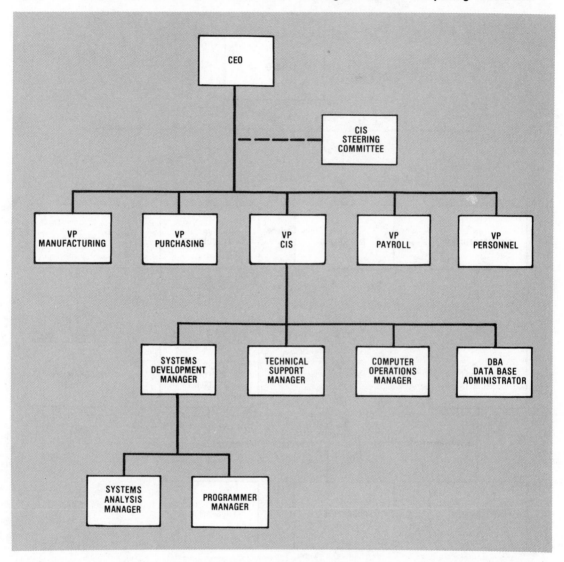

served and allocated cautiously. It also became apparent that misuse of the data assets could cause calamities ranging from employee frustration to loss of earnings to complete enterprise failure.

Data management became a specialty. Data base management systems (DBMS) with a managing data base administrator (DBA) are now commonplace. Data have come to be viewed as a vital corporate shared resource to be controlled and coordinated by a central authority within the organizational hierarchy. The data are "owned" by the corporation (with CIS as the caretaker) and all usage is to be carefully coordinated.

Although the organizational structure shown in Figure 5-2 is still fairly common, a new movement is clearly on the horizon. This new realignment has been triggered by three factors: (1) a new explosion in computing technology, (2) a backlash to complete data centralization, and (3) the realization that expensive computing solutions generally and the concentration of CIS corporate power and prestige specifically are not guarantors of corporate success.

The new explosion of computing technology is characterized by the proliferation of powerful microcomputers across the corporate landscape. The absolute data processing and storage capabilities of mainframe, mini-, and microcomputers have become blurred with recent innovations. In addition, the advent of networking and data communication has had a profound effect on how users view computing solutions. Concurrently, a variety of software systems has been developed that allow relatively unsophisticated users to implement highly complex computer functions. End-user computing (EUC) is becoming more commonplace.

In making use of these new hardware and software advances, departments and users have found centralized CIS data base configurations to be cumbersome — technologically, logistically, and politically. Frustrations regarding these problems have led to a retreat from CIS centralization. Individual users want easy access to data in order to use their new computing power.

Corporate entities have also begun to question the ultimate value of extensive and expensive computer solutions. It has become increasingly evident that producing large, complex computer systems in house is extremely risky and costly. Systems that do work often are not used. Ones that are used often do not justify their expense. In short, centralized CIS as a vital corporate function is being challenged.

Figure 5-3 shows the effect of these influences upon CIS in the corporate hierarchy. The picture of a multi tiered environment may be emerging. CIS still has a shared corporate role, but a diminished one. More and more CIS data and functions are being distributed to the departmental and user level within the organization. (The CIS corporate function is being further diminished by a new reliance upon third-party computing solutions and consultation. Vendors now exist who will supply relatively generic data processing solutions, such as payroll or accounts receivable, at attractive prices. More specific computing solutions may be provided through consulting services.) Both inter- and intra-departmental minicomputers are being used for the sharing of unit-level common data and processing. Individual users share resources via microcomputers linked into local area networks (LAN). These processing levels may be linked to each other via bridging mechanisms. Organizationally, this arrangement is a compromise between the alignments displayed in Figures 5-1 and 5-2.

Along with this new CIS organizational perspective comes a slightly different data perspective. Data at different levels in this scheme will have different value and different ownership. They will no longer be strictly a corporate asset. In fact, the ultimate value of data, like that of CIS, is being questioned. Does the corporation really need all these data? A new corporate reality is being

Figure 5.3. An organized structure with a modified CIS function.

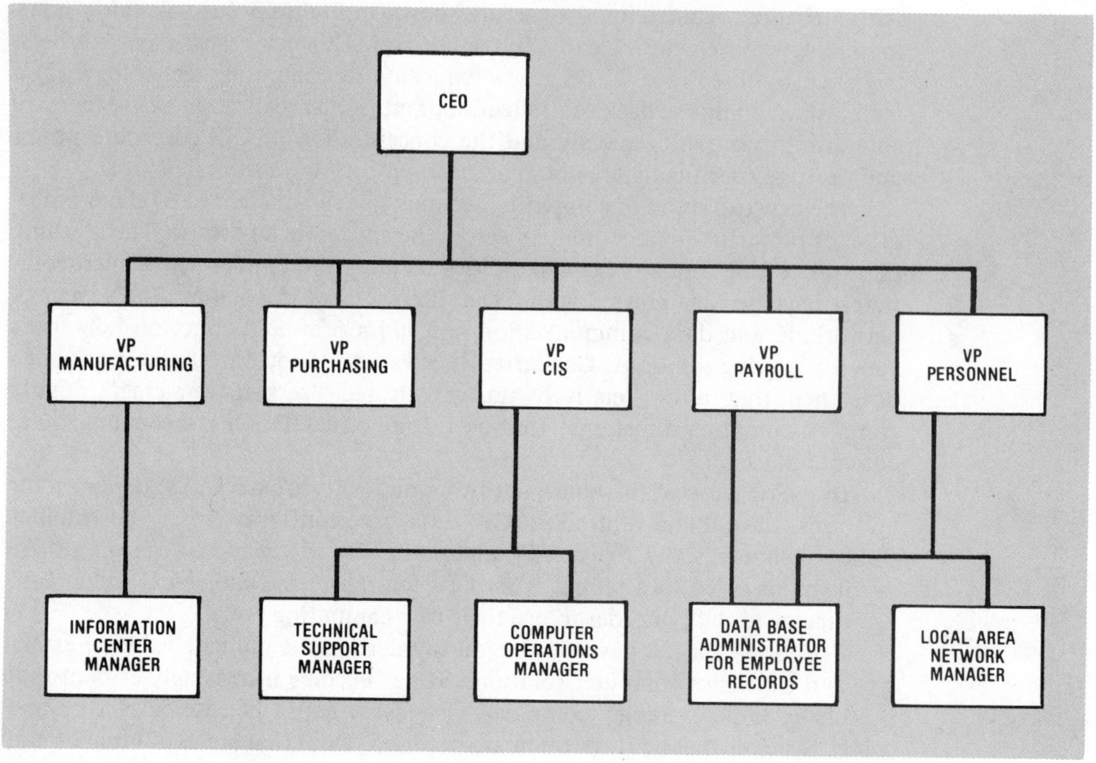

shaped that can be characterized by the phrase "just good enough (JGE)." Viewing data as a capital asset implied that more was always better. This new JGE view implies that the value lies in whether or not the data makes a difference at the corporate, departmental, or user level. Meeting short-term objectives combined with long-range goals will be critical. The sheer magnitude of computing solutions and data will no longer be valued in and of itself.

HOLISTIC DATA MODELING

Holistic data modeling involves a systematic data driven approach to systems development. The organization is viewed at various levels from a largely data, as opposed to process, perspective. The various data requirements of each level of the overall enterprise combine to form a synergistic data system. A **synergistic system** is one in which the combined interaction of individual components produces more than the sum of the individual components.

Data-Driven Design Perspective

Some methodologies emphasize a data driven systems development approach. **Data-driven** design refers, in its most simple definition, to modeling processes that focus primarily upon the data objects, instead of the functions, of a system. Data-driven design methodologies may be concerned with data input and output objects such as records, reports, or screens or with entities for which data are either currently or potentially recorded or stored. Some common data-driven modeling techniques are data-structured design, object-oriented methods, and entity-relationship models. Data-structured design provides a symbolic modeling tool to record and develop data input, output, and transformational structures. Object-oriented methods view systems as a collection of class-derived **objects** from which messages are received and sent (see feature at the end of this chapter). **Entity-relationship diagrams** are models that define system data entities and their corresponding relationships. Data **entities** are objects within businesses, such as customers or parts, for which information is to be accumulated. Relationships are logical **association** between entities, for example, "customers *purchase* parts." Contrast these methods to techniques discussed in Chapter 4. Using data flow diagrams (DFD) for process analysis emphasizes functionality and movement of data. Functions or processes are isolated, and the data exchanged between them are specified in detail. DFDs are thus process or function oriented. Data-driven design is data or object oriented.

Initially, data-driven design seems less ambiguous than a process or function orientation because data objects are easier to isolate than functions within organizations. For instance, it is easier to determine the existence of the purchasing records without having to specify what it is that purchasing does. Determining the relationship between purchasing records and personnel records, on the other hand, will require more investigation. Eventually the line where relationships end and functions begin will become blurred. Complete analysis will ultimately require a combination of both data- and process-analysis techniques.

Enterprise Modeling

The evolving role and value of organizational data, combined with new computing technologies, require modeling techniques that view data from multiple perspectives. The significance and priority of an individual piece of data will vary substantially as they are observed from the various corporate levels. As an organizational resource, data must be modeled with respect to:

1. the enterprise as a whole,
2. a specific business area,
3. essential departmental functions, and
4. individual user views.

Complete data analysis must determine how the informational needs and perspective of one level affect all others.

Viewing the enterprise is much like visualizing the context model in a DFD. Here the data object to be modeled is the entire business concern. As the overall system in a context DFD is connected to external entities, so is the enterprise linked to other data objects. Think of a large multinational and multipurpose corporation. On a regular basis it must interact with outside corporate entities, regulatory agencies, governmental bodies, the consumer public, and the banking system, as well as others. The enterprise has relationships with these external objects. These relationships have data needs and requirements. Modeling at this level should be relatively general, with more specificity being provided as successive levels are viewed. A very high level enterprise data model is thus derived. Figure 5-4 illustrates a context level data flow diagram as a conceptual view of an enterprise model.

Figure 5.4. *A data flow diagram showing a conceptualized view of an enterprise model.*

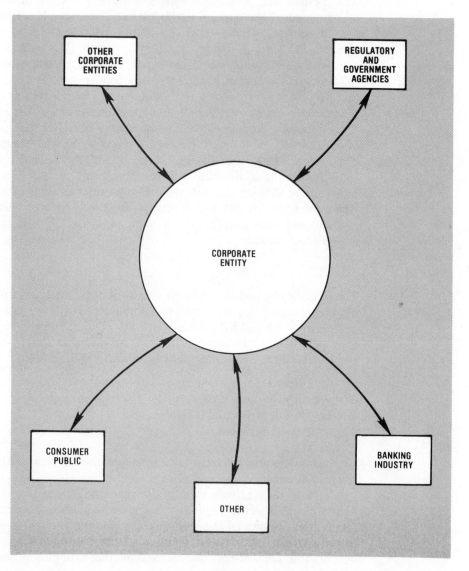

Part 2   Systems Analysis Modeling Techniques

This high-level view of data requirements needs to be linked to the long-range strategic goals and objectives of the enterprise. This is to ensure that informational expenditures are directly related to the enterprise strategic planning.

Within the enterprise as a whole, there will be specific business areas. The enterprise may deal with a variety of products, product lines, or services. These business areas should be defined and isolated. The connections or **relationships** between the business areas need to be established. At this level, data needs will still be somewhat aggregate. The data shared between these objects are likely to be entire databases residing on mainframe computing systems. Figure 5-5 illustrates a business-area view model.

Within each business area a variety of departmental functions can be isolated. Some of these functions may be shared with other business enterprises. Some of them must be replicated. For example, it may be possible for business areas to share a common payroll department but impossible for them to share

Figure 5.5.   A business-area view model.

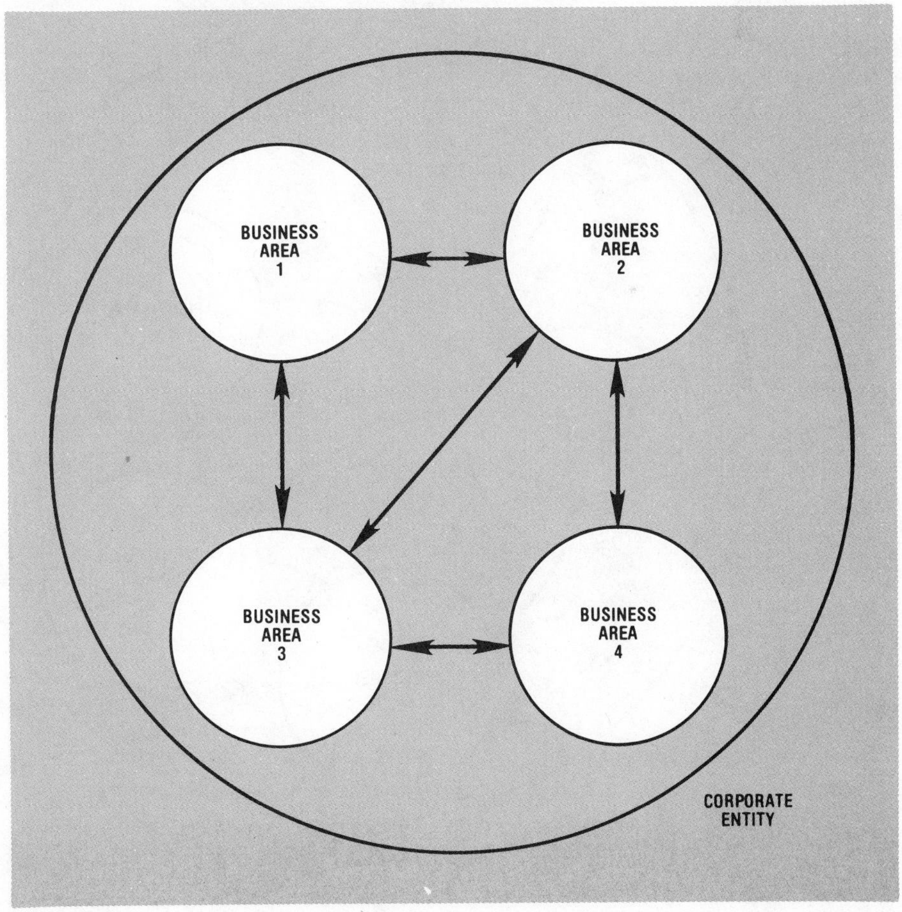

inventory functions. These departmental views of the enterprise are those most closely associated with actual individual computer information systems. Thus it is at this level where data and process modeling begin to interact. The data relationships between these entities (departments) require fairly detailed specificity, probably to the record level. Figure 5-6 illustrates a departmental view model.

Finally, within departments there will be user views. These views of the data are those that individual persons or project teams must regularly deal with. The detail of data at this level for the relationships between user views must be to the very specific input/output requirements such as the field and character levels of reports or records. The user views will be the foundation for the data model throughout the enterprise. Figure 5-7 illustrates a user view model. This is also the level of most concern for this text. However, successful CIS development will

Figure 5.6. ***A departmental view model.***

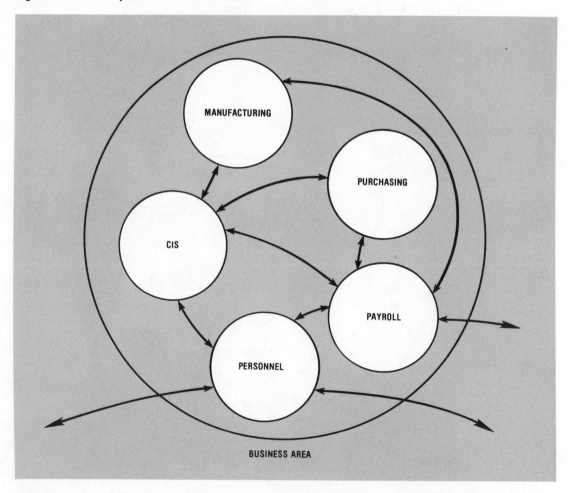

Part 2 Systems Analysis Modeling Techniques

Figure 5.7.   A user view model.

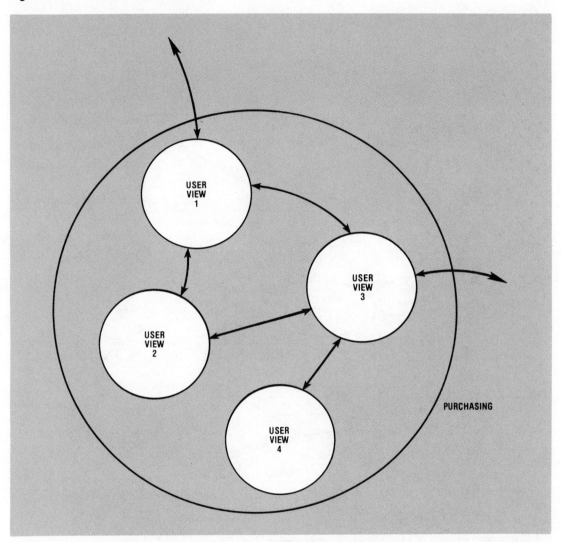

result only with sensitivity to the impact of new or revised systems upon all enterprise levels. Figure 5-8 illustrates a complete hierarchical view of the entire enterprise.

More and more emphasis is being placed upon data modeling and data relationships in the systems development process. Some methodologies go so far as to ignore process or functional analysis (and thus data flow diagrams) entirely. Others wait until data modeling is complete. Data modeling in these methodologies thus becomes the driving development force and the primary analysis tool. This text will emphasize the importance of both (data and process) types of modeling and attempt to balance the significance of each.

Figure 5.8. Hierarchical view of enterprise.

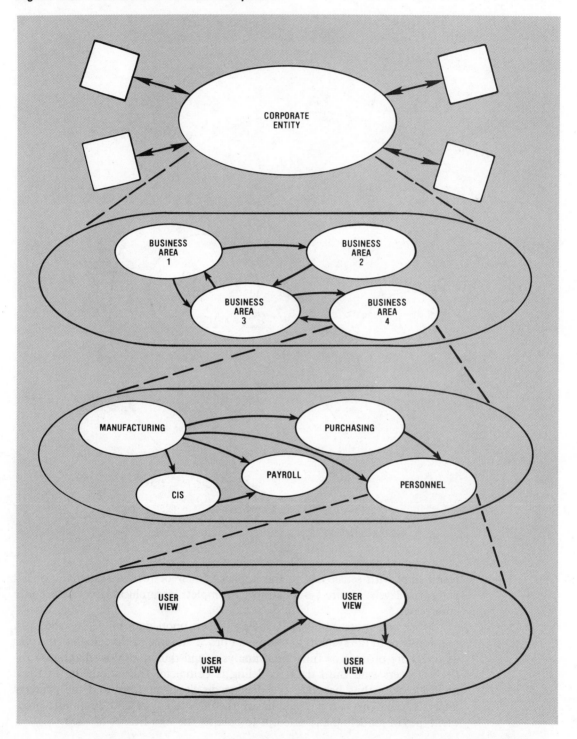

Part 2   Systems Analysis Modeling Techniques

Synergism and Modeling

Conceptual enterprise modeling is holistic in approach. Holism assumes an importance of the whole entity and an interdependence among its components. Holism also implies synergism, that is, the value of the functions of the components of a whole can be greater the a simple summing of the parts. For example, consider the new potentials and possibilities brought about by the addition of enhanced connectivity technologies to existing computing resources. The result is not merely more of the same but provision for completely new ways of thinking about business relationships. In other words, the enterprise operating as an holistic entity can be more productive than merely adding up the production of individual employees, departments, and business areas.

Holistic data modeling assumes an approach that is sensitive at each enterprise level to the needs of the other levels. When defining user views, questions must be asked that relate back to enterprise-wide strategic planning. A departmental decision to discontinue a specific file must consider other potential users of that file. The entire enterprise must be in some way linked with every data decision.

This perspective is different from traditional systems analysis techniques. Usually, systems analysis is thought of as (1) breaking the whole into component parts, (2) providing solutions for the individual components, and (3) assembling the component solution into a whole solution. Traditional systems analysis concentrates upon the component solutions. It often neglects the enterprise while solving a component part. This (along with the reasons identified in Chapter 2) is why so many system development projects are unsuccessful. Holistic modeling adds a dimension of concern for the entire enterprise while solving individual components.

ENTITY-RELATIONSHIP (E-R) DIAGRAMS

The **entity-relationship (E-R) diagram** is a tool for doing data modeling. E-R diagrams may be used to supplement the DFD as means of better understanding the system's data requirements.

The E-R Development Process

E-R modeling, like other aspects of the system development process, involves certain basic principles in order to be successful. These principles as described in Chapter 2 are:

- Iteration
- Hierarchical decomposition or layering
- Evolutionary scope and objective
- Use of graphic tools
- Use of models
- Understanding, imagination, and creativity

The E-R modeling process is iterative in nature. Initially, in the analysis of a system, certain broad categories of data will become evident. For example, in a college registration system it will be obvious upon the development of the preliminary data flow diagram that information about students, instructors, courses, and the registration process will need to be collected, stored, and recalled. Items identified as **data stores** on the DFD are data objects or "entities." But at this early stage the precise elements of data and their organization will not be evident. A preliminary E-R diagram may be built, but it is unlikely that complete data structures will exist. As the analyst probes deeper into the details of the system, more data about the data of the registration system will be collected. This process, like that of building the data flow diagram, will require user involvement, understanding, and agreement. Users should be continuously consulted during E-R modeling to insure that all current and potential data entities and relationships are being considered. Collecting these data may at times seem needlessly repetitive, but it is critical to the usefulness of the eventual database.

Likewise, E-R modeling involves hierarchical decomposition and layering. From the large categories of data entities in the registration system (students, instructors, courses, and registration), structures or records will be partitioned. These data structures, or records, will be further decomposed into individual **data elements**, or fields. Finally, precise characteristics about each field must be defined. For example, should the field be a key; should the data be numeric, character, picture, or something else; is the field required data? These and other field-specific questions will be answered and documented in the data dictionary. Each iterative view will take the analyst through succeeding levels in the data hierarchy. As the investigation progresses, however, the analyst must give attention to preceding levels to analyze how new information has impacted previous analysis efforts.

The scope and objectives of the data modeling are evolutionary by nature. Early in the development process, a preliminary understanding about the system database may describe such issues as who "owns" the data; which departments must interact with the data; and what are the sheer magnitude and complexity of the data? As data modeling progresses, the understanding of these issues will evolve until a "final" resolution is reached for project purposes. (In reality there is no final resolution of these issues, as they continue to evolve long after system development.)

Graphic tools can be used to model data in greater detail than simply the recognition of data stores on the data flow diagrams. These graphic data representations will help insure clear communication between the analyst and the user about the specific nature, structure, and relationships of the data base. The entity-relationship diagram is a commonly used tool to provide graphic representations of data entities and their relationships.

The data model developed using a graphic tool like an E-R diagram must be supported by a data dictionary. The data dictionary will contain all of the detail necessary to implement the conceptual data system into an actual functioning data base. The model, however, is a component in the overall system model.

Successful system development will require an integration of a variety of tools and documentation to present a complete system portrait.

As is true of systems development in general, data modeling requires understanding, imagination, and creative thinking of the analyst. The data analyst must understand the relationship between the overall system objectives and the data configuration if all the data constituencies are to be satisfied. For example, in the case of the college registration system, a campus administrator may see a high priority for a data organization that minimizes computer processing and storage requirements in order to save costs. However, such an organization may mean that the actual registration process is cumbersome and causes long lines and excessive waits for schedules. Students might thus be frustrated and unhappy with this solution. Obviously, the objectives of efficiency and budgets must be balanced with convenience and timeliness if the system is to be truly successful.

Such solutions do not always appear out of thin air or even as the result of exhaustive investigation. Often such solutions are only discovered through imagination and creative thinking. New ideas and approaches should be developed and explored. The more stores, structures, and elements required in a data base, the more potential data configurations are possible. The analyst should not be confined to the current data organizations.

The purpose of E-R diagrams is thus to:

1. verify accuracy and thoroughness of data design, current and new, with users.
2. organize and record organizational data entities, relationships, and scope through decomposition and layering.
3. enhance the overall communication between development project team members, system technicians, management, and users with the use of graphic models.
4. generally simplify and bolster the creative data design process.

DEFINITIONS OF E-R DIAGRAMS

Entity-relationship (E-R) diagrams are graphic illustrations used to display objects or events within a system and their relationships to one another. E-R diagrams model data in much the same way that data flow diagrams (DFD) model processes and data flow. However, in DFDs processes are first identified and then the data that flow between them are isolated or derived. Thus the processes are the focal point of the DFD. In E-R models, entities are isolated and the relationships between them are defined. The entities in E-R diagrams are usually data-related objects or events, and the relationships are typically common data associations or linkages between the entities. Thus the focal point of E-R models is data, not processes.

The process of developing E-R models also requires attention to the actual data being modeled. As the graphic representation is being built, data structures or tables and elements must be identified and recorded. These data about data will become the organizational "base of data" and should be faithfully documented in the ongoing data dictionary. Much of the data will have been provided during the development of the DFD. The "base of data" is the data or information available to any organization used for implementation of both short- and long-term objectives. It is the necessary information required to achieve the organizational mission or function. The application of structure, coherency, and organization transforms the "base of data" into the "database."

An **entity** in an E-R model represents an object within the business unit or enterprise that warrants sufficient interest to have data about it captured, stored, maintained, and/or reported. Such entities endure over time. Examples of such entities at a college or university would include such objects as the faculty, students, and courses offered.

Relationships are logical **associations** or **events** that share commonality between entities. An example of an association is the relationship between the students (entity) and the instructor (entity) assigned (relationship) to a particular course. If a college computer system is to maintain the knowledge of which instructors are assigned to which courses, then obviously this relationship must be reflected in the overall base of data. An example of an event which shares commonality between entities would be when a student (entity) registers (event) for courses (entity) for a given semester. Again the act of registration and information about it must be recorded if the college is to carry out its daily operations.

It is often difficult to distinguish between entities and relationships or associations and events. Analysts will often disagree about which is which. For example, is a course which lasts a semester an event or an entity? Similarly is the relationship of an instructor's assignment to a particular course an association or an event? While the initial decision may have some effect upon the initial appearance of the E-R model, if the vital data about the objects and their relationships are recorded and logically organized, then the resulting overall data model will be successful. The important thing is to utilize the modeling tools to record and organize vital organizational information.

E-R models typically illustrate entities and relationships. A box symbol is often used to represent entities and a diamond for relationships (see Figure 5-9). Generally speaking, the more "event-like" a relationship is, the more likely it will be to require a unique data structure or data table. Many times, significant and complex events seem so important that they will eventually be modeled as entities.

Figure 5.9   E-R graphic symbols.

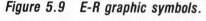

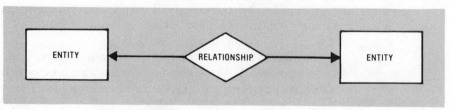

Many times, simple associations between entities require no unique data to be collected and maintained. For example, the association between an instructor record and a courses offered record requires only that each contain a common key data element. Figures 5-10 and 5-11 show two alternative ways of maintaining the association between the instructor and courses offered. In Figure 5-10, the instructor key, instructor-number, is maintained in the courses-offered structure. To find the instructor of a course given a course-offered record, you would use the class-instructor as the key to search the instructor file. In Figure 5-11, the course-offered key, class-number, is maintained in the instructor structure. To find the instructor of a course given a course-offered record, you would find a match of class-number to instructor-class in the instructor file.

Conversely, complex events sharing commonality between entities are examples of relationships that will probably require unique data structures to maintain and fully functionalize the relationship being expressed. For example, the

Figure 5.10. *Association of courses offered to instructor.*

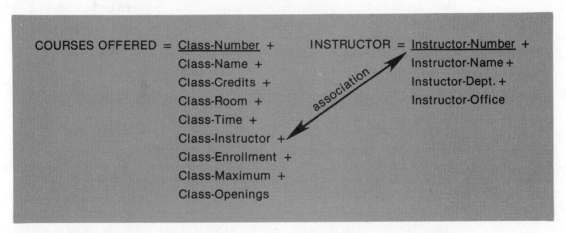

Figure 5.11. *Alternative association of courses offered to instructor.*

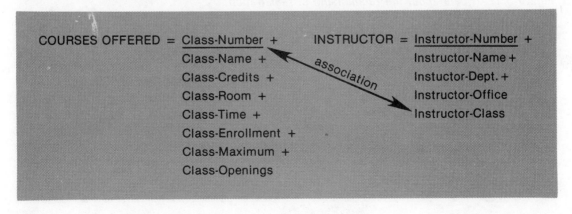

event of registration for courses by students will probably require a great deal of very specific information in order to provide the necessary utility required of the data base. Figure 5-12 shows data which may be required about the relationship of registration. Storing these data in the student record would be inappropriate for many reasons. For instance, the student record would have to be expanded each semester that a student enrolled for classes in order to keep an accurate history. (While it is obvious that a student history or "transcript" must be maintained, it is not logical to store this information in a student structure. These data are not specifically about a student, but rather about a registration event concerning a student.) Also processing student records for other purposes, like printing the campus phone book, would be made unnecessarily complicated by the presence of registration structures within the student record. Likewise, keeping the registration information within the class lists makes absolutely no sense from either a logical or functional view of the database.

Types of E-R Relationships

There are three basic **types of relationships** modeled between entities on an E-R diagram, one-to-one, one-to-many, and many-to-many.

A **one-to-one relationship** signifies that items in one of the associated entities has exactly a one-to-one correspondence to items in the other entity. Given a value in entity A there exists only one value in entity B associated with it and vice versa. Figure 5-13 shows a simple one-to-one relationship between two entities as displayed on an E-R diagram. In this example instructors (entity) are assigned (relationship) to courses (entity). This scenario assumes that each instructor is assigned to one course only (per term) and that one course has only one instructor. (Obviously, this is usually not the case.) Sample data structures or tables are illustrated in Figure 5-10 for these entities.

For this type of relationship, no additional or unique data need to be collected to maintain the association. This type of relationship may be resolved by maintaining a data link or association between the data elements of the two tables. However, the data element CLASS-INSTRUCTOR in courses offered

Figure 5.12. Data about the relationship of registration.

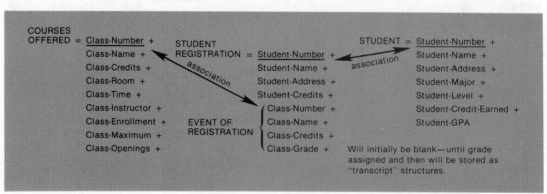

Part 2   Systems Analysis Modeling Techniques

Figure 5.13. A one-to-one relationship.

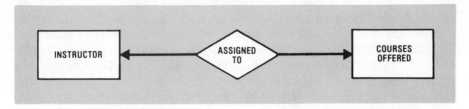

and INSTRUCTOR-NUMBER in instructor must be available in both tables to continue the relationship or linkage. Figure 5-10 shows an example of a data link.

Many times, a one-to-one relationship can be resolved by a merging of the entities. For instance, in the example here if the instructor were always assigned the same course term after term, year after year, it may be useful to merely merge the entities, and thus the tables, for instructors and courses. Thus a potential alternative to this relationship is the table displayed by Figure 5-14. Notice that the key in this case will refer to either the course or the instructor since the instructor always teaches the same course.

However, in this particular case this is probably not a wise decision because an instructor is not likely to teach the same course forever. In fact, it is not even likely that the instructor would teach only one course. As soon as an instructor teaches more than one course in any given term, this becomes a **one-to-many relationship**, thus precluding any possibility of merging the entities. As a rule, never merge any entities where it seems possible for a one-to-one relationship to become a one-to-many. Also, from a processing viewpoint, there are many situations in this scenario wherein the course or the instructor information would be needed independent from each other. For example, a report listing students registered for the course would not need a great deal of information about the instructor.

Figure 5.14. Merged instructor and courses offered tables.

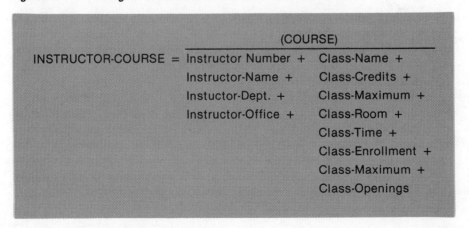

	(COURSE)	
INSTRUCTOR-COURSE =	Instructor Number +	Class-Name +
	Instructor-Name +	Class-Credits +
	Instuctor-Dept. +	Class-Maximum +
	Instructor-Office +	Class-Room +
		Class-Time +
		Class-Enrollment +
		Class-Maximum +
		Class-Openings

Assuming the one-to-one relationship is not merged and the relationship between the entities is maintained, then the analyst should be clear about the precise method of association. As illustrated in Figure 5-10, the relationship between the instructor and the course is maintained by the **key** (underlined) INSTRUCTOR-NUMBER in the instructor table with the data element CLASS-INSTRUCTOR in the courses-offered table. Another possibility here would be to have the courses-offered table key COURSE-NUMBER (let's not deal with multiple sections for the moment) also available in the instructor table as the element INSTRUCTOR-CLASS (Figure 5-11). This solution, however, may not be practical because it would then be difficult to add new courses to the instructor file without altering the instructor table format and size. The solution suggested in Figure 5-10, on the other hand, would allow for insructors to be assigned to multiple courses without a file structure change.

A one-to-many relationship implies that more than one item in one entity may be associated with one item in another. One item in an entity refers to many items in another, but not vice versa. Figure 5-15 displays the instructors assigned to courses-offered example, now assuming that an instructor may be assigned to many courses but each course would be assigned to only one instructor. The symbol displaying the many relationship is the double arrow. The double arrow is placed on the entity that may be associated in multiple with the other. In this case, there may be multiple courses assigned to an instructor.

Figure 5.15.   A one-to-many relationship.

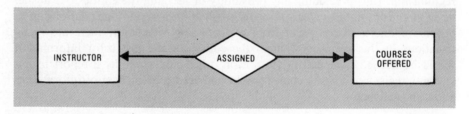

The data tables needed to display this association, illustrated in Figure 5-16 (a) are identical to those in Figure 5-10. As previously discussed, the one-to-many relationship can be provided by maintaining the association of the INSTRUCTOR-NUMBER in the instructor table with the CLASS-INSTRUCTOR in the courses-offered table.

A **many-to-many relationship** implies that each item in an entity may be associated with many others in another entity. One item in an entity refers to many others in another and vice versa. Figure 5-17 displays the relationship represented by students registering for courses. Each student may sign up for many courses and each course may have many students. The act of registering is obviously an event requiring a unique data table to maintain the relationship. In this case, the data table is the event of student registration as displayed in Figure 5-18.

Figure 5.16. *Tables of one-to-many relationships.*

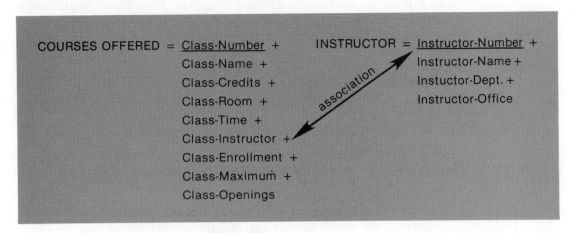

Figure 5.17. *A many-to-many relationship.*

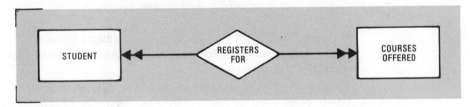

Figure 5.18. *Data table showing the event of student registration, a many-to-many relationship.*

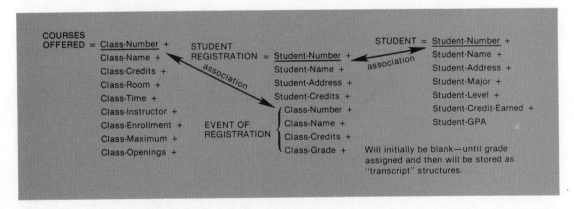

Many-to-many relationships may be resolved by producing an intermediary table for the relationship. An analyst may wish to further "entify" such relationships. To entify a many-to-many relationship means to decompose it in such a way that only one-to-one or one-to-many relationships remain. The process of

entification would thus turn the registration relationship like the one shown in Figure 5-17 into an entity like a schedule of courses. The schedule would have a one-to-one relationship with the students (one student has one schedule) and a many-to-many relationship with course offerings (many courses listed on one student schedule and the same course listed on many students' schedules as displayed in Figure 5-19). The many-to-many relationship of the schedule to course offerings could be further entified.

STEPS IN BUILDING AN E-R DIAGRAM

Keeping in mind the principles of E-R development as discussed earlier, there are several specific steps to follow in building an E-R diagram. They are:

1. Determine the data entities.
2. Generate a list of potential entity relationships or "pairings."
3. Determine the significance (if any) and the relationship between the entity pairings.
4. Analyze the significant entity relationships.
5. Develop an integrated E-R diagram.

This process will result in a thorough, systematic investigation of the existing system. Also, it should help focus both user and analyst upon potential new data entities and/or relationships.

Step 1. Determine the data entities. The data entities, as defined previously, are those objects within the system which seem likely candidates to have infor-

Figure 5.19. Entification of student-to-courses-offered relationship.

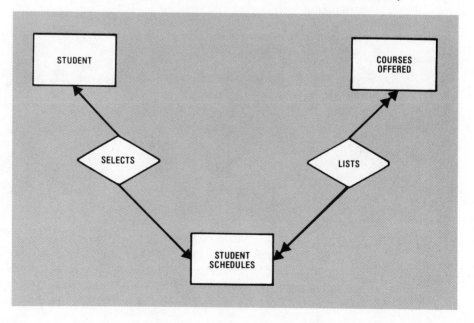

mation about them stored. Another way to think about data entities is to ask "what things within the system are likely to be data files?" A good place to start is the preliminary data flow diagrams. Obviously the data stores on a data flow diagram are likely candidates for data files and, thus, entities on an E-R model. A list of the entities should be defined, always subject to change, as development progresses. Figure 5-20 displays a preliminary DFD for a campus registration system. To simplify the example, let's select only four of the identifiable entities on the DFD, students (student file), instructors (instructor file), student schedules (registration file), and courses offered (class file).

Step 2. Generate a list of potential **entity pairings**. In other words, what is the maximum number of potential combinations among individual entities — or how many "pairs" of entities may be defined from the given entity set? In order to generate a list of pairings, one simply creates all possible combinations of the entities. In the registration example, there are four entities: students, instructors, student schedules, and courses offered. From these four entities, six potential combinations may be derived. These are:

Figure 5.20. Data flow diagram for student registration system.

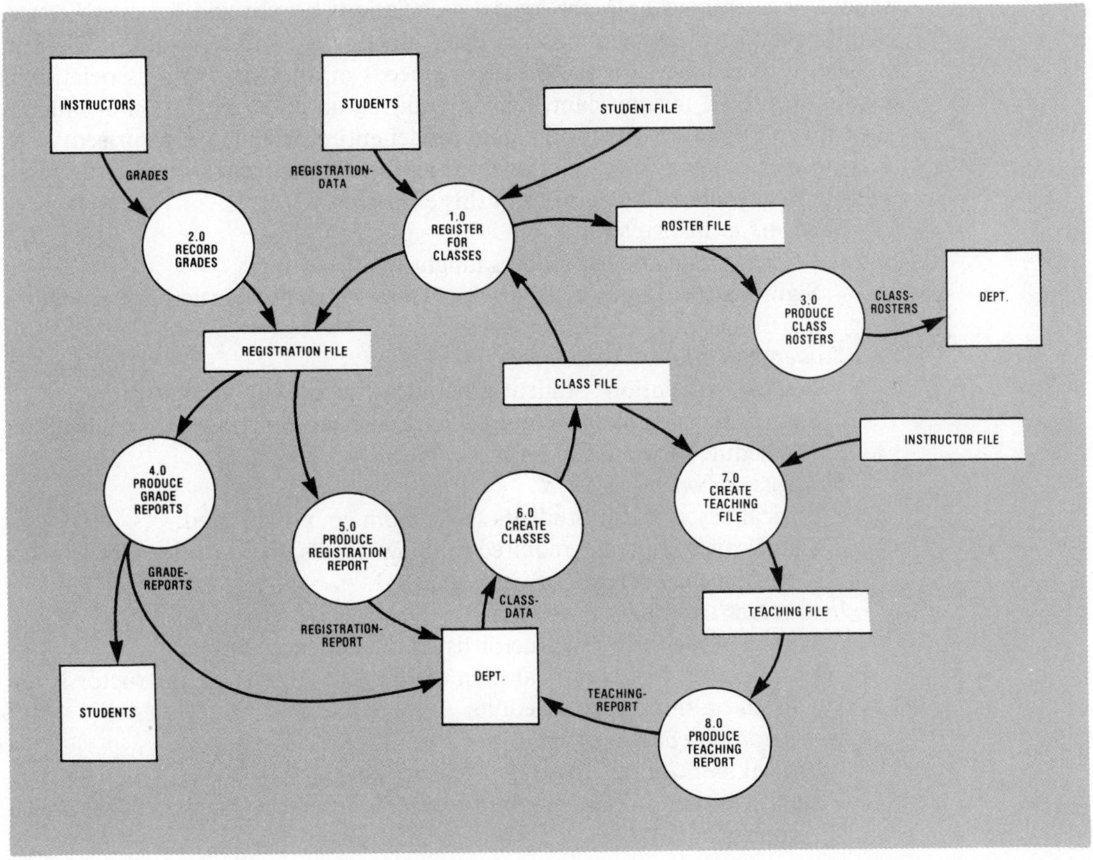

Students to instructors
Students to student schedules
Students to courses offered
Instructors to student schedules
Instructors to courses offered
Student schedules to courses offered

Obviously the more entities defined the more potential pairings. One more entity would have meant 10 potential entity combinations. The formula for determining the number of possible pairings is:

$$\sum_{i=1}^{N-1} i$$

where N is the number of entities defined. It should also be noted that some entities may relate to others in more than one way. Thus, the absolute number of relationships can be greater than the derived number of pairings.

Step 3. Determine the significance (if any) and the relationship between the entity pairings. Once these pairings are generated, the relationship of each should be examined both for logical associations nature and for significance. Significant logical associations are determined when some portion of data in one entity is required for the processing needs of another. If an association is determined to be insignificant, that is requiring no data integration or linkage, then it can be removed from the data model entirely. Don't be surprised, however, to reexamine deleted relationships as the development process continues. Let's look at each of the pairings in this example.

Students to instructors
　Logical association: Students taught by instructors.
　Significance: Linkage required to know to which instructors a student is
　　assigned.

Students to student schedules
　Logical association: Student generates schedule (upon registration).
　Significance: Linkage required to know which courses a student has
　　scheduled for a given term.

Students to courses offered
　Logical association: Students select from courses offered.
　Significance: Linkage required to know details about courses for which a
　　student may register or has registered.

Instructors to student schedules
　Logical association: Instructor listed on student schedule.
　Significance: Not significant. In the current system the instructor is not
　　listed on the course schedule.

Instructors to courses offered
　Logical association: Instructor teaches course.
　Significance: Linkage required to know which instructor teaches which
　　courses.

Student schedules to courses offered

Logical association: Student schedules list selected course offerings.

Significance: Linkage required to know for which courses a student has registered.

Step 4. Analyze the significant entity relationships. The next step will then be to analyze the relationship of the significant pairings developed above. For each significant pairing, the type of relationship (one-to-one, one-to-many, many-to-many) should be determined. A single E-R diagram should be developed for each significant pairing. A method of resolution should be provided for each relationship. Continuing with the registration example, there are:

Students to instructors

Relationship: Many students may be taught by an instructor. Many instructors may teach a student. Hence the relationship is many-to-many. See Figure 5-21.

Figure 5.21. Relationship of students to instructor.

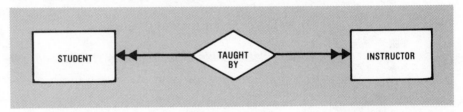

Resolution: This relationship may be resolved by another data table (roster file shown in Figure 5-20) which contains a list of students assigned to a class.

Students to student schedules

Relationship: The relationship is one-to-one because a student generates a student schedule and a student schedule is generated by a student. See Figure 5-22.

Figure 5.22. Relationship of students to schedules.

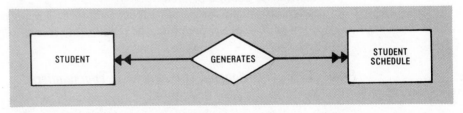

Resolution: This relationship may be resolved by keeping a student number on each schedule.

Students to courses offered

Relationship: Many students register for each course offered and a student may register for many courses offered, therefore the relationship is many-to-many. See Figure 5-23.

Resolution: This relationship may be resolved by the data entity student schedules (registration file—shown in Figure 5-20) which contains the classes for which a student registers.

Figure 5.23. **Relationship of students to courses offered.**

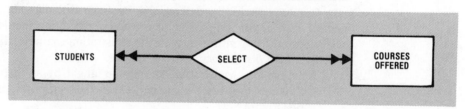

Instructors to student schedules

Relationship: The relationship is many-to-many because many instructors may be listed on a course schedule and many student schedules may list an instructor. See Figure 5-24.

Figure 5.24. **Relationship of instructor to student schedule.**

Resolution: Since the system requirements do not include detailed instructor information to be included on the schedule, there is currently no significant relationship between these entities. Further user discussion may reveal, however, some relationship such as that assigned instructors will be listed on student schedules.

Instructors to courses offered

Relationship: An instructor teaches a course and many courses are taught by an instructor, therefore, the relationship is one-to-many. See Figure 5-25.

Figure 5.25. **Relationship of instructor to course offered.**

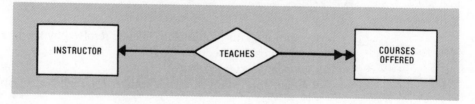

Resolution: This relationship may be resolved by the data element linkage between CLASS-INSTRUCTOR in the class file and INSTRUCTOR-NUMBER in the instructor file.

Student schedules to courses offered

Relationship: Many student schedules list course offerings. Many course offerings may be listed on a student schedule. Hence the relationship is many-to-many. See Figure 5-26.

Figure 5.26. *Relationship of schedules to courses offered.*

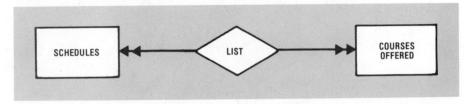

Resolution: This relationship may be resolved by the CLASS-NUMBER in the course offerings file and the CLASS-NUMBERs in the registration file (schedules).

Step 5. Develop an integrated E-R diagram. Finally, an E-R diagram may be assembled to represent all the relationships defined above. See Figure 5-27 (a). As we have seen, the relationship of registration (student to course offerings) is maintained by the entity of student schedules (actually an entification of the registration relationship). Thus the registration relationship is redundant on this diagram and can be removed. The diagram displayed in Figure 5-27 (b) now represents the data relationships for the four entities (students, instructors, student schedules, and course offerings) of the partial registration system.

FEATURE: OBJECT ORIENTED DESIGN

A rapidly developing design methodology is that of object oriented design or object orientation. From an applications viewpoint, object oriented design combines both data and process development methods. Recall that systems development methodologies traditionally utilize either a functional or a data orientation. Thus analysis using data flow diagrams begins with the delineation of the major system functional components or processes. Analysis using entity-relationship diagrams begins with the delineation of the various data entities. Object oriented design combines, conceptually, aspects of both the process and data orientations. An object in object oriented design contains both specified activities (processes) which it may perform and the necessary information (data) to carry out those activities.

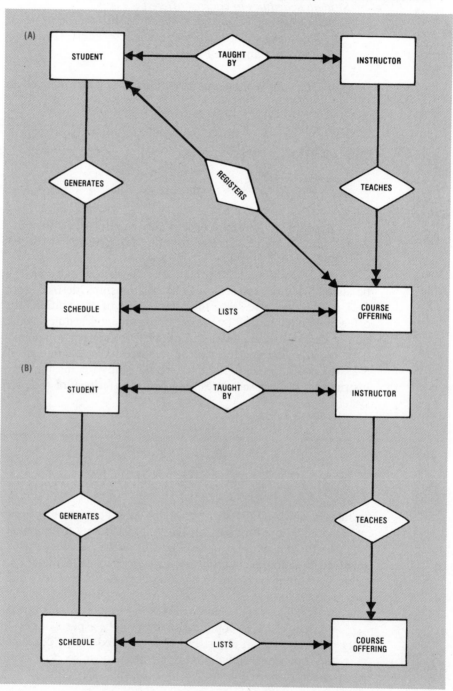

Part 2   Systems Analysis Modeling Techniques

Feature figure. *Object oriented design—class object and initiated objects.*

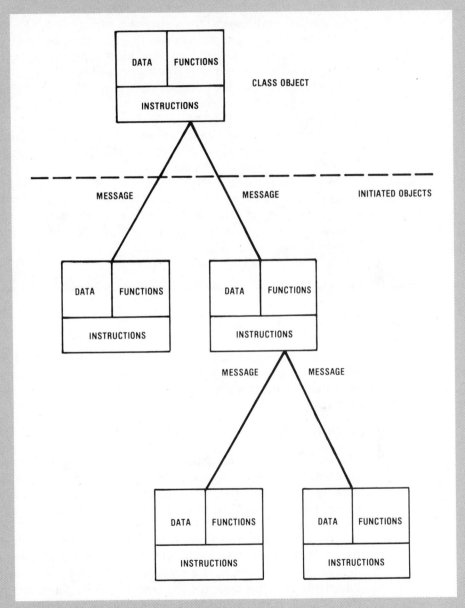

Object oriented design involves both the definition of objects and the subsequent interactions between objects. The definition of objects involves the concept of class and inheritance. A class is a general category of similar objects. Classes are created with well-defined sets of attributes, i.e., specific functions or data. Objects designated within a class inherit the attributes of the class and also contain specific processing characteristics.

Once object classes are defined, implementation involves the specification of multiple objects and their corresponding interactions. These interactions are configured in such ways as to meet system requirements. Objects may act upon other objects, be acted upon by other objects, or act on behalf of other objects. Interactions are executed through "messages" between objects. Messages may be simple on/off switches or may contain detailed processing information. Execution involves the dynamic initiation of objects, each inheriting the attributes of its class and each containing specific processing details as well as message information.

Since object oriented design produces modular, self-generating and reusable codes, the time it takes to do complex software development can be greatly reduced. Also, object orientation provides an extremely flexible operating environment, thus reducing costly maintenance. This type of development methodology is relatively resource intensive because of its highly graphic interface nature. However, as computer hardware becomes more powerful and memory expands greatly, look for more and more applications development to take on an object orientation.

LOGICAL DATA ANALYSIS

Once data stores and data structures have been isolated and defined, the next step is to examine and refine the actual organization of the data stores. **Logical data analysis** provides a means for organizing logically simple and efficient data stores.

Analyzing Data Stores

The development of the data flow and supplemental entity-relationship diagrams will provide a fairly complete portrait of the current system function and data configuration. Also, new requirements of the system function may have caused addition, deletion, or transfiguration of the current data stores, structures, or elements.

The contents of data stores have, up to this point, been defined intuitively by considering the output produced by the transformations that are fed by those data stores. For example, if a report is generated by a particular process, the underlying data that comprise the report must be derivable from the input to that process. If the input source is a data store, the components of the report must be components of the data store or derivable from them. Further, for data to be extracted from a data store, they must have been put there in the first place. Therefore, data flows into data stores must account for all required elements. Tests of reasonableness are applied throughout data flow analysis to make sure that all data are accounted for and are available at the requisite points within the system.

The motivation for modeling the system and analyzing data flows is to be sure that data are available to carry out the identified transformations to produce the desired outputs or to maintain required relationships between data objects. No focused effort is made at this point to assure that the components and organization of the data stores are designed properly. Even if assurance exists that particular data stores support system processing and maintains entity relationships, it does not necessarily follow that the components and organization of those data stores are the best that could be specified. Direct consideration must be given to designing data stores that can be packaged into physical files or databases that most effectively support system processing.

Logical data analysis provides a means for deriving the logical data structure of a system. The logical data structure refers to the organization of system data into data stores that are simplest in structure and minimal in content. Logical data analysis will determine *how* the required data will be stored structurally and logistically (still independent of the specific hardware environment).

Logical Data Structure Criteria

Two main criteria may be applied to data stores to determine whether their components and organization are optimum for the system they support. One criterion is **simplicity**. Organization of and access to data within a data store should be as simple as possible. As a general rule, the goal is to structure a data store so that it can be implemented as a simple sequential or direct-access file. That is, the components of the data store should be referenced only by a primary key, and there should be no repeating groups of data within the data store. (A key is one or more data elements that identify uniquely the occurrence of a data structure in a data store.) Thus, for example, a data store is simpler if it does not have alternate keys or pointers to link records and if it does not require implementation of variable length records. One criterion for logical data organization is always simplicity over complexity. This is true whether the data stores for a particular application will eventually be implemented as conventional files or packaged into one or more databases. Just as with systems processing design or software design, the simplest, most straightforward structure is nearly always the best.

The second criterion for logical data design is nonredundancy. **Redundancy** occurs, in part, when the same data element has been placed within two or more data stores. Redundancy can threaten the integrity of a system. If the value of a data component in one file is changed, the same element must be changed in all other files. Problems arise if files with redundant data are not all processed at the same time. In such cases, special processing runs may be needed to update the redundant components. This, in turn, means that adequate records must be kept to process these special runs. To avoid these problems, it is simpler to attempt to minimize redundancy.

Redundancy also occurs when the same data appear in different forms within the same data store—when two or more data components within a data store provide the same information. For example, within a student record system at a college, each record within the student file might contain the three data fields: course hours attempted, credits earned, and overall grade point average. There is no logical reason for including the grade point average. As long as the hours attempted and the credits earned are required as separate data elements, the grade point average can be calculated at any time and is thus unnecessary within the data store. Minimization of redundancy within a data store simplifies the file structure and leaves fewer data elements to be processed and updated.

The task at hand, therefore, is to derive a logical structure for the proposed system. The result will be a set of data stores that contain minimal redundant data elements, that are organized for simple access, and that support the processing functions of the system.

Advantages of Data Normalization

The procedure used to derive this logical structure is called **normalization**. In general, normalization produces the simplest, most straightforward organization of data elements into component data stores. Normalization should produce a set of data stores containing nonredundant data elements accessible through use of unique primary keys. The advantages of normalization are ease of understanding, ease of use, ease of implementation, and ease of maintenance.

Ease of Understanding. Normalization presents data structures in a way that can be understood easily by operational and management users. The structures of data are presented in simple two-dimensional tables that do not require technical understanding on the part of users and owners of the data.

Ease of Use. Data structures can be partitioned further, or joined through relationships (as described earlier), to permit any number of different logical viewpoints to be represented. Different structures can have different file organizations to allow efficient access for primary applications yet be accessible for many other secondary applications. That is, attributes from different files can be related with little complexity.

Ease of Implementation. Normalized structures can be implemented as simple files set up for either serial or direct access. In addition, the structures can be implemented within database systems.

Ease of Maintenance. Nonredundancies in the attribute files reduce problems while keeping all files up to date. If an attribute must be added to, changed, or deleted from a file, there is assurance that no other file will require the same maintenance. All attributes that are not primary or secondary keys appear only one time and in one place within the overall system data structure.

The Process of Normalization

Recall the data flow diagram for the student registration system as shown in Figure 5-28. The part of the system shown here contains several data stores, some used to maintain data over a period of time and others used as transitional stores for the production of reports. During the modeling process, each data store was designed to support a particular transformation. The components of these data stores are shown in the partial data dictionary in Figure 5-29. (The

Figure 5.28. Data flow diagram for student registration system.

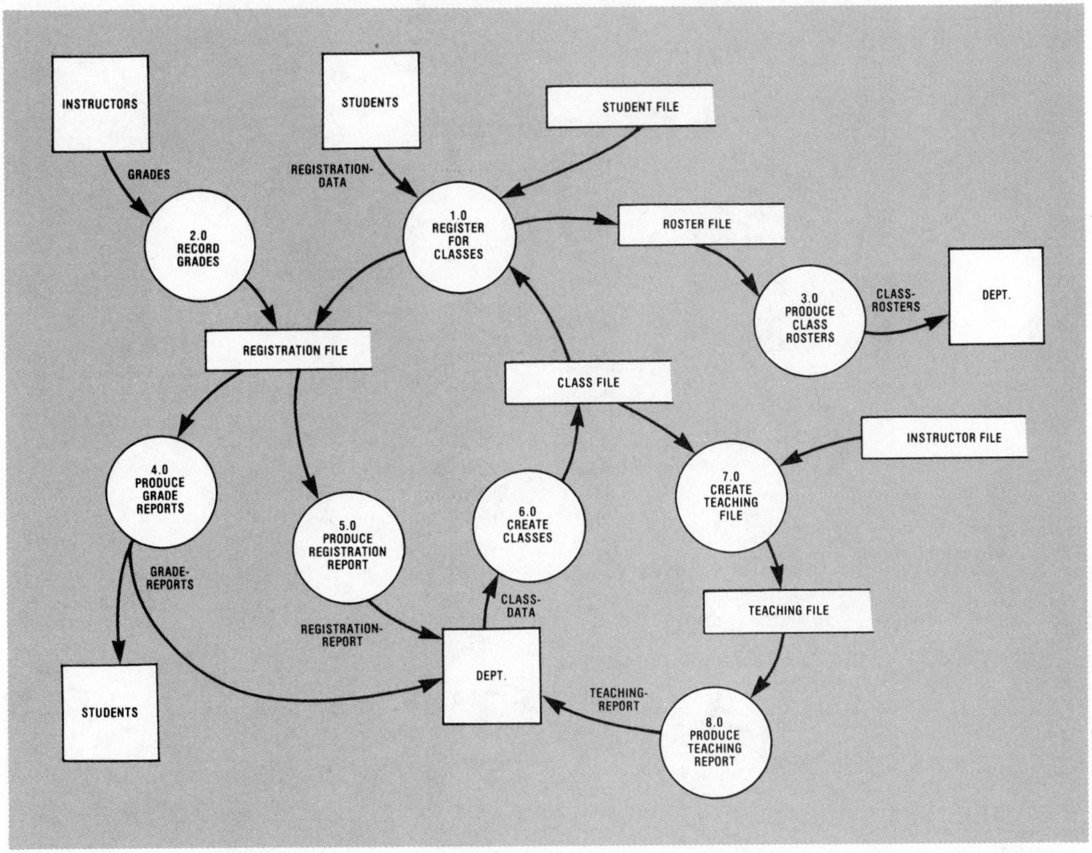

data elements that make up the key for each data store are underlined.) Note that each data store is an iteration of a data structure. Thus, the normalization of data stores is essentially equivalent to the normalization of a set of data structures. The normalization process explained in this text will result in a set of data structures said to be in the **third normal form**. (Some methodologies may carry the level of normalization further.) There are essentially three steps in this process:

Step 1: Partition each data structure that contains repeating groups that accomplish the same purpose. This step places the set of data structures (or stores) in a state known as the **first normal form**.

Within the data dictionary in the student registration example, there are three current data stores that contain repeating groups. The REGISTRATION-FILE contains a schedule of classes for each student. The ROSTER-FILE contains, for each class offered, the names of students enrolled in the class. The TEACHING-FILE contains, for each instructor, a list of courses taught.

Figure 5.29. Partial data dictionary for student registration system.

```
        CLASS-FILE              = {CLASS} All classes offered where
        CLASS                   = Class-Number +
                                  Class-Name +
                                  Class-Credits +
                                  Class-Room +
                                  Class-Time +
                                  Class-Instructor +
                                  Class-Enrollment +
                                  Class-Maximum +
                                  Class-Openings


        INSTRUCTOR-FILE         = {INSTRUCTOR} All instructors where
        INSTRUCTOR              = Instructor-Number +
                                  Instructor-Name +
                                  Instructor-Dept. +
                                  Instructor-Office


        REGISTRATION-FILE       = {STUDENT-REGISTRATION} All students where
        STUDENT-REGISTRATION    = Student-Number +
                                  Student-Name +
                                  Student-Address +
                                  Student-Credits +
                                  ⎧ Class-Number + ⎫
                                  ⎪ Class-Name +   ⎪
                                  ⎨ Class-Credits + ⎬
                                  ⎩ Class-Grade    ⎭  All classes for student


        ROSTER-FILE             = {ROSTER} All classes where
        ROSTER                  = Class-Number +
                                  Class-Name +
                                  Class-Credits +
                                  Class-Room +
                                  Class-Time +
                                  Class-Instructor +
                                  Class-Enrollment +
                                  ⎧ Student-Number + ⎫
                                  ⎨ Student-Name +   ⎬
                                  ⎩ Student-Level    ⎭  All students in class


        STUDENT-FILE            = {STUDENT} All students where
        STUDENT                 = Student-Number +
                                  Student-Name +
                                  Student-Address +
                                  Student-Major +
                                  Student-Level +
                                  Student-Credits-Earned +
                                  Student-GPA


        TEACHING-FILE           = {INSTRUCTOR} All classes where
        INSTRUCTOR-ASSIGNMENT   = Instructor-Number +
                                  Instructor-Name +
                                  Instructor-Dept. +
                                  Instructor-Credits +
                                  ⎧ Class-Number + ⎫
                                  ⎨ Class-Name +   ⎬
                                  ⎪ Class-Credits + ⎪
                                  ⎩ Class-Enrollment ⎭  All classes taught by instructor
```

Each of these data stores is a composite of other stores used in the printing of special reports. For example, the REGISTRATION-FILE combines data elements from both the STUDENT-FILE and the CLASS-FILE. Although the same data are contained in two different data stores, those data have been brought together within the REGISTRATION-FILE as a means of relating classes with students. Also, the ROSTER-FILE relates students with classes and the TEACHING-FILE relates classes with instructors. These composite data stores were created originally to produce relations that did not exist within the set of separate class, instructor, and student files.

Figure 5-30 shows the result of the first step in normalization. For each data structure that contains a repeating group, the repeating group has been removed and set up as a separate data structure. The key for this new structure is formed by **concatenating** (adding) the key for the original data store with the key for the repeating group. The key for the original file is retained as the key for the data structure without its repeating group. For example, consider the two derived structures named REGISTERED-STUDENT and STUDENT-CLASS that are based on the original STUDENT-REGISTRATION structure. REGISTERED-STUDENT is the STUDENT-REGISTRATION structure with the repeating group removed. Its key is the same as the key for the original structure. The new structure, STUDENT-CLASS, is formed from the repeating group. Its key is the combination STUDENT-NUMBER and CLASS-NUMBER. A concatenated key is needed for this new structure because the class data contained in the structure pertain to a particular student. Without the STUDENT-NUMBER appended to the CLASS-NUMBER key, there would be no way of relating a particular student, as was implied in the original file.

The fact that the two derived data structures contain the same information as did the original STUDENT-REGISTRATION structure can be verified by the presentation in Figure 5-31. The STUDENT-CLASS structure contains the courses in which each student has enrolled. Each class is uniquely identified by the concatenation of the STUDENT-NUMBER and the CLASS-NUMBER. The REGISTERED-STUDENT structure contains only student-related data on each student enrolled in a class, keyed to the STUDENT-NUMBER. The motivation for having the original REGISTRATION-FILE was to produce a report that lists, by students, all classes for which those students have registered. If such a report is to be generated through use of these new data structures, two data stores must be accessed: First, the store containing the STUDENT-CLASS structures is accessed to locate those classes taken by a particular student. Then, using the STUDENT-NUMBER portion of the concatenated key, the store containing the STUDENT-REGISTERED structures is accessed to locate corresponding names and addresses. The relationships among the data elements in the original file are maintained—even after separating its repeating groups into a file by themselves. The concatenated key describes the relations among these new data stores.

The same procedure is followed for the ROSTER and the INSTRUCTOR-ASSIGNMENT structures. Both structures have repeating data groups that must be removed and placed in a second structure identified by a concatenated

Figure 5.30. Conversion of student registration data structures into first normal form.

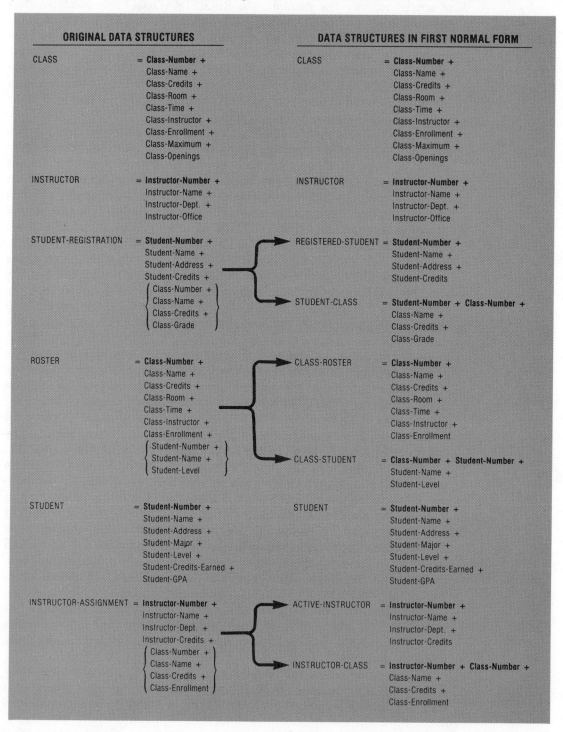

ORIGINAL DATA STRUCTURES

DATA STRUCTURES IN FIRST NORMAL FORM

CLASS
= **Class-Number** +
Class-Name +
Class-Credits +
Class-Room +
Class-Time +
Class-Instructor +
Class-Enrollment +
Class-Maximum +
Class-Openings

CLASS
= **Class-Number** +
Class-Name +
Class-Credits +
Class-Room +
Class-Time +
Class-Instructor +
Class-Enrollment +
Class-Maximum +
Class-Openings

INSTRUCTOR
= **Instructor-Number** +
Instructor-Name +
Instructor-Dept. +
Instructor-Office

INSTRUCTOR
= **Instructor-Number** +
Instructor-Name +
Instructor-Dept. +
Instructor-Office

STUDENT-REGISTRATION
= **Student-Number** +
Student-Name +
Student-Address +
Student-Credits +
{ Class-Number +
Class-Name +
Class-Credits +
Class-Grade }

REGISTERED-STUDENT
= **Student-Number** +
Student-Name +
Student-Address +
Student-Credits

STUDENT-CLASS
= **Student-Number + Class-Number** +
Class-Name +
Class-Credits +
Class-Grade

ROSTER
= **Class-Number** +
Class-Name +
Class-Credits +
Class-Room +
Class-Time +
Class-Instructor +
Class-Enrollment +
{ Student-Number +
Student-Name +
Student-Level }

CLASS-ROSTER
= **Class-Number** +
Class-Name +
Class-Credits +
Class-Room +
Class-Time +
Class-Instructor +
Class-Enrollment

CLASS-STUDENT
= **Class-Number + Student-Number** +
Student-Name +
Student-Level

STUDENT
= **Student-Number** +
Student-Name +
Student-Address +
Student-Major +
Student-Level +
Student-Credits-Earned +
Student-GPA

STUDENT
= **Student-Number** +
Student-Name +
Student-Address +
Student-Major +
Student-Level +
Student-Credits-Earned +
Student-GPA

INSTRUCTOR-ASSIGNMENT
= **Instructor-Number** +
Instructor-Name +
Instructor-Dept. +
Instructor-Credits +
{ Class-Number +
Class-Name +
Class-Credits +
Class-Enrollment }

ACTIVE-INSTRUCTOR
= **Instructor-Number** +
Instructor-Name +
Instructor-Dept. +
Instructor-Credits

INSTRUCTOR-CLASS
= **Instructor-Number + Class-Number** +
Class-Name +
Class-Credits +
Class-Enrollment

Figure 5.31. *Components of student registration data structures in first normal form.*

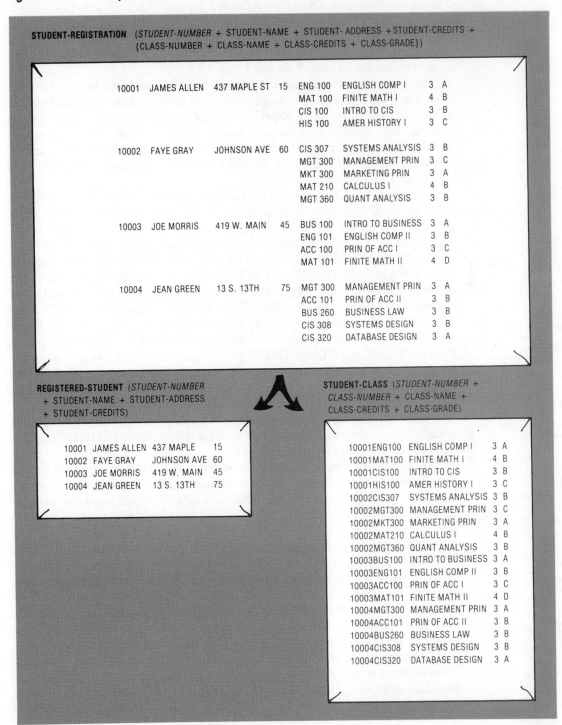

STUDENT-REGISTRATION (*STUDENT-NUMBER* + STUDENT-NAME + STUDENT- ADDRESS +STUDENT-CREDITS + {CLASS-NUMBER + CLASS-NAME + CLASS-CREDITS + CLASS-GRADE})

10001	JAMES ALLEN	437 MAPLE ST	15	ENG 100	ENGLISH COMP I	3	A
				MAT 100	FINITE MATH I	4	B
				CIS 100	INTRO TO CIS	3	B
				HIS 100	AMER HISTORY I	3	C
10002	FAYE GRAY	JOHNSON AVE	60	CIS 307	SYSTEMS ANALYSIS	3	B
				MGT 300	MANAGEMENT PRIN	3	C
				MKT 300	MARKETING PRIN	3	A
				MAT 210	CALCULUS I	4	B
				MGT 360	QUANT ANALYSIS	3	B
10003	JOE MORRIS	419 W. MAIN	45	BUS 100	INTRO TO BUSINESS	3	A
				ENG 101	ENGLISH COMP II	3	B
				ACC 100	PRIN OF ACC I	3	C
				MAT 101	FINITE MATH II	4	D
10004	JEAN GREEN	13 S. 13TH	75	MGT 300	MANAGEMENT PRIN	3	A
				ACC 101	PRIN OF ACC II	3	B
				BUS 260	BUSINESS LAW	3	B
				CIS 308	SYSTEMS DESIGN	3	B
				CIS 320	DATABASE DESIGN	3	A

REGISTERED-STUDENT (*STUDENT-NUMBER* + STUDENT-NAME + STUDENT-ADDRESS + STUDENT-CREDITS)

10001	JAMES ALLEN	437 MAPLE	15
10002	FAYE GRAY	JOHNSON AVE	60
10003	JOE MORRIS	419 W. MAIN	45
10004	JEAN GREEN	13 S. 13TH	75

STUDENT-CLASS (*STUDENT-NUMBER* + *CLASS-NUMBER* + CLASS-NAME + CLASS-CREDITS + CLASS-GRADE)

10001ENG100	ENGLISH COMP I	3	A
10001MAT100	FINITE MATH I	4	B
10001CIS100	INTRO TO CIS	3	C
10001HIS100	AMER HISTORY I	3	C
10002CIS307	SYSTEMS ANALYSIS	3	B
10002MGT300	MANAGEMENT PRIN	3	C
10002MKT300	MARKETING PRIN	3	A
10002MAT210	CALCULUS I	4	B
10002MGT360	QUANT ANALYSIS	3	B
10003BUS100	INTRO TO BUSINESS	3	A
10003ENG101	ENGLISH COMP II	3	B
10003ACC100	PRIN OF ACC I	3	C
10003MAT101	FINITE MATH II	4	D
10004MGT300	MANAGEMENT PRIN	3	A
10004ACC101	PRIN OF ACC II	3	B
10004BUS260	BUSINESS LAW	3	B
10004CIS308	SYSTEMS DESIGN	3	B
10004CIS320	DATABASE DESIGN	3	A

key. At this point, the resulting set of data structures is in first normal form. That is, the structures contain no repeating groups.

Step 2: Verify that each nonkey data element in a first normal form structure is fully functionally dependent on the primary key. This step places the set of data structures in second normal form.

This step involves only those structures that are identified by concatenated keys. The work of this step is accomplished by verifying that each nonkey data element in a data structure is dependent on the full concatenated key, not just on a partial key. That is, each element should require the entire key as a unique identification. If rather, a data element is determined uniquely by only a part of the key, the element should be removed from the structure and placed in a structure of its own.

For example, consider the STUDENT-CLASS data structure that was identified through first-order normalization of the STUDENT-REGISTRATION structure. As shown in Figure 5-30, this structure consists of a STUDENT-NUMBER + CLASS-NUMBER concatenated key along with the data elements CLASS-NAME, CLASS-CREDITS, and CLASS-GRADE. Neither CLASS-NAME nor CLASS-CREDITS is fully functionally dependent on the entire key. Both are uniquely determined by the CLASS-NUMBER portion of the key. That is, given the CLASS-NUMBER, the CLASS-NAME and CLASS-CREDITS can be identified. The STUDENT-NUMBER portion of the key is superfluous—it is not necessary to have the STUDENT-NUMBER to find the CLASS-NAME and CLASS-CREDITS. (This example assumes all classes are for fixed credit and that there are no variable-hour classes.) CLASS-GRADE, on the other hand, is fully functionally dependent on the concatenated key. Knowing only the STUDENT-NUMBER or knowing only the CLASS-NUMBER is insufficient information for knowing the CLASS-GRADE. The grade relates to the particular student in a particular class, and therefore, both parts of the key are required to define it.

To place structures in **second normal form**, the data elements that are not fully functionally dependent on the concatenated key are removed from the relation and set up in separate data structures with corresponding keys. Thus, in Figures 5-32 and 5-33, the STUDENT-CLASS relation is broken out into two separate structures: CLASS-REGISTERED contains the CLASS-NAME and CLASS-CREDITS data elements that are dependent only on the CLASS-NUMBER portion of the key. The GRADE relation contains the CLASS-GRADE element, which is dependent on the entire key. Similar steps have been taken for the CLASS-STUDENT and INSTRUCTOR-CLASS structures. Note in Figure 5-30 that, in the last two cases, one of the resulting structures contains only key information. These structures are not likely to become physical files except in environments that utilize flat files exclusively. In database management systems, these relationships are maintained through software functions. However, it is important to document such relationship so that they are not neglected at implementation time. The CLASS-STUDENT structure establishes the relation between a given class and its students. In other words, given a

Figure 5.32. *Conversion of student registration data structures into second normal form.*

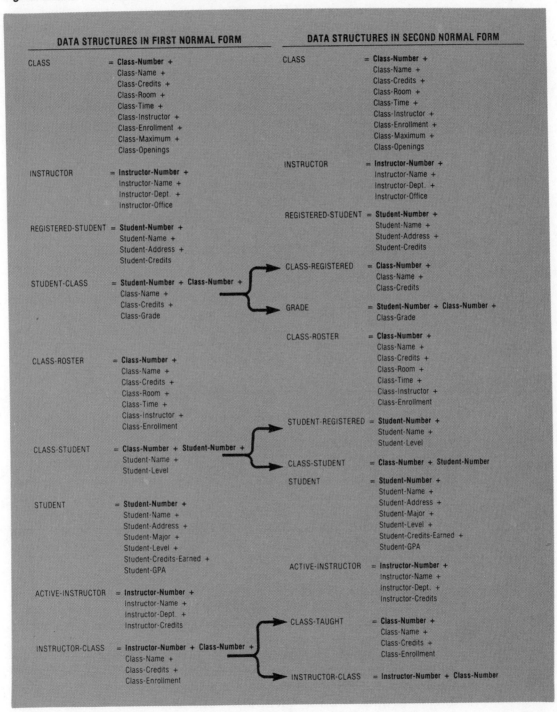

particular class number, the student numbers for the students in that class are available. Similarly, the INSTRUCTOR-CLASS structure relates individual instructors to classes taught.

Step 3: Verify that all nonkey data elements in a second normal form data structure are mutually independent of one another. After the data structures have been converted to second normal form, each structure is checked to verify that each nonkey data element is independent of every other nonkey element in the relation. In other words, there is a check for redundancy within the relation. Duplicate data elements or elements that can be derived from other elements are removed to place the relation in third normal form.

Within the structure labeled CLASS in Figure 5-34, the data element CLASS-OPENINGS is redundant with the two elements CLASS-ENROLLMENT and CLASS-MAXIMUM. That is, the number of openings in a class can be derived by subtracting the CLASS-ENROLLMENT value from the CLASS-MAXIMUM value. In effect, CLASS-OPENINGS appears twice in the relation, once explicitly as a named data element and once implicitly as a derived value. Therefore, the element CLASS-OPENINGS has been removed from the data structure.

Within the STUDENT relation, STUDENT-LEVEL is redundant with STUDENT-CREDITS-EARNED. Assuming that class level is given by the number of credits earned by the student, total credits earned is simply another way of representing the class level. Therefore, the data element STUDENT-LEVEL is unnecessary and is removed from the relation.

Minimization of Redundant Data Elements among the Data Structures

After the set of data structures has been put in third normal form, there are likely to be redundancies among the normalized structures. For example, in Figure 5-34, several data structures share the same data elements. Class data appear in the CLASS relation as well as in the CLASS-REGISTERED, CLASS-ROSTER, and CLASS-TAUGHT relations. Student data are located in the REGISTERED-STUDENT, STUDENT-REGISTERED, and STUDENT relations. Finally, instructor data are found in two different relations—INSTRUCTOR and ACTIVE-INSTRUCTORS. Since one of the primary purposes of logical file design is to eliminate redundancy, the structures with common data elements should be collapsed into a single structure.

Figure 5-35 shows the components of the data structures after those with common elements have been joined and duplicate elements removed. In making the decision about which structures should be assembled into a composite structure, the analyst is guided by a sense of what the object of a structure is and by what the attributes of that structure are.

In general, the object of a data structure is the entity to which the structure pertains. The attributes of an object are items of data characterizing that object. Thus, the object of the structure CLASS is classes taught. Its attributes are CLASS-NAME, CLASS-CREDITS, CLASS-ROOM, CLASS-TIME, CLASS-INSTRUCTOR, CLASS-ENROLLMENT, and CLASS-MAXIMUM.

Figure 5.33. Components of student registration data structures in second normal form.

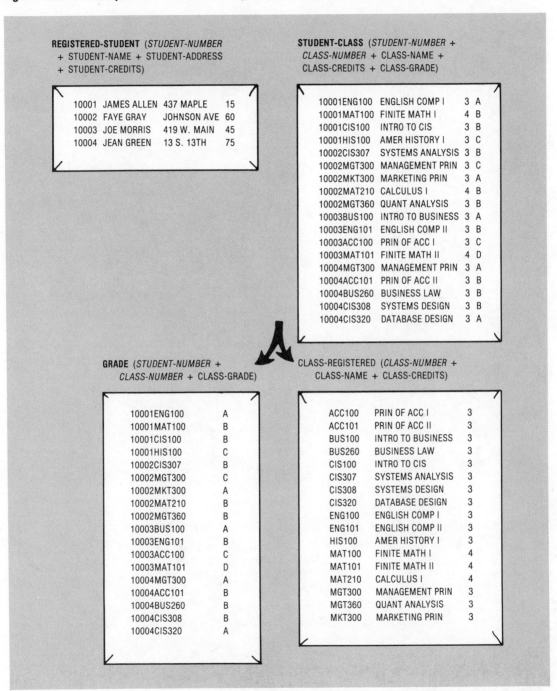

REGISTERED-STUDENT (*STUDENT-NUMBER*
+ STUDENT-NAME + STUDENT-ADDRESS
+ STUDENT-CREDITS)

10001	JAMES ALLEN	437 MAPLE	15
10002	FAYE GRAY	JOHNSON AVE	60
10003	JOE MORRIS	419 W. MAIN	45
10004	JEAN GREEN	13 S. 13TH	75

STUDENT-CLASS (*STUDENT-NUMBER* +
CLASS-NUMBER + CLASS-NAME +
CLASS-CREDITS + CLASS-GRADE)

10001ENG100	ENGLISH COMP I	3	A
10001MAT100	FINITE MATH I	4	B
10001CIS100	INTRO TO CIS	3	B
10001HIS100	AMER HISTORY I	3	C
10002CIS307	SYSTEMS ANALYSIS	3	B
10002MGT300	MANAGEMENT PRIN	3	C
10002MKT300	MARKETING PRIN	3	A
10002MAT210	CALCULUS I	4	B
10002MGT360	QUANT ANALYSIS	3	B
10003BUS100	INTRO TO BUSINESS	3	A
10003ENG101	ENGLISH COMP II	3	B
10003ACC100	PRIN OF ACC I	3	C
10003MAT101	FINITE MATH II	4	D
10004MGT300	MANAGEMENT PRIN	3	A
10004ACC101	PRIN OF ACC II	3	B
10004BUS260	BUSINESS LAW	3	B
10004CIS308	SYSTEMS DESIGN	3	B
10004CIS320	DATABASE DESIGN	3	A

GRADE (*STUDENT-NUMBER* +
CLASS-NUMBER + CLASS-GRADE)

10001ENG100	A
10001MAT100	B
10001CIS100	B
10001HIS100	C
10002CIS307	B
10002MGT300	C
10002MKT300	A
10002MAT210	B
10002MGT360	B
10003BUS100	A
10003ENG101	B
10003ACC100	C
10003MAT101	D
10004MGT300	A
10004ACC101	B
10004BUS260	B
10004CIS308	B
10004CIS320	A

CLASS-REGISTERED (*CLASS-NUMBER* +
CLASS-NAME + CLASS-CREDITS)

ACC100	PRIN OF ACC I	3
ACC101	PRIN OF ACC II	3
BUS100	INTRO TO BUSINESS	3
BUS260	BUSINESS LAW	3
CIS100	INTRO TO CIS	3
CIS307	SYSTEMS ANALYSIS	3
CIS308	SYSTEMS DESIGN	3
CIS320	DATABASE DESIGN	3
ENG100	ENGLISH COMP I	3
ENG101	ENGLISH COMP II	3
HIS100	AMER HISTORY I	3
MAT100	FINITE MATH I	4
MAT101	FINITE MATH II	4
MAT210	CALCULUS I	4
MGT300	MANAGEMENT PRIN	3
MGT360	QUANT ANALYSIS	3
MKT300	MARKETING PRIN	3

Figure 5.34. Conversion of student registration data structures into third normal form.

DATA STRUCTURES IN SECOND NORMAL FORM		DATA STRUCTURES IN THIRD NORMAL FORM	
CLASS	= **Class-Number** + Class-Name + Class-Credits + Class-Room + Class-Time + Class-Instructor + Class-Enrollment + Class-Maximum + Class-Openings	CLASS	= **Class-Number** + Class-Name + Class-Credits + Class-Room + Class-Time + Class-Instructor + Class-Enrollment + Class-Maximum
INSTRUCTOR	= **Instructor-Number** + Instructor-Name + Instructor-Dept. + Instructor-Office	INSTRUCTOR	= **Instructor-Number** + Instructor-Name + Instructor-Dept. + Instructor-Office
REGISTERED-STUDENT	= **Student-Number** + Student-Name + Student-Address + Student-Credits	REGISTERED-STUDENT	= **Student-Number** + Student-Name + Student-Address + Student-Credits
CLASS-REGISTERED	= **Class-Number** + Class-Name + Class-Credits	CLASS-REGISTERED	= **Class-Number** + Class-Name + Class-Credits
GRADE	= **Student-Number** + **Class-Number** + Class-Grade	GRADE	= **Student-Number** + **Class-Number** + Class-Grade
CLASS-ROSTER	= **Class-Number** + Class-Name + Class-Credits + Class-Room + Class-Time + Class-Instructor + Class-Enrollment	CLASS-ROSTER	= **Class-Number** + Class-Name + Class-Credits + Class-Room + Class-Time + Class-Instructor + Class-Enrollment
STUDENT-REGISTERED	= **Student-Number** + Student-Name + Student-Level	STUDENT-REGISTERED	= **Student-Number** + Student-Name + Student-Level
CLASS-STUDENT	= **Class-Number** + **Student-Number**	CLASS-STUDENT	= **Class-Number** + **Student-Number**
STUDENT	= **Student-Number** + Student-Name + Student-Address + Student-Major + Student-Level + Student-Credits-Earned + Student-GPA	STUDENT	= **Student-Number** + Student-Name + Student-Address + Student-Major + Student-Credits-Earned + Student-GPA
ACTIVE-INSTRUCTOR	= **Instructor-Number** + Instructor-Name + Instructor-Dept. + Instructor-Credits	ACTIVE-INSTRUCTOR	= **Instructor-Number** + Instructor-Name + Instructor-Dept. + Instructor-Credits
CLASS-TAUGHT	= **Class-Number** + Class-Name + Class-Credits + Class-Enrollment	CLASS-TAUGHT	= **Class-Number** + Class-Name + Class-Credits + Class-Enrollment
INSTRUCTOR-CLASS	= **Instructor-Number** + **Class-Number**	INSTRUCTOR-CLASS	= **Instructor-Number** + **Class-Number**

Figure 5.35. *Data structures of student registration system after combining of common elements from third normal form.*

The data structure contains the attributes that pertain to one and only one object. A similar rationale can be applied to the INSTRUCTOR, STUDENT, and GRADE data structures. No superfluous data elements appear in the relations, and no elements appear as attributes in any other relations.

The structures CLASS-STUDENT and INSTRUCTOR-CLASS are special cases in that these structures contain only key attributes and, as mentioned earlier, are not likely to become physical files. These key attributes are primary keys to the other data structures and the attributes of those structures. These special structures are called **correlations**, relating objects identified by the composite data structures. Thus, the structure CLASS-STUDENT is used to relate the attribute CLASS structure with attributes in the STUDENT structure. Similarly, the correlation INSTRUCTOR-CLASS relates INSTRUCTOR with CLASS.

As an example of how such correlative structures are used, recall that the student registration system is to produce class rosters. This report, therefore, combines STUDENT attributes with CLASS attributes. Access to the data stores corresponding to the CLASS and STUDENT data structures alone, however, cannot produce the report. Nothing is in the CLASS structure to indicate which students are enrolled; there are no attributes in the STUDENT structure to point out the classes taken. The independence of these two structures is to be expected; it merely indicates their preferred "single-mindedness." The relationship between the CLASS and STUDENT structures is given in the correlative structure, CLASS-STUDENT. For a given CLASS-NUMBER, the CLASS structure provides information on that class, the CLASS-STUDENT structure provides the STUDENT-NUMBER for each student in the class, and this, in turn, leads to the STUDENT structure.

Another form of redundancy may result when correlations are defined. For example, in the INSTRUCTOR structure shown in Figure 5-36, the **attribute** INSTRUCTOR-CREDITS is not necessary. This data element gives the total number of credits taught by an instructor. This same information can be derived from the CLASS structure accessed through the INSTRUCTOR-CLASS correlation. The INSTRUCTOR-NUMBER in the INSTRUCTOR data structure can be matched against the INSTRUCTOR-NUMBER in the INSTRUCTOR-CLASS correlation. Then the corresponding CLASS-NUMBERS can be used to access the CLASS-CREDITS attributes in the CLASS structure. INSTRUCTOR-CREDITS, therefore, can be derived by summing the individual class credits for each class taught by the instructor.

In a similar way, STUDENT-CREDITS, recorded in the STUDENT structure, can be derived. The STUDENT-NUMBER is used to access the GRADE structure, and the corresponding CLASS-NUMBER provides access to the CLASS structure containing CLASS-CREDITS. The class credits values are totaled for each class taken by the student. As shown in Figure 5-36, the INSTRUCTOR-CREDITS and STUDENT-CREDITS attributes have been removed from the respective data structures.

Finally, the CLASS-INSTRUCTOR attribute has been removed from the CLASS structure and set up as a separate correlation identified as CLASS-

Figure 5.36. *Data structures of student registration system after redundancies among data structures have been eliminated.*

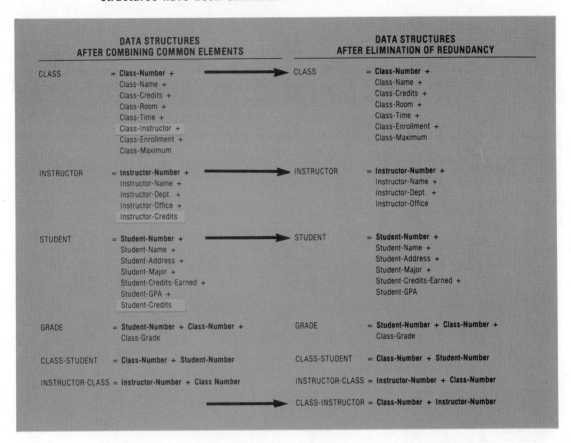

INSTRUCTOR. This situation is a case in which an attribute of one structure, the structure INSTRUCTOR, is an attribute of another structure, CLASS. However, the redundant element cannot simply be dropped from CLASS; if CLASS-INSTRUCTOR were eliminated from CLASS, there would be no direct way of knowing what classes were taught by which instructors. Yet, the information needed would be available if there were a correlation between classes and instructors, as there is between instructors and classes. Therefore, the CLASS-INSTRUCTOR correlation is established and replaces the redundant attribute. Another reason for this change is to establish a general correlation between classes and instructors. The correlation provides the same information as does the CLASS-INSTRUCTOR attribute within CLASS; however, the correlation gives additional information.

Now, all of attributes of INSTRUCTOR can be related to all attributes of CLASS. For example, the information is available and accessible to determine which departments have instructors teaching particular classes. Class numbers can be related to instructor numbers, which, in turn, can be related to instructor attributes that include the department identifier.

Effect of Normalization upon DFD and Data Dictionary

As a mechanical step, the revisions made to the set of data stores must be reflected in the data flow diagram and data dictionary. The data flow diagram shown in Figure 5-37 is a revision of Figure 5-28. Note that transformation 7.0 CREATE TEACHING FILE has been eliminated from the system. Also, only

Figure 5.37.   Revised data flow diagram for student registration system.

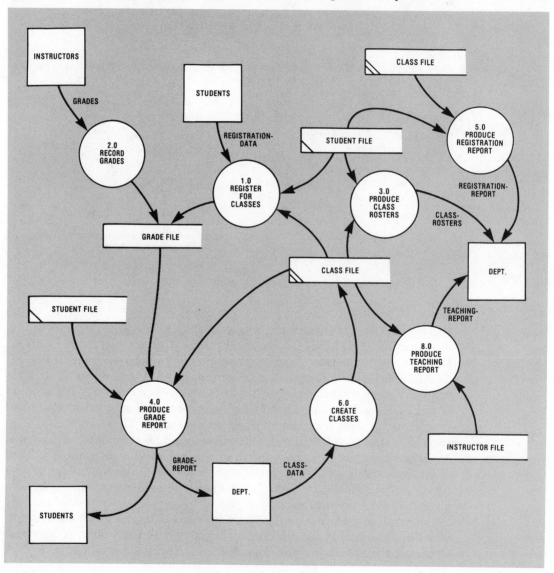

Part 2   Systems Analysis Modeling Techniques

the attribute files are presented on the revised data flow diagram. Correlative files are internal to the system and need not be shown for system processing clarification. Figure 5-38 gives the data dictionary entries for the new file structures.

Figure 5.38. **Data dictionary entries for revised file structure for student registration system.**

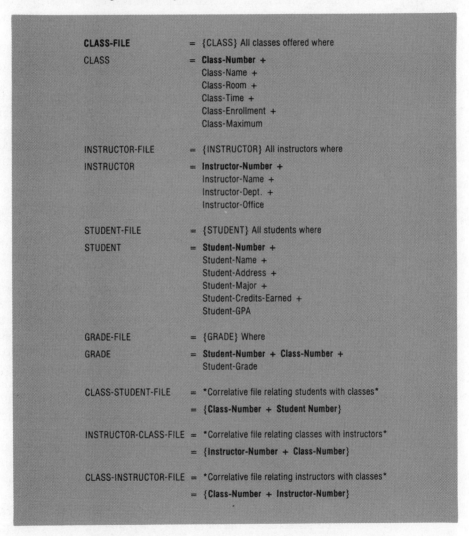

```
CLASS-FILE              = {CLASS} All classes offered where
CLASS                   = Class-Number +
                          Class-Name +
                          Class-Room +
                          Class-Time +
                          Class-Enrollment +
                          Class-Maximum


INSTRUCTOR-FILE         = {INSTRUCTOR} All instructors where
INSTRUCTOR              = Instructor-Number +
                          Instructor-Name +
                          Instructor-Dept. +
                          Instructor-Office


STUDENT-FILE            = {STUDENT} All students where
STUDENT                 = Student-Number +
                          Student-Name +
                          Student-Address +
                          Student-Major +
                          Student-Credits-Earned +
                          Student-GPA


GRADE-FILE              = {GRADE} Where
GRADE                   = Student-Number + Class-Number +
                          Student-Grade


CLASS-STUDENT-FILE      = *Correlative file relating students with classes*

                        = {Class-Number + Student Number}


INSTRUCTOR-CLASS-FILE   = *Correlative file relating classes with instructors*

                        = {Instructor-Number + Class-Number}


CLASS-INSTRUCTOR-FILE   = *Correlative file relating instructors with classes*

                        = {Class-Number + Instructor-Number}
```

SUMMARY

The value and nature of organizational data are evolving toward a multifaceted role. While no longer viewed as having absolute value or utility, data remain a vital corporate, departmental, and individual asset.

Holistic data modeling emphasizes the necessity to view data from an enterprise perspective. An enterprise consists of a collection of specific business areas composed of essential departmental functions provided by individual users. Data must be modeled and refined at each organizational level if they are to have a positive synergistic effect upon the corporate mission.

Data analysis occurs simultaneously with process and data flow analysis in the overall modeling process. The data and data flow models will be combined during physical system implementation.

Entity-Relationship (E-R) diagrams are data-oriented models that display the data-significant entities of an organization and the relationships between them. To be successful, E-R modeling must involve the same basic principles as system modeling generally, that is, iteration; hierarchical decomposition and layering; evolutionary scope and scale; use of graphic tools and models; and understanding, imagination, and creativity.

There are basically three types of relationships on an E-R diagram: one-to-one, one-to-many, and many-to-many. Implementation resolutions for these relationships must be provided to maintain data linkages between entities.

One of the main tasks of systems analysis is data flow analysis, aimed at assuring that data are available to carry out the processing transformations needed to produce the desired outputs.

The two main criteria applied to data stores are simplicity and nonredundancy. Simplicity relates to the type of file organization and access method that can be used to get to the data. Redundancy refers to the duplication of the same data components within two or more data stores. Redundancy also occurs if the same data appear in different forms within the same data store. A proper data structure should contain no redundancy. Each data element should appear only once within the set of data stores. Another incidence of redundancy occurs when two or more data components within a data store provide the same information.

Advantages of placing data structures in third normal form include ease of understanding, ease of use, ease of implementation, and ease of maintenance.

The procedure used to derive this logical file structure, called normalization, replaces a set of existing files with an equivalent set containing nonredundant data elements accessible only through primary keys. Normalization includes four basic steps.

The revisions that have been made to the file structure after normalization must be reflected in the data flow diagram, the E-R diagram, and the data dictionary.

KEY TERMS

1. association
2. attribute
3. concatenating
4. correlations
5. data driven
6. data element
7. data store
8. enterprise modeling
9. entification
10. entity
11. entity-relationship diagram
12. entity pairing
13. event
14. first normal form
15. functionally dependent
16. holistic data modeling
17. key
18. logical data structure
19. logical data analysis
20. mutually independent
21. types of relationships
22. normalization
23. object
24. pointer
25. redundancy
26. relationship
27. second normal form
28. significance of a relationship
29. simplicity
30. third normal form
31. trident

REVIEW/DISCUSSION QUESTIONS

1. How has the value of data changed over time?
2. What is meant by the term *holistic data modeling?*
3. Explain the difference between data driven and process driven design methodologies.
4. How are data viewed from an enterprise perspective?
5. What is an entity-relationship (E-R) diagram? What is the purpose for developing this type of diagram?
6. Explain the symbols used in an E-R diagram. Give an example.
7. What are the three relationship types of E-R diagrams?
8. What are the steps for building an E-R diagram?
9. How many potential pairing combinations exist for a system with five identifiable entities?
10. When is the double arrow symbol used on an E-R diagram?
11. What two criteria are applied in the analysis of data stores and why is each important?
12. What are the advantages of normalization?
13. Explain the steps in the data normalization process.
14. What are two types of redundancy?
15. In what cases would a new data structure contain only key information and no data elements?
16. Discuss the general rule concerning merging entities.
17. What is the effect of normalization upon the data flow diagram?
18. How do data flow diagrams and E-R diagrams relate to one another in the analysis process?

19. Would there be situations in which normalization of data would not be an advantage?
20. What are your predictions for data modeling in the future?

6

Using the Techniques: the Modeling Process

Learning Objectives

On completing the reading and other learning assignments in this chapter, you should be able to:

■ Describe the use of process and data modeling techniques in information systems planning.

■ Describe the goal and end results of the systems analysis process.

■ Describe logical and physical models, their purposes, and the differences between the two types of models.

■ Explain the use of a logical model as a base for design and derive a logical model from the physical model of an existing system.

■ Describe the four step analysis process and the use of logical and physical models to support the process.

■ Explain the use of data modeling techniques in the systems analysis process.

■ Explain the iterative nature of the analysis process and how this iteration occurs in the context of the system development life cycle.

THE BIG PICTURE: ENTERPRISE TO APPLICATION SYSTEM

The purpose of this chapter is to discuss the application of the process and data analysis techniques presented in the prior two chapters.

The central focus of this book is on the procedures and techniques used to build information systems and on the analysis and design skills needed to support this work. However, this development work and the resulting application systems fit in a larger context: the business enterprise. It is important to understand this context in order to understand the application of the modeling techniques studied in Chapters 5 and 6.

Historically, the process of building information systems to support an enterprise has been fairly uncoordinated. Major application systems have been built one at a time, with each new system attempting to interface as necessary with those already in place. This activity took place over time, without an overall architecture to guide the work. The result in most organizations is a collection of application systems that have overlapping functionality, redundant data, and overly complex interfaces.

More recently, an organization is likely to have recognized the need for a long-range information systems plan based on the organization's business plan that establishes several enterprise-wide architectures:

■ *A data or information architecture*, expressed in terms of E-R models, provides a stable framework on which to organize the individual data elements, thereby reducing redundancy.

■ An *application architecture*, expressed in terms of very high level data flow diagrams, provides a framework for identifying the individual systems and the interfaces between them.

■ A *technology architecture* provides a model of the major hardware components and communication networks needed to support the applications.

■ A *management architecture* provides a model of the CIS organizational structure needed to support the data resource, the various business application areas, and the geographical processing units.

Once these architectures are in place, they form the enterprise model against which new development work can take place.

Before addressing the systems development process, note that both modeling techniques apply to long-range information systems planning as well as development — data modeling more than process modeling.

As part of the planning activity, the key business functions (high-level processes) are modeled. They are eventually partitioned into major information systems to form the application architecture. The result is expressed using data flow diagrams, but at a very high level. The data are also modeled — both in their own right and as needed to support the key business functions.

There is, however, a major difference between the data models and the process models built during planning: Processes can be partitioned into (relatively) nonoverlapping application areas. As a result, process analysis can remain at a high level. Data cannot be partitioned in this way. They are used by many processes. The E-R models around which the data are organized will necessarily span multiple application areas. Consequently, the data analysis must be somewhat more detailed and complete.

In this chapter, as the application of the modeling techniques to the process of developing an individual system is discussed, the concentration will be more on the process modeling described in Chapter 4. The data modeling techniques of Chapter 5 are also important; but, as noted, data analysis tends to span application areas and is, therefore, more directly applicable to building the enterprisewide information architecture during planning than to modeling an individual system during development.

A small case example will illustrate the sense in which data modeling impacts—but is more far reaching than—the modeling of a single application system.

■ ■

MINICASE:
DEEP POCKETS INSURANCE COMPANY

Deep Pockets Insurance (DP) sells a full line of insurance products—both life and property-casualty. Their main processing systems are organized around their products. Years ago, DP's first major automated system was one to process their auto insurance business. Systems followed to process homeowner and life insurance products, as well as other minor lines of business.

The basic file structures created for the auto system were replicated for the other products. The policy was the focal point. There was an auto master file, keyed on policy number, that contained data about the customer and data about the auto (used to determine insurance rates) and data about the coverages (such as collision, comprehensive, medical payments, etc.). There was also a billing file and a claims file, each keyed on policy number. As illustrated in Figure 6-1, there were separate sets of files for each product. Over the years as the systems were enhanced, the files were modified slightly. When on-line query capabilities were added, auxiliary files were created to increase processing efficiency. But the basic underlying E-R model remained much the same.

For simplicity, consider the data as organized around four key entities:

- *Policy*, including rating and coverage attributes.
- *Customer*, including name, address, and personal attributes.

Figure 6.1. *Deep Pockets Insurance Company master files organized around the policies.*

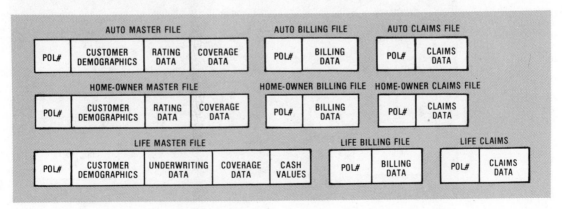

- *Bill*, including billing and payment attributes.
- *Claim*, including loss attributes.

Figure 6-2 presents an E-R model that illustrates the relations between these entities in Deep Pockets' original systems. Actually, there is a separate model for each insurance product—auto, homeowners, or life. Note the dominant role of the policy entity. The model has a number of inadequacies—a fact that became apparent to Deep Pockets over time.

As competition in the insurance industry became more intense, Deep Pockets became more interested in cross-selling their products to existing clients and expanding their customer base. They needed to know who their customers were and what products they already owned. Given the data view in Figure 6-2, there is a single association of customer with policy. Thus, DP would not even know if a client had two auto policies, to say nothing of an auto policy and a homeowners policy.

Customer service was another problem for DP. A customer with a question about a policy or the status of a claim often would not know the policy number. There needed to be a way to get from the customer name to the policy number.

The result was the DP "alpha file." It was essentially an inverted list—a file with one record for each customer, keyed on customer name, containing a list of all policy numbers owned by that customer. In essence, this alpha file represented a

Figure 6.2. E-R model embodied in the design of the original processing system for Deep Pockets Insurance Company.

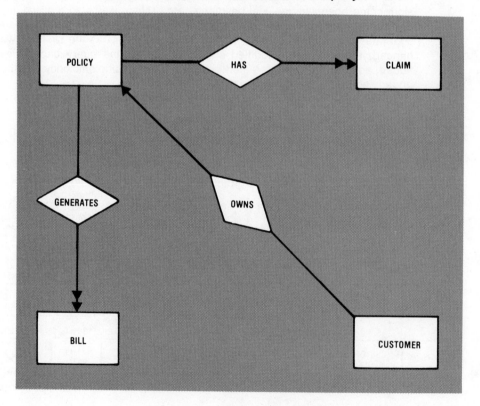

Part 2   Systems Analysis Modeling Techniques

relationship entity between the policy and customer entities (see Figure 6-3). It is interesting to note that the awkward names that must be given to the relationships reflect the fact that the alpha file is not a true business entity. It is itself an awkward means of dealing with an enterprise data model that no longer supports the business.

Over time, as Deep Pockets faced stiffer competition, they sought to extend their customer services. They now offered mutual funds and wanted to extend that to a full customer account/funds management service. The service would permit a customer to be billed in equal installments—monthly or quarterly—for all policies. It would permit some policy premiums to be paid with the proceeds of a mutual fund account or with dividends from a life policy. There was also a desire to be able to combine all bills for a given household on a single billing statement.

Figure 6.3. *E-R Model with Deep Pocket's "alpha file" serving as a relationship entity linking customers to policies.*

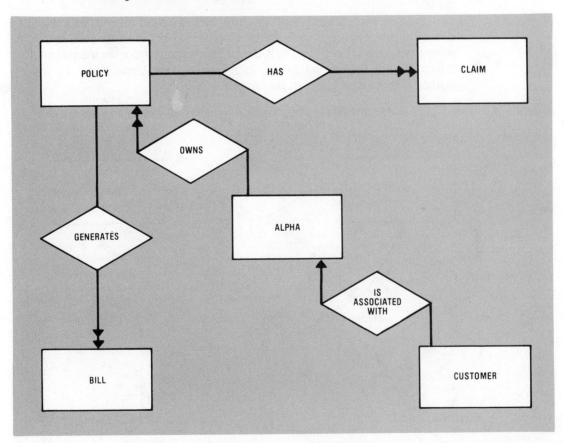

Deep Pockets hoped to be able to create a new billing system that could be used by all the product-based systems (e.g., auto, homeowner, life), bypassing the billing functions within each system. They expected significant application development work in building the new billing system, but they were unprepared for the implications to their data base. The E-R model for the environment they wished to create is shown in Figure 6-4. The impact of this model goes far beyond the new billing system. It touches each of the main product systems as well.

■ ■ ■ ■ ■ ■ ■ ■ ■ ■ ■ ■ ■ ■ ■ ■ ■ ■ ■

The Complexity of Real Life

As noted, data modeling—since it spans multiple application systems—is an activity that should occur before developing a given application system. Ideally, a planning engagement would have already been done. Then it would be possible to use that portion of the E-R model that spanned the application system to be developed. At most, only additional detail would need to be added to the model.

There are two problems with this approach. First, in many cases a planning effort will not have preceded the development effort. In this case, it will be necessary to at least create an E-R model broad enough to span the system. The master files of the current system can form an initial entity list. This is explained in more detail later in the chapter.

Figure 6.4.   E-R Model to accommodate Deep Pocket's proposed new billing system.

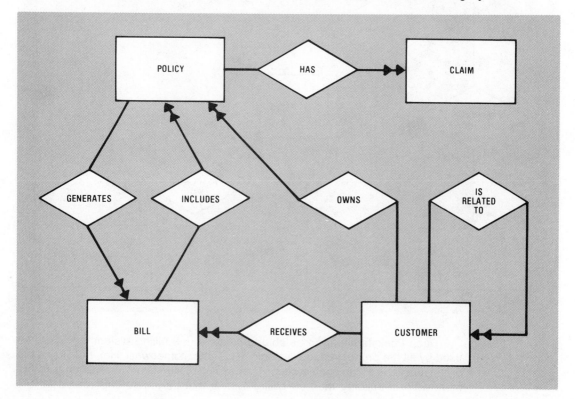

The second problem is more complex. Picture an organization that over the past thirty years has automated most of its key business processes. Application systems overlap. Redundant data abound. System health varies — some systems are technically obsolete, some no longer fit the business, others are reasonably adequate. The organization conducts a long-range information systems planning study and creates the four architectures described above.

The problem is that the organization is not in a position to scrap all current systems and replace them with new systems that are consistent with the architectures. Rather, there must be a development plan. The plan is more likely to be driven by business need than by architectural purity. Suppose a decision is made to replace the general ledger and financial reporting system. There are two major complications: This system is (and will be) heavily interfaced with many of the other application systems, and a software package with its own data architecture probably will represent about two-thirds of the final system.

What good is the data architecture that was developed? How does its existence impact the systems development work that must be done? It at least forms an ideal model that can be emulated as closely as possible. As the new system is designed, physical files can be designed that are consistent with the model when possible. And programs can be designed that will be easy to update should the physical data base be improved later.

THE GOAL OF ANALYSIS

The analysis process discussed here takes place during the first two phases of the system development life cycle presented in Chapter 2. It carries through the life cycle until there is a general design for the new system. In order to understand the process, it helps to first understand where you are headed. What is the goal during these analysis and general design activities?

New System Design Specification

The ultimate goal of the analysis and general design work is to produce a **general design specification for the new system**. This specification should be sufficiently detailed to

- Ensure the feasibility of the proposed design.
- Support an estimate of the cost to implement the system to within 10 percent accuracy.
- Serve as a basis for doing detailed technical design, program design, and implementation work.

This design specification will contain a leveled set of data flow diagrams, process specifications, and a complete data dictionary. It will also contain a recommended database design in the form of a normalized set of data stores with keys and access paths identified.

The specification will document the physical design decisions necessary to ensure that the user's technical and operational requirements will be met. The ultimate goal of analysis and general design, then, is the **new system design specification** document. But what should this design be based on?

User Specification

In the final analysis, the new system design specification is necessarily dependent on today's technology and the physical organization of the user area. But these are not a stable base for the design. Both the technology and the organization will change over time. It would be good if the design could be based on the data and the processes or functions that are inherently part of the business. Being less likely to change over time, they form a more stable base for design.

To do this, a **user specification** is created as a basis for—and to serve as input to—the new system design specification. The user specification focuses on "what" the organization is doing; the new system design specification focuses on "how" it is to be done.

The user specification also contains data flow diagram models, but they are models that emphasize the business functions rather than the physical limitations of today's technology and organizational structure. They are referred to as logical models.

THE LOGICAL MODEL: A BASE FOR DESIGN

Understanding what logical models are and how to derive them is key to understanding the structured analysis process. An analogy may help.

Just as data flow diagrams form an abstract model of reality (in this case a system), so too maps are used to form an abstract model of reality (the geographic world). Maps can be used to zoom in, providing various levels of detail. If you are driving from New York to Los Angeles, a high-level map of the interstate system is fine until you reach California. Then you may wish to switch to a more detailed map of the state, then the county, and finally the city of Los Angeles. A leveled set of data flow diagrams provides the same type of zoom capability with respect to system detail.

Maps have another important modeling characteristic. By changing their features, we can use them to serve very different audiences. Road maps serve the traveler. On the other hand, maps that suppress the road details and highlight the topography better serve the geographer. This is exactly the same for "data flow diagram-based" models. The physical models studied in Chapter 4 serve the detailed system designer. They are used in the new system design specification. When the features of these physical models are changed, logical models are created to serve a different audience—the end user. Logical models suppress the physical characteristics of the system and highlight the business functions and data inherent in it. They are more easily understood and verified by the end-user and they serve as a stable base for beginning design work.

As stated above, a logical model highlights the data content and handling, regardless of methods used to provide them. Thus, the logical aspects of a system are those elements that are the same whether the work is done with pencils and paper or by a computer.

By contrast, a physical model tends to identify the aspects of the system that are dependent on how the processing is currently or will be done—the people who are involved in the processing, the forms used, the computerized processing, and so on. Logical models, then, concentrate on *what* the system does, while physical models stress *how* the job is done.

A model is not necessarily completely physical or completely logical. Models, however, may have certain characteristics that tend to be more physical and others that tend to be more logical. These characteristics are summarized in Figure 6-5, which identifies some traits of systems and the ways in which they are presented in physical and logical models. Figures 6-6 and 6-7, which present a simple model of a student course registration system, illustrate some of the differences between logical and physical models.

Notice the sequential nature of the processing in the more physical diagram, Figure 6-6. The processes to check prerequisites, available seats, and student credit are presented in sequence. There is no organizational—or logical—rule

Figure 6.5. Summary of key differences between physical and logical models.

MAJOR CHARACTERISTICS OF MODELS		
	Physical	**Logical**
Viewpoint	How processing is done	What the system does
Processes	Sequential	Often parallel
Names	Documents, people, forms	Underlying data and processes
Data flows	Excess (tramp) data	Only data used or produced by the process
Controls	Includes controls for crossing man-machine boundaries	Limited to essential business controls

Figure 6.6. Data flow diagram that emphasizes physical characteristics of a student registration system.

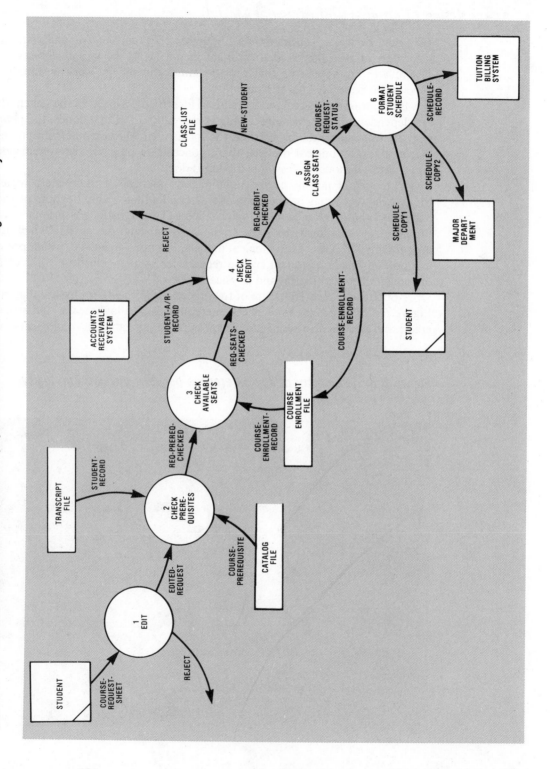

Figure 6.7. Data flow diagram that emphasizes logical characteristics of a student registration system.

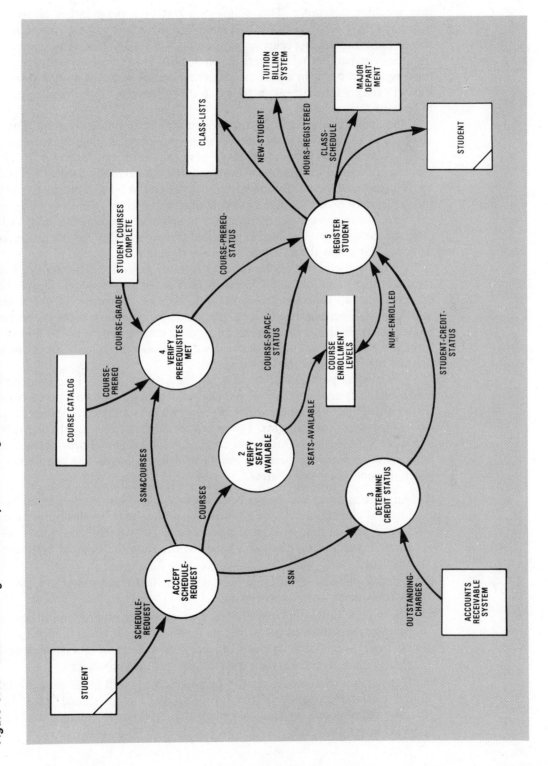

that specifies this order. This diagram is merely a presentation of the way processing happens to be done currently. The more logical view, in Figure 6-7, shows these processes occurring in parallel. A model that shows processes occurring in parallel when there is no logical, or business, reason that the processes must occur in a specific sequence stresses what the system does and leaves flexibility for the designer to match the sequencing to the design approach to be used.

The names in the more physical diagram tend to refer to actual, physical objects and records while the names in the more logical diagram refer to the actual data, with no implication about physical packaging. Moreover, the data flows in the logical diagram transport only the data actually used or produced by the processes covered. By contrast, the entire course request is drawn through the sequence of processes in the physical diagram, with each process using only that part of the request that pertains to its operation. Again, the more logical diagram stresses what the system does and leaves flexibility for the designer to determine later how the data and processes should be packaged.

Finally, the controls in the logical diagram, processes 2 through 4, being critical business controls, are a necessary part of the logical model. The physical diagram has two other controls — the edit and the formatting of the student schedule — that pertain strictly to the man-machine boundary. If the system were implemented physically in a different way, these controls might not be necessary. Since these controls are not concerned with the essential rules of the business, they are not included in the logical model.

The starting point for understanding the existing system is to construct a model of the system based on a physical understanding of how processes are performed. This initial model will tend to exhibit more of the physical characteristics of the data flow diagrams. The reason for moving from this physical model to a more logical one is simple, but crucial: *A **logical model** provides a firmer foundation on which to base the design of a new system.* The key points on which this concept is based are:

- An existing system is always bound, limited, and ultimately shaped by its physical constraints. These physical constraints may be hardware, departmental boundaries, or even the people themselves. The constraints often result from tradeoff decisions made at the time the original system was developed.

- Existing physical constraints may result in inefficient — even incorrect or logically inconsistent — processing.

- The logical processing requirements of a system — the essential business processes that must be performed no matter how the system is implemented physically — are fairly stable. The physical aspects of a system tend to change more frequently than the essential business processes.

- If the design of a new system can be based on a logical model that captures the essential processes of the business, that design should result in a more maintainable system — a system that is easier to enhance during its operational life.

Much of the processing that takes place in an existing system may actually have grown over time to compensate for shortcomings in the physical system. It may not be at all essential to the business being conducted. As a dramatic example, consider an actual finding at a large government agency in Washington.

Analysts were studying a paperwork processing system throughout this large bureau to determine manpower and equipment needs of a major business data processing system. On the basis of a purely physical study, they determined that the request from one of the departments to expand its personnel by 20 percent was probably justified.

As the next step in the project, however, the analysts converted this physical model into a logical one, and another group of analysts reviewed the flow of data on a logical basis. This analysis revealed that the overworked department did not have to be expanded; in fact, it wasn't needed at all. It turned out that the functions of this department were redundant with operations being performed elsewhere. Under a strictly physical review, there was no way of telling what was happening, logically, to the data. Under a logical review, physical duplication came quickly to light.

Creating a Logical Model

The value of the logical model as a more stable base on which to create the design for a new system has been stressed. A process for deriving a logical model of a current system from a physical model of that system will be described here. Then, in the following section, this activity will be placed in the context of the overall systems analysis process. Note that the process of deriving a logical model from a physical model of a current system can open up important insights and opportunities.

First, the building of a logical model may lead the systems analyst to uncover processes, outputs, or inputs that are part of the system but were omitted from the physical model. In providing information for the building of a physical model, users commonly forget one or more procedures or processes. The discipline of building a logical model almost invariably catches these problems by requiring analysis of business processes rather than system steps.

Second, this business emphasis also leads to a more specific understanding of why system functions are performed and what results are expected. With this understanding, it is often possible to simplify, even to eliminate, some existing processing steps that really aren't needed to conduct the business.

Finally, the creation of a logical model forces the analyst to concentrate on the business objectives of the organization. A clear understanding of these objectives provides a basis for evaluating requirements for the new system, as they are identified during the second step of the analysis process.

As stated earlier, a logical data flow diagram models the data and the processing that are essential to the business. In other words, a logical model presents those features of the system that would have to exist no matter what physical processing methods were adopted. Given a **physical model**, the transition to a logical model can be accomplished by following a series of orderly steps:

Step 1. Replace upper level parent bubbles with child diagrams. Do this in one or more large, expanded data flow diagrams. As a general rule, lower-level diagrams tend to be more logical. These very large diagrams, while not satisfactory for documentation and communication purposes, are very effective working models for team members who are deeply involved in the project.

Step 2. Remove nonlogical processes. These are the processes that

- Edit data. Usually, edit functions are applied to data flows of manually captured input.
- Audit. Typically, data being output for users are audited through machine processes before reports or displays are generated.
- Move data within a system without transformation.

The reason for removing these processes is that they are entirely physical. They are totally dependent on how the system is implemented physically. They perform no logical function upon the data. (These processes will, of course, be replaced as necessary in the construction of the physical model of the new system.)

Step 3. Remove nonlogical data stores. These are data stores that exist as intermediate or holding files. They are not necessary to the logical processing of the data.

Step 4. Connect system fragments. Fragments resulting from the deletions in the previous steps will need to be reconnected.

THE ANALYSIS PROCESS

Systems analysis is a process that involves repeating, or iterating, a series of process steps to build an understanding of current systems and procedures and to define new systems. Intuitively, the process is quite simple and straightforward. Four key steps are repeated with increasing levels of detail and understanding:

- Understand the existing system. (Where are we today?)
- Identify changes in user requirements. (Where do we want to be?)
- Specify one or more possible solutions. (How can we get there?)
- Evaluate the feasibility of the proposed solution. (Will it work?)

Logical and physical models are used to support this process.

Overview of the Analysis Process

The analysis process, supported by data flow diagram-based models, is listed below.

1. Understand the existing system.

■ Construct a physical model of the existing system.

■ Evaluate the physical model.

■ Derive a logical model from the physical model.

2. Identify changes in user requirements.

■ Document business processing (logical) requirements.

■ Document technical and operational (physical) requirements.

3. Specify a new system solution.

■ Create a logical model for the new system. Use the logical model of the existing system and the changes in processing (logical) requirements.

■ Create a physical model for the new system. Use the logical model for the new system and the changes in the technical and operational requirements.

4. Evaluate the feasibility of the proposed new system.

This modeling process is illustrated in Figure 6-8. Beginning in the upper left corner, a physical model of the existing system is created. Then, a logical model

Figure 6.8.   The use of data flow diagram models in the analysis process.

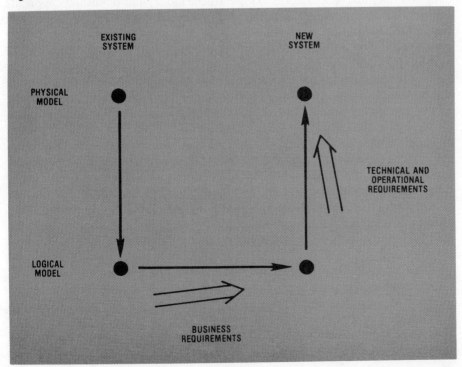

of the existing system is derived from the physical model (lower left). The business requirements for the new system drive the creation of a logical model for the new system (lower right). Finally, the technical and operational requirements for the new system drive the creation of a physical model for the new system (upper right).

This process, starting with the logical model of the existing system, is illustrated by the series of abstract models beginning in Figure 6-9.

Figure 6-9 shows an abstract, idealized, data flow diagram. Assume that it represents a logical model of an existing computer information system. A systems analyst would use this type of data flow diagram to establish agreement about the essential business processing in an existing system. That is, user managers would be asked to review this type of data flow diagram and to agree that it does, in fact, represent what is happening now.

The analyst then modifies the existing model to reflect the changing business situation. The result is a marked up version of the data flow diagram of the existing logical system, as shown in Figure 6-10. In effect, the analyst has noted changes in both data and processes to reflect new and future business needs.

As a next step, the analyst develops a data flow diagram that reflects these business changes. This produces a logical model of the new system, as shown in Figure 6-11. This logical model of the new system is then the basis for planning the new physical system, as shown in Figure 6-12.

Note that the designation of physical aspects of the new system in Figure 6-12 has been accomplished by overlaying processing boundaries on the logical data flow diagram. The effect is to separate the model into physical components on the basis of equipment and timing. Portions of the data flow diagram in Figure 6-12 fall outside the human-machine or computer boundaries that have been drawn. The portions of the system external to these boundaries are the manual functions.

These diagrams are, of course, greatly oversimplified. Models for an actual system would involve an entire set of diagrams modeling complex processing and supported by a collection of process specifications and a complete data dictionary. At the outset, the analyst begins with the physical model and builds an understanding of the logical system from that base. A logical model becomes the working base for the identification of requirements and the design of a new system. That is, the logical model of the existing system is updated and used as a basis for a logical model of the new system. In the final design of the new system, work progresses from the logical to the physical. Thus, the initial process of analysis has been reversed. At the outset, the transition was from physical to logical. As systems analysis proceeds, the progression is from logical to physical.

This basic four-step process of systems analysis is repeated, or iterated, throughout the first two phases of the systems development life cycle, becoming increasingly deeper at each iteration. By the time the full, iterated process has been completed, users have a graphic model of the new system as they will see it. This model then becomes the basis for understanding and for agreement on how the new system should function.

Before looking at each of the four analysis steps in more detail, note that the process is explained and illustrated using a case example in Chapters 19 and 20. Those chapters are part of a section that explains the flow of the entire development process; they can be read and understood at this point in the text.

Understanding the Current System

The analysis process begins with the construction of a physical model of the current system. A technique for creating this model, based on critical events within the system, was presented in Chapter 5. Using that technique, a context diagram is created very early as a means of confirming the scope of the system under study. Then, as information is collected about the current system, fragment diagrams are constructed as a way of organizing the information. Next, the event analysis is used to create a Diagram 0. Lower-level diagrams and process specifications are added as more information is gained.

This so-called **physical model** need not be overly physical. The real interest is to get to the logical model. Typically, only enough physical data are included in the existing physical model to be able to verify with operational people that the model is correct and to be able to perform a quick analysis of the physical deficiencies of the existing system. These deficiencies might include such items as:

- bottlenecks in processing.
- inability to handle certain transaction types.
- heavy exception processing.
- excessive manual procedures and controls.
- complex or convoluted processing flows.

The physical model need not have complete detail. Lower-level processes can be added while moving from the physical to the logical model of the existing system.

The process for deriving the logical model from the physical is outlined in a previous section. The steps presented there *can* be mechanically applied. However, the experienced analyst, understanding the eventual goal, will tend to begin creating models with many of the characteristics of a logical model as soon as possible. The mechanical steps, then, will just be used as a final verification that the model is as logical as possible.

Identify Changes in User Requirements

The second step in the analysis process is to identify user requirements for the new system. These are most often expressed, at least in part, as changes to the current system. That is, rather than obtaining an exhaustive list of requirements, the tendency is to focus on what the new system should do differently. This, by the way, emphasizes the need for a complete and detailed logical model of the existing system. Without it, critical business functions and processing rules could be overlooked.

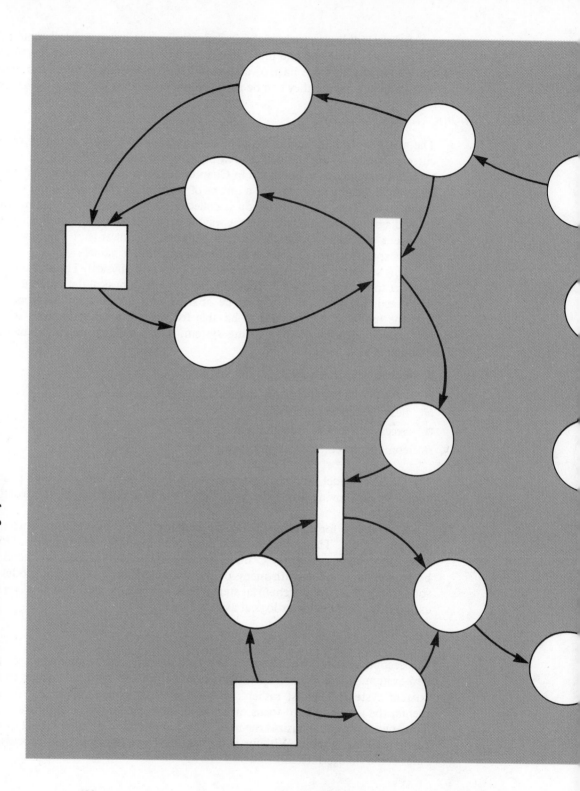

Figure 6.9.   Logical model of an existing system.

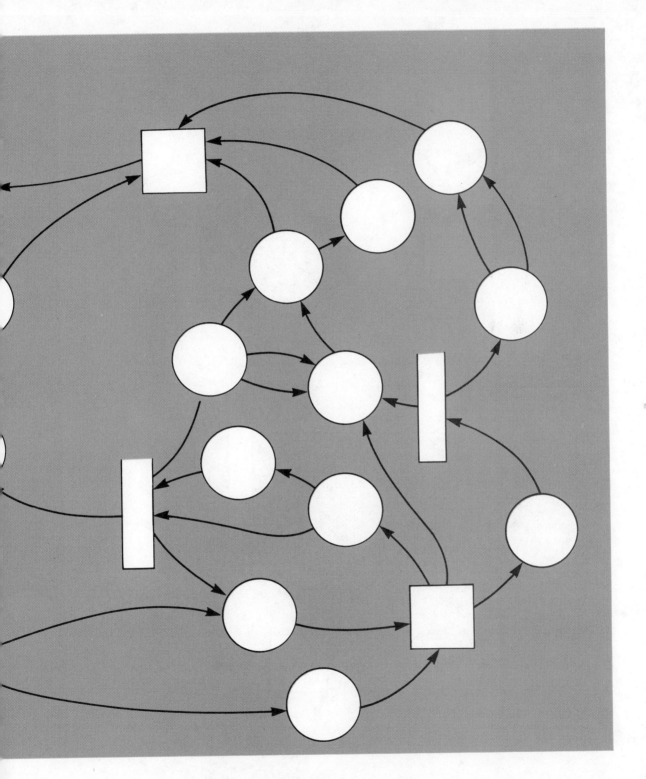

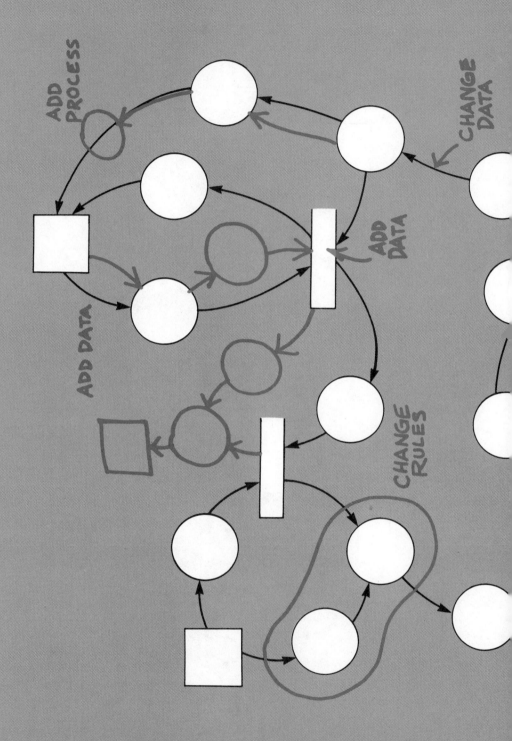

Figure 6.10. Logical model of an existing system—as modified by business requirements.

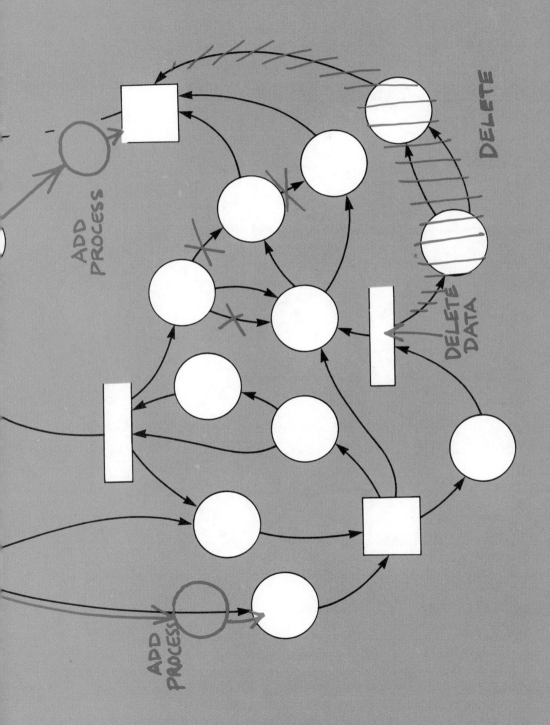

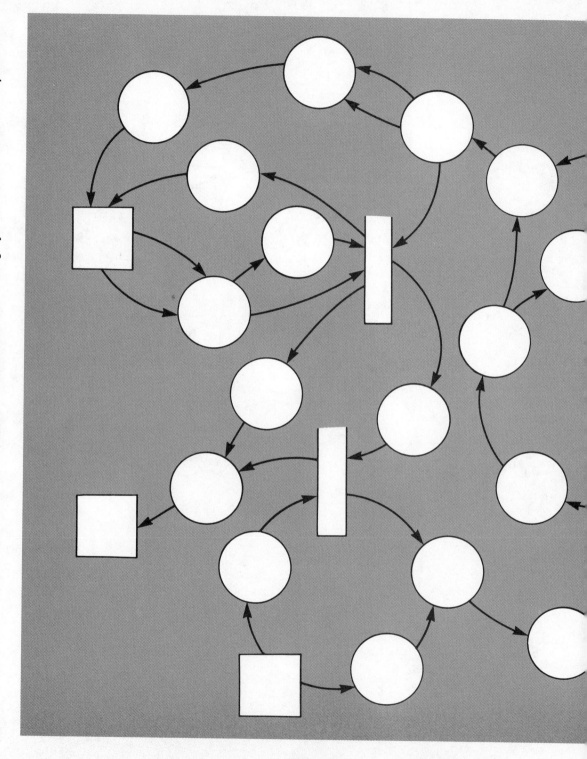

Part 2   Systems Analysis Modeling Techniques

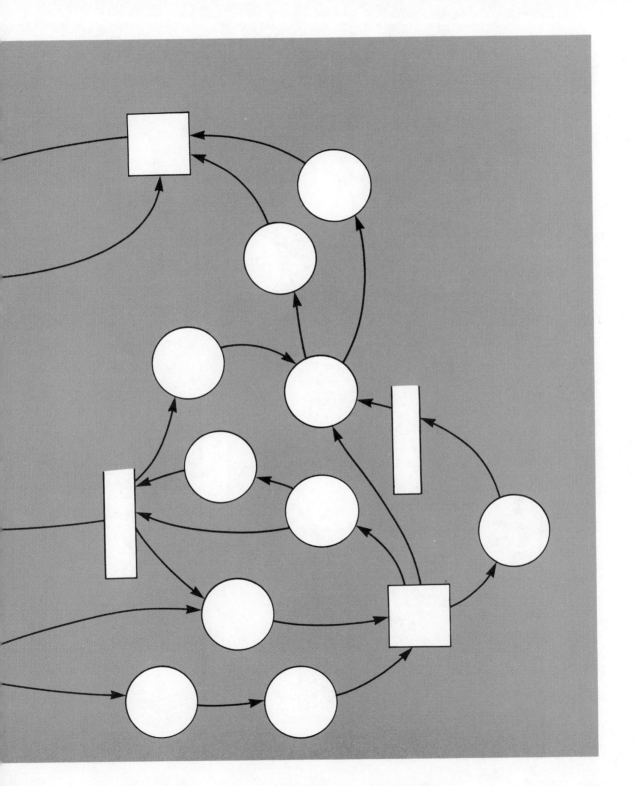

Figure 6.12. Physical model of new system—derived from logical model of new system and new physical (delivery-oriented) requirements.

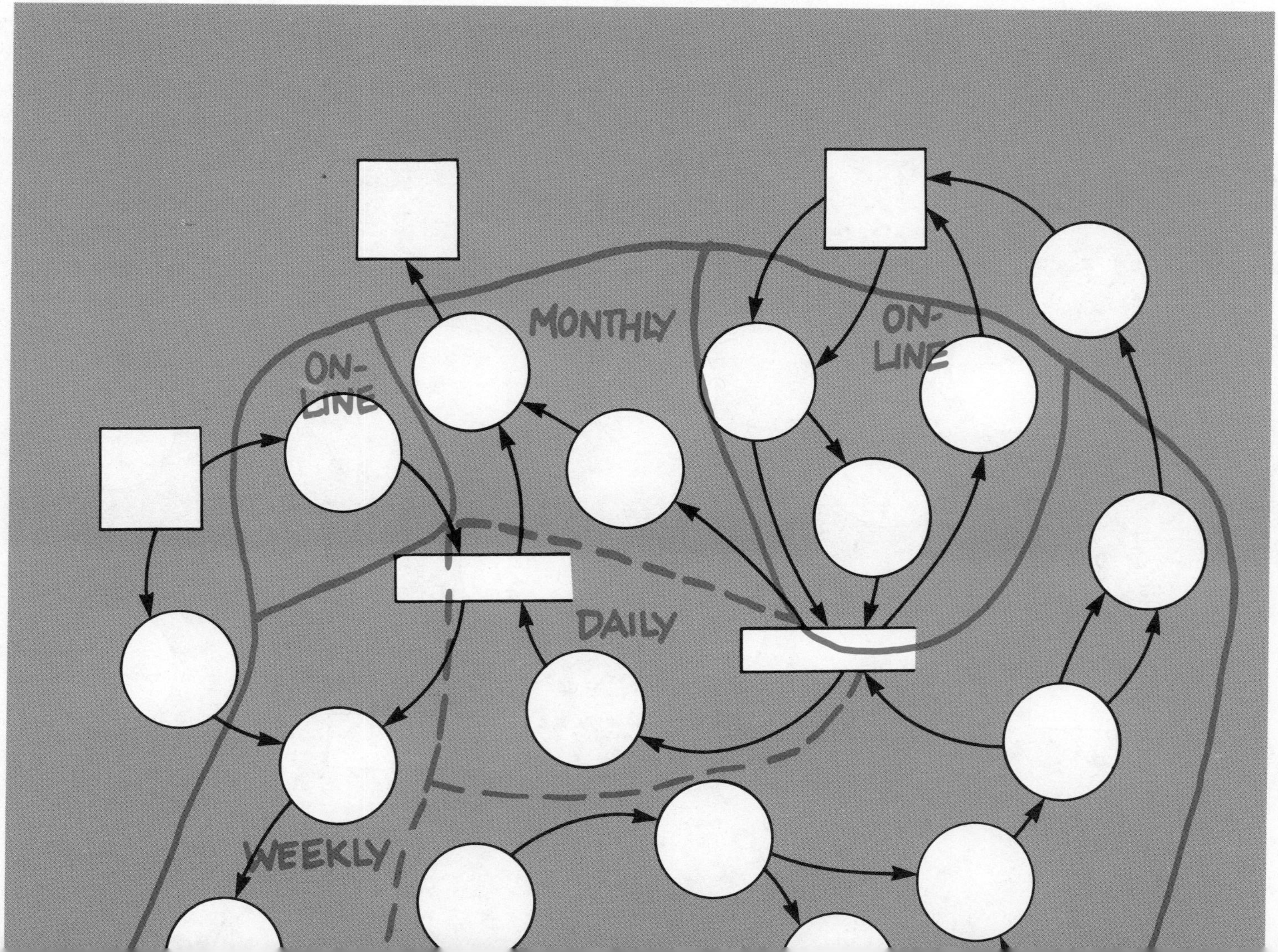

Part 2 Systems Analysis Modeling Techniques

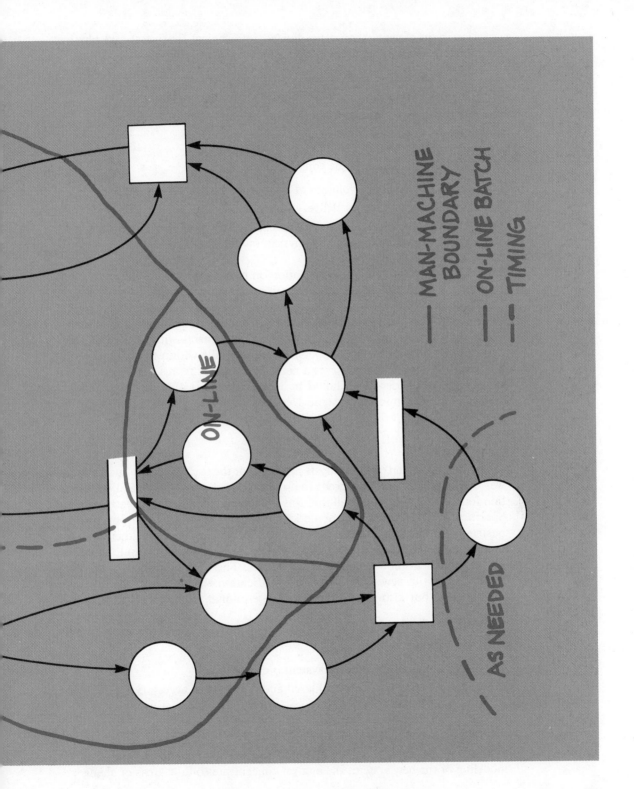

MAN-MACHINE
BOUNDARY

ON-LINE BATCH

TIMING

ON-LINE

AS NEEDED

User requirements should be divided into logical (business) and physical components. Logical requirements are found by identifying:

■ New or changed organizational goals or objectives.
■ Changes or additions in data processed within the system.
■ Changes or additions in business policies that affect processes.
■ Changes in system scope.

Physical factors that should be considered include:

■ Changes in timing or volumes of transactions within the system.
■ Changes in methods for delivery of results.
■ Changes to address the physical deficiencies of the current system that were identified when analyzing the physical model.

Throughout the gathering of information on user requirements, the analyst has to apply professional judgment. Determinations must be made as to whether a stated requirement represents a read need of the organization or simply a desire on the part of an individual. This distinction can be made by applying a simple principle: Compare each statement of user requirements with the overall goals and objectives of the organization. If a request falls within the organization's goals and objectives, it represents a need. If a request represents an interpretation of what the user feels should be included, this is a desire. Needs should always be covered by a new system. Desires should be evaluated on their merits.

Specify a New System Solution

It is in this third step of the analysis process that the overall goal of analysis that was discussed earlier is achieved: the production of a general design specification for the new system. Recall that this is accomplished by first creating a User Specification, based on a logical model of the new system and incorporating the business requirements for the new system. This logical model is then a stable foundation on which to make general system design decisions, resulting in one or more physical models for the new system. These physical models are then the basis for the new system design specification that incorporates not only the business, but also the technical and operational requirements for the new system.

In the course of specifying the new system solution, then, the use of models proceeds through three stages:

■ A logical model for the new system is created.
■ The new logical model is evaluated and modified as necessary.
■ One or more physical models are created for the new system.

Create a Logical Model of the New System. The logical model of the new system evolves from the logical model of the existing system. In beginning the modeling of the new system, the analyst concentrates on the areas of change:

- Determine whether each change represents a modification or an extension of capabilities.
- Determine the effect of each change in terms of processing activities, data flows, data store contents, data access capabilities, or process definitions.

During the process of identifying needs or requirements for the new system, individual changes may be modeled separately, in fragments, or mini-models. Each of the changes is then reviewed carefully in walkthroughs with the user. Next, the model fragments are incorporated into the logical model of the existing system, modifying that model to produce a logical representation of the new system. The new model is then used to communicate a complete understanding of what processing capabilities the user expects from the new system. This process is illustrated graphically in Figures 6-9 through 6-11. This series of figures, of course, represents an idealized situation. In practice, the modifications will be performed on a set of large, expanded data flow diagrams representing the logical model of the current system. The result is a set of large data flow diagrams that represent the lower, or more detailed, levels of processing for the new system.

The final step in creating the new logical model is to reorganize these diagrams by grouping logically related lower-level processes and forming a hierarchical set of data flow diagrams. Attempts should be made to create these logical groupings using some of the criteria identified for constructing the first model of the existing system. Identify key business events such as:

- The production of a major system output.
- The acceptance of a major system input.
- Major functional processes that occur within the system.

These logical groupings are important, for they will tend to influence the ultimate packaging or design of the new system. These mid-level groupings may well represent individual computer programs, for example. It will be better to have this organization based on events that are inherently part of the business than on things like today's organization structure. The resulting logical model, then, includes a hierarchical set of data flow diagrams, a complete data dictionary, an entity-relationship model, a normalized data model, and a set of process specifications.

Evaluate the Logical Model of the New System. After the logical model of the new system has been constructed, a thorough set of walkthroughs should be conducted to assure the quality of this model. One review should test for simple mechanical correctness. Tests to be applied in this review could include:

- Are all components named?
- Are all of the names meaningful?
- Are the proper symbols used throughout?
- Are all levels of the data flow diagram consistent and balanced?
- Are the outputs from each process properly supported by the available input data?

■ Are all data stores updated and also used as sources for data? Is there a balance between data accessed and data input to a data store?

Upper-CASE tools can handle a number of these tests.

In addition to mechanical checks, the model itself should be checked to be sure that it is an accurate and complete representation of the business. Formal walkthroughs, during which analysts and users review each model in detail, should verify that the model is clearly readable, understandable, and correct.

Finally, there can be at least an informal evaluation of the quality of the logical grouping decisions that evolved the hierarchical set of data flow diagrams from the large, expanded diagrams first produced. Two important design evaluations for the higher-level process organization are:

■ Coupling.
■ Cohesion.

Coupling refers to the number of data interfaces between two higher-level processes, as represented by the number of data flows that connect them and the volume and type of data transferred. The goal is to minimize the coupling between the processes. This results in processes that are more independent and, hence, more easily maintained. With minimal coupling, a change to one process is less likely to affect other processes. Clearly, different decisions about how to group lower-level processes into parent processes will influence the degree of coupling between the parent processes.

For example, one common mistake is to create a parent process called UPDATE FILES within which is grouped all of the update processing for all input to the system. A similar error is to create a parent process labeled WRITE REPORTS. In both cases, many processes that have no particular business relationships are lumped together, thereby increasing the coupling of this parent process with a variety of other unrelated parent processes.

Consider, for instance, the abstract data flow diagram fragment in Figure 6-13, representing a portion of a "middle-level" diagram. The process P7, UPDATE FILES, is responsible for the actual updating of three totally unrelated data stores. The result is that this process is heavily coupled with all the others for no business reason. The organization shown in Figure 6-14, on the other hand, is preferable. It permits the construction of the more natural higher-level diagram illustrated in Figure 6-15.

Cohesion refers to the internal strength or singularity of purpose of a process. A process has a high level of cohesion if it is directed toward achieving a single business purpose. A high level of cohesion is desirable and usually goes hand in hand with a low level of coupling between processes. A process called WRITE REPORTS, for example, has a very low level of cohesion. It draws together a large number of lower-level processes that have no business relationship to one another. On the other hand, a process such as PREPARE CUSTOMER BILL, while it may have twenty or more processes in an expanded child diagram, has a singularity of purpose—a high level of internal cohesion. There would be a minimal amount of coupling with other, outside processes.

Figure 6.13. *Portion of data flow diagram illustrating heavy coupling—caused by a general update files process.*

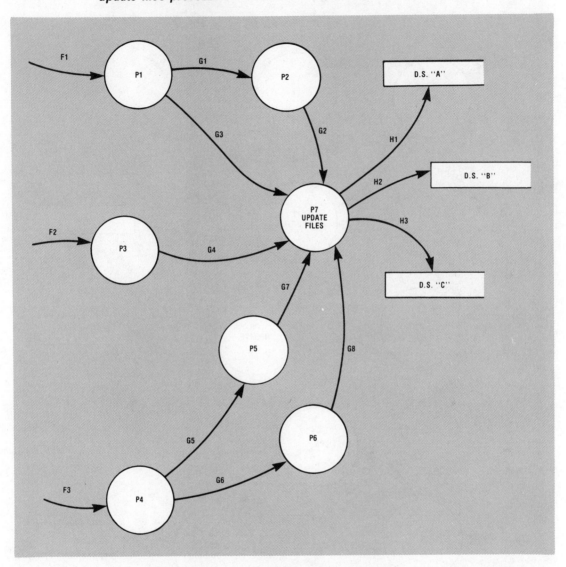

As indicated above, the payoff for creating models with minimal coupling between higher-level processes and high levels of cohesion within these processes is greater system maintainability. If a system design is based on a model with these characteristics, any change that occurs is likely to relate to only one or two of the high-level processes. Modifications can be made to the affected processes without impacting others.

Create a Physical Model of the New System. In building the logical model of the new system, concentration is on *what* processing should be done. In

Figure 6.14. Portion of a data flow diagram showing the same functions as Figure 6-13 with less coupling among processes.

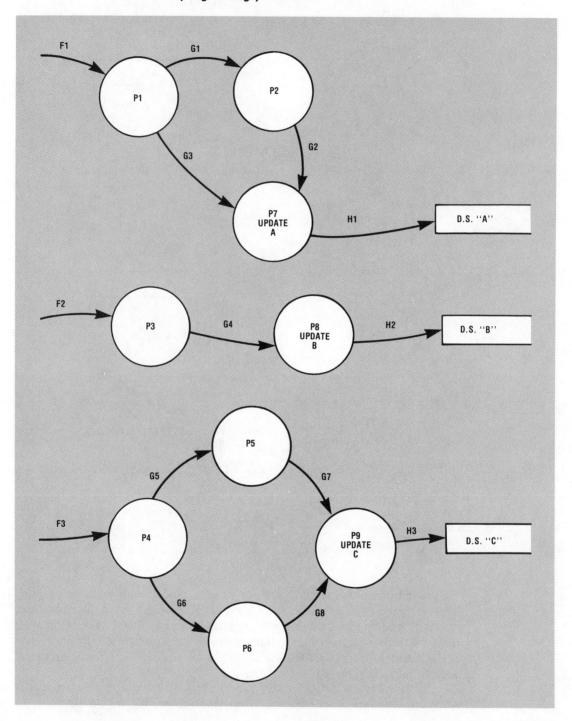

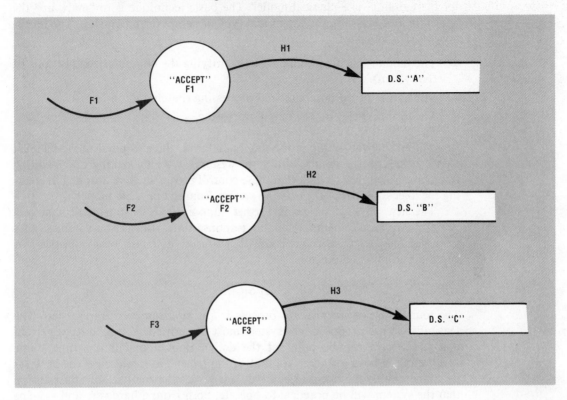

creating the physical model, emphasis shifts to *how* these functions are to be performed. The physical considerations will impact heavily the feasibility of the proposed system.

In building the physical model, it is necessary to deal with many tradeoffs. Among these are determinations of the type of processing to be used. What portion of the processing should be computerized and what should remain manual? Within the computer processing, which processes should be interactive and which should be batch? What should be the basic nature of the human-machine interface? What are the critical performance requirements in terms of throughput, response time, and so on? Decisions relating to these questions will impact costs as well as other feasibility considerations.

Where users make requests about features of the system, tradeoffs have to be evaluated in terms of importance of the request, cost, effectiveness, efficiency, and so on. It is often appropriate to develop multiple physical models representing different levels of user support.

The physical model constructed at this point must have sufficient detailing to show how the system actually will operate from the user's point of view. This level of understanding cannot be built with logical models alone.

Figure 6-12 illustrates a technique used in evolving from a logical to a physical model. The logical data flow diagram of Figure 6-11 is used as a basis for the building of a physical model. The basic technique is to "mark up" the logical model, showing the extent and type of computer processing. The resulting diagram indicates:

- The human-machine boundaries (identifying the computerized portions of the system).
- The nature of the computerized processing (batch and on-line).
- The timing cycles for the batch processing.

In addition to establishing processing boundaries, the new physical model must identify the control points within the system at which editing and auditing functions are applied. Recall that these control processes were dropped in creating the logical model of the existing system from the physical model.

The new physical model is further supported by a statement of system performance requirements, including response time, transaction volumes, data store volumes, and anticipated growth patterns, and also rough formats for computer inputs and outputs.

Evaluate the Feasibility of the Proposed System

The fourth step of the analysis process is an important verification step. The feasibility of the proposed new system must be verified. You need to be certain that the system can be built for the dollar amount and in the time frame specified. You need to be certain that, if implemented, it will meet the business need and enable the users to achieve their targeted benefits. You must ensure that the system will be practical to operate, both from a hardware and systems software point of view and from a people processing perspective. Finally, the political aspects of the proposed system must be evaluated. Given proper training, will the system be acceptable to the operating people in the user community, or might there be a serious threat of sabotage?

As a final check, this step might involve evaluating the feasibility of two or more proposed designs. It is not uncommon to create multiple design proposals for a new system. One might combine the use of a software package with custom programs. Others might present various levels of automated support, moving beyond base-level requirements or needs and into the category of "nice to have" features. The feasibility analysis, then, provides the basis for the selection of one of these options.

In addition to representing a final global check, feasibility evaluations also occur at a micro level throughout the design process. Design is really a series of tradeoff decisions. Which functions to automate and which to leave manual, which should be on-line and which batch, how extensive the editing should be, which file or data base structures to use, and dozens of other questions must be answered. For each decision, one from among several options must be selected. The feasibility of each of these options is evaluated at a micro level as the design decisions are made.

The Iterative Nature of the Analysis Process

The point has been made several times that analysis is an iterative process. Now that you understand the basic four-step analysis process, this point can be expanded.

Rather than viewing analysis and general design as a mechanical, front-to-end, four-step process, view the four steps as a cyclical process that can be repeated or iterated with gradually increasing levels of detail and understanding. Figure 6-16 (a) illustrates the cycle and 6-16 (b) superimposes the modeling steps on this cycle. Figure 6-17 illustrates the increased layers of detail with successive iterations.

Understanding the natural iteration and layering of detail that occurs during analysis is the key to successfully dealing with large, complex systems development efforts. It is a necessity for a successful analyst. This is also where the real power of data flow diagram models comes into play.

One of the major challenges with a large, complex system is the tremendous amount of detail that must be understood, documented, analyzed, and reorganized. You must be able to recognize both data elements and processes that are redundant in the system, those that are missing, those that are incorrect, and those that, while correct, are unnecessarily complicated. This demands that you have a means of moving quickly and accurately from highly detailed to more global views of the system and back again. Since a large system contains more detail than any one person can readily understand, the tendency is to get trapped in the detail of only one aspect of the system. It is very much like quicksand. The more detail you obtain, the stronger the pull to get into even more detail and the more difficult it is to lift back up to a less detailed, but more comprehensive, view. In the end, while a team of five to ten analysts may have correctly documented all the detail of the system, they may have no means of recognizing redundancy in different parts or of streamlining broad processes and making them less complex.

By following an iterative analysis process and documenting results by using a leveled or hierarchical set of data flow diagrams, you can partition the system into nonoverlapping parts and maintain intermediate levels of detail to help pull back up to more global and comprehensive views of the system. At the highest level, begin with a context diagram. After one or two iterations of the analysis process, results can be documented in a Diagram 0. In fact, when the creation of a Diagram 0 was discussed in Chapter 4 using major event analysis, recognition was given to the fact that this resulted in a mechanism for smoothing out the amount of detail that had been collected—for suppressing those details that were unnecessary at this point and highlighting those areas that were not well understood.

Diagram 0, then, effectively partitions the system into major parts, perhaps subsystems, represented by the individual processes. If each of the individual processes in Diagram 0 is viewed as a context diagram in its own right, the analysis process can be repeated individually within each context diagram, creating a next level of diagrams. Then, these individual pieces can be brought back as part of the whole and a more global analysis of the results can be done.

Figure 6.16. *The four-step analysis process viewed as a cyclical process.*

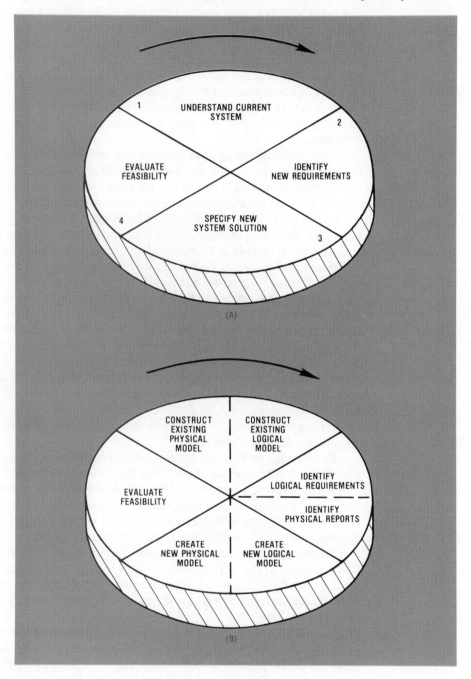

Part 2   Systems Analysis Modeling Techniques

Figure 6.17.   The iteration and layering inherent in the analysis process.

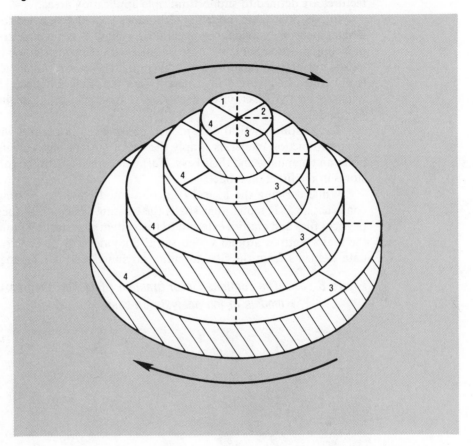

    This gives a sense of the iterative process that can continue to as many layers of detail as required. In practice, of course, it is not so orderly. Experienced analysts will tend to focus more on those parts of the system that appear to be more complex or that have been more volatile in the past. Nonetheless, the basic four-step analysis process *is* repeated or iterated, detail *is* suppressed during the initial iterations, and data flow diagrams *are* used as a means of controlling the level of detail and a technique for lifting above the detail to achieve more global views of the system.

DATA MODELING AND THE ANALYSIS PROCESS

Up to this point, the focus has been more on process modeling than on data modeling. Acknowledgment was given at the beginning of the chapter that data modeling tends to span multiple application systems. Hence it tends to be used heavily to support systems planning efforts, where comprehensive data architectures are defined to support multiple application areas.

In addition, these modeling techniques should be carried forward into the development of individual application systems. It is possible to define a data modeling process that can run in parallel with the construction of physical and logical models and can provide a higher quality new system physical model. This is illustrated in Figure 6-18, where a data modeling sequence has been superimposed on the function or data flow diagram modeling sequence shown in Figure 6-8.

The existing physical data model, constructed in parallel with the existing physical function model, is simply the list of current physical files—both computer and manual—and their keys. This will coincide with the collection of data stores in the function model.

While deriving the logical (function) model for the existing system, also construct an E-R model that spans the existing system. Use the list of current physical files and entities external to the system as a starting point to determine the major entities around which the E-R model will be constructed. Map all data elements from the files to entity attributes and use the logical (function)

Figure 6.18. The combination of function (data flow diagram) and data models in the analysis process.

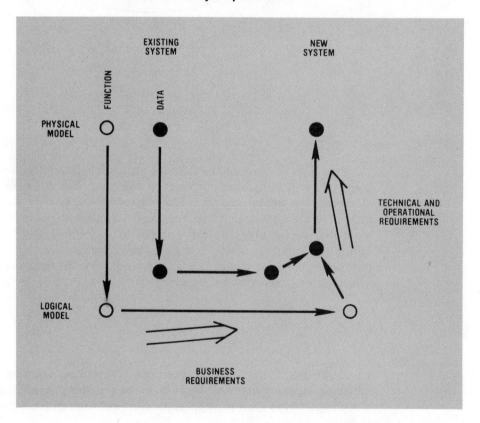

model to verify relationships. This constitutes the existing logical data model in the lower left corner of Figure 6-18.

Next construct the logical data model for the new system. New business requirements may or may not drive the definition of new entities. But they will almost certainly dictate a change in the relationships, and probably in the attributes as well. Recall the situation with Deep Pockets Insurance Company. Their attempt to build a customer funds management system caused fundamental changes to the relationships among their key entities. If the process has been followed correctly, a "nearly normal" set of data stores should exist that contain all of the data elements in the new logical (function) model. Verify that this is the case and update as necessary.

You are now ready to merge the two logical models—function and data—into a combined logical model for the new system. Do this by replacing the data stores that have been carried along in the function or data flow diagram-based models with the normalized set of data stores from the logical data model and adjusting data flows as necessary. In practice, it is a good idea to do this merge using fairly low-level data flow diagram models, then create the intermediate-level parent diagrams.

It is this merged logical model for the new system than can serve as the base for constructing the physical model for the new system. One thing that happens during the construction of this physical model is the identification of the actual physical data bases to be used in the new system. This is discussed further in Chapter 12. It is desirable to preserve, as much as possible, the logical data model created here. Sometimes that is not possible. If a software package is part of the solution, it will have its own physical data base structure which may not be consistent with the logical model. In addition, in those cases where data must be shared with other existing application systems, certain existing master files may need to carry forward unchanged. Despite these problems, the logical data model is still useful. Since it represents the ideal model (or at least a slice of it) for the future, file interfaces can be designed in order to minimize system maintenance when changes to the physical files are made in the future.

THE ANALYSIS PROCESS IN THE SDLC

In Chapter 2 a system development life cycle was discussed as a framework in which to learn the various skills presented in this book. The modeling process presented in this chapter is used during the first two phases of that life cycle: the investigation phase and the analysis and general design phase. Recall that the investigation phase consisted of two activities, a fairly rapid initial investigation followed by a feasibility study.

Initial Investigation

The iterative analysis process begins with the initial investigation activity. Based on a request for a new or improved system, the analysis process is used to probe for just enough information to establish the scope of the project. The analyst's documentation identifies some important aspects of what the new system will look like if it is developed. These include:

- Major outputs.
- Major inputs.
- Major processing functions.
- Relationships to other computer information systems.

Along with gathering this information, the analyst also builds an understanding of the objectives that lie behind the request for new system development. In a short time, the analyst should be able to answer several key questions:

- What do we have?
- What is needed?
- What could we deliver with the resources available to us?
- Does the project have sufficient potential to justify further investigation and development?

Modeling is minimal at this stage. During the initial investigation, the primary modeling result will probably be a context diagram. Depending on the size of the project, there may or may not be a need to take the time or effort necessary to develop a Diagram 0.

Feasibility Study

During the feasibility study activity, the same four steps in the analysis process produce a result drawn to greater detail. Typically, the analyst will develop a Diagram 0 for the current system and will make some attempt to distinguish between the logical and the physical aspects of the system.

Within the feasibility study, also, the analyst will identify the key requirements of the new system — those that represent changes from the way things are being done under the existing system. Within this context, the analyst will begin to distinguish between the logical and physical aspects of the new requirements — between the actual business requirements and the methods for delivering them.

As a final analysis procedure during the feasibility study, one or more potential solutions, or new systems, will be outlined at a general, Diagram 0, level. This preliminary look at the new system potential will also include evaluation of the possibility of using application software packages. The reason for looking at software at this point is that program development can represent up to 50 percent of the cost of a new system. If a cost saving solution is apparent at an early stage, this can affect projections of feasibility for the new system.

Analysis and General Design Phase

The major portion of time spent on the iterative modeling process occurs during the analysis and general design phase. The four-step analysis cycle illustrated in

Figure 6.19.   Gantt chart for analysis and general design phase.

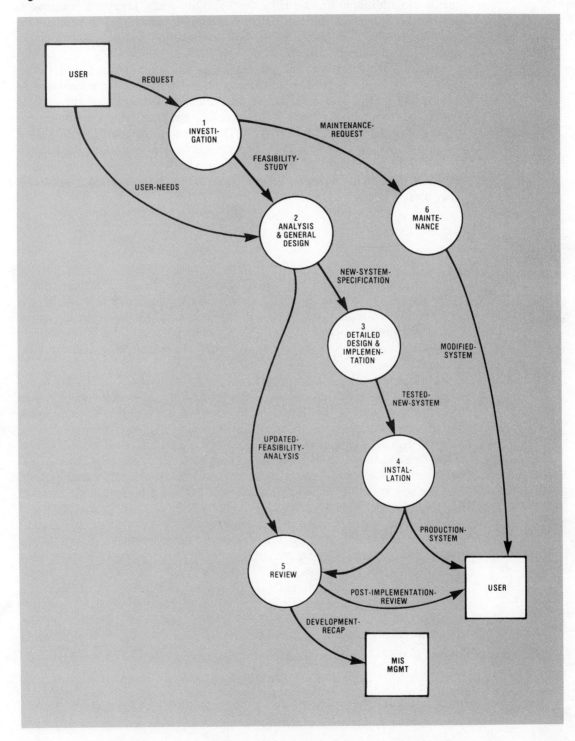

Figures 6-16 and 6-17 was completed once during the initial investigation and one or two additional times during the feasibility study. Iterations continue as necessary in this phase until sufficient understanding is gained to produce the two main products of the phase: the user specification and new system design specification discussed earlier.

Recall that the analysis and general design phase consists of four activities illustrated in Figure 6-19. The first step of the analysis process, understanding the existing system and creating physical and logical models of the existing system, corresponds to activity 3. The second step, identifying changes in user requirements, corresponds to activity 4. The third step, specifying a new system solution, corresponds to activity 5. And the fourth step, evaluating the feasibility of the proposed system, feeds activity 6. Clearly, because of the iterative nature of the analysis process, these activities cannot be completed in sequence. They must overlap.

SUMMARY

The work to develop an individual application system fits in the broader context of the business enterprise. Ideally, a systems development effort should be preceded by an information systems planning effort covering the entire enterprise. Data modeling techniques help establish the overall data architecture during planning. Data models typically extend beyond the bounds of a single application system.

The central goal of systems analysis is the development of specifications for a new system that meets user needs. These specifications—the user specification and the new system design specification—are the primary results of analysis. The user specification presents a complete model of the new system as the user will see it. The new system design specification encompasses both the user specification and all specifications of hardware, software, procedures, and documentation needed for actual design and implementation of the new system.

The new system specifications are based on the use of logical and physical data flow diagram models. A logical model is a general overview presentation of what the system does, regardless of the methods used. A physical model focuses on how the processing actually takes place, in sequence. Included are people, forms, and manual or computerized processing. To understand an existing system, a systems analyst begins by building a physical model. The next step is to derive a logical model of the existing system and from that to develop a logical model of the new system. A logical model provides a firmer foundation on which to base the design of a new system, unhindered by the physical constraints and assumptions of the existing system. Finally, a physical model of the new system is created.

Systems analysis as a process involves four steps that are repeated, or iterated, at levels of increasing detail and deeper understanding. These steps are: (1) understand the existing system; (2) identify changes in user requirements; (3) create a new system solution; and (4) evaluate the feasibility of the proposed solution. Both data flow diagram models and data models are used to support this four-step analysis process.

The four-step analysis process fits naturally into the first two phases of the system development life cycle. The steps are performed once, at a very high level, during the initial investigation activity. One or two additional iterations occur during the feasibility study activity. Then additional iterations, at increasing levels of detail, are performed during the analysis and general design phase.

KEY TERMS

1. data or information architecture
2. application architecture
3. technology architecture
4. management architecture
5. new system design specification
6. user specification
7. logical model
8. coupling
9. cohesion
10. physical model

REVIEW/DISCUSSION QUESTIONS

1. What architectures are created during information systems planning?
2. How are data flow diagram models and data models used in this planning process?
3. Explain why data models tend to cross application system boundaries.
4. What is a user specification and what is its function in systems development?
5. What is a new system design specification? How is it related to the user specification? What role does it play in the overall systems development life cycle?
6. What is the difference between a physical model and a logical model? How do data flow diagrams reflect these differences?
7. Describe the process for deriving a logical model from a physical model for an existing system.
8. Explain the four-step analysis process.
9. Explain the way in which logical and physical models support the analysis process.
10. Why is it important to develop a logical model of the existing system before starting to design a new system?

11. Describe criteria for evaluating the logical model of the new system.
12. What is involved in creating a physical model for a new system from the underlying logical model?
13. Explain the use of data modeling techniques during systems analysis. How do they relate to the process modeling techniques using data flow diagrams?
14. Explain the manner in which data flow diagram-based models naturally support the iteration of the four-step modeling process.
15. Discuss how the iterative analysis process is carried out in the context of the system development life cycle.

PRACTICE EXERCISES

1. A data flow diagram need not be exclusively logical or physical. Rather, diagrams often include both physical and logical characteristics. Consider the diagram in Figure 6-20, modeling a simplified catalog ordering process.

   a. Which elements of this diagram are particularly logical?
   b. Which elements of this diagram are particularly physical?
   c. How might this diagram be modified to make it as logical as possible?

   Certainly, a more detailed knowledge of the business is required to be able to answer these questions fully. However, a great deal can be inferred from the diagram alone.

2. The following narrative describes briefly the order-entry processing for a small manufacturing company. Many details are omitted.

   "Sally opens the mail and checks orders for completeness. Incomplete orders are given to Nancy in customer relations. Complete orders are taken to accounting by Pete, the messenger. Accounting checks the customer rating. If it is okay, the order is sent on to sales, which checks to see if the item is in inventory. If it isn't, sales backorders the item and informs Nancy. If it is, sales prepares a three-part packing slip and sends it to shipping. Shipping pulls the item and ships it to the customer with the first copy of the packing slip. The second copy of the packing slip goes to accounting, which bills the customer. The third copy is used to update the inventory records."

   Using this narrative:

   a. Construct a physical data flow diagram modeling the order entry processing. Use question marks to indicate those points where more detailed knowledge is needed.

Figure 6.20. Simplified data flow diagram containing both physical and logical aspects of a catalog ordering process. (For use with exercise.)

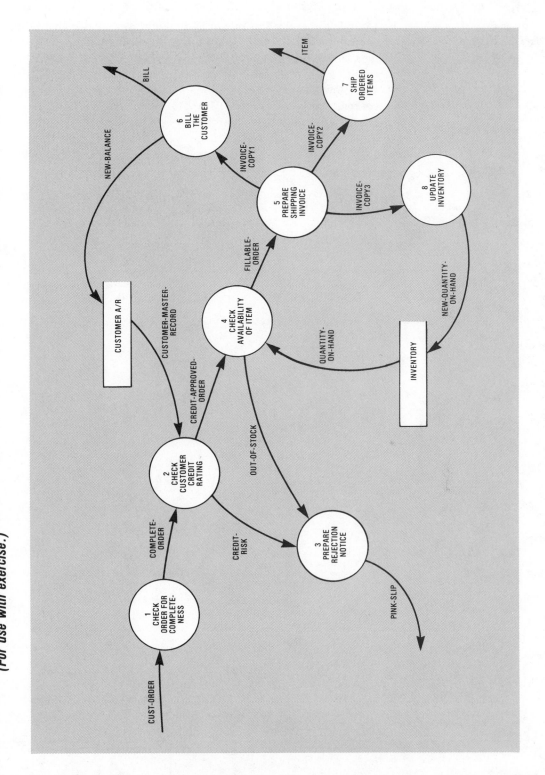

b. Complete the physical model by making some reasonable business assumptions to answer the questions raised in the building of the physical data flow diagram.

c. Create a set of data dictionary entries for the data stores and major data flows, again making reasonable business assumptions concerning content.

d. Derive a logical model from the physical model.

7

Computer-Aided Software Engineering

Learning Objectives

On completing reading and other learning assignments for this chapter you should be able to:

- Adequately define the support functions and the components of typical CASE systems.
- Describe how the integrated function of a CASE system may assist an analyst in the development of a system design specification.
- Give the potential benefits that may result from incorporating a CASE environment into a data processing shop.
- Describe how the incorporation of a CASE system may impact the participants and process of a systems development life cycle.
- Explain why CASE systems are not more widely utilized.
- Explain what is necessary before CASE systems will be more widely adopted in business and industry.

WHAT IS CASE?

Computer-Aided Software Engineering (CASE) provides automated assistance to the analysts, designers, and builders of computer systems through the implementation of the tools, techniques, and methodologies of systems development. CASE tools are analogous to CAD/CAM in a manufacturing environment in that they provide the potential for support of production as well as design activities.

Systems Development Methods and Tools

Like most professional disciplines, systems analysis and design require both a "methods" and a "tools" component. Methods instruct professionals in "what" to do and "how" to perform a task, while tools provide a means for actually performing the task. Traditionally, systems analysis and design techniques emphasize the methods of systems development. These techniques demonstrate the philosophies, heuristics, and strategies of such concepts as structured analysis and design, data flow modeling, a system development life cycle, data design, process definitions, prototyping, and the like.

The actual implementation and incorporation of these concepts into physical systems documentation and "working" models has largely been left to individual analysts. The "tools" component of the systems analysis and design profession has in the past been lacking. For example, in order to develop the various system representations, like data flow diagrams or system flowcharts, many data processing professionals have utilized combinations of tools such as typewriters, word processors, generic computerized graphic, generators and templates. Producing working models or actual systems has been done either by programmers or more recently with the use of fourth-generation languages (4GL). Until recently analysts were provided very little assistance or automation to produce the products of their trade.

The computing industry has realized that truly good systems are those that are well conceived, designed, and documented as well as implemented. Structured analysis and design methodologies have thus become widely accepted and practiced. As these methodologies have become more refined and standardized, the need for better tools has greatly increased. As a result Computer-Aided Software Engineering (CASE) is now an important and rapidly expanding area of computer technology.

Definition of CASE

CASE refers to a category of automated tools available to assist the systems development and software engineering processes through computerization. In its most narrow definition, CASE provides documentation support only for the systems analyst. More broadly speaking, however, CASE provides development support from early in the requirements specification stage to eventual systems maintenance. CASE systems incorporate typical systems analysis and design methodologies with integrated software packages to provide analysts with tools similar to **Computer Aided Design (CAD)** for industrial technologists. While the verdict is still to be determined regarding its ultimate impact, CASE technology provides system developers with the promise of higher productivity and greater system longevity.

The analogy of CAD as well as **CAM (computer aided manufacturing)** is a good one to explain the broad functions of CASE. CAD provides support for the specification and design of machine parts and processes. CAM assists in the actual production of machine parts and/or end products. Integrated, CAD/CAM forms an automated method of manufacturing that greatly improves the productivity, maintainability, and flexibility of the entire manufacturing process. Similarly, the ultimate promise of CASE is not merely to assist in analysis and design but to create actual production systems. Thus, while CASE systems were initially developed to meet largely documentation needs of data processing professionals, these products now include components that span the entire systems development life cycle.

Computer-Aided Software Engineering (CASE) systems are rapidly becoming a common means of supporting software development efforts. Although commercial CASE systems vary, all consist of a variety of somewhat integrated components that seek to enhance software analysis, design and implementation techniques at different stages in the development life cycle. These systems attempt to improve overall computer systems development effectiveness.

THE COMPONENTS OF CASE

The functions or support provided by CASE components can be generally grouped into four categories. Those are documentation assistance, analysis enhancements, project coordination, and application generators.

Documentation Assistance

Early CASE tools provided basic **documentation assistance** to the systems development process. Systems documentation, particularly graphic representations, is often difficult to produce and maintain. Analysts and designers utilize a variety of representations to model different aspects of computer systems. For example, data flow diagrams model processes, external entities, and data stores and map the data which flows between them. Entity-relationship diagrams model data objects and their relationships. A system flowchart models the sequencing of individual jobs and the data sets that combine to form a computer system. Structure charts model the relationship of individual program modules. Many other representations may be necessary to fully illustrate a complicated computer system. This graphic modeling, while extremely valuable, is difficult to produce and correct by manual means such as templates or freehand drawings. A pencil-and-paper version of a data flow diagram will often have to be completely redrawn to reflect a minor system change.

The use of graphic modeling has not replaced the need for written documentation in systems development. Systems documentation still requires a great deal of verbal editing. Examples include specifications about processes, files, screens, procedures, and the like. A variety of written reports is also required for communicating system development status and progress to the project's interested constituencies, such as users, managers, and technicians. Before the introduction of word processors, analysts used typewriter or handwritten material to provide this documentation.

Finally, documentation is necessary to illustrate the outputs of a computer system. As early as is possible in the development process, screen and report layouts should be reviewed with system users. Paper layout forms have been utilized for producing such layouts in the past. Correcting such layouts is as tedious as correcting graphic presentation.

The basic CASE documentation assistance tools are graphics generator, data dictionary, word processor, and report and screen designer.

Graphics Generator. The **graphics generator** is used for modeling such system representations such as data flow diagrams, structure charts, entity-relationship diagrams, system flow charts, program flowcharts, and structure charts. This component is probably the most widely used and valued feature of CASE products. Usually a variety of symbols is readily available to model these representations. Figure 7-1 shows typical symbols and representations included in most CASE graphic generators.

CASE graphic generators are essentially drawing boards in which the user selects from predetermined symbols and draws connecting lines and arrows to produce system representations and diagrams. Graphic generators usually include mouse or light-pen support for easy and fast symbol manipulation. The types of manipulations provided by the graphic tools include such functions as repeats, moves, deletions, possibly sizing and grouping, and other **"cut and paste"** maneuvers. Some graphic generators may even provide a means for producing original symbols for subsequent use. Some degree of text may be added to the representations in order to label symbols, lines, or diagram portions. Figure 7-2 shows a data flow diagram, probably the most common of systems development representations, produced by a CASE graphics generator.

Besides merely producing graphics, these systems provide layering capabilities of the various representations. For example, a process bubble on a data flow diagram may be **exploded to a lower-level** group of processes, which jointly comprise the original process. Conversely, a group of processes may be **imploded to the higher-level** diagram they represent (see Figure 7-3). In this manner, system representation may be linked to display hierarchical or other relationships. Also, linkage can usually be established from the graphic diagram to a data dictionary.

Data Dictionary. The **data dictionary** serves as a central repository for all information concerning databases, files, structures, and elements, as well as specifications for processes, programs, reports, or screens. It is probably the next most common and utilized feature of CASE products, after graphic generators. The data dictionary may be as simple as a standardized file-naming scheme or it may be implemented through some sophisticated file-management software. The dictionary can usually be accessed through its own function or through other CASE components. For example, you could reach the process specification for a process on a DFD through a linkage provided by the graphics generator component as illustrated in Figure 7-4. The data dictionary is particularly useful to team projects because several team members may be sharing or updating any of the project information.

Figure 7.1. *Typical CASE symbols.*

KEY TO GRAPHICS

DFD - DATA FLOW DIAGRAMS   SH - SCREEN HIERARCHY
SFC - SYSTEM FLOW CHART   SS - STRUCTURE CHART
PFC - PROGRAM FLOW CHART   ERD - ENTITY RELATIONSHIP DIAGRAM

NAME	GRAPHIC	REPRESENTS	SYMBOL
BOX 1	DFD	EXTERNAL ENTITY	
	SH	SCREEN	
	SS	MODULE	
	SFC	PROGRAM	
	ERD	ENTITY	
	PFC	PROCESS	
BOX 2	DFD	EXTERNAL ENTITY	
	SH	SCREEN	
	SS	MODULE	
	SFC	PROGRAM	
	ERD	ENTITY	
	PFC	PROCESS	
BOXDIA	PFC	INPUT / OUTPUT	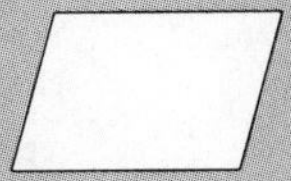
BUBBLE1	DFD	ORDINARY PROCESS	
	SFC	TAPE	
BUBBLE2	DFD	HIGHLIGHTED PROCESS	
DASD1	SFC	ON-LINE STORAGE	
DASD2	SFC	ON-LINE STORAGE	

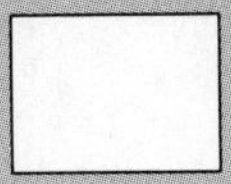

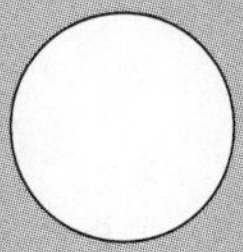

DFD - DATA FLOW DIAGRAMS   SH - SCREEN HIERARCHY
SFC - SYSTEM FLOW CHART   SS - STRUCTURE CHART
PFC - PROGRAM FLOW CHART   ERD - ENTITY RELATIONSHIP DIAGRAM

NAME	GRAPHIC	REPRESENTS	SYMBOL
DIAMOND1	PFC ERD	DECISION RELATIONSHIP	
DIAMOND2	SFC ERD	SORT RELATIONSHIP	
DISPLAY	SFC SH	TERMINAL DISPLAY SCREEN	
DOCUMENT	SFC	OUTPUT DOCUMENT	
DOUBBOX	ERD	ENTITY	
CROWFOOT	ERD	MULTIPLE RELATIONSHIP	
ELLIPSE	ERD SFC	ATTRIBUTE, DATA ELEMENT TERMINAL	
LINK	DFD OTHERS	LINK TEXT TO SPECIFICATION LINK TEXT TO SPECIFICATION	

KEY TO GRAPHICS

DFD - DATA FLOW DIAGRAMS
SFC - SYSTEM FLOW CHART
PFC - PROGRAM FLOW CHART

SH - SCREEN HIERARCHY
SS - STRUCTURE CHART
ERD - ENTITY RELATIONSHIP DIAGRAM

NAME	GRAPHIC	REPRESENTS	SYMBOL
RBOX	DFD	ORDINARY PROCESS	
RECTANG1	DFD	DATA STORE, FILE	
RECTANG2	DFD	DATA STORE, FILE	
SEMIBUB1	PFC	BEGIN CASE	
SEMIBUB2	PFC	END CASE	
OFFPAGE	SFC SH SS PFC	OFF-PAGE CONNECTOR	
DATADN	SS	DATA FLOW	
DATAUP	SS	DATA FLOW	
SWITCHDN	SS	DATA FLOW	
SWITCHUP	SS	DATA FLOW	

Figure 7.2. Data flow diagram from CASE tool.

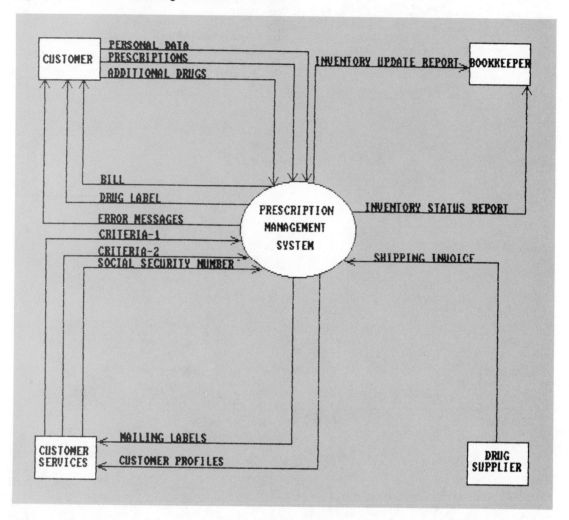

REPOSITORY

A recent evolution in systems development technology is the concept of the repository. A *repository* is like a super data dictionary. It contains all the components of a data dictionary, information about data elements, structures, stores, and the like, as well as various types of system specifications. In addition, the repository contains actual source and object code previously housed in separate system libraries. Modules, programs, macro instructions, and system

Figure 7.3. **Hierarchical explosions and implosions of CASE graphic generator.**

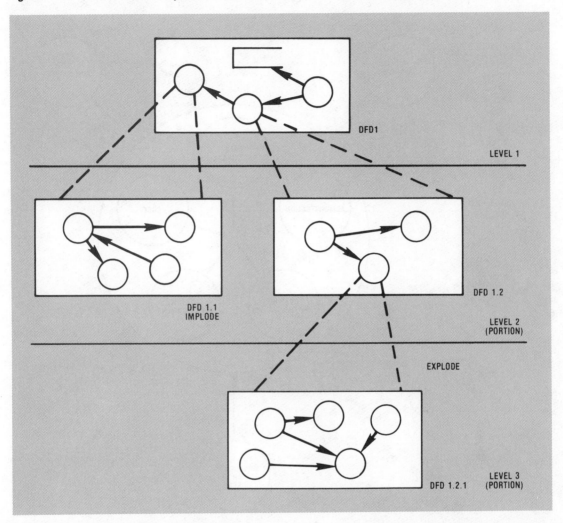

protocols would be accessible through it. Graphic representations are also part of the repository, as are data flow diagrams, entity-relationship diagrams, system flow charts, structure charts, and screen or report layouts.

The repository would thus store and integrate all system development data produced by full-featured CASE systems. In additional, administrative information could be generated and accumulated through the repository. Information about security guidelines, corporate standards, accounting procedures, audit trails, and development or performance histories would be produced and maintained (see Feature figure). Potentially, information about hardware speci-

Feature figure.   Information repository directory system.

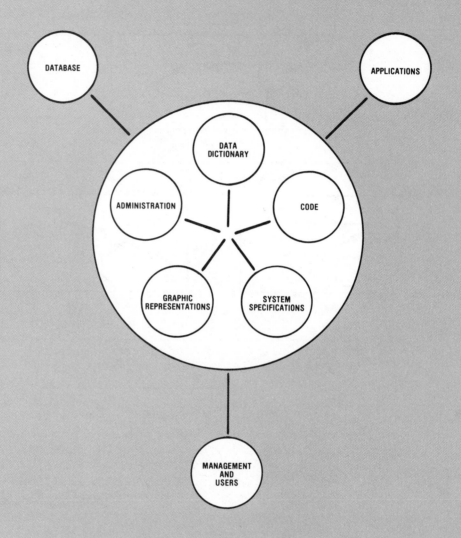

fications, capabilities, and requirements could also be stored. Eventually, as they become more common, image, video, and audio data might be included as well.

All this information would be linked and coordinated in much the same way as actual corporate data in a database management system (DBMS). Inter-related specifications, data dictionary items, graphic representations, and actual codes would be dynamically altered as components were changed. All items included in the repository would be cross-referenced to all other appropriate items. The repository thus would become an interactive system development and maintenance tool. As such, it would be a directory for management, application, and data base functions. This interactive functioning directory, often called an Information Repository Directory System (IRDS), could become an integral part of the corporate information resource management scheme.

The natural tendency of software productivity tools, like CASE systems, is to be more inclusive of all system components, to provide more integration between the components, and to be more responsive to all stages in the system life cycle. The concept of the IRDS is a major step in that direction.

Figure 7.4. Access to specification through CASE graphic generator.

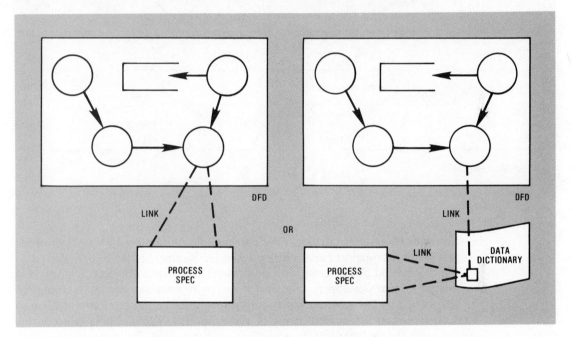

Word Processing. Usually some text editing capabilities are included in CASE products, often in the form of a relatively simple **word processor**. The primary function of the editor is the preparation of written documentation such as the various design specifications for process files, structures, records, and layouts. Usually, "forms" are provided for specifications. These are simply word-processing templates with predetermined formats to be filled in regarding the various design entities. Often these templates are part of the data management package provided by the data dictionary, making the templates and all the items on them available for management activities, such as a listings or sorting of similar or identical items. Figures 7-5 and 7-6 illustrate several blank processing templates, in this case a PROCESS and a DATA STORE specification. The word-processing capabilities may also be used for the various report-writing

Figure 7.5. *Typical CASE word-processing template—PROCESS specifications.*

```
                    PROGRAM/PROCESS SPECIFICATION


PROCESS NAME:
_____

SYSTEM NAME:                        DATE:

PROCESS NO.:                        PREPARER:

DESCRIPTION:
_____

INTERFACES:
            INPUT                        FROM
            _____

            OUTPUT                       TO
            _____


_____

DEFINITION:
```

functions necessary in project development. In addition, many CASE products provide import-export capabilities to popular commercial word processors.

Report and Screen Designers. The **report and screen designers** are provided so that system developers may easily design reports and "paint" screens for verification by users. These input-output layouts are also an important form of documentation for implementers of the proposed system. These components constrain the designer to actual working circumstances, for example, appropriate column length and row width. More sophisticated tools may be coordinated through the data dictionary to generate initial layouts from design specifications. Similarly, the designer tool may generate design specifications from newly created layouts. Figures 7-7 and 7-8 illustrate these functions.

The documentation assistance displayed in Figure 7-9, is currently the most common, useful, and widely utilized function of the CASE products. The further integration of these components provided by a CASE tool allows the complete documentation or system specification to become an interactive blueprint for the system design. For example, you may start at a high-level data flow diagram and explode a particular process for more detail. Then you may wish to interact with the data dictionary and word processor to complete the output specification for a data flow on the lower-level data flow diagram. Once this

Figure 7.6. Typical CASE word-processing template—file specification.

```
                    DATA STORE/FILE SPECIFICATION


   FILE NAME:
   _____

SYSTEM NAME:                          DATE:
   FILE NO.:                          PREPARER:
    ALIASES:
 STRUCTURES:
   _____

DESCRIPTION:

DEVICE TYPE:                    ORGANIZATION:
RECORD SIZE:       (BYTES) AVERAGE VOLUME:        (RECORDS)
PEAK VOLUME:                    GROWTH RATE:
     KEY(S):
            PRIMARY                     SECONDARY
            _____



  RETENTION:
   _____

ACCESSED BY:
            PROCESS(ES)           UPDATE        ACCESS METHOD



     BACKUP:
INSTRUCTIONS:
```

task is completed, you may use that specification to generate the initialization of a screen layout with the screen designer. Using a screen designer, you may then complete the screen layout. All these functions may be provided conveniently through a CASE package.

Some CASE systems may contain many more complex and dynamic components. These are likely to be widely utilized as these products become more popular.

Figure 7.7.   Initial report layout generated by design tool using output specifications.

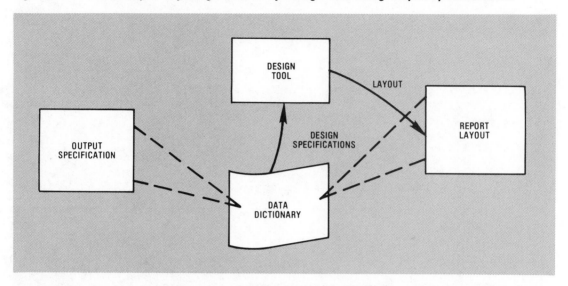

Figure 7.8.   Initial data specification generated by design tool using screen layout.

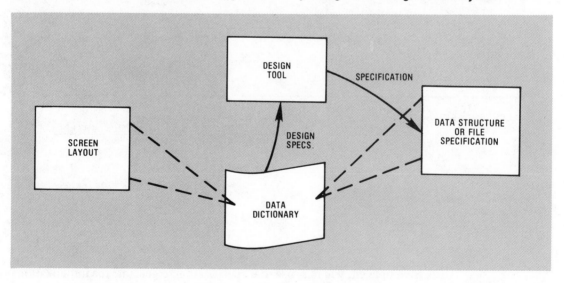

Analysis Enhancements

Some of the CASE components actually may support the analytical capabilities of an analyst or designer. For example, the initial creation of input-output layout designs from specifications, as discussed earlier, is a task usually thought of as analytical. Many products provide verification features which check

Figure 7.9. CASE documentation assistance.

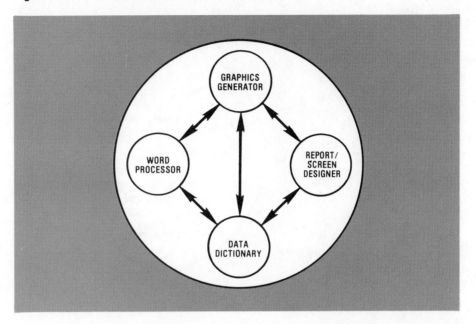

models and the data dictionary for obvious errors or inconsistencies. Some offer features that take design specifications and create efficient system data designs and in some cases, the actual programs and data file structures. Other tools may provide a visual system simulation or prototype of the proposed system to compare to user expectations. Typical **analysis enhancement** components are verification processes, data optimization, and prototyping as illustrated in Figure 7-10.

Verification Processes. CASE tools often check for simple errors or inconsistencies in or among the documentation items. For example, a DFD may contain a data store with a particular data element or field that has never actually flowed in from any source on the entire model. A structure may be labeled on the DFD but not further documented by a required design specification. These situations may be flagged or automatically corrected by some verification process. These types of processes can be likened to debugging functions of programming language compilers. Like programming some of the methodology of systems analysis and design can be so systematic and straightforward that the computer can actually determine questionable circumstances. In this situation, the CASE system may use inherent "intelligence" to verify the accuracy or correctness of a design solution, usually a function solely the concern of the human designer.

Data Optimization. There is a variety of systematic modeling and normalizing techniques that may be performed on the system's collection of files and data. The more systematic these processes are, the more potential for computer assistance. Thus a feature of some CASE products is the optimization of the

Figure 7.10. CASE analysis enhancements.

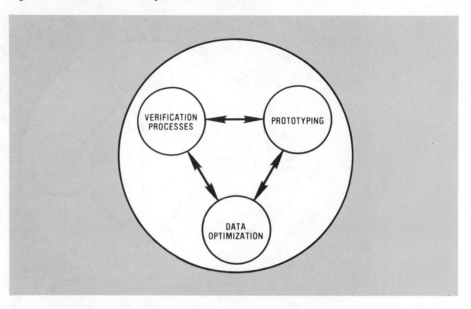

system's database. That is, the overall collection and organization of the files, records, and fields of the system database may be configured by the computer to maximize logical efficiency and minimize redundancy.

Prototyping. The **prototyping** of a potential system refers to a visualization or actualization of a working system model. The prototype, or working model, of the system is a convenient illustration to be developed jointly with users to insure the large-scale effectiveness and completeness of the system design. In the most fundamental sense, report and screen layouts are prototypes of the actual system outputs. In a broader characterization, however, a prototype is an actual operational system model capable of performing all the actual functions of the proposed system. This type of prototype may eventually be the system, thus highlighting the extraordinary potential of this type of feature. In between these extremes, a CASE system may have the ability to organize system screen layouts in an order that might arise from eventual menu selection. This feature is very useful for presentations to user and management groups. All CASE systems thus provide some prototyping capabilities, if only report and screen layouts.

Project Coordination

Many of the CASE components help with project coordination. For example, the communication between all interested parties in the development project may be augmented by the presentation capabilities of the CASE tool. Some components may help facilitate the performance of a work-group or system management. For example, project management techniques as discussed in Chapter 3, may be implemented through such components. One purpose of these features is to keep group members informed of the ongoing developments made by other members and the subsequent effect of their work upon the overall system documentation project status.

Another purpose is to coordinate as closely as possible the specific system design specifications, such as record layouts and entity names, with the eventual production environment. Also, many of the commercial CASE products may be implemented in a networked situation, thus providing coordination for systems development hardware devices and data. Typical CASE coordination components are presentation facilities, project management, and application interfaces, as illustrated in Figure 7-11.

Presentation Facilities. During the development process, project team members will need to produce a variety of presentations to keep team members, users, technicians, and management informed about ongoing progress. These presentations may encompass any part of the system design in varying quantity, quality, and depth and may be aimed at widely differing audiences. Most CASE tools offer a broad range of **presentation capabilities**. Graphic and textual software, in addition to that available in the graphics generator and word-processing components, may be provided. The data dictionary may also help to organize, summarize, and print from the many graphic and textual materials developed in the other CASE components. For example, a report to management may require portions of a high-level data flow diagram, a great deal of written project summary, and perhaps a graph displaying project activity status. Programmers may need only specifications on modules, screens, files, records, and the like. Presentations to system users may display a project over-

Figure 7.11. CASE project coordination.

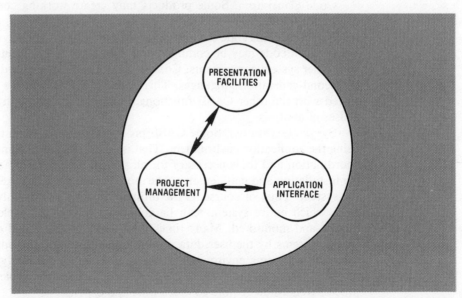

view and possibly a portrait of the user interface in the form of screen designs and hierarchy.

Project Management. **Project management** features provide tools to implement the techniques for planning, controlling, and monitoring systems development projects as discussed in detail in Chapter 3. PERT and GANTT charts may be available as well as detail on specific team member responsibilities and project activity status. These are particularly useful components, enabling project leaders and managers to reallocate resources as necessary during the development process. This becomes a very powerful and convenient tool when actually integrated into the production activities of the CASE system.

Application Interface. Very sophisticated CASE products provide an interface to specific operating environments. For instance, record and field specifications may be constrained to formats compatible with specific application languages, like COBOL, PL/I, C, dBASE, or a 4GL. A more sophisticated CASE product might have a data dictionary that is the actual device used in the production environment, thus ensuring consistency and coordination with the eventual production applications. Changes made to design elements then automatically become changes to the production elements.

Application Generators

The long-range promise of CASE technology is to provide development assistance from requirements to installation, maintenance and beyond. Thus a key component in CASE is the ability to actually generate working applications. These applications run the gamut of simple code generators to complete system generation and fourth-generation language (4GL) interfaces. Typical application generators thus are code generators, system generators, and 4GLs as illustrated in Figure 7-12.

Code Generators. Some products may create working computer pseudo-code, code, modules, or programs directly from design models, prototypes, and specifications. This code then becomes the basis for eventual system implementation. Such code may be compiled and used directly in an integrated fashion with other system components. Code generators have been produced for almost all second-generation languages. This code is more useful the more it is integrated with the other CASE functions, particularly those utilized in the early phases of analysis.

System Generators. Some CASE products are capable, in limited ways, of being the application environment. That is, the CASE environment provides the coordination and tools necessary for all system development activities, including installation and maintenance. The model created by the CASE tool becomes the system. This, of course, is the ultimate in CASE, an analyst's workbench from which entire systems can be conceived, designed, implemented, maintained, and monitored. Many times these features are added on to packaged CASE systems by the user data processing shop to accommodate their highly divergent operating environments. These systems may actually be transparent to users. That is, they would be developed without the typical development processes that now require so much time and expense.

Figure 7.12. CASE application generators.

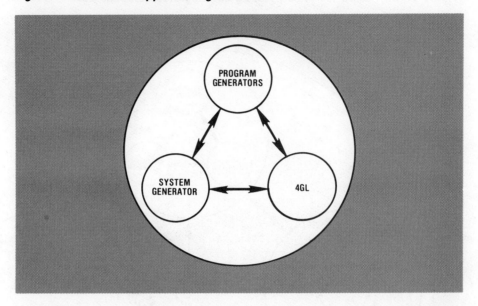

Fourth Generation Language (4GL) Interface. **Some CASE products provide an interface to a 4GL. That is, a relatively nonprocedural language may be integrated in combination with the data dictionary and a database management system. The total package thus provides the means to provide a working application with relatively little coding effort. These systems are particularly useful for situations involving reporting or querying of stored data.**

The "perfect" CASE system would provide an integrated workbench of tools to coordinate all aspects of systems development efforts, from requirements specifications to system installation and beyond. Although many such individual CASE components may exist, few actually provide a complete, integrated tool for the entire systems life cycle as depicted in figure 7-13.

Upper and Lower CASE

The following list summarizes the major components of CASE systems.

Upper CASE

- Documentation assistance
  - Graphics generator
  - Word processor
  - Data dictionary
  - Report and screen designer
- Analysis enhancements
  - Verification processes
  - Data optimization
  - Prototyping

Figure 7.13. **CASE tool incorporating all integrated components.**

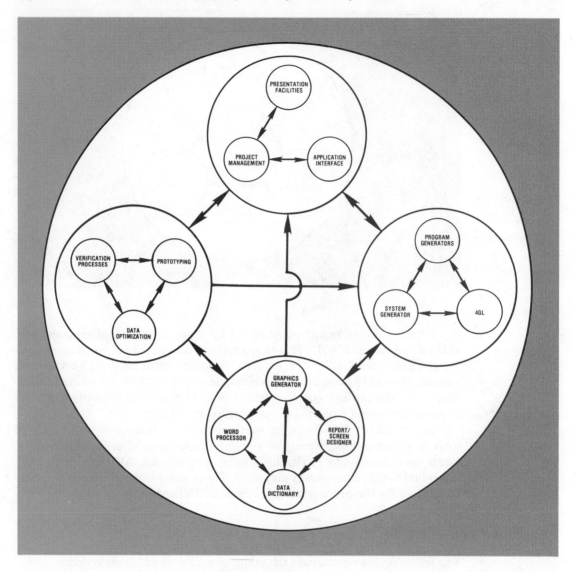

■ Project coordinators
  — Presentation facilities
  — Project management
  — Application interface
■ Application generators
  — Code generators
  — System generators
  — 4GL

Lower CASE

Those at the top of the list, usually the documentation assistance tools, are often called **upper CASE** referring to the fact that they assist most with the front end of systems development, requirements, and needs specification. Those at the bottom of this list, usually, the application generation tools, are often called **lower CASE**, referring to their assistance to the outputs of the development process, the actual programs and systems.

The ultimate usefulness of any CASE system may actually be in how well components of upper CASE are integrated to lower CASE components. The more integrated and transparent the transition between these components, the more useful the CASE tool. Keep in mind, however, that while CASE systems may be able to assist the analyst in a variety of system development activities and in certain limited applications may actually replace many programming activities, the mental skills and capacities of the analyst are irreplaceable. CASE systems merely provide the analyst with a computerized tool by which specific systems analysis and design methodologies may be employed in conjunction with personal skills. CASE systems *do not* analyze or design systems. Analysts and designers analyze and design systems. CASE systems merely assist this process.

THE PROMISE OF CASE

The ultimate goal of a CASE system is increased productivity. But what is productivity? One measure of systems development productivity used in the past was the number of lines of code produced. For example, how many lines of code could a programmer produce in an hour? To increase productivity thus meant to increase the number of lines of code produced in an hour. The obvious fallacy in this type of measurement of productivity is that the lines of code produced may not solve the problem at hand or that a simpler design resulting in a better system may have required fewer lines of code. This type of productivity measure applied to analysis and design activities then might look at the number of bubbles on a DFD or screen layouts produced by an analyst in an hour. CASE systems, particularly through the graphics generator and screen designer, would unquestionably enable analysts to produce more DFD bubbles and screen layout per hour. But, like increasing the lines of code, speeding the production of these items may not improve the actual system. So what then is productivity?

The measures just mentioned actually refer to system development efficiency, that is, end products produced in some time frame. These measures are used primarily because they are easy to quantify and summarize. However, they probably have very little to do with overall system performance. Perhaps a better way to measure system development productivity would be in terms of effectiveness. Effectiveness refers to how well a system meets the needs and objectives of the users, or how well it suits the short- and long-range strategic goals of the organization. CASE systems offer hope for application developers in that they may be able to build more effective systems through their use. While measures of effectiveness are certainly more difficult to quantify than efficiency, they will certainly be more relevant to the eventual system user and organization. (Try telling a disgruntled and disillusioned user that the incomprehensible system you produced was coded at 250 lines an hour.)

Thus, if CASE systems are to have benefits for the organizations which employ them, they must enhance the overall systems development effectiveness. Some of the ways in which effectiveness may be evaluated are uniformity of development end products, maintainability of development end products, enhanced communication of project participants, reduced development time, and improved system quality.

Uniformity of Development End Products

Although CASE systems vary somewhat among themselves, once adopted within an organization, they have the effect of standardizing the analysis and design end products. All members of development teams or staffs will follow the methodology, guidelines, and formats inherent in the adopted CASE system if they are consistently required. Specifications will all follow predetermined formats and contain identical characteristics. Output layouts will be uniformly constrained. Graphic models and diagrams will be bound by steadfast rules and verified by consistent and systematic processes. Thus there will be a common ground of understanding for all members of development groups to embrace across projects or teams. A person shifted from one project or team to another during ongoing development will operate under similar ground rules and consequently be productive more quickly. Although many data processing environments may now stress such standards regardless of their use of CASE, enforcement is often difficult. CASE should make the enforcement of uniformity and standardization easier.

Maintainability of Development End Products

Through standardization and computerization, CASE systems make the documentation much more easily maintainable than did previous methods. One of the problems with employing systems development methodologies has been the difficulty in updating or correcting systems documentation, particularly graphic representations. Because of these difficulties, systems documentation is often not used or not maintained when necessary, thus making it either nonexistent or wrong. With CASE systems, documentation products are stored in computer files, making the maintenance of system specifications much less a burden. While discipline is still required to adequately maintain documentation, both during a system's development and later in its life cycle, CASE systems provide the analyst and system maintainer with a very convenient and maintainable system specification.

Also, since some CASE systems have dynamic **integration** among some components, fewer actual changes will be necessary. For example, the removal of a specific file on a data flow diagram may automatically remove its reference in the data dictionary and any corresponding inclusion in a library of file specification. The overall system database may also be automatically adjusted or reoptimized to reflect such changes. Likewise, the removal or change to a particular field in a record layout may require only a change to a record specification for the entire system specification to be adjusted accordingly. Such capabilities could make the tedious job of documentation maintenance much more likely to be accomplished.

Enhanced Communication of Project Participants

Initially, the value of CASE systems will be measured by their worth as communication tools. The methodological activities of analysis and design are worthless in a vacuum. Communication is of utmost importance. The ideas developed or discovered by the analyst must be clearly understood by users, by the programmers and technicians, and by management. The uniformity and maintainability of CASE systems all help make it an exceptional communication tool. Graphic representations can isolate or highlight broad concepts to users. Detailed specifications and report or screen layouts can provide essential information to programmers. Management can be kept abreast of development status through system documentation and CASE-generated presentations. The analyst, as the hub of a communication network during systems development, may use CASE systems to tie all the critical communication components together.

In order to clearly communicate a computer information system, a clear and visible portrait of that system must be made available for all involved parties to evaluate and comprehend. It is the accuracy, insight, and elegance of this portrait that may eventually determine the success or failure of a system development project. This portrait is essentially a set of documentation that clearly communicates the system with enough detail for user comprehension, programmer direction, and management approval. CASE systems can help make the products of systems analysis and design more visible. The portrait an analyst can paint using this type of tool can be more complete, accurate, and elegant. It can both look better and be better. CASE systems may permit more specific visions of future systems than do traditional means.

Reduced Development Time

As mentioned earlier, the potential of CASE lies in more than documentation. CASE can offer support facilities that range from complete requirements definition to system maintenance. In the future, CASE systems may be capable of generating complete computer systems. A traditional systems development life cycle is illustrated in Figure 7-14. An investigation determines feasibility and defines user requirements. The user requirements are transformed into design specifications, including specific output layouts and system models or prototypes. These specifications are implemented by programmers or technicians who write and test computer programs. The system is installed in its technical environment, where it will be maintained until it becomes obsolete. When major changes in the system are required, the entire cycle must be initiated. That is, the requirements must be defined, specifications generated, programming completed and tested, and changes installed in the production system.

Figure 7.14. Traditional systems development life cycle.

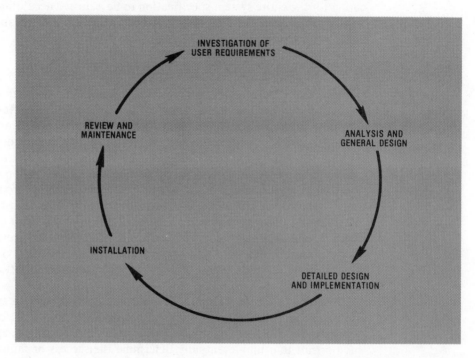

CASE systems offer the promise of a shortened development life cycle. Maintenance of the system documentation may be less time consuming as a result of the integration of facilities. But beyond this feature, CASE may actually alter the typical development life cycle. In a future CASE environment, as illustrated in Figure 7-15, systems may be generated after requirements specification. Programs, modules, and computer "language" will be transparent to the system developers. Implementation will be computer initiated. Since the CASE system will be part of the production environment, little installation will be required. Complete systems generated through requirements specification may be maintained by changing the initial specifications rather than the end products. Thus maintenance will entail changes to original specification only. All other maintenance activities will be computer generated. In such an environment, development time for both new systems and major maintenance projects will be greatly shortened. Response to changing organizational and competitive circumstances will be swift.

Improved System Quality

In the final analysis, more effective systems will be those of improved quality. *Quality*, as defined here, means the extent to which the goals and objectives of the organization are furthered by the computer system. Quality is thus the measurement of effectiveness. CASE systems have the potential of increasing

Figure 7.15. Potential CASE development life cycle.

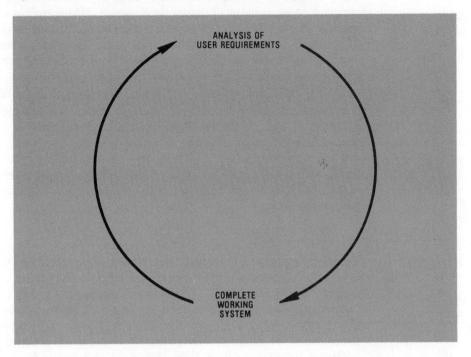

the system effectiveness in all of the areas. The potential of increased standard-ization, ease of maintenance, enhanced communication, and reduced develop-ment time will hopefully result in more flexible, error free, and correct systems. Also, in this type of environment, the requirements of users and the visions of the designers may more quickly and thoroughly be combined into one system image. The resulting system image should more accurately reflect the ever more transient and fluid user and business needs. Tailoring of the actual system could be swift and transparent.

THE STATE OF CASE

Although CASE promises to have tremendous impact on data processing envi-ronments in the near future, adoption of this technology has been painstakingly slow. Organizations have incorporated CASE systems selectively and experi-mentally. These products must improve, and organizations must prepare their environments for CASE adoption before they will become widely utilized.

Current CASE Usage

Although the projected CASE market is expected to top $1 billion by 1990 and there are now literally hundreds of CASE products available commercially or developed in-house, the actual usage of CASE technology is quite low. CASE is being used in only about 5 percent of large organizations most suitable for its adoption. Among many of those organizations, CASE has not been fully implemented. Either it is still considered experimental or it is being used on a project-by-project basis rather than as an organization standard. Many of those currently using CASE tools either plan fewer future CASE purchases or plan to try different products. Those CASE products actually in use are not being utilized to their fullest extent. Typically, the heaviest use of CASE products concentrates upon the use of the graphic generators, the data dictionary, and the design aids; that is, the documentation assistance, much of which could be accomplished through less sophisticated means. Also, code generators and 4GLs are becoming more common, though not in a way that is closely integrated with upper CASE concerns. Thus despite its great potential, CASE has not really become a major thrust in the data processing environments of business and industry.

Factors Inhibiting CASE Usage

There are several reasons for the reluctance of organizations to adopt CASE. One factor is that it is unclear who in the corporate structure is responsible for the selection, operation, and evaluation of this type of product. CASE systems are meta-systems—they transcend the ordinary boundaries of the organizational functional hierarchy. The most advanced CASE system would provide a working environment for systems development from requirements specifications to installation and maintenance. Who should be responsible for such a large-scale innovation: those in development, those in database administration, those in technical service, those in operation? A fully equipped CASE system must overlay all of these areas in order to provide the greatest potential advantage for the organization. Careful organizationwide planning must accompany CASE adoption.

Conversely, CASE adoption on a smaller and more localized scale might provide benefits to any or all of the areas mentioned, but the full promise of CASE would not be realized. Localized organizational adoption may lead to a host of incompatibilities, including conflicting formats, standards, and methodologies. Inevitable organizational "turf" battles resulting from such an adoption strategy might actually slow the usage of CASE.

Another factor inhibiting CASE usage stems from the observation that the most likely customers for CASE are large mainframe MIS shops. Because large multistaff, multihardware systems are to be found in such places, they have the greatest potential for gain and improvement. These environments, however, have not yet fully incorporated personal computer technology or intelligent workstations. Since most CASE products are personal-computer oriented, the large MIS shops would have to radically adjust their hardware architecture to adopt them. The fully developed CASE products themselves may function adequately in personal computer environments, but they may not have the sophistication to provide the complete array of components for the mainframe world. This is another reason documentation assistance is the most widely used CASE support.

Perhaps the primary reason for the reluctance on the part of MIS shops to incorporate CASE is its strict adherence to a methodology. CASE products force standardization and uniformity upon all areas that incorporate it. While CASE products are flexible enough to accommodate a variety of methodologies, some methodology must be the foundation if CASE is to be successfully implemented. For all of the supposed benefits of analysis and design methodologies, many companies have not yet completely adopted them. Use of such techniques like diagramming and prototyping are performed largely on an ad hoc basis. Methodology training is primarily an on-the-job enterprise. Until a business strictly enforces a methodology which incorporates analysis, design, and strategic planning of organizational computer systems, CASE technology can not (and should not) be adopted.

Conditions for Future CASE

Despite the current usage and the problems involved in implementation, the future of CASE remains bright. This is due to the allure of the ultimate promise of CASE technology. The promise of a systems development environment wherein projects can be planned, designed, monitored, controlled, implemented, installed, and maintained all under the same centralized and integrated facility is too great to ignore. As long as CASE has the potential of making higher-quality, more productive, and generally more effective computer systems, it is likely to interest data processing shops everywhere. But for CASE to truly realize its potential, several conditions must be met. These conditions are better CASE systems, organizational commitment, and adoption of a foundation methodology.

Better CASE Systems. The CASE systems must improve so that they can fully achieve their promised impact on the development life cycle. To do this, future CASE systems must incorporate expert system components and possibly utilize "object-oriented" techniques (see Chapter 12). CASE products must also be made more transportable among micro-, mini-, and mainframe computer architectures and provide greater integration and flexibility among features and operating environments. All the components must fit into the computing environments typical of large MIS shops. CASE systems must be readily capable of more than documentation assistance on microcomputers.

Organizational Commitment. The adoption of CASE requires steadfast management commitment. To realize the full potential of CASE requires the coordination and adjustment of all aspects of the computer system's life cycle. Successful adoption must be approved, enforced, and regulated by the highest levels of management. Benefits from the use of CASE are unlikely to materialize on a short-term basis if derived using typical efficiency measurements. Therefore, in order to realize the improved systems effectiveness promised by CASE, a long-term commitment must be made. This commitment must be made apparent in the way CASE is positioned, staffed, and budgeted in the organizational hierarchy.

Adoption of a Foundation Methodology. Before CASE can be implemented in any organization, a development methodology must already be in place. More and more, this methodology must include organizational strategic planning as well as traditional analysis and design tools and techniques. Strategic planning refers to tying the organizational goals and objectives directly to specific projects, such as computer systems. Enterprise modeling is becoming more common, and CASE products should be tailored to facilitate this activity. This usage will allow computer systems to be more readily evaluated on the basis of overall strategic effectiveness as well as traditional efficiency standards. Thus in order for CASE to be accepted, a corporate foundation methodology needs to be expanded and completely internalized.

INFORMATION ENGINEERING

CASE tools have developed to the point which they can truly be considered *power tools* for the system developer. This, in turn, has made *information engineering* viable as a system development approach.

Information engineering spans an entire development life cycle from planning through analysis and design to the construction and implementation of the system. It encompasses an *integrated set of formal techniques* for creating enterprise models, data models, and process models. Equal emphasis is given to four aspects of the enterprise: data, process, technology, and management issues (see Figure 7-16).

Figure 7.16. *Information engineering is a collection of techniques that (a) are integrated across all stages of the development life cycle from planning through construction and (b) encompass the four key views of an organization.*

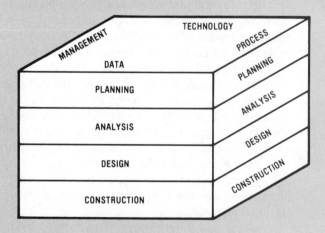

A key to information engineering is the concept of an encyclopedia or *knowledge base*. This is a data base in which the various models created using planning and analysis activities (E-R models, data models, data flow diagrams, and process specifications) are stored. Later, the products of design, including screen and report design and program design, are incorporated into the knowledge base. The concept of a knowledge base is contained within the concept of a repository.

The knowledge base is the foundation for automating the system development process. It is not simply a passive repository of old models and specifications. Rather, it is an active encyclopedia that the CASE tools can access and update. The creation of analysis models can be automated, using in part the results of planning that are stored in the knowledge base. Various aspects of the design process can be automated, using in part the results of analysis that are stored in the knowledge base. And finally, detailed designs and code can be automatically generated, using the results of analysis and design stored in the knowledge base.

CASE tools are integrated across the phases of the systems development process and access and update a common encyclopedia or knowledge base, resulting in the ability to apply engineering rigor to the building of systems. The collection of integrated techniques, automated tools, and knowledge base is referred to collectively as information engineering.

SUMMARY

Software development requires both methodology and the tools that help implement that methodology.

Computer-Aided Software Engineering, CASE, refers to a category of software products that provides automated support for the various systems development activities.

CASE products are similar to industrial CAD/CAM in that they have the potential for assisting both the design and the production of computer information systems.

Types of support provided by typical CASE products include documentation assistance, analysis enhancements, project coordination, and application generators. When integrated, these support functions can have a profound impact upon the system development life cycle and the organization itself.

Examples of typical tools of documentation assistance provided by CASE products include graphics generators, word processors, data dictionaries, and report or screen designers.

Examples of typical analysis enhancement tools include verification processes, data optimizers, and prototyping devices.

Examples of project coordination include presentation facilities, project management, and application interfaces.

Examples of typical application generation tools include code generators, system generators, and 4GLs.

Documentation assistance tools are often referred to as *upper CASE* and application generation tools as *lower CASE*.

CASE systems have the potential for improving systems development effectiveness and efficiency. System effectiveness refers to how well it meets user needs and organizational objectives.

The benefits that may be derived from the adoption of a CASE development environment include uniformity and maintainability of development end products, enhanced communication among development participants, reduced development time, and improved system quality.

Complete and sophisticated CASE systems are capable of altering the system development life cycle so that development and maintenance may be accomplished merely by specifying user requirements, which automatically generate system solutions.

Although the promise and future of CASE are considerable, few organizations have currently fully adopted its usage into development activities.

The factors inhibiting the adoption of CASE technology include organizational and operating architectural incompatibility, as well as a lack of a foundation methodology among potential CASE users.

For CASE systems to be more fully adopted in the future, they must be improved in terms of integration, flexibility, and transportability, and organizations must be genuinely committed to their implementation and provide a foundation methodology.

KEY TERMS

1. analysis enhancements
2. application interface
3. CAD/CAM
4. CASE
5. code generators
6. cut-and-paste maneuvers
7. data dictionary
8. data optimization
9. documentation assistance
10. exploded to a lower level
11. foundation methodology
12. graphics generator imploded to a higher level
13. lower CASE
14. presentation facilities
15. project management
16. prototyping
17. report and screen design
18. system generators
19. system integration
20. upper CASE
21. verification features
22. word processor

REVIEW/DISCUSSION QUESTIONS

1. Define the term CASE and discuss the three main components of a typical CASE system.
2. Compare CASE systems to CAD/CAM systems.
3. What are some of the typical tools of documentation assistance provided by CASE products?
4. What are some of the typical tools of analysis enhancement provided by CASE products?
5. What are some of the typical tools of application interface provided by CASE products?
6. What is meant by *lower CASE* and *upper CASE?*
7. What are the potential benefits of incorporating a CASE environment into a data processing shop?
8. Of what importance is a foundation methodology in the use of CASE?
9. Give specific examples of ways a CASE system would assist an analyst.
10. Are CASE systems widely utilized at present? Explain why or why not.
11. Explain what is necessary before CASE systems will be more widely adopted.
12. How does the presence or absence of PCs in a mainframe environment affect CASE use?
13. What are some reasonable predictions concerning the use of CASE?

Systems Analysis:
General Tools and Techniques

Objectives

Part III covers the nonmodeling tools and techniques used throughout the systems development life cycle. The main objectives of this part are (1) to present and discuss the techniques of gathering information about existing and desired information systems, (2) to discuss the need for and techniques of communication as it is related to the systems development effort, and (3) to present a method for evaluating requests for systems development. The feasibility analysis phase will result in a recommendation for one of four courses of action:

■ Continue systems development into the next phase of the systems development life cycle.

■ Enhance an existing system through a maintenance project that modifies and enhances a system that is already in place rather than developing a new system.

■ Use an alternate approach in which new processing procedures are implemented through the use of fourth generation languages, possibly with the assistance of staff in the corporate information center.

■ Do nothing, tabling or actually rejecting the request. The proposed system is not considered feasible, at least at this time.

ACTIVITIES

The only activity among these three processes that is part of the systems development life cycle (SDLC) is the feasibility study. Information gathering is present throughout the SDLC, but it is very important in the first four of the fifteen activities, which are aimed primarily at building an understanding of the business problem to be solved and the nature and content of the business operations themselves. Obviously, effective information gathering is critical to the success of these activities.

Similarly, communication is not an activity of itself, but it is a part of every other activity within the SDLC. The oral and written communication skills of the systems analyst can have a critical impact on the potential success of an information systems development project. Communication includes such tasks as (1) conducting problem-solving sessions, (2) performing technical walk-throughs, (3) preparing oral and written reports for management groups, (4) creating procedure and training manuals, and (5) making oral presentations.

The activities in the investigation phase are the initial investigation and the feasibility study. The *investigation phase* begins with a request for service. This normally comes from the user area, although it could come from another management group. The main objective of this phase is to determine what to do with the request for service. The recommendation may be to develop a whole new system, to modify the existing system to meet the users' information requirements, or to leave the existing system alone for the present time. The initial investigation is completed quickly, usually in a few days or certainly in less than two weeks, depending on the scope of the project.

If the recommendation is to consider the development of an entirely new system, management will want a better understanding of how the proposed system might work, its benefits, and its costs before they commit to undertake the project. These answers are provided as a result of activity 2, the *feasibility study*. Five basic types of feasibility are investigated. They are:

- Operational feasibility—will the system work from a people processing point of view?
- Financial feasibility—what are the development as well as the ongoing costs of this project and how do these compare to the benefits that will be derived from the project?
- Technical feasibility—does the appropriate information systems technology exist to undertake this project successfully, and is it affordable?
- Human factors feasibility—if we build this system, will the user community "embrace it" and "use it" or will they "resist it"?
- Schedule feasibility—can the proposed system solution be implemented in the time available?

The activities that make up the first phase of the systems development life cycle are shown in an exploded format in Figure III-1.

END-PRODUCT

The end-product of the first phase of the systems development life cycle is a feasibility report. It contains a recommendation about whether the system can be developed and implemented successfully. The three main types of feasibility, financial, technical and operational, are the primary focus of this report.

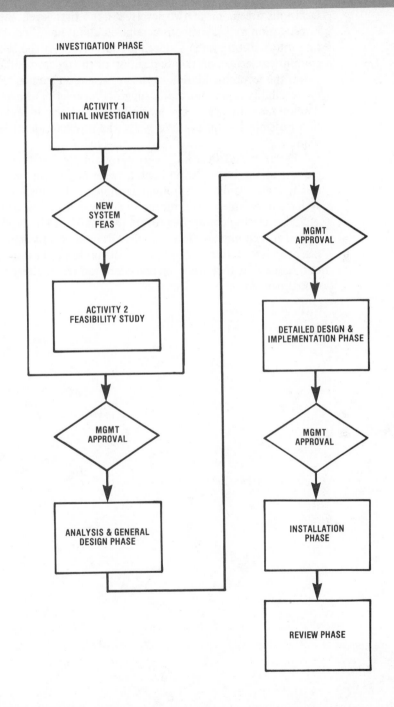

Decisions are made at two levels. At the first level, the team performing the investigation makes a recommendation about handling the request to the corporate information systems steering committee. At the second level, the steering committee decides on the disposition of the recommendation.

If the recommendation of the investigation team is to develop a new system, the feasibility report normally suggests completing the next phase in the systems development life cycle. The feasibility report also includes a general description of a possible system that will solve the problem identified in the initial service request.

If the initial decision is to maintain the existing system or to refer the request to the information center, there might not be a feasibility report. Instead, there would be a joint recommendation by users and the information systems department on a mutually acceptable course of action.

The steering committee would then have the choice of accepting or rejecting whatever recommendation is made. Other alternatives might be to table or delay the proposed action, or simply to do nothing. The steering committee might also request further study or consideration of an alternative other than the one recommended.

Information Gathering

Learning Objectives

After completing the reading assignments and practice exercises for this chapter, you should be able to:

- Explain the importance of information gathering in a systems development project.
- Identify four categories of information that should be gathered and describe the relevant types of information within each category.
- List several types of existing documentation that may be important sources of information.
- Name four basic methods of information gathering and state the advantages and disadvantages of each.
- Describe the steps involved in preparing for and conducting information gathering interviews.
- Discuss the characteristics of a good questionnaire.
- Identify five basic types of questionnaire items and explain how each is used.
- Describe the observation method of information gathering.
- Explain the meaning of work sampling and its use in systems analysis.
- Identify external electronic sources of information about the economy, new technologies, and competitors.

IMPORTANCE OF INFORMATION GATHERING

The first four of the fifteen activities in the systems development life cycle are aimed primarily at building an understanding of the business problem to be solved and the nature and content of the business operations themselves. In other words, the early part of a systems development project is devoted to studying and learning about particular portions of a business and about the information processing systems that currently support that business activity.

Tasks connected with these analysis activities therefore involve special challenges in gathering necessary information. There are no books or road maps to lead you to perceived business problems or opportunities. There is probably very little in the way of documentation to tell you what is happening within a current information system. The documents that do exist are probably spread out across the length and breadth of the organization, with some additional items tucked away in the desk drawers of persons doing the work. Before any studying or learning can take place, the information itself must be assembled.

Even after existing documentation has been located, the information gathering job may have just begun. It is common for systems analysts to collect complete sets of documentation for existing systems and procedures, only to find that they are out of date—that people don't do things that way anymore. The information gathering tasks then extend to making the contacts and observations necessary to update information on what really is happening. Locating and putting together the needed information is often likened to the work of a private investigator.

In summary, information gathering during the early activities of a systems development project is neither routine nor easy. At the same time, however, the job of information gathering is absolutely vital. Without an understanding of the business and its present activities, design and development of new computer information systems simply cannot go forward.

This chapter overviews some of the basic sources of information about existing systems as well as some of the techniques that are used for gathering that information.

CATEGORIES OF INFORMATION

One of the first requirements in the gathering of information about systems is to figure out what you are looking for and where to find it. In starting this search, it can be valuable to have a checklist covering the types of documentation needed and some possible locations. A sample checklist is shown in Figure 8-1. The items shown on the list, along with descriptions of the documents involved and their importance in systems analysis, form the basis of the following discussion.

This checklist and accompanying explanations are intended to serve as general guidelines only. No attempt has been made to assign relative importance to the various categories or to suggest the amount of effort that should be

Figure 8.1. *Categories of information checklist.*

_____ Information about the Organization

    _____ Goals of the company

    _____ Organizational structure

    _____ Objectives and purposes of functional units

    _____ Policies

_____ Information about the People

    _____ Authority and responsibility relationships

    _____ Job duties

    _____ Interpersonal relationships

    _____ Information needs

_____ Information about the work

    _____ Tasks and work flows

    _____ Methods and procedures for performing the work

    _____ Work schedules and volumes

    _____ Performance criteria

    _____ Control mechanisms

_____ Information about the Work Environment

    _____ Physical arrangement of work areas

    _____ Resources available

devoted to each; nor should it be assumed that each category of information will necessarily be required in all cases. It should also be noted that the list is not all-inclusive. Other categoreis of information may exist that are not on this list. These decisions are judgmental, varying with the nature and complexity of the individual system. One of the basic challenges of information gathering lies in determining where to look, how much is enough, and when to stop.

Goals, objectives, and policies are closely interrelated, expressing the direction the organization wishes to pursue in increasingly specific terms. Goals are broad statements of the purposes of the organization. Objectives are milestones of accomplishment along the way toward those goals. Policies are specific rules or procedures for reaching those objectives. Since an information system implements policies—and policies, in turn, implement objectives and goals—the basic purpose of an information system is to facilitate achievement of the organization's mission.

Therefore, any request for systems services must be evaluated in light of its contribution to company goals and objectives.

Goals of the Company. Most large companies, and many medium-sized organizations, have formal statements about their reason for being in business and the goals of their management. **Goals** are long-term in nature and are often covered by formal statements of company strategy. These statements of goals represent management's image of what the organization should look like in the long term—five to seven years into the future. Such statements may be contained in orientation pamphlets given to new employees or in annual reports. In other cases, there may be a less formal, typewritten list of management goals. The value of having such a statement of goals is that it sets the tone and direction for much of the systems analysis and development work that will follow. An information system supports an organization. An organization is a group of people and resources that are headed in a known direction. Because these goals orient the organization, they may also provide a frame of reference for the systems development project.

Organizational Structure. A company's organizational structure, like its statement of goals, is an indication of management intentions and directions. It is a basic principle of management that setting goals comes first. Then the company is organized to meet those goals. In many companies, formal organization charts will be readily available. If they do not exist, less formal, but perhaps more accurate, charts should be drawn on the basis of inputs from top-level and user department managers. If actual lines of communication and responsibility differ from those shown on existing documents, the actual situations should be noted. An organization chart is an achievement-oriented structure. An information system is a tool for supporting that organization. Therefore, an understanding of the organization is a prerequisite to information systems development. This understanding should encompass the workings of the organization as an integrated, high-level system. In the course of gathering information, one thing to watch for is a correspondence between statements of goals and organizational structures. If the organizational structure does not appear to support the top-level goals of the enterprise, some further data gathering and clarification of intent are indicated.

Objectives and Purposes of Functional Units. Functional units are subsystems of the overall organization. As such, each separately identifiable group, division, or department of an organization should have its own **objectives** and purposes. Logically, these should match and support the goals of the organization as a whole, though this is not always the case. Again, it is important to understand how the objectives established for subsystems mesh with—or fail to mesh with—those of the overall system. Information systems will frequently cross organizational boundary lines. Therefore, an understanding of the purposes established for the parts of the organization will help direct the content and flow of information.

Policies. **Policies** are rules or guidelines for the conduct of business. These policies should implement overall goals and objectives. Again, it is important to find out how the policies relate to the goals and objectives of the organization. An information system is a direct implementation of policies. Therefore, policies and the relationships of policies to goals and objectives represent the prospective needs that an information system should be meeting. Any exceptions to policies encountered in the course of information gathering should be noted, along with the impact of these special conditions on the conduct of the business.

Information about the People

Information must be gathered about people to identify authority and responsibility, relationships, job duties, interpersonal relationships, and information needs. This information is necessary to fully understand the proposed role of the new information system in the organization.

Authority and Responsibility Relationships. In some cases, information about authority and responsibility relationships will simply fill out and enlarge upon existing organization charts. In many cases, however, actual working relationships will be vastly different from those represented in organization charts. Individuals with natural leadership may have assumed responsibility or taken on authority simply because others to whom it was assigned were too hesitant or timid. In other words, the idea at this point is to learn how an organization actually operates at the people level, rather than the formal view presented by an organization chart. The information gathered, which may be kept confidential, should provide the project team with an understanding of who really makes the decisions and who can be enlisted to help when it is really important to get something done. The success of any systems development project ultimately depends on management support. Therefore, it is important to identify leaders who can and will make the commitment of the company resources (i.e., people, equipment, money) necessary to guarantee the success of the project.

Job Duties. In reviewing existing methods and procedures, an analyst must understand what each person actually does in connection with the ongoing operation of the existing system. Available documentation, including manuals or formal procedures for task performance, should be collected. Gathering documents, however, may not be the same as pulling together information and understanding what is really going on. There are frequently differences between formal written procedures and the way the work is actually done. Several of the information gathering methods discussed later in this chapter provide techniques for uncovering work procedures that have not been formally documented. Here, as throughout the systems development process, the job of information gathering is to learn what is really going on.

Interpersonal Relationships. Information gathered about interpersonal relationships serves either to validate or to correct impressions established by formal organization charts. Within any organization, informal personal relationships will be built. People take shortcuts. People prefer to deal with their friends. People do whatever they have to do to get the job done most conveniently for them, in the least time. In the process, the actual flow of information may differ both from organization charts and from existing systems designs. The systems analyst needs to find out what is really happening, rather than simply collect documents about what is supposed to be going on. Another reason for studying interpersonal relationships is to identify key people who can assist in "selling" the new system to peers. Many people resist change, and a new system introduces changes that may be unsettling to them. If influential persons can be identified and convinced of the value of the new system, their peers can be more easily influenced to accept the necessary changes.

Information Needs. For each person in every job, information requirements should be assessed. This assessment should include a study of what information is actually being received. Frequently, there will be shortfalls: People need more information about the organization than they are actually getting if they are to do their jobs efficiently. The converse may also be true: People may be so swamped with unneeded information that a lot of time is wasted. They suffer from information overload. The purpose, at this level, is to find out what each person really needs. Then, systems analysis techniques can be applied to compare information requirements with the information received. These results will be used later to evaluate and balance the flow of data through the system.

Information about the Work

To completely understand the existing and proposed information systems, the systems analyst must obtain information about tasks and work flows, the methods and procedures for performing the work, work schedules and volumes, performance criteria, and control mechanisms.

Tasks and Work Flows. The objective of gathering information about tasks and work flows is to find out how data flow through the system and how they are transformed by the system. In part, this information can be gathered by collecting forms that include actual entries made at each point in the system. Note that the emphasis is on processing points rather than on individual persons. There may be processing steps that center around the personalities, skills, or experience of individuals. If this is the case, information gathering should uncover those situations in which existing systems are personality-dependent. In general, however, the focus is on the data and content changes within data structures. One graphic means of capturing this type of information is a document flowchart of the kind shown in Figure 8-2.

Methods and Procedures for Performing the Work. The focus of gathering information about methods and **procedures** for performing work is on the physical processes that exist within the system. The information gathering job

Figure 8.2. Flowchart showing the handling and control of forms documents.

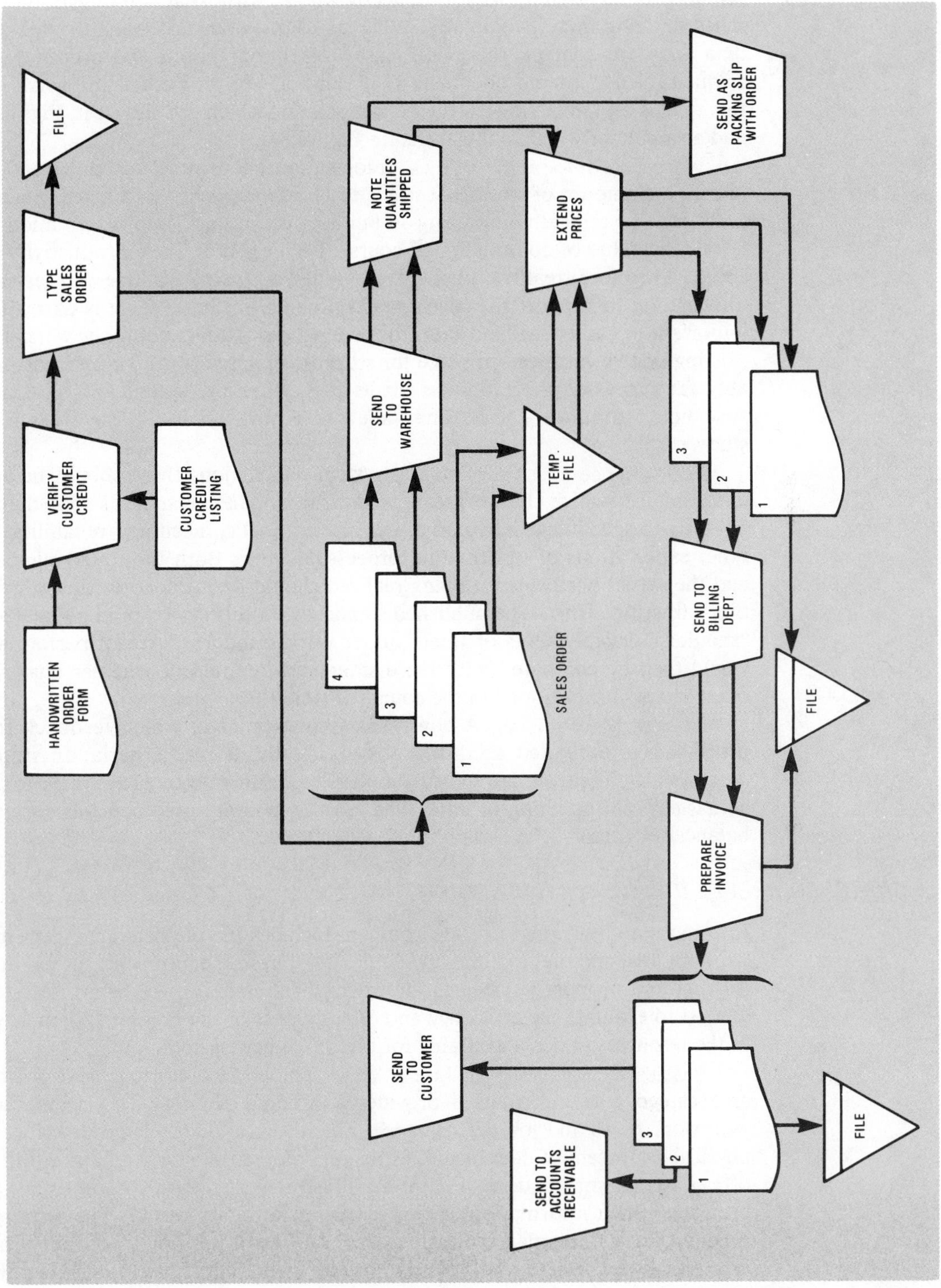

centers around learning what is done, by whom, with what equipment, on what schedules, and under what rules. Whereas the previous task concentrated upon data and data content, this one focuses closely on actions and procedures. A frequently encountered document that can help supply needed information of this type is a system flowchart, the symbols for which are shown in Figure 8-3 and a sample of which is illustrated in Figure 8-4.

Work Schedules and Volumes. Information about work schedules and volumes—the amount of work that needs to be accomplished in a given period of time—can be critically important in building computer-based information systems. The value of computers, of course, lies largely in their productivity and speed. Therefore, realistic ideas of schedules and work volumes are essential information to support the development process. In this area, it is particularly important to gather realistic data from the people actually doing the work. If an existing system has been in place for some time, actual work volume has probably far surpassed the estimates made at the time the system was instituted. Also note variations—peaks and valleys—in work loads for the areas under study.

Performance Criteria. For any system-related job, there should be standards against which the work can be measured. These standards should apply not only to schedules and volumes but also to quality, accuracy, reliability, and other expectations of information processing work. Both the stated standards and the actual performance being realized should be included in this information gathering effort. The published standards, in this case, would be treated as "shoulds," or statements of intent about work standards. Actual performance would then be compared with these standards to find out whether quality or other factors have slipped in the course of time.

Control Mechanisms. A control is a checkpoint at which feedback from processing is evaluated according to specifically defined criteria. In systems development, controls are always applied separately from procedures for the actual physical handling of data. The most commonly used controls are input balances or totals.

Information about the Work Environment

Information about the work environment includes the physical arrangement of the work area and the resources available (i.e., physical equipment) for use in the existing and proposed systems. Knowing what these are will help the systems analyst to evaluate the efficiency and effectiveness of the present system as well as the resources that are available for use in the new system.

Physical Arrangement of Work Areas. The physical-arrangement-of-work-area category of information provides additional physical details associated with work flows and job performance. The information gathered describes the physical movement of documents, forms, people, or transmitted data within the offices where work is done. Figure 8-5 illustrates a method for capturing and presenting such information, a flow diagram for a work area. The result will generally be a floor plan indicating desks and work positions, with a series of arrows showing where and how data move in the course of processing. This

Figure 8.3. **Common system flowcharting symbols.**

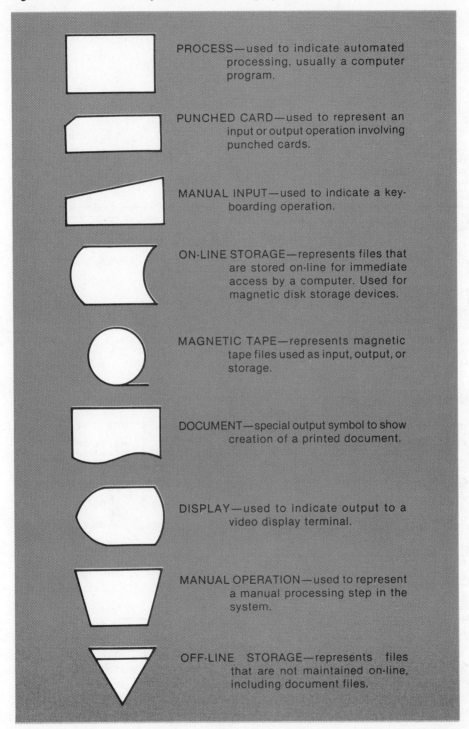

PROCESS—used to indicate automated processing, usually a computer program.

PUNCHED CARD—used to represent an input or output operation involving punched cards.

MANUAL INPUT—used to indicate a keyboarding operation.

ON-LINE STORAGE—represents files that are stored on-line for immediate access by a computer. Used for magnetic disk storage devices.

MAGNETIC TAPE—represents magnetic tape files used as input, output, or storage.

DOCUMENT—special output symbol to show creation of a printed document.

DISPLAY—used to indicate output to a video display terminal.

MANUAL OPERATION—used to represent a manual processing step in the system.

OFF-LINE STORAGE—represents files that are not maintained on-line, including document files.

Figure 8.4. Sample systems flowchart.

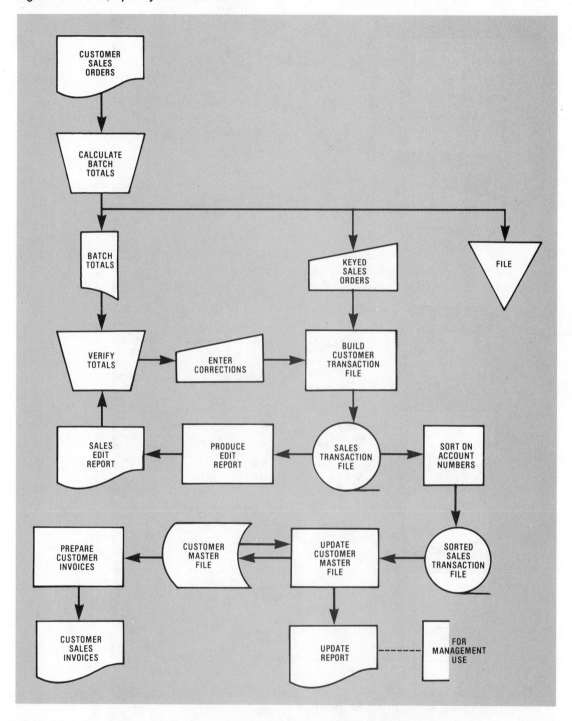

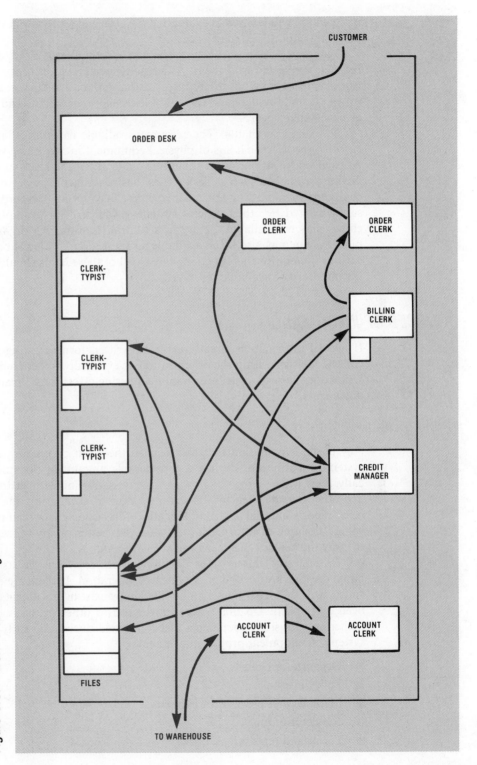

Figure 8.5. Work area flow diagram.

Chapter 8   Information Gathering

information will be used in evaluating the efficiency, effectiveness, and degree of control within the existing system.

Any new system is likely to disrupt existing work flows and the human contacts connected with them. As a result, social relationships and comfortable work patterns may be upset. Information gathered at this stage will help the project team to understand these problems and to anticipate and deal with them as new systems evolve.

Resources Available. The resources-available category of information focuses on the specific items of physical equipment in use, along with their costs. At each work station, notes should be made about the kinds of equipment and facilities available, such as desks, files, business machines, personal computers, computer terminals, or other items. These task-specific resources are generally supplemented by other, general systems resources. For example, copying machines may be available for use in a central location. An organization's computer system may also be an available resource, even if it is not being used in the existing system for this functional area. All of these items should be included in the inventory of available resources.

SOURCES OF INFORMATION

If needed information already exists in written form, existing documents are collected, either within the organization or externally. Where reliable documentation does not exist, the information gathering effort must create the necessary documents.

Existing Documentation

Any business operation that has reached the point of needing an information system probably already has a considerable amount of documentation. Typically, there will be a regular flow of paperwork dealing with customers, vendors, and other outside agencies, as well as a flow of accounting, management, and other reports internal to the organization. These documents can be an extremely valuable source of information because, for better or for worse, they describe the way the business has been operating to date.

In gathering this type of documentation, try to assess its completeness, based on your knowledge of the business operation. If there are evident gaps or "missing links," see if these can be filled in by existing documents that may have been overlooked. Do this before moving on to other methods of information gathering. Existing documents to be gathered during the early activities of a systems development project may include:

- Organization charts.
- Policy manuals.
- Methods and procedures manuals.
- Job descriptions.
- Forms and reports.

- Document flow and work flow diagrams.
- Systems flowcharts.
- Computer program documentation.
- Data dictionary listing.
- Computer operations manuals.

System Users and Managers

Information can be gathered from people as well as from documents. Techniques for gathering information through personal contacts with users and managers are identified and described in the section on methods for gathering information.

External Sources

For some systems, it will be necessary to gather information from outside the organization itself. In particular, in examining alternatives for new systems, analysts may need to consult external information sources to find out what is available and, if appropriate, how well individual methods are working elsewhere. These external sources include:

- Other companies.
- Equipment and software vendors.
- Business and information system publications, seminars, workshops, or visits to showrooms or other companies for demonstrations.
- Access to on-line data services (i.e., CompuServe, Dow Jones).

METHODS FOR GATHERING INFORMATION

Four representative, commonly used methods for gathering information through contacts with people have been selected for discussion in this chapter:

- Interviews.
- Questionnaires.
- Observation.
- Work sampling and measurement.

The interview method involves interaction between an interviewer and a subject. The questionnaire method involves development of a written instrument that encourages the subject to present information independently of any external prompting. In the observation method, data are also gathered unilaterally, this time by the collector rather than the subject. Work sampling involves statistical techniques for gathering information about a large volume of work by studying a carefully selected portion of the total. Other methods can be used, including combinations of these, but these four represent a basic cross section of information gathering methodologies.

Interviews

An *interview* is a planned meeting between a data gatherer and one or more subjects for the express purpose of identifying information sources and collecting information. Interviews are used to gather information in situations in which it is particularly valuable to allow a systems analyst or other team member to apply judgment and to respond to observed situations. This is because, with the interviewing technique, the data gatherer is on the scene and can respond to situations as they arise. Interviews are also interactive. The interviewer has an opportunity to guide the efforts and contributions of information providers. Further, an interviewer can probe, as necessary, to seek needed information.

Identifying Information Sources. The first step in an interview program for information gathering is to identify the sources of information. During the early stages of a project, interviews will typically concentrate on managers and supervisors who have an overview perspective on the business, its problems, and its information needs. As the project moves on, more detailed information may be needed about operational functions. As these needs arise, the emphasis will probably shift from managers to operational personnel.

A further advantage of this top-down approach is that the project gains top management support before interviews are conducted at the lower levels of the organization. Thus, people at the operational level know that their supervisors and managers have already lent their support to the study by participating in it.

No matter at what level the interviews are conducted, advance identification of sources makes it possible to allocate the time and other resources to be expended in information gathering. Without advance planning, there is no way of knowing the extent of the information to be gathered or the cost of gathering it. Thus, planning includes both the identification of subjects and the allocation of interviewer time, as well as other costs.

Preparing for the Interview. To prepare for the interview, the interviewer must have an idea of exactly what this interview is to accomplish. The interviewer should begin by writing down one or two basic objectives which should be explained to the subject when an appointment for the interview is made and again at the start of the interview session.

Next, the interviewer should prepare a written outline of points to be covered in the interview. This will not be a formal list of questions, since all possible questions cannot be anticipated, but should be an outline of topic areas to be discussed. Often, points raised by the subject will lead the interview in unexpected directions. The outline of topics helps keep the discussion in perspective and on target and lets the interviewer fit the responses into the framework of what needs to be known. An outline that can serve as an interview guide is shown in Figure 8-6.

Once sources have been identified and the objectives and interview topics have been established, the next step is to contact prospective interview subjects

SOME COMMENTS ABOUT INTERVIEWS

When using interviews to gather data for a business report, you are likely to use one of the following interview types: persuasive, information-giving, or information-gathering. Persuasive interviewing might be conducted to encourage students to take part in an experiment; information-giving interviewing might be used to instruct selected subjects in how to function during an experiment. In terms of data gathering, however, you are most likely to use the information-gathering type of interview. Here are some points to ponder when you consider using interviews to gather data:

- Sometimes only one individual (or only a few) needs to be interviewed. This is particularly true when the individuals are experts. The opinion of one dietitian may be far more valuable than the opinion of many employees about the nutrition of cafeteria food.

- If many people need to be interviewed, do you need a random sample? Must you meet the criteria of random sampling? If you are sampling and interviewing many people, are you conducting a scientific experiment in which you are required to meet all the relevant scientific criteria? Not all studies need to be scientific.

- Since interviews are such obtrusive data-gathering techniques, should you consider an alternative collection method? Would questionnaires or observation suffice?

- Is interviewing, which is individualized and flexible, able to justify the sometimes extensive personnel time and effort it requires?

- Would telephone interviewing, which has its own strengths and weaknesses, serve better than face-to-face interviewing? Telephone interviewing can gather more honest answers than face-to-face interviews since the interviewee does not have to look you in the eye. But be careful—for the same reasons telephone interviewing yields honesty, it can result in dishonesty. Telephone interviewing usually takes longer to conduct than you plan. Wrong numbers, busy signals, no answers, and number changes are part of the time to account for in telephone interviewing.

to set up appointments. These contacts should, if possible, be handled by phone. If all of the parties work for the same company, telephone contacts are usually adequate. If the organization or the study is relatively large, however, it is often desirable to follow up with a written outline of the information to be gathered. Source personnel should always be advised, either orally or in writing,

Figure 8.6. Outline of interview objectives and topic areas.

<u>Interview Subject</u>

Cliff Mason, Office Manager, Sales Order and Billing Department

<u>Objectives</u>

The purpose of this interview is to determine the current procedure for processing customer sales orders. The need is to confirm that the procedures followed parallel those documented in the procedures manual. Also, it will be determined whether the current system is adequate for the volume and nature of orders received and for management reporting.

<u>Topics</u>
1. Nature of orders. Methods for original writing of orders that are placed through standard order forms, over the telephone, or in person. Estimates of the proportions of orders taken via these methods. Number of orders processed daily and staffing required to handle the orders.

2. Credit procedure. Estimated proportion of orders that require credit verification or approval. Time spent on credit approval and availability of credit evaluation sources. General policy on credit sales. Proportion of credit-approved orders that result in bad debts.

3. Sales volume. Estimated dollar average of sales orders. Proportions of sales volume accounted for by ordering methods. Percentage of volumes resulting in bad debts.

4. Inventory checking. General procedures for checking stock availability. Availability of up-to-date stock lists. Estimated proportion of back-ordered items per order.

5. General satisfaction with order entry procedure. Problem areas.

6. Management reporting. Availability of reports to facilitate management of order entry procedures.

about the objectives of the interview, the topics to be covered, and the types of documents that might be needed. An example of a memo requesting an interview appointment and outlining the purpose and topics of an interview is shown in Figure 8-7.

Enough lead time should be allowed to let subjects prepare themselves. An unprepared subject greatly diminishes the value of an interview. Similarly, it is crucial that needed documents or other information be on hand at the time of the interview to avoid the necessity for additional visits to cover the same topic.

An effective interview program involves mutual cooperation. Cooperation, in turn, is improved through understanding and preparation. The interviewer should prepare by learning about the person to be interviewed and his or her responsibilities. Preparation should also include a review of any existing documentation about the system or portion of the business being surveyed.

Conducting the Interview. Staging can be important to the success of an interview. If at all possible, the interview should be held in the subject's own office or department. It is best that the subject be on familiar ground, where reference materials or support personnel are available as needed. To the extent possible, time should be blocked so as to avoid interruptions during the interview. Also, to the extent possible, interviews should be conducted one-on-one. Unless additional parties have specific roles to play, their presence should not be encouraged.

As a general rule, the best interview is one during which the interviewer says the least. At the very most, an interviewer should talk perhaps 15 or 20 percent of the time. The interviewer cannot learn anything as long as he or she is talking. Therefore, interviews should be devoted to listening. Comments or questions should be limited to those specifically designed to get the subject to provide information.

Listening tactics should be responsive. That is, as the subject talks, the interviewer should make it clear that he or she understands what is being said. An effective technique is simply to restate, or paraphrase, what the subject has just said. Thus, the interviewer might say, "Just to make sure I understand the point you are making, let me give you my understanding of what you have said." The restatement that follows should simply paraphrase the information provided, in neutral terms and from the subject's own point of view. Other tips for good listening include not interrupting and maintaining a genuine interest in the statements of the interviewee.

Above all, the interviewer's comments should be noncommittal. They should express neither approval nor disapproval of what is being said—only comprehension. As long as the purpose is information gathering, the interviewer should not argue with the subject. Nor should facial expressions or tone of voice betray strong positive or negative reactions. Because the interviewer's own reactions can have the effect of distorting the information presented, interviewers must try to be as unobtrusive as possible.

Because of the overriding need to be noncommittal, many inexperienced interviewers go to the other extreme and say nothing at all. They just listen, making notes as appropriate. Total silence from the interviewer, however, can be

Figure 8.7. *Memo confirming interview appointment and outlining the topics to be covered.*

Date: February 15

To: Cliff Mason, Office Manager, Sales Order and Billing

From: Bob Underwood, Systems Analyst, CIS

Re: Interview Appointment

This memo will confirm our phone conversation of last Monday regarding the
interview scheduled for next Tuesday, February 22. I will be at your office at
9:30 a.m. We should plan on spending no more than an hour on the topics listed
below.

As you are aware, the CIS Department is responding to a request from Diane
Morris, Administrative Assistant, to look into the sales order processing
system. It has come to her attention, primarily through customer letters and
phone calls, that delays in processing and delivering orders are becoming a real
problem. It is likely that the growth we have experienced over the past two
years has placed a burden on our current manual order processing system. There
is interest in investigating the possibility of implementing automated
procedures to support these increased sales volumes.

Over the next two-and-a-half weeks, I will be speaking with most of the managers
and supervisors who oversee the various aspects of order processing and
delivery. The purpose of these interviews is to gain a basic understanding of
the current procedures that are followed and to uncover any problems that might
account for delays in processing orders.

Your assistance is needed in the following areas. Please give some thought to
these topics prior to our meeting and, if possible, bring along any
documentation and statistics relevant to them.

1. Order writing procedures, including staffing levels and volumes of orders.

2. Credit verification procedures, including delays caused by the procedures
    and problems in controlling bad debts.

3. Inventory verification. Problems with stock-outs and backorders.

4. Management reporting procedures pertaining to above areas.

intimidating in itself. It is far better to acknowledge what is being said and to provide some indication of comprehension. Responsive listening of this type encourages the presentation of more information.

Note taking during the interview should be kept to a minimum. Extensive note taking or recording of the interview can be intimidating to the subject, who may not be willing to speak as freely as in informal discussions. Summary or reminder notes are usually sufficient to help the interviewer recall the information obtained during the interview. Immediately following the session, these summary notes should be reviewed to capture all the important information gathered during the interview.

To the extent possible, the subject should be able to set the pace and pattern of the interview. The interviewer should be careful not to ask questions that seem argumentative or that break the subject's train of thought. Remember, the subject has had advance notice and knows what the interview is expected to accomplish. He or she has prepared, mentally at least, the information to be presented. Any question that interrupts or upsets this established thought pattern may be resented or simply ignored. It is far better to let the subject go ahead and make the statements he or she has prepared. After that, probing questions can be asked. These should be referenced within the framework of statements already made by the subject. If a question must be asked that is totally unrelated to the subject's previous statements, the interviewer should make it clear that this question represents a change of subject and content.

Above all, the interviewer should never forget that the interviewee is the one providing the information. It can be tempting to get into a discussion with the person being interviewed, making comments or asking questions that demonstrate the interviewer's own command of the subject. Remember that this doesn't collect any information—it just slows the process down. Comments by the interviewer should be limited to whatever is needed to encourage the presentation of information by the person being interviewed.

The following is a checklist of potential pitfalls to be avoided, along with some suggestions for avoiding them:

- Beware of leading questions. Leading questions can bias an interview by establishing expectations that can influence responses. Avoid questions that begin with "Isn't it true that . . ." or "Don't you agree that . . ."

- Avoid premature conclusions. If a subject makes a positive statement, it can be tempting to draw a conclusion, thus closing off further discussion of the topic. For each topic, be sure to give the subject a full hearing. Ask questions that require more than yes-or-no answers.

- Be careful, conversely, not to accept negative responses too readily. Particularly in situations in which change is anticipated, people are bound to be upset. Change, by its nature, begets resistance. Accept and understand negative responses, but don't overreact to them.

- Don't be so impressed or awed by a person such as a top-level manager that the interview loses its objectivity. Interviews associated with systems development projects frequently involve persons at the top levels of their organizations. A "halo effect" can easily set in. The interview, even the entire project, can be distorted in an effort to please a top-level executive rather than to identify the facts needed to solve a problem.

■ Beware of interview subjects who try too hard to please. Many people in large organizations become politically motivated. They may be tempted to say what they think the interviewer wants to hear rather than to analyze what is really happening and to present relevant information. By the same token, the interviewer should avoid stereotyping interview subjects. Remember, the purpose of the interview is to gather information. This purpose is thwarted if the interviewer is thinking: "He's just a clerk," or "She's only a secretary."

In summary, the interviewer must maintain control over the interview. A balance must be struck between letting the subject do the talking and ensuring that relevant and useful information is obtained. Maintaining this type of balance and control is the basic challenge involved in conducting a successful interview.

Follow-up. Persons who cooperate by participating in interviews should receive the courtesy of some follow-up that acknowledges the productivity of the time and effort they have expended. One simple method of follow-up is to send information collection summaries to interview subjects. Another practice, as time permits, is to send thank-you notes or memos to those who have been interviewed. A memo recapping an information-gathering interview is shown in Figure 8-8.

If formal summaries of individual interviews are prepared as part of systems documentation, these should be shared with interview subjects. Interviewees should be encouraged to comment on drafts of these summaries. They may have additional information to add or points to clarify or correct. Remember, the idea is to gather information. Information acquired as a follow-up to an interview is just as valuable as data from any other source.

Advantages of Interviews. The principal advantage of interviews lies in the personal contact involved. A person gathering data from another person face to face can be flexible and adaptive. This is bound to produce more information of higher quality than can be obtained by alternate, impersonal methods.

Interviews can probe to greater depths than are possible with any other information-gathering method. Conversely, if an interview subject is not sufficiently informed or is hostile, the interview can be terminated quickly with relatively little time wasted. In other words, the interview provides a controlled opportunity for information gathering.

Disadvantages of Interviews. Interviews are time-consuming. For this reason, they are generally the most costly means of information gathering. Evaluation of the information gathered through interviews may also be more difficult than the tabulation of comparable results produced by questionnaires or other more highly structured methods. Interviews also carry with them the danger of a biased interviewer. If the interviewer has made up his or her mind in advance about the results to be derived, the resulting information will be biased.

Figure 8.8. *Memo following up on interview including a summary of the findings.*

Date: March 1

To: Cliff Mason, Office Manager, Sales Order and Billing

From: Bob Underwood, Systems Analyst, CIS

Re: Interview Summary

Thank you for sharing your time and expertise during these opening phases of the systems study on the order processing systems. Your insights will be valuable in our efforts to improve customer service and to provide you with information needed to manage the order processing function.

Below are listed the main points that I was able to glean from our conversation. Please take a few moments to review this listing for accuracy and to check that these statements represent your general viewpoint. If I have misstated or misinterpreted your ideas, call and we can discuss any discrepancies.

1. The current procedure has been in place for approximately 7.5 years. During this time, sales volumes have risen from an average of 80 to an average of nearly 150 orders per day. Orders themselves have increased from an average of 4 items per order to 10 per order. Most orders (about 60%) are mail orders, with the remaining order methods being nearly equally divided between phone and in-person orders. The average order amount is $265, up from $58 7.5 years ago.

2. Regular order writing staff include 7 full-time clerks. Their job is primarily to transcribe orders onto standard order forms. This is done manually. Checking of stock availability is done by having the clerks reference an inventory list during order writing. This list is shared by the clerks and is updated every few days as time becomes available in the warehouse.

3. Credit checking is performed by the credit officer. All orders not accompanied by payment are forwarded to this person, who checks the credit status against a listing of customers provided by the accounts receivable area. Approximately three-quarters of all orders are from repeat customers with established credit ratings.

4. The staff of order writers is pressured by the volume of orders to be processed. Errors result from hurried transcription of orders and from inaccessibility of up-to-date inventory lists.

5. There is a general feeling that backorders are excessive. However, there are no data available to support this assumption and there is no general policy on acceptable volumes of backorders. It is difficult to anticipate stock-outs in advance, since inventory lists may be outdated.

6. The credit officer spends most of her time checking credit status of customers with acceptable credentials and track records of on-time payment. Bad debts are almost nonexistent among repeat customers and are even very low among new customers. Processing delays occur because of excessive credit check efforts. Orders stack up on the credit officer's desk (delays run as long as two days) awaiting checks. The company would be better served by accepting a higher level of bad debts in exchange for expedited orders.

7. No regularly scheduled reports are provided.

LISTENING IS A TEN-PART SKILL

White-collar workers, on the average, devote at least 40 percent of their work time to listening. Apparently they earn 40 percent of their salaries for listening. Yet tests of listening comprehension have shown that without training these employees listen at only 25 percent efficiency.

This low level of performance becomes increasingly intolerable as evidence accumulates that it can be significantly raised. The component skills of listening are known. They boil down to this:

Learning through listening is primarily an inside job—inside action on the part of the listener. What is to be done to replace some common present attitudes with others? Recognizing the value of effective listening, many companies have added courses in this skill to their regular training programs. Some of the pioneers in this effort have been American Telephone & Telegraph Co., General Motors Corporation, Ford Motor Company, The Dow Chemical Company, and Minnesota Mining & Manufacturing.

Warren Ganong, of the Methods Engineering Council, has compared trainees who have been given a preliminary discussion of efficient listening with those not provided such discussion. On tests at the end of the courses, the former achieved marks 12 to 15 per cent higher than did the latter.

A. A. Tribbey, general personnel supervisor of the Wisconsin Telephone Company, in commenting on the results of a short conference course in which effective listening was stressed, declared: "It never fails to amaze us when we see the skill that is acquired in only three days."

The conviction seems to be growing that upper-level managers also need listening skills. As Dr. Earl Planty, executive counselor for the pharmaceutical firm of Johnson & Johnson, puts it: "By far the most effective method by which executives can tap ideas of subordinates is sympathetic listening in the many day-to-day informal contacts within and outside the work place. There is no system that will do the job in an easier manner. . . . Nothing can equal an executive's willingness to hear."

A study of the one hundred best listeners and the one hundred worst listeners in the freshman class at the University of Minnesota has disclosed ten guides to improved listening. Business people interested in improving their own performance can use them to analyze their personal strengths and weaknesses. MIS professionals, especially systems analysts, are constantly involved in gathering information from users about a proposed or existing system. The old saying is very true, you can't obtain information when you are talking; you obtain information when you listen. Here are the ten guides to good listening:

1. Find an Area of Interest. All studies point to the advantage of being interested in the topic under discussion. Bad listeners usually declare the subject

dry after the first few sentences. Once this decision is made, it serves to rationalize any and all inattention.

Good listeners follow different tactics. True, their first thought may be that the subject sounds dry. But a second one immediately follows, based on the realization that to get up and leave might prove a bit awkward.

The final reflection is that, being trapped anyhow, perhaps it might be well to learn if anything is being said that can be put to use.

The key to the whole matter of interest in a topic is the word *use*. Whenever we wish to listen efficiently, we ought to say to ourselves: "What is the speaker saying that I can use? What worth-while ideas has the speaker? Is the speaker reporting any workable procedures? Anything that I can cash in or with which I can make myself happier?" Such questions lead us to screen what we are hearing in a continual effort to sort out the elements of personal value. G. K. Chesterton spoke wisely indeed when he said, "There is no such thing as an uninteresting subject; there are only uninterested people."

2. Judge Content, Not Delivery. Many listeners excuse their inattention to a speaker by thinking to themselves: "Who could listen to such a character? What an awful voice! Will the speaker ever stop reading from notes?"

The good listener reacts differently. A good listener may well look at the speaker and think. "This person is inept. Almost anyone ought to be able to talk better than that." But from this initial similarity, a good listener moves on to a different conclusion, thinking "But wait a minute. . . . I'm not interested in personality or delivery. I want to find out what the person knows. Does this person know some things that I need to know?"

Essentially we "listen with our own experience." Is the conveyer to be held responsible because we are poorly equipped to decode the message? We cannot understand everything we hear, but one sure way to raise the level of our understanding is to assume the responsibility, which is inherently ours.

3. Hold Your Fire. Overstimulation is almost as bad as understimulation, and the two together constitute the twin evils of inefficient listening. The overstimulated listener gets too excited, or excited too soon, by the speaker. Some of us are greatly addicted to this weakness. For us, a speaker can seldom talk for more than a few minutes without touching on a pet bias or conviction. Occasionally we are roused in support of the speaker's point; usually it is the reverse. In either case, overstimulation reflects the desire of the listener to enter, somehow, immediately into the argument.

The aroused person usually becomes preoccupied by trying to do three things simultaneously: calculate what hurt is being done to one's own pet ideas; plot an embarrassing question to ask the speaker; and enjoy mentally all the discomfort visualized for the speaker once the devastating reply is launched. With these things going on subsequent passages go unheard.

We must learn not to get too excited about a speaker's point until we are certain we thoroughly understand it. The secret is contained in the principle that we must always withhold evaluation until our comprehension is complete.

4. Listen for Ideas. Good listeners focus on central ideas; they tend to recognize the characteristic language in which central ideas are usually stated

and they are able to discriminate between fact and principle, idea and example, evidence and argument. Poor listeners are inclined to listen for the facts in every presentation.

To understand the fault, let us assume that a person is giving us instructions made up of facts A to Z. The person begins to talk. We hear fact A and think: "We've got to remember it!" So we begin a memory exercise by repeating, "Fact A, fact A, fact A . . ."

Meanwhile, the person is telling us fact B. Now we have two facts to memorize. We're so busy doing it that we miss fact C completely. And so it goes up to fact Z. We catch a few facts, garble several others, and completely miss the rest.

It is significant that only about 25 percent of persons listening to a formal talk are able to grasp the speaker's central idea. To develop the skill to do so requires an ability to recognize conventional organizational patterns, transitional language, and the speaker's use of recapitulation. Fortunately, all these items can be readily mastered with a bit of effort.

5. Be Flexible. Research has shown that our hundred worst listeners thought that note taking and outlining were synonyms. They believed there was but one way to take notes—by making an outline.

Actually, outlining would work only if all talks followed some definite plan of organization. Unfortunately, fewer than half, even of formal speeches, are carefully organized. Few efforts are more frustrating than trying to outline an unoutlineable speech.

Note taking may help or may become a distraction. Some persons try to take down everything in shorthand; the vast majority of us are too voluminous even in longhand. While studies are not too clear on the point, there is some evidence to indicate that the volume of notes taken and their value to the taker are inversely related. In any case, the real issue is one of interpretation. Few of us have memories good enough to remember even the salient points we hear. If we can obtain brief, meaningful records of them for later review, we definitely improve our ability to learn and to remember.

The hundred best listeners had apparently learned early in life that if they wanted to be efficient note takers they had to have more than one system of taking notes. They equipped themselves with four or five systems and learned to choose the one suited to the organizational pattern, or the absence of one, in each talk they heard. If we want to be good listeners, we must be flexible and adaptable note takers.

6. Work at Listening. One of the most striking characteristics of poor listeners is their disinclination to spend any energy on listening. College students, by their own testimony, frequently enter classes all worn out physically; assume postures that only seem to give attention to the speaker; and then proceed to catchup on needed rest or to reflect on purely personal matters. This faking of attention is one of the worst habits afflicting us as a people.

Listening is hard work. It is characterized by faster heart action, quicker circulation of the blood, and a small rise in body temperature. The over-relaxed listener is merely appearing to tune in and feeling conscience-free to pursue any of a thousand tangents.

For selfish reasons alone, one of the best investments we can make is to give each speaker our conscious attention. We ought to establish eye contact and maintain it, to indicate by posture and facial expression that the occasion and the speaker's efforts are a real concern to us. When we do these things, we help speakers express themselves more clearly, and we in turn profit by better understanding of the improved communication we have helped them achieve. None of this necessarily implies acceptance of their points of view or favorable action upon their appeals. It is, rather, an expression of interest.

7. Resist Distractions. Good listeners tend to adjust quickly to any kind of abnormal situation; poor listeners tend to tolerate bad conditions and, in some instances, even to create distractions themselves.

We live in a noisy age. We are distracted not only by what we hear but by what we see. Poor listeners tend to be readily influenced by all manner of distractions, even in an intimate face-to-face situation.

A good listener instinctively fights distractions. Sometimes the fight is easily won by closing a door, shutting off the radio, moving closer to the person talking, or asking the person to speak louder. If the distractions cannot be met that easily, then it becomes a matter of concentration.

8. Exercise Your Mind. Poor listeners are inexperienced in hearing difficult expository material. Good listeners apparently develop an appetite for a variety of presentations difficult enough to challenge their mental capacities.

Perhaps the one word that best describes the bad listener is *inexperienced*. Although poor listeners spend 40 percent of their day listening to something, they are inexperienced in hearing anything tough, technical, or expository. They have for years painstakingly sought light recreational material. The problems they create are deeply significant, because such people are poor producers in factory, office, or classroom.

Inexperience is not easily or quickly overcome. However, knowledge of our own weakness may lead us to repair it. We need never become too old to meet new challenges.

9. Keep Your Mind Open. Parallel to the blind spots that afflict human beings are certain psychological deaf spots that impair our ability to perceive and understand. These deaf spots are the dwelling places of our most cherished notions, convictions, and complexes. Often, when a speaker invades one of these areas with a word or phrase, we turn our mind to retraveling familiar mental pathways crisscrossing our invaded area of sensitivity.

It is hard to believe in moments of cold detachment that just a word or phrase can cause such emotional eruption. Yet with poor listeners it is frequently the case; and even with very good listeners it is occasionally the case. When such emotional deafness transpires, communicative efficiency drops rapidly to zero.

Among words known thus to serve as red flags to some listeners are mother-in-law, landlord, redneck, sharecropper, sissy, pervert, automation, clerk, income tax, communist, Red, dumb farmer, pink, "Greetings," evolution, square, punk, and welsher.

Effective listeners try to identify and to rationalize the words or phrases that are most emotionally upsetting to them. Often the emotional impact of such words can be decreased through an open discussion of them with friends or associates.

10. Capitalize on Thought Speed. Most people talk at a speed of about 125 words a minute. There is good evidence that if thought could be measured in words per minute, most of us could think easily at about four times that rate. It is difficult—almost painful—to try to slow down our thinking speed. Thus we normally have about 400 words of thinking time to spare during every minute a person talks to us.

What do we do with our excess thinking time while someone is speaking? If we are poor listeners, we soon become impatient with the slow progress the speaker seems to be making. So our thoughts turn to something else for a moment, then back to the speaker. These brief side excursions of thought continue until our mind tarries too long on some enticing but irrelevant subject. Then, when our thoughts return to the person talking, we find the speaker is far ahead of us. Now it's harder to follow the speaker and increasingly easy to take off on side excursions. Finally we give up; the person is still talking, but our mind is in another world.

The good listener uses thought speed to advantage by constantly applying spare thinking time to what is being said. It is not difficult once one has a definite pattern of thought to follow. To develop such a pattern we should:

■ Try to anticipate what a person is going to talk about. On the basis of what has already been said, ask yourself: "What is the speaker trying to get at? What point is the speaker going to make?"

■ Mentally summarize what the person has been saying. What points have been made already, if any?

■ Weigh the speaker's evidence by mentally questioning it. As the facts are presented and illustrative stories and statistics are given, continually ask yourself: "Are they accurate? Do they come from an unprejudiced source? Am I getting the full picture, or is the speaker telling me only what will prove a point?"

■ Listen between the lines. The speaker doesn't always put everything that's important into words. The changing tones and volume of voice may have a meaning, as may facial expressions, the gestures made with hands, and the movement of the body.

Not capitalizing on thought speed is our greatest single handicap. The differential between thought speed and speech speed breeds false feelings of security and mental tangents. Yet through listening training, this same differential can be readily converted into our greatest asset.

Source: Ralph G. Nichols, Department of Rhetoric, University of Minnesota, Minneapolis.

Questionnaires

A **questionnaire** is a special-purpose document that requests specific information from respondents. Compared with an interview, a questionnaire is an impersonal, often mass-produced method for gathering the same information from many people. Questionnaires are particularly appropriate in information gathering situations involving large populations of source people whose responses can be tabulated quantitatively. A questionnaire is best suited to situations in which respondents are asked to make limited numbers of factual comments.

Characteristics of Good Questionnaires. To be an effective information gathering instrument, a questionnaire should have certain basic characteristics, including:

Validity:	This means, simply, that the questionnaire does the job it was intended to do. The validity of a questionnaire can be difficult to judge. The usual means of determining validity is to compare the tabulated results of the questionnaire with other known measurements. For example, the results of a questionnaire can be compared with the findings of interviews, with the results of observation, or with predetermined expectations of managers and systems analysts. If the result of all is similar, validity is indicated.
Reliability:	Measures of reliability are built into the structure of questionnaires themselves. That is, the same information is sought in different ways through the use of multiple questions. Then, the responses to these redundant questions are compared for consistency of information. In some questionnaire situations, inconsistent responses on key questions can result in a downgrading of the confidence placed upon individual responses or even on the survey as a whole.
Face validity:	In appearance and content, a questionnaire must establish credibility with the respondent. That is, on reviewing a questionnaire, the respondent should get the feeling that the persons who developed the instrument knew what they were doing and had a valid purpose for including the items they did. Given the stated purpose of the questionnaire, the questions should appear to the respondent to be authentic and purposeful.
Ease of administration and scoring:	Directions to respondents should be stated clearly and should be easy to follow. Questions should be arranged in a logical order, according to subject matter. The physical appearance of the questionnaire should

be orderly—it should not appear difficult to follow or to complete. Questions should be as simple as possible to answer, and the length of the questionnaire should be manageable. If appropriate, and if the numbers are great enough, the questionnaire may be structured for machine scoring.

Planning for a Questionnaire. In considering the use of a questionnaire, the first planning step is to determine the exact purpose of the information-gathering activity. Once this purpose has been clearly defined, a decision should be made about whether a questionnaire is the best tool to use.

Questionnaires are an effective means of identifying specific facts, opinion choices, perceptions of a subject on a multiple-choice basis, or respondent attitudes. In general, a questionnaire will be most useful if:

- The number of respondents is large.
- The same information is required from all respondents.
- It is impractical to gather the information by any other means.
- A mechanism exists to count and tally responses.

The next step is to identify the *respondents*—those who will receive questionnaires. The total group of persons who are potential information providers is known as the **population** to be surveyed. In some cases, it will be both practical and desirable to provide questionnaires to all members of this population.

If the number of potential respondents is very large, however, some subset of the total group must be chosen to receive questionnaires. This group is known as the **sample**. Selection of a sample must be made using special techniques to assure that the responses of the sample group accurately represent those of the entire population.

Next, a decision must be made on how the questionnaire is to be administered. The basic choices are personal delivery with scoring done by interviewers, mail distribution, or telephone survey. Each of these alternatives has its own productivity and cost tradeoffs.

Finally, decisions must be made about the form of the questionnaire and the methods to be used in analyzing the results. Again, a number of options are available. If extensive use is to be made of a questionnaire, qualified specialists should be consulted.

Writing Questionnaires Items. A number of choices are available in the types of questions that can be written and the types of responses that can be solicited:

- **Open-ended questions** offer no response directions or specified options. A question is asked, and space is provided for writing in any answer the respondent wishes. This type of question can be used only if a questionnaire has extremely limited distribution or is to be used as an interview guide. A large number of questionnaires with open-ended questions would require too much time to score. For examples of such items, see Figure 8-9.

Figure 8.9.   Open-ended questionnaire items.

```
a.   What one specific improvement would you seek to improve the flow of
     paperwork across your desk?

b.   What do you feel is the major reason for the increased number of product
     returns that has occurred during the past six months?

c.   Describe briefly your opinion of the proposed policy changes concerning the
     accounts receivable discount rates and periods.
```

- **Fill-in-the-blank questions** are generally used to solicit specific facts. This type of question seeks specific, finite, factual answers. But responses are not restricted to a given set of choices. Numeric responses are often totaled and divided by the number of respondents to determine an average response (see Figure 8-10).

Figure 8.10.   Fill-in-the-blank questionnaire items.

```
a.   What is the name of your immediate supervisor?

     _____

b.   How many sales orders do you write on the average day? _____

c.   What is your estimate of the percentage of invoices that are paid in full
     within the first 10 days?

          _____ %
```

- **Multiple-choice questions** provide the respondent with a series of specific choices. These choices are finite and limit the response content. Often, one response is provided that permits the respondent to disqualify himself or herself if the question is inappropriate to his or her specific situation (see Figure 8-11).
- **Rating scales** are a type of multiple-choice question. Rather than providing a series of different answers, however, the rating scale offers a range of responses along a single dimension. For example, a user might be asked to rate the satisfaction level of an existing system on a scale of 1 to 5. Alterna-

Figure 8.11.   Multiple-choice questionnaire items.

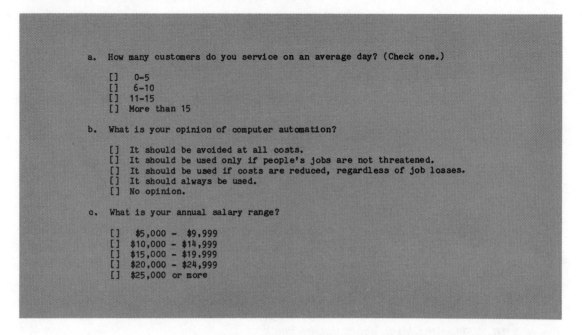

```
a.  How many customers do you service on an average day? (Check one.)

    []   0-5
    []   6-10
    []   11-15
    []  More than 15

b.  What is your opinion of computer automation?

    []  It should be avoided at all costs.
    []  It should be used only if people's jobs are not threatened.
    []  It should be used if costs are reduced, regardless of job losses.
    []  It should always be used.
    []  No opinion.

c.  What is your annual salary range?

    []   $5,000 -  $9,999
    []  $10,000 - $14,999
    []  $15,000 - $19,999
    []  $20,000 - $24,999
    []  $25,000 or more
```

tively, a series of satisfaction ratings might be provided, offering a number of choices ranging from completely satisfied to completely unsatisfied (see Figure 8-12).

■ **Ranking scales** ask respondents to rank a number of items in order of preference or in order of their importance. For example, users might be asked to rank a list of suggested improvements in the order in which they would find them most helpful (see Figure 8-13).

No matter which types of questions are used, certain rules must be followed in the preparation of questionnaire items:

■ Each item on a questionnaire should be limited to a single topic.

■ Each item should be appropriate for the respondents who will receive the questionnaire. Relevant considerations include the educational level of the respondents, the special jargon of their industry, their area of work, and the ready availability of the information requested.

■ Items should be designed for easy scoring, in keeping with the method of analysis to be used.

■ Questions should be worded precisely and accurately. Simple sentence structures that avoid biased or negative wording should be used. Any alternatives given should be mutually exclusive. That is, there should not be two overlapping response choices for a single question.

■ Items should be grouped on the questionnaire for similarity of information content, with some logical order among groups of questions.

Figure 8.12. **Questionnaire items using rating scales.**

```
a.  What is your general level of satisfaction with each of the following
    aspects of your job?  (Circle your response.)

                                  Very                        Very
                                  Dissatisfied                Satisfied

    1.  Salary                    1     2     3     4     5     6     7
    2.  Co-workers                1     2     3     4     5     6     7
    3.  Work environment          1     2     3     4     5     6     7
    4.  Supervisor                1     2     3     4     5     6     7

    b.  Rate your supervisor along the following dimensions by placing an (X)
    along the scale.

    1.  Helpful        ___:___:___:___:___:___:___ Unhelpful
    2.  Well organized ___:___:___:___:___:___:___ Disorganized
    3.  Decisive       ___:___:___:___:___:___:___ Indecisive
    4.  Friendly       ___:___:___:___:___:___:___ Unfriendly
```

Advantages of Questionnaires. Questionnaires are generally the most economical method of gathering data from large groups of people. A questionnaire program can be implemented and administered quickly and easily. Results can be tabulated rapidly and analyzed readily.

Disadvantages of Questionnaires. Effective questionnaires can be difficult to construct. If the subject matter is complex, several drafts (and possibly trial mailings) may be necessary before the final instrument is ready to be administered.

Questionnaires produce only specific, limited amounts of information in direct response to the questions that are included. There is no mechanism for adapting to a subject's responses or for probing more deeply as answers are received.

Questionnaires frequently suffer from very low return rates; therefore, little confidence can be placed in the results.

Observation

Observation is a method of information gathering in which a qualified person watches, or walks through, the actual processing associated with a system. Data are gathered, and the observer's report is based on what is seen without discussing the operation with users.

For example, in studying the flow of work through an office, a trained observer might follow the paperwork from the time a source document is created, through the various work stations where data are added to or gathered from the document, until the document is finally filed away permanently. The work flow would be documented on special forms, which could then be studied for possible improvements in the physical layout of the office.

Figure 8.13.   Questionnaire items using ranking scales.

a. Rank each of the following aspects of your job in order of importance to
   your satisfaction with your work. (1 = most important, 5 = least
   important)

   _____ Salary

   _____ Benefits

   _____ Co-workers

   _____ Work environment

   _____ Supervisor

b. What proportions of your time are spent on the following activities during a
   normal working day. (Percentages should total 100%.)

   _____% In meetings

   _____% On the phone

   _____% Answering correspondence

   _____% Meeting with subordinates

   _____% On break

   _____% Other duties

Observation programs can be structured to varying degrees. A highly structured program would use specialized data gathering instruments similar to questionnaires as tools for observing and noting specific data about a given operation. Only predetermined functions within the system would be reviewed and recorded.

A semistructured approach can also be used. Under this method, an observer does not make any notes during the observation. Rather, the observer watches what is happening for a specified period of time, such as one hour. Notes are then recorded on a special form after the observation has been completed.

An important characteristic of observation as an information-gathering method is that highly trained people are needed. Observers usually have to be experienced systems analysts or, in some cases, industrial engineers.

Advantages of Observation. A major advantage of observation is that the information gathered relates directly to the observed performance of system-related tasks. That is, the observer sees firsthand just what is happening in the operation of a system. Thus, information obtained by observation can be of much higher quality than is possible through secondhand reports gathered from interviews or questionnaires.

Another advantage is that data are collected on a real-time basis. Information is generated in the process of observation. There are no instruments to be evaluated or reports to be prepared, as is the case when questionnaires or interviews are used. Finally, data gathered by observation are highly believable; they have high face validity.

Disadvantages of Observation. Observation techniques can present logistical problems. For example, the observer must be on the scene when a specific function is being performed. Thus, if an operation takes place only in the middle of the night, observation could become highly inconvenient.

Another potential disadvantage is that the performance of the people being observed may be affected by the very presence of an observer. People may not perform the same way when they are being watched as they do in the normal course of system processing activities.

A final disadvantage is that specially trained people are needed for observation assignments. These people may not be readily available. Even if they are available, the need for specialists may limit the extent of the observation that can be conducted.

Work Sampling and Measurement

Sampling is a methodology used to gather information about a large population of people, events, or transactions by studying some subset of the total. For example, before an election, a sample of voters will be questioned about their preferences. These data are then projected to predict the outcome of the election.

Similar methods can be used to gather information about the operation of an existing system. Representative transactions are selected and studied, and statistical methods are used to infer characteristics of the entire population of transactions from which the sample was drawn.

One sampling technique, for example, is simply to write a program that causes the computer to select a sample of transactions or file records. Another sampling technique might be to select random batches of manually processed transactions or to select, say, one transaction document out of every twenty or thirty processed.

These methods produce limited, specific, but potentially valuable results. One application for sampling techniques is a review of error rates and error distributions. All clerical functions within all information systems are subject to errors. In establishing controls and exception-handling procedures for computer information systems, it can be important to derive a reasonably accurate estimate of the rate and distribution of errors. This information makes it possible to design control and corrective procedures, to identify the points at which controls must be established, and also to estimate the cost of corrections.

Another potential use of sampling techniques is to study transaction distributions. For example, a company may want to know where transactions will originate for a given system. This distribution may be geographic, or it may be departmental within the organization. In either case, the information is needed as a basis for specifying the location and number of terminals to be installed, the types and capacities of communication lines, and other system elements.

Sampling programs require the services of qualified individuals with experience in research design and statistics. These specialties are beyond the scope of this text. If sampling activities are contemplated, appropriate qualified persons should be consulted.

Measurement, like sampling, deals primarily with the number and types of transactions processed by the system. It is a classification of the various different types of transactions along with their respective volumes at particular points in time. For example, Christmas is a high-volume period for sales transactions and February and March are normally low-volume periods.

SUMMARY

An information system exists to support a specific organization. To understand an existing system or to develop a new system, the systems analyst needs to gather information about the organization itself, the people who make up the organization, the work they do, and the environment in which they work.

Essential information about the organization includes its goals, its organizational structure, the functional objectives that support its goals, and the policies and procedures designed to achieve those objectives. Important information about people includes their authority and responsibility relationships, their job duties, their interpersonal relationships, and their information needs. Information about the work of the organization includes a description of tasks and work flows, methods and procedures for performing the work, work schedules and volumes, performance criteria, and control mechanisms. Information about the work environment includes the physical arrangement of work areas and the resources available to those who work there.

Information can be gathered from existing documents, including organizational charts, policy manuals, methods and procedures manuals, job descriptions, forms and reports, document flow and work flow diagrams, systems flowcharts, computer program documentation, data dictionary listings, and computer operations manuals. Information can be gathered from people by means of interviews, questionnaires, and observation. Information, particularly on new systems, can also be gathered from sources external to the organization, including other companies, equipment and software vendors, business publications, seminars, and workshops. In addition computerized databases from public or private sources such as the Census Bureau or McGraw-Hill can provide helpful information concerning competitors and the general economic climate.

The most common methods of gathering information that have not already been documented are interviews, questionnaires, observation, and work sampling. An interview is a planned face-to-face meeting between a data gatherer and one or more subjects for the express purpose of collecting information. Interviews have the advantage of personal contact, enabling the interviewer to probe for information. Disadvantages include the time and expense of interviewing, difficulty of evaluation, and the possible bias of the interviewer.

Steps in preparing for an interview include identifying the subjects to be interviewed, preparing a list of objectives and an outline of topics to be covered, and setting up appointments. In conducting the interview, the interviewer should listen responsively, indicating interest and comprehension, while remaining as noncommittal and unobtrusive as possible. The interviewer should let the subject do the talking yet maintain control over the interview to ensure that relevant and useful information is obtained.

A questionnaire, a document that solicits specific responses, is an impersonal, often mass-produced method for gathering the same information from many people. Questionnaires have the advantages of low cost, ease of administration, and rapid tabulation when collecting data from large groups of people. Disadvantages include the difficulty of constructing effective questionnaires and the inability to adapt to or probe responses as they are received.

The characteristics of a good questionnaire are validity, reliability, face validity, and ease of administration and scoring. Questionnaire items may include open-ended questions (for a questionnaire of limited distribution), fill-in-the-blank items, multiple-choice questions, rating scales, and ranking scales. The questionnaire should be logically organized, appropriate to the respondents who will receive it, and designed for easy scoring and analysis.

Observation is a method of information gathering in which a qualified person watches, or walks through, the actual processing associated with a system. Data are gathered on the basis of what is seen, without discussing the operation with users. The major advantage of observation is that the observer sees firsthand what is actually happening, thus obtaining information of the highest quality, on a real-time basis, and with maximum credibility. Disadvantages include inconvenience, the possibility that people may perform differently under observation, and the need for specially trained observers.

Work sampling is a method of gathering information about a large number of transactions by studying a small subset of the total. Sampling techniques are used to select representative transactions for study, and statistical methods are used to infer characteristics of the entire population of transactions from which the sample was drawn. In systems development work, sampling techniques can be used to study the geographic or departmental distribution of transactions or the rate and distribution of transaction errors. Use of these techniques requires the services of specialized personnel with experience in research design and statistics.

Many corporations utilize on-line access to economic and research databases as sources of information about the state of the economy, new technologies, and specific activities in certain industries. This information is often useful when evaluating the feasibility of a system development project.

KEY TERMS

1. interview
2. questionnaire
3. validity
4. reliability
5. face validity
6. goals
7. population
8. sample
9. open-ended question
10. fill-in-the-blank question
11. multiple-choice question
12. rating scale
13. ranking scale
14. observation
15. sampling
16. policies
17. procedures — not defined
18. objectives

REVIEW/DISCUSSION QUESTIONS

1. What is the role of information gathering in systems development?
2. What kind of information does the systems analyst need to know about the organization with a CIS problem or requirement? Why?
3. Name the three major sources of information in a systems development project.
4. What are the advantages of interviews over questionnaires as a means of gathering information? What disadvantages do interviews have?
5. Why is it generally a good idea to interview managers and supervisors before interviewing operational personnel?
6. How does an interviewer go about preparing for a series of interviews?
7. Describe the basic rules and tactics for conducting a successful interview.
8. Under what circumstances is a questionnaire likely to be the most appropriate method for gathering information?
9. What are the four basic characteristics of a good questionnaire?
10. What are the main advantages of observation as a method of information gathering? What are the main disadvantages?
11. Under what circumstances is work sampling likely to be a useful technique?

PRACTICE ASSIGNMENTS

1. For each of the following information needs, suggest an appropriate data gathering technique and describe how and why it is suitable. Also for each need, identify a primary and a secondary source of information that could be sought if the primary source is not available.
   a. The formal structure of responsibility and authority within a major department of a large organization.
   b. The company policy on the assignment of credit ratings to new customers.
   c. The job duties of an accounts receivable clerk within a small company that has only one accounting staff member.
   d. The amount of time spent by a secretary on various job duties.

e. The average number of errors made by a billing clerk in calculating invoice totals.

f. The reason for preparing a three-part purchase order form to buy merchandise to replace inventory stocks.

g. The best arrangement of desks and other fixtures within an office.

h. Modifying a computer-generated management report by rearranging the columns of information.

i. The general level of satisfaction among fifty employees in the warehouse.

j. The computerized procedure for selecting suppliers and producing purchase orders for merchandise.

k. The type of information collected about job applicants.

l. The cost to the company of having the office manager spend time in responding to customer complaints.

2. Figure 8-14 is a memo that was sent to the head of an accounting department as an interview request. Critique this memo.

Figure 8.14. Sample interview appointment memo.

```
Date:     March 14

To:       Dennis Warren, Accounting Supervisor

From:     Anne Paige, Analyst

Re:       Interview

I would like for you to come to my office next week sometime to
discuss the very serious problems that you have in your department.
It seems that many of the other managers are upset that their reports
are late and never up-to-date.

I will be discussing the following topics:

1.  How many people work for you?  What are their salaries?

2.  What are the exact duties of each of your employees?

3.  Why do they make so many errors?

4.  What procedures are followed by the data processing department to
    keep your files up to date?

5.  What kinds of reports do the other managers need?

6.  How will your staff feel if we automate the entire accounting
    function and have to lay off the unproductive workers?

I will use this information in coming up with some better ways of
doing the work in your area.  I already have some idea of the
changes I would like to see and hope you will agree with them.
If I am not in my office when you come by, please wait, as I will
probably return soon.
```

3. Construct questionnaire items to solicit the following information items. The gathered information should be easy to tabulate.
   a. The amount of time an office worker spends: (1) answering the phone, (2) filing, (3) typing correspondence, (4) typing reports, (5) writing memos, and (6) performing other duties.
   b. The degree of importance each of the following job dimensions plays in the job satisfaction of an average worker: (1) salary, (2) fringe benefits, (3) coworkers, (4) work environment, (5) amount of supervision, (6) amount of work, and (7) other factors.
   c. The salaries of workers paid between $10,000 and $25,000.
   d. The relative importance of each of the following reasons for customer complaints: (1) late deliveries of orders, (2) stock-outs, (3) damaged merchandise, (4) misbillings, (5) discourteous service, and (6) high prices.

Communication

Learning Objectives

After completing the reading and other learning assignments for this chapter, you should be able to:

- Explain the importance of communication in a systems development project.
- Discuss the seven myths and realities of communication.
- State the basic principles of audience identification and effective communication.
- Identify the primary interests and the major information needs of the different groups involved in the systems development process.
- Use the five basic steps in problem solving as a basis for management-type presentations on information systems.
- Describe a problem-solving work session and explain its use in the system development process.
- Describe a technical walkthrough—including personnel, procedures, and end-products—and explain its role in systems development.
- List and describe briefly the steps involved in preparing a written report or an oral presentation.
- Explain the purpose and organization of a management summary.
- Describe the content items that would be present in an effective procedures manual.
- Explain the purpose of a training manual.
- Choose the most appropriate communication style for a given situation.

THE NEED FOR COMMUNICATION

A CIS project enlists the participation of a broad range of individuals, including multiple levels of management, a wide range of user personnel, and an equally wide range of IS professionals. These people have different backgrounds. They come from different disciplines. They may speak virtually different languages and use widely varying jargons.

A CIS project may be so extensive, in terms of the number of people involved and the elapsed time required, that all of the people who work on it may not even get the chance to meet one another. In effect, a group of total strangers may be asked to produce a coordinated, integrated, responsive system. To pull all these diverse people and interests together, the IS project needs effective communication programs directed to the specific information requirements of all involved parties. Identifying some of these people may help to illustrate the problem:

- Users participate in a project because they have business problems to solve. They may have little or no knowledge of computers or of the process involved in developing information systems. But users need to understand the process of systems development at least enough to appreciate the application of this process to their own requirements.

- Computer professionals, including systems analysts, programmers, and technical support personnel, may be knowledgeable about systems development but have limited knowledge of how the business functions. They need to gain an understanding of organizational objectives and business functions, as well as of the specific problems they are being asked to solve.

- Computer professionals must also be able to communicate meaningfully with each other. In particular, systems analysts must be able to present information so that designers and programmers can work quickly and effectively and so that technical support personnel will understand hardware and systems software requirements.

- Top level managers, including members of the corporate IS steering committee, need to look at a project in terms of the importance of the business objectives to be met and also in terms of the investments that must be made and the projected returns on these investments.

- All parties associated with a systems development project must gain an understanding of top-level corporate policies and guidelines that apply to their efforts.

Although communication needs are diverse, responsibilities are clear. The project leader must create a communication structure that delivers the information that people need to do their jobs. Systems analysts are at the hub of this communication network. They are positioned as a vital communication link between users on the one hand and designers, programmers, and technical support staff on the other. Because of their role, systems analysts must be aware of the communication needs of all the people with whom they deal.

SEVEN-MYTHS AND REALITIES CONCERNING COMMUNICATION

Several myths about communication exist. Here is a discussion of seven of these myths along with their respective realities.

Myth 1: We only communicate when we consciously make an effort to do so.
Reality: We frequently communicate messages we are not aware of communicating.
Myth 2: We communicate as if words had specific meanings.
Reality: Words do not have meanings; rather, meanings are within people based on their experiences.
Myth 3: We communicate primarily with words.
Reality: The majority of the messages we communicate are based on the nonverbal aspects of communication.
Myth 4: Nonverbal communication is silent language.
Reality: Some nonverbal communication is silent, but much of it is not silent.
Myth 5: We communicate as if communication were a one-way activity.
Reality: Communication is a two-way activity in which feedback from the other party is crucial.
Myth 6: The message we communicate is identical to the message received.
Reality: The message finally received by the listener is never identical to the message sent.
Myth 7: You can never give someone too much information.
Reality: People can be given too much information. An information overload can be just as much of a problem as not having enough information.

EFFECTIVE COMMUNICATIONS REQUIRES BOTH SENDING AND RECEIVING SKILLS

LACK OF SKILL IN SENDING

Many people consider oral communication to be as natural as breathing, eating, and sleeping. They maintain that with maturity one naturally develops into a proficient communicator. Each day we can observe many walking examples of the falsity of that position.

The ability to communicate ranks high among those attributes that employers seek in a potential employee. Business leaders frequently bemoan the lack of this ability among many college graduates. Workers often cite an inability to communicate as a prime shortcoming of their superior.

LACK OF SKILL IN RECEIVING

Until recently people did not recognize that the receiver plays an important role in the communication process. Popular opinion held that if information were transmitted properly, there would be effective communication. If not, the communicator was at fault. Now most people realize that, whether the message is spoken or written, getting the desired response from the receiver depends partly on whether it is received as intended.

We spend almost 50 percent of our average work day listening to others. Listening ability can be improved, and several tape-recorded courses are available for this purpose. Listening is also the subject of many training courses conducted in business and governmental organizations.

Since Brenda enjoyed working with numbers, she was especially pleased when hired as a payroll clerk. That job was an eye-opening experience for her, however. She had always thought that a payroll clerk spend most of the day working with numbers.

After six months on the job, Brenda said, "I like my work but it's different from what I expected. At least half of my time is spent getting and giving information. Mathematical ability is important to do this job, but the ability to communicate with others is just as important."

Educators regularly express alarm at an apparent national decline in reading abilities. Some companies provide remedial reading instruction for employees who are unable to read and to comprehend at an acceptable level. Certain employers consider reading to be so important that they provide this instruction completely at company expense. The worker attends these classes at full pay.

Companies and individuals daily pay the price for problems caused by a lack of skill in receiving information. The drill-press operator who did not listen carefully to the supervisor explain how to work with the new alloy destroyed $300 worth of drill bits and wasted $1,000 worth of raw materials. When provisions of the group health insurance plan were changed, a memo detailed the changes. It became apparent several weeks later that the maintenance workers had misunderstood the memo. An inability to receive information accurately contributes greatly to communication problems and partially explains the great importance now attached to communication.

IDENTIFYING AUDIENCES

A key responsibility of the systems analyst in any systems development project is to identify the audiences to whom messages must be communicated—as well as the information needs of these audiences. If communication is to be effective, messages must be shaped to meet the specific information needs of selected individual persons or groups.

Communication needs of individual audiences are easy to recognize, once the matter is given some thought. The point to be made here is that the needs of the audience must determine the content of the message. All effective communication is, first and foremost, *to* an audience. The content of messages delivered *about* a subject must be tailored to the audience that is to receive it.

The principles involved are logical and straightforward: Know your audience; understand their interests or motivation, as well as their information needs; then shape your message to meet those needs. Following this simple approach will result in more efficient and more effective communication in any systems development project.

The communication activities of systems development projects fall into three broad categories:

■ Problem-solving work sessions.

■ Technical reviews (walkthroughs).

■ Reports (written and oral presentations).

PROBLEM-SOLVING SESSIONS

Systems analysis is problem solving. A computer information system solves a business problem. This is a basic definition of why systems are developed and what they do. In practice, the overall problem being solved consists of scores, probably hundreds, of smaller subproblems. Members of the project team, particularly systems analysts and user managers, will typically address one or more of these problems during each working day.

The main requirement in dealing with and defining potential solutions for problems lies in being objective. Problem solvers should avoid being drawn into the details or personal frustrations of information system problems. In looking at a problem objectively, the analyst can separate symptoms from fundamental causes, moving logically toward identifying alternatives, or logical solutions.

Objectivity will also save time. An objective problem solver will not become swamped in irrelevant details that prevent identifying solutions. Objectivity in problem solving can be assured by following a relatively simple five-step process:

Step 1: State the problem clearly, separating large problems into individual, smaller ones.

Step 2: Analyze the problem for its probable cause.

Step 3: Identify alternatives for eliminating the cause.

Step 4: Consider the consequences of these alternatives.

Step 5: Choose the best alternative.

This problem-solving model is simple and direct. The best way to apply it is simply to remember the steps, then follow them when problem solving or decision-making situations arise.

To find alternative solutions, project team members should think as creatively as possible. Alternatives offered as possible solutions *should not* be restricted to the capabilities of current systems or even to technologies that have been discussed.

A significant feature of the problem-solving process is that solution alternatives are generated initially without consideration of their consequences. Consideration of the consequences of each alternative as it is listed introduces inhibitions. Emphasis should not be on acceptance or rejection without full consideration. Otherwise, the concentration of participants is interrupted, and creativity is diminished.

At the next step, when consequences are considered, the job should be done thoroughly. For each alternative, both advantages and disadvantages should be identified. A scenario should be played out under which it is assumed that the solution has been implemented. The projected system solution should then be compared with current methods to identify possible improvements or new problems. Consideration of consequences, in effect, makes it possible to model the results of potential solutions before time and money are expended to implement them.

The choice of which alternative to implement may be relatively easy to make on the basis of cost-benefit analyses. The point is that this process can lead to the identification of a clearcut need that could be reported to management in easily understood terms. There may be no need to involve managers, or even other members of the team. Rather, the problem could be identified, its cause pinpointed, and logical alternatives made available for decision making by managerial and technical personnel.

Sometimes defective decisions are reached in small groups because of certain characteristics of individuals. For example, powerful individuals sometimes dominate groups and keep others from actively participating in the group process; poor decisions often result. You may encounter a group member who disagrees and consumes valuable group time talking about unrelated topics. On other occasions individuals in the group may press for a quick decision because all the important aspects of the problem have been carefully considered. In numerous other ways, individuals can dilute the decision-making potential of groups.

TECHNICAL REVIEWS (WALKTHROUGHS)

A **walkthrough** is a quality review applied to such systems development products as data flow diagrams, program structure charts, pseudocode listings, collections of proposed input documents, collections of proposed output documents, and test plans.

A walkthrough of a systems development product can be compared to a quality inspection of a manufactured product. At manufacturing plants, there are points at which inspectors review all of the work done in a given department or set of work stations. They make sure that wires are connected correctly, that the parts of the product actually function, and so on. A manufactured product is a system made up of parts that have to work together. With computer information systems, the component parts are analysis, design, and implementation products.

As is the case with a manufactured product, the people doing the walkthrough simply identify problems. There is a separation between quality inspection and actual production. Inspectors don't fix things, they just find errors or problems. People who conduct walkthroughs are not expected to conduct detailed analyses of the errors or to fix them. Their job is simply to identify any errors or problems where they exist, referring the work back to the responsible developer.

Within a systems development project, a technical review, or walkthrough, should be conducted any time a product is developed. For this purpose, a product is any portion of the system that can be identified as a separate unit and that has the capability of introducing errors into the system. Project management procedures should be set up to check each such product with a walkthrough by qualified personnel.

Walkthrough Participants

A walkthrough is conducted by enough people to do the job thoroughly but not so many that the whole process becomes bogged down. Typically, three to five persons will be involved in reviewing any particular product. The key person is the *author*, or developer, of the product. The author must decide when the product is ready for a walkthrough. The nature of the product will shape the selection of other members of the review team.

If the project is relatively large, one or more experienced systems analysts may be appointed as **administrators** of walkthroughs. The administrator schedules walkthroughs, as requested by authors, and monitors their progress. It is part of the administrator's job to make sure that all reviewers have copies of the document to be examined in advance of the meeting. During the meeting, the administrator resolves any conflicts or disputes that may arise. The administrator must keep in mind that the purpose is to identify errors, not to correct the errors or to argue about matters of personal approach or style. Thus, the administrator has the authority to cut off any discussion that is no longer productive, moving the group on to its next topic.

The administrator also checks the document itself to make sure that the walkthrough job will be manageable. Product reviews should be relatively small tasks, short enough so that a walkthrough can be completed in a concentrated period, usually 30 to 60 minutes.

Each walkthrough should have someone appointed as recorder. This individual's job is to write a summary of identified errors or questions that are raised. From these notes, the recorder prepares a walkthrough report that is distributed, promptly, to members of the walkthrough team. A separate, abbreviated version is distributed to project management. The recorder must have a thorough understanding of the product being examined. Therefore, the recorder should be a professionally qualified member of the project team.

Two or more persons serve as reviewers of the technical document during a walkthrough. Their job is, clearly and simply, to spot problems or errors in the product under review.

Walkthrough Structure

A walkthrough is not a general informal meeting but rather a constructive analysis session in which all parties should participate as equals. The plan for a walkthrough should recognize that the participants are busy people. For a walkthrough to be productive, the rule about simply identifying problems, not solving them, should be strictly enforced. Ideally, the walkthrough will trace the product from beginning to end, completing this task in a short, concentrated effort. Participants should complete their work without interruption.

The session should be planned so that all members of the review team receive copies of the product to be reviewed a sufficient time in advance. At the session itself, the author should describe the product. Reviewers should then present their concerns and questions. After all of the questions have been identified, the author traces through the document. Starting at the beginning, each question or criticism is addressed. Some questions may be resolved with on-the-spot answers. Others, however, may be identified as requiring further work by the author. In addition, the discussions may raise new questions. All problems, together with their resolution or agreement that further work is needed, should be noted and described by the secretary.

Walkthroughs should be conducted in a businesslike way. Personal remarks or personal criticisms of team members are counterproductive. If such statements are made, the discussion should be brought back into its main channel immediately. Comments should focus on questions of accuracy, conformance to standards, following of specifications or objectives, maintainability of the software being reviewed, and the general quality of work. Ideally, minor mechanical errors should be covered in separate written comments submitted before the walkthrough takes place. This will improve the efficiency and productivity of the walkthrough session.

To the extent possible, members of a walkthrough team should have different experience levels. Junior members have the opportunity for a valuable learning experience as they work with more experienced people. At the same time, junior personnel can bring fresh approaches into these sessions.

If rework requirements are identified, additional walkthroughs may be scheduled. The review process is continued until all identified problems have been fixed.

Walkthrough End-Products

As indicated, a walkthrough produces two end-product documents: the walkthrough report and the management report.

Walkthrough Report. This is a brief, factual document. It should identify the product involved, the author, the date, and the names of all persons who participated. The outcome of the walkthrough should be noted. The three possible outcomes are:

- The product is accepted.
- The product will be considered accepted when specific, identified revisions have been made.
- Another walkthrough will be necessary after identified problems have been corrected.

The main report content consists of any concerns raised during the walkthrough or submitted in writing. This report should be completed and submitted to walkthrough participants as soon as possible after the session.

Management Report. This report summarizes the walkthrough report. It contains the identifying information and walkthrough outcome, but not the detailed list of errors or concerns. The management report is submitted to the IS supervisor responsible for the project and also becomes part of the permanent documentation about the product. If the outcome is full or conditional acceptance, participants sign the report to indicate acceptance of the product reviewed. By signing, the participants share responsibility for the quality of the product they have certified.

Avoiding Common Pitfalls in Walkthroughs

When walkthroughs are conducted expertly and professionally, they can serve a valuable quality control purpose. They can help to mold a highly professional team committed to producing a quality system. For success in the conduct of walkthroughs, however, it is important to recognize that they will not be successful automatically. Potential problems and pitfalls exist that should be anticipated and avoided.

One common problem is that a walkthrough team is given too large a product to review. The session takes too long. People lose their concentration and begin to worry about other things they should be doing. The administrator should apply his or her experience to assure that the products selected for review can be covered in a relatively short time.

Another problem can occur if participants do not receive copies of the document to be reviewed in time to prepare themselves. Of course, no matter how much time is allowed, it is possible that participants will be unprepared. An atmosphere should be created in which reviewers understand the necessity to prepare themselves for a walkthrough session. At minimum, each participant should have read through the document being reviewed carefully before the walkthrough takes place.

Constructive criticism should be encouraged and supported. However, care must be taken to avoid letting criticism deteriorate into arguments or personal attacks. The product must, at all times, be separated from its author. At the same time, people should not be so inhibited that they are afraid to criticize anything. Solid, professional criticism helps improve a product. It takes judgment and experience to know the difference between professional comments and personal insults. Professional criticism is necessary. Dwelling on personalities is unacceptable.

REPORTING

The reporting function is a major component of any communication structure for a systems development project. Reports deliver messages to identified audiences. Each message must be:

- To an audience.
- About a clearly identified subject.

The needs of the audience shape the content of the message.

Organizing a Message

To help assure that written reports or oral presentations meet the needs of their audiences, a relatively simple process, or set of steps, can be followed:

Step 1: Collect all information first. Relevant information should be gathered and reviewed first. This becomes the basis for the content of the message. Thus, information gathering is a key first step.

Step 2: Identify audience needs. Given a body of information that is ready for presentation, the needs of the audience or audiences should be identified and defined. On the basis of these needs, priorities should be established that rate the importance of the information items to the audience. In a relatively long document, information items can be listed, then numbered in the order of their priority.

Step 3: Start the presentation with the most important item, then support this initial statement. The beginning statement in any report or message should contain the information most important to the identified audience. After that, information items should be arranged in order based on their importance. At the same time, the ordering of information items should be logical. That is, if a recommendation or finding is presented at the beginning of the message, the items that follow should support the initial statement. These items should follow a logical progression.

Step 4: Analyze and criticize the content of the message. If the full message seems incomplete or doesn't make sense in its entirety, it may be necessary to review the initial statement or even to gather more information.

Step 5: Use only enough time or words to deliver a message that meets the information needs of the audience. It is not necessary to put all available information into every message. Part of the skill of efficient writing or presentation lies in deciding what to leave out. Again, the needs of the audience should shape the message.

This approach to organizing and preparing messages works equally well in either of the two main types of reporting that occur within a systems development project: written reports and oral presentations.

To the extent possible, documents produced in a systems development project use graphic techniques or are structured to meet specific communication needs. Examples include data flow diagrams, structure charts, process specifications, and data dictionaries.

Each of these structured documents, however, requires at least a brief narrative description as an overview. Further, management reports that serve as the basis for project decisions require carefully prepared management summaries.

In addition to these basic working documents, systems development projects are expected to produce considerable volumes of written documents in the form of procedures manuals and training manuals.

In each case, thought must be applied to tailor the information content of the written messages to the needs of its audiences.

Management Summaries. Managers use summary reports as a basis for making resource decisions. From the manager's point of view, this is a problem-solving situation. A sound technique for organizing management summaries, therefore, is to follow a problem-solving model.

Earlier in this chapter, a methodology for problem solving was presented. In writing a summary report to managers, assume that they will be going through this problem-solving process as they review the information presented in your report.

A good way to begin a management summary, then, is to describe the problem being solved. This description should make it clear that the problem or decision situation has been analyzed and that causes have been identified. That is, reporting should be done as though the problem-solving process had already been applied successfully, without having to pause for each analytical step.

The next portion of a management summary should identify the alternatives that were considered. Those that obviously didn't fit can be discarded with brief explanations about why they were rejected. The consequences of the most likely alternatives can then be reviewed in somewhat greater depth.

Obviously, since management summaries are recommendations, no decision can actually be made. Rather, the summary should end with a recommendation to the management group. If the presentation has been structured carefully, the recommendation should come as a logical conclusion to the report. If, for any reason, the conclusion does not seem fully supported by the presentation, revision should be considered.

This type of structuring is basic to management reporting. Managers don't want to be presented with problems. They want recommendations for solutions and for actions. By structuring reports in this way, members of the project team make it clear that they have thought about the situation and are ready to make a commitment to deliver results if they receive management support in the form of a favorable decision.

Some report-writing guidelines suggest that management summaries begin with a recommended decision then support the recommendation with factual presentations. This type of format is used and can work. However, the report structure suggested here, which follows the decision-making process, seems to relate more closely to the requirements and thought processes of this particular audience: Identify the problem, briefly state and evaluate the potential solutions, and recommend a course of action. In oral presentations to management groups, discussed later in this chapter, the situation is somewhat different. In this environment, after the group has seen the documentation, the opposite approach can be used: Begin with a recommendation, then go through the written report in support of the recommendation.

In following the problem-solving model for management reporting, remember the basic principle of problem solving: Large problems are solved by partitioning them into a collection of smaller problems. The problem-solving process should then be applied separately to the individual subproblems, no matter how closely related they may be to one another. Thus, if a management summary covers a complex situation involving multiple problems or decisions, each should be summarized individually. A collective summary on the total recommendation can then be placed in the report, either at the beginning or at the end, depending on the length of the document and the nature of the group that will receive it.

In general, a management summary should be limited to one or two pages. If the summary is longer than that, it defeats its own purpose. Any further detailing required to support the recommendation should be contained in separate sections of the management summary. They might also be included as appendices.

Policy Statements and Procedure Manuals. As you pursue your career in information systems, you will most likely be involved in writing policies and procedures in one of three instances: (1) when a new system begins; (2) when a new policy or procedure is needed; or (3) when old policies or procedures are being rewritten. You'll probably have a chance to write policies and procedures about a variety of topics. Many systems organizations have policies and procedures for the following topics:

1. Documentation.
2. Gaining user approval for system specifications.
3. Evaluating employee performance.
4. Communication protocols.
5. User and information staff responsibilities in the systems development process.
6. Procedures for technical walkthroughs.

Policies and procedures normally are concerned with the internal operations of a company. Some general guidelines that may help you in preparing them are presented below.

Guideline 1:   Answer All Possible Questions
                Your job as a writer of policy and procedure statements will be to answer these six questions:

- Who: All the people who are to act.
- What: Exactly the action that should take place.
- When: At what point in time actions are to occur.
- Why: The justification for the action.
- Where: The locations to be affected.
- How: The procedures involved.

Usually, the why is answered in the policy statement itself.

Guideline 2: Follow a Specific Format

First, the written statement should be free of errors in grammar and format. After this, two characteristics pertain to an effective policies and procedures format:

1. Policies appear first, then procedures.
2. Procedures are listed step by step.

As you write policy and procedure statements, you will often find that more than one policy is covered by a given procedure. If this is the case, you should list all of the relevant policies first then follow them with the procedures.

Guideline 3: Orient the Message to the Receivers

Your analysis of the person who will implement the policy and procedure statements will affect the document. The policy or procedure should be *readable* at the appropriate level. It should also be *tactful*. Don't emphasize the superiority of the company over the individual with such words as "will" or "shall." For example, Don't say, "systems analysts shall document all files with the appropriate file-layout sheet." Try to be *concise* where possible. Don't say "may be prepared" or "shall be decided" say "prepare" and "decide."

Policies and procedures are guides to decision making. They are intended to help a business meet its objectives by providing guidelines for more consistent decision making. Few people want to consult a policy or procedure manual, but they'll be more inclined to do so if, when you write your policy and procedure statements, you apply the three guidelines.

Procedure manuals, as the term is used here, are documents that direct people in performing manual procedures within a computer-based system. In effect, manuals do for people what programs do for computers. However, people and computers are different. Manuals should reflect those differences.

These guidelines are important, but the guiding principle in developing a manual should be that people are in the system because they are able to apply judgment. Any functions that can be automated completely would be done by a computer. Thus, emphasis in the procedures manual should be on those points in the system at which people assure quality or apply judgment. Care should be taken to explain the reasons for doing things in the ways that have been specified.

This type of presentation helps to convince people that the jobs they are doing are worthwhile. A well-executed procedures manual should have the effect of selling the person doing the work on the value and importance of the job. Unfortunately, many procedures manuals give the impression of talking down to the people who actually do the work, of emphasizing the steps taken rather than the importance of the results. Such manuals, rather than guiding and helping people, encourage feelings of boredom and futility. Thus, they defeat their own purpose, contributing to a lack of quality rather than assuring that standards are met.

Some content items within procedures manuals that can help build human understanding and interest are:

- Explain the purpose and value of the overall system of which the individual is a part.
- Identify the customer, or user, of the outputs produced by each task.
- Describe specifically what successful performance will look like and what will be expected from the person handling each task.
- Describe any and all quality standards that should be met within the context of the job description itself.
- In describing procedures, cover the steps to be taken in sequence. Be sure to identify the starting and completion points for each step, as well as the overall continuity between steps.
- Whenever a judgment or decision is to be made by a human operator, emphasize the value of this judgment and its contribution to the success of the system. Follow the decision-making model in identifying what is to be decided, what alternatives are available, and the conditions under which each alternative should be selected.
- Encourage people to apply judgment. That is why they are part of the system. Include instructions about how individuals can make suggestions to improve the system or to streamline the work flow.

The same guidelines apply in developing procedures manuals for computer console operators. The more a manual can do to help make an operator feel important because of the ability to apply judgment, the more effective that manual will be. Conversely, the more a manual tends to treat a person as an attendant waiting upon a machine, the less effective that manual will be.

Training Manuals. The job of training operators and users for installation and use of a new system should be approached with some humility. When it comes to using computer information systems, experience is still the best teacher. There is no way that a trainer, no matter how skilled, can impart all of the knowledge and experience needed for smooth, continuous operation of a computer information system. This kind of skill and experience can only be acquired on the job.

Therefore, materials and presentation programs for training sessions should be prepared with the full knowledge that it will be almost impossible to complete the job of training personnel during the brief classroom sessions that are made available. Recognizing this, the training program should concentrate on teaching people to meet needs or solve problems on the job. This is a more practical approach than undertaking a probably impossible task of teaching all of the operations, functions, and skills that will be needed on a relatively complex job.

The purpose of training materials is different from that of procedures manuals. Training manuals should be designed as easy-to-use references. Thus, for example, it is perfectly acceptable to have a reference in a training manual that simply tells an operator what page of the procedures manual to turn to for instructions on a given job. The training manual can then offer hints aimed at helping the operator to master the functions described in the procedures manual. It is not necessary to duplicate all of the procedures manual content in a training manual. Rather, the idea is to help the operator feel comfortable with the procedures manual so that it can be used as a job aid.

In a CIS environment, there are many opportunities to use the computer itself as a training aid. This is particularly true in the training of operators working at video display terminals. Many "user friendly" systems build in options in which operators can ask for prompting or help from the computer itself. Under one option, for example, the operator simply enters a question mark at the beginning of a line on the terminal, then presses the return key. The computer is directed to display a menu for assistance routines that the operator can call up.

Another common technique used in data entry systems is to display help information at the top of the screen. This help information identifies the codes or formats to be used by the operator. As the operator learns the job, this display can be eliminated.

Above all, effective training programs *teach operators to learn*. A training effort should never downgrade people to the level of machines by attempting to simply "program" them to make the correct responses.

Oral Presentation

There are many points within any systems development project at which complete sets of information must be considered, organized, assembled, and presented orally rather than in written reports. The process of organizing information for oral presentation is much the same as that described for written reports. However, the emphasis or pattern of presentation may differ.

Oral presentation situations that arise in systems development projects fall into three broad categories, project management reviews, status reviews, and acceptance reviews.

Project management review sessions involve reports by members of the project team to team leaders or project managers. The content of the reports may be either technical or general, depending on whether the work is done by computer professionals or user members of the team. Usually, these meetings are held periodically, as often as the project manager considers necessary to manage or control the development process. Topics for these meetings may include reports of progress during the current week, completion of tasks, time remaining for tasks in process, reviews of particular problems encountered, or tasks that are about to begin.

Status review meetings are conducted periodically, usually weekly or bi-weekly, throughout a project. Their purpose is to keep user management current on the progress of the project. Status reviews are information sessions, not sales meetings. They do not necessarily culminate in approval or acceptance of work done. Rather, they are a means of achieving communication, of keeping project management and key user managers in touch with each other to assure a continuity of understanding. Participants in these meetings are usually the project leader, key user managers, and, possibly, members of the project team with special contributions to make.

Acceptance reviews are sessions in which the project team goes before some management group to present information about a phase, activity, or interim product for which approval is needed. One of the most important types of acceptance review during a project is the phase report presented to the steering committee recommending commitment to the next phase of the system development life cycle. In addition to the steering committee sessions, acceptance reviews may be held with user managers who are asked to review a set of output reports, business forms, data entry formats, a model for the new system, or some other product of the systems development process. Meetings of this type may also be held with auditors who review the reliability and auditability of the procedures being designed. The common denominator of such meetings is that brief, formal documents are usually prepared in advance and provided to the decision makers. The oral presentation then explains and supports the written document, with the intent of securing approval for recommendations made.

As stated previously, many of the guidelines for preparing written reports apply equally to oral presentations. However, certain special considerations also apply in the case of oral presentations. These include visual support and certain questions of organization.

Visual Support. Wherever possible, an oral presentation should be supported by visual aids of some sort. The number and type of visual materials used will depend on the situation. At a management review, for example, the visual focus may be on the forms or products being analyzed. A programmer reviewing the design of a module might provide copies of his or her structure charts for all persons attending the meeting. The same would be true for systems analysts presenting data flow diagrams for analysis of existing or proposed systems.

At larger meetings, different types of visuals might be appropriate. For example, if ten or more persons are attending an acceptance review, it could be distracting if each of them was expected to leaf through a set of loose pages. It is more effective, in a case like this, to use slides or overhead transparencies to project summary notes onto a screen. In this way, the attention of participants is focused on one specific topic at a time.

Whatever method is used, the principle is the same: Meetings devoted to reviews of project content should be supported by some sort of visual device that focuses the attention of participants on the topics being discussed. Further, each participant should be able to take away a set of notes that will serve as reminders, or reinforcement, of the discussions held.

Organizing Oral Presentations. As is the case with written messages, a safe practice for oral messages is to structure information content according to the decisions to be made. However, some modification may be necessary to cover situations in which participants have already seen the summary report about which the oral presentation will be based. It certainly is not acceptable simply to stand up and read a report that people already hold in their hands.

Thus, if the audience has already seen the report, it is best to begin with a statement of the recommendations. Then, brief references can be made to the content of the report in support of the recommendation.

In oral reports associated with written summaries, interaction with the audience is essential. Listeners should be left with the feeling that a thorough job has been done of analyzing the topic. They should feel that the decision that they make is soundly supported. Audience participation is essential to establishing this feeling.

Provision should be made for dealing with questions from the audience. If no questions materialize during the presentation, two techniques may help. One is to identify, before the presentation, questions that members of the audience ought to have. Then, during the presentation, these questions can be raised and answered on the spot. Another, somewhat more aggressive approach is to ask questions and require answers from members of the audience. In any case, audience participation should be encouraged throughout the presentation, rather than waiting until the end to invite questions.

To illustrate how participation can be stimulated at an acceptance review, suppose a group of top-level users is checking out a training plan for a new system. The person presenting the plan sees nothing but nodding of agreement from the audience. To stimulate participation, some priming questions are in order. For example, as a summary point during the presentation, the speaker might ask: "As you can see, we are planning to train four people at a time from your department. Can you spare this number of people at any given time? Will this rate of training keep up with the installation program you have planned?"

At a steering committee meeting, priming questions might deal with interdepartmental interfaces in a system under development. Assuming that the heads of two or more departments who will use the system are present, it is always a good tactic to ask these individuals whether the planned interfaces within the system reflect their ideas of how the system should work.

In summary, systems development work is done by project teams. Teams, in turn, are bound together by common commitments and common understandings of a shared purpose. The development of this singleness of purpose and unity of effort among the many and diverse people involved in a systems project does not happen automatically. It requires a carefully defined communication structure, made up of many elements and serving a wide range of information needs.

IDENTIFYING YOUR COMMUNICATION STRENGTHS

Effective communication often depends on assuming the most appropriate style for the communication task at hand. The key is to analyze the situation and to choose a communication style that will work in that setting. There are four alternative communication styles that might be chosen: blaming, directing, persuasive, and problem-solving.

A person who uses the **blaming** style is attempting to find fault or discover who is to blame for a problem. This approach evokes negative feelings and for that reason should be avoided.

A directing style involves telling others, particularly subordinates, how to do their jobs or how to approach problems. Discussion is minimized and communication is predominantly one-way. This approach can be effective in certain situations. Computer programmers who refuse to document their work might be directed to do so before they move on to the next program or program module.

The persuasive style employs information sharing and acceptance techniques. Instead of directing the audience to do something, the message is presented for their evaluation and active acceptance. You want to convince the audience to select a particular course of action because they believe that it is the correct approach. Often the very persuasive person can identify a personal need in the receiver and then present a plan of action that meets that need. Because the recipients make the decision, there is a much greater acceptance of the action than is the case with the blaming or the directing approaches.

The problem-solving style seeks mutual acceptance from both the sender and receiver of the final action; compromise is very common. Two-way communication is required, and ideas are jointly explored and evaluated. Personalities may emerge, but they are not used in determining the final decision. This style is the most effective in the systems development process.

The blaming and the problem-solving approaches, from the sender's viewpoint, are opposites. Similarly, the directive and the persuasive approaches are at opposite ends of the spectrum. Further, the blaming and the directing techniques have little feedback while the persuasive and the problem-solving approaches build on this interaction. Figure 9-1 indicates the extent of participant

Figure 9.1   Four communication styles compared by extent of participant involvement.

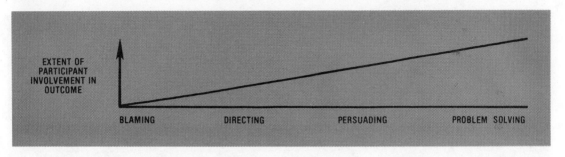

involvement among the four communication styles.

If you know which style is your dominant style, you can better prepare for an occasion (e.g., acceptance review) with the correct style, whether it is your first choice or another one. The self-assessment instruments in Figures 9-2 and 9-3, when completed and scored, can tell you your dominant communication style.

In Figure 9-1, blaming is opposed to problem solving; therefore if blaming and problem solving styles can be evaluated, it should be possible to determine abilities on the two styles. It should also be possible to determine abilities on the other two styles between the extremes. This evaluation instrument measures the tendency to use blaming and problem solving styles.

If your score for the left column in Figure 9-3 is between 21 and 28, you are probably a moderate blamer, a score of 29 or higher suggests that you rely somewhat heavily on the blaming style. Examination of such a communication style is necessary. The communicator who uses it is not likely to be a successful project leader.

If your score for the right column is from 21 to 28, you fall in the moderate problem-solving style category. A score of 29 or higher indicates a strong leaning toward problem solving as your dominant technique. You have good project leader communication skills.

Don't assume that blaming is always bad and problem solving always good. There are occasions when you need to be directive and perhaps even to blame. Problem solving can be both tedious and time consuming; it is not a panacea for all ills. Become familiar with the four styles and with your own strengths and weaknesses, then try to select the appropriate style for each occasion.

Figure 9.2.   Self-assessment of communication style.

	Very Little	Little	Some	Great	Very Great
1. Make judgments early in the conversation.	_____	_____	_____	_____	_____
2. Share my feelings with others.	_____	_____	_____	_____	_____
3. Talk about the issues.	_____	_____	_____	_____	_____
4. Have analyzed others' motives.	_____	_____	_____	_____	_____
5. Talk about the person.	_____	_____	_____	_____	_____
6. Use clear and precise language.	_____	_____	_____	_____	_____
7. Decide on the action before the conversation.	_____	_____	_____	_____	_____
8. Encourage the other person to discuss feelings.	_____	_____	_____	_____	_____
9. Am open for new information.	_____	_____	_____	_____	_____
10. Ask questions which seek agreement with me.	_____	_____	_____	_____	_____
11. Talk the majority of the time.	_____	_____	_____	_____	_____
12. Ask questions which get others to describe events.	_____	_____	_____	_____	_____
13. Talk half the time or less.	_____	_____	_____	_____	_____
14. Others defend their position to me.	_____	_____	_____	_____	_____

Source: Sandra E. O'Connell, *The Manager as Communicator*, (San Francisco: Harper & Row, 1979), p. 25. Reprinted by permission of Harper & Row Publishers, Inc.

Figure 9.3. Self-assessment of communication style.

Item No.	Score	
1	_____	
2		_____
3		_____
4	_____	
5	_____	
6		_____
7	_____	
8		_____
9		_____
10	_____	
11	_____	
12		_____
13		_____
14	_____	
Totals	_____	_____

Total column 1 _____

Total column 2 _____

Interpretation of scores: very little = 1 point, little = 2 points, some = 3 points, great = 4 points, and very great = 5 points

Source: Sandra E. O'Connell, *The Manager as Communicator* (San Francisco: Harper & Row, 1979), pp. 25–26. Reprinted by permission of Harper & Row, Publishers, Inc.

SUMMARY

An information systems project may involve many people, with widely varying backgrounds and interests. Communication with all of these individuals and groups must address the specific requirements of each. The systems analyst is responsible for filling these information needs. The systems analyst must identify each audience, its primary interests or motivation, and its information needs. Messages can then be shaped to meet the specific interests, as well as the information needs, of selected individuals or groups.

The communication activities of systems development projects fall into three broad categories: problem solving work sessions; technical reviews or walkthroughs; and reports, both written and oral.

Effective problem solving requires objectivity. This objectivity can best be assured by following a step-by-step problem-solving process. First, state the problem clearly, separating large problems into individual, smaller ones. Then, analyze the problem for its probable cause. Next, identify as many alternatives as possible for eliminating the cause. Then, after all alternatives have been identified, consider the consequences of each. Finally, choose the best alternative.

A walkthrough is a quality review applied to such systems development products as data flow diagrams, program structure charts, pseudocode listings, collections of proposed input documents, collections of proposed output documents, test plans, and others. The purpose of a walkthrough is to identify errors or problems, which are then referred to the responsible developer for analysis and correction.

All members of the review team should receive copies of the product to be reviewed at least one day in advance. The review session itself should be focused, businesslike, and brief—a maximum of 30 minutes or so. Constructive criticism should be encouraged, but personal remarks or arguments are out of place. A walkthrough report should be prepared and delivered to all participants as soon as possible after the review session. A separate management report should state the outcome but omit the detailed list of errors or concerns.

In preparing written reports or oral presentations, it is best to follow an established, step-by-step process. First, collect all relevant information. Next, identify and define the needs of the audience and establish information priorities. Then, prepare the presentation, starting with the item most important to the identified audience and arranging other items in their order of importance. Next, analyze and criticize the content of the message, making sure that the presentation is orderly, logical, and complete. Finally, be sure you have included enough information—but not too much—to meet the specific needs of this audience.

Management summaries are used as a basis for decision making, which is a form of problem solving. Therefore, management summaries are most effective if they follow the basic problem-solving model reviewed earlier. Procedures manuals are documents that direct people in performing manual procedures within a computer-based system. Care should be taken to explain the reasons for following established procedures and the importance of quality information to the organization as a whole.

Training materials should be aimed at teaching people to meet needs and solve problems on the job. With appropriate software, the computer itself can also be used as a training aid.

Oral presentations are often required in connection with project management reviews, status reviews, and acceptance reviews. Wherever possible, oral presentations should be supported by visual aids to help focus the attention of participants. Members of the audience should be encouraged to ask questions and participate actively in the discussion. Identification of your dominant communication style and choosing the most appropriate style for a given situation will enhance your effectiveness as a communicator.

KEY TERMS

1. walkthrough
2. administrator
3. management report
4. procedures manual
5. management summary
6. training manual
7. project management review
8. status review
9. acceptance review
10. blaming

REVIEW/DISCUSSION QUESTIONS

1. Explain the importance of communications in the systems development process? What groups need to communicate effectively if a project is to succeed?
2. List several of the myths of communication. Is it true that people communicate in verbal or written forms only? How else would a person communicate?
3. How can problem solvers help to ensure that they are being objective?
4. Technical reviews are "quality reviews." What documents or processes in the systems development process are reviewed for quality? Who participates in these quality reviews?
5. What are some of the mistakes that can be easily made when conducting a technical walkthrough (review)?
6. Written reports and oral presentations are a vital part of the systems development efforts. What process can be used to organize both types of messages?
7. What are the three basic guidelines to follow in preparing policy or procedure manuals?

8. Distinguish "policies" from "procedures." How are these two things different from one another?
9. Describe the basic purposes of the three types of oral presentations: (1) project management reviews, (2) status reviews, and (3) acceptance reviews.
10. There are four communications styles. Which of these should never be used and why? Why is it important for presenters to vary the communication style they use?

Feasibility Analysis

DETERMINING FEASIBILITY

Something that is *feasible* can be done. There is also an implication of practicality associated with feasibility. A systems development project that is feasible can be done within the budgets and time schedules established by management.

The term **feasibility study** implies some additional meanings:

When a feasibility study is completed, it is assumed that the original problem or need has been understood and that alternative solutions to the basic need or problem have been considered. The feasibility lies in the solution, not in the problem itself.

It is assumed that a feasibility study will encompass at least two, perhaps more, prospective solutions to the stated need or problem. This does not mean that two or more separate systems are designed, then the best one is selected. Rather, it means that several alternatives will be considered before a project focuses on the one that appears best for the situation under study.

A feasibility study should conclude with a clear-cut recommendation. That is, a definite course of action should be proposed. At a minimum, this recommendation will indicate whether the project should be continued or abandoned. Feasibility-study recommendations also establish dollar values for the benefits to be derived from systems development projects. One of the results of the feasibility study will be a projected budget indicating the cost of developing the new system. Thus, the recommendations not only imply that a project is feasible but also indicate the associated cost and potential payback of proceeding with it.

Feasibility Analysis Considerations

Feasibility considerations covered during this activity should include financial feasibility, operational feasibility, technical feasibility, schedule feasibility, and human factors feasibility.

These are presented again in Chapter 19; but in preparation for a discussion of some of the tools and techniques for evaluating feasibility, each type of feasibility is briefly defined.

Financial Feasibility. *Financial feasibility* is the most often used method for evaluating proposed computer information systems. It is sometimes called a cost-benefit analysis. The idea is to determine savings and other benefits that would result from implementation of a new system. These benefits are then compared with costs. If the benefits come out far enough ahead, the decision is positive. If not, there must be other compelling reasons for the development of a new system to be justified. Financial considerations are only one aspect of feasibility, but they are important.

Operational Feasibility. An operational CIS should meet business needs or solve business problems. Therefore, one of the considerations in evaluating the feasibility of a proposed system is whether the organization can gear up to handle the manual processing efficiently. In other words, the question centers on whether the system will work from a people processing—rather than from a computer processing—point of view. This is known as **operational feasibility**.

Any new information system will impact the way in which people perform their jobs. How well a specific CIS matches the people in the user and management group constitutes another view of operational feasibility. Do the work tasks that are now required as a part of the new system comply with the existing job descriptions for the individuals involved? In some cases job descriptions may have to be rewritten. If this is the case, various union personnel or government regulations may have to be consulted for either notification, approval, or compliance.

Another issue concerns how the new CIS will affect or fit in with the existing organizational structure. Information systems often cross organizational boundaries, and therefore they can cause various organizational units to communicate to a greater or lesser extent or in different ways than was the case under the old system. These changes may require changes in the existing organizational structure in order for the new CIS to operate effectively. These are the types of operational feasibility issues that must be investigated before recommending the continuation of any CIS project. In short how will the proposed system affect the workers, their managers, and the organization as a whole?

Technical Feasibility. Considerations of **technical feasibility** center around the existence of computer hardware and software capable of supporting the system being studied. The concern is whether the equipment and software that an organization has, or can justify financially, are capable of processing the proposed application. Although financial considerations are related, this concern is primarily technical.

One frequent reason for the lack of technical feasibility lies in unreasonable suggestions received from users who are not acquainted with the limitations of computers. When people see computers doing complex things, such as sending people to the moon and back or looking for income tax evaders, they get the idea that computers can do almost anything. In particular, since people can read natural language, puzzling out incomplete sentences and fragments of handwriting, they may see this as an easy task for computers.

To deal with such situations, it is extremely important that systems analysts themselves have a background in computer programming. Systems analysts who are not experienced in computer programming may come up with ideas and suggestions that are technically infeasible for computer application. This not only diminishes the credibility of the systems analyst but also wastes time and resources that could be allocated to other, more productive projects.

Schedule Feasibility. The question of **schedule feasibility** arises when a systems development request is accompanied by a specific, possibly inflexible, deadline. The question then becomes: Can the proposed system solution be implemented in the time available?

By the same token, the systems analyst who knows what software really does may find ways to modify and reuse existing software. This can lead to a proposed solution that saves both time and money through the utilization of existing resources rather than the development from scratch of entirely new programs.

The question of schedule feasibility highlights one of the important intangible factors associated with a feasibility study. That is, each of the feasibility considerations may affect others. As a result, tradeoffs may be required in evaluating the feasibility of a new system. In some situations, scheduling or deadlines may not be a factor. However, it always pays to investigate the issue, just to be sure.

Human Factors Feasibility. New or modified computer information systems are vehicles of change. People are, by nature, resistant to change. Thus, there is always a potential for conflict in the development and implementation of a computer information system. For this reason, a feasibility study should evaluate the dimension of **human factors feasibility**. An estimate should be made as to whether the reactions of people to a new system might impede or obstruct its development or implementation. If so, an evaluation should be performed to determine the extent of such obstructions and to devise measures to eliminate or work around them.

It is commonplace, for example, for the implementation of major computer information systems to trigger extensive employee turnover. The classic example is a person who has been doing one job one way for perhaps twenty years. Under a proposed computer information system, the tasks that this person will perform are to be changed significantly. This can create severe trauma, possibly resulting in an inability or unwillingness to perform at all. Other concerns may center on changes in social or work group patterns, changes in management or management style, threats to economic security, and the feeling that the challenge will be removed from the job. Other workers may fear a loss of status or an altered or lost career path. All of these fears are part of human factors feasibility.

Such reasons should be anticipated and plans should be made to allay unfounded fear or concern. In fact, systems have been delayed or not developed at all because of the prospect of human trauma. This type of decision may be a sound one. People who are afraid of or resistant to change may actually, though perhaps unwittingly, work actively to sabotage any system that appears to threaten them.

Evaluating Feasibility

The responsibility of the project team that performs a feasibility study is to make a recommendation to the steering committee. It is important that this responsibility be clearly understood. The project team does not make the feasibility decision. Rather, the project team makes recommendations and lives with decisions made by others, usually the information systems steering committee of the organization.

Identifying Benefits and Costs

Costs and benefits can be either recurring or nonrecurring. Recurring costs and benefits are happening either continuously or periodically during the life of a system. Nonrecurring items happen only once, usually at some point during the life cycle of the project. Most costs and some benefits can be measured in dollars and cents. These quantifiable items are called either *tangible costs* or *tangible benefits*. Certain costs and benefits are difficult or impossible to quantify and so are labeled either *intangible costs* or *intangible benefits*.

Benefits fall into one of two categories. *Performance benefits* include the positive returns directly associated with the implementation of a system. For example, replacing a typewriter with a word processor that increases the productivity of a secretary is a performance benefit. A *cost-avoidance benefit* is achieved when implementation reduces an existing cost. For example, if an organization can decrease its printing costs by 20 percent, it has achieved a cost-avoidance benefit.

Costs can be classified as direct or indirect. **Direct costs** are directly associated with using existing labor and resources to install and integrate a new system into the existing working environment. This would include the costs of hardware, software, programmers, analysts, telecommunications, managers, and anything else that would be required to build the new system. In some form, they would probably be charged against an alternative. **Indirect costs** are costs that cannot be directly associated with the construction of a new information system. For example, in the case of a new word-processing system, operators would need to be trained on the hardware and software. This activity would most likely be identified and charged as an indirect cost. That is, regardless of the alternative—except for maintaining the current operating environment—the operators must be trained.

Regardless of classification, costs may be fixed or variable. A *fixed cost* associated with a system does not change with the volume of production or its use. For example, the funds used to purchase a new printer represents a direct fixed cost whether that machine is used for one hour or twenty-four hours a day.

On the other hand, *variable costs* increase (or decrease) as the organization raises (or lowers) the system's volume of production or use. If the newly acquired printer were not used at all, the affiliated labor cost would be zero. If the machine were used for only one shift, the labor costs would equal the typical wages of the operators supporting it. The cost of labor is variable; as you increase the use of the printer, you experience an increase in the cost of labor. Variable costs may fall with a system's increased production or use; this is common with industrial utility rates, in which more power used results in a lower cost per unit.

A system's **tangible benefits** consist of any advantageous reasons for pursuing a project that can be quantifiably measured. Tangible benefits include more profit, less expense, more customers, less waste, increased performance, and less error.

The tangible benefits of a product are always emphasized during the sales pitch by a vendor representative. In fact, the salesperson usually brings up the tangible benefits first. Unfortunately, the benefits are always a projection. For example, a salesperson may state that XYZ Computer has increased productivity by 90 percent for every one of his customers. But there is no proof that it will increase productivity 90 percent for the organization he is addressing. For this reason, financial and systems analysts are suspicious of marketing statistics.

When conducting an economic feasibility study, the analyst should try to identify all the tangible benefits of each of the project's alternatives. But one cannot quantify any benefit without knowledge. The more information the analyst can amass about the effect of an alternative on the organization, the better the decision concerning the project. To gain all of the necessary information, the analyst should:

■ discuss the alternative with the user. User management is an excellent resource for verifying tangible benefits.

■ conduct the appropriate research. Evaluation of products and services often can be found in many trade journals.

Once all the tangible benefits have been identified, the analyst must then quantify each. The value of the benefit must be realistic. Some benefits are clearcut, for example, removing the old tape drives may save the organization $24,000 annually in maintenance expenses. If the analyst needs to estimate the benefits value, he or she should be conservative. If the analyst is too optimistic, the risk of falling short will be greater.

Intangible benefits are reasons an alternative plan should be implemented: to promote goodwill, a better work environment, or the general welfare of society. These are the benefits that the system will bring to the organization and its affiliates that are often impossible to quantify. Examples of intangible benefits are increased customer satisfaction with the organization, a reduction in overall global pollution, and an increase in employee morale.

Although the intangible benefits are important, they do not make their way into the number-crunching mechanics of financial analysis. If an alternative threatens an existing intangible benefit of the organization, for example, employee morale, it may be immediately rejected as operationally infeasible. If an alternative is marginally attractive financially, the intangible benefits may convince management to adopt the proposal.

Tangible costs for an alternative fall into one of the following categories:

■ **Research and development costs.** These nonrecurring costs are incurred from the preliminary investigation through the post implementation review of a project. When in-house systems are designed, these expenses may be extensive and cannot be ignored.

■ **Hardware costs.** Hardware costs, which are often nonrecurring, represent the initial purchase of a computer and its related peripherals. These costs are usually fixed. It is general practice to use the total cost of the hardware, including delivery, installation, and sales tax if applicable.

■ **Software costs.** Software costs, like hardware costs, are usually nonrecurring fixed costs. They represent the full cost of a purchased product and possibly its installation if it is done by the vendor.

■ **Labor costs.** In most situations, labor is a recurring variable cost, for greater production usually results in increased labor costs. If an alternative is added that actually hastens the correct completion of an activity, labor may actually decrease, becoming a cost-avoidance benefit. When an alternative offers improvement in an individual's performance with no change in labor, the financial strategy used to evaluate the project may convince the analyst to classify the labor issue as an intangible benefit. For example, assume that the introduction of a microcomputer into a secretary's work environment decreases the work load to a more comfortable pace. The computer should lessen the stress on the secretary and, as a result, boost productivity.

■ **Maintenance costs.** Maintenance costs may be either fixed or variable recurring costs. Some project alternatives allow for the purchase of a *service contract* from the vendor. A service contract sets the terms for corrective maintenance at an established fee. The contract may be for a short term or a long term, depending on the negotiations between the organization and the vendor. If it is for a short term (for example, for one year), it may be viewed as a semivariable cost because it will change periodically during the life of the hardware or software. But if a contract is purchased for the entire life of the asset, maintenance costs will be considered fixed. If no maintenance contract is available or an application system is developed in-house, the maintenance of the system will be a variable cost, in which case the organization pays for repairs when a breakdown occurs.

■ **Overhead costs.** Overhead costs are the recurring variable and fixed costs associated with the physical facility that will house the hardware, software, supplies, and labor associated with the project being considered. This includes the fixed cost of the square footage of the building for the physical equipment, office space for the personnel necessary to operate the system, and workstation furniture. Overhead recurring variable costs include air conditioning, heat, and other utility costs necessary to enable the system or application to exist in the organization.

■ **Facility costs.** Facility costs are nonrecurring startup costs. These fixed costs include wiring, new floors, antistatic carpeting, cubicles, air conditioning installation, and security and fire protection equipment.

■ **Operational costs.** Operating costs are associated with the day-to-day operations of the system or application. These are often variable costs such as the operators' wages, paper, media, and office supplies.

Intangible costs may be viewed as the opposite of intangible benefits, the only similarity being that they, too, cannot be quantified. These costs include loss of customer base, operational slowdowns, and degradations in the workplace.

TECHNIQUES FOR EVALUATING FINANCIAL FEASIBILITY

Several techniques can be used to evaluate the financial feasibility of a system. The most common technique is cost-benefit analysis. Other techniques include payback analysis, return on total assets, net present value, and breakeven analysis.

Cost-Benefit Analysis

The purpose of **cost-benefit analysis** in a feasibility study is to summarize the relevant costs and benefits of the proposed project in sufficient detail to permit management to decide whether to proceed any further with the project. Costs and benefits can be both tangible and intangible.

In the feasibility study, many of the estimates are probable ranges of costs and benefits. Management should not expect precise estimates at this stage because there is still much that is not yet known about the costs of installing and operating a proposed system. Each additional phase of the development allows a more accurate cost-benefit analysis as more detail is gathered. Estimating has been likened to "trying to guess what the core of an onion will look like as you peel off its outside layers." The various types of development and operating costs are depicted in Figures 10-1 and 10-2.

The general format of a cost-benefit analysis is illustrated in Figure 10-3. The following information is needed before the analysis can be prepared:

- An estimate of the cost of operating the current system.
- An estimate of the cost of operating the proposed system.
- An estimate of costs for subsequent phases of the development project.
- A description of intangible benefits.
- A basis for estimating how the above costs and benefits will change over the next few years (e.g., assumptions regarding volume increases, inflation).
- An identification of the risk associated with either doing or not doing the project.

Different organizational units should assume primary responsibility for the various components of the cost-benefit analysis under the overall coordination of the project team leader.

Economic analyses prepared at the completion of the design phase are much more comprehensive than this analysis, though the format is essentially the same. The following characteristics apply to feasibility study cost-benefit analyses:

- **State the cost-benefit analysis conservatively.** In subsequent stages of the systems development life cycle, experience has shown that the costs of installing and operating a new system tend to exceed the estimates made in feasibility studies while realized benefits tend to be less than those estimated. The project team should present ranges of probable costs and benefits. One technique is to assign the user responsibility for estimating savings and benefits from the installation of the new system and be sure that this responsibility is noted in the feasibility study document. When users are made aware that they will subsequently be held accountable for achieving savings or benefits, they will tend toward conservative estimates. The IS department should be responsible for estimating the cost of developing the system and of the information technology to be used when the system is in operation.

Figure 10.1. Typical development cost elements.

Personnel
  Analysts
    Interviewing
    Preparation of reports
    Documentation
    Contemplation
    Preparation of procedures
    System test
    Inspections, walkthroughs
    Training—operators
    Training—clerical people
    Consultations—users
    Consultations—pilot operation
    Supervision—file conversion
    Forms design
    Formal presentations

  Programmers
    Coding
    Documentation
    Debug
    Inspections, walkthroughs
    Customizing purchased programs
    Consultations—analyst
    Consultations—programmers
    Formal presentations

  Operators
    Conversion
    Training
    Programmer support
    Consultations—analyst

  Clerical personnel
    Conversion
    Training
    Consultations—analysts

  Management
    Supervision
    Consultation—analyst

  Other
    Data entry
    Art—forms design
    Technical writer—documentation

Equipment
  Capital expenditures
    New equipment
    Packaged software
  Equipment installation
  Equipment test and debug
  Existing equipment use
    Test and debug time
    Disk space
    Tapes
    Other supplies
  File conversion
  System test

Materials and Supplies
  Publication of procedures
  Paper, forms, cards
  Preparation—new forms
  Copies

Overhead
  Management support
  Secretarial support
  Heat, light, space

External
  Consulting fees
  Special training

■ One risk of trying to be conservative in a cost-benefit analysis is that users and IS departments may be so conservative that nothing gets done. The executive steering committee must make sure that this does not occur.

Figure 10.2.   Typical operating cost elements.

Personnel
    Operator support
    Clerical support
    Programmers—maintenance
    Direct management support

Hardware
    Computer residency time
    Main memory space
    I/O operations
    Secondary storage space
    Maintenance

External
    Leases
    Rentals
    Subcontracting
    Auditing

Materials and Supplies
    Forms
    Paper, forms, cards
    Tapes
    Disk packs
    Scrap
    Inventory carrying cost

Overhead
    Management support
    Secretarial support
    Heat, light, space

Periodic reviews by qualified outsiders, for example, will give the steering committee assurance that internal estimates are in line.

■ **Make assumptions for financial projections.** Feasibility study cost-benefit analyses require that certain assumptions be made about the behavior of future costs and activities. Assumptions can be made about inflation, interest rates, volume increases, wage increases, and the like. In most organizations, similar assumptions are made as a routine matter in medium- and long-range financial plans. The project team's best strategy is to use the same assumptions in its cost-benefit analysis as those used in an organization's financial plans. Thus, assumptions in the cost-benefit analysis will be consistent with the other financial projections that members of the executive steering committee review when they carry out their other responsibilities.

■ **Assess the elements of project risk.** Some proposed projects are inherently more risky than others. Risky projects are likely to exceed their estimated costs of installation and operation; they may take much longer to install than predicted; the technology suggested may not be appropriate or work effectively; users may not accept the system once it has been installed; and business operations may be disrupted. Such a list could go on and on, and unfortunately, many real-life examples could be furnished for each item on the list. Often, IS professionals in particular are aware that a proposed

Figure 10.3.   Preliminary Cost-Benefit Analysis.

ABC INVENTORY SYSTEM
COST-BENEFIT ANALYSIS

Estimated initial cost of new computer system
Cost of site preparation $10,000
Analysis and programming of basic
applications 25,000
Cost of training, file conversion, parallel
operations, etc. 8,000

Total one-time costs $43,000

Estimated annual operating costs
Computer and related equipment lease or
amortization and maintenance $12,500
Software lease 2,500
Analysts and programmers 8,500
Operating personnel 4,000
Space charges, supplies, power, etc. 4,000
Total operating costs $31,500

Annual savings (displaced costs plus value
of operation efficiencies) $82,000

Net annual savings
(annual savings less annual operating $50,500
costs)

Other intangible benefits (list)
1. Higher employee morale
2. Better customer service

project carries a higher-than-normal degree of risk but have not found a way to convey that awareness to the executive steering committee at the feasibility study stage.

F. Warren McFarlan developed a framework for assessing **project risk** that consists of three components:

1. The familiarity of the company with the technology proposed for the project.
2. The project "structure," i.e., the extent to which user requirements are known at the outset.
3. The size of the project relative to those normally undertaken.

Figure 10-4 illustrates the way these three factors can relate to create an overall project risk profile. McFarlan also discusses techniques for managing projects with differing risk profiles. Project risk is an important concept to consider in the feasibility analysis, not only because it can be an important element in evaluating whether to proceed but also because it puts the executive steering committee on notice that this particular project will require close scrutiny as it goes forward.

The concept of project risk also applies to a group of projects. As pointed out by McFarlan, a group of systems development projects can be examined for their collective risk when all the projects are considered at one time.

Figure 10.4. **Project implementation risk.**

	High Structure	Low Structure
Low Company-Relative Technology	Large size— low risk	Large size— low risk (very susceptible to mismanagement)
	Small size— very low risk	Small size— very low risk (very susceptible to mismanagement)
High Company-Relative Technology	Large size— medium risk	Large size— very high risk
	Small size— medium-low risk	Small size— high risk

Source: Cash, J., McFarlan, F., and McKenney, J. *Corporate Information Systems Management: The Issues Facing Senior Executives*, 2nd Edition (Homewood, Ill.: Richard D. Irwin, 1988), p. 165.

Return on Total Assets

This profitability measure looks at the amount of resources needed by the firm to support its operations. **Return on total assets (ROTA),** which reveals the effectiveness of management in generating profits from the assets it has available, is perhaps the single most important measure of return: When applied to a proposed information system, it is computed as follows:

$$\text{ROTA} = \frac{\text{Net income from the project}}{\text{Total assets invested in the project}}$$

$$\text{for example: } \frac{\$18,005}{\$338,620} = 5.3\%$$

Because both the net return from the project (net profit margin) and asset productivity (total asset turnover) are embedded in ROTA, it provides a clear picture of a company's managerial effectiveness and the overall profitability of its resource allocation and investment decisions. In the example above, the company earned 5.3 percent on its asset investment of $338,620.

A **required rate of return** is the percentage rate that an investment must earn in order to be financially attractive. For example, if temporary investments yield 9 percent, an organization may fix its required rate of return at this amount. If this is the case, a project alternative must show a return of 9 percent or more to be considered financially rewarding. From a strictly financial point of view, if a system alternative yields less than 9 percent, there is no need for the organization to undertake the project. The project will fall below the required rate of return, and financial advisers would recommend that the company invest its money in other areas.

Payback Analysis

Payback analysis is a simple way to assess whether a business should invest in a proposed information system on the basis of how long it will take for the benefits of the system to pay back the costs of developing it. The analyst computes the **payback period** by dividing the cost to develop by the average annual savings that are the result of the new system:

$$\text{Payback} = \frac{\text{Original investment (cost to develop)}}{\text{Average annual return on investment}}$$

For example, assume a new system costs $75,000 to develop and the resulting average annual operational benefits (savings) are $20,000. The payback would be 75,000/20,000 or 3.75 years.

Since this is a popular way to assess alternative investments, businesses typically have a set time period for payback assessments (three years, for example). This is something you can find out from the accounting personnel within your firm.

The previous example was simplified to introduce the concept of payback analysis. It is more typical for the investment (cost to develop) to be spread across two or more years. Operational savings also usually vary from year to year over the life of a system. Figure 10-5 shows a more typical application of payback analysis. Note the cumulative costs and cumulative benefit columns. The payback period is the last year that cumulative costs exceed cumulative benefits plus the cumulative costs/cumulative benefits proportion of the year in which cumulative benefits exceed cumulative costs. The system illustrated in Figure 10-5 has a payback of 4.95 years.

If the proposed system has a projected payback of six years in a company that adheres to a three-year maximum payback on projects involving fast-changing technology, the project will be rejected.

Net Present Value

A limitation of the payback analysis is that it does not consider the time value of money (NPV). For example, assume that investment alternatives A and B both have initial costs of $100,000 and ten-year lives. Analysis of investment proposal A shows that it would have a zero cash flow (benefits or savings minus costs) for Years 1 through 3 and a $50,000 cash flow for Years 4 through 10, resulting in an average annual net savings of $35,000 ($7 \times 50,000 \div 10$). The payback period would be 2.86 years. Analysis of investment proposal B shows an even cash flow of $35,000 over the ten years. The payback for Proposal B would also yield a payback period of 2.86 years; but because of the timing of the payments, the two alternatives are not identical at all.

In Figure 10-6, system costs total $120,000 over four years and benefits total $180,000. Therefore, we might conclude that benefits outweigh the costs. However, benefits only started to surpass costs after the second year, and dollars in the fourth year will not be equivalent to dollars in year one.

Figure 10.5. An example of payback analysis.

Year	Costs	Cumulative Costs	Benefits	Cumulative Benefits
0	48,000	48,000	0	0
1	5,000	53,000	20,000	20,000
2	5,000	58,000	20,000	40,000
3	6,000	64,000	14,000	54,000
4	6,000	70,000	14,000	68,000
5	8,000	78,000	14,000	82,000
6	10,000	88,000	14,000	96,000
7	10,000	98,000	14,000	110,000
8	10,000	108,000	14,000	124,000

$$\text{Payback period} = 4 + \frac{78,000}{82,000}$$

$$\text{Payback period} = 4 + .95$$

(cumulative benefits exceed cumulative costs between years 4 and 5)

For instance, a dollar invested at 9 percent today will be worth $1.09 at the end of the year and will double in approximately eight years. The present value, therefore, is the cost or benefit measured in today's dollars and depends on the cost of money. The cost of money is the opportunity cost, or the rate that could be obtained if the money invested in the proposed system were invested in another (relatively safe) project.

The present value of $1.00 at a discount rate of i is calculated by determining the factor:

$$\frac{1}{(1+i)^n}$$

where n is the number of periods. Then the factor is multiplied by the dollar amount yielding present value as shown in Figure 10-6. In this case the cost of money (i.e., discount rate) is assumed to be .10 (10 percent) for the planning horizon. Present value multipliers are calculated for each period: $n=1$, $n=2$, ... $n=4$. The present value of both costs and benefits can then be compared to determine the comparable dollars. A net present value must be calculated for each project alternative that appears feasible. The one that yields the highest net present value will be the most cost effective.

Figure 10.6. *Tables showing net present value analysis.*

ABC Inventory System (without considering present value)					
	Year				
	1	2	3	4	Total
Costs	40,000	40,000	20,000	20,000	120,000
Benefits	30,000	50,000	50,000	50,000	180,000

ABC Inventory System (considering present value and a discount rate of .10)					
	Year				
	1	2	3	4	Total
Costs	40,000	40,000	20,000	20,000	
Multiplier	.91	.82	.75	.68	
Value of costs	36,400	32,800	15,000	13,600	97,000
Benefits	30,000	50,000	50,000	50,000	
Multiplier	.91	.82	.75	.68	
Value of benefits	27,300	41,000	37,500	34,000	139,800

Break-Even Analysis

By comparing costs alone, break-even analysis allows the systems analyst to determine the break-even capacity of the proposed information system. The point at which total costs of the current system and those of the proposed system intersect represents the **break-even point**, where it becomes profitable for the business to get the new information system.

Total costs include the costs that recur during operation of the system plus the developmental costs that occur only once (e.g., one-time costs of installing a new system)—that is, the tangible costs that were just discussed. Figure 10-7 is an example of break-even analysis on a hardware store that maintains its inventory using a manual system. As volume rises, the costs of the manual system rise at an increasing rate. A new computer system would cost a substantial sum up front, but the incremental costs for higher volumes would be rather small.

Figure 10.7. Break-even analysis for the proposed automated inventory system.

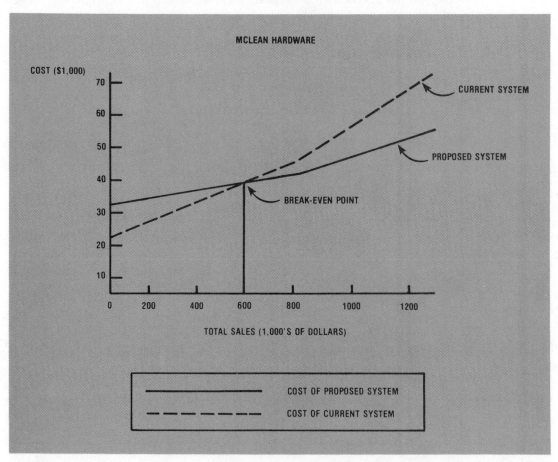

Part 3   Systems Analysis: General Tools and Techniques

TECHNIQUES FOR ASSESSING SCHEDULE FEASIBILITY

To determine if the project can be completed within a given time frame, two key factors must be determined. First an estimate must be made of the resources and time necessary to complete the project on schedule. Estimating the resources was also a part of the cost-benefit analysis technique. Second, these needs must be compared to the available resources, primarily personnel and equipment. This comparison will determine the feasibility of meeting any given schedule.

The resources available for any given project are a function of the quantity and types of resources the organization has available and the proportion of these resources that are now available or will become available to be used in constructing this system. Resources should never be pulled from an existing project to start a new one, although this is a management decision and often out of the control of the project team actually doing the work. Every MIS group should already have an inventory of existing resources. Various resource categories are presented in Figure 10-1. In some cases adding additional personnel to a systems development project can speed up the process of completing the system. Programming and systems design activities, however, are only partially divisible tasks. This means that doubling the number of programmers on a task will not mean that the task will be completed in half the time. The reason is that the necessary communication that must take place to allow the new project team members to be productive and contribute takes time. Frederick Brooks, a leader in the computer science field even went further when he stated, "Adding additional people to a late software development project makes it later." His theory is that to educate additional project team members and communicate the necessary information to them would actually require more time than would be gained by having a larger project team.

TECHNIQUES FOR ASSESSING HUMAN FACTORS, TECHNICAL, AND OPERATIONAL FEASIBILITY

Interviews, observation, and questionnaires are the three techniques that can be used to assess the human factors feasibility of the new system. Questionnaires can be particularly effective because they can maintain the anonymity of the respondent. They also can provide feedback from a larger and more diverse group of potential users. These techniques are discussed in detail in Chapter 8.

Technical feasibility is again assessed by comparing the company's technical resources (i.e., people, skills, equipment) to the technical requirements of the proposed system. If the company does not possess the necessary technical resources and the steering committee still wants to pursue development, management must be prepared to acquire the resources outside the organization. This may mean using outside consultant organizations or purchasing the necessary hardware and software, and possibly hiring new employees.

Operational feasibility is also assessed primarily via interviews, questionnaires, observation, and in some cases statistical measurement. The only way to find out if the organization can accommodate the manual processing required in the new system is to observe the existing manual procedures and talk to the people performing them. Once the new systems procedures have been determined, it will be the individuals who will actually perform the work and their supervisors who can best assess the operational feasibility of the new system.

FUNCTION-POINT METRICS AND PROJECT ESTIMATING

Estimating the time and personnel required to develop an information system is a difficult job. Historically, most estimating approaches have been bottom-up: attempt to construct a task-level work plan, estimate the time required for each task, and sum the estimated hours.

Bottom-up estimating techniques work reasonably well for four- to six-week windows. Beyond that, a work plan is hard to predict. Standard task lists can be used, but later tasks are heavily dependent on the results of near-term tasks. Phase estimates on large projects can be highly variable, and estimates covering multiple phases are nearly worthless.

There is a great deal of interest in devising top-down techniques that can derive estimates based on external characteristics of the system to be developed and an evaluation of the soft characteristics of the development environment—the skill of the people, the automated tools available, and the internal political characteristics of the organization.

The concept of function points, developed by A. J. Albrecht at IBM in the late 1970s, is beginning to have some impact on this problem. Albrecht created an abstract metric based on five external characteristics of a system: its files, outputs, inputs, queries, and interfaces with other systems. Each characteristic had a relative weighting factor (see figure below). Albrecht also allowed each

Feature figure. **Sample function point calculation for a system.**

Item	Number	× Weight	= Total
Files	5	10	50
Outputs	15	5	75
Inputs	7	4	28
Queries	10	4	40
Interfaces	3	7	21
		Total Function Points	214

amount to be increased or decreased by up to 25 percent to account for relative complexity.

The total of function points associated with a system is merely an abstract number; but research has shown this number to be a relatively stable predictor of development effort—all other things being equal. Thus, over time, metrics could be established by an organization to measure, on the average, the number of development hours required to produce a function point. This begins to provide a base for top-down estimating.

Of course, the problem is that all things are never equal. The soft characteristics of the development environment create high degrees of variability in estimates. Eventually, there will be expert systems capable of combining function point type metrics with environment characteristics to produce reasonably accurate top-down estimates of development time.

SUMMARY

Feasibility means that a project is possible, practical, and realistic. Factors to be considered in evaluating feasibility are financial, operational, technical, scheduling, and human.

Completion of a feasibility study means that the original problem or need has been understood, alternative solutions have been considered, and the best one has been recommended for evaluation. A feasibility study should conclude with a clearcut recommendation as to whether the new system should be developed, along with a projected budget for the systems development project.

An evaluation of financial feasibility results in a cost-benefit analysis, weighing projected benefits against the costs of developing and operating the new system. As with any other capital investment, development of an information system must be justified in terms of its projected payback period and its return.

Operational feasibility involves the question of whether the organization can gear up to handle the manual processing involved in a given systems operation efficiently.

Technical feasibility involves the availability of computer hardware and software capable of supporting the proposed system. A related concern is whether the equipment and software that an organization has, or can justify financially, are capable of processing the proposed application. A third related issue concerns the technical competency of the proposed project team.

The question of schedule feasibility arises when a systems development request is accompanied by a specific, possibly inflexible, deadline. If the proposed system solution cannot be implemented in the time available, alternative solutions may need to be considered.

An evaluation of human factors feasibility involves estimating the reactions of people within the organization who might impede or obstruct development or implementation of the new system. Human factors considerations may be important in the planning process and even in the decision about whether to proceed with development.

Evaluating the feasibility of a proposed system can be a complex job, depending on the factors involved. A major complication can be the need to establish values for intangible benefits.

The principal end-products of the feasibility analysis are a feasibility report to the steering committee, a project plan to be implemented if the steering committee authorizes continuation of the project, and a preliminary set of working papers for the next phase of the project.

Benefits can be classified as performance benefits, which are the positive returns directly associated with the implementation of a system; cost-avoidance benefits, which reduce an existing cost; tangible benefits, which are quantifiable; and intangible benefits, which are not measurable in absolute quantifiable terms. A tangible benefit might be the maintenance costs that would be saved if the new CIS employed a smaller, more reliable, but just as powerful piece of hardware. Old hardware often costs more to maintain then state-of-the-art hardware. Intangible benefits would include such items as promoting the general welfare of society and increased employee morale.

Several techniques for evaluating financial feasibility are discussed in this chapter including cost-benefit analysis, payback analysis, return on total assets, net present value, and break-even analysis. In cost-benefit analysis, the relevant costs and benefits of the proposed project are detailed so that management can decide whether to proceed any further with the project. Payback analysis is used to determine how long it will take for the benefits of the system to pay back the costs of developing it.

Return on total assets is a ratio which relates the net income from a project to the total assets invested in that project. Net present value analysis helps the systems analyst to present management with the time value of the investment in the information system as well as the funds flow, which is available through payback analysis. Break-even analysis can be used to relate the total costs for the new systems development and operation to the total cost of operating the existing system. The break-even point is the level at which it becomes profitable for the business to develop the new information system.

Costs and benefits can be either recurring or nonrecurring. Recurring costs and benefits happen either continuously or periodically while nonrecurring items happen only once. Costs can also be classified as direct, which means they can be tied to the development and installation of a new CIS, or indirect, which means that they will be incurred regardless of the system alternative chosen. A third method for classifying costs is to determine whether they are fixed or variable. Fixed costs do not change with the volume of production or usage of the CIS while variable costs increase (or decrease) as the usage of the system changes. Several techniques for addressing schedule, human factors, technical, and operational feasibility are also briefly presented in this chapter.

KEY TERMS

1. feasibility study
2. cost-benefit analysis
3. operational feasibility
4. technical feasibility
5. schedule feasibility
6. human factors feasibility
7. cash flow
8. direct costs
9. indirect costs
10. tangible benefits
11. intangible benefits
12. project risk
13. return on total assets
14. required rate of return
15. payback period
16. break-even point

REVIEW/DISCUSSION QUESTIONS

1. Why is it important for a systems analyst to know the fundamentals of cost-benefit analysis?
2. What is the difference between a tangible benefit and an intangible benefit?
3. List the four kinds of tangible development costs.
4. What is a required rate of return? Is it the same for every organization? Explain your answer and provide an example.
5. Define opportunity cost and give an example.
6. The original investment in PCs will be $25,000 and will give the organization an average annual return of $2,400. What is its payback period?
7. What is the purpose of break-even analysis? What is the break-even point?
8. Define schedule feasibility and human factors feasibility.
9. What is the difference between cash flow and payback period?
10. Project risk is a function of a number of different variables. Discuss these factors.

PART 4

Systems Architecture: Bridging the Gap between Analysis and Design

During the analysis portions of a systems development project, emphasis is almost entirely upon the business objectives and specific requirements of the application being developed, in other words, the logical system model. Accordingly, the activities of analysis are nontechnical in nature as implementation details are purposefully avoided. The analysis activities define "what" the system is to accomplish; the design activities must define "how" the system is to accomplish its mission.

In practice, the boundary between analysis and design is not distinct. Concerns about the system's physical configuration cannot completely be ignored during analysis. Likewise, design efforts and physical constraints may lead to necessary changes in the system's original requirements. Also, many of the activities of design are simply continuations and expansions of analysis work at a much greater level of detail.

As the project life cycle moves from analysis to design the activities performed necessarily become much more technical. The realities of the physical or technical environment have to be faced. These factors may force design accommodations to the existing hardware and software within the organization.

The physical or technical environment, the system architecture, may permit — or even require — the introduction of new technologies, including hardware such as microcomputers, laser printers, or graphics terminals or software such as office automation, data base management, or data communication systems. The overall configuration of these components will be known as the system architecture. The capabilities within any given computer installation may represent either new opportunities or unforeseen constraints in the development of designs to implement user specifications. The challenge in design is to configure a technical architecture and computing solutions that accurately reflect the user functional and data views but can be delivered on time given current system physical constraints and installed within reasonable budgets.

More specifically, the overall system architecture will include computing processors and data communication systems, database management systems, and applications software systems. The blueprint for this architecture is accomplished as a transitional activity between analysis and design.

Generally, technical support specialists will assist analysts and designers in developing the technical architecture. Particularly the areas of processors, operating systems, and data communications require technical specialists to insure adequate system capabilities for proposed software designs. Also, the systems analyst needs a basic understanding of the central issues of the centralization versus distribution of data processing components but does not necessarily need the technical expertise for implementing this distribution. The data base and application design components of the overall technical architecture, while also requiring specialized expertise, usually require more attention by system analysts.

From this perspective, Chapter 11 includes a discussion, in general terms, of computing processors, data communications, and the issue of centralization. Chapters 12 and 13 include a discussion, in greater detail, of database and applications software design, respectively.

Developing the Physical Environment: The Technical Architecture

---

Learning Objectives

On completing reading and other learning assignments for this chapter, you should be able to:

- Explain the evaluation sequence and methods applied in matching new system requirements to existing technical capabilities.
- Describe design alternatives for data capture, input, storage, processing throughput, and output.
- Explain the basic functional differences between mainframes, minicomputers, and microcomputers.
- Describe concerns in designing data communication capabilities for individual applications.
- Explain how systems may be centralized or decentralized and the design considerations inherent in the degree of distribution.
- Give hardware and system software considerations associated with different levels of distribution.

MATCHING THE LOGICAL REQUIREMENTS TO THE PHYSICAL DESIGN

During systems analysis, quantitative data are gathered about transaction volumes, file sizes, response times, expected growth, and processing volumes for the new system. Analysis may apply rigor to accumulating these data. However, until actual design begins, little is done about matching these requirements with the realities of existing capabilities.

In other words, as systems design is begun, evaluations must be made to determine where and how a new system can fit into the organization's overall processing environment. The normal data processing cycle can provide a structure for matching the requirements of individual systems with the data and throughput capacities of the environment in which it will exist. The evaluation sequence can run the following course (see Figure 11-1):

- Data capture.
- Storage.
- Processing throughput.
- Output.

Figure 11.1. Design evaluation sequence.

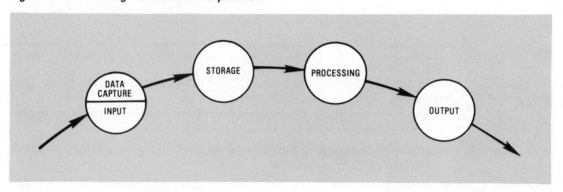

Data Capture

There is little that a designer involved with an individual systems development project may be able to do to impact decisions about the makes or models of the installation's mainframe computer(s) or communications backbone. However, selection of data capture and entry devices can be expected to fall within the decision responsibilities of an individual project team.

Data capture refers to the initial recording of data and their subsequent entry into a machine readable format. Data may or may not be captured in paper form. Once entered, however, the data will be captured on an electronic medium.

There was a time when systems designers assumed routinely that source data would be captured on source documents and that some transcription step would be necessary for data entry. This assumption is no longer true. Today, data capture can be regarded as a frontier for innovation in the design of computer information systems. For example, many supermarkets have installed scanners at checkout counters to read the universal product code on each item's packaging. Key entry at the cash register terminal by the checker is reduced greatly but not eliminated completely. This innovation speeds up the checking process and reduces errors.

Data capture has become more customized through the technological advances of recent years. Once data entry meant transmitting captured data to a central point for reading into a computer system on high-speed devices. Today, the rule is that users should control and operate the entry function as close to the point where data capture takes place as possible, unless there is a compelling reason to do otherwise.

Local control of the data capture and entry functions is a clearcut trend. Statistics gathered by the U.S. Department of Labor, for example, show data entry operators as the only job category within the data processing field for which diminishing demand is anticipated. It makes sense, given today's technologies and continuing improvements expected in the future, to incorporate the capture and entry functions within single transactions rather than to require separate, centralized data entry functions that are costly, time consuming, and error prone.

One compelling reason for placing the capture and entry functions within the user group is that responsibility accompanies performance. That is, users who handle their own entry also are responsible for verifying the accuracy and reliability of the data they enter. By controlling the quality of data entry, users also help to assure the quality of results they will receive. If all other things were equal, quality assurance alone would be enough to justify decentralization of data entry.

Also, given the low cost and efficiencies of microprocessor-based captive and entry devices, substantial savings usually can accrue from decentralization of data entry.

Today data capturing equipment is small enough and inexpensive enough that almost any business-related application can support individual selection of equipment in this area. In the era of microprocessors, this opportunity means that the systems designer can have a profound impact upon system capabilities through selection of locally installed devices used for data capture and possibly also for direct input to and receipt of output from a system.

Storage

Many alternatives also exist today in the area of data storage. Data are among an organization's most valuable and volatile resources. To be useful to the organization, data must be stored in structures and formats that are planned, predictable, controllable, and readily available. Data resources must be carefully safeguarded to assure continuing availability and integrity. Further, there must be compatibility of data resources throughout an organization.

Therefore, in the data storage area, the challenge lies in, first, identifying existing resources that can be of value to a new application and, second, making sure that the new data elements developed in support of the new application are compatible with the organization's overall database. Remember, data structures emulate the organization they support. Constraint and discipline are essential in planning for and maintaining data resources.

Processing Throughput

Processing throughput refers to the overall workload of the computing processor. That is, what processing "power" is needed in order to transform system inputs into outputs.

The systems designer, working with technical specialists, must develop an understanding of the current and planned computer installation and be responsible for accommodating the new system to it. The application under development will become, in effect, a customer of the processing facility. As a representative of the customer organization that will use these services, the systems designer is responsible for making the best deal possible for his or her own application. To do this, the systems designer must be able to present, factually and intelligently, the processing requirements of the individual application to members of the technical staff who will be responsible for developing support services.

Since the system under development is likely to be a replacement, it is natural to compare its processing throughput requirements with the current ones. The objectives will be to determine the impact of the new system upon the current system architecture. Specific types of information that should be reviewed with the technical and operations personnel would include activity volumes, pattern of activity, processing time per activity, mix of processing activities, and on-line response time.

Activity Volumes. The number of transactions for both on-line and batch processing and the frequency of processing, especially of batch jobs, will affect resource requirements directly. Volumes should include highs, lows, and averages. An increase in the volume usually will accompany the new system.

Pattern of Activity. Volumes alone do not tell the entire story. The pattern of activity will identify peak and lull times. This measure is important for determining the maximum times needed for resource support. In addition, it indicates lull times during which unneeded resources may be shared. For all subsystems, the activity patterns should specify seasonal trends (such as holiday sales) and calendar trends (such as heavy end-of-fiscal-year reporting). For on-line systems, the pattern of transactions throughout the day should be specified.

Processing Time per Activity. Certainly, the longer it takes to complete a processing activity, the fewer such activities can be completed within a given period of time and with a given processing resource. This fact applies to both on-line transactions and batch job streams. Various components must be included in determining the processing time of an activity. These timings include CPU processing, data transfer to and from storage devices, printing or other output, and data transfer across communication lines. Terminal operators' response and fatigue factors also should be addressed.

Mix of Processing Activities. Because a system's processing will comprise a mix of different activities, the use of resources will vary, depending on that mix. For example, processing the company payroll may need to be done at the same time as the processing of accounts receivable. These systems may be executed on the same processor and thus compete for storage and throughput. If both have similar priorities and time schedules, storage and throughput must be sufficient to accommodate them.

On-Line Response Time. Although related to all of the above, performance of an on-line subsystem, and terminal response times in particular, are important enough to be highlighted. The timeliness of computer feedback at a terminal, in response to an operator striking the <ENTER> key, will impact, in turn, the performance and productivity of the user. The level of acceptable and desired response times will vary. A range usually is specified. Tradeoffs weigh heavily here in the design of the technical configuration, including CPU memory sizes, disk access speeds, and data communication transfer rates.

These factors are major considerations in evaluating designs for processing throughput capacities. Although interwoven tightly, they can be combined to determine minimum and maximum impact on the installation.

Output

New output options also are emerging. Traditionally, the predominant output method was to create either an inquiry file or voluminous documents at a central location and provide results as needed through on-line or physical delivery.

Today, although centrally printed reports or standard terminal displays still may be at the heart of system outputs, there are other options. In a three-campus student records system, for example, a remote facility might maintain files for its own class schedules, combining this information with course descriptions from a central source. Individual departments or faculty members may have their own microcomputers connected to remote minicomputers. The central computer would remain a universal resource, but each faculty or staff member also might have the ability to tailor the delivery of outputs to specific needs. That is, users of such a system would not be limited to a standard menu of inquiries or to fixed content in reports. Rather, the capability exists to tailor outputs to individual needs.

In many instances, the same microcomputers or intelligent terminals that make it possible to control inputs remotely also can format and generate tailored outputs. For example, an investment of just a few hundred dollars will add a printer to virtually any microcomputer. For this relatively small sum, a user is able to document individual inquiries or to be selective about the data to be incorporated into a report. It usually is preferable to allow creation of selective reports remotely instead of requiring users to wade through large volumes of paper distributed universally.

Other options include the ability to accept and manipulate data at local terminals, to use graphic outputs, to incorporate data into a word-processing document, to synthesize data and produce audio outputs, or even to install devices that create documents in a variety of typefaces.

To summarize, the systems designer no longer should feel constrained to the limitations of report or screen layout forms. Rather, the context of user operations can be matched closely with available, affordable output operations that already exist and are proliferating rapidly.

In general, computer processing equipment and related system software can range from large mainframes to minicomputers, microcomputers, and dependent terminals. Recent technological innovation has blurred the absolute distinction among these devices. In fact, an argument can be made that the distinction between these devices is more one of control, access, and specialization than of processing capabilities. Systems and application software will drive these processors to deliver the computing solutions required by the user areas. These differing types of processors may need to be interconnected in varying manners to support user applications and requirements and to share data files. Data communication systems must be utilized to combine processing units into functional and strategic networks.

For each type of configuration, the system must have an appropriate design. Individual applications may use a full range of equipment, from mainframes to microcomputers, connected with sophisticated communication and networking apparatus and supported by a variety of application and operating software. They may therefore require programs and procedures to deal with all of these.

Processors

Mainframe Considerations. **Mainframes** reflect functions at the highest level of the corporate entity. Processing options and data available on mainframes may be shared organization wide.

Processing to be done on a large mainframe assumes extremely short cycle times. Cycle time refers to the speed with which input is transformed into output. Also, large throughput capabilities and the availability of technical experts and mass storage are required to support processing. Also assumed is system software with extensive utilities and multi-tasking capabilities. A large mainframe system can be assumed to have both batch and on-line capabilities. There usually are large batch applications to justify the kinds of processing power delivered by such equipment. However, many large processors exist just to deliver on-line applications.

With mainframes the emphasis is on high-volume productivity. The designer has to anticipate and avoid situations that can cause program execution to abort entirely. Rather, the idea is to plan for and deal with exceptions before they occur, making provision within programs for noting exceptions for later resolution without interrupting the main flow of processing. As units of processing equipment get smaller, systems become increasingly dependent upon human intervention. The smaller and less sophisticated a hardware device becomes, the greater the provision that has to be made for manual procedures covering recognition and resolution of exception situations or problems. On a mainframe, it is possible to have literally millions of transactions processed without involving people in resolution of exceptions. Exceptions may not even surface until the end of a business day or possibly the end of a week. On a microcomputer, by contrast, each exception may need a human response.

The system software supporting a large mainframe will be structured to implement some sort of priority scheme. A mainframe installation typically serves many departments of an organization and may, at any given time, be processing dozens of different applications. Potentially hundreds of terminal devices, including microcomputers, may be attached to and operating from a mainframe at any given time.

Usually, a modern mainframe installation will be isolated from users through physical security measures. Hardware devices will be in enclosed rooms accessible only through locked doors. Individual equipment units may be in locked enclosures of their own. For example, many installations keep the central processor separate from file peripherals and printers. If there is a centralized data entry facility, it is segregated from all of the other equipment components.

A processing center built around a large mainframe can be regarded as an information factory. The designer must recognize that users and operators associated with any given application will have little impact upon the processing or scheduling of jobs in such an environment. Because production delays are costly, the heavy volume makes it vital that programs anticipate and incorporate recovery capabilities for every imaginable contingency. In some critical applications, duplicate or redundant CPUs may be used to insure nonstop processing with automatic cutover, or switching, from one host to another, if one processor fails.

Minicomputer Considerations. **Minicomputers** typically are maintained, utilized, and controlled within a department or business area of the enterprise. Most minicomputers are designed specifically for use in an interactive environment. Many of the minicomputers now being offered are larger and more powerful than the largest mainframe of a decade ago. Therefore, many of the large minicomputer systems have, essentially, all of the processing capabilities of mainframes. That is, even though minicomputers may be installed largely for interactive use, they probably will be capable of handling batch jobs as background work with considerable efficiency.

The minicomputer fits a wide range of business environments, from the first-time user who needs a system with expansion room to the large, sophisticated user who employs minicomputers in an extensive communication network. Today's minicomputer can serve quite adequately as the sole host for centralized processing systems in small- to medium-sized corporations. Although a minicomputer typically may service between twenty-five and fifty users, smaller configurations are not unusual for resource-intensive applications. In larger firms, departmental systems often are off-loaded to a minicomputer located within the user's area. Personnel, purchasing, and corporate legal counsel often are examples of areas where minicomputers are found doing CIS applications. Many minicomputers also are designed for the fast "number-crunching" needs of engineering or scientific research firms.

Microcomputer Considerations. **Microcomputers** have proliferated beyond anyone's expectations in recent years. These machines typically handle personal or user-level data and processing. Microcomputers are being incorporated into medium- and large-scale information systems with increasing frequency. These devices have moved rapidly from the arena of video games and hobby uses into the realm of serious business tools. For the systems designer, a decision to incorporate microcomputers in an application can present some special problems. For one thing, a microcomputer is a fully integrated computer system. Thus, a microcomputer needs its own operating system and its own application software, regardless of what other provisions have been made for application or system software within the overall configuration. A microcomputer also has its own secondary storage that probably is physically incompatible with the storage devices or schemes used by other computers within the same overall system.

These conditions create some special challenges:

- Each microcomputer must be regarded as a stand-alone processing system, with plans and designs structured accordingly.

- Within a distributed processing environment, the microcomputer must be configured for compatibility with central capabilities and other distributed processors, through data communications, as a remote terminal or by direct attachment.

- The microcomputer offers additional, stand-alone processing capabilities that can support branch or remote offices, possibly through applications independent of the one under development.

- Microcomputers are highly communications oriented. They can be linked into data communication networks using either leased lines or dial-up connections.

- The expanding presence of microcomputers is well known. First-time users and experienced professionals are among the purchasers. There already exists a rapidly expanding arsenal of program and application software for microcomputers. Among the more popular are database and file management, spreadsheet, graphics, data communications and word processing. It is entirely possible that existing software can be used to support input or local processing functions performed on microcomputers, reducing overall software development costs for a new application.

- Recent technological advances in areas such as optical storage minituarization and .high-speed processing have transformed the idea of "desktop mainframe" from fantasy to reality. These mainframe micros will present special challenges to system designers. The temptation will be to distribute more and more processing from the corporate and departmental levels to the individual one. This shift in processing responsibility will require a kind of user different from the one who sends processing requests to mainframe or minicomputers.

This proliferation of microcomputers is one of the major concerns for organizations and for the systems designer in particular. Because microcomputers are attractively priced and in some organizations are status symbols, many systems already may have been acquired. Thus, as a new system is developed, incongruities can arise quickly. Software under development likely does not run on all machines; and consequently, either new equipment must be purchased to replace nonstandard processors, or dual sets of software must be maintained. Data communication capabilities also will vary, possibly precluding attachment to a network. Training also poses a problem as relatively novices take total control over systems distributed to personal computers. These conditions represent roadblocks to the project and major challenges to the designer. A management policy decision is required that states which configurations will be supported. Supporting multiple systems is extremely expensive.

Data Communications

A data communication link or **network** is nothing more than another way to join the equipment components that form a system configuration. Looking at data communications in this way can impart a valuable perspective to the design of applications that will use distributed processing capabilities.

A computer processing system is an integrated entity. Any computer processing system, be it in a single room or in multiple sites around the world, consists of interconnected devices that can be used in coordination to produce a desired result. If all of the components of a system happen to be at the same site, the components probably are connected by cables that operate at system speed. Such devices are said to be **hardwired**. If the individual components are dispersed geographically, the connections are data communication links that usually operate at slower speeds. In addition to slower speeds, the data communication links impose requirements for controls over completeness and integrity of data transmissions.

Given this relatively straightforward distinction, a decision to investigate data communication capabilities opens a Pandora's box of alternate options and configurations. An information systems designer need not be an expert in the technical details of these alternatives and options. However, the designer must understand the basic concepts and tradeoffs and know when to draw on whatever specialized technical expertise is available to the project team.

When elements of a processing system are connected through communication links, the choice of communication method to be applied depends mainly on a few critical factors. These factors include volume of data to be transmitted, frequency of transmission, and the importance of privacy or secrecy of data. For all systems, controls must be applied to assure that all transmitted data are received and verified.

By thinking of a communications-supported computer system as a single entity that just happens to be spread out geographically, much of the mystique often introduced in this field can be eliminated. With this outlook, the same kinds of processing options and services can be obtained from a distributed network as are available in a single installation. That is, processing options tend to center around batch or interactive capabilities. Remote, communications-supported sites can accumulate transactions and send those transactions to a central facility in batches. Remote sites also can do local batch processing. The same is true for interactive service. On-line users can interact with a central computer, or they can use a local minicomputer or microcomputer for interactive processing. Even though a specialist would likely be consulted for any significant connectivity implementations, the analyst should be generally familiar with several aspects of data communications in order to design high-level distributed systems. The analyst should have a working knowledge of networking options and components, transmission methods and media, and communication design consideration.

Networks. Networks are multiple-user interconnections for data communication purposes. Virtually all **dial-up** and **wide-area telephone service (WATS)** traffic is carried over network systems operated by communications utilities or other specialized companies. A growing trend has developed in the establishment of private networks by large corporations or governmental organizations. Private networks serve multiple points within individual user organizations. Many companies that have gone into distributed data processing have implemented these capabilities through private networks.

Generally, networks fall into one of two categories, **local area networks** (LAN) or **wide area networks** (WAN), although recent advances in technology have blurred their definitions. LANs usually are thought of as short-range communication schemes totally within the control and ownership of the user enterprise. LANs serve building-to-building, user-to-user type applications. Some define a LAN simply as any network serving within a fifty-kilometer radius. LANs are most widely used to share common data and application programs and for communication services such as electronic mail (E-Mail). WANs typically cover larger geographic areas, usually requiring the crossing of public rights of way and often using the circuits of a common carrier, such as a utility.

Within any given network, there will be two or more computers serving as data communication processors. These processors, in turn, will be connected, through modems or transmission links, to each other and to terminals, microcomputers, or a variety of input and output devices. In a multiple-computer network, the processor that serves as a control point, monitoring and logging transmission traffic and storing shared data and applications, is known as a server. Usually a server will have greater storage capacity than other devices, or nodes, on the network. A server that is a mainframe or minicomputer is usually referred to as a "host" processor. A server or host is a hub that services terminals or other user devices.

The transmission and receipt of data communication traffic are governed by sets of rules known as **protocols**. Implementation of protocols has been described as electronic handshaking. The protocols establish the bit, character, or message synchronization between communicating devices. Synchronization signals exist to facilitate the recognition and correction of errors and to determine how devices can access a network. Protocol standards serve to govern the formation of strings of bits into characters and groups of characters into fields and records. In transmissions, entire messages are assembled under control of these protocols. Each character is validated on both transmission and receipt, giving rise to the allusion to handshaking.

Protocols also serve a security function, since they establish the access paths and passwords that will be honored. If different types of user devices are linked into a network, protocols establish the code formats and patterns that create the needed compatibility. If devices operate on different protocols, the devices cannot be used together.

Data communication networks are set up, generally, under two types of configurations or topologies. **Topologies** are physical patterns of interconnections between nodes. A network can consist of a series of nodes functioning as peers, or the nodes can be controlled centrally by a host computer that switches network traffic.

The peer organization method uses a decentralized organization scheme. One common configuration, illustrated in Figure 11-2, is the **ring structure**. Under this approach, any number of processors can be connected in a continuous path. Messages, or packets of data, are routed continuously around the circular configuration of a ring structure. Each node accepts and assimilates the data packets intended for its users, passing along those that belong to others.

Under a centrally controlled organization, all data go through a central point, usually a mainframe or minicomputer, that performs all housekeeping functions associated both with data transmission and information control. A **star network** structure, the most common point-to-point network, is diagrammed in Figure 11-3. Another such topology, the bus network, links nodes serially from a central server as shown in Figure 11-4. The central switching

Figure 11.2.   A ring network.

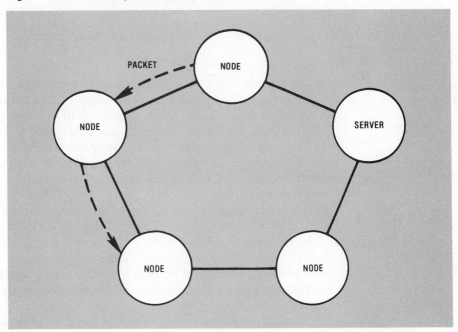

Figure 11.3.   A star network.

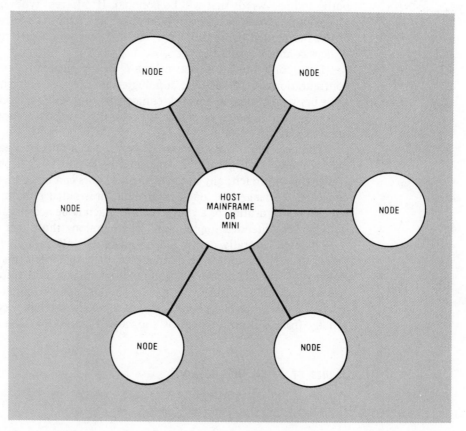

equipment logs all receipt and retransmission of messages. Housekeeping software initiates monitoring and control messages to all user points. These messages are used as verification that all transmissions were processed and received as directed. Data can be sent from one secondary node to another by routing through the central controller. Under a point-to-point network, it is no longer necessary to circulate packets of data, passing them through all points to arrive at the desired point. Rather, a message goes directly from origin to central controller to destination.

Between various networks in a configuration are connecting devices or systems. Bridges are devices that connect similar networks or form intranetwork connections, as illustrated in Figure 11-5. Gateways may connect different types of networks or different computing devices, as illustrated in Figure 11-6. A series of gateways, themselves forming a network, connecting large components of the enterprise physical architecture is known as a system backbone. (See Figure 11-7.)

Transmission Methods and Media. Data communication is the movement of encoded information from one point to another by means of electrical transmis-

Figure 11.4.   A bus network.

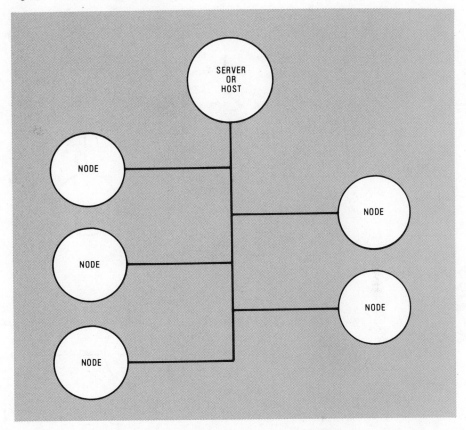

sion systems. Computers communicate with on-off electrical signals, or binary digital pulses, as shown in Figure 11-8 (a). Much long-distance communication between computer devices occurs over telephone transmission lines. One problem is that many telephone transmission lines are designed to carry continuously variable, or analog, signals, as shown in Figure 11-8 (b), rather than discrete pulses. However, modern communication systems are being installed to carry voice, data, and sometimes image, all in digital format, possibly on the same medium.

When data are transmitted between the central processor of a computer and an attached, hardwired terminal, the signals form a series of bits in a digital mode. When remote communication across analog telephone lines is needed, it is necessary to take the digital pulses and impress them onto an analog signal that varies by changes in the value of the information pulses. This translation step must take place before data transmission can take place.

There must be a device at each end of a communication link to translate computer digital code into analog code for transmission and back into the digital code at the other end. Devices that handle these functions are called

Figure 11.5. Ring networks connected by a bridge.

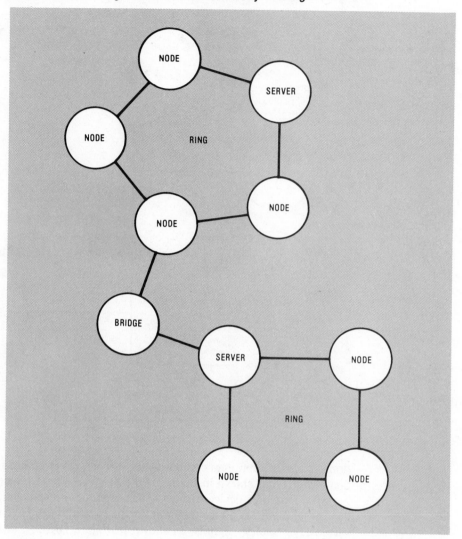

modems. This term is an abbreviation of modulator-demodulator, which describes the functions performed. On transmission, the modem modulates the digital signal, creating binary analog code. On receipt, the device demodulates the signal, translating the code back into digital format. If digital telephone service is available, a modem is not necessary. The action of a modem is diagrammed in Figure 11-8 (c).

Rates of data transmission are measured in terms of **bits per second (bps)**. Communication line speeds also are measured by *baud rate*, which refers to the number of times per second that a line signal can change its status. The term **baud** is an abbreviation of the name Baudot, the Frenchman who developed the

Figure 11.6.   Gateway between ring and bus networks.

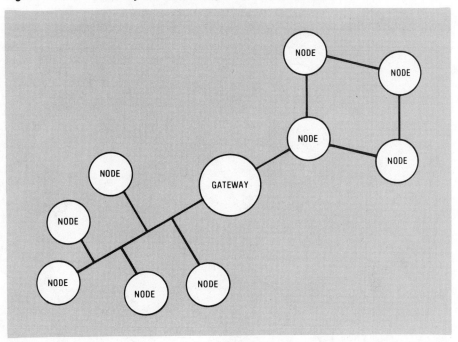

coding scheme for machine telegraphy. Baud rates are not the same as bps. Speed expressed as a baud rate is lower than the equivalent expression in bits per second.

Transmission rates are related to the capacities of the transmission media used. For example, traditional teletypewriter lines have transmission rates of 1,200 bps. These are single lines connecting two points. A normal, voice-grade telephone connection like those normally used in point-to-point dialing systems has a maximum capacity, with special conditioning, of 9,600 bps. Coaxial cables like those used for television systems can be equipped for transmission rates of up to 16 million bps. Similar capacities are available through microwave and satellite transmission systems, both of which use radio transmission principles. In addition, high-speed transmission is now coming into the marketplace through the use of fiber optics and laser methods, both of which use coherent light as a transmission medium and are capable of transmission rates upwards of 100 mbps or mega (million) bits per second. These light-oriented carriers, which have the advantage of being relatively independent of weather or environmental interference, will undoubtedly be the transmission medium of choice in the near future.

Typically, the greater the distance traversed the greater the capacity required of the transmission media. An enterprise will therefore be likely to choose a satellite, microwave, or dedicated digital phone medium for site-to-site communications requiring greatest capacities. Satellite transmission can span inter-

Figure 11.7. Backbone formed by series of gateways.

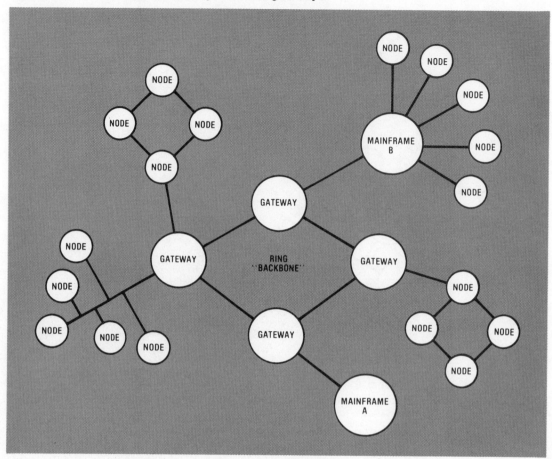

continental distances. Microwave is used for high volume over relatively short distances, often site-to-site communications over rough terrain. Dedicated phone lines provide service where costs are otherwise prohibitively high, probably resulting in transmission capacity tradeoffs. Between buildings at a site, the medium of choice will probably be either a wiring scheme of relatively high bandwidth, such coaxial, or fiber optics. Within buildings, the transmission media may range from fiber to coaxial to twisted pair to ordinary phone lines, depending upon capacity required and costs.

Costs are dictated by both the medium itself and its termination points. *Termination points* refer to the connections at which the medium must accommodate a node device, a change in medium, or a split. For instance, although fiber cable is likely to be an all-round wiring solution of the future, costs currently are somewhat prohibitive. The cost of the fiber itself has been continually dropping, but the termination point hardware is still excessively expensive. As the termination point hardware becomes more widely manufactured and

Figure 11.8. Waveforms of signals used in data communications.

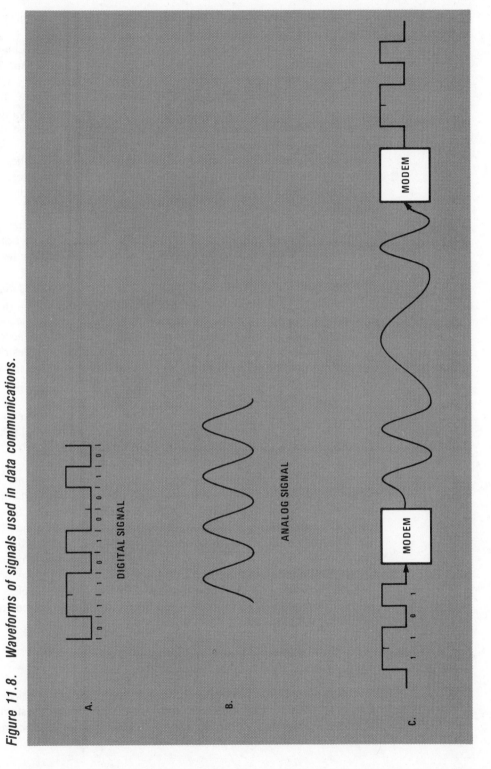

A.

‖0‖1‖1‖‖0‖1‖‖0‖1‖0‖1‖‖1‖0‖1‖

DIGITAL SIGNAL

B.

ANALOG SIGNAL

C.

1 1 0 1

MODEM

MODEM

utilized, the costs of a fiber solution for more types of applications will drop and they will become common.

Systems Design Considerations. In the design of individual applications that use data communication capabilities, concerns include speed, cost, accuracy, access, and compatibility.

These factors are not considered in isolation any more than any other factors associated with systems design. Rather, they are highly interrelated. For example, speed of transmission is related directly to the cost of service; the greater the speed, the higher the cost. Therefore, tradeoffs lie in identifying the costs of different communication capacities then measuring these costs against known volumes. These figures, in turn, become criteria for determining whether data transactions will be transmitted as they are created or volume jobs will be held for batch transmission during idle overnight hours.

Accuracy also relates to cost and to speed as well. High-speed service requires dedicated communication lines. The main enemy of accuracy in data transmission is electronic interference, or **noise**. Dedicated, or **leased, lines** can be conditioned to be less noisy than dial-up connections.

The question of access is of special concern to the systems designer. Access can be controlled through hardware and software measures. In a leased-line system, for example, access is controlled by the dedicated connections. In a dial-up system, extensive user passwords are necessary to control access. If privacy or confidentially of data is an important factor, it may be desirable to install special devices that scramble signals on transmission, then unscramble them on receipt of messages. This **encryption** guards against either inadvertent or purposeful connection into lines by unauthorized persons.

Security in designing interconnected systems is a major concern, particularly if a WAN utilizing a public transmission medium is employed. Besides the issue of privacy, such systems are at risk to potentially destructive elements, such as computer viruses.

Compatibility of data becomes a concern and a systems design factor largely because data communication makes possible the transmission of data between computers with different data formats or binary structures. The binary formats of multiple makes or models of computers can be rendered compatible by controls, known as **protocol emulation** software, that can be built into data communication systems. From the designer's standpoint, technical compatibility should be thought of as a checklist item. Wheneer communication capabilities are considered, code formats or protocols should be checked for compatibility. Conversion requirements should be identified and implemented.

CENTRALIZATION VERSUS DISTRIBUTION

With almost any application under development today, technical implementation must consider the decentralization, or distribution, of system capabilities. System capabilities are centralized when a single computer system processes all applications and contains all data.

Data from remote locations can be processed through teleprocessing, or data communications over telephone lines, which expands the reach of the central system. Whether processing is done off-line (batch) or on-line, data are input via a remote device, transmitted to the central processor, acted upon by one or more application programs, transmitted back to the remote location, and displayed or printed.

Distributed systems occur when system components are separated geographically and application processing is done on more than one processor. Further, the application programs and supporting data are not necessarily the same at all locations. The distributed systems may be connected in a variety of configurations, including various data communication relationships.

Many large organizations are configuring their data processing architectures to take advantage of the strategic capabilities of connectivity between mainframes, minicomputers, and microcomputers. A typical configuration, as illustrated by Figure 11-9, might have an installation mainframe(s) contending with organization-wide data and applications. This mainframe would be connected to departmental minicomputers, standalone terminals, and remote sites in a star communications configuration. The minicomputers might then be connected to individual microcomputer users in star, ring, or bus networks. This physical architecture might reflect the corporate functional hierarchy. The success of this configuration will depend upon the distribution or centralization of specific applications.

Areas of Distribution

In determining whether (or how much) to decentralize any given application, the main considerations relate to the organization itself. Corporations, for example, tend to be either centralized or decentralized in their management philosophies and leadership styles. The more centralized the outlook of a given management group, the more likely it is that a centralized system will be implemented. Conversely, the more vigorously a company has subdivided itself into operating divisions or geographic entities, the more likely it is that information systems will be decentralized. As time passes, the systems designer needs to be aware of changes in management philosophies. Such changes, if they occur, may or may not be dramatic. The degree of centralization or distribution can be applied in three separate areas for any given application or system: data, processing, and control.

Data. Distribution of data resources can be carried out in a wide range of options of varying degree or extent. The design decisions made here will have broad significance. Since data represent a primary corporate resource, processing and control designs will follow data. Questions of centralization or distribution of the data resource focus on the location of data, level of detail of data at each location, timeliness of data, and the handling of redundancies.

Centralization of data exists when computerized files or databases are housed and maintained in a single location under the custody of a single operating unit. Centralization exists even though on-line inquiry capabilities to those data resources may be worldwide. Conversely, distribution of the data resource is

Figure 11.9. A typical large-organization computer network architecture.

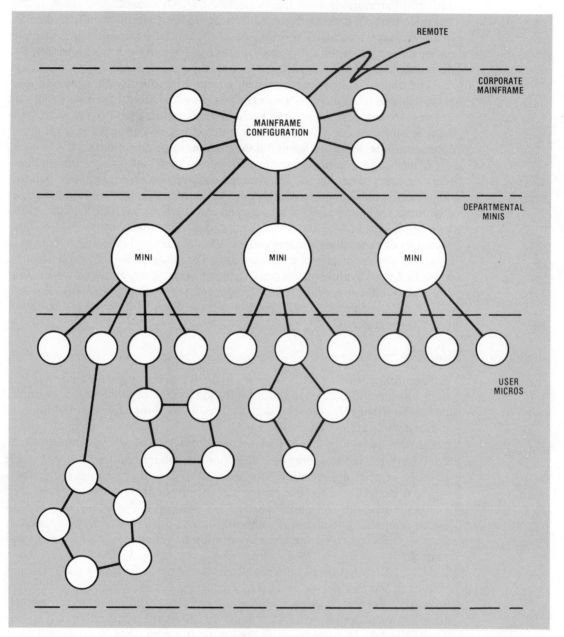

measured by the physical location of files or databases on computer systems that are separated from a single central facility.

To illustrate, the implementation of a three-campus student records system might call for a distribution of data. Data elements common to all three campuses would be centralized. Data elements individual to specific campuses would be distributed. Thus, each campus would have a separate set of files dealing with its schedule of classes, location and time of classes, and faculty assignments for those classes. However, since the courses offered are accredited and uniform throughout the system, the course catalog files could be centralized.

An example of how decisions concerning level of detail affect distribution of the data resource can be seen in the financial recordkeeping aspects of the university system. Files could be designed, for example, so that each campus would keep detailed records of its own payrolls, purchases, and revenues. Summaries of these financial detail files could be prepared periodically and used to update a master budgetary data base at the central facility. The data in the central system, then, would reflect the statewide status of the university budget. Should exceptions develop, inquiries could be initiated for references to the detail files on the individual campuses.

Having data files that are current depends upon the frequency of data communication between centralized and distributed files. For data that are maintained in the central office and needed also in the distributed locations, the entire updated data file, or just changes, can be **downloaded**, or transferred from the host, on a periodic basis. The frequency of this transmission will depend on the volatility of the data and how up-to-date the data need to be at the remote location. Often, these batch transmissions are done nightly or weekly. The scope of data sent depends upon the percentage changed. In a student records system, data updates to courses with prerequisite changes probably would be sent annually. By contrast, an entire file of closing stock prices could be distributed nightly to offices of a brokerage firm. Communication of data from distributed locations follows similar considerations. In some instances, such as an order-processing system, transmission may occur throughout the day. Local order files are maintained, and orders that cannot be filled locally can generate an order to the central file site immediately.

Data communication costs are reduced if data are located at each site or where needed for processing. For common (shared) data, redundancy of data would be introduced by this approach. An extreme approach, of course, would be to replicate all files at all locations, provided processing and reference volumes supported these expenditures. This level, or degree, of distribution of data resources would call for specific procedures to maintain, distribute, and protect those resources.

Maintenance of the data would be likely to occur at a single site. Procedures are necessary to provide periodic distribution of data to recreate data at all sites. As is the case with any distributed-site data, backup and recovery procedures must be developed for each site. In this case, such procedures are simplified because data simply can be transmitted from the maintaining site. However, depending on the volume of data and capacity of the communication network, this transfer can be an expensive and time-consuming process.

If files are maintained at a local site and are not replicated at the central facility, the design of the system must assure that the decentralized files are protected adequately, reproduced periodically, saved at remote locations, and safeguarded generally against major disaster. The same assurance steps, of course, are necessary for central files that are shared with terminals in multiple locations.

Processing. The distribution or centralization of processing follows functional lines and the handling of data. Separate decisions are made for such areas as data capture, entry, mainframe processing, storage, and output. Decisions conform to corporate policies or positions while attempting to meet user needs or desires.

As a general principle, for example, it is considered desirable today, to incorporate data capture and, if possible, entry functions within user source transactions. Following this principle, an increasing number of systems assign data capture and entry responsibilities to the organization's customers themselves, making customers part of the processing cycle. An excellent example of this practice can be seen in the automatic teller machines installed by many banks. The customer making a deposit or withdrawal actually is posting the bank's files as part of the transaction. Similarly, a student records system might call for students to use terminals and enter their own requests for courses during registration.

Decentralized data entry of this type, however, does not necessarily call for decentralization of processing or record storage. Processing functions can be subdivided in almost infinite combinations. For example, an automatic teller machine may function completely under control of a central computer that develops all account balances and simply transmits funds-disbursement codes and transaction ticket information to remote stations. Alternatively, the processing can take place within the teller machine. The decentralized processor then computes balances and transmits information back to the central computer for file updating. Thus, a bank with one hundred teller machines in place conceivably could process transactions on all of the machines simultaneously, queuing file update or access transactions at a central computer.

Part of such centralization or distribution decisions centers around questions of equipment configuration. For example, assuring continuous service to a network through a central site would require two or more central mainframes. If the active mainframe experienced an interruption of service, the processing load would be switched automatically to a standby unit. The standby unit might have been used for program development or batch processing tasks, which now are delayed. To continue providing network service, other tasks may have to be rescheduled. However, if processing capabilities are incorporated at the distributed processors, it may be possible to continue processing even though service to the mainframe is interrupted.

There are many options for centralizing or distributing computer processing. Particularly in a world that is populated increasingly by microprocessors, there are no hard-and-fast rules—just a vast number of available solutions.

Control. Control becomes an increasing concern as the extent of distributed processing within a system increases. As a basic principle, it is easier and safer to apply controls at a single location and have a single point for all transactions. Additional measures are needed as the number of entry points into or processing points within a system increases.

In general, controls are either operational or systemic. *Operational controls* deal with access, authorization, or verification. *Systemic controls* deal with hardware configurations and software updating to assure that functional compatibility and data comparability are maintained throughout the system.

Among operating controls, access deals with entry into and use of a system. For example, in a student registration system, access to the computer system could be gained through entry of a valid log-on code and student identification number. Authorization, then, would be applied by controls within the system itself. These controls are used to restrict access to functions and data. Further, authorization codes are invoked within applications to control processing. For student registration, authorization also would take place when the system checked its financial records to verify that there were no outstanding bills for the student attempting to register. Verification typically is achieved by communication from the system to the user. The intent is to verify to the user that processing was completed successfully. In a student registration system, verification could take place with a display or a printout listing the classes for which registrations have been accepted. This verification method would satisfy the user that desired results have been achieved. In the same way, an automatic teller machine typically prints a transaction summary each time a depositor uses any device within the system.

Systemic controls are designed to make sure that the system is geared to implement policy or design decisions. With a distributed system, data updates may need to take place at different locations within the network. Consequently, controls must be built-in to address the possibilities of failure in communication to, or in processing at, another location. Usually, verification data are returned for display or printing at the initiating processor to indicate completion of processing or transmission. Procedures must be designed to restore data if partial updates occurred, to retry communications, or to accumulate data for later transmission or processing. Without such controls, the system's integrity is damaged. In a student registration system, it would be necessary to update accounts receivable files in the system with each transaction. If, for example, a central file showed that the student had paid a balance in full while a remote file showed that the balance was still due, an authorized student might not be able to register. Thus, if there are multiple files, multiple updates may be necessary. The same need for updating would apply to modifications in application programs. That is, each time a procedural change was made, all copies of software affected by the change would have to be updated concurrently.

In addition, system controls must be incorporated to prevent concurrent updates of a particular data file or record. For data in a centralized system, the second update transaction can be locked out from processing. However, such controls become much more complex if the data being updated are redundant on several processors.

Centralized Systems

If an organization operates with a single centralized computer facility, it elects, in effect, to put all of its eggs in one basket. On the positive side, considerable computing power can be assembled through concentration. Conversely, however, this type of concentration increases dangers from mechanical, electronic, or accidental disruption of service.

An advantage of centralization lies in the relative ease with which resources may be controlled. All data files and equipment are in one place. Thus, it is easier to monitor the updating of files and the supervision of data libraries. Further, it becomes easier to coordinate with equipment vendors to be sure that preventive maintenance measures are applied as scheduled and that any equipment failures are handled immediately. In a large centralized facility, it is easier to store and plug in spare, or backup, devices to maintain service. If installations are large enough, and if most of the equipment in a given installation is provided by a single manufacturer, it may be possible to have full-time vendor maintenance personnel stationed at an installation.

At the same time, centralized facilities are highly visible and considerably more vulnerable than systems distributed over multiple sites. Because of the financial value of the assets and the vulnerability that comes with centralization, special security measures must be applied to a centralized facility. Most computer rooms have access systems for physical security. Provision must be made for remote storage of backup files that would be used for recovery if originals were destroyed. Further, arrangements must be made for backup processing capabilities that could be used on an interim basis if an emergency situation arose. When teleprocessing capabilities are present on the system, telephone lines are used for data communication, and the entire system is vulnerable to unauthorized access.

Distributed Systems

In any review of the impact of distributed systems upon any given application, one of the first considerations should be the scale of distribution, including the size and capacity of individual processing **nodes** within the overall system. Distributed systems typically result from attempts to off-load processing from the central system. Especially with teleprocessing applications on the central computer, increased demands and activity volumes create a bottleneck on throughput. Performance of on-line systems may be degraded noticeably. The introduction of distributed processors often provides improved user services. With increased purchases of software systems by users, additional computer processors are acquired for running these applications. Finally, distributed systems are developed to bring resources closer to the user and to provide user control over processing of the data. Tradeoffs exist in costs. The individual computers may cost less than expanding the mainframe, but the need for an extensive data communication network may offset that advantage.

Concerns also center around the maintenance and protection of data resources. Today, storage devices available for mainframe and minicomputer systems are highly reliable. On the other hand, these capabilities do not exist generally, at this time, for microcomputers. To illustrate the risk, devices that read and write data on diskettes are far less reliable, at least at this time, than hard-disk equipment. Evaluation of the methods and relative reliability for recording, storing, and manipulating files at remote sites is essential in planning for the ongoing continuity and reliability of a new application. If data developed and maintained at remote sites are essential to a system, some provision should be made for creating off-line backup files or for transmitting the data to the central facility on a regular basis and incorporating them into master files.

Although distributed data processing gets around the inherent problem of having all of an organization's computer eggs in one large basket, there are also potential problems with the operation of multiple smaller installations. The operations personnel at remote locations are likely to be less experienced and have less training in dealing with exception or emergency situations. Unavoidably, there will be a lower level of maintenance for a site that has a small minicomputer or microcomputer than is available for a large central facility. Spare equipment or spare parts may be in shorter supply at individual distributed sites. In a distributed network, it may be necessary to ship small units of equipment to central points for maintenance and to maintain a central store of backup units. In such networks, each equipment failure does mean some degree of service interruption at the remote point.

Maintaining, diagnosing, debugging, and updating software can be a lot more complex if an overall processing system is spread out over multiple sites. Even though processing is decentralized, all elements of the network still must be planned for, supported by, and managed by a centralized CIS staff.

Because distributed sites often will not have technical support at the location, the system support must be provided through remote log-on capabilities. These capabilities permit access to a distant system, using the communications network, so that it may be unnecessary to dispatch personnel to the site in case of trouble. Problems can be recreated, diagnosed, and corrected from a central support location. Both hardware and software can be addressed. Software modifications usually can be downloaded over the network. Hardware problems, though, will require sending an engineer to the site to do the actual repairs.

Although there is some inherent safety in dispersing processing facilities, there are also some exposures to risk. Instead of one massive backup or recovery plan, for example, a company may need multiple plans, depending upon the extent of distribution. The primary concern is ensuring that the plans are executed properly at each site. Even though the exposure at any individual facility is smaller than it is for a central location, destruction of resources is a possibility at each location — a contingency that must be planned for in advance.

There are also some security and privacy consequences involved in distribution processing that should be considered in designing each individual application. One frequently used precaution for application programs is to establish a rule that only object code will be located at remote sites. Greater security assurance is the result if the source code is maintained only at a centralized data processing development site. If the source code is distributed, there is a temptation by remote sites to modify applications without corporate authorization or awareness. This may lead to disastrous consequences.

For the systems designer, there is little that can be done to impact the decision about whether a company's overall facility should be centralized or decentralized. Rather, the responsibility lies in evaluating the existing facility and providing the most practical measures available for assuring users continuing reliable service. The needs of a given application for file protection and recovery plans will vary in differing technical environments. Even though the individual designer may be able to do nothing about the technical environment, an understanding of that environment can have a strong impact upon the quality of an individual system.

SUMMARY

An awareness of the technical environment within which a system will function should be thought of as a prerequisite to further design efforts. That is, the environment should be studied and understood as a basis for selecting and applying a strategy for application software design.

The capabilities within any given computer installation may represent either new opportunities or unforeseen constraints in the development of designs to implement user specifications.

As systems design is begun, evaluations must be made of existing technologies and capabilities to determine where and how a new system fits into its overall processing environment. The sequence of evaluation can follow the data processing cycle, including data capture, storage, processing, throughput, and output.

As a general rule, users should control and operate the data capture/input functions as close to the point where transactions take place as possible, unless there is a compelling reason to do otherwise.

To be useful to the organization, data must be stored in structures and formats that are planned, predictable, and readily available. Systems designers must be concerned about identifying existing resources for data storage and assuring compatibility of the new application with those resources.

In order to determine the overall impact of a proposed system upon the current technical architecture, the systems designer should review with technical specialists the following new system characteristics: activity volumes, pattern of activity, processing time per activity, mix of processing activity, and on-line response time.

The capability exists either to tailor outputs at a central facility or to bring records from a central facility to a remote location where tailoring can take place. The systems designer should not feel constrained by the limitations of universally applied report or screen layout forms.

Key areas of concern to the system designer in planning the integration of the new application with the existing technical environment include computer processing hardware alternatives, data communications, and the centralization or distribution of CIS resources.

Depending upon the degree of distribution, separate alternatives and considerations exist for the utilization of mainframes, minicomputers, and microcomputers.

Data communications should be thought of as an alternate method of linking computer hardware units. Systems design concerns for data communications include speed, accuracy, access, compatibility, and cost.

Local area networks (LANs) are high-speed communication systems designed to service localized business needs. Wide area networks (WANs) service remote business concerns and usually employ public data transmission systems. Three network physical patters, or topologies, are star, bus, and ring. Bridge devices provide connections between like networks. Gateway devices provide them for dissimilar networks.

Degrees of distribution can be applied in the areas of data, processing, and control. Design considerations relating to distribution include the level of service to be provided, uniform application of software versions throughout the system, compatibility and uniformity of data files, difficulty of servicing hardware or software problems, and provisions for recovery.

KEY TERMS

1. local area network (LAN)
2. wide area network (WAN)
3. teleprocessing
4. download
5. work station
6. mainframe
7. minicomputer
8. microcomputer
9. hardwire
10. poll
11. demand
12. modem
13. bits per second (bps)
14. baud
15. point-to-point
16. dial-up-service
17. wide area telephone service (WATS)
18. noise
19. leased line service
20. network
21. node
22. protocol
23. topology
24. ring structure
25. packet
26. star network
27. encryption
28. protocol emulation

REVIEW/DISCUSSION QUESTIONS

1. What is the role of the project team in making decisions on data capture and input methods?
2. Describe several data capture/input method alternatives.
3. In general, where should the input function be placed and what is the rationale for this guideline?
4. What type of information is important regarding the design of processing requirements for an individual application?

5. Describe several output-method alternatives.
6. Explain the basic differences between mainframes, minicomputers, and microcomputers.
7. What alternatives exist for work stations?
8. What are five concerns in designing data communication capabilities for individual applications?
9. Define briefly the two categories of networks.
10. Describe the two basic types of network configurations, or topologies.
11. The degree of CIS resourses centralization or distribution can be applied in what three general areas?
12. What issues are involved in deciding upon the degree of centralization or decentralizatiion appropriate for a given CIS?
13. What are some of the concerns regarding the proliferation of microcomputers in organizations for the systems designer?
14. How does an organization's management style relate to the issue of CIS centralization or distribution?
15. How does the centralization-decentralization issue affect back-up procedures?

12

File and Database Design

Learning Objectives

On completing reading and other learning assignments for this chapter, you should be able to:

■ Identify the different types of application support files.

■ Explain how an organization's files incorporate entities, attributes, and relationships.

■ Tell how data structures may be derived as a basis for file design decisions.

■ Show the use of E-R and access diagrams in file and database design.

■ Give the principal methods of file organization and access.

■ Tell how files are implemented physically for different file organization and access methods.

■ Give the key concerns for the systems designer in designing files.

■ Explain the difference between hierarchical, network, and relational database models.

■ Describe the general organization and main advantages of database management systems.

OVERVIEW

It has been said that an organization's collection of files, its database, models the organization itself. At the very least, files require structures that parallel the structure and functions of the organization. This correspondence should exist because the organization depends upon the database for operational, supervisory, and planning support. In turn, the components of files are the data that represent and reflect the key assets of the organization, including its customers, its inventory, its production, its employees, and other assets or entities important to the functioning of the business.

For the database to be useful, the relationships among the organization's assets also must be reflected in the relationships among the data fields, records, and files within the database. File design, therefore, requires a modeling of the relationships and functions that exist within the organization. Establishing this replication between files and the organization that will use them represents a major challenge in the design of computer information systems.

In order to complete the physical data model necessary to fully implement the overall technical architecture, many aspects of the file and database design must be further developed. The various support files for systems applications must be identified by combining and integrating data stores and entities isolated on the DFD and E-R representations. For each file identified, access methods and organizational and handling techniques must be derived which will support any of the various applications that utilize the files. Finally, the specific hardware, software, and storage media must be determined that will be capable of implementing the overall data model. Traditional file management systems or a database management system (DBMS) may be chosen for implementation. Constraints of the existing file handling system may have to be incorporated into the logical data model, thus resulting in a less-than-perfect, yet optimal, physical solution.

APPLICATION SUPPORT FILE TYPES

The first step in designing the database to support a system is to identify the different types of files needed and their basic content. Much of the information needed to accomplish this task has been accumulated during systems analysis. The starting point is a set of normalized data stores prepared as part of the physical DFD and completed **E-R diagram**. Any given application may require any or all of several types of files. File types include master files, transaction files, reference files, archival files, backup files, and transaction log files.

Master Files. Master files contain basic information about identified entities. For, example, in a university registration system there would be separate master files for students, instructors, classes, and so on. A master file contains one record for each entity occurrence, for example, one for each student or instructor included in the system. Certain types of fields within master files tend to be static or unchanging. For example, the student name or number would be unlikely to change over time. On the other hand, some fields within the master files would change on the basis of transaction data on a periodic basis. For example a student's GPA may change each academic term. Master files are thus cumulative as well as relatively permanent.

Transaction Files. Transaction files are dynamic. Transaction files, containing records of source transactions of an organization, are used to update master files. Transaction files thus reflect specific, timely incidents in the business operation. Examples of transaction files might include payroll earnings records or cash receipts in a business, grade assignments or course sign-ups in a university.

Reference Files. Reference files contain constant data used each time an application program is run. These data are used, along with data from transaction files, to update master files. These are relatively stable data; stable enough that they need not be part of the transaction record but with sufficient potential for change that the values should not be coded in the actual programs. An example of a reference file is a data table on federal withholding taxes, indexed to employee earnings. Tables of this type are searched each time payroll records are updated.

Archival Files. Archival files are files retained after they have been processed. Such files are used largely for historical reference or special search. For example, a hospital might keep transaction files detailing treatments of patients for many years. These files could provide the basis for research on the incidence and treatment of specific diseases.

Backup Files. Backup files consist of several physical copies of transaction and master files retained for the specific purpose of reconstructing and recovering a company's records in the event of disasters or other irregularities that interrupt normal processing. For example, copies of last week's payroll earnings records, together with copies of last week's employee master records, would be saved and protected as a backup in the event of damage or loss of current files. Several generations of such records would be saved as part of an overall backup plan.

Transaction Log Files. Transaction log files are, in effect, master accounting records that serve as a journal. Typically, this type of file is kept on a running basis as part of an on-line processing system. All transactions entered into the system are logged, usually on two or more tapes or disks, in sequence, as the transactions occur. These logs assure auditability of computer records. In effect, these logs are the starting point on an audit trail for business transactions. The files could also be used for recovery if master or transaction files were inadvertently destroyed.

LOGICAL DATA ORGANIZATION AND IMPLICATIONS

During analysis, the initial file or database design is established. Documentation is developed that outlines a logical structure for files. User specifications will include identification of data stores, data elements within those stores, and relationships among the data stores to be maintained by the system under development.

Logical File Structure

The logical data structure that supports the processing of a new system is derived through use of normalization techniques. **Normalization**, which is described in depth in Chapter 6, is a systematic process that results in a comprehensive set of data stores in which redundancy among component data items has been minimized. Also, access to records has been built around a series of primary keys, and fields within the data records have been identified to define relationships among those records. Normalization produces data structures that can be packaged physically as two types of files, attribute and correlative.

Attribute files contain data components that describe an identifiable entity or object of importance to the organization. In a sense, attribute files correspond to master files that will be maintained in support of processing.

Correlative files establish relationships between attribute files through key values that associate records in one attribute file with those in another attribute file. Correlative files establish access paths, that is maintain data relationships among attribute files so that data elements in physically separated files without common keys can be related logically for integrated use within information systems.

Correlative files can be implemented in several different ways. In a traditional file environment, correlative files can be packaged separately as direct-access files that can be searched randomly to find associated keys. Also, the correlations can be maintained within internal tables held in memory during processing. If attribute files are organized as indexed-sequential files (described later in this chapter), correlations can be implemented as secondary keys, fields used to define alternate relationships associated with the files. In a database environment, the database management software formats the files to allow the relations among attribute records, thus eliminating the correlative file.

E-R and Data Access Diagram

Figure 12-1 shows an E-R diagram for a portion of the normalized data stores that might be defined for a university registration system as developed in Chapter 6. The attribute files are illustrated in the E-R diagram as entities, whereas the correlative structures are designated in this case as relationships or associations.

Four main entities are represented by the files—STUDENTS, CLASSES, INSTRUCTORS, and GRADES. The STUDENTS data structure contains information to identify the students and to keep track of academic progress. The CLASSES structure contains identification information, along with data elements that keep track of the availability of openings in each class. The INSTRUCTOR structure contains basic instructor information and identifies each instructor's departmental association. The GRADES structure relates students with classes for the purpose of maintaining grades earned in each class. These four structures can be packaged as attribute files that store basic information associated with the entities represented by those structures.

Using the E-R diagram has some advantages over use of data flow diagrams alone. With data flow diagrams, the emphasis is on the flow and transformation of data. The data stores and access play a background, supporting role. The E-R diagram, on the other hand, allows the user and analyst to concentrate on the ways in which data will have to be accessed in the new system. Theoretically, these accessing relationships, as a product of the normalization process, should

Figure 12.1.   E-R diagram for student registration system.

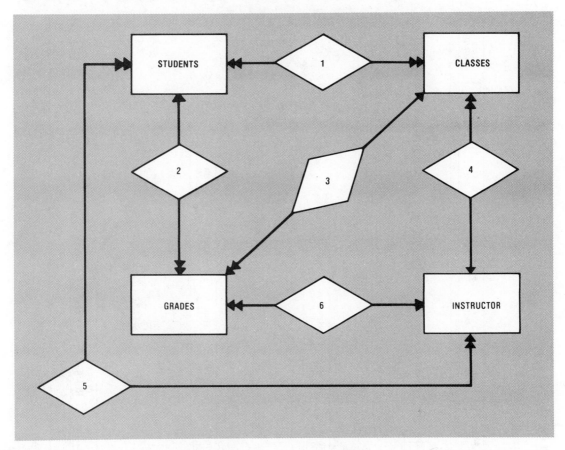

be complete. In practice, however, a careful study of the E-R diagram often leads to the specification of new access paths and, as a result, new system outputs that may have been previously overlooked. Ultimately, the entities represented in the E-R diagram will have to be implemented physically to support the desired access relationships.

Each entity will become an attribute file with records comprised of fields representing entity attributes. The attribute key or keys will become key fields within the records. Each correlative structure will be implemented as a direct-access file whose primary key will be the first attribute key in the relation. The correlative file will resemble a table to be searched for matching values.

Figure 12-2 is a **data access diagram** showing the formats of the files and the corresponding relationships, or access paths, for the student registration system. The arrows indicate the paths from one attribute to another, either directly through the same key or through the relations established in the correlative files. The data access diagram represents the appropriate documentation format to support the transition from logical to physical file design. It communicates

Figure 12.2. Data access diagram for student registration system.

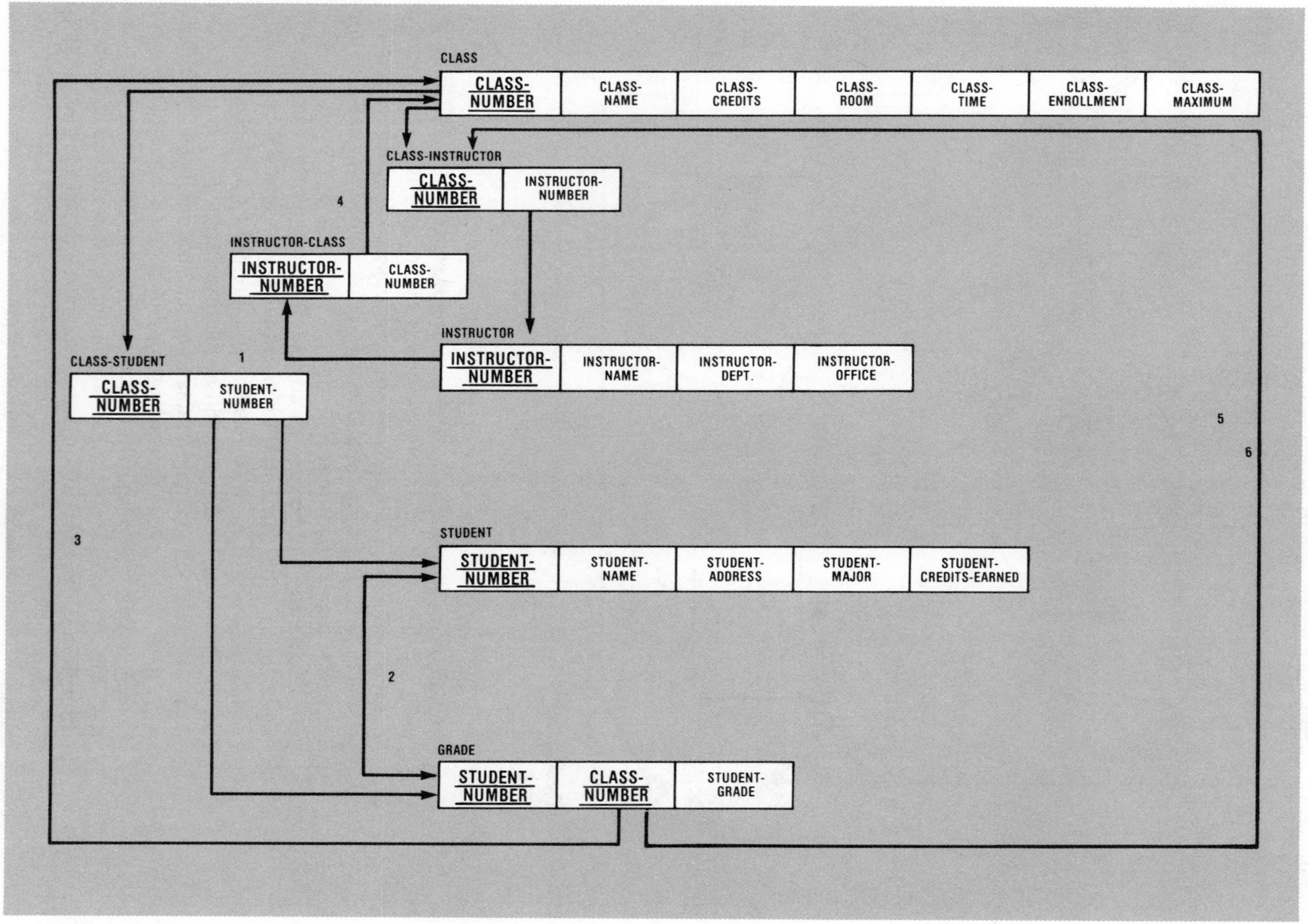

clearly to the designer the precise data and accessing capabilities required. (Note that on this particular data access diagram, the data access paths are cross-referenced to the relationships shown on the E-R diagram in figure 12-1.)

Suppose, for example, that class rosters are to be prepared for each of the classes represented in the CLASS file. (See Figures 12-1 and 12-2 for access path and relationship number 1. First access would be to the CLASS file to extract class identification data. Then, the CLASS-NUMBER field within this record would be used as a partial key for searching the CLASS-STUDENT file to find the STUDENT-NUMBER of students enrolled in the class. These numbers, in turn, provide access to the STUDENT attribute file for extracting student identification data to be printed on the rosters.

Data Structure and File Design

Being able to identify entities important to the organization and to define the attributes associated with those entities is an essential feature for enhancing the flexibility and maintainability of an information system. The motivation is to structure data so that those data represent the business organization rather than supporting specific processing urgencies of any given moment. Unless the organization changes its line of business, the entities with which it deals will remain relatively stable. There may be need, over time, to expand or contract the sets of attributes that represent these business entries. In general, however, the entities will remain the same.

Processing needs, however, probably will change. In a business organization, new reporting obligations will have to be included within the system to meet changing business needs and government regulations. Different report formats will be solicited from users of the information system. Additional processing steps will be inserted into work procedures to reflect changing business policies. These and other changes are to be expected, since organizations are dynamic and are evolving new methods of operation continually.

The data structures that support an organization, therefore, also must be adaptable to processing changes. This adaptability is built into the structure of attribute files through the correlations established between those files. Note in Figures 12-1 and 12-2, for example, that all four attribute files are interrelated. A relationship has been established between each entity and the other three entities through their primary keys. Thus, any new processing need that requires access to any combination of attributes from any of the files can be serviced without changing the file structure. In other words, the overall data structure can support any particular logical viewpoint or processing need involving these attributes.

It should be remembered that a normalized data structure is an idealized solution to an organizational problem. Although it represents the optimum design for supporting that organization, a given normalized data structure may not be the most efficient design for any one processing need. For example, note in the STUDENT data structure in Figure 12-2 that no grade point average (GPA) attribute is included. The GPA can be calculated from the values in fields of the STUDENT and GRADES structures. To include the GPA within the structure would be redundant from the standpoint of a strictly normalized structure.

Suppose, however, that this structure were to be implemented as a file to support on-line inquiry and that the grade point average would be displayed. For each access to the file, the GPA would have to be calculated. If, in a high-volume situation, the computer time necessary for this calculation caused a degradation in service, it might be best to include the GPA separately within the data structure.

An opposite situation, however, also might occur. Suppose the GPA were to be retained as a separate data element both for the overall average for each semester and as an accumulated GPA at the end of each semester. In this case, a grade change would require a considerable amount of recalculation during file updating. Tradeoffs must therefore be considered between the idealized data structure and its processing efficiencies. Usually, these tradeoffs impact the attributes associated with particular entities rather than the entities themselves or the relationships among them.

The final data structure for an organization or a subset of that organization can be packaged physically in one of two ways. In a traditional file-oriented environment, the attribute and correlative structures are implemented as traditional sequential, direct, or indexed-sequential files; the designer determines the appropriate organization methods and establishes the formats of data fields within the records. In a database environment, a database administration (DBA) group works closely with the designers to implement the data model with database software.

File design decisions include determinations about whether on-line file maintenance capabilities will be used, whether transactions against the files will be batched, whether inquiry capabilities need to be supported, whether access times are sufficient to support proposed applications, and whether the hardware and systems software available have the capacity to store the files and handle the transaction volumes. A number of tradeoffs must be considered in connection with these decisions.

As such considerations arise during systems design, they are reflected in the systems flowcharts that describe the physical packaging of systems into jobs, job steps, and on-line procedures. When systems flowcharts first are prepared at the end of the analysis and general design phase, they reflect the designer's best initial estimate of the physical structure of programs and files that will support processing (see Chapter 13). As these design efforts are reviewed and carried to a more detailed level early in the detailed design and implementation phase, some of the assumptions may be modified to allow for hardware, software, and processing constraints.

FILE ACCESS METHODS AND OPTIONS

File access is a term describing the ways data maintained by a system can be sought, extracted from, and replaced within data files. A file access technique represents the user's outlook on data as a resource. That is, file access represents the way data will be used.

File Access Methods

There are three basic file access methods, physical sequential (serial), logical sequential, and direct.

Physical Sequential (Serial) File Access. Physical sequential access, or serial access, represents, in a sense, a chronological approach. That is, records in a file are read or processed in the same order the data were recorded initially. An example of a file that usually is accessed serially is a transaction file of weekly payroll records captured from time cards or time clocks. Another example might be data entries recorded at the point of sale in a retail store. Both types of files are built chronologically, as data are generated.

Logical Sequential Access. Logical sequential access follows a keyed sequence. That is, records are read in order, according to a logical identifier, or key. Keys that drive logical sequential access functions are data fields within the records that contain the data. Payroll master files, commonly organized and accessed successively by employee number, represent a typical example of logical sequential access.

Direct Access. Direct access is also known as *random access*. These names come from the fact that access is direct to the record being sought, without regard to the storage sequence. Given any key value, the corresponding record can be found at random from within a collection of records that comprise a file. Virtually all on-line or interactive systems require random access capabilities.

File access methods are determined during the analysis and general design phase of the systems development life cycle. These methods represent the user's requirements for accessing data and having files available for processing. Thus, file access is a logical consideration in the development of information systems. At this point, little concern has been given to the physical design of files to support the access needs. As development moves into the detailed design stages, an important decision relates to how data files will be placed on storage devices to support these needs.

Storage Media

Sequential access devices read and write records in order, one after the other. These devices, therefore, require that data records be organized in either physical or logical sequence, corresponding with the access method to be used. Magnetic tape drives are the most popular type of sequential access device.

Direct access devices make it possible to process records either sequentially or at random. The physical constraint of sequential access devices, requiring correspondence between organization and access methods, is removed. Records can be accessed in the physical order in which they are recorded on the file, in logical sequence according to keys within the records, or on a random basis, without access to any preceding or succeeding records. The most common secondary storage device for direct access is the magnetic disk drive.

Record Formats

Application programs process files of logical records. A **logical record** is the combination of data fields presented to a program for processing in a single READ operation. The fields in a logical record represent a set of attributes concerning one of the organizational entities about which information is stored.

A **physical record**, on the other hand, consists of one or more logical records grouped to conform to the storage and processing requirements of the computing environment. A physical record is the unit of data that is either written or accessed by the central processing unit at any one time. The physical record, or block, is brought into primary storage in the main CPU at processing time from secondary storage one block at a time. The primary storage area, which houses the block, is called the **buffer** because of its strategic positioning between the file on secondary storage and the application program running on the CPU. There may or may not be direct correspondence between physical and logical records. That is, a physical record area may contain one or more logical records, depending upon the file organization preferences of the system designer. Whereas a single logical record is made available for program processing with each READ operation, one or more physical records may be accessed by the systems software. Figure 12-3 illustrates the blocking function. In this exam-

Figure 12.3.   Logical records groped in file with a blocking factor of 3.

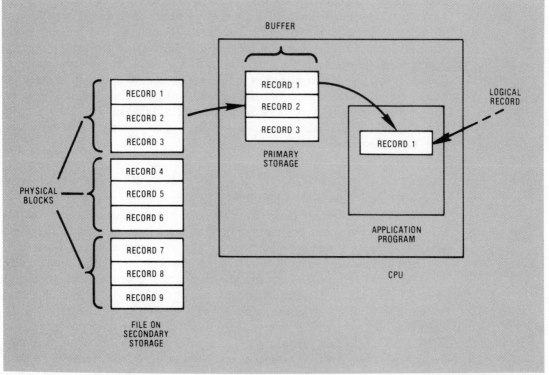

ple, three logical records comprise one physical block. Each block is brought into primary storage, and then each individual logical record is accessed by the application program with single READ operation.

File design involves consideration of the physical sizes of records residing on secondary storage devices. These physical records, or **blocks**, can take on various sizes, depending upon the characteristics of the devices and on needs for processing efficiency. Thus, one decision that must be made by the systems designer relates to the blocking factor, or logical records per block, for records in a file.

Record blocking is designed to optimize computer throughput. Thus, the blocking of records can lead to more efficient processing of any given application program. As a general rule, the larger the block size, the more efficiently the file can be processed. This is because of the relatively costly overhead associated with moving chunks of data from secondary to primary computer storage. The larger the blocks, the fewer the number of data movements. Similarly, the larger the block size, the more efficiently any given file will use its storage media — up to a limit (track size). Considerable space on file media is occupied by **interrecord gaps (IRG)** and **interblock gaps (IBG)**. In the case of magnetic tape, the logical records themselves may occupy less space than the gaps that set them apart. The tradeoff is that the larger the block size, the more primary storage is used during an application program run. Consequently multiple programs, with large record and block sizes, may "hog" CPU storage allocations. Therefore, blocking decisions can be important elements in file design in large mainframe systems where many programs may be running at the same time.

When all records in a given file are assumed to contain the same number of fields and to be of the same overall length, they are known as **fixed-length records**. It is also possible to vary the number of fields within records or the length of individual fields. The result is a **variable-length record**. Within variable-length records, record sizes are established by setting up a field that tells the system the length (in bytes) of the overall record.

Obviously, it can be more difficult to establish buffers, memory areas, or file allocations for variable-length records than for fixed-length records. For this and other reasons, the normalization process that establishes the data model upon which the file design is based identifies and eliminates repeating fields within records. Thus, all records within normalized files are assumed to be of fixed lengths.

FILE ORGANIZATION AND HANDLING TECHNIQUES

File organization refers to the physical patterns in which data are recorded on storage devices. The organization scheme chosen for packaging the logical data structures into physical files can either support or constrain access capability. For example, of the commonly available methods for organizing files, some provide serial, sequential, and random access while others provide only serial and sequential access. A challenge of design, therefore, is to match file organization with logical file access requirements.

Whereas file access represents the user's viewpoint about processing data, file organization must represent the system's viewpoint; a computer system manages data according to their physical arrangement on storage devices. Therefore, file design involves determination of how data will be placed on these devices and how they will be made available by the computer system to provide needed user access. There are three basic file organization methods; sequential, direct, and indexed-sequential.

Sequential File Organization

Sequential file organization is common to all computer systems. Under this method, records are written onto a storage medium, either tape or disk, contiguously, one after another, in the chronological sequence in which they are presented to the system. Sequential files support serial access. This organization scheme also can support logical sequential access, as long as the records were placed in the file in a physical order corresponding with the logical order of keys embedded within the records. Figure 12-4 illustrates this organization. It is up

Figure 12.4. Sequential file organization.

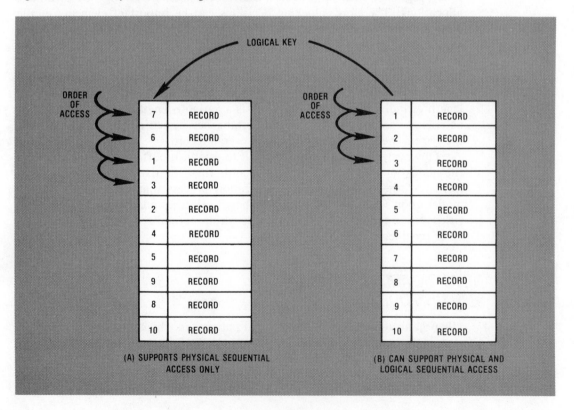

to the user, or programmer, to be aware of the physical organization of the file and to make sure that records are ordered to meet processing demands.

When sequential files are processed, records are made available in the order in which they appear on the storage device. Thus, if processing requirements dictate a different order of access, it becomes necessary to create intermediate files through use of sorting routines. If sequential files are used in support of file updating or maintenance, it is necessary to make sure that both the master file and the transaction file are in the same physical and logical sequence. Compatible sequences assure that updating can take place in a single pass through both files. Figure 12-5 illustrates a typical master file update using a sequential file organization. The transactions are originally captured in their order of occurrence and then sorted to a new sequential file by logical key order. This logical order corresponds to the order of the master file. The master and transaction file are then accessed sequentially for processing in the update program.

Updating a sequential file necessitates the creation of an entirely new master file, regardless of whether tape or disk is used. Usually, the new file is established as the current version, with the source file retained as a backup.

Sequential files frequently are stored on magnetic tape. Magnetic tape devices are popular partly because the media and the equipment are both relatively inexpensive. In addition, tape processing, involving the writing of new files as master files are updated, provides a built-in backup mechanism to protect data resources.

Disk media are appropriate for the storage of sequential files under certain conditions. One of these is for small files, such as tables, that are used frequently by one or more processing routines. Small numbers of records can be stored efficiently in sequential order on disks and can be accessed and updated easily.

In addition, disk storage is appropriate for sequential files that are sorted or re-sorted frequently. Disk devices present effective sorting capabilities. Tape files that require sorting often are transferred to disk for these functions. If the files are stored on disk in the first place, the transfer operations are avoided entirely.

In some situations, disks may be the only available media. This is particularly true for microcomputers, which typically are provided with diskette drives as standard storage devices.

Sequential file organization is appropriate for applications in which either serial or logical sequential access is necessary. Most often, this requirement occurs when the majority of the records in a file will be accessed during each program execution and when it is possible to anticipate the order in which records must be made available. A payroll master file with employee number as key, again, is a common example. Each time the file is processed, most of its records will be accessed and used in processing. Further, it is both convenient and efficient to sequence transaction files so that they correspond with the key sequence of the master file. Thus, it is possible to process transaction records

Figure 12.5. Master file update using sequential file organization.

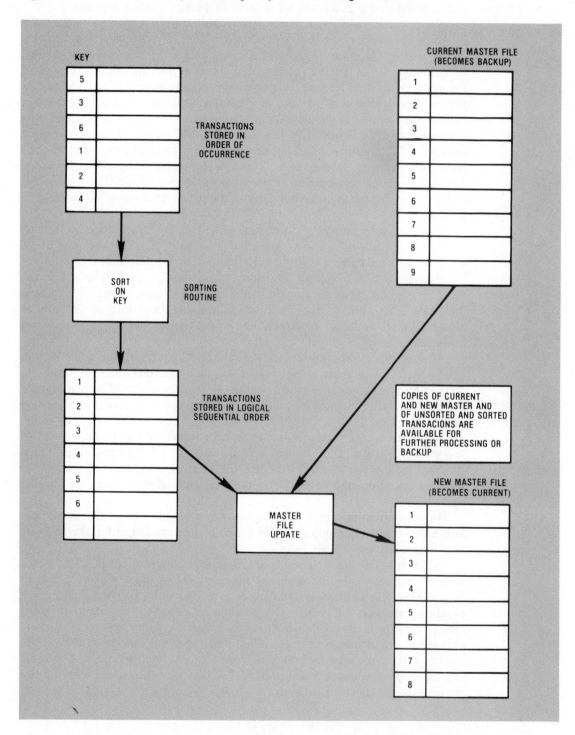

master records to update the file. For these reasons, many payroll files use sequential file organization.

Direct File Organization

Direct file organization is a method in which the physical location, or address, of a record in a file is determined by the value of its key field. Typically, a mathematical formula is applied to the key value to determine an address in the file. With availability of this address, the system can access the record directly, without the need to search through the file in physical sequence to locate the desired record. Although the file may be accessed serially, the physical sequence of records on storage media may have no logical meaning since the records are not necessarily ordered according to keys. Figure 12-6 illustrates a direct file organization.

A direct file organization is applicable where there is a need for immediate, rapid access to records in the file and where it is impractical or impossible to anticipate the order in which records will be processed.

Direct files are used to support random processing. In random processing, the order in which records are processed cannot be predicted in advance. Further, access requests often are processed individually. That is, it is impossible or impractical to batch transactions so that all processing can take place at the same time. The nature of this usage eliminates the potential for using sequential organization. For example, to process each random access request with a tape file would require reading sequentially from the beginning of the file through the

Figure 12.6.   Direct file organization.

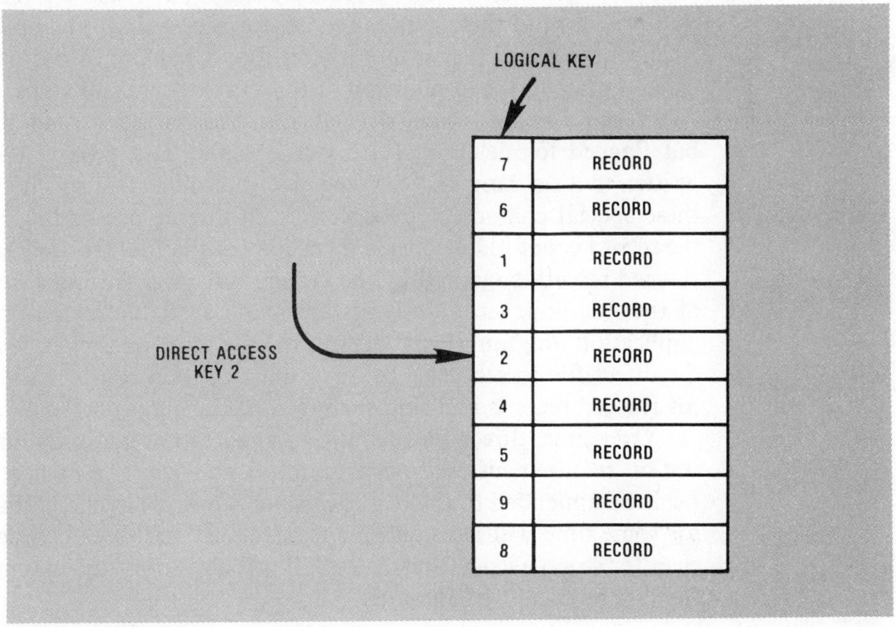

records to the point where the required record has been recorded. This access method is inefficient and, essentially, unworkable. An important feature of direct files is that they make possible rapid access to individual records without this type of sequential search.

Under a direct file organization scheme, the location, or address, of a record in the file is often expressed in terms of its position relative to the first record in the file. When this type of addressing is used, direct file organization is known also as relative file organization. Although there is a relationship between the record keys and the positions of the records in the file, there is no requirement that these relative addresses correspond with the logical order of keys.

Direct files tend to be convenient to process. For example, many access functions involving direct files are for user inquiries. The user simply enters a record key. The system finds the desired information and prints or displays the record. There is no impact upon the content of the file.

Record updating in a direct file occurs in place. That is, after one or more fields are modified by the update program, the record is written back to its address in the file, replacing the original record. Thus, file updates are destructive to the original information contained in the records. For this reason, updating nearly always involves creation of a transaction log. For example, when a given record is updated, the transaction that was applied to it may be written to the log file. Thus, if the direct file is destroyed inadvertently, it becomes possible to reconstruct it using a backup copy of the direct file and the log file. Either magnetic tape or disk can be used to maintain log files. Figure 12-7 illustrates a typical master file update using a direct file organization. The transactions are captured in order of occurrence and sent immediately to a log which records them contiguously. As they occur, the transactions are also sent to the application program, in this case an update, for processing. The update transaction is applied directly to the current master file. A backup of the master file has been created prior to the application of this current series of transactions.

When a record is to be deleted from a direct file, it is not removed physically but flagged for deletion. In this case, a **flag** is a group of special characters written to a field appended to the record to indicate a specific condition. When these special characters are encountered during processing, they indicate that the record is not to be considered as part of the file. During random access, this flagged record is ignored by the system software. During sequential processing of the file, however, all records are made available to the program. Thus, an application program that processes the file sequentially — say, a program to sort the direct file in sequence by key — must contain routines to check specifically for flagged records and skip such records during processing.

Over time, direct files require reorganization and rebuilding. The reorganization requirement may occur because a new application requires additional fields be appended to the records. More often, a direct file that has been in use for some time will have had many additions and deletions and become inefficient for storage usage and access. This is a result of the manner in which direct files are physically maintained.

Figure 12.7. *Master file update using direct file organization.*

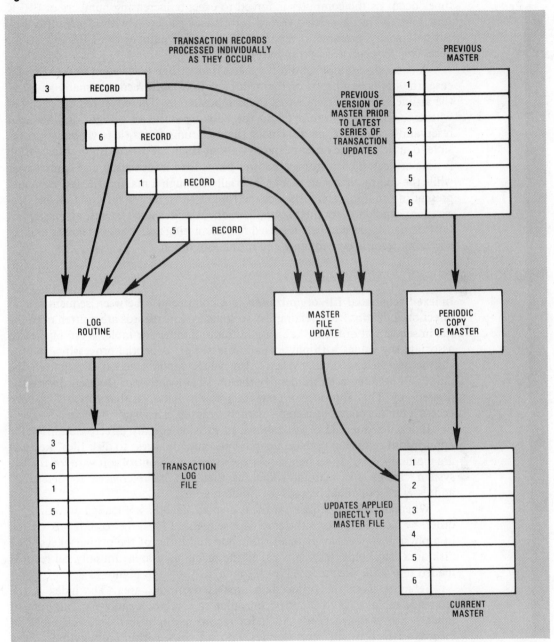

One way to determine whether direct file needs reorganization is to consider run times or access times. Many operating systems include packages that keep track of access times and other operating statistics involving use of direct files. A sure way to tell that a file is losing efficiency is a steady, though usually gradual, increase in access time experienced by users. These increases in access times occur as the computer is forced to execute increasing numbers of SEEK functions to find a needed record. Statistical packages within operating systems, typically, are able to report on the average number of SEEK executions necessary for each access transaction.

A common example of direct file use is an airline reservation system. In this case, the file is composed of flight information, with records usually keyed to the airline and flight number as the composite key. These records are accessed whenever customers inquire about the booking status of a flight or when seat reservations are to be made. Under these circumstances, it is virtually impossible to anticipate the order of inquiry about flights. Further, flight information is time-critical. The customer requires immediate information and cannot wait while the computer system searches serially through a massive file to locate and present information about the desired flight. Thus, airline information files are excellent candidates for direct organization. Within these systems, airline identification and flight numbers are used for calculating addresses of records and for accessing records immediately and in random order.

Indexed Sequential File Organization

Indexed sequential file organization is a compromise between sequential and direct organization. To oversimplify to some extent, records are written onto the file in sequential order, by key. In addition, an index, or table, is established to associate key values with physical addresses. For sequential processing, the file can be accessed in order by key. Also, where random access is required, the index can be referenced to identify the physical location of the record with the desired key. This approach represents a compromise, in that supporting both access methods comes at a cost—namely, trading efficiency for access.

Indexed sequential organization can provide equally effective support for applications requiring both sequential and random access to disk files. Records are maintained in key sequences. At the same time, control software for the file system creates and maintains indexes that can be referenced to determine addresses of individual records for random access.

When an indexed sequential file is created, records are loaded onto disk, in order, by record key. As is the case with sequential files, the records are written in a physical order that matches the sequential order of the primary keys. The disk area that holds this file is called the prime data area. Initially, all records loaded into a file are recorded in this area, as shown in Figure 12-8.

Separate from the prime data area is the index area. The index is the reference table used to identify, or point to, record locations in support of random access instructions. An index record is established for each block of records—which usually corresponds with a track—within every cylinder on a disk drive. This index is keyed to the highest value for any record in the corresponding block.

Inquiries or changes for indexed sequential files can be handled either in sequential or in random order. Sequential transactions are processed in record key order, as would be done with an ordinary sequential file. Random inquiries

Figure 12.8. *Indexed sequential file organization.*

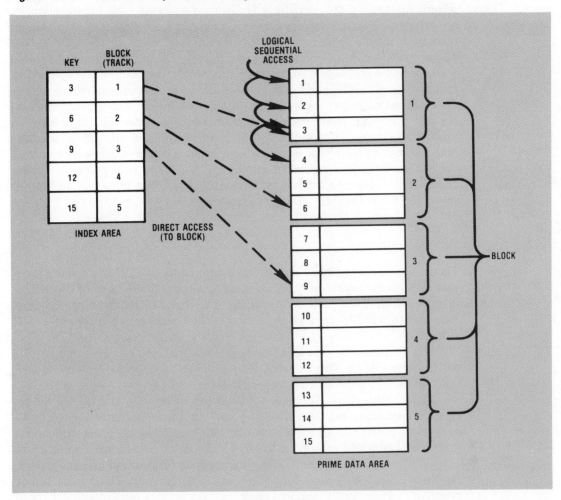

or change transactions are referred first to the index, which then points to the block location of the record. That block then is searched sequentially to find the record that is to be referenced or changed. When changes are made, the new data are written in place over the existing record.

Like direct files, indexed sequential files lose efficiency over time. Response times experienced by users deteriorate as the number of deleted records increases and as the complexity of pointer chains within overflow areas also increases. Overflow areas accommodate changes to the file that would not fit into the prime area. When access times are degraded to an unacceptable level, the file must be reorganized by building a new file. Reorganization involves copying all existing records, in sequence, into the prime area of the new file, updating the index area, and allowing for a new overflow capacity. Utility programs are available to handle these reorganizations.

Obviously, applications in which both sequential and random access to records are desired are candidates for indexed sequential file organization. A typical example is an inventory control system. Such a system is used in keeping track of merchandise on hand and for ordering and restocking depleted goods. The primary file in such a system is an inventory file in which product records are kept. As merchandise is removed from stock, the records are updated to reflect withdrawals. When merchandise is restocked, the corresponding records are modified to reflect the additions. Since withdrawals and replacements do not take place in a predetermined order, it is necessary for this file to support random processing. However, in support of other applications, such as preparation of inventory listings or merchandise reports, it becomes necessary to access the file sequentially by product number. Thus, an inventory control system demands both random and sequential access capabilities for which an indexed sequential file is the appropriate mechanism.

FILE DESIGN DECISIONS

The design of files involves identification and consideration of alternatives involving formats, organization options, and controls. These areas of file design, in turn, produce decision criteria to be considered in determining the exact characteristics of files for a given application and deciding where those files will reside.

The discussion in this section, then, deals with the elements of final file design decisions. In effect, the list of topics in this section provides a checklist that can be used as a guide in decision making.

The decision-making process itself involves identifying alternatives for access, organization, and control, then evaluating these alternatives against corresponding costs, values, or compliance with requirements. These evaluations involve tradeoffs that are unique in each organization and for each application. Thus, this discussion does not offer a prescription for decision making. Rather, the intent is to identify areas for concern and consideration. These areas include processing requirements, required response time, activity rate, volatility, backup requirements, and file device capacity.

Processing Requirements

Data files generally support applications that will be processed either on a batch or on an interactive basis. In some cases applications may involve combinations of batch and interactive processing.

Batch processing often involves the accumulation of an entire transaction file that is entered as a unit and processed against a master file. In most cases, the efficient organization method for such files will be sequential. For sequential processing, both the transaction and master files have to be in the same order. Matching records then becomes rapid and efficient, as long as a high percentage of master file records is to be updated with each processing of the file.

A typical batch application is payroll, as described earlier in this chapter. Other typical applications supported by sequential files include logs, backup or protection files, and archival files. A typical logging application, for example, would be electronic journaling. Electronic journaling is a chronological listing of all transactions processed within an installation. These files can be used as audit trails or for reconstruction of files under recovery procedures. A backup or archival file is a sequentially created copy of a master file. The original files themselves may or may not be sequential.

To illustrate file usage in an interactive manner, consider the airline reservation application. A reservation system requires direct access to information about individual flights. Therefore, there would be no way to anticipate the order in which transactions are presented to the system or to organize transactions so that they correspond with the sequence of a master file. Thus, with a lack of correspondence between the ordering of transactions and master file records, a direct file organization becomes the only way to support such an application.

In some instances, applications require a mixture of accessing and processing capabilities. For example, transactions might be processed sequentially against a master file, but it might also be necessary to support an on-line reference application that uses the same file. Such a mixture of processing methods is implemented by many banks. Processing of checks written by depositors typically is done sequentially. The checks are sorted in account-number order, then these transaction files are processed against customer master files in batches. The same file, however, also can be referenced directly, at random, by bank officers and tellers who need status information.

Tradeoffs in processing, therefore, consider such factors as the type of access (serial, logical sequential, or random) that must be supported, whether batch or on-line processing is required for conformance with processing cycles, and the types of relations that must be established between files. As these considerations become evident during the analysis and general design phase of the systems study, they are used as the primary criteria for choosing a file organization and access method. In some cases, processing requirements dictate clearly the type of organization scheme that must be employed. In other cases, two or more options will exist. Additional criteria must then be applied in choosing the appropriate organization method.

Required Response Time

Consideration of **response time** applies to direct access applications only. The volume of inquiries and the response time required must be taken into account in determining what equipment and what organizational approach to use.

For example, an airline reservation system represents a high-volume application in which there is a real, monetary value associated with rapid response time. A direct file organization with direct access provides the fastest method of getting at needed records. By contrast, if an indexed sequential file were used for airline reservations, access time could be at least twice that for a direct file.

This extra time under the indexed sequential approach is needed because the computer must perform an extensive search of an index before it can even initiate a record access operation.

Activity Rate

The **activity rate** of an application refers to the frequency with which records are accessed by the application. For example, a payroll application would have a high activity rate, or hit rate, because most records are processed on every processing run. By comparison, checking account updating applications would have a lower hit rate because only a relatively small percentage of account holders write checks on any given day.

Normally, sequential processing and access methods are appropriate when hit rates are high because sequential processing represents the fastest method for accessing each record in a file. By contrast, occasional reference to records within a file would make on-line, direct access more efficient.

Volatility

The **volatility**, or rate of change and expansion, of master files should be taken into account in determining the organization to be used. If additions to, and deletions from, files are to be relatively great, it is often best to use a sequential organization plan. An excellent example can be seen in billing programs for transient classified advertising in newspapers. These advertisements are called in by telephone. Usually a classified ad runs for a few days and then is dropped. Its customers are one-time or occasional users. When a bill is paid, the customer name is dropped from the accounts receivable file. Thus, there are large volumes of additions to, and deletions from, the file every day. If such a file were organized for direct access, the entire file would have to be restructured almost every day. Under sequential processing, structuring is routine. That is, a sequential file is rewritten every time it is processed. Thus, additions or deletions present no problem; sequential files are volatile by nature.

Special user requirements, of course, can have an overriding effect on the selection of file organization method. To illustrate, highly volatile files are used by law enforcement agencies to record stolen cars or wanted persons. Content of these files changes rapidly. If batch processing were possible, this application would lend itself well to sequential files. However, on-line reference is a must. Therefore, the application itself dictates a direct access capability. Thus, even though greater processing efficiency might be attainable with sequential files, it is virtually necessary to use an indexed sequential or direct file organization.

Backup Requirements

Every system needs backup and recovery procedures. If master files are destroyed or if an error occurs during update processing, there must be some method for restoring the files to their proper state. Backup files provide a starting point. Recovery procedures specify a plan for restoring the files.

Sequential files have an advantage in that such files automatically create backup files, because a new file is written during each update processing run. Thus, the input file and the transaction file become backup files for each newly created file.

When direct access files are used, special backup procedures must be developed. The protection is needed because master records are updated in place. Transactions are usually logged as they occur, but transaction records are only valuable as related to a current version of the master file. Master records may be written to an update log file before and after updating, providing a basis for file restoration if something goes wrong during the update processing. It is also good practice to make a backup copy of the master file before a direct update is performed.

File Device Capacity

While not a characteristic of the application itself, the proposed file organization should be reviewed to be sure that the file devices available can handle the files to be created. For example, there might be enough room on a disk file to handle a sequential file application. However, it might turn out that there isn't enough room to accommodate the space overhead of a direct or indexed sequential file. Additional storage capacity, and corresponding additional cost, may be necessary. In general, one of the checkpoints that should be covered is to make sure that the storage devices to be used can accommodate the files to be created.

DATABASE MANAGEMENT SYSTEMS

The term **data management** refers to the hardware and software technology necessary for data organization, storage, retrieval, and presentation for processing. Data management facilities in most computer installations are provided by traditional file management systems. That is, data are organized within logical groupings called records; these records are grouped within sequential, direct, or indexed sequential files; and files of similar record types are placed on secondary storage devices such as magnetic tape or disk for convenience of retrieval.

For the most part, data management has been designed to allow access to data through applications programs. In fact, files frequently are organized to support specific applications and written in a specific programming language. Data records and their relationships, therefore, often become application dependent; that is, the file organization supports the viewpoint of a limited number of users who are serviced by the application.

Data management systems, on the other hand, are collections of generalized file management software with the purpose of taking over many of the common processing functions that traditionally have been implemented through applications programs. These systems include report writers and report generators, sort packages, file creation and updating facilities, and basic inquiry processing and data manipulation functions. The purpose of data management systems is to allow users to perform many recurring data processing functions without the time and effort required to develop specialized programs. Data management software provides a convenient interface between the user and data organized under traditional file organization methods.

A **database management system (DBMS)** is a combination of data organization and access techniques that extend the capabilities of data management systems. In general, a DBMS is capable of integrating and managing data to serve the needs of a variety of users with a variety of viewpoints. A DBMS overcomes the constraints imposed in traditional file-oriented environments by organizing data independently of applications.

Multiple Data Views

A database management system supports three viewpoints about how data are stored in a database: physical view (internal), logical view (conceptual), and user view (external).

Physical View. The physical view of data refers to the way data actually are organized and stored on secondary storage devices. For the most part, direct and indexed file organization techniques are used along with methods for relating data maintained in physically separate files.

Logical View. The logical view of an entire database is called the **schema**. A schema is composed of the set of entities, attributes, and relationships that describe the logical organization of data necessary to support all users of the database. The schema is derived through normalization techniques and documented with data access diagrams.

User View. The logical view of a single user (user view), may require a subset of the database. This subset, **subschema**, is comprised of the collection of attributes drawn from the schema to support the processing needs of a user or application program. Whereas a database has a single schema, it is capable of supporting any number of subschemas.

The data access diagram in Figure 12-9 repeats a portion of the schema shown in Figure 12-2 for one of the databases that could be defined to support a university registration system. The entities within this portion of the database are STUDENTS, CLASSES, and GRADES, each with its own attributes, or data elements. Through various keys, relationships have been established between the entities. The schema has been designed to support user needs for accessing different combinations of attributes for various applications.

Figure 12-9 shows two potential subschemas that can be derived from the schema. Subschema A represents the collection of attributes required to produce class rosters. This subschema may represent the viewpoint of an application program that will generate the rosters at the beginning of a term. Subschema B, on the other hand, represents a different viewpoint. In this case, the combination of attributes can be used to produce grade reports that will be made available at the end of the term. In each case, a single schema is the basis for the application. It is not necessary that separate files be established to support the different applications.

The schema is a global view of the entities important to the organization, the attributes that characterize these entities and that will be made available to

Figure 12.9. *Schema and subschemas to support processing within a student record system.*

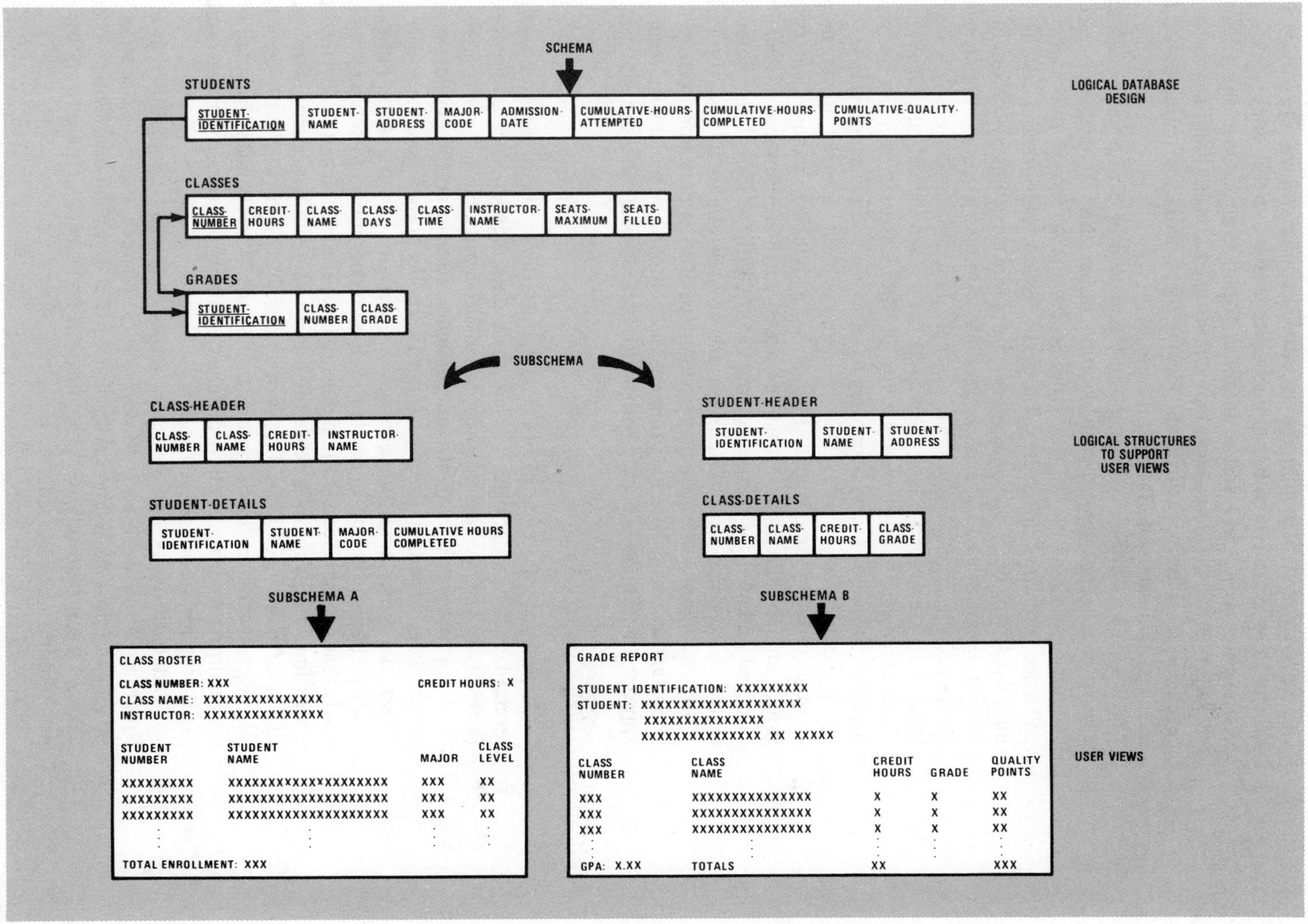

different users, and the relationships that must exist for maneuvering through the database and accessing the required attribute values. Definition of this schema may be one of the responsibilities of the systems analyst, working in conjunction with users and a database administrator. Once the schema and subschemas are defined and documented, a database administrator or other technical database specialist will format the schema for maintenance by the database management system software.

Within a DBMS environment, determination of data organization and access is primarily a logical consideration rather than a physical one. During systems analysis activities, the database schema is derived and modeled as a collection of entities, attributes, and relationships. This schema may have to be integrated with other schemas representing other systems in the organization. During design, specialists such as database administrators assist in creating and formatting the physical database through data description or data definition languages. These special languages, peculiar to each individual DBMS, communicate the logical data structures to the DBMS so that the data can be organized on devices to allow access according to various subschemas, or views.

It should be noted that a DBMS, in and of itself, does not provide assurance of quality data management. In a sense, a database management system is simply another file organization and access method. However, it does provide extended potential for managing data resources if the logical viewpoints represented in schemas and subschemas are of high quality. Thus, the technical aspects of database management systems are of secondary importance. What is important in a database environment, as well as in a file environment, is the appropriateness and accuracy with which these logical views are modeled.

Benefits of a DBMS

With an appropriate data model and the availability of database software, several benefits can accrue. These include data independence, nonredundancy, flexibility of access, data integrity, and data security.

Data Independence. **Data independence** means that the physical organization of data is not tied directly to specific applications programs or user needs. The data are insulated from changes in processing requirements. For example, in a traditional file environment, files may be organized to support processing needs that are in effect at the moment. Data are bound physically to the programs that use them. Whenever there is a change in processing requirements, files must be changed by additions or deletions of fields within the records, and all programs that process those files also must be changed. In addition, the restructuring of a file to allow different methods of access propagates changes to all programs that use the file.

Database technology, however, allows convenient adaptability to change. Programs define data needs through logical references to database subschemas rather than through references to physical file organizations. Thus, processing changes mean that only the program with the particular subschema viewpoint would need to be changed.

Nonredundancy. The principle of **nonredundancy** requires that entity attributes appear only once in a database. Although some redundancy may be preferable for enhancing database performance, the goal is to keep the number of identical attributes at a minimum. In a file environment, redundancy is virtually unavoidable in providing different programs with different views of data. In these situations, if a program changes the value of an attribute in one file, special arrangements must be made for updating the attribute in all the other files containing the same field. Although the process of normalization helps in avoiding excessive redundancy, file processing methods still can produce duplications of fields that lead to maintenance problems. In a database system, replication of data elements is at a minimum. Applications can share common attributes without being bound together by common physical views of data. Thus, programs can operate independently.

Flexibility of Access. **Flexibility of access** means that extraction and processing of data contained within a database need not be limited to specialized applications programs. In addition, the database can be referenced through higher-level, nonprocedural languages that give the nontechnical user access to data. Normally, database management systems are supported by query languages, report writers, and other generalized software that permit natural-language-type inquiries of the database. In effect, database technology allows as many different applications as can be modeled through subschemas.

Data Integrity. **Data integrity** refers to the preservation of a high degree of consistency and quality of data. By its very nature, a database system maintains data integrity. The characteristics of data independence and nonredundancy help assure control over data resources. The DBMS helps reduce the need for users to coordinate their use of data that will be changed, replaced, or linked with other data through new relationships.

Data Security. A database system helps provide security of data resources or **data security**. Through elaborate software mechanisms, the system can establish accessibility limits on data and permit only authorized users to gain access to the data defined by the users' personal subschemas. In effect, a DBMS places data resource control into the hands of data administrators and takes it out of the hands of technical persons with the know-how to access the data.

DBMS Tradeoffs

Performance of the database management system represents a tradeoff in three areas: application processing efficiency, processing overhead, and disk storage space.

A DBMS presents multiple logical views, or subschemas, of the data to multiple users. Yet, these views are all based on a single set of physical files that implement the overall schema. It is not surprising, then, that some application programs might run very efficiently, while others do not. Normally, the underlying physical files are "tuned" so that they provide the most rapid and efficient support to the most critical programs. In this way, the applications that must run most efficiently or have the most stringent response time requirements receive the better service.

The very ability of a DBMS to provide different views of the data to different users, as well as different access paths for different applications, creates a great deal of "behind-the-scenes" complexity. Data maintained in a DBMS typically require significantly more storage space than would be used in traditional file processing environments. There is also a heavy processing overhead required to maintain the various access paths as the database is updated.

These disadvantages can be more than offset, however, by the long-term flexibility provided by a DBMS environment. As business needs change and new application requirements arise, such requirements often can be accommodated by simply developing a new logical schema and/or subschema, rather than by restructuring the entire database and the programs that use it.

Database Models

A data model is a systematic, logical representation of the various views of the organizational data. The model provides a blueprint for implementation of the system's logical data structures, entities, and relationships into a functional, physical DBMS. A model provides an underlying structure upon which to map the actual logical data schema. Three common models form the foundation for most commercial DBMS products. They are hierarchical, network, and relational.

These models provide a framework for organizing the logical data structures and relationships. They do not deal with concepts for implementation such as language syntax, indexes, link lists, or pointers. Each specific DBMS product, based on one of the models, will provide a data definition language (DDL) that will actually operationalize those structures and relationships.

The Hierarchical Model. The **hierarchical**, or sometimes called tree-structured, data model represents the database as a series of structures in a hierarchy or tree diagram. Commercial products based upon the hierarchical model include IMS and SYSTEM 2000. The fundamental data structure in a hierarchical model is called a record. A record is a grouping of data elements that describe one kind of object or thing. For example every student record might have the same data elements, such as NUMBER, NAME, ADDRESS, etc.; but there would be different values for each element. The hierarchical relationship of different types of records within the database form the data model.

In the hierarchical model, each type of record exists in a "parent to child" relationship to other records of different types. The model begins from one source or "root" record, which is drawn at the top of the tree structure. Other records are joined by lines or arcs, denoting their subordination or superordination to each other. Figure 12-10 depicts a simple hierarchical or tree diagram for the university registration system.

To access data in a hierarchically based DBMS, you must follow the branches from the root through the tree to the appropriate data location. This model seems natural for typical business data management situations because of the hierarchical nature of those organizations. For example corporate structure, inventory, billing, and other business entities are organized in a hierarchical manner. However, access to data is constrained along the branches of the tree.

Figure 12.10.   Hierarchical data model.

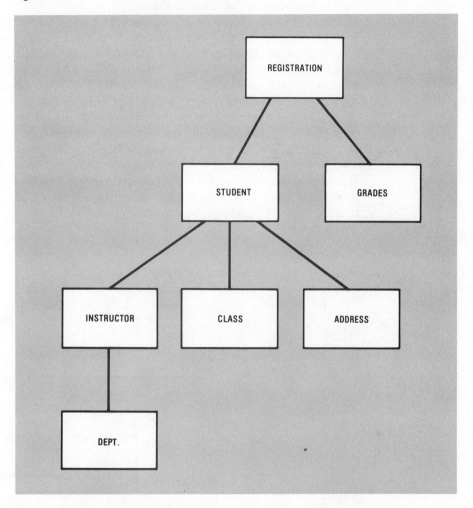

Therefore this model may be inappropriate for systems experiencing excessive and changing circumstances or numerous queries aimed at low levels on the diagram.

The Network Model. **Network data models** are similar to hierarchical models in that the major data structure is called a record and the overall schema expresses the relationships between records of different types. The most common commercial products employing a network model include DBMS-10, IDMS, and DMS 1100. The database model is composed of "instances" or "occurrences" of records linked together in a network fashion.

In the network model, relationships among record types are much more flexible than in the hierarchical model. More complex and less ordinary relationships are easier to define. Records of the database are organized into one or more designated "sets." The sets describe the relationship between record types.

One record in a set is designated as the "owner" and all others are "members." This is known as an "owner-coupled set."

Many sets may be defined in the network model. Each record type may be both an owner or a member of multiple sets. Thus a wide variety of possible relationships can be developed with the network model. Specific DBMS packages further define rules which specify set relationships and various other data alignments such as order or composition. Figure 12-11 represents a network model using the record types from the university registration system. A set is illustrated by the student to instructor network connection, the student being the owner and the instructor being the member in this example.

Accessing data in a network-based DBMS typically involves beginning with an owner of a set, finding a member who in turn may be the owner of another set. Also, successive members of a particular set may be accessed, for example all of the instructors for which a particular student has enrolled in a course. All of these types of operations in a network model are known as "navigating" the database.

Figure 12.11.   Network data model.

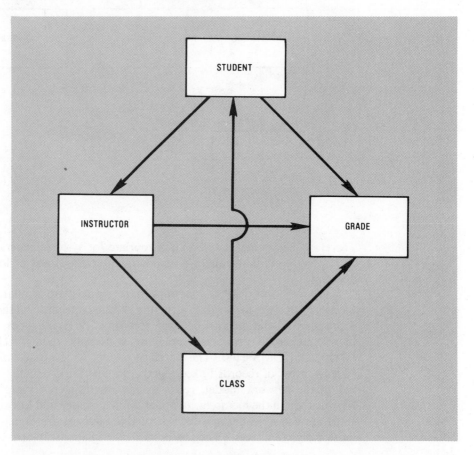

The advantage to a network-based DBMS is the many alternative ways in which paths can be specified to specific data for different user views. This model is highly efficient in well-structured and standardized operations wherein every transaction falls within a large number of predetermined categories. Compared to the hierarchical model, the network model provides a greater flexibility and performance. The tradeoff, however, is that the network model's multiple relationships among records requires a great deal of system overhead in the form of storage and processing capability.

The Relational Model. The **relational model** expresses the data structures and relationships in the form of a table, that is a collection of data values or occurrences organized in rows and columns. Mathematically, this form is known as a *relation*, hence the name. Some of the most common commercial products implementing a relational model are SQL/DS, INGRES, DB2™, and ORACLE®.

Each table or relation in the database model is given a unique name, usually referring to the object or entity being described. Each column in the table, called an attribute, also is assigned a name. Each row of the relation, called a *tuple*, contains a value for each column. Figure 12-12 depicts two relations from the university registration system, STUDENT and GRADE. STUDENT NUMBER is an attribute of both relations. The set of values represented by attributes of one entire tuple describes on object or entity, or in this case, a particular student or a grade.

Operations provided by relational DBMS products originate from mathematical set operations. Typical set operations include select, project, and join.

A *select* operation allows the selection of certain specified rows from a relation. For example, all students (or rows) with grades above 2.00 may be selected or all students within a particular major may be selected.

The *project* operation allows the formation of a new relation from columns of an original one. For example, STUDENT NAME, CREDITS EARNED, and GPA might be projected from the STUDENT relation for inclusion on a grade report.

The *join* operation allows the formation of a new relation from two or more existing ones. The rows of the new relation are formed by joining the rows of the existing relations that have the same values for certain attributes. For example, a new relation might be formed from STUDENT and GRADE wherein the grade information (from the GRADE relation) of a student for a particular course would be joined with the student information (from the STUDENT relation.)

Combinations of select, project, and join operations, as well as other types of relational operations, allow the most flexible and adaptable query and reporting operations of these database models. Relational model DBMS products do not usually store all relationships explicitly, rather they allow the formulation of new relationships and associations on an ad hoc basis. This is obviously the most advantageous of the models in situations where unplanned, changing circumstances are normal systems application.

Figure 12.12. *Relational data model.*

STUDENT RELATION

ATTRIBUTE ▼

STUDENT NUMBER	STUDENT NAME	ADDRESS	MAJOR	CREDITS EARNED	GPA
TUPLE ➤ 451–32–1060	Smith, Bob	___	___	___	___
519–21–1111	Jones, Sue	___	___	___	___
391–44–3321	Blair, Robin	___	___	___	___
496–12–9310	Alvarez, Juan	___	___	___	___
___	___	___	___	___	___
___	___	___	___	___	___
___	___	___	___	___	___

GRADE RELATION

ATTRIBUTE ▼

STUDENT NUMBER	CLASS NUMBER	STUDENT GRADE
TUPLE ➤ 451–32–1060	___	___
519–21–1111	___	___
___	___	___
___	___	___
___	___	___

Database Models and Files

Even with traditional file environments, techniques using the database style for organizing data can be applied to produce similar benefits. The process of normalizing files to reduce redundancy, to eliminate the need for variable-length records, and to permit access through primary keys can produce systems that emulate database environments. Although processing inefficiencies may result for any particular application, system efficiency will be enhanced. The integrity of the data will improve and adaptability of the system to future needs will increase.

Generally, the collection of data managed by an organization remains fairly stable. Applications that process the data, however, change and expand. If a system design, especially its file structure, is modeled after those applications, a change in processing requirements will dictate a change in the file structure, with corresponding modifications required in all software that accesses those structures. If, on the other hand, a system design is anchored to the data structure rather than to the processing structure, the impact of changes is reduced. Files organized according to business needs rather than to computer processing needs serve long-term organizational goals as well as immediate data processing objectives.

Thus, determination of file organization methods should be preceded by careful modeling of the data. This modeling, in turn, should borrow from schema development techniques that are applied in database environments. The result will be a file structure that is generally applicable to both the current processing environment and to planned changes and contingencies.

SUMMARY

In the building and use of computer information systems, files are the major focal point. It has been said that to be successful an organization's database must model the organization itself.

Application support file types include master, transaction, reference, archival, backup, and transaction log files. A given application may include any or all of such file types.

File design involves the process of normalization, which produces ideal data structures that can be packaged physically as attribute or correlative files.

E-R diagrams are useful to the analyst and designer in file design because they focus on data and relationships in a systematic, exhaustive way, which is not necessarily true of a data flow diagram. Each entity may be ultimately packaged as a file, and the relationships identified between the entities will be operationalized as access paths.

A data access diagram illustrates the necessary data access paths for the implementation of application programs' use of the normalized files. This is the appropriate documentation for the transition between logical and physical file design.

The overall data organization should, if at all possible, model the business organization rather than merely support specific processing urgencies. The business organization should remain fairly stable, as should the data organization, whereas specific processing may change erratically.

Although normalized data structure and design are an ideal, they may need to be compromised to meet specific processing requirements and existing hardware or software constraints.

File access methods include physical sequential (serial) access, logical sequential access, and direct (random) access.

In general, sequential file access can be accomplished with magnetic tape storage media, but direct access must be implemented with magnetic disk storage media.

A distinction is made between logical and physical records. Files which are blocked will bring multiple logical records into the CPU buffer during an application program execution. The larger the block, the more efficient the I/O processing but the greater the CPU memory usage.

File organization methods include sequential, direct and indexed sequential. A sequential organization will support serial and logical sequential access; a direct organization will support random access; and indexed sequential will support all access methods.

Direct and indexed sequential file organizations require periodic reorganizations to remain efficient.

Areas of concern in the process of file design include processing requirements, response time, activity rate, volatility, backup requirements, and file device capacity.

Beyond traditional file management systems are database management systems (DBMS) which allow multiple views, based on subschemas, of a single database, based on a schema.

A DBMS may benefit a data organization by greater data independence, nonredunancy among files, accessing flexibility, data integrity, and added data security.

The three most common data models upon which specific database schemas are based are hierarchical, network, and relational models. The relational model adds the greatest degree of flexibility in defining associations between data structures.

KEY TERMS

1. E-R diagram
2. data access diagram
3. normalization
4. attrribute file
5. correlative file
6. file access
7. physical sequential (serial) access
8. logical sequential access
9. direct access
10. file organization
11. sequential file organization
12. indexed sequential file organization
13. direct file organization
14. sequential access device
15. direct access device
16. logical record
17. physical record
18. block
19. interblock gap (IBG)
20. interrecord gap (IRG)
21. buffer
22. fixed-length record
23. variable-length record
24. flag
25. access count field
26. response time
27. activity rate
28. volatility
29. data management system
30. database management system (DBMS)
31. schema

32. subschema
33. data independence
34. nonredundancy
35. flexibility of access
36. data integrity

37. data security
38. hierarchial model
39. network data model
40. relational model

REVIEW/DISCUSSION QUESTIONS

1. List the six types of files needed to support a system and explain the basic content of each.
2. What are the three principal methods of file access?
3. What are the three principal methods of file organization?
4. Explain the meaning of the terms logical record and physical record.
5. Into what two categories may storage devices be grouped and what specific type of hardware typically is associated with each?
6. What tradeoffs are associated with the use of magnetic tape?
7. How does file organization relate to the type of storage device used?
8. What are six key concerns in the process of file design?
9. Explain the three viewpoints about how data are stored in the database under a database management system.
10. What are the advantages of a database management system?
11. What are the disadvantages or tradeoffs of a database enviroment?
12. Explain the differences between hierarchial, network, and relational database models.
13. What are the roles of normalization, E-R diagrams, and data access diagrams in file and database design.
14. Explain the differences between a sequential update and a direct update.
15. What is the role of the system flow chart and what types of changes may occur during the file design process.

PRACTICE ASSIGNMENTS

For each of the following file requirements, determine an appropriate file organization and access method. Provide a justification for your recommendations.

1. An employee payroll file will be accessed once a week to calculate the company's payroll and to issue paychecks. Records in this file contain employee identification, pay rate, and withholding information. This is a master file against which a transaction file containing data from weekly time cards is processed. The file will be accessed in order by employee number. Between 90 and 95 percent of all records will be processed.
2. An airline reservation file contains passenger flight information used in booking passengers and issuing tickets. It is keyed by the flight numbers of the airline. Rapid access to this file is important so that customers can receive flight information while they wait at reservation counters or on the telephone. Bookings take place immediately. Thus, the flight records are updated as soon as passengers ask for reservations.

3. An inventory file contains product information about all merchandise held in stock. Each record contains product descriptions, prices, quantities on hand, and reorder points. Whenever an item of merchandise is withdrawn from stock or stock is replaced, the record is updated to maintain a current record of product availability. Also, periodic inventory reports are prepared for management. These list, in sequence by product number, the quantities of merchandise in inventory. Also, customer inquiries about the availability of stock require that the product records be accessible immediately through on-line terminals.

4. A file of federal withholding tax tables is used for determining withholding amounts during payroll processing. This file is loaded into program tables when the payroll program is run. The program then searches the in-memory tables to locate withholding amounts. No maintenance or updating is required of this file. It is a reference file that is built one time, at the beginning of the year.

5. A transaction log file is written as part of the on-line updating procedure for master file maintenance. Additions, changes, and deletions applied against a customer master file are processed interactively through on-line terminals. These transactions are recorded in a log file and include the date on which the change took place, an identification of the master record that was affected, and a notation about the type of maintenance activity and the field change that was completed. This journalizing technique provides an audit trail through which the transaction can be traced from its point of origin through its appearance in the master file.

Constructing a General Application Design

Learning objectives

On completing reading and other learning assignments for this chapter, you should be able to:

- Describe the role of software design in the systems development process.
- Describe the characteristics of a "good" application design.
- Discuss some trends affecting the design of software and delineate the scope of design efforts.
- Understand the function of a system flowchart and flowcharting symbols.
- Be able to package a system data flow diagram into a system flowchart using appropriate packaging criteria.
- Explain the options available to implement system software components.
- Describe when application packages may be an appropriate implementation option and how they may be evaluated.
- Describe the implications of a decision to do custom programming.
- Explain what program development considerations are associated with custom programming for on-line systems vs batch systems.
- Describe tradeoff issues involved in selecting options for the implementation of an application design.

THE PURPOSE OF SOFTWARE DESIGN

Systems design deals with overall requirements and results in a specification of the input, processing, output, and data resources that will interact to provide the needs stated as a result of analysis. In a sense, systems analysis can be likened to an architect's rendering of a building to be constructed. The viewer can tell what the building will look like; but before construction can begin, sets of extremely detailed plans and specifications, a blueprint, must be developed. These plans serve as the basis for actual construction, or implementation, of the original rendering. The blueprint is thus the design of the rendering.

A user specification for a new system plays the same role and serves the same basic purpose as an architect's rendering for a new building. That is, a specification document provides an overall picture of what an information system will look like and what it will do. Beyond that, a series of detailed technical designs must be produced for a system under development. These specifications will become the blueprint guiding the implementation effort. The three categories of system design that require detailed specification are the physical system architecture, the file and database, and application software.

Concerned mostly with application software, software design is one step in the preparation of a total system design. Systems analysis takes a complex business problem and breaks it down into a system of data and processing components. This resulting logical system is then organized into jobs, job steps, and individual interactive procedures. Software design then takes one of the system components—the processing function—and bridges the gap between its broad, general specifications and the myriad lines of program code that fulfill those specifications.

As in any phase of technically oriented design, software design takes an overall assignment that is too complex to deal with in its entirety and breaks that job down into a series of smaller parts that can be understood and handled individually. The skills and methods for identifying what those smaller parts are, how extensive each of the parts is to be, and how all of the parts relate to one another, is the crux of software design.

TRENDS AFFECTING SOFTWARE DESIGN

As computers have become more generally available and have grown in capacity and capability, the systems that can be planned and implemented have become more extensive. Thus, complexity of applications is, in a sense, an outgrowth of the success achieved by the builders of computers and by developers of system software. The extended capabilities of hardware and software have, in turn, been passed along into the application area.

Unfortunately, trends in applications software development have not kept pace with trends in the hardware and systems software areas. Design methodologies that were sufficient when hardware and software constraints limited the application of the computer to rather simple data processing systems are no longer adequate for building the systems of today. There is an order of magnitude difference between designing and developing a basic accounting system of 5,000 to 10,000 lines of code and a management information system of, say, 300,000 lines of code. The degree of complexity inherent in the latter type of system places analytical demands on the designer that were not even considered in earlier systems.

Another difference between the systems being developed today and those of a decade ago relates to the types of users who operate and are serviced by the systems. Data processing systems traditionally have been batch-oriented systems run by computer professionals. All data entry, processing, and output took place within the confines of the computer room, which was considered off limits to the eventual user of the information produced. Within such a highly controlled environment, data processing was the responsibility of the computer specialist, who designed systems more in accordance with machine constraints than with user needs. Today, however, the clients of information systems have become more knowledgeable about computer processing. They request—often demand—increasingly complex processing services and expect those services to be delivered.

Computer power also has moved out of the computer room and on to the shop and office floors. Users are performing more of the data entry and data processing operations that once were closeted within the computer department. Therefore, systems today must be designed for use by nontechnical people. Thus, input and output facilities become increasingly important, and human-machine interfaces have become the focal points for design. Extensive editing and other preprocessing functions must be built on to the front ends of applications, and more flexible "user friendly" formats must be designed into the outputs.

Business itself has become more competitive and dependent upon computer power for survival. Although the computer still performs valuable bookkeeping and record-keeping functions, these services are overshadowed in importance by the need to meet competition. The use of management information systems and growth in the use of decision support systems signals the integration of the computer into the management structure of many organizations. These types of systems perform valuable management control services, business simulations, and performance projections that require access to comprehensive data bases of information and elaborate software to search, extract, and manipulate the data. The effectiveness of software designs in this environment is judged, in the final analysis, on the ability of the organization to reach its goals, not just on the accuracy and timeliness with which business records are maintained.

These and other developments have made software design an exacting and demanding skill. Software design now must proceed with an eye on flexibility, generalizability, and maintainability. In this environment, software is extremely complex, and change has become inevitable. Today's systems increasingly are susceptible to changes in user needs and to changes dictated by a volatile business and technical environment. Thus, software design has become an extremely dynamic area of endeavor. There are no firm, positive prescriptions for how best to design applications software. The field has, as yet, written no "cookbooks" about how to develop these products. However, certain trends are clear.

One of these trends is marked by a term that has been applied with some acceptance to the entire area of application software development—software engineering. In effect, this acceptance means that software developers are attempting to apply the disciplined, relatively standardized procedures found in the engineering of structural, mechanical, electrical, and electronic systems to the construction of software products.

In principle, the approach is based on the use of functionally independent, integrated components. That is, software design attempts to subdivide problem solutions into software modules, or pieces of code, that implement specific, identifiable processing components organized to produce minimal connections among those components. In effect, software design principles recognize that most systems are much too complicated to be considered in detail in their entirety. Thus, a software system is divided into interrelated programs. A large program is broken down into smaller and smaller modules. At succeeding levels within this hierarchy of programs and modules, functions and interconnections are defined. Further, design proceeds downward from a relatively broad definition of processing requirements to exacting operational details at the lower levels. This process brings order and simplicity to design. Each component of the software system has a functional identity. It stands apart from other components in terms of detailed design considerations; yet, it interfaces easily with other modular components. Such characteristics contribute to flexibility in design, ease of implementation, and reduced problems in long-term maintenance.

Another dimension to software design lies in communicating solutions to the people involved in implementing those solutions. In effect, the paperwork products of application software designers are the blueprints for software systems in the same way that blueprints developed by construction specialists are the guides followed by plumbers, electricians, and other craft specialists. Graphic techniques have been developed both to guide the design process and to communicate design solutions clearly to those who will implement software systems. CASE tools, discussed in Chapter 4, are sometimes used to implement these graphic techniques.

CHARACTERISTICS OF A "GOOD" DESIGN

An application software package is likely to be in use for a long time, possibly longer than the people who develop it. Though highly technical in nature, software quality ultimately involves the same criteria which affect other key business decisions. The fastest and most elegant piece of software is still worthless if it performs or enhances no strategic business requirement. And like other business decisions, easy, quick-fix, short-term solutions should not outweigh long-term organizational goals. Therefore, quality, strategic, and cost-effective standards must be met.

To be considered good, such application software must work correctly, meet specifications, be reliable, be maintainable, be easy to use, be easy to implement and test, use computer resources efficiently, and be on time and on budget. Here is a closer look at what each of these means.

Work Correctly. It goes without saying that a software product must work. Obviously, a program that produces incorrect output has no value to the organization. Thus, the first criterion is correctness.

Meet Specifications. Besides working correctly, the software must conform with expectations established by and for the users and documented in the user-approved systems specification. The designer and programmer have little, if any, latitude in modifying those specifications. The software must solve the "right" problem correctly. Any proposed changes should be approved by users and reflected as new specifications.

Be Reliable. The software product must work correctly and meet specifications over time and under changing circumstances. It must be dependable to produce results consistently for as long as it remains in production. Reliability also implies robustness. That is, the system must be able to deal with expected and unexpected situations inevitably arising from use by nontechnical users.

Be Maintainable. Software products have relatively long useful lives over which changes in requirements are inevitable. Across the operational life of a system, more effort and time are likely to go into modifying the system to meet these changing requirements than went into its original development. Thus, the software design must contribute to convenience and ease in performing maintenance work.

Be Easy to Use. Programs developed for use by managers, workers, and other nontechnical personnel must be easy to use and should not require technical expertise. Systems must conform as nearly as possible to the normal work patterns of people rather than require people to adapt to the technology. Helpfulness, consideration, and tolerance for human error are watchwords for the designer.

Be Easy to Implement and Test. Without compromising the above criteria, the software must be designed to make efficient use of development time and resources. It must be structured for ease of programming and testing. The designer must recognize that development teams, rather than an individual, typically will be involved in implementation. Further, the designer must consider that multiple programs and data files will require interfacing and coordination.

Use Computer Resources Efficiently. Although not as important as it was when computer hardware was relatively expensive and the need to optimize its use was critical, the need to use the technology efficiently is still an important consideration. This is especially so with small computer systems such as minicomputers and microcomputers. Specifically, efficiency relates to CPU and memory usage, as well as to auxiliary storage space utilization and access.

Be on Time and on Budget. Careful and systematic planning is required for all successful business endeavors. Computer system development is no exception. The realities of delivering a viable computer system within time and financial constraints is a complex chore, particularly with large scale and long range projects. The successful designer must be able to make decisions weighing and juggling all such factors. Estimating task expense and completion times are required skills.

It should be evident from the above list that design "goodness" is related primarily to human factors rather than to technological ones. The expense involved in developing and using an information system results mainly from the cost of personnel required to analyze, design, implement, use, and maintain the system. Maintenance is by far the largest cost of any software system over its entire life cycle. Hardware costs continue to decline rapidly, while personnel costs continue to escalate. Similarly, the effectiveness of a system is primarily contingent upon the time, effort, and success people have in using it.

PACKAGING TO APPLICATIONS: THE SYSTEMS FLOWCHART

General design is an interim procedure performed once a full set of DFDs is available. The full detailing of the design does not take place at this point. Rather, a single **black box** known as a system is broken down into a set of interrelated black boxes, or subsystems. The black boxes interrelate at the subsystem interfaces through communication (data) flow, and this is a major measure of compatibility. One of the things accomplished in this breakdown of black boxes is that the overall system becomes more understandable. Further, each subsystem is easier to implement with detailed designs than a larger system; the larger system would require complex operations and programs that are difficult to manage. Thus, general design produces the overall structure for how the system will work, in preparation for detailed design. The process subdivides large systems into a series of smaller units that can be dealt with at lower, more technical levels. A primary tool for documenting the results of general design at this stage in development is the systems flowchart.

Purpose of the System Flowchart

The starting point for software design is the set of **systems flowcharts** that defines the programs and data files to be used. The systems flowcharts also specify how the programs and data files will be integrated within a job or processing procedure.

A systems flowchart has multiple roles in the design process. Broadly speaking, a systems flowchart is a way to represent a design of the computerized part of the system in terms of sequences of black-box processing steps and controls among those black boxes. A systems flowchart is an overview document. The detailing of what goes on inside the black boxes is done with the aid of software design tools (i.e., structure charts) that are identified and delineated further in subsequent chapters.

The systems flowchart represents the relationships between jobs and job steps in the overall application system job stream. Each **job** usually represents one identifiable processing function. A computer job may involve on-line, interactive processing or off-line, batch processing. A job may contain one or more job steps. Batch jobs usually are divided into separate job steps. A **job step** is a single processing function performed by a single computer program or load unit. It is the conceptual black box, interacting with one or more input or output files. A job, thus, is a sequence of job steps and a **job stream** a sequence of jobs.

The overall sequence of jobs in the system flowchart becomes the road map for the designer for further technical specification. The black boxes represented in each job step of the system flowchart will require more detailed modular decomposition. The files outlined here will be completely implemented. Because most of the overall system sequence and naming conventions are illustrated on a system flowchart, it becomes a convenient guide from which to write system Job Control Language (JCL) or other such macro instructions. Also, because of these factors and their relation to JCL, system flowcharts may often become the first line of emergency documentation for maintainers and operators of the eventual production system.

As an important link between the analysis and design development processes, the system flowchart thus will continue to provide critical documentation throughout the system's life cycle.

System Flowchart Symbols

System flowcharting is a vehicle of communication that can be used by anyone interested in a system. It can serve as a universal language, largely because of its simplicity. The entire language of system flowcharting can be expressed in a few basic symbols, as illustrated in Figure 13-1. As shown in this illustration, these symbols are designed to communicate only down to the black-box level in describing systems. The rectangle representing a computer function or processing unit, in effect, becomes a black box. The remaining symbols describe peripherals of the system, or system inputs and outputs. It is the black box that, at later stages, will be subdivided using software design techniques into a hierarchy of less comprehensive black boxes. These subsequent black boxes, or modules, and their supporting documentation are used in writing actual programs. This subdivision, or partitioning, into **structure charts** is discussed in detail in Chapter 15.

Figure 13-2, page 414, displays a simple computer job illustrated with system flowcharting symbols. Note that the arrowed lines on the system flowchart represent flow of control, not flow of data as is shown on a data flow diagram. In this example, the flow of control is passed in succession to the three job steps, each being executed once in a single job run. Each job step has one executable program, load unit, or utility and may have any number of input and output devices. In Job Step 1 of this example, an off-page connector cross references the original tape input (Tape1) from its previous creation or update

Figure 13.1. Common systems flowcharting symbols.

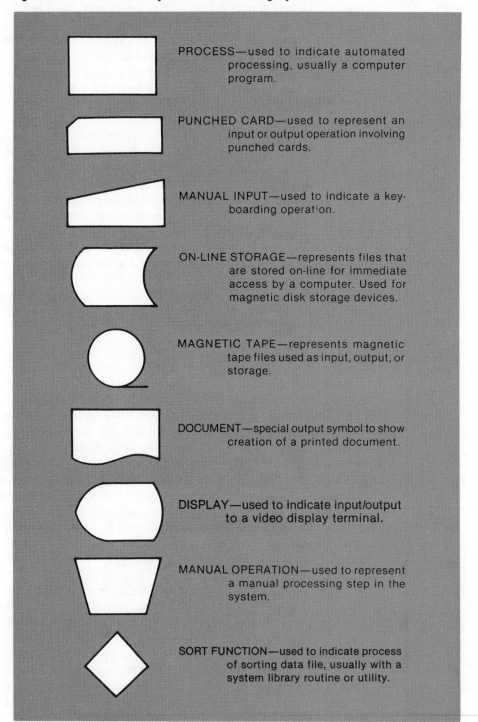

PROCESS—used to indicate automated processing, usually a computer program.

PUNCHED CARD—used to represent an input or output operation involving punched cards.

MANUAL INPUT—used to indicate a keyboarding operation.

ON-LINE STORAGE—represents files that are stored on-line for immediate access by a computer. Used for magnetic disk storage devices.

MAGNETIC TAPE—represents magnetic tape files used as input, output, or storage.

DOCUMENT—special output symbol to show creation of a printed document.

DISPLAY—used to indicate input/output to a video display terminal.

MANUAL OPERATION—used to represent a manual processing step in the system.

SORT FUNCTION—used to indicate process of sorting data file, usually with a system library routine or utility.

Figure 13.1. Common systems flowcharting symbols (continued)

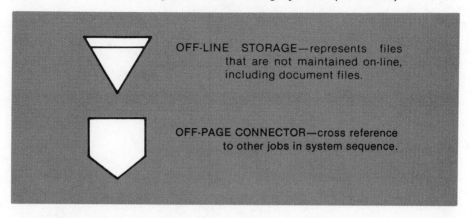

OFF-LINE STORAGE—represents files that are not maintained on-line, including document files.

OFF-PAGE CONNECTOR—cross reference to other jobs in system sequence.

job (Job3). Likewise, the next utilization (Job6) of the resulting disk file (File2) in Job Step 3 is cross-referenced to Job6.

Packaging into Jobs and Job Steps

The physical data flow diagram and the processing requirements completed during analysis combined with the constraints and utility of the current system operating architecture will form the basis for packaging the various system components into jobs or job steps. This packaging will take place in two distinct stages. First, the system will be partitioned into the components of the initial system flowchart largely on the basis of the physical boundaries which have been illustrated on the completed physical or implementation-dependent data flow diagram. Second, once more technical details become clear, usually after programs have been further decomposed into modules or routines, additional criteria may be applied to adjust the original partitioning. These stages are by no means mutually exclusive, since constant refinement is an ongoing development activity. The discussion to follow will identify some of the criteria that should guide both first- and second-stage packaging design efforts.

First-stage partitioning criteria include person-machine boundaries, hardware boundaries, geographic boundaries, processing-type boundaries, and timing cycles.

Person-machine boundaries. Divisions will be noted which separate processes to be performed manually from those to be accomplished through computerization.

Hardware boundaries. Certain processes may be carried out on different computer processors or processor types. For example, some functions may be designated to execute upon a mainframe and others upon microcomputers. This will require separate processing components.

Geographic boundaries. Processing that is required at different sites will also involve separate system jobs. For example, consider the case in which a serial transaction file created in an on-line mode from several

Figure 13.2. Job 4—Example of job illustrated with flowchart symbols.

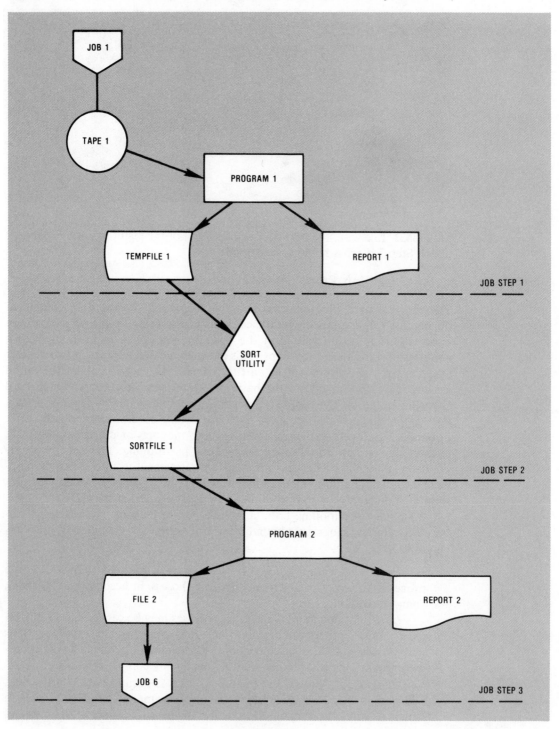

remote sites will be collected and used to update a master file in batch mode. Transactions are logged as they occur. After this file is built, it is applied against the master file on a batch basis. Thus, there is a processing boundary requiring a separate job step or job between the data collection function and the file updating function .

Processing-type boundaries. **Batch** processing refers to the handling of records or transactions in groups or batches. It usually involves little user interaction except maybe for job initiation (possibly done on-line). **On-line** processes are those in which transactions or records are dealt with one at a time until complete, prior to handling the next transaction. On-line systems involve a user interaction, usually with a screen terminal or monitor. The user responds to the consequences of the system processing. Real-time systems are those which contain elements of immediacy and continuous self-monitoring. These systems have the ability to interrupt current processing to complete more urgent, dynamic requests or to respond to changing environmental circumstances. Each of these processing types requires a separate job.

Timing Cycles. Processes intended to operate on different timing cycles generally require separate jobs. Thus daily, weekly, monthly, or yearly system functions will be grouped into individual jobs.

The criteria listed above represent information readily available at the end of the analysis phase of systems development when a physical, or implementation-dependent, data flow diagram is complete and corresponding documentation has been gathered.

Once a more rigorous decomposition of the system black boxes has occurred and more technical details are considered regarding the constraints and utility of the existing system technical architecture, a second round of partitioning should occur. This will be most useful toward the end of the system design activities, although the system flowchart may be adjusted as soon as such details become apparent.

Second-stage partitioning criteria include run times, volume requirements, equipment limitations, availability of utility software, and security requirements.

Run Times. Decisions may be based upon how large or extensive an individual processing function may be, as determined by its projected **run time**. The designer determines the size of the file or files to be processed, the amount of processing to be applied to each record, the output functions, and the corresponding time requirements. Based on these factors, the designer estimates potential job run times. An inadvertent interruption in processing a lengthy job could mean that all of the time and effort applied up to the interruption is wasted. When processing is resumed, the task might have to be restarted from the very beginning.

One of the objectives of systems design is to keep run times for tasks within manageable boundaries. For example, the designer might deem it wiser to establish, say, four job tasks of one hour each, creating files of intermediate results, rather than one job requiring four hours to complete.

Volume Requirements for the Job. In some batch cases, it may not be practical, or preferable, to design computer jobs for processing complete file content on any one run. On the one hand, volume demands may contribute directly to excessive run times, as described above. In addition, processing large volumes of data during single runs may degrade processing control capabilities. For example, it is common practice to establish processing checkpoints through the use of batch control totals. Record counts, hash totals, and other batch totals are developed for each batch of transaction records. During processing runs, these totals are compared with check totals developed by the program performing the processing. Discrepancies require resolution of problems, followed by reruns of affected input batches. If many batches of transactions are submitted for processing within a single job run, correction and resubmission of erroneous batches may become time consuming and tie up substantial amounts of computer time.

Equipment Limitations. Constraints can be placed upon systems design by the capabilities or limitations of units of equipment. For example, if a large report is to be printed, a designer may want to set up a separate program to handle this task rather than perform printing as part of a file update run. Separate runs would make it possible to use special programs that operate the printer as background work while other, more time-critical processing continues.

In other cases, the limited capacity of storage devices may constrain the amount of processing that can be accomplished on any computer run. Consider, for example, a large file which requires sorting as part of a file update run. If available disk work space is inadequate to handle such large sorting requirements, it may be necessary to partition the file into two or more logically related subfiles. The subfiles would then be sorted separately into intermediate files, which would be processed in separate job steps.

For on-line processing, constraints usually result from data communication speeds, CPU memory size, and data access times for storage devices. All these factors affect the response time to a user's processing request. Thus, equipment limitations have an effect on both the equipment configuration design and the software design.

Many such device-related constraints can develop. General design specifications rarely can be elaborated routinely into ideal technical designs. Hardware barriers often require "shoehorning" an application into a given physical environment.

Availability of Utility Software. If special systems software or utility programs are available, the flowcharts may be structured to take advantage of their capabilities. For example, in designing for the classic job of creating a transaction file to be used in updating a master file, the sorting of records is a requirement for sequential batch updating. In most computer installations, this sort would be handled through utility software provided by the computer manufacturer. Thus, the job stream creates a transaction file as the transactions are entered and recorded. This serial file of transactions would be input to the sort utility and sorted to create the sequential transaction file as output. Then, this sorted file would be processed against the master file.

This approach would create a job stream with three separate job steps—a data entry and serial file creation job step, a sort process that builds the transaction file, and an update job step to apply the transactions against the master file. In practice, all three processes could be combined into a single job. However, the design and processing complications of combining the processes, along with the availability of a sort utility, suggest a three-step approach as most appropriate.

The availability of database, data management, and report-writing software for large numbers of modern computer systems has made it possible to develop many traditional data processing applications without ever writing custom programs. If specialized processing applications are not needed to meet user requirements, job steps and processing tasks can be defined by available processing utilities.

Security Requirements. Jobs or job steps may be created to accommodate business audits and ordinary backup requirements. More on this topic is covered later in this text.

System Flowchart Examples

To illustrate how a system flowchart may be derived from data flow documentation, consider Figure 13-3. Here a lower-level data flow diagram represents a portion of a corporate sales-processing system. This diagram shows processing functions, data stores, and data flows, as well as physical boundaries between on-line and batch processing and timing cycles.

Salespersons phone in SALES-RESULTS at any time during the working day. Each time a call is received, a clerk will immediately enter the SALES-RESULT using an on-line process (4.1). At the end of the day, the sales data from all of the incoming calls will be edited for entry errors (4.2). INVALID-SALES-TRANSACTIONS with errors will be rejected, and an ERROR-REPORT will be produced (4.3). The next morning the clerk will examine the ERROR-REPORT and reenter the corrected transactions in the same manner as any other SALES-RESULTS. VALID-SALES-TRANSACTIONS will be collected and used to update the SALES-MASTER-FILE at the end of the week (4.5). A report will be produced (4.7) for management, showing weekly sales activity. An error report will also be produced (4.6), showing any discrepancies between the SALES-MASTER-FILE and the incoming SALES-TRANS-ACTIONS. Notice that this diagram displays the intermediate files, DAILY-SALES TRANSACTIONS and VALID-TRANSACTIONS. These are required primarily because of timing considerations of the processes. Also, a sorting process (4.4) and file (SORTED-TRANSACTIONS) are necessary because the transactions have been entered as they have been phoned in and the master file update (4.5) is assumed to be performed sequentially. Processes such as data entry, updates, and sorts may not be appropriate on original data flow dia-

Figure 13.3. *Data flow diagram for portion of sales processing system with physical boundaries.*

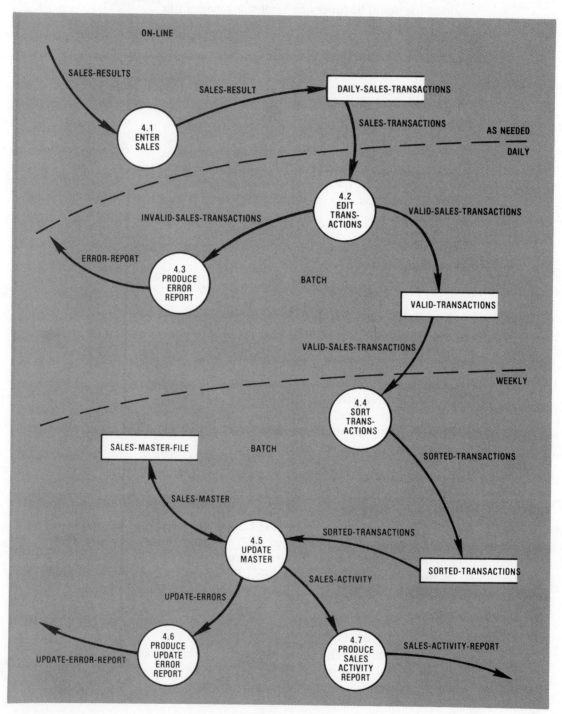

grams. However, adding such details may help the designer complete the system flowchart.

The physical boundaries displayed on the data flow diagram will act as guides in the partition to jobs and job steps. There are several rules of thumb to follow in this process. Generally you should try to minimize the number of jobs and job steps in the system flowchart. Therefore, unless there is a reason to do otherwise, the job stream will contain the minimum number of jobs and each job will contain the minimum number of job steps. The minimum number of jobs can be largely determined by the physical boundaries, or first-stage criteria, of the data flow diagram. Reasons to further partition usually involve the second-stage packaging criteria mentioned above such as run times, volume requirements, or use of system library utilities.

To illustrate, Figures 13-4 shows the system flowchart derived from the system data flow diagram represented in Figure 13-3. Since the data flow diagram is partitioned into three distinct physical sections, resulting from on-line, batch, and timing boundaries, the minimum number of jobs would be three. Again second-stage packaging criteria may dictate more jobs, but the minimum will be three.

Figure 13-4A illustrates Job 1 in this job stream. The SALES-RESULTS are entered through terminal input and stored on to file F1, DAILY-SALES-TRANSACTIONS using program P1. A double arrow is displayed from P1 and the terminal symbol, SC1, because the same program in which data are entered must also produce the data entry screen. File F1 is cross referenced with an off-page connector to Job 2 in the job stream since this will be the next usage of this file in the ordinary flow of events. File F1 is appended with each SALES-RESULT as they are entered.

Job 2 in this job stream is illustrated in Figure 13-4B. The data flow diagram section in Figure 13-3, displaying processes 4.3, PRODUCE-ERROR-REPORT, and 4.2, EDIT-TRANSACTIONS, is transformed into one job with one job step since no apparent reason to do otherwise is noted. A cross reference illustrating that F1 was last updated or created in Job 1 is displayed. Program P2 creates Report R1, ERROR REPORT, and file F2, VALID-TRANS-ACTIONS. File F2 is cross referenced to Job 3.

Figure 13-4C illustrates Job 3 in this job stream. Here two job steps are required in order to take advantage of a system utility sort routine. Notice also that five versions of file F2, VALID-TRANSACTIONS, are represented as each version would indicate a working day's batch of transactions. F3, SORTED-TRANSACTIONS, is created in job step 1 to be used to update F4, SALES-MASTER, in job step 2. Since the newly created SALES-MASTER in job step 2 will become the current (to be updated) file in the next run of this job, a current version and a new version of F4 are illustrated. Usually this can be accomplished through an operating system or file handling utility. Other job steps may have been required for this job if, for example, the report output could have been accomplished through a more convenient (other than programming) reporting utility.

An additional factor at this stage in the design process would be backup

Figure 13.4. System flowchart derived form the systems data flow diagrams in figure 13.3.

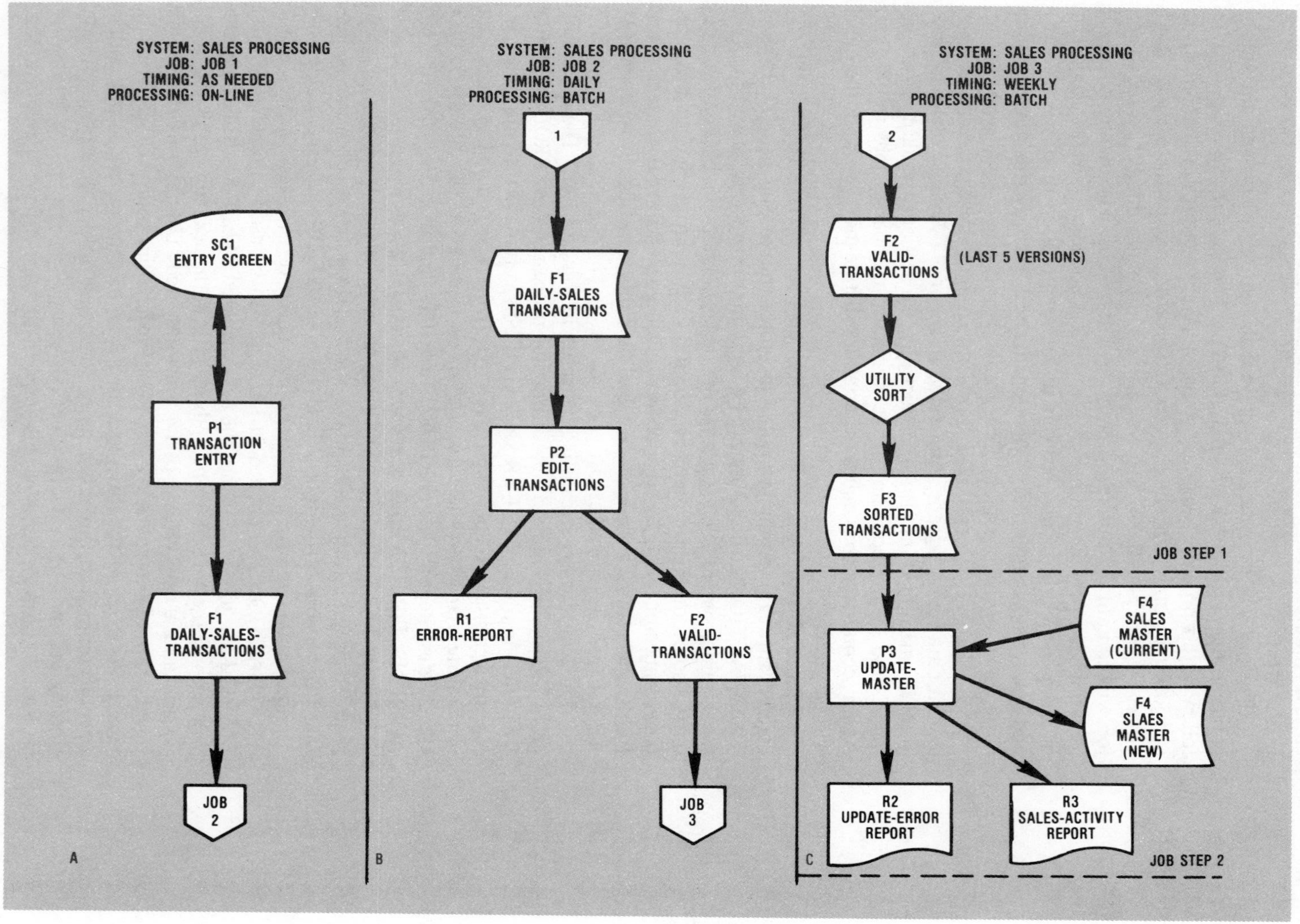

SYSTEM: SALES PROCESSING
JOB: JOB 3
TIMING: WEEKLY
PROCESSING: BATCH

SYSTEM: SALES PROCESSING
JOB: JOB 2
TIMING: DAILY
PROCESSING: BATCH

SYSTEM: SALES PROCESSING
JOB: JOB 1
TIMING: AS NEEDED
PROCESSING: ON-LINE

considerations. Each file and the output from each job must be reproducable in the event of a system failure of any kind. How much backup and for what length of time is largely an analysis issue that should be documented at this point in development. Backup or copying of files may be done either before or after a file is altered with a job run. This would usually mean adding job steps to jobs where appropriate. One means of creating backups would be to copy all such files to another portion of reserved on-line storage such as a disk drive or off-line storage such as tapes. These decisions are usually made because of urgency of the data in question, equipment limitations, and off-site security requirements.

The value of a systems flowchart is less dramatic and apparent in documenting the design of on-line processing. In batch systems, separate programs or load units exist for all of the separate job steps. Usually, interfaces between these programs are defined by intermediate files. As described above, natural processing boundaries exist between processing functions within a batch system. Within on-line systems, on the other hand, several processes are encompassed within a single processing procedure, or program. Processing boundaries do not show up as transitional files or differences in timing requirements. Typically, somewhat independent, smaller-scoped groups of processes are brought together into an on-line job. Thus, the single processing box shown in a systems flowchart for an on-line system may imply several processing steps — from data entry and editing through updating, retrieval, and display.

For example, the data flow diagram illustrated by Figure 13-5 represents basically the same logical functions shown in Figure 13-3. In Figure 13-5, however, all of these processes are contained in the same physical section of the data flow diagram. In this case the SALES-RESULTS are entered on line, edited, verified and randomly updated individually rather than in batches to the SALES-MASTER file. Error messages and update activity are reported via the terminal to the system user. Therefore, no intermediary file, such as DAILY-TRANSACTIONS or VALID-TRANSACTIONS is apparent.

The system flowchart derived from this data flow diagram is illustrated in Figure 13-6. All processes occur within a single job step in one job. Since the master file update is through random access, only one version of SALES-MASTER is displayed. All messages which had been produced on batch reports now return to the user with a terminal display.

The typical approach in designing on-line components of a CIS is to group several business tasks or functions under an "umbrella." Each function is based on a type of event that might take place in the business. For example, a sale is made; a new employee is added to the staff; an adjustment is made to an incorrect sale record; or a specific report is required. The process illustrated in Figures 13-5 and 13-6 may be but one of a range of on-line options. These events may be disjointed from one another except for their tie to a common database of information. The umbrella is implemented through a menu program, that is a terminal display of processing options. Each option reflects a business function. Figure 13-7 illustrates a sample menu for the sales-handling system described above. Functions from other portions of the overall system data flow diagram

Figure 13.5. *Data flow diagram for sales processing system, example two.*

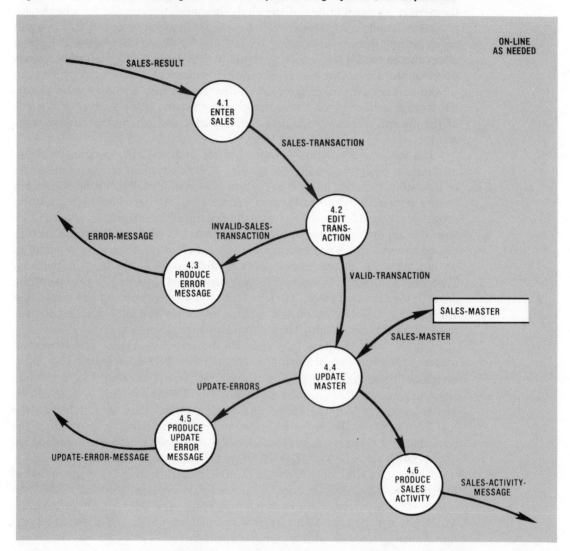

may be included for convenience. The system user selects an option and appropriate processing is initiated.

Backup and recovery of data require more sophisticated approaches in an on-line system than in batch processing. Because the system is needed on a continuing basis for sending and receiving timely information, special concern must be given to such problems as addressing program failure, interruption of power, and loss of communications.

Also, fewer details will be apparent on the data flow diagram and the initial system flowchart for such systems. For example, in the on-line sales processing system, a log file of the daily transactions would be necessary to recreate a given

Figure 13.6. System flowchart for sales processing, example two.

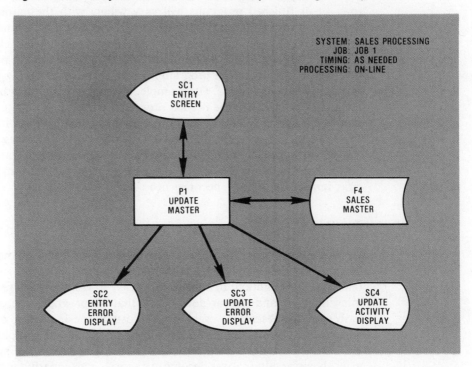

Figure 13.7. Main menu for sales processing system.

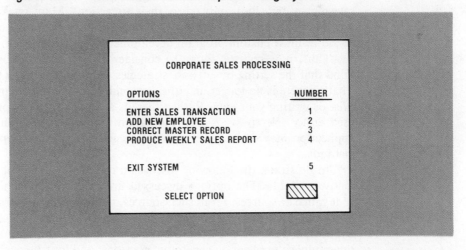

day's activity in the event of system failure. While this may be obvious to experienced programmers, it is not apparent on these representations. Conversely, in the batch example of the sales processing system a file has already been identified which captures the DAILY-SALES-TRANSACTIONS.

The scope and extent of activities involved in going from systems flowcharts to a set of finished programs will vary widely with the nature and types of programs involved. In some instances, a systems flowchart delineates a program to an extent that application software design becomes relatively routine. This occurs in situations, for example, in which there are many precedents — and much experience within a programming group — for designing and developing certain types of programs. For example, existing modules may be reworked and hung together to form the needed program. Again, an analogy with construction is appropriate. Some houses are mass-produced and, in effect, wheeled in from a factory to place on a prepared foundation. In other cases, every aspect of a house is custom tailored. For programs that are opening new areas of information processing applications or using new technologies, custom tailoring — specific, innovative design — becomes necessary.

STRATEGIC OPTIONS

Certain strategic options are available by which system jobs and job steps may be implemented. Application software development practices should fulfill a plan that is thought out in advance. It is easy to assume, from reading programming manuals and similar documents, that all programs are developed originally and from scratch, every time. Most of the literature, and most texts, understandably, place emphasis upon original design and complete development of programs. Students need this practice. In the real world of systems development, however, alternatives become attractive — particularly for executives faced with the reality of modern programming costs and delays involved in the preparation of original programs. For example, off-the-shelf packaged programs may save money, but this is only one of their attractions. Many packages also make it possible for users to implement programs months ahead of the schedules that would result if custom program development were undertaken.

Thus, it is realistic today to consider all available options first. Bear in mind that the setting of software strategies today is far from a binary situation. That is, there is no longer an either-or condition between buying programs that exist or writing your own. Rather, there is a whole range of options that can be used either selectively or in combination. Thus, the programs for any given application may derive from as many as four, five, or six separate sources or methods.

To illustrate, the following discussion covers only some of the options currently available. The options discussed are extensive enough to illustrate the wide range of sources. From such sources, the designer can formulate a strategy to provide a solution that meets the user's specifications. These options include application packages; custom programming; library routines, utilities and skeleton modules; application generator programs; and fourth-generation languages.

Application Packages

Application packages fall into two broad categories — industry applications and generic applications.

Special industry applications have proliferated as quickly as needs have been identified. Today, there are thousands of application packages, available from hundreds of suppliers. In some cases, regulatory conditions serve to make standardized application programs a hands-down choice. For example, consider the case of common-carrier trucking companies that operate interstate. These organizations must report mileage to government agencies. Since this is a standard requirement for large numbers of companies, many highly efficient application packages have been developed and marketed. Today, it would be a questionable practice for a trucking company to develop an application program from scratch.

There are also many generalized packages which have been developed for such industry-specific applications such as law offices, manufacturing firms, distributors, wholesalers, retailers, banks, and insurance companies. Many such packages are available for micro, mini, and mainframe devices or combinations thereof. The marketing of software application packages is a billion-dollar, growing industry and each year accounts for a higher percentage of all computer systems in use.

The same basic principles have been brought to bear in a number of generic application areas. For example, it would have to be an unusual situation, indeed, for a company to develop its own payroll program from scratch in today's marketplace. There are so many payroll packages available, with so many options, that it simply doesn't pay any more not to consider packaged options. Similarly, if a new system involves analysis of financial data, it now is almost axiomatic to consider use of "electronic spreadsheet" packages.

EXPERT SYSTEMS

A type of application package becoming extremely popular as well as economically viable is the expert system "shell." Expert systems are the subset of artificial intelligence (AI) which seems to hold the most promise for business applications in the foreseeable future. AI refers to a wide and varying range of computer systems which attempt to simulate more fully the functions of human beings. For instance, applications are being developed in AI which would allow mechanized optical sensing devices to visually differentiate between and recognize various specific objects, i.e., a tree or an incoming enemy warhead. Another such applications of AI seeks to provide a computerized means of recognizing, translating, and responding to human speech.

Expert systems, as the name implies, deal with the knowledge of experts. A common and reoccurring problem for many businesses is the individual and collective loss of expert knowledge through retirement, transfer, death, job or career change, or other forms of personnel attrition. This phenomenon is sometimes called "institutional memory loss." Often the knowledge required to carry out specific decision-laden activities is too complex to be fully documented by corporate procedures and regulations. Some decisions seem to require an expert with years of experience to know just what to do in every circumstance. For example, a doctor is able to correctly diagnose a patient's ailment through a combination of medical knowledge and clinical experience. Similarly, the processing of a complicated insurance claim or bank loan application may require an experienced business expert.

An expert system attempts to capture the expert's knowledge and to simulate his or her decision process so that others may imitate that process. Thus the medical profession has tried to make use of expert systems for many years, with varying degrees of success, to assist in diagnostic procedures. Business applications of expert systems might assist in the acceptance or denial of an insurance claim or a loan application.

Although expert systems may be developed in house, more often an expert system shell is acquired and tailored to the specific application. A shell is a generic program into which is entered the application knowledge and set or rules necessary to make decisions. The process of capturing such expert knowledge can be long and tedious, usually requiring a series of interviews between the expert and an information specialist known as a "knowledge engineer."

Computer software applications of expert system shells are typically composed of four components: the user interface, the development engine, the knowledge base, and the inference engine (see figure below). The user interface provides a means for the knowledge engineer to enter the expert information and the access by which subsequent users of the system may seek decision

Feature figure.   Typical components of an expert system.

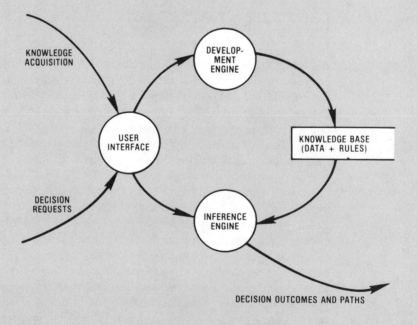

guidance. The development engine is the functional component which allows the knowledge engineer to collect the expert data and to establish a rules set between the data. The rules set becomes the foundation upon which decisions will be based. Often the rules set takes the form of a hierarchical series of IF-THEN-ELSE statements. The knowledge base is a database containing the expert data and the rules hierarchy. The inference engine is the functional component that allows users of the system to access the knowledge base with a particular set of circumstances in order to arrive at a specific decision outcome. The inference engine may also display the decision paths detailing how the decision was determined.

Not all decisions can be derived from the expert system. Like all computer systems, an expert system is only as good as the information with which it is programmed. Once a situation arises that no one could initially foresee or there are changes in corporate policy or legislative requirements, a human being must intervene in the process. Thus such systems must be carefully monitored and human backups be available. Also, a note of caution must be expressed. Many people fear that such systems will remove the element of human responsibility from important decision making. In the worst case, a medical diagnostic system may provide an incorrect analysis, and allow a patient to die. Such a tragic outcome cannot be blamed on a computer system, but must rather rest with human beings.

Thus, the greatest benefit from expert systems will be to free humans from the most mundane of decision processes, consequently freeing them for more challenging and critical ones.

Application packages are available for virtually every major function of most organizations and businesses. Typical examples include general ledger reporting packages to produce financial statements, inventory reporting and replenishment systems, invoicing systems, accounts receivable systems, accounts payable systems, payroll systems, and income tax computation programs.

Advantages and Disadvantages of Application Packages. The most obvious potential advantage of application packages is that, if they fit, they can save substantial time and money. A software package that requires little modification can be installed in less time than custom development of a system would require. Users can realize a financial benefit from a more timely answer to their business needs. In addition, a CIS department with already stretched resources probably can afford more readily the expense of package selection and installation. This approach can provide better service to the user department and to the company in general.

There also is a degree of assurance — since other users have applied and found success with the package — that the programs are workable and of relatively high quality. Such programs may present an opportunity for a high-quality solution to a problem that is complex from a business view or is technically difficult to solve.

The main disadvantage is that, if the package does not represent an exact fit with identified needs, either the purchased package or the procedures of the user organization may have to be modified. To use the package, the company may find that it has to trade off desirable system features or change some of its procedures. In some instances, the user may have to take the system as it is or not at all. Also, with packaged software, the interface with other parts of the system or related systems may not be straightforward. If the mismatch is great, portions of programs may have to be revised or rewritten to tailor them to the specific user needs.

Another potential disadvantage of purchased software is that maintenance may be a problem. Maintenance can be performed internally or can be provided by the software vendor. Since the programs were not written within the organization, different standards may have been applied in designing, coding, or documenting the programs. Further, program designs may be too inflexible to change readily. Even if the package is of generally high quality, time and money will have to be committed to training one or more CIS staff members to maintain it. Typically, a maintenance contract may be purchased that covers error correction and continuing enhancements to the package. This needed resource, though, is outside the direct control of the CIS department; and consequently, timeliness of response may be a concern.

Packaged programs cannot be purchased and installed just anywhere they seem to fit. Rather, before a decision is made to use packaged application software, careful study and evaluation are necessary.

Evaluating Application Packages. In considering the potential and appropriateness of application packages, the new system specification provides a good basis for evaluation. In the new system specification, requirements are described in terms of data and functions—at a highly logical level. Physical requirements usually have been addressed only to the user's view of interacting with the system.

Thus, on the basis of processing and data retention requirements alone, it is possible to set and weight priorities for the desired features of any given application software program. These weighted values can be checked against the specifications for a variety of available application packages. Though this type of evaluation may be too simplistic for final decisions, it is possible simply to combine weighted values assigned to each package, coming up with a total and buying the one with the highest rating. Thus, it is critically important to be sure that the package is capable of handling the data and functions specified. In practice, there are many qualitative factors that also would be considered. But this weighting approach can be a basis for identifying candidates.

Evaluation should be based also upon a number of other factors, including these:

- The reputation of the software house or vendor.
- The extent to which the vendor supports the software package.
- Verification that the software will run on existing, planned, or acceptable hardware.

- The advice of an impartial user of the package, particularly if implemented on a similar hardware configuration.
- The software vendor's policy and willingness to customize or enhance a package to match the specific user's needs.
- Quantitative measures which represent the package's ability to provide the necessary capacity, throughput, and performance relative to the proposed system specifications.
- Difficulties that may occur during installation.
- The completeness and quality of documentation.
- The overall flexibility of the design, architecture, or actual system programs.

Using the new system specification that contains both logical and physical needs, it is possible to compare individual data elements, key processing functions, and even specific process narratives to those of a software package. Those comparisons and the above considerations will assist the evaluation of whether an available package fits both the system and the organization. If the fit is not exact, the evaluation either will disclose what needs to be done to adapt the package or will reach the conclusion that custom development is necessary. There usually is no exact match between organization and user needs and available software packages.

Ultimately, specialists trained in other package acquisition issues should be consulted prior to any final purchase decisions. These specialists should assist in the intricacies of potential modification agreements, legal ramifications, pricing options and strategies, and contract negotiations.

Custom Programming

Despite the extensive growth in the use of application software packages, the amount of **custom programming** done for business-related packages will continue to be considerable. Although software firms or consultants are retained to develop unique or custom software, much of this effort is still done by an organization's own CIS staff. Indeed, custom programming is the central focus of this text. In general, there are three major reasons why CIS organizations develop their own programs.

First, although there is considerable breadth to the offerings of application packages, software is not available to satisfy all applications in all industries. Further, what is available may not be acceptable to an organization after an evaluation of the above factors. In such cases, custom development is the only remaining option.

Second, in-house development may be preferred for compatibility with other existing systems and business practices. A given company may have adopted a philosophy or unique set of standards for all of its application software. If so, management may feel that continuing compatibility is important enough to override any convenience or economy available through packages.

Third, some systems people are simply more comfortable developing their own application software. Others may be skeptical about programs they did not invent or develop themselves. In general, this line of reasoning can be seen as a do-it-yourself syndrome. If this preference is strong enough, and if the manager who holds the preference has enough influence within his or her organization, in-house programming will prevail.

Additional considerations must be taken into account depending on whether the custom program to be developed is an on-line or batch processing system.

Library Routines, Utilities, and Skeleton Modules

It has been a longstanding practice of computer manufacturers to provide programs known as utilities to perform standard functions, such as sorting, collating, and reporting. In addition, most installations have software modules that are usable across different applications. As programs have been developed and refined to meet these needs, many systems or operations managers have set up what are known as **library routines** to preserve these standard program modules for reuse. Included can be data editing routines, programs to establish tables, and so on.

Utility programs are used by the designer to handle typical, mundane tasks. For example, report-writing packages can be used to generate both standard reports and unique, one-time reports. After defining the files being used, such tools provide for the entry of criteria by which records can be selected for reporting. Report or screen display formats then can be specified in a manner much simpler than with usual programming languages. Data elements to be displayed and their format are specified, as are sorting and level summary totals. Thus, reports can be prepared with relative ease.

So-called **skeleton programming** is an extension of the same principle. These skeletons may also be created locally or be vendor supplied. In this case, a designer has available precoded programs that serve as the framework to which specific applications are added. These programs may range from a listing of all the necessary headings in the four divisions of a COBOL program to the actual coding of certain high-level modules, lacking only application-specific names. For example, the design and implementation of a sequential, batch master file update is a standard task. A skeleton program could be derived so that all file descriptions are copied and the main level processing logic is already present. All that is needed are the details of each transaction's processing.

The objective of these tools is to provide the designer with building blocks for the development of a system. The tools are then housed in system libraries for "checkout" or duplication when necessary. Such an approach has the advantages of improving productivity, using proven, tested components, and focusing custom efforts on unique parts of the system.

Application Generators

An **application generator** is a level of program development above that of a compiler or translator. Such generators may be components of an integrated CASE tool or they may be stand-alone products. Application or code generators produce source code in an intermediate, high-level language. For example, there are generators that produce source code in such languages as COBOL or BASIC. This source code then can be used as though it had been written by programmers, modified as necessary, and compiled for execution.

Another characteristic of generators is that their users deal in parameters, or specifications, rather than in writing code in executable sequences. Typically, forms or screens are provided in which the user specifies functions to be performed, file sizes, record sizes, and field sizes. Given sufficient specifications, the generator then produces a source program.

The most obvious advantage of a program generator is that programming time is reduced. Unquestionably, the computer can generate code faster than a person can. Overall programming time is reduced because it is possible to go directly from design documentation into coding without actually writing lists of instructions.

Programming tradition holds that, while program generators add convenience and reduce costs for the creation of programs, the programs produced are not as efficient, in terms of processing throughput, as those that are coded by experienced programmers. Thus, in the past, there has been a tendency to use generators primarily for programs or applications that are either run infrequently or involve minimal processing. As part of an evolving trend, these programming tools continue to improve and gain acceptance.

Fourth-Generation Languages (4GL)

Fourth-generation languages (4GL) are end-user oriented. Nonprocedural in nature, they typically require that parameter input be supplied to generate applications. This structure permits higher productivity and more closely resembles natural language. Such languages become especially helpful to end-users in developing distributed applications.

Another characteristic of 4GLs is that they usually are designed around functions associated with files or data bases. Most 4GLs provide a capability for defining input parameters that can express such file concerns as editing and validation criteria and major and minor file keys. Often, they contain facilities for maintaining, updating, querying, or reporting from files. In fact the distinction between 4GLs and data base management systems (DBMS) is becoming more and more insignificant.

Many organizations have created "information centers" around 4GLs and DBMSs. The information center may be staffed by one or more data processing professionals or sophisticated user personnel. Such centers can respond quickly to one-of-a-kind, imprecise, or spontaneous application requests. Oftentimes they may actually provide solutions for ongoing production work. These services take pressure off DP staff for such requests and benefit users by providing speedy turnaround for special processing situations, which are often relegated to a low long-range priority status but may nevertheless be of high concern to users.

TRADEOFFS

Setting a strategy for application design, as with any other aspect of systems development, involves a number of potential options and tradeoffs among those options. In general, the options lie between custom development for specific needs and the so-called "short-cuts" offered by application packages or by special programming tools such as utilities, skeleton modules, code generators, or 4GLs. The issues to be faced include productivity, costs, timeliness, and compromise of business requirements.

Productivity

Emphasis on productivity stems from a continually increasing demand for information systems to support organizations. The greatest demand is for packages, tools, and techniques that provide quality solutions with a minimum investment in time. Proven, tested solutions are attractive in the light of otherwise long development schedules. Specifically, the writing and testing of program code is time-consuming. Thus, anything that significantly reduces, or even eliminates, the writing of code enhances programming productivity.

On the other hand, there is another dimension to productivity that has to be considered—the actual effort and cost required to install a "short-cut" and the productivity of the job once it is running. It could be ultimately wasteful to save a small percentage of programming cost at the outset, only to double development time or to multiply other problems once the job is in use.

Further, productivity also extends to maintenance of operational programs. This dimension, too, should be considered as part of the tradeoff in establishing an application design strategy. This productivity factor can have an effect lasting several times the length of the development cycle.

Costs

Costs, too, should be examined fully. Saving money at the front end may be an illusory advantage if increased costs of using and modifying programs are encountered later.

In considering application packages particularly, total costs of acquiring the system, putting it on-line, maintaining it, and securing other services from the vendor should all be taken into account. As one example, a systems organization may consider acquiring a package because a part of it fits the needs of a system under development particularly well. The decision may involve buying some elements of a package that will not be used. Further, in buying a package, a company may be undertaking to update and maintain those parts that will never be used. Thus, costs should be projected and evaluated over the full estimated life of the system.

Timeliness

Sometimes, a system has to be up and running by a given date, no matter what the circumstances. If deadlines are real and must be met, decision criteria should center around achieving these goals with the least wear and tear upon the people and the organizations involved. If timeliness is a paramount factor, concerns over cost may have to be disregarded almost entirely.

When timing is critical, it is also important to look to available resources within the organization. It may, for example, be possible to finish a program in time—if all of the existing staff is thrown at the job. However, if there is any question about meeting the deadline, or if the people involved are already committed to other important projects, packages may wind up being the only solution.

Compromise of Business Requirements

There are different schools of thought about compatibility of computer programs and business functions. One classic outlook is that the automated system must adapt itself always to the needs of a business, regardless of other situations or circumstances. Under this outlook, there is heavy pressure within an organization to design all applications from scratch, tailoring the programs to the stated needs of users.

Another outlook holds that business procedures usually have a greater potential for flexibility than operating managers are willing to admit. Persons who hold this view look at an automated system and its implementation as a totality. It is felt that programs and procedures that do the best job in terms of all factors—cost, productivity, availability, maintainability, and so on—should be adopted. If business processes or procedures must be modified to accommodate the best overall solution, changes may be both justified and desirable.

In the real world, compromise tends to be a way of life. Decisions rarely go all one way or another. Rather, tradeoffs are considered and compromises are established to fit individual situations. Users can expect to modify their lives to some extent if they become involved in development of new automated systems. Similarly, technical purists who would like to optimize every system, in every way, are given the opportunity to do so only rarely. Design strategies, in the end, represent a compromise in favor of what has to be done and the best way to do the job.

SUMMARY

A system's design provides a detailed blueprint from which the system will be implemented.

Software design methodology has not kept pace with the growth in complexity and magnitude of today's required computer systems. Combined with the more sophisticated nature of the software user, exploding hardware capabilities, and increasing business competitiveness, software design issues have become increasingly difficult.

The characteristics of a "good" software design require that it work correctly, meet specifications, be reliable, be maintainable, be easy to use, be easy to implement and test, use existing computer resources efficiently, and be on time and within budget.

Systems analysis produces a model for a new system expressed in terms of functional processes and data transformations. A new system remains a black box at the time when systems design is launched.

General design produces a set of technical specifications identifying which computer programs interact with input, storage, and output devices, in which sequence, and at what times to perform processing.

A primary tool for implementing and expressing the results of general design is the systems flowchart. The system flowcharting language is designed to communicate only down to the black box level in describing systems.

Software design starts with data flow diagrams as major inputs. Designers create flowcharts that serve to document their decisions. Systems flowcharts identify jobs and job steps. A job is composed of job steps and a job step is a processing function that is controlled by a single computer program interacting with one or more input or output devices.

The system flowchart provides both a guide for further design efforts and critical documentation for eventual system operators and maintainers.

Criteria that may be applied to partition the data flow diagram into the jobs and job steps of the system flowchart include person-machine boundaries, hardware boundaries, geographic boundaries, processing-type boundaries, and timing cycles. When more technical details are known and black boxes further decomposed into structure charts, then additional packaging criteria may be considered such as job run times, volume requirements, equipment limitations, availability of utility software, and security requirements.

For on-line systems, delineation of functions often occurs with the preparation of structure charts rather than of flowcharts. The structure chart documents, in detail, the separate procedures that comprise the system that may not be apparent on the system flowchart.

An application software design may be implemented through a whole range of options that can be used either selectively or in combination. These options include application packages, custom programs, library utilities and skeleton modules, code generators, and fourth-generation languages.

Custom programming may be preferred in some CIS shops for compatibility with existing systems or because management is prejudiced in favor of in-house development.

Tradeoffs involved in selecting in-house program development include productivity, costs, timeliness, and compromise of business requirements.

KEY TERMS

1. system flowchart
2. job
3. job step
4. job stream
5. run time
6. black box
7. batch
8. on-line
9. application packages
10. custom programming
11. library routines
12. utility programs
13. skeleton programming
14. application generators
15. fourth-generation languages

REVIEW/DISCUSSION QUESTIONS

1. Compare information systems and software design strategies of today with those of ten years ago.
2. What are characteristics of a "good" design?
3. What is the purpose of the system flowchart?
4. Describe considerations that should influence the partitioning of a DFD into separate jobs.
5. What options are available to implement system software components?
6. When might application packages be an appropriate implementation option?
7. What factors should be considered in the evaluation of application packages?
8. Why is custom programming still a popular option for some CIS shops?
9. Explain the major tradeoffs between custom development and the so called "short cuts."
10. Discuss the differences between the system flowcharts for a master file update done in batch processing for a master file using direct access versus a master file using sequential access.

Software Design:
Technical Design Specifications

Once a system architecture has been conceived and a decision has been made to develop custom, in-house programs, further technical design specifications are required. These specifications will focus upon both the external and internal perspectives of the desired software.

The external software design is largely a user-level view of the proposed system. That is, what will the system look like to the user? How will the user communicate with the system, and how will it communicate with the user? To be successful, a "friendly" interface must be created between the user and the underlying computer programs. Friendly software design involves attention to the human characteristics, or factors, of the interactions between users and computer programs.

Although many interface design guidelines remain constant, often differing human users will necessitate concern for differing human factors. The external software design specifications will ultimately become the user's vision of the proposed system.

The internal software design is largely a programmer-level view of the software. That is, how do the various pieces of the software puzzle fit together, and why? Why is one configuration of the pieces better than another? To implement successful application programs, as defined in Chapter 13, several strategies can be employed. These strategies suggest how one approaches the structuring of the internal components of the software programs. Designs resulting from such strategies can be "fine-tuned" using various evaluative criteria such as a desire for low module "coupling" and high module "cohesion." Also, internal software design specifications must implement the external user view of the system. These specifications will become the blueprint for software construction.

Chapter 14 discusses the external technical design issues, or the human factors of software design. Chapters 15 and 16 discuss the internal issues of design strategies and evaluation criteria, respectively.

The Human-Computer Interface Design

Learning Objectives
After completing the reading assignments for this chapter, you should be able to:

- Discuss the objectives of input and output design.
- Discuss the various types of output.
- Discuss how output can become biased.
- Discuss the guidelines for designing input including both forms and screens.
- Discuss the guidelines for designing effective output.
- Identify and discuss the goals of human factors design.
- Discuss the diversities among human decision makers, managers, and other computer users.
- Present and discuss the guidelines for dialogue, data display and data entry design.
- Discuss the proper role of system messages.
- Discuss the importance of response time in on-line, interactive systems.

INPUT AND OUTPUT DESIGN

Prior to the discussion of human-computer interface design, the issue of designing effective input and output for a computer system should be addressed. This is an often-overlooked design issue because it seems so simple; but, in fact, the first point at which the human-computer interface should be considered comes during the design of specific input and output.

Input Design

The old saying, "GIGO (garbage in, garbage out)" is very true. The higher the quality of the input data, the more likely that the user will receive high quality output from a computer system. The forms and visual display screens can have a positive or a negative impact on the quality of input data.

Input Design Objectives. Any input design should meet several objectives including (1) accuracy, (2) effectiveness, (3), consistency, (4) ease of use, and (5) simplicity. If an input design can be completed correctly by an experienced person or a novice then it meets the criterion of accuracy. Effectiveness refers to the issue of whether the input screens or forms serve a useful purpose in the information system. If no purpose can be cited, then they are probably neither needed nor effective. Consistency refers to the practice of always grouping data in the same manner from application to application. Ease of use means that the screens and forms are simple and straightforward to interpret and utilize. This relates to the fifth objective, simplicity, which refers to keeping the screens purposefully organized and uncluttered so that the user can readily determine how to enter the data into the system. A discussion of the dialogue between the MIS and the user is provided later in this chapter.

Input Form Design Guidelines. Many systems involve the use of forms as both an input and an output. Input forms are typically preprinted documents that require the user to fill in responses in a standardized way. They are often source documents used for data entry into a system such as a sales order. Four guidelines should be kept in mind when designing forms: (1) make sure the forms are easy to fill out; (2) design the form to assure its accurate completion; (3) make the form as attractive as possible; and (4) ensure that the form meets the purpose for which it was designed.

To reduce error, speed completion, and facilitate the entry of data, it is essential that forms be easy to fill out. This guideline is based on more than well-placed empathy for the user. The cost of the forms is minimal compared to the cost of the time employees spend filling them out and entering the data from them into the computer. Forms should be designed such that they flow from left to right and top to bottom. This is a requirement because in our western civilization one reads anything in this manner. Any other flow will take additional time and frustrate the user. For example, any form that requires the user to search for a space at the bottom and then return to the top to complete another item is poorly designed. Figure 14-1 illustrates a sample order form with the proper flow.

A second technique that will make forms easier to fill out correctly is the logical grouping of information. Seven main sections are included in most forms. They are the heading, an identification, instructions, body, signature and verification, totals, and comments.

The heading section should include the name and address of the business originating the form. The identification section includes all the codes that may be used to file the form and gain access to it at a later date. This is important for forms that must be kept for a long period of time for reference purposes.

Figure 14.1.   Sample order form with the proper flow.

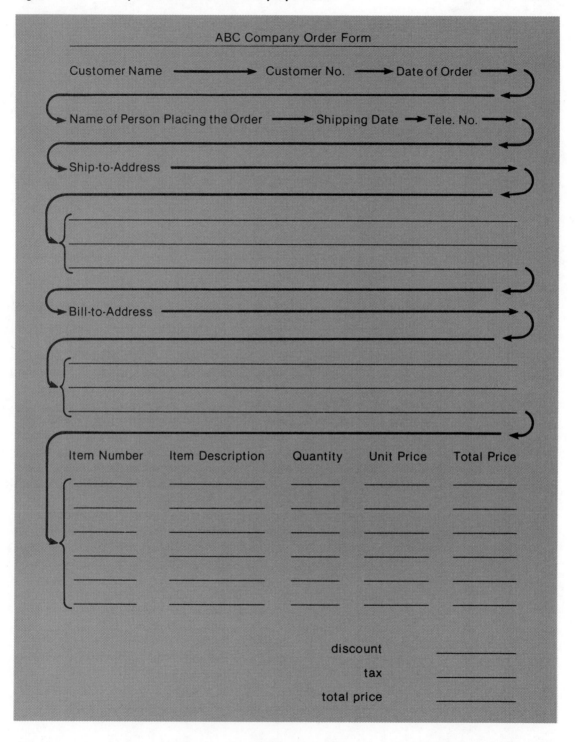

The instructions section tells people how the form should be filled out and where it should be sent when completed. The middle of the form is called the body and it usually requires the most detail and attention from the person filling it out. It often contains very specific (i.e., item number on an order) and variable (i.e., quantity ordered) data.

The bottom quarter of the form is composed of three sections: signature and verification, totals, and comments. By requiring a signature in this part of the form, the designer is echoing the design of other familiar documents, such as letters. Requiring ending totals and a summary of comments is a logical way to provide closure for the person filling out the form. Figure 14-2 presents the logical grouping of information on a form.

Figure 14.2. The seven sections in a typical form.

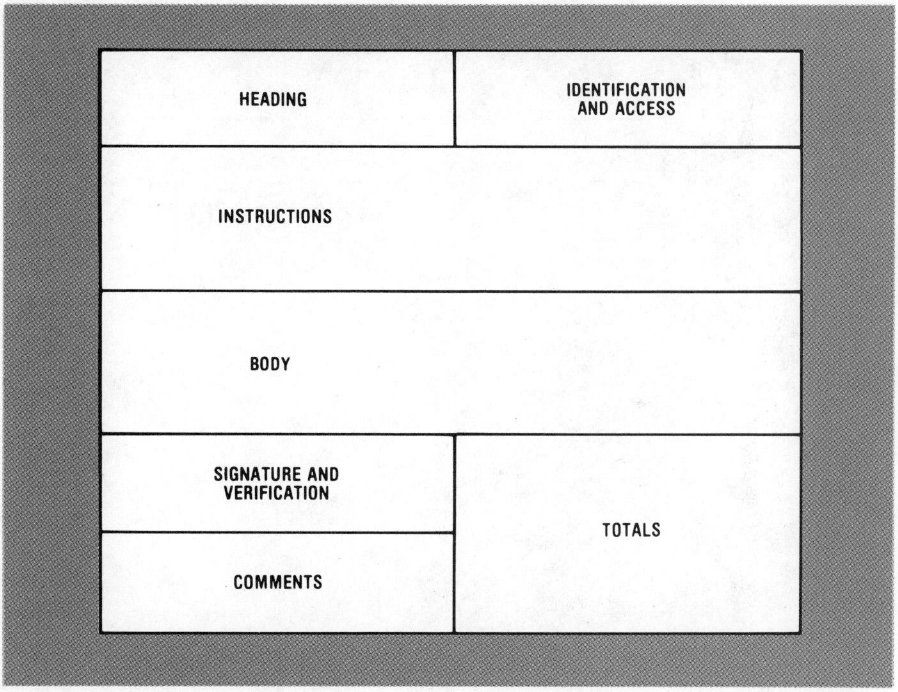

One final technique for ensuring that a form is easy to work with is the use of clear and precise captions. Captions tell the person completing the form what to place in a blank line, space, or box. Several types of captions are presented in Figure 14-3. Line captions can either be to the left or below the lines. Checkoff captions can be either vertical or horizontal. Boxed captions are very popular, especially if a box is subdivided into an exact number of smaller boxes, one for each character. Table captions are also quite useful. Combinations of these captions can also be used very effectively.

Figure 14.3. Captioning alternatives.

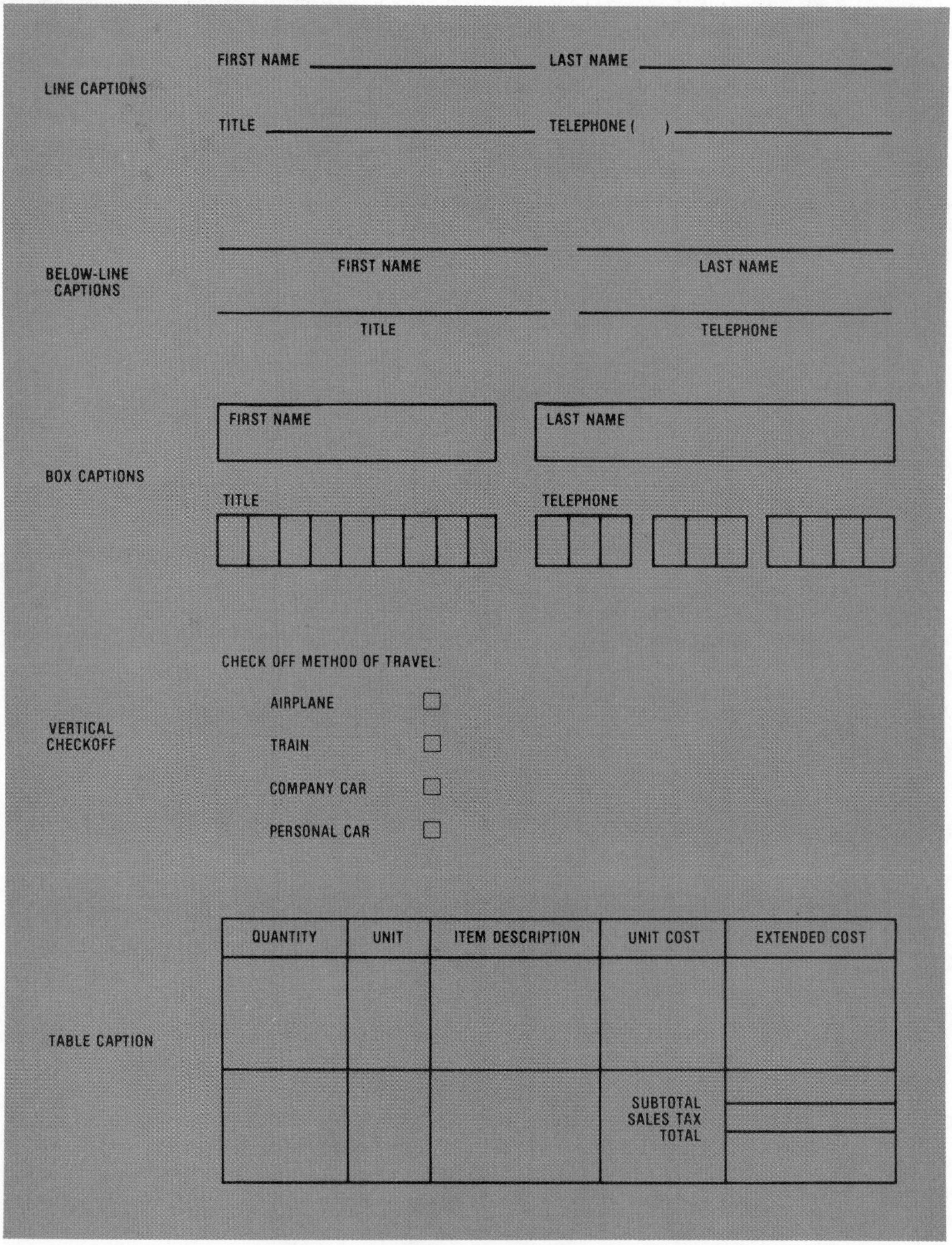

LINE CAPTIONS

FIRST NAME _____ LAST NAME _____

TITLE _____ TELEPHONE (   ) _____

BELOW-LINE
CAPTIONS

_____ _____
FIRST NAME   LAST NAME

_____ _____
TITLE   TELEPHONE

BOX CAPTIONS

FIRST NAME   LAST NAME

TITLE   TELEPHONE

VERTICAL
CHECKOFF

CHECK OFF METHOD OF TRAVEL:

AIRPLANE   ☐

TRAIN   ☐

COMPANY CAR   ☐

PERSONAL CAR   ☐

TABLE CAPTION

QUANTITY	UNIT	ITEM DESCRIPTION	UNIT COST	EXTENDED COST
			SUBTOTAL SALES TAX TOTAL	

The design of a form is important in assuring that people will complete it accurately, whether they use the form frequently or not. The form should flow properly, use clear captions, and include a logical grouping for information. If the form includes totals which can be cross-checked, this feature should be implemented in the form. Figure 14-4 presents a sample expense form for employees that would facilitate accurate completion.

Figure 14.4. **Sample expense form.**

TEXAS TECH UNIVERSITY
EMPLOYEE EXPENSE VOUCHER

EMPLOYEE NAME _____   DATE _____

EMPLOYEE SSN _____

DEPARTMENT _____

OFFICE NUMBER _____   OFFICE PHONE _____

LIST EXPENSES FOR EACH DAY SEPARATELY. ATTACH RECEIPTS FOR ALL EXPENSES EXCEPT MEALS, TAXIS, AND MISCELLANEOUS ITEMS.

DATE 19___	PLACE CITY, STATE	MEAL EXPENSES	LODGING EXPENSES	AUTOMOBILE		MISCELLANEOUS		TAXI COST	TOTAL COST
				MILES	COST	DESCRIPTION	COST		
TOTALS									

I CERTIFY THAT ALL THE ABOVE INFORMATION IS CORRECT

_____   _____
SIGNATURE OF CLAIMANT   DATE

_____   _____
APPROVED BY   DATE

Making a form attractive does not and should not mean spending a lot of money on the form. Multicolored forms with fancy logos are not the issue. Rather the issue is organization and clarity. The form should appear uncluttered. It should provide enough space for responses. A general rule of thumb is to allow for seven typewritten or five handwritten characters per inch. Having a logical layout and the proper flow contributes to any forms attractiveness. Separating sections of the form with heavy lines can also help organize it and make it more attractive to the user.

Output Design

The information system delivers the end product "information" to the user. The effective interpretation of this output information will depend to a great extent upon its design. Output can take many forms including hard-copy printed reports, microfilm or microfiche, audio, and the most common medium the video display screen. Users evaluate the CIS almost solely on the quality and effectiveness of the output it delivers. The proper methods for designing video (data) displays are discussed later in this chapter. Designing the other forms of output is discussed after the objectives for effective output design are presented.

Output Design Objectives. Output should be designed to (1) serve the intended purpose, (2) fit the user, (3) deliver the proper quantity of output, (4) use the most appropriate output media, (5) provide timely output, and (6) provide the output to the individuals and departments that need it.

All output should have a purpose. It is not enough that a report or screen be made available to users because it is technologically possible to do so. During the information requirements determination phase of analysis, the systems analyst finds out what purposes must be served. Output then is designed based on those purposes. If the output is not functional, it should not be created, since there are time and materials costs associated with all output from the system.

Designing output to fit particular users is difficult. There are often hundreds of CIS users for a single application, and they may disagree among themselves about the type and form of output they prefer. The users are part of the design team; and all users should have the opportunity to comment on and suggest changes in the design of the output. When a suggested change is supported by a large number of users, it should be quickly evaluated and possibly implemented. More often than not, the output will be designed for the position (e.g., controller, director of personnel, purchasing agent) rather than the individual who occupies that position. It is more likely that a decision support system would be designed for a specific individual. One final point, it is more necessary than ever before to design flexibility, especially in terms of the output, into the system such that the inevitable requests for changes can be more easily accommodated.

The task of designing output is in part a task of deciding what quantity of output is correct for users. This is a very difficult task, since information requirements are continually changing. A useful rule of thumb is that the system must provide what people need to complete their work. However, this is still far from a solution since it may be appropriate to display a subset of that information at first, and then provide a way for the user to access additional information easily. For example, rather than cluttering a screen with an entire year's sales, each of twelve successive screens might provide a month's sales with subsequent months and summary information available on separate screens. The key factor in determining the appropriate quantity of information is to avoid overloading management personnel with information. One popular technique is to give them the summary report on the screen first, with a method to retrieve the underlying detail if they need it.

As mentioned earlier, output can take many forms including printed paper reports, information on output display screens, audio with digitized sounds that simulate the human voice, and microfilm. Choosing the right output media for each user is another objective in designing output.

For many people, output conjures up the vision of stacks of computer printouts, but this is changing rapidly. With the movement to on-line systems, much output is now exclusively on display screens. The analyst needs to recognize the tradeoffs involved in choosing an output method. Costs differ, as do the flexibility, life span, distribution, storage and retrieval possibilities, transportability, and overall impact on the user.

Providing the output at the proper time is essential if it is to be used effectively in the management and decision-making activities of the organization. The timing depends on the function being performed. It is the systems analyst's and the user's responsibility to determine the proper timing. Some outputs will be produced daily, others only monthly or yearly. Information that is needed frequently is often provided on request through some type of CIS retrieval system.

Output is often produced at one location, for example at a centralized data center, and then distributed to the users. For the CIS output to be of value, it must be directed to the appropriate user. Most systems have substantial printed output, which is the primary type of output that requires distribution.

Output Design Guidelines. Designing output is unique to every system. The media, timing, content, and format for the output depend upon the nature of the CIS and specifically the purpose and objectives of the overall system. What is appropriate for one system in one organization may not be appropriate for the same type of system in another firm. Guidelines for designing effective output include (1) choose the most appropriate media, (2) match the output content and form to the user's needs, and (3) utilize as unbiased an output presentation as possible.

Choosing the most appropriate media depends on the system objectives, the user's preferences, and the various costs of implementation of the media for a given system. The options for output media include printers, data displays, audio, and microfilm (microfiche). The advantages and disadvantages of these media are presented in Figure 14-5.

Matching the output content and form to the user's needs is actually part of the design process. The intended purpose for which the output is to be used will influence its form and content as well as the output media that are chosen. Many printed outputs utilize preprinted forms that contain the company's

Figure 14.5. *Advantages and disadvantages of several output media.*

Method	Advantages	Disadvantages
Printer	affordable for most organizations flexible in types of output, location, and capabilities handles large volumes of output reaches many users inexpensively highly reliable with little down time	may be noisy compatibility problems with software may require special expensive supplies still requires some operator intervention depending on model, may be slow
Display screen	interactive works in on-line, real-time transmission through widely dispersed network quiet takes advantage of computer capabilities for movement within databases and files good for frequently accessed, ephemeral messages	requires cabling and setup space still may require printed documentation can be expensive if required for many users
Audio output	good for individual user good for transient or ephemeral messages that will be acted upon immediately and then discarded good where worker needs hands free for other tasks good if output is highly repetitive	is expensive to develop need dedicated room where output will not interfere with other tasks has limited applications is not yet perfected
Microform	handles large volumes of information reduces space required for storage preserves fragile but frequently used materials avoids problems of paging through physically cumbersome reports	requires special software for easy accessibility needs special equipment for printing hard copy can be expensive initial investment

name, address, and other information. Customer bills are a good example of this type of output. These outputs may also contain preprinted heading information and instructions for the customers about how they can pay their bills. Some portion of the bill is often returned with the payment. This type of form is called a *turnaround document* because the output from one stage of processing becomes the input for the next, when a customer returns part of the document with a payment. Examples include credit card bills and all types of utility bills. These output forms are based primarily upon the system specifications and the needs of the users.

In cases where preprinted forms are not used, reports are created with computer-generated descriptions to accompany the numeric information. The information contained in the report may be highly summarized such as the monthly income statement a chief executive officer (CEO) might receive. It could also be highly detailed, such as the list of deliveries a truck driver is supposed to make on a given day. The intended purpose of the report again determines its content and form. To fully determine the intended purpose of the output, several specific questions must be addressed. They include these:

Who are the intended users of the output? Hard copy is appropriate for salesmen who must carry the output with them, while customer service representatives are best served by video display output.

How many people will use the output? If only one person at a time uses the output, the video display, microfilm, or even voice output would be appropriate. If several users should receive the output, it is more appropriate to print it. When several users require the output at different times, a video display in conjunction with an on-line CIS is the preferred output method.

Where is the output needed? Printed output is most appropriate when it can be distributed locally. When output is to be used at locations physically far away from where it is produced, it is better distributed electronically. It can be printed or displayed at the remote locations again, depending on the purpose it is to serve.

How often will the output be accessed? Output that is infrequently utilized is most appropriate for computer output microfilm or microfiche. This is especially true if large volumes of output are involved.

How long must the output be retained? Printed output deteriorates with age while output to microfilm or microfiche is less likely to deteriorate as quickly. Therefore to store output for long periods, it may be necessary to use microfilm. Government regulations, such as tax laws, often are the determining factors of how long an output document should be kept. In other cases it may be organization policy or common sense.

What special rules govern the output that is produced? The federal government, for example, requires W-2 forms to be printed rather than microfilmed.

In what kind of environment will the output be produced and used? Printed output for invoices may be appropriate in a lumber company to give the customer a record of his bill and payment even when the environment for the printer itself may not be ideal. Lumber yards are often dusty, hot, and humid. Printers work best in dry and cool environments.

Bias in Output. Bias is present in everything that humans create. This is not to say that bias is bad but to make the point that it is inseparable from what we (and consequently our systems) produce. The concerns of systems analysts are to avoid unnecessarily biasing output and to make users aware of the possible biases in the output they receive. There are three main ways in which presentations of output are unintentionally biased: how information is sorted; the setting of acceptable limits; and the choice of graphics.

Bias is introduced to output when the analyst makes choices about how information is sorted for a report. Common sorts include alphabetic, chronological, and cost.

Information presented alphabetically may overemphasize the items that begin with the letters A and B, since users tend to pay more attention to the information presented first. This is in part why companies choose names like "AAA Plumbing"—so that they will be listed first in the telephone directory.

Bias is also unintentionally introduced into reports that are arranged chronologically. Once again, the user's attention is drawn to the events listed first, which are those things that occurred first. So in reviewing the use of computing time, an MIS manager who uses output presented chronologically may be biased toward examining usage for January, February, and March and underemphasize the figures for November and December. A third type of sorting, by cost, may also bias the output. Presenting information by cost alone (or any single factor) can be extremely misleading.

A second major source of bias in output is the predefinition of limits for particular values being reported. Many reports are generated on an exception basis only, which means that when limits on values are set beforehand, only exceptions to those values will be output. Exception reports make the decision maker aware of deviations from satisfactory values. There are two general problems with setting limits that may bias output: (1) setting limits either too high or too low and (2) making the range of exceptions either too narrow or too wide.

Limits that are set too low for exception reports can bias the user's perception. For example, an insurance company that generates exception reports on all accounts one week overdue probably has set too low a limit on overdue payments. The decision maker receiving the output will be overwhelmed with "exceptions" that are not really cause for concern. The one-week overdue exception report leads to the user's misperception that there are a great many overdue accounts. A more appropriate limit would be accounts thirty days overdue, with an exception report generated for them. Users can also be biased by output that is printed in exception reports when too high a limit is to be met before information is included. An example might be the reporting of overdue accounts only once a year. For the information to be useful, limits on allowable defects must be tightened. The resultant bias of setting too high a limit is that a false sense of security is generated. In fact, there is little, if any, output when allowances are set at unrealistically high limits.

The second way that setting limits can introduce bias is if the range of information output in an exception report is set too narrowly or too broadly. For example, selecting expense accounts that have included dinner items with charges greater than $400 will net so few accounts that the data will probably not be useful.

Conversely, setting too wide a range for information output on an exception report can also bias users. For example, if the water company generates an exception report on its residential users, but employs a range of all residential customers using between 1000 and 1,000,000 gallons per month, the output will be overwhelming.

Output is subject to a third type of presentation bias, which is brought about by the analyst's choice of graphics for output display. Bias can occur in the selection of the graphic size, its color, the scale used, and even the type of graphic.

Graphic size must be proportional, so that the user is not biased as to the importance of the variables presented. For example, Figure 14-6 shows a column chart comparing the price of a stock on December 31 with its price on the same date a year later. Notice that the vertical axis is broken, and it appears that the price in the second year is twice what it was in the first year, when actually the price has gone up only slightly. Choice of graphic color is also important so that the user is not unduly biased by it. The analyst needs to be aware that any colored output naturally claims more user attention than black and white printed or displayed output. The type of graphic chosen for output is also a potential source of bias for users. A pie chart is inappropriate if percentages of a whole are not the point. Bar and column charts can overexaggerate differences between variables.

Figure 14.6. **An example of a bias in a graphic setting.**

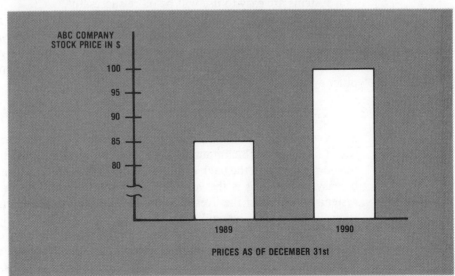

If more than two variables are to be shown over time, it is more appropriate to depict them on a line chart rather than on a bar chart. A poor choice of graph along with an inappropriate presentation can bias the user as to the meaning of the output.

There are several strategies that can be used to avoid any bias in the output. These are the most important:

Be aware of the sources of bias — the analyst and the user must recognize the areas where bias may influence the interpretation of the output.

Solicit user feedback — the analyst must obtain feedback from the user concerning the appropriateness of the output; this may require several iterations.

Create flexibility in the output — users and the systems analyst can avoid some degree of bias by allowing limits to be modified at the discretion of management.

By applying these three techniques, you will avoid output bias.

HUMAN FACTORS DESIGN GOALS

Computer-based information systems have frustrated computer users for decades. Although software in most cases is the problem, we all know it is possible to place too many users on the same system at the same time, which of course results in slow "response times" and frustration. In many cases, it is not slow response times or simply errors in the computer programs that cause the problem, it is poor systems design. Menu's may be difficult to interpret, error messages may be displayed incorrectly or in the wrong place on the display screen, or the written documentation may not be correct and complete. Software should be designed with the user in mind. Designers are realizing that information systems are easy to use will be more successful.

Providing a high-quality user interface to a system will result in greater employee productivity, better decision making, and a higher-quality working environment. Everyone wins and no one loses; what could be nicer? Let's consider the consequences of not considering the user when designing a new computer system.

Why Consider Human Factors Design?

The recent interest in human-factors design results in part from the frustrations we all have had with computer systems. These include little things like placing the power switch in the back of the machine rather than the front where it would be easy to find if it is the very first time you have looked for it. Information systems now impact the lives of 70 percent of the work force in modern industrialized nations. Why can't they work as they should, "efficiently and effectively"? Well, they can; and what's more, it is critical that they do. Why?

First of all, many information systems are essential to the safety and comfort of citizens. Air traffic control, patient monitoring systems, manned spacecraft, and military radar systems are examples of systems that could be life-critical. IBM Corporation was granted a $3.6-billion contract to redesign the air traffic control system in the United States in 1988. It is expected that the project will take ten years to complete. These types of systems are expensive, but they must have the greatest degree of reliability. Mistakes cannot be tolerated; therefore the users have to be well trained, and their performance must be periodically tested. Training sessions may often simulate emergency situations. This happens in the case of space shuttle astronauts many times prior to every mission.

Some systems may not be life-critical, but they can save costs or provide additional revenues. These could include any business computer application such as credit card processing, inventory control, production scheduling, and point-of-sale terminal systems. These systems are typically less expensive than life-critical systems and less reliable. Operator training is expensive; therefore, the software must be extremely easy to use. At McDonald's restaurants, for example, the cash registers have pictures of the products, not words, so that the operator is less likely to make a mistake. Reducing the time it takes to take one order by just one second could save McDonald's hundreds of thousands of dollars per year, maybe even millions. And because a mistake will result in even more time spent with a customer, the fewer mistakes magnify the benefits of the system substantially.

A third source of interest in human factors stems from the increase in microcomputer applications both at home and in the workplace. Software houses must create personal computing packages that are easy to use, have low error rates, and work quickly. They must also be simple so that first-time users can understand them easily. If voluntary users meet with difficulties using an electronic spreadsheet, calendar, or word processor, they will be unlikely to buy it or to use it if it has already been purchased.

The package should also provide a command language level of operation so that an experienced person can bypass the menus a novice would use and directly enter the command of choice. This is called a layered design because there are several ways to employ the system depending on the user's level of expertise. Most packages will sell at a relatively low cost; but because of the necessity for reliability, the packages are well tested. This cost can be spread over a large number of users (i.e., customers).

The fourth factor influencing the current interest in human-factors design is the increased use of knowledge-based systems. Many computer systems today are being developed to support intellectual and creative pursuits. Creative environments include writers workbenches, computer-aided design software for engineers and architects, and even systems designer workbenches such as Excellerator and BriefCASE, which is used in conjunction with this text. Expert or knowledge-based systems may also be created for specific purposes such as medical diagnosis, credit approval, or oil exploration. In both cases (supporting creativity and solving specific problems), users are likely to be highly motivated novices at using computers in general and the specific software package in particular. The degree of usage therefore, varies widely among users.

Understanding the physical, mental, and personality differences among users is critical to designing a satisfactory human-computer interface. The physical design of workplaces, whether they involve interaction with a computer or not, is termed **ergonomics**. The physical differences between users is so great that to say "average user" is a contradiction in terms because there is no such thing.

Physical human variances that will affect the way in which people use computer systems are often related to the user's vision. These include response time to visual stimuli, depth perception, motion sensitivity, night or low-light vision, peripheral vision, ability to read text, color vision, visual fatigue, eye disorders, and corrective lenses. Other important senses are the sense of touch, which is important for keyboard, touch sensitive screen, or mouse use, and hearing, which is important for detecting audible tones and for voice input/output devices. These human diversities help determine the characteristics of the computer workstation area. Many factors are considered in workstation design: work-surface height; clearance for the operators legs under the workstation; back rest and lumbar support; illumination levels and glare minimization; chair casters, height adjustments, and angles; and work surfaces among others. The more comfortable people are at the computer workstation, the more productive and satisfied they will be in their jobs. Uncomfortable chairs, poor lighting, or inadequate space for legs can significantly reduce worker productivity. Remember the most elegant screen design or help system may not overcome an uncomfortable environment. One final comment, the room layout may also impact worker productivity. If workers often work in teams or collaborate on jobs, it may be advantageous to group several workstations closely together. Students in a lab setting will learn as much or more from each other than they will from an instructor. It is truly a collaborative learning environment when the lab is physically designed to foster student interaction.

Cognitive and perceptual abilities also vary widely among users. How quickly a human being can identify changes on the monitor and initiate some type of corrective action will often determine the success or failure of a particular task. Humans are diverse in terms of the following cognitive characteristics: short- and long- term memory capacities, problem-solving ability, ability to search and scan, time perception, problem solving, and decision-making capabilities.

These differences should have a significant effect on the design of most interactive systems. One's knowledge of the task and the computer application system, along with the previously discussed cognitive factors, is the best predictor of performance.

Personality differences constitute the third category of human diversities. Some people inherently like technology, computer or otherwise, while others don't. Even those who like computer technology may vary in terms of their preferences for a style of interaction (i.e., fast or slow, detailed or summary, and tabular or graphic). Personality differences are inherent in all of us, the question is which specific characteristics are important with regard to the proper design of the human-computer interface.

Further research will be required to determine general or standardized rules for the design of the human-computer interface. All we as systems designers can do now is interview the systems users to determine their preferences and then design the specific system accordingly. It is clear however that a better understanding of all human diversities, physical, cognitive, and personality, can be helpful in designing systems for a specific community of users.

GUIDELINES FOR HUMAN FACTORS DESIGN

Some of the basic guidelines for the design of the human-computer interface are discussed in this section. Guidelines are presented concerning the dialogue between the user and the system, proper data display and data entry techniques, error detection and control, and finally some suggestions concerning acceptance testing are made.

Dialogue Design

Schneiderman in his text, *Designing the User Interface: Strategies for Effective Human-Computer Interaction* (Reading, MA: Addison-Wesley, 1987), suggests eight rules that apply to designing an effective dialogue between the user and the system.

1. Strive for consistency. Consistent sequences of actions should be required in similar situations. The terminology used should be identical in menus, prompts, commands, and help screens. Any exceptions to this consistency rule should be limited in number, such as allowing an abbreviation for a delete file command when in all other instances the command is not abbreviated. In other words, don't confuse or frustrate the user by being inconsistent.

2. Enable frequent users to use shortcuts. As users become more experienced with a system, they want to increase the pace of interaction. Prompts and intermediate menus are less important to this type of user. Frequent users will appreciate special function keys that accomplish several commands automatically, provide abbreviations for commands, or offer the ability to bypass menus and simply issue a command. Shorter response times and faster display rates are also attractive to experienced users.

3. Provide informative feedback. Each operator interaction should result in some type of system feedback. A limited response is all that is required for frequent operator actions, but for infrequent or major actions (i.e., ERASE) the system response should be substantial (i.e., ARE YOU SURE? (Y/N)).

4. Design dialogues to yield closure. Each series of actions should have a beginning, a middle, and an end. An operator needs feedback in order to know that one sequence of tasks has been successfully completed and the next can now begin.

5. Provide simple error handling. First attempt to design the system so that the user cannot make a serious error. If an error is made, the system should detect the error and offer a simple method for correcting it. The user should only have to correct the portion of the command that is in error; and if an error is made, the state of the system should be left unchanged. If the system is changed, instructions should be provided to restore the system to its correct state.

6. Permit easy reversal of actions. Actions should be reversible wherever possible. This relieves anxiety since the operator knows that errors can be undone. It also encourages exploration of unfamiliar options.

7. Maintain an internal locus of control. Experienced operators want to feel that they control the system and that the system responds to their commands. Any lack of flexibility in obtaining needed information or using the system frustrates the user.

8. Reduce short-term memory load. Humans have a limited amount of short-term memory. Most experts agree that five to nine symbols are the optimum number for codes that must be recalled. This means that commands should be kept as simple as possible. Multiple–page displays should be consolidated; and if a complex sequence of actions is necessary, adequate training should be provided along with an on-line help function.

Although these underlying principles are relevant to most human-computer interface situations, they must be interpreted and tailored to the individual system. These principles will aid system designers in providing a user interface that will increase productivity while enhancing the users' satisfaction with the system.

Data Display

Data display guidelines have been developed by several groups including Dumas [1987], Lockheed [1981], and Smith and Mosier [1984]. A guidelines document can help by promoting consistency among multiple designers. Here are several general guidelines for the display of data:

1. *Consistency* — all terminology, formats, and abbreviations contained in displays should be standardized and controlled by a data dictionary.

2. *Efficient user assimilation* — All formats should be in a form that is familiar to the users. This means that alphabetic data should be left-justified, numeric data should be aligned on decimal points, spacing should exist between data fields, and appropriate labels should be provided. Data should be relevant to the task at hand. Only the information the user needs should be displayed.

3. *Minimal user memory requirements* — Users should not be required to remember information from one screen for use on another screen. Tasks must be arranged such that completion occurs with three or fewer commands if possible, minimizing the probability of forgetting to perform a step. Again labels and common formats should be employed.

4. *Data display and data entry compatibility*—The format for displayed information should be clearly linked to the format for data entry.
5. *Flexibility*—The users should have control over the data display formats, in order to receive the information in the most convenient form for the task they are working on.

These general guidelines are a useful starting point, but more specificity is often required. Some more specific rules of thumb for designing data displays include these:

■ Place a descriptive title on each screen.

■ Indicate on each screen how to exit from the screen.

■ Left-justify text but leave a ragged right margin.

■ Avoid hyphenation of words between lines.

■ When displays continue over multiple screens, the screen should indicate where the user is in the display.

■ Use abbreviations only when they are easily understood by the user and significantly shorter than the full text display.

■ Arrange items in a table or list in an order recognizable to the user.

■ Break up long strings of alphanumeric characters into smaller groups of three or four characters each.

■ Use blinking lights or audible tones to highlight only critical information that requires an immediate response from the user.

Figure 14-7 depicts a poorly designed menu screen, and Figure 14-8 presents an improved version of the same screen.

Figure 14.7. *An example of a poorly designed menu screen.*

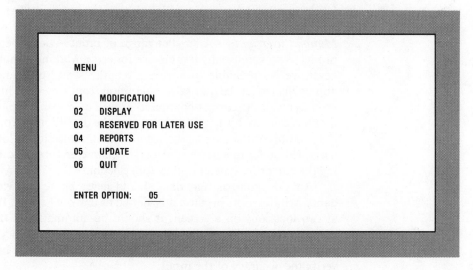

Figure 14.8.   An improved menu screen.

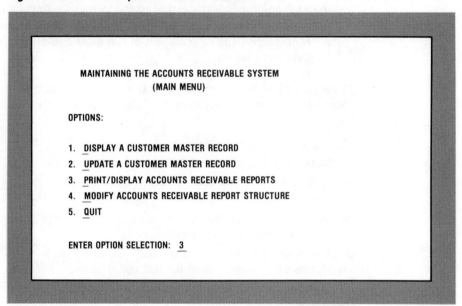

```
          MAINTAINING THE ACCOUNTS RECEIVABLE SYSTEM
                         (MAIN MENU)


     OPTIONS:


     1.  DISPLAY A CUSTOMER MASTER RECORD
     2.  UPDATE A CUSTOMER MASTER RECORD
     3.  PRINT/DISPLAY ACCOUNTS RECEIVABLE REPORTS
     4.  MODIFY ACCOUNTS RECEIVABLE REPORT STRUCTURE
     5.  QUIT


     ENTER OPTION SELECTION:  3
```

Data Entry

Data entry tasks can occupy a substantial fraction of the users time, and they can often be a source of frustration and errors. Input errors are a primary reason why many transactions are processed incorrectly and many management reports contain erroneous information. Some general guidelines for data entry include these:

1. *Consistency*—Similar sequences of actions under all conditions, similar labels, similar delimiters, similar abbreviations are all desirable features in a new system.
2. *Minimal user input*—A smaller range of input actions means greater user productivity and usually less chance for error. Making a choice with a single keystroke is preferable to keying a lengthy string of characters. Another approach is to let the user select an option from a menu. This eliminates the need to recall the correct command as well as possible typing errors. If the user has to move his hand to a mouse or the directional arrow keys to adjust the position of the cursor, the value of menu selection is lost. Experienced users will prefer to enter a six-to-eight character command instead of moving the cursor to a menu option for selection.

   Another point is that data should never be keyed twice. This redundancy irritates users because it is viewed as a wasted effort. If data is needed at two locations on a screen, it should be automatically transferred. The user can always change the data by overtyping. Redundancy has value only from a control standpoint. That is, critical data fields may be keyed twice to verify the accuracy of the input.

3. *Minimal user memory requirements*—The system should reduce the need for users to remember long codes or complicated commands.
4. *Data display and data entry compatibility*—again the format for data entry should be closely linked to the format of displayed information.
5 *Flexibility*—Experienced operators often prefer to enter information in a sequence they can control. Flexibility and consistency can contradict each other; therefore, the flexibility concept must be employed cautiously.

These are very general guidelines for data entry. Some specific principles include the following:

■ When the user must transcribe data directly from a paper form to the screen, the layout of the screen should correspond to the form.

■ Areas of the screen not needed for data entry, should be made inaccessible to users.

■ Allow users to move freely through the fields on the data entry screen.

■ Automatically justify data entries, alphabetic entries to the left and numeric entries to the right with the automatic adjustment of all decimal points.

■ Allow the users to leave the data entry screen without filling in all of the data fields.

■ Never require users to enter information already available elsewhere (e.g., in the database).

■ Display default values in data fields when appropriate.

Figure 14-9 is an example of a poorly designed data entry screen. Figure 14-10 shows how it can be improved.

Figure 14.9.   *An example of a poorly designed data entry screen.*

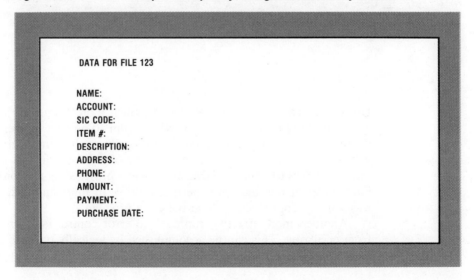

DATA FOR FILE 123

NAME:
ACCOUNT:
SIC CODE:
ITEM #:
DESCRIPTION:
ADDRESS:
PHONE:
AMOUNT:
PAYMENT:
PURCHASE DATE:

Figure 14.10. *An improved data entry screen.*

```
                        ABC AUTO PARTS COMPANY

                          ORDER ENTRY SCREEN

ACCOUNT NO: __-_____-__ SIC CODE: __-_____ DATE OF PURCHASE: __-__-__

COMPANY NAME: _____ PHONE: _____-_____-_____

STREET ADDRESS:_____

CITY: _____ STATE: _____ ZIP: _____-_____

                             ITEMS ORDERED

Item No:            Item Description         Qty Ordered          Price

_____        _____        _____     $ _____.___
_____        _____        _____     $ _____.___
_____        _____        _____     $ _____.___
_____        _____        _____     $ _____.___

FORM OF PAYMENT (X): CASH__          TOTAL AMOUNT DUE:    $ _____.___
                       CC__          AMOUNT PAID     :    $ _____.___
                    CHECK__          BALANCE DUE     :    $ _____.___
```

Error Control

Users of software systems make errors much more frequently than might be expected. They make mistakes anywhere from 10 percent to over 40 percent of the time they use a system, depending primarily on the complexity of the system and the experience of the user. One method of reducing the loss in productivity due to errors is to improve the **error messages** provided by the computer system. Superior error messages are specific, positive in tone, and clear in telling the user what to do, not simply that there is a problem.

Another, more effective approach to error control is to prevent the error from occurring. This can be accomplished by logically organizing screens and menus, designing commands and menus to be distinctive, making it difficult for users to undertake irreversible actions, and providing feedback about the state of the system. Specific techniques for ensuring correct actions include these:

1. *Correcting matching pairs* — This is a common problem, which includes matching a right parenthesis with a left.
2. *Completing sequences* — Sometimes an action requires several steps or commands to reach completion. Systems should accomplish as many tasks as possible with a single action. For example, users of a data communications system seldom need to know how to load necessary communication files, or to power on the system; these tasks are accomplished automatically with a single command.
3. *Correcting commands* — Typical errors with commands include requesting a file that does not exist, selecting a menu option that is unavailable, or entering a data value that is not acceptable. These errors are often typographical — misspelling a command or omitting a space. Error messages may not be explicit enough for the user to determine what the problem is and how to correct it. One approach is to minimize the number of keystrokes (the fewer the keystrokes the less the chance for making an error, especially if the keystrokes require the use of special keys like shift, control, or upper case characters). Some systems offer automatic completion of a command when the user types the first few letters, some may provide a menu of options. Some systems also allow users to point to menu selections rather than utilizing the keyboard, again eliminating another possibility for error.
4. *Establishing limits* — Limits should be set for the format and magnitude of all entries. In a payroll system, for example, an hours-worked entry might be limited to a range of 10 hours to 80 hours for a single week.

Figure 14-11 presents several examples of poor error messages along with improved versions.

Acceptance Testing

An **acceptance testing** plan should be written before the design is made final. Both hardware and software test plans are regularly included as part of the system specifications. The extension of this to the development of an appropriate and effective human interface is very logical. Schneiderman suggests that before preparing a human interface plan the systems designers should first determine the relative importance of five human factors: retention over time, subjective satisfaction, error rates of users, time to learn, and speed of performance. Once the relative importance of each of these quality criteria has been determined, specific measurable objectives should be established to inform customers and users and to guide designers. An example of a retention-oriented acceptance test would be:

> After one week, student dBASE III PLUS programmers will be comfortable enough with the system to avoid using the ASSISTANT menu option.

Figure 14.11. *Examples of poor error messages and improved error messages.*

POOR ERROR MESSAGE	IMPROVED ERROR MESSAGE
1. ERROR D159	A RECORD WITH THE KEY 472–58–9999 CANNOT BE FOUND IN THE ACCREC.BAK FILE
2. PROTECTED FILE	THE ACCREC.MAS FILE YOU REQUESTED IS PROTECTED: SEE THE DATA BASE ADMINISTRATOR
3. YOU IDIOT, TYPE THE DATE AGAIN IN THE CORRECT FORMAT	THE DATE SHOULD BE TYPED IN THIS WAY: XX/XX/XX (example: 07/09/89)
4. WRONG SELECTION	PLEASE TYPE AN OPTION FROM THE MENU
5. RETYPE THE COMMAND	RETYPE THE SERVICE YOU WISH TO ACCESS: THE LEGAL SERVICES ARE COBA1, COBA2, ACS1, ACS2 AND CRAY

These types of acceptance tests constitute the definition of user friendliness for the system. They are actually one criterion for determining the degree to which the system is a success. The presence of a precise acceptance test will focus more attention on the human-machine interface during the design phase. It will help ensure that pilot studies are run to determine if the project can meet the test plan goals. Objective criteria is often used, such as, "20 out of 30 production supervisors should be able to correctly enter 24 hours of production control data within ten minutes." Suggestions from participants in the pilot tests and subjective reactions of satisfaction with the system will also be recorded.

INTERACTION STYLES

After the task analysis has been completed and the necessary performance standards have been specifically identified, the systems designer must then choose the most appropriate interaction style. The most common of these include menu selection, command language, direct manipulation, and forms fill-in.

Menu Selection

In **menu selection**, the users read a list of items and select the one most appropriate to their task, usually by highlighting the selection and pressing the return key or by keying the menu item number. If the terminology and meaning of the items are completely understandable, users can accomplish the desired tasks with little memorization and few keystrokes. Because this interaction style provides maximum structure for using the system, it is very appropriate for novices and infrequent users. It can also be appropriate for frequent users if the menu display and selection processes are very rapid.

Menu selection systems require a very complete and accurate analysis of user tasks to ensure that all of the necessary functions are supported with clear and consistent terminology. Dialogue management tools to support menu selection are a valuable tool in ensuring consistent screen design and validating menu completeness.

Common problems that can occur with the menu selection interaction technique include (1) the danger of incorporating too many different menus in the system, (2) the fact that frequent users will feel as though they are being slowed down, (3) domination of much of the available screen space, and (4) the need for a rapid display rate.

Command Language

For the frequent user, the command language provides a feeling of "control" over the system. Users first learn the appropriate syntax, then create their own commands and initiate a process to accomplish an objective. This flexible interaction style encourages initiative on the part of users, who often create complex user-defined "macros" (i.e., programs built with an internal command programming language). There are some problems with this interaction style including these drawbacks: (1) error handling is difficult because of the diversity of possible causes of the error, and (2) this technique requires a substantial amount of training and memorization.

Direct Manipulation

Direct manipulation provides a visual representation that allows the user to directly manipulate the objects of interest. Keyboard entry of commands is replaced by cursor motion devices (using the directional arrow keys, using a mouse, or using a touch-sensitive screen) or perhaps by voice activation to select from a visible set of objects and actions. Direct manipulation is appealing to novices, easy to remember for intermittent users, and (with careful design) fast enough to satisfy the frequent user.

Forms Fill-in

If users are required to perform data entry, the **forms fill-in** interaction technique is very useful. The other techniques have some serious deficiencies for user data entry. Command language requires too much prior learning; menu selection is too cumbersome; and direct manipulation is not appropriate because keying the data is necessary. With the forms fill-in approach, users see a display of related fields and move the cursor to the desired field to enter the input data. The data entry operators must recognize the labels on the data fields. This means that some training will normally be required. This approach is most appropriate for intermittent and frequent users.

XEROX PARC'S NOTE CARDS: CREATING A HYPERTEXT USER INTERFACE

Hypertext (also know as nonlinear text) is an approach to information management in which data are stored in a network of nodes connected by links. Data can take the form of text, graphics, or video, as well as source code. The user can view the nodes, and in some systems the network itself, through an interactive, graphic browser. The user typically employes a mouse as the primary input device. Furthermore, he or she can manipulate these nodes through a structure editor.

In his survey on hypertext, Conklin [1987] identifies the following items as necessary features of a somewhat idealized hypertext system:

The database is a network of textual nodes, i.e., processing of quantitative information, although possible, is not a primary objective of hypertext.

The windows displaying the node contents may contain any number of link icons, which represent pointers to other nodes in the databases.

The user may create new links to new nodes (e.g., annotation) or to existing nodes (for establishing new connections).

Standard window system operations must be supported, i.e., both window and icon position and shape are visual cues to remembering the window contents.

Hypertext is certainly not new. By some accounts, it is at least twenty years old. However, with the relatively recent surge of interest in computer support of collaborative professional work, hypertext technology has started coming out of the computer science–software engineering closet and into the management support systems (MSS) mainstream. One example of this is the NoteCards system built by Xerox Corporation.

The original motivation in building NoteCards was to explore the development of an information analyst's support tool, one that would help gather information about a topic and produce analytic reports at regular intervals and on demand. It was observed that the general procedure that such analysts used was (a) reading sources (news reports, scholarly articles, etc.), (b) collecting clippings and filing them (in actual shoe boxes!), and (c) writing analytic reports. It was also observed that throughout the process, analysts formed analyses and conceptual models in their heads. The research goal of the PARC team was to develop technology to aid the analyst in forming better conceptual models and analyses and to find better expressions of these models and analyses. A "programmer's interface" makes NoteCards an open architecture that allows users to build (in Lisp) new applications on top of NoteCards, including making it easy to customize the browser. NoteCards allows easy creation of new types of nodes. Forty of fifty such specialized node types have been created to date, including text, video, animation, graphics, and actions. The new version also allows several users to work in the same Notefile at the same time.

Part of NoteCards' success is due to the fact that it was developed and used on Xerox D series Lisp machines, which are such powerful work stations that they allow rapid creation and browsing of many hypertext nodes, as well as having a high resolution screen that allows windows and link and node icons to be displayed in excellent resolution (see below). There are currently between 50

Feature figure. *A sample of the NoteCards screen showing NoteCards and File Boxes.*

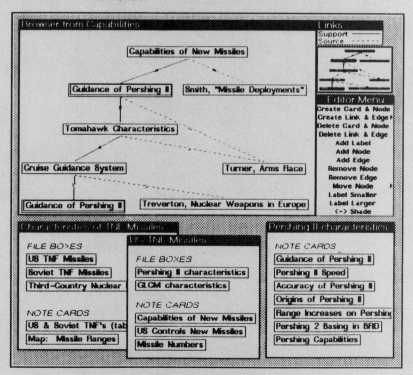

and 100 users of NoteCards, many of them outside of Xerox, even though it is not a supported product; and several of these users have constructed very large databases in the system (e.g., 1600 nodes with 3500 links between them). Unfortunately, the Xerox D machines are quite expensive, and they are the only delivery vehicle for NoteCards at this time.

Conklin, J. "A Survey of Hypertext," MCC Technical Report Number STP-356-86 Rev. 2, December 3, 1987.

OTHER CONSIDERATIONS

Designing an effective human-computer interface is not an easy task. Several other factors that may have an effect on this process are discussed in this section, including the use of system messages and printed materials, the importance of tutorials and help functions, and the importance of response times.

System Messages

Developing effective **system messages** means pilot testing them with actual users. Messages should be evaluated by several people in an environment as realistic as possible. In addition, the frequency with which errors occur should be recorded. If errors occur too frequently (i.e., one in every twenty transactions), the systems programs should be modified to correct the problem. Users will always recall the one time they encountered difficulty with the system and forget the twenty times when it worked correctly. Guidelines that may help the systems professional when designing messages include these:

- Be as specific and precise as possible.
- Use a positive tone; avoid condemnation.
- Be constructive; indicate what needs to be done.
- Be consistent with terminology, abbreviations, and grammatical form.
- Consider multiple levels of messages.

Printed Materials

All users of interactive systems will require some training; and this, in turn, will require the use of some type of printed materials, including:

1. User Manual — This document describes the features of the system. It often includes an alphabetical listing of commands, a quick reference card with concise presentations of syntax, and a tutorial for the first-time user.
2. Computer-based Material — This may include an online user manual. Basically this is an electronic version of the traditional user manual. It also often includes an online help facility and an online tutorial system.

Guidelines to be employed in the preparation of user manuals include:

- Keep the writing style clean and simple.
- Pilot test the manual before implementing it system wide.
- Show numerous examples.
- Include a complete and understandable list of error messages.
- Provide a table of contents, index, and glossary.
- Provide a complete, detailed index with cross references to terms used interchangeably.
- Utilize diagrams to illustrate important points and the transition from one section to another.
- Provide meaningful illustrations of sequences of commands.
- Always let the user tasks guide the organization of the document.

Tutorials and Help Functions

It is often appealing to systems designers and users alike to make technical manuals available on the computer. The advantages of such **on-line tutorials** include these: (1) the information is available whenever the computer is available; (2) users do not have to allocate work space for opening printed manuals; (3) information can be electronically updated; (4) specific information can be located rapidly if the on-line manual offers electronic indexing or text searching (i.e., it is easier to find 1 page in a 2000-page manual on a computer than it is to do it manually); and (5) computer screens can show graphics and animations that may be helpful to users in understanding a specific part of the system.

On-line help functions usually offer concise descriptions of the command syntax and semantics. These are most useful for the person who is somewhat knowledgeable about the software but is not an expert. Novices would usually require more of a tutorial. The most common approach is to design an interactive tutorial environment. One introductory tutorial displays the exact keystrokes the user must employ to perform a particular task. Users can either type the exact keystrokes or they can keep pressing the space bar to speed through the demonstration. Some users find this approach too restrictive because it prevents individual exploration. Many beginning users benefit greatly from on-line tutorials for three primary reasons: (1) the user does not have to keep shifting attention between the terminal or PC and the instructional material; (2) tutorials allow the user to practice the skills needed to use the system; and (3) the users can work alone at his or her own pace and without the fear of embarrassment about mistakes made before other students and an instructor. The best approach for evaluating an online tutorial or help system is to pilot-test it and refine it where necessary.

In conclusion, paper manuals, on-line help, and tutorials all play an important role in the success or failure of a software system. Several guidelines for smoothing communication include these:

- Write on-line instructions in plain English.
- Address the user directly as "you."

- Be as specific as possible in describing the cause of an error, do not use error codes.
- Be consistent in the format, wording, and placement of messages on the screen.
- Include memory aids in the prompt to make formats, infrequently used processes, or exceptions to normal practice clear.
- Provide a direct route back to the application task.
- Do not expect the user to read more than about three screens of help at one time.

The Importance of Response Time

When delays in obtaining the necessary information to do a job occur, many people become frustrated, annoyed, and eventually angry. Slow response times and display rates produce these reactions from computer users. This can lead to a lack of users, dissatisfaction with the system, and more frequent errors. Even if the users accept the situation as it is, they don't like being slowed down by the system and prefer to work more quickly if only the system would allow them to do so.

System **response time** is the number of seconds it takes from the moment a user initiates activity, usually by hitting the return key, until the system begins presenting the results on the display screen or the printer.

Research tells us that in most situations response times of less than a second lead to higher productivity. Satisfaction with the system also increases as the response time is shortened, but it can also induce stress in the user if the pace is too rapid. As users pick up the pace of the system, they may make more errors. If these errors can be easily detected and corrected, then the productively will generally increase. If the errors are difficult to detect or very costly, then a moderate pace is preferred. The optimal response time for a specific application and user community can be determined by measuring the productivity, cost of errors, and cost of providing a short response time. Productivity is measured by correctly completed tasks, not the total number of tasks completed in a given time period. Therefore managers must remain alert to changes in the work style as the pace quickens.

Novices will usually prefer a slower pace then will experienced users. If technical feasibility or costs prevent response times of less than a second, each class of commands should be assigned to a response time category: for example < 1 second, 1–3 seconds, and > 3 seconds. Response time is defined here as the time between the point when the return key is hit and the point when the output begins to appear. Variations in response times around the average response time can be tolerated if they are kept within plus or minus 50 percent of the mean. Within this range the variation will have very little impact on performance. If larger variations occur, they should be accompanied by some type of informative message. If the response is too rapid rather than too slow, an alternative solution is to intentionally slow the response time. **Display rates** are faster than human reading speeds; therefore if the full text must be read and comprehended before the user takes action, the system must intentionally be slowed. For tasks that do not require full text reading, faster display rates will speed performance but may lead to an increase in errors. Faster display rates (within the constraints discussed here) are preferred.

THE FANTASTIC VOYAGE: CHARTING A HUMAN-COMPUTER INTERFACE

Skip Walter clapped his hands together loudly, startling several people in the front of the meeting room.

Walter, Digital Equipment Corp's manager of business office services and applications and the "father" of All-In-1, was making a point.

He was telling the attendees at a recent industry executive forum about some of his explorations into the nature of communications, explorations that could eventually lead to the design of new and radically different office information systems.

Sophisticated Methods

Right now, he said, the computer-human interface is primarily visual and character based. It works fairly well. But every day, in the simplest person-to-person interchanges, human beings use far more sophisticated methods of assimilating, sorting, and communicating information.

To illustrate, Walter recalled a financial officer at DEC who used an interesting analogy to explain why substantial cash reserves were necessary for a fast-growing company.

It is like driving down a highway, the man said, in a car marked Income. Right behind you is another car with Expenses painted in big red letters on the side.

Now you know, for safety's sake, there should be a car's length of distance between your car and the car behind you—the safety zone. That is your cash reserve.

Now if you're driving at a sedate 10 mph, you don't need much space between vehicles. But here you are clipping along the thruway at 60 mph in your souped-up, fuel-injected, income sports car. If you're without adequate cash reserves, you're racing down the highway with the expenses car a mere four inches from your rear bumper. If your income falters for even an instant, what happens? Wham! Here Walter clapped his hands together, making his listeners jump.

The story, he explained, took a dry accounting idea and made it understandable and memorable by appealing to all the senses we use to assimilate information—the visual (you can see the cars), the auditory (the hand clap), and the kinesthetic (you can feel yourself speeding down the road and sense in your gut the wrenching impact of two crashing vehicles).

What people want, Walter explained, is communication, not information. "I receive 100 mail messages a day," he said. "That's 600 to 700 pages of information. I can't physically scan, much less read to understand, all the trade publications and books I need to. Or talk, with all the people I need to. I don't need more information; what I need is a way to capture and share knowledge. A way to communicate with others and with myself about the meaning of facts—not moving these facts back and forth."

Walter was delving into difficult questions. He was probing that often-explored but little-understood arena where people, processes, and technology combine to form what he characterizes as a living, intelligent structure.

Writing about the modern scientific reductive method, which attempts to understand a process by chopping it up into separate pieces, William Wordsworth said, "We murder to dissect." The point is that the intelligence of the structure cannot be isolated. It is enmeshed in the total structure.

To communicate knowledge across this living network of people, processes, and technology, new and innovative methods of presenting information must be developed. They must involve our visual, auditory, and kinesthetic senses.

To illustrate his point, Walter unveiled some proprietary research on which his group is working. He showed several short videotapes about a mundane subject—database design.

But the tapes were far from mundane. The attendees saw the data elements in three dimensions and in color. Elastic connectors, fine white filaments, stretched between the data elements, visually indicating the web of relationships. It was reminiscent of the film *Fantastic Voyage*, in which the characters, miniaturized by technology, enter a man's body and use a tiny submarine to sail through the uncharted regions of his body.

Shifting Relationships

In the DEC video, you move in three dimensions among the data, changing them, rearranging them, retrieving them, observing in real time how the relationships between elements shift. More important, because of the way the data are presented, you are able to bring your intuitive faculties to bear as you roam this digitized landscape.

The videotapes are rudimentary, but the possibilities are fascinating. Imagine adding sound and a joy stick. You could zoom among the towering structures that you have built like an intergalactic fighter pilot from *Star Wars*. Others could join you in this network of information and ideas, and, like explorers mapping uncharted territory, you together could discover new relationships, new roads to explore. This is simulation rather than real life. If you fall off a cliff, it's not fatal; you simply push the rest button and try again.

As Walter sees it, the next step is deceptively simple but hard to realize: the design of human interfaces that use sound, pictures, and movement. As this approach develops, we will be making the first tentative steps toward tapping the tremendous capabilities latent in the partnership between man and technology.

SUMMARY

Computer software must be designed from the user's perspective if the system is to function in an optimal way. The objectives of an effective human-computer interface include increased user productivity, fewer errors, and higher levels of user satisfaction with the system.

Designing the best possible input and output should be the first objective in providing an effective human-computer interface. Input forms and input screens are the two most common forms of computer input. Input forms are preprinted documents that require the user to fill in responses in a standardized way. Forms should be designed such that they flow from left to right and top to bottom. This is because one reads everything in this manner. Forms should also group the data they contain in a logical manner. To do this, most forms have seven sections, which include a heading, an identification, instructions, body, signature and verification, totals, and comments. Clear captions can also be an aid to users in accurately and easily completing forms.

Output can include printed reports, microfilm, audio, and the most common medium—the video display screen. Output should have a specific purpose; it should be flexible enough to be easily modified to meet the needs of different managers; it should utilize the most appropriate media (e.g., print, audio, display); and it should be presented at the proper time to be effectively employed by management.

The output of every system is unique. It is the systems analyst's and the user's responsibility to choose the appropriate media, correctly match the output content and form to the user's needs, and utilize as unbiased an output as is possible.

Unclear or derogatory error messages, cluttered display screens, and confusing sequences of operations must be avoided if software systems are to truly succeed. This chapter has attempted to provide some guidelines in designing several aspects of the human-computer interface including input form and output design, dialogue design, data display, data entry, error control, acceptance testing, interaction styles, system messages, tutorials, and help functions.

KEY TERMS

1. turnaround document
2. direct manipulation
3. natural (command) language
4. menu selection
5. form fill-in
6. dialogue design

7. response time
8. ergonomics
9. human diversities
10. task profiles
11. acceptance testing

12. on-line tutorials
13. error messages
14. display rates
15. system messages

REVIEW/DISCUSSION QUESTIONS

1. What is meant by maintaining an internal locus of control in a dialogue design?
2. What are some common problems that can occur with the menu selection interaction technique?
3. What factors might be considered in workstation design?
4. What is an acceptance test and when is it used?
5. What is a pilot study and when is it used?
6. What advantages do on-line help functions have over paper documentation?
7. Are traditional user manuals ever preferable to on-line help and tutorial functions? If so, under what circumstances is this the case?
8. What are the keys to effective screen design?
9. Should display rates ever be slower than they could be? If so, why?
10. What is response time, and why is it important?

15

Software Design Strategies

Learning Objectives

On completing reading and other learning assignments for this chapter, you should be able to:

- Tell how software may be structured by statements, modules, and program control structures.
- Describe the attributes of modules in terms of function, logic, and interfaces.
- Explain the use of program control structures for sequence, repetition, and selection.
- Describe graphic representation tools used in software design.
- Describe the use of such software design strategies as functional decomposition, transform analysis, and transaction analysis.
- Describe the relative strengths and weaknesses of the three software design strategies presented in this chapter.
- Tell how design approaches may be applied to achieve a single coordinated software design strategy.

THE STRUCTURE OF SOFTWARE

The activities of the software designer have as their main purpose the definition and structuring of the components that will comprise the set of programs required to make a software design operational. Thus, the software designer considers the question of which program functions should be interconnected, and in what ways, to meet processing specifications. The resulting design, then, becomes the blueprint for the programmer, who elaborates the design into sets of computer operations that perform requisite input, processing, output, and storage functions.

Statements and Modules

At the fundamental level, software is constructed from two basic components: statements and modules. These two elements, or primitives, are the basic building blocks from which application programs are built. Program **statements** are the elementary computer operations that are selected and organized to perform problem-oriented processing functions. Statements form the lowest level of operation that can be carried out under a specific programming language. Groups of statements are arranged in a structure that causes the computer to complete a processing sequence; that is, accepting inputs and producing prescribed outputs. It is the structure, the arrangement, and the relationships among the statements that introduce a quality dimension to design.

At the software-design level, the main design component is the module. A **module** is a collection, or organized grouping, of source code statements. Statements are organized within modules so that the modules can be linked to form programs. The task of the designer includes determining software functions and the manner in which those functions are related logically. Taken together, these software functions — packaged as modules — make up the program. Characteristics of a program module include:

- A module consists of a group of statements that are physically contiguous and that are executed as a unit.
- The group of statements that form a module have identifiable beginnings and endings.
- In most cases, the group of statements has a single entry point and a single exit.
- The group of statements that form a module can be referenced collectively within programs by a specific mnemonic, or assigned name.
- Modules are identified by standard programming terms, such as a COBOL section, paragraph, or subprogram; a BASIC subroutine; a PL/1 procedure or task; or a FORTRAN function or subroutine. Thus, a module can be either a separately compiled program or subprogram or an identifiable internal procedure within a program.

Attributes of Modules

All modules have three basic attributes, function, logic, and interfaces.

Function. **A module's function** is the data transformation that takes place when the module is executed. A function can be described as the black-box behavior of a module. In other words, the function of a module consists of the results that can be discerned externally without looking inside the module. The nature of this examination is implied by the term **black box**. Functions of a black box are deduced by an understanding of its inputs and outputs. For example, a stereo receiver has a music source and electricity as input and high fidelity music as output. The owner of the stereo is not overly concerned about how it works, but expects high quality output given the appropriate inputs.

Thus at the software design level, a reference to a module is also a reference to its function. The problem-oriented function of the module as described on the systems flowchart is expanded into a hierarchy of processing-oriented functions that accomplish its purpose. Normally, concern with the module's logic is limited to consideration of its activation sequence. Little or no interest is taken in the detailed computer operations required to implement its function.

In representing software designs graphically, a module is depicted as a box with a label describing its function. The name assigned to each module both describes its function and encompasses collectively functions of subordinate modules that contribute to its execution. The collection of modules that represent a design usually are documented within a structure chart.

Logic. The **logic of a module** is a description of, or specification for, the actual processing that takes place within the module. The logical description of a module has been likened to a white box or clear box. With the logic exposed, it becomes possible to understand the inner workings of a module.

At the programming level, concern is mainly with the logic of a module. Processing algorithms are designed to transform the inputs into outputs, and these algorithms are translated into statements. Design, therefore, centers on the statement as the basic building block of algorithms. The function of a module is the given. By the same token, the logic of a module is the result.

Interfaces. **Interfaces** are the connections or couplings between modules. Module interfaces serve to establish paths across which control is transferred from one module to another. For example, in a COBOL program, the transfer of control between modules takes place on execution of a PERFORM statement or a subroutine CALL. Transfer of data, then, occurs through identification of the data elements to be passed from one processing module to another or through reference to a data structure common to both modules.

Therefore, connections between modules serve two main purposes: (1) the transfer of control from one module to another and (2) the passing of data from one module to another. The effectiveness of a software design depends largely on how effectively control is transferred between modules and the method used to pass data from one module to the next.

Program Control Structures

Software design takes place at two levels: logical and physical. At the logical level, the processing modules required for an application are defined and organized into a hierarchy. This hierarchy represents the problem-related connections among the software components. It documents the processing activities that will be implemented and shows how these activities are related to one another in terms of their data interfaces. A structure chart prepared to describe this problem solution provides documentation of the overall logical structure of the software.

Once a logical solution is devised, it must be adapted for computer processing. Thus, at the physical, or implementation, level, consideration is given to the execution structure of the software. This consideration involves determining the sequencing of computer operations within and between modules.

The importance of recognizing this difference between the logical, problem-related structure of a piece of software and its physical, execution-control structure cannot be overemphasized. Initial design activity takes place at the logical level. The designer attempts to model a software structure that mirrors the structure of the problem to be solved. At this point, little (if any) consideration is given to the possible execution structure. Modules are designed to correspond with processing functions implicit in the problem structure; connections between modules are modeled after the relationships existing in the problem structure.

Once the logical structure of the solution is determined, it then is packaged for implementation. The physical constraints of the computer system are taken into account as the design is modified to include execution control structures.

In the interest of simplicity of design, structured design, like structured programming, emphasizes a restricted number of ways in which to construct relationships between program components. The minimum set of **logical (program) control structures** necessary and sufficient for controlling the activation sequence of processing components within a program and between program modules are sequence, repetition (iteration), and selection.

Sequence. The activation **sequence** of program modules is controlled through use of language statements like PERFORMs or CALLs within the source program or, alternately, by the physical placement of modules to correspond with execution sequence. In the structure chart drawn to indicate the execution structure, modules usually are organized to reflect this sequence. Processing operations within a module normally are carried out in the physical sequence in which they appear. Unless it is instructed otherwise, the computer will execute statements in this top-down order. Sequences, therefore, represent the natural order of processing as viewed from the standpoint of the computer.

Repetition. Another valid type of control structure for modules and statements is **repetition**. A repetition is the continued activation of a module or a set of statements for as long as a stipulated condition exists. With each execution of a repetition, a condition test is first applied. If the condition for ending the loop has not occurred, the processing is repeated. When eventually the condition is found to exist, repetitive processing terminates and control passes to the next statement in sequence.

Selection. A **selection** control structure implements processing decisions. That is, based on comparative tests applied to data being processed, control is passed to any one of two or more modules or sets of statements. Typically, a selection is invoked with an IF command. Selection control structures often are referred to **as case constructs** whenever three or more alternative processing activities are included within the structure. Some programming languages have command structures specifically utilizing case designations. In other languages, case constructs are contrived by using multiple IF statements or nested IF-THEN-ELSE statements.

GRAPHIC REPRESENTATION OF SOFTWARE

Typically, modules or groups of modules are represented within **structure charts**. Structure charts, in turn, are used as a means of communication about software designs. There are several generally accepted notations or conventions used to represent modules and the interconnections among modules within structure charts. The differences between these conventions are such that anyone who can read one style of notation should have no trouble deciphering and dealing with others. To illustrate, two popular notation methods are presented in Figures 15-1 and 15-2.

Figure 15-1 presents a typical structure chart that often is used to document program designs. Modules are arranged in an activation hierarchy (**module**

Figure 15.1. *One system of notation for structure charts illustrates the modules in a program and their hierarchical relationships, and optional includes identification of data passed between them and the types of control structures used to relate them.*

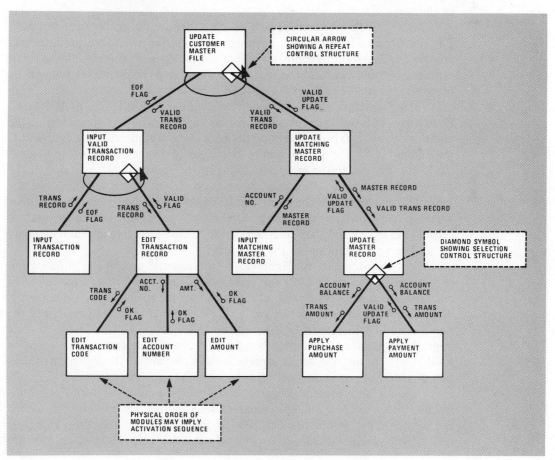

hierarchy) in which lower-level modules, **subordinates**, are executed from their immediate **superordinates**, the modules on the next higher level of the hierarchy.

Figure 15-1 again illustrates the distinction that must be made between the logical design of a piece of software and the final physical design that can be implemented on a computer. Logical design considers the hierarchical structure of processing functions with only minor concern given to modeling the execution structure. Therefore, the structure chart seldom, if ever, includes initialization and termination modules or documentation of specific programming techniques. The structure chart shows only the logical relationships among modules that perform major processing functions.

Within limitations that do not encompass actual machine execution, activation sequences — implemented with the three control structures discussed earlier — are documented on the chart. Although the order of activation, or sequence, cannot be inferred directly from the arrangement of modules, there is often an implied sequence from top to bottom and from left to right. Symbols representing repetition and selection have been added to Figure 15-1 to show the control structures that relate the modules. The circular arrows represent the repetition and the diamond symbol represents the selection of subordinate modules.

Other symbols are used to show the data that are passed between modules. The small, named arrowheads document the interfaces between modules and provide confirmation that proper inputs are available to the module and that expected outputs can be produced. The white arrowheads depict data to be processed that relate to the problem itself. The darkened arrowheads depict flag data, or information about the condition of the data itself, i.e., EOF, VALID FLAG, etc. If a particular module will be implemented as a subprogram, the notations refer to explicit pieces of data, or data arguments, that are passed. Depending upon the programming language of implementation, individual modules may refer to the same data items by different names. As a rule, if the subordinate and superordinate modules use different names internally for the same data element, then the name displayed on the structure chart will be that which the superordinate uses. If the module will be implemented as an internal subroutine, the named data interfaces refer to data elements available globally for all internal subroutines of the program.

The structure chart in Figure 15-2 contains the same basic information as the one in Figure 15-1. In this case, data interfaces between modules are documented in a separate table of input-output parameters. The table then is cross-referenced to the structure chart. These input-output relationships of the parameters is defined with respect to the called module. This interface table might be expanded to include other data details such as data type, length, or valid values. Again, the actual structure chart documents the logical organization of processing modules, not necessarily the physical organization.

These methods present programs and program modules in terms of hierarchical structures. Further, structured representations are modeled on a top-down basis, first from a logical view of the software components and their relationship, and eventually to a physical view that can be translated directly

Figure 15.2. *An alternate style of structure chart optionally is supported by a table of input and output interfaces between modules.*

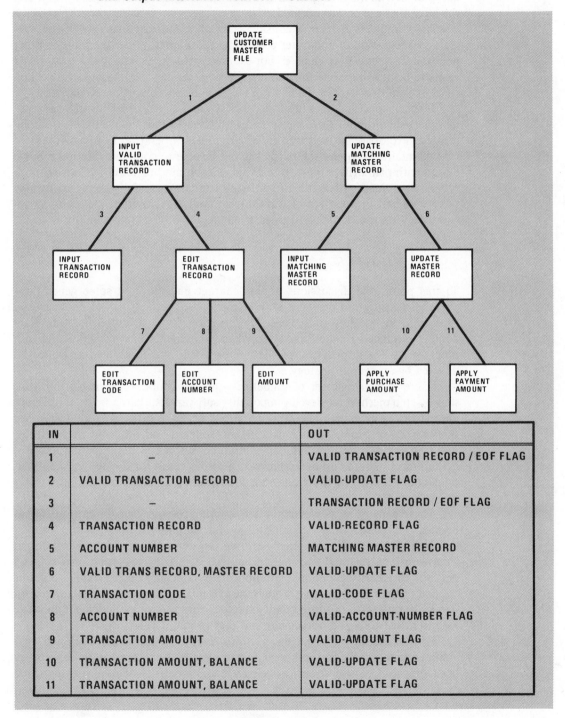

IN		OUT
1	–	VALID TRANSACTION RECORD / EOF FLAG
2	VALID TRANSACTION RECORD	VALID-UPDATE FLAG
3	–	TRANSACTION RECORD / EOF FLAG
4	TRANSACTION RECORD	VALID-RECORD FLAG
5	ACCOUNT NUMBER	MATCHING MASTER RECORD
6	VALID TRANS RECORD, MASTER RECORD	VALID-UPDATE FLAG
7	TRANSACTION CODE	VALID-CODE FLAG
8	ACCOUNT NUMBER	VALID-ACCOUNT-NUMBER FLAG
9	TRANSACTION AMOUNT	VALID-AMOUNT FLAG
10	TRANSACTION AMOUNT, BALANCE	VALID-UPDATE FLAG
11	TRANSACTION AMOUNT, BALANCE	VALID-UPDATE FLAG

into code. Any method that presents these program design concepts clearly is acceptable. The method is less important than the thought that goes into it and the ideas that are communicated.

As design moves from a consideration of the logical structure of the software to integration of computer processing techniques, either the same or other notational systems may be used. For example, structure charts can be expanded easily to include initialization and termination routines. In fact, structure charts can be taken to a level of detail from which code can be produced directly.

Further specification, however, should not be excessive. Ideally, program designers should not be too concerned with "how" a particular module is implemented. Professional, well trained programmers, operating in an environment that maintains adequate standards, should be able to complete internal module design with primarily a black box vision of each module and its relationship to others, combined with critical functional details. These functional details may be represented in a variety of ways during analysis activities, including narratives, decision tables, decision trees, pseudocode, or structured English.

SOFTWARE DESIGN STRATEGIES

To this point, the discussions in this chapter have covered some general approaches to program design and implementation, as well as the elements and tools used in building programs. The question to be answered is: "How are designs produced that effectively package statements into modules and into programs?" The application of these approaches and tools, in turn, must be directed by an overall strategy.

There is no single set of guidelines—no cookbook—covering a uniform, step-by-step method for developing quality software. Rather, a series of different approaches is evolving. The representations here are offered as guidelines for thinking about problems that may be encountered and solutions that will unfold. No set of prescriptions can guarantee automatic high-quality software development. Three design strategies will be discussed for the design and development of programs—functional decomposition, transform analysis, and transaction analysis.

These general strategies approach software design from slightly different perspectives. Functional decomposition, for example, focuses on the identification of functional components through systematic top-down partitioning. Transform analysis and transaction analysis also include a top-down strategy but look to identify functional components by focusing on the transformations applied to data as they flow through the system. In all cases the design motivation is the same—to produce quality software that is easy to implement and test, easy to modify, easy to document, and easy to maintain.

For these design approaches, a uniform set of assumptions is applied. It is assumed that, before design begins, a complete set of system specifications has been prepared. These specifications include statements of user requirements, including definitions of output reports, input documents, transaction documents, files, and databases, and any other data sources and destinations. Also included would be a multi-leveled data flow diagram design complete with process specifications for describing the data transformations at the lowest logical levels. A further assumption is that a systems flowchart has been prepared. This flowchart describes jobs and job steps in a batch job stream or single on-line program that may include several on-line procedures selected through menu choices. First cut packaging, as described in Chapter 13, must be completed.

FUNCTIONAL DECOMPOSITION

Functional decomposition represented the first attempt, during the 1970s, to produce a set of procedures that could be followed in developing quality software products. At that time, there was an awareness of the benefits that could accrue from using structured programming techniques. By applying these standards, the task of programming was made more manageable at the coding level. So, functional decomposition applied the same rationale at the design level. That is, not only could the concept of a minimum set of control structures guide the structuring of code, but it also could be applied to the design and structuring of modules. By breaking a program down into modular components and relating those modules with sequence, repetition, and selection control structures, order could be brought to the design task.

Prior to functional decomposition techniques, attempts at establishing modularity in programs were outgrowths of flowcharting, or algorithmic, approaches to design. That is, programs were designed in a linear fashion, beginning with input and following sequential processing steps, continually transferring program control, up to output.

In breaking up flowchart organizations of programs into modules, subdivisions were rather arbitrary. Modules were defined as often by size criteria related to hardware constraints as by their individual processing functions. Consequently, no real progress was made in developing designs that were minimally sensitive to change. Maintenance was a continuing problem because the structure of the software bore little resemblance to the structures of the problems to which that software was applied.

Functional decomposition was a first attempt to deal directly with this correlation at the design level. It presented a strategy for systematizing the development process, providing a problem-based rationale for decomposing programs into modules and into statements, and for relating modules with standard program control structures. The process of functional decomposition is also called stepwise refinement because the partitioning process carries the design through increasing levels of detail, beginning with an abstract statement of the program function and ending with a set of operational details that implement the function.

Functional Decomposition Technique

Functional decomposition begins with identification of a top-level module representing the overall function of the program to be developed. At the second level, submodules representing major subfunctions that make up the overall program function are defined. These subfunctions are defined at an additional level of detail beyond the program function. As these and successive levels of modules are identified, additional levels of functional details are required for implementation.

The top-level module is primarily a control module, accomplishing the processing functions by calls to second-level modules. The manner in which these business functions are decomposed at subsequent levels has the effect of breaking down a large, complex job into a series of smaller, more manageable tasks. Tasks at successively lower levels contain more processing details than those tasks at higher levels.

Obviously, considerable judgment must be applied in the decomposition process. The designer is faced with the problem of determining which functions should be partitioned into what subfunctions. Also, in working downward through the levels of partitioning, the context of design changes. At the top levels, decomposition is carried out in light of the business functions that are to be performed. However, at lower levels, these business functions must be translated into computer processing techniques. Therefore, there is a transformation of the design from basically a problem-related, logical, structure to a machine-related, physical one.

Functional Decomposition Example

The process of functional decomposition can be illustrated by the following example. An on-line updating program is to be designed. This program will input transaction records interactively and post amounts contained within the records to corresponding master records. As in most on-line systems, a transaction log will be maintained. That is, a summary of the transaction will be written to a file that will serve as an audit trail of evidence that the transaction has been posted against the master. The partial system flowchart shown in Figure 15-3 describes the procedure in terms of its major input and output files.

Functional decomposition begins with the definition of a top-level module that represents the entire updating procedure. This module would be a control module that calls upon subordinates to carry out detailed processing. First-level partitioning then would identify the major processing functions making up this overall function. At this point, however, functional decomposition offers little guidance about exactly how to partition. The criterion is simply that subordinate functions should be identified and modules defined to carry out the processing.

The experienced designer will recognize that in the typical on-line update system three common functions appear. First, the transaction record must be input and edited to ensure that only valid transactions are applied as updates to the master file. Second, the actual posting of amounts to the file will take place.

Figure 15.3. *Annotated system flowchart for master file updating.*

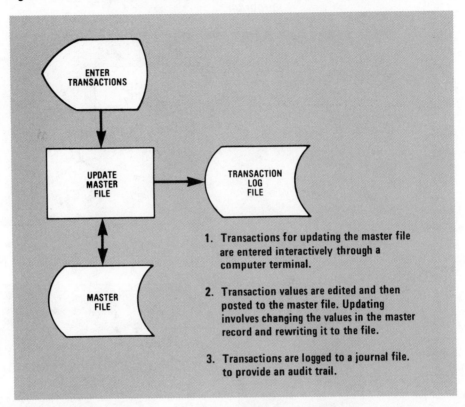

1. Transactions for updating the master file are entered interactively through a computer terminal.

2. Transaction values are edited and then posted to the master file. Updating involves changing the values in the master record and rewriting it to the file.

3. Transactions are logged to a journal file. to provide an audit trail.

Finally, a journal record will be written to the log file. Therefore, a first cut at a structure chart for this program might appear as shown in Figure 15-4 (a). The top-level module, UPDATE-MASTER FILE, calls upon three subordinate modules – INPUT VALID TRANSACTION RECORD, POST TRANS-ACTION RECORD, and WRITE TRANSACTION LOG – to perform the major processing tasks in the system.

In thinking about the computer processing steps necessary to implement these functions, it becomes apparent that the structure shown in Figure 15-4 (a) will need to be modified. The modules POST TRANSACTION RECORD and WRITE TRANSACTION LOG will not be activated for every input transaction; these modules will be executed for valid transaction records only. Also, the last transaction may be a signal from the terminal operator indicating that no more transactions are to be input and that processing is complete. This suggests placing these two modules subordinate to a control module, PROCESS VALID TRANSACTION RECORD, which, in turn, will be governed by a selection control structure. That is, processing will take place only on input of a valid transaction record that is not an end-of-processing indicator.

These considerations are reflected in the structure chart shown in Figure 15-4 (b). Here, the modules have been reorganized to represent the structure

Figure 15.4. *Structure charts for initial partitioning of master file update program.*

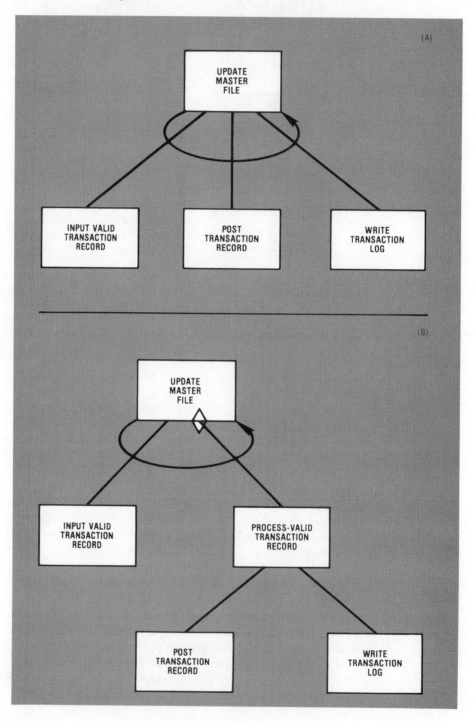

Part 5 Software Design: Technical Design Specifications

under which processing will take place. The major program control structures have been superimposed over the problem requirements to indicate how the functions must be presented to the computer for processing.

The next step in the design process is to decompose these initial modules into their subordinates. Design has not yet reached a level at which it can be translated conveniently into program code. Additional refinement is necessary as shown in Figure 15-5.

Consider the INPUT VALID TRANSACTION RECORD module. This module will require partitioning into two subordinate modules. It is assumed that transaction input will take place on-line. An operator seated at a terminal will enter transaction values that will be edited and then used in updating a master record. For each transaction, the program will display a data entry screen. Labels will be displayed to guide the operator through the data entry session. For example, prompts will be given for the master record key that identifies the record to be updated along with prompts for each of the data fields that represent update amounts. Therefore, routines will be needed to display the initial data entry screen and to input the transaction fields. These requirements are shown in Figure 15-5 as modules DISPLAY INPUT SCREEN and INPUT VALID TRANSACTION FIELDS.

The INPUT VALID TRANSACTION FIELDS module also has been partitioned into two submodules—ACCEPT VALID MASTER KEY and ACCEPT REMAINING VALID FIELDS. This partitioning is necessitated by the structure of data fields that make up the transaction record. The transaction record must contain a key that corresponds to one of the records in the master file. Therefore, one of the requirements is to input and validate the master key. This operation involves moving the key that is input to a master file search-key data area and randomly accessing the master file. If the corresponding master record is in the file, the remaining transaction fields are input. If there is no matching key, an *invalid key* condition exists, in which case the program prompts for another key value. Thus, the routines to input the key are repeated until either a valid key is input or the operator decides to terminate the updating session. It is assumed that the end of the session is indicated when the operator bypasses entry of a key, leaving the field with a null, or blank, value.

If a valid master key is input, the module named ACCEPT REMAINING VALID FIELDS is called. This module directs the acceptance and editing of each of the data fields that contain updating values. In the current example, it is assumed that a transaction record is composed of three data fields, FIELD-A, FIELD-B, and FIELD-C. These are numeric fields that can be edited independently of the master record.

As shown in Figure 15-5, a separate module is defined for each of these input routines. The logic of these modules is similar to that of the master key input module. That is, the operator enters a value in response to the field prompt. The input value then is edited to verify that it is reasonable and within an expected range of values. If so, data entry continues with the next field. If the input value does not pass the edit, however, an error message is flashed on the screen. The message can be displayed alongside the entered value. To high-

Figure 15.5. **Structure chart for partitioning of INPUT-VALID-TRANSACTION-RECORD procedure of master file update program.**

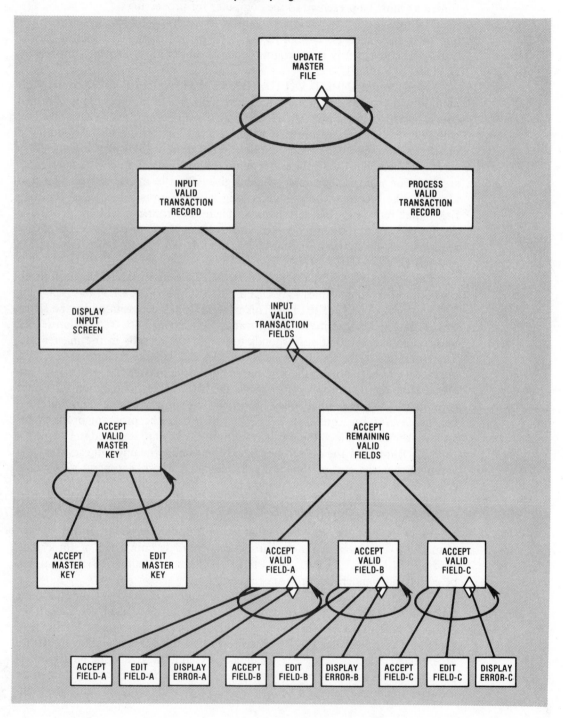

light the error condition, the incorrect value may be displayed again in reverse video or blinking. The operator then must enter another value. The accept and edit routines are repeated until the entered value passes the edit.

Following the data entry session, control returns to the module UPDATE MASTER FILE with either a valid transaction record or a flag indicating the end of the session. If a valid record is present, the module PROCESS VALID TRANSACTION RECORD is called; otherwise, a null, or blank, master key was input, an end-of-session flag has been set, and the program is terminated.

Because the input branch of the program is designed to pass only valid transaction records to the update branch, updating and logging are relatively straightforward processes. Figure 15-6 shows the structure chart expanded to include this further partitioning.

First, the image of the master record prior to updating is written to the log file. Next, the amounts fields containing values are added to develop a transaction total. This total, as well as the individual amounts, will be added to the master record. Then, the transaction amounts are posted to the master record. The update total is posted to the file in all cases. The transactions fields, however, are posted only if they contain numeric values. Thus, each of the field-update modules is governed by a selection control structure. Following updating, the master record is rewritten to the file. Finally, processing is completed with the writing of a transaction to the transaction log file.

At this point, the program design identifies the basic set of modules necessary to perform processing. Their structure generally parallels the structure of business activities required to edit, post, and log transactions. Furthermore, a general computer processing model has been superimposed over the problem structure. Thus, functional decomposition attempts to model a program on the basis of the problem structure and, at the same time, recognizes that the design must facilitate computer processing. Integration of program control structures within the structural design of the software is a common approach.

The design, however, is still not in final form. For example, files must be opened and closed, flags must be initialized, and other pre- and post-processing activities must be added to the design to bring it closer to an operational model. Nevertheless, a formal, logical model of processing has been developed. The design is in a form that can be expanded easily to include these operational details.

TRANSFORM ANALYSIS

Transform analysis, or as it is sometimes called, the *data flow approach*, has been derived, generally, from functional decomposition approaches. In addition, it provides methods for identifying and organizing program functions that more closely model the structure of the problem than functional decomposition. It is offered as an adjunct to functional decomposition for determining just how to decompose a problem structure and derive a corresponding program structure.

Figure 15.6. *Structure chart for partitioning of PROCESS-VALID-TRANSACTION-RECORD procedure of master file update program.*

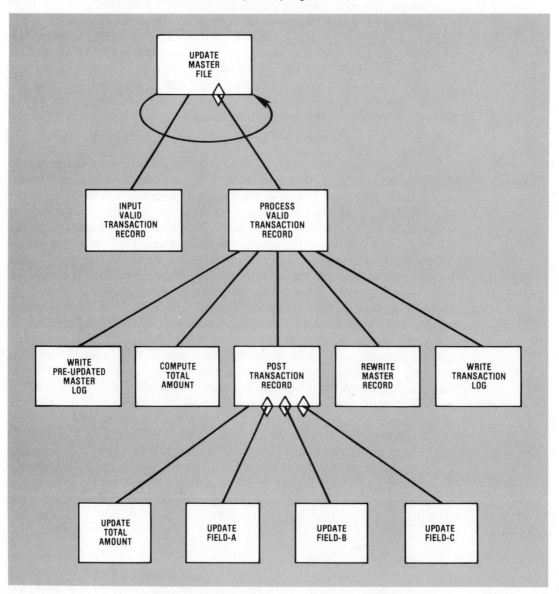

Transform Analysis Technique

Transform analysis makes use of data flow diagrams to model the problem and to bring understanding about its structure. Design activity then translates that business model into a hierarchical organization of software modules that preserve the model of the original problem.

Program structures are identified through data flow analysis. That is, the flow of data through a system and the transformations applied to those data are used in determining the overall relationships among problem functions. The structure of functions becomes the basis for the structure of software to implement those functions.

As a basis for software design, it may be possible to use data flow diagrams developed during the analysis and general design phase of the systems development life cycle. If the specifications prepared during analysis are not based on data flow diagrams or if the diagrams are incomplete, the designer will have to develop low-level diagrams to model the system being implemented. The specifications for the new system, whatever their format, should be reviewed to make sure that all data streams are traced thoroughly and that all major data transformations are represented by clearly identifiable bubbles on the diagram.

Transform Analysis Example

As an illustration of the design process, first an abstract example will be used. Figure 15-7 presents the data flow diagram that might have been drawn to model this abstract problem. This data flow diagram represents a portion of a larger system which has been packaged into a system flow chart black box or program using first-stage packaging guidelines as prescribed in Chapter 13. Each bubble in the data flow diagram represents a successive transformation that is applied to the data as they flow through the system.

As in functional decomposition, design based on data flow begins with identification of a top-level control module that represents the program function as a whole, labeled ABSTRACT EXAMPLE in Figure 15-8 (B). At this point, the data flow diagram for the application is analyzed. A determination is made

Figure 15.7.   Abstract data flow diagram modeling a portion of a system to be implemented as a computer program.

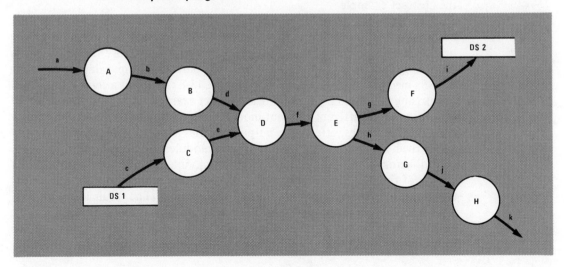

of the major processing branches of the system. Analysis involves the identification of three types of branches from the program level control module. These are afferent, efferent, and central transform. For each major processing branch, a control module is defined subordinate to the top-level module.

Afferent branches encompass inputs to the program. An afferent, or input, branch is identified by those transformations that translate physical inputs into logical inputs ready for the main business processing functions. A physical input is a record or data item that resides in a file, that has been captured on some type of input medium, or that is being entered through a terminal keyboard or other type of direct-entry device. To be in a form acceptable for central processing functions, this physical input first must be stripped of its physical characteristics (through deblocking of files or construction of text from words, for example). Next, the input requires preparatory editing, validation, sorting, or other transformations to put it in proper format for processing. Thus, an afferent branch of a data flow diagram includes all transformations applied to inflowing data up to the point at which the data are available and in the proper format for processing. Figure 15-8 (A) shows two afferent branches composed of process bubbles A, B, and C for the abstract example.

Efferent branches of the data flow diagram encompass the movement from unstructured, unformatted output data produced by the system through the series of transformations that generate physical outputs. Thus, efferent data flows move outward from the main processing functions of the system. Efferent branches are identified by tracing backward from final system output up to the points at which output data (or unformatted results) initially appear; that is, where the central business processing seems to be occurring. Data are created by the main business process in a purely logical form. The program must transform these logical data into physical formats for display on a terminal, a report, or perhaps even a graphic audio display. Depending on the particular application under study, there may be two or more efferent branches. For example, Figure 15-8 (A), shows two efferent branches composed for processes F, G, and H for the abstract example.

The portions of the system not included in the afferent or efferent branches — everything that is left — are part of the **central transform** branch or branches. This portion of the system, which is responsible for the main business processing functions of the application is the part where input data streams are transformed to create output streams. Figure 15-8 (A) shows a central transform comprising processes D and E for the abstract example. As a general rule for all structure charts, afferent or input modules are positioned to the left and below their superordinates, efferent or output modules are positioned to the right and below their superordinates, and transform modules are positioned in between.

In factoring at the first level, a control module is defined for each afferent branch of the data flow diagram, for each efferent branch, and for the central transform (or for each logical group of transforms). The result is a high-level input-processing output model of the system. As illustrated in Figure 15-8 (B), each of these first-level control modules is responsible for carrying out the transformations required in each branch of the system. For example, the mod-

Figure 15.8. *Partitioning of data flow into afferent, efferent, and central transform branches, and a resulting top-level structure chart.*

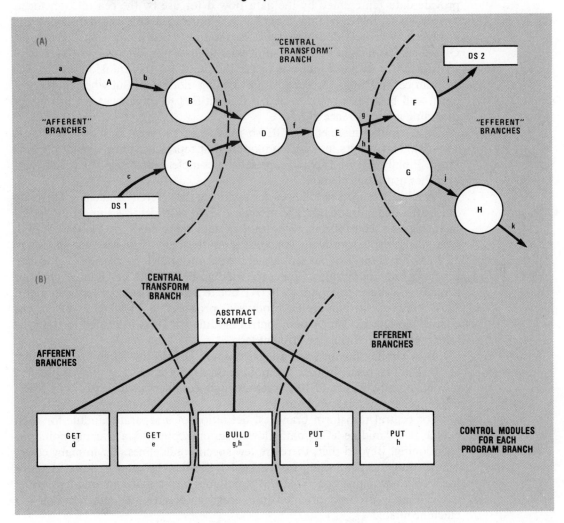

ules GET-d and GET-e are the control modules for the two afferent branches. The modules named PUT-g and PUT-h are defined to oversee processing in the two efferent branches. The central transform branch is controlled by the module BUILD-g,h.

Once the top-level structure of the system is derived, factoring proceeds iteratively, in top-down fashion, for each branch of the structure chart. Each succeeding bubble of the data flow diagram becomes the basis for the next set of lower-level modules of the structure chart. Factoring then ends at the lowest levels of the respective branches, where physical inputs or outputs can be identified.

The process for factoring each afferent branch is shown in Figure 15-9. The module GET-d was identified in the first-level factoring as a control module to provide data represented by the data flow d for use by the central transform. According to the data flow diagram in Figure 15-8 (A), the data flow d is produced by process B, and that process requires a b as input. Thus the module GET-d can be factored into two processes as shown in Figure 15-9 (A), one to transform a b into a d and one to get the input for this transformation. The afferent control module receives a d by calling module B. But when calling B it must send b. A new module GET-b is identified to implement the process of providing an occurrence of b.

In a similar manner the GET-b module is factored as shown in Figure 15-9 (B). This results in a GET-a module that represents some type of physical input. Finally, Figure 15-9 (C) represents a complete factoring of both afferent branches using this method.

A related process is followed for factoring the efferent branches. These are illustrated in Figure 15-10. The module PUT-h was identified in the first level factoring as a control module to output data represented by the data flow h from the central transform. According to the data flow diagram in Figure 15-8 (A), the data flow h is sent along the output branch by process G, and that process produces output j. Thus, the module PUT-h can be factored into two processes as shown in Figure 15-10 (A), one to produce j and one to dispose of j. PUT-h sends h to module G. Module G produced a j and returns it to the control module PUT-h. A new control module PUT-j is identified to continue the process of factoring the efferent leg.

In a similar manner, the PUT-j module is factored as shown in Figure 15-10 (B). The result is a PUT-j module that represents some type of physical output. Finally, Figure 15-10 (C) represents a complete factoring of both efferent branches using this method.

For central transform branches, definition of a separate module for each bubble in a "middle-level" data flow diagram represents a starting point for partitioning. Beyond that, there are few specific guidelines. So, in many cases, central transform branches are factored following the same process used for functional decomposition. That is, the designer has to make a transition from a model that is problem oriented into program designs that are more closely machine related.

However, there are some rules of thumb that can be applied to determine when decomposition has gone far enough. Decomposition is complete when

- There are no further identifiable subtasks to be added at lower levels.
- A standard, or library, routine can be applied to accomplish the functions for which a module has been identified.
- Modules are so small that they have reached a level at which coupling, cohesion, and sizing guidelines described in Chapter 16, would be violated by further partitioning.

Figure 15-11 represents the "first-cut" structure chart that results from applying the transform analysis process. In a real example, this structure chart then

Figure 15.9. Factoring of afferent branches.

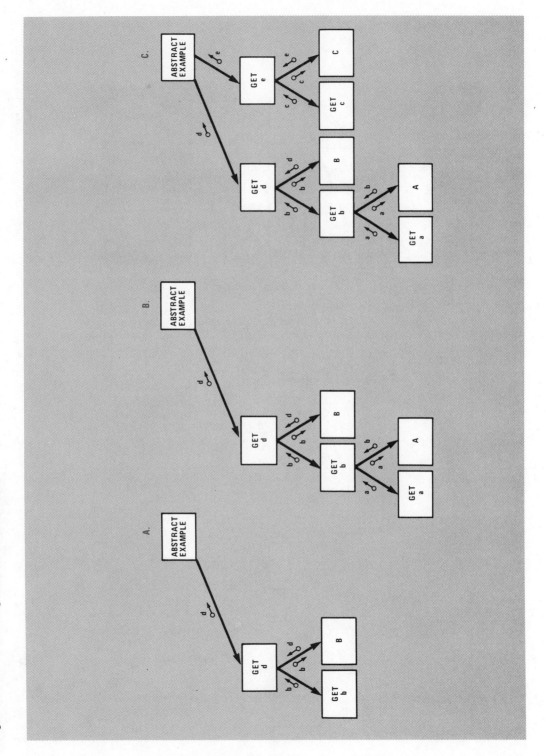

Figure 15.10. *Factoring of efferent branches.*

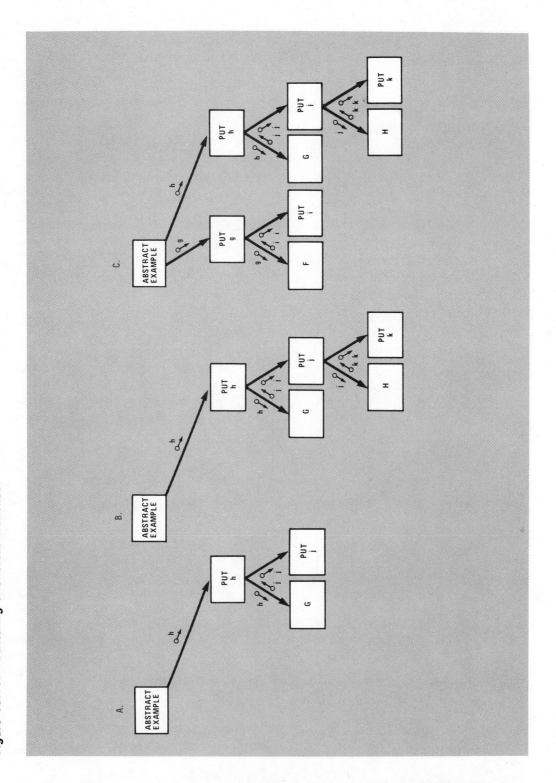

Figure 15.11. "First-cut" structure chart based on transform analysis.

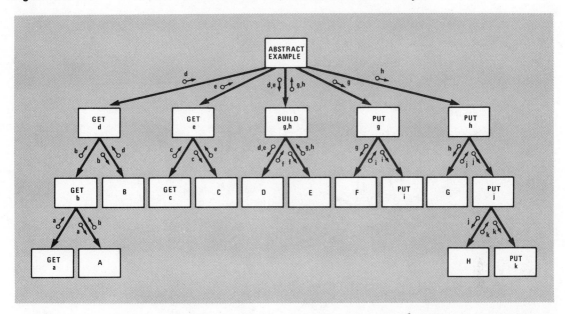

would be modified using some of the evaluation criteria discussed in Chapter 16.

Consider, now, the transform analysis process applied to a real example. The data flow diagram in Figure 15-12 models a loan quotation application. The task is to design a program to produce loan quotations. Figure 15-13 contains the relevant data dictionary entries.

The LOAN-REQUEST portion of the quote request specifies a desired loan type (auto or home, for example), the amount to be borrowed, the maximum payment the customer can afford, the frequency of payments and interest compounding, and a range of possible payback periods. For example, a home-loan quote request might specify a range of payback periods from 25 to 30 years. In this case, the resulting LOAN-QUOTATION produced by the program actually would contain six sets of loan summaries: One each for payback in 25, 26, . . . 30 years.

Process 1: EDIT SYNTAX simply does individual field editing and cross-field editing. A cross-field edit determines if a particular field is reasonable, given information contained in another field. For example, a cross-field edit might determine if a particular LOAN-TYPE falls within a specified range of PRINCIPAL amounts.

Calculations are done in Process 2: VERIFY LOAN PAYABLE to verify that the desired loan actually can be paid off in each requested payback period using the CURRENT-RATE and the MAX-PAYMENT. The CURRENT-RATE, is read from a table and depends on the LOAN-TYPE, PRINCIPAL, and PAYMENT-FREQ.

Process 3: CALCULATE MAX LOAN AMOUNT determines the amount that the bank is willing to loan, based on the LOAN-TYPE, the FINANCIAL-

Figure 15.12. (A) shows data flow diagram for loan quotation application.

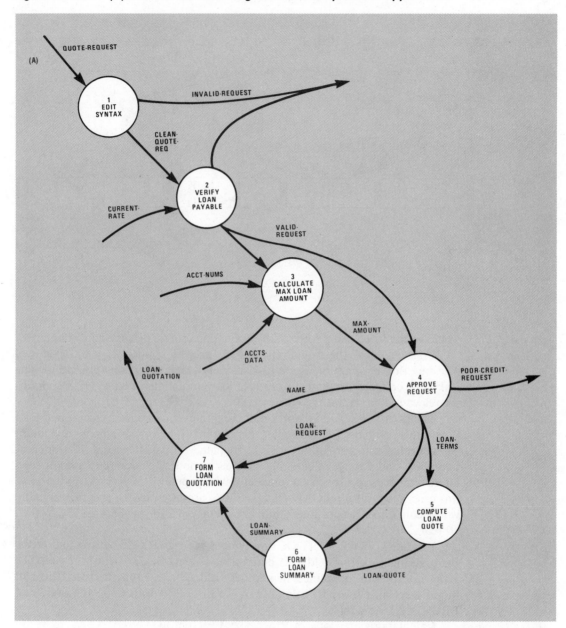

DATA submitted as part of the request, and the status of the various other accounts the customer has with the bank. The customer's Social Security number is used to access the set of account numbers for the customer's various accounts, and each ACCT-NUM is used to obtain the status information for that account.

Figure 15.12. (B) shows diagram partitioned into afferent, efferent, and central transform branches.

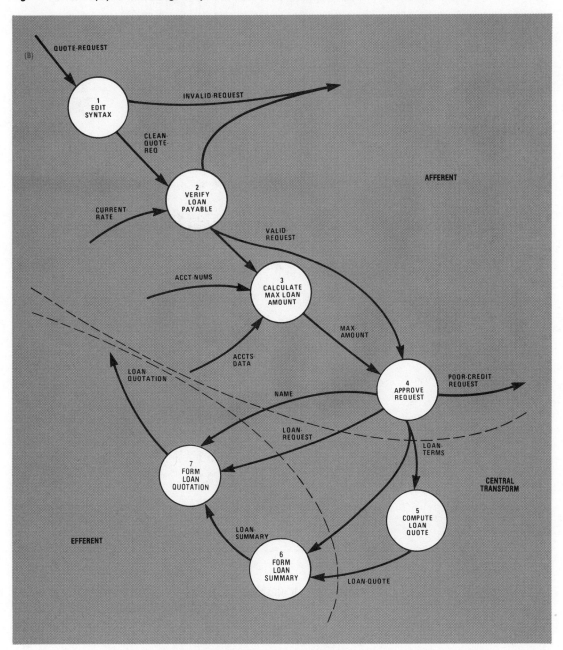

If the MAX-AMOUNT is less than the requested principal, Process 4: APPROVE REQUEST reduces the principal and accepts the request only for that portion of the payback period range for which the loan is payable. Using the resulting LOAN-TERMS for each payback period, Process 5: COMPUTE

Figure 15.13. Data dictionary entries for loan quotation application.

```
QUOTE-REQUEST =        SSN
                       + NAME
                       + LOAN-REQUEST
                       + FINANCIAL-DATA

LOAN-REQUEST =         LOAN-TYPE
                       + PRINCIPAL
                       + MAX-PAYMENT
                       + PAYMENT-FREQ
                       + PAYBACK-PER-RANGE

VALID-REQUEST =        QUOTE-REQUEST
                       + CURRENT-RATE

APPROVED-REQUEST =     VALID-REQUEST

LOAN-TERMS =           PRINCIPAL
                       + CURRENT-RATE
                       + PAYMENT-FREQ
                       + PAYBACK-PERIOD

LOAN-QUOTE =           PAYMENT-AMOUNT
                       + TOTAL-INTEREST-PAID
                       + TOTAL-AMOUNT-PAID

LOAN-SUMMARY =         LOAN-TERMS
                       + LOAN-QUOTE

LOAN-QUOTATION =       NAME
                       + LOAN REQUEST
                       + {LOAN-SUMMARY} PAYBACK-PERIOD-RANGE
```

LOAN QUOTE does the calculations necessary to produce the corresponding LOAN-QUOTE details. Process 6: FORM LOAN SUMMARY combines the LOAN-TERMS and LOAN-QUOTES into LOAN-SUMMARIES. Finally, Process 7: FORM LOAN QUOTATION assembles the several summaries into a single LOAN-QUOTATION.

The first step in applying the transform analysis process to this problem is to determine the afferent, efferent, and central transform branches of the model. There is little doubt that Process 1 is part of a single afferent branch and that Process 7 is part of the single efferent branch. The remaining questions are: How far forward does the afferent branch extend and how far back does the efferent branch extend? In other words, what remains is the central transform. Figure 15-14 (8) displays a partitioning of the LOAN-QUOTE data flow and assumes that the afferent branch consists of Processes 1–4, the efferent branch consists of Processes 6 and 7, and the central transform consists of Process 5.

Figure 15-14 presents a "first-cut" structure chart for this program. A program control module (QUOTE LOANS) is created which controls the three main module branches. The structure chart results from a mechanical application of the transform analysis process. Notice that the new VALID-REQUEST, labeled APPROVED-REQUEST on the structure chart, contains the necessary input, NAME, LOAN-REQUEST and LOAN-TERMS required by the central transform and efferent program branches.

A closer look at the problem may suggest changes in the structure chart. The input leg may be simplified by including the GET-CLEAN-QUOTE-REQ module in its parent and by letting the VERIFY-LOAN-PAYABLE module get the current interest rate for the particular loan type. In addition, superfluous data are being passed to GET-MAX-AMOUNT. The only data required are: SSN, FINANCIAL-DATA, and LOAN-TYPE. These changes are made in Figure 15-15.

When considering the two modules with heavy computation—VERIFY-LOAN-PAYABLE and COMPUTE-LOAN-QUOTE—a significant overlap is observed. The calculation COMPUTE-PAYMENT-AMOUNT has been factored out of these modules into a single computation module that, in turn, can be called by the other two modules. This change also is included in Figure 15-16.

Finally, the output leg in Figure 15-14 is awkward. For example, NAME and LOAN-REQUEST must be sent to PUT-LOAN-QUOTE on the first call for a customer, but not on subsequent calls because all quotations for one program execution will be from the same customer. In Figure 15-15, the top module, QUOTE LOANS, calls PUT-REPORT-HEADING to output the NAME and LOAN-REQUEST. QUOTE LOANS has also been made responsible for collecting the individual LOAN-QUOTEs and forming the LOAN-SUMMARY. Many of these types of decisions are based on the designer's previous experience.

It is helpful to understand clearly what the transform analysis process does—and does not—accomplish. The process separates the modules that deal with input and output from the main processing modules. Transform analysis further helps to organize the input and output legs. However, this technique does little for factoring the central transform. Also, this approach clearly depends on the level of detail in the data flow diagram. If a very hierarchically low level of the data flow diagram is used, the result is too many small modules. On the other hand, a high-level data flow diagram probably will result in an incomplete factoring of the central transform. Thus, transform analysis does not provide a mechanical process that will result in optimum factoring of the central transform. However, basing the factoring on a middle-level data flow diagram does provide good initial guidance.

Figure 15.14. "First-cut" structure chart for the QUOTE LOANS program.

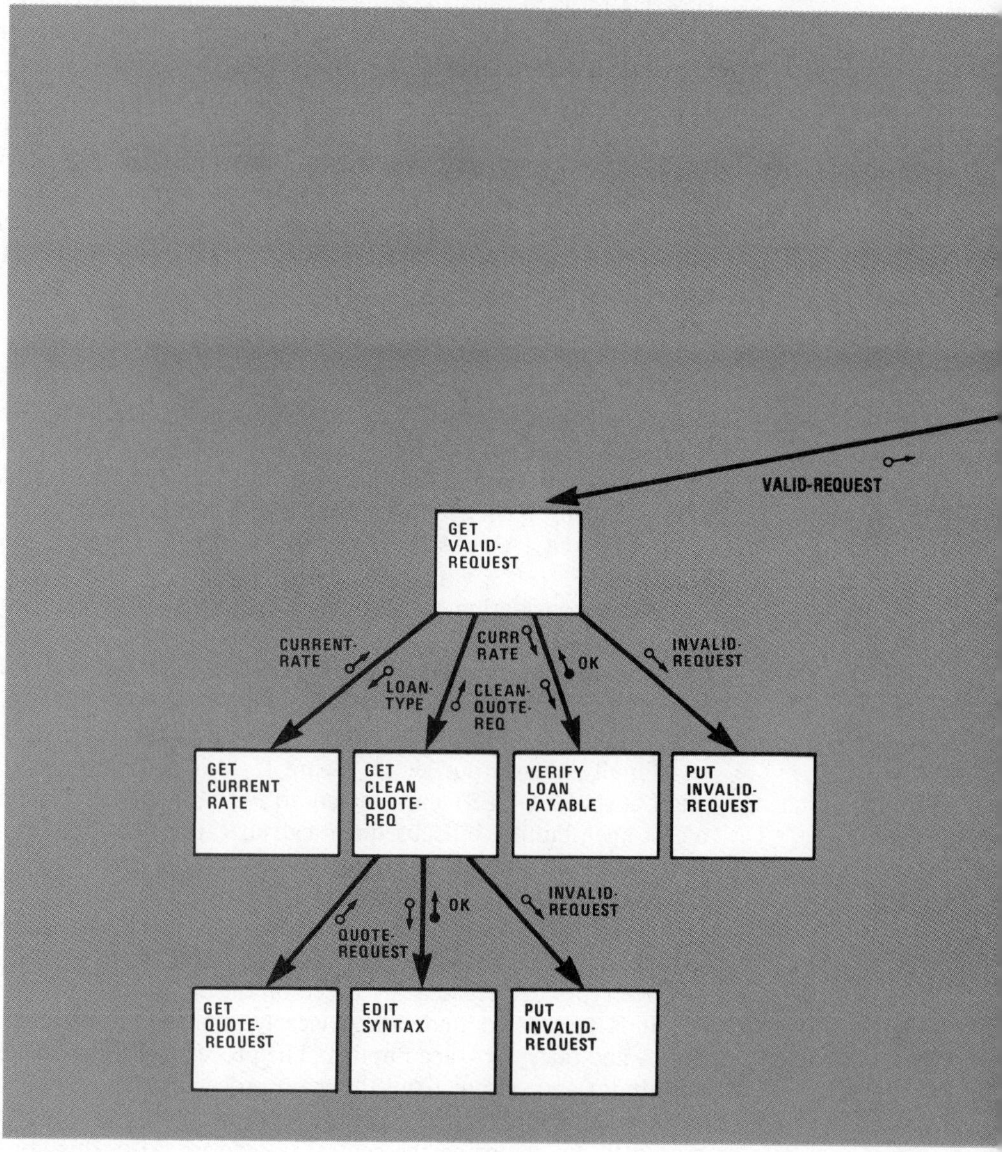

TRANSACTION ANALYSIS

Often a program must process multiple types of transactions with extensive similarities in processing. A tempting design approach is to maximize the amount of common code by emphasizing these processing similarities and treating differences as exceptions. However, this approach can create maintenance

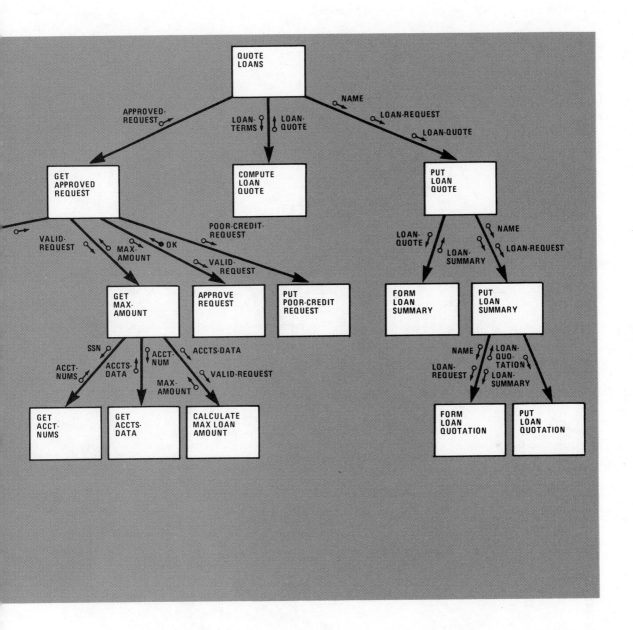

problems because business changes tend to center around the transactions, not around the processing similarities. Thus, if a transaction is changed, large portions of the program also may have to be changed. **Transaction analysis** is a data-flow-oriented design process that organizes the design around the transactions in the higher-level modules and recaptures processing similarities using common lower-level modules.

Figure 15.15. **An improved structure chart for the QUOTE LOANS program.**

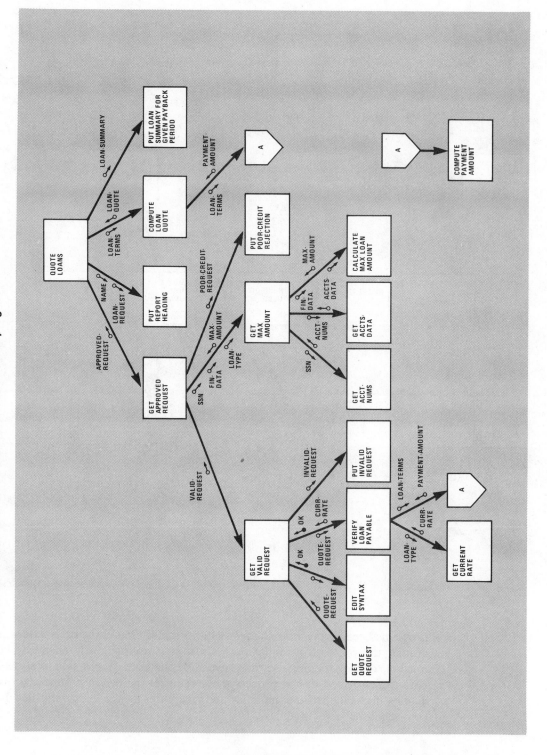

Figure 15.16. General structure for a transaction-centered design.

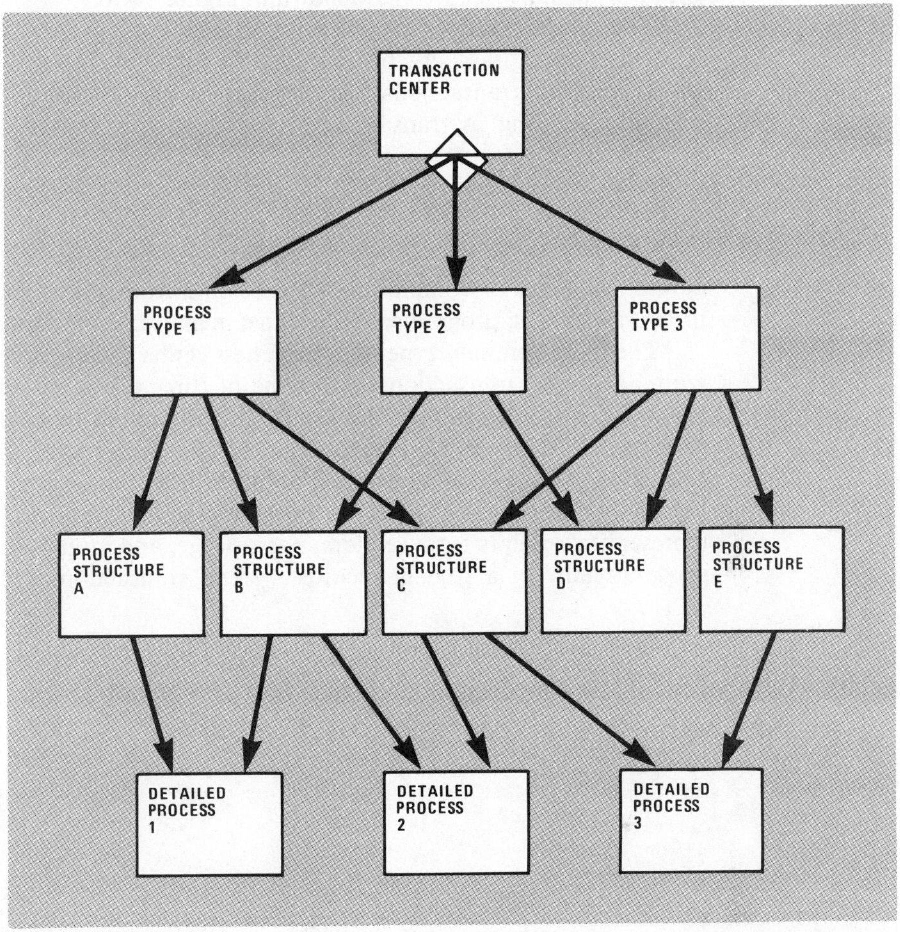

Transaction Analysis Technique

The general structure of a transaction-centered design is shown in the partial structure chart in Figure 15-16. The top module simply recognizes the transaction and routes it to the appropriate processing module. Each processing module knows the detail of that particular transaction—its data and the processing steps that must occur—but is unaware of the other transactions. The actual processing of the transactions is done by a third level of modules that process individual data structures. It is at this level that some benefit from processing similarities may start to occur. Thus, common detailed processes may be factored out of the third level modules to achieve even greater benefit from processing similarities.

The data flow diagram corresponding with a transaction center typically will show a data flow that branches where parallel processes handle each transaction type. Figure 15-17 shows a portion of a data flow diagram corresponding with the partial structure chart shown in Figure 15-16.

The process of deriving the structure chart from the data flow model is straightforward. Basically, the designer must be able to recognize situations in which multiple transactions are an inherent part of the logical or business-related processing. A transaction in this sense is any data structure that can assume one of a number of types.

Transaction Analysis Example

Several examples of common data processing transactions include file update programs; editing programs; and on-line, menu driven programs.

The most common type of **transaction center** occurs in a file update program. An input transaction can be one of three types: an add transaction to insert a new record in the file, a change transaction to modify values in an existing record, or a delete transaction to remove a record from the file. The single input stream would be routed to one of three processing routines, depending on the transaction type. An inventory system may process transactions representing receipts from vendors, parts usage, and inventory adjustments in a single stream. In a student records system, transactions for adding a class,

Figure 15.17. *Partial data flow diagram corresponding with Figure 15-18.*

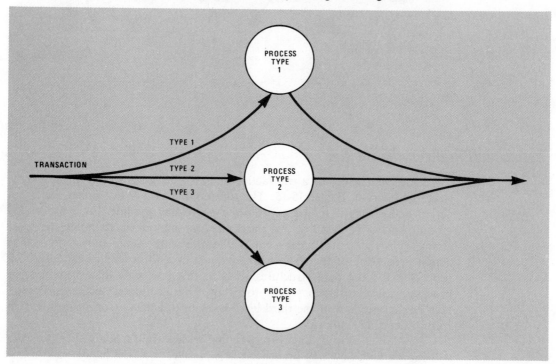

Part 5   Software Design: Technical Design Specifications

dropping a class, and changing registration status between regular grading and pass-fail may be processed together.

Edit programs typically process transactions of several types in a single input stream. While different transactions will have fields in common, the edit program should have a transaction center that calls separate modules to control the editing of each transaction type. These modules, in turn, may call some of the same modules to process the common fields. The edit module for a single record type also can be considered a transaction center with each field in the record treated as a separate transaction type.

On-line, menu-driven applications represent another common setting for transaction-centered design. A typical example is shown in Figure 15-18. A function menu allows the user to select one of four functions, each treated as a transaction: inventory receipt, part usage, inventory adjustment, and part status query.

Transaction centers of the type described above can appear within any of the branches of a data flow diagram. Editing routines, for instance, often will take the form of a transaction center located in the afferent branch. File update routines involving additions, changes, and deletions are common within the central transform branch. Reporting routines that print under alternative formats usually would appear in an efferent branch.

Figure 15.18. *Structure chart for an on-line inventory program that presents a menu of transactions for the user.*

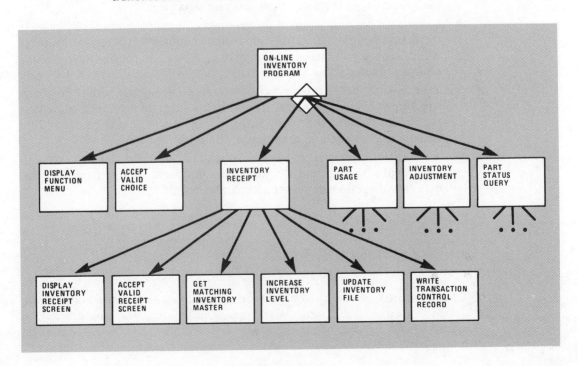

In general, the criteria used to guide partitioning are the business functions that are to be implemented. Even so, different designers may come up with vastly different designs depending on their perspectives on the business problem. Unfortunately, functional decomposition does not provide clear, exacting guidelines for how to go about partitioning. Thus, a lack of consistency in producing designs has been felt to be a weakness of this approach. There is no guarantee that two designers working on the same problem will develop the same solution or even similar solutions. The design seems to depend on the experience and perspective of the individual designer.

A strength of the functional decomposition approach is that it is built upon sound principles. Use of top-down design techniques, procession through various levels of abstraction, identification of business functions, and use of the minimum set of program control structures to govern processing are all proven methods. However, the lack of formal guidelines for applying these techniques can make implementation of this strategy relatively inexact and inconsistent.

Both transformation and transaction analysis present a number of advantages, including:

- Hierarchical designs are produced through top-down methods similar to the outcomes of functional decomposition.

- Because designs are based on an identification of business processing functions and their relationships, connections between program modules will have similar structures. Changes in the business functions can be traced easily to changes required in the program structure.

- Criteria for decomposition of afferent and efferent branches are included in the design strategy. In effect, input and output procedures are localized within separate branches of the system, thereby improving maintenance efforts and effects.

- There is assurance that the program structure corresponds with the problem structure as nearly as possible. The data flow diagram provides a convenient method for defining the major business functions to be carried out and for organizing the system in accordance with these functions.

- A design consistency is enforced because of uniform partitioning criteria. It is reasonable to assume that two or more designers working from the same data flow diagram will deliver comparable results.

Data Driven Design

Data structured, or data driven, software design is another method of program design. This approach, particularly popular in Europe, was pioneered by an international trio: Jean-Dominique Warnier of France, Michael Jackson (not the singer) of England, and Ken Orr of the United States. This methodology assumes that the best software is data structured, that is, the structure of the software programs should match closely the structure of the data organization of the outputs of the program. Thus data driven design techniques rely heavily upon careful and precise exposition of the system outputs prior to program design. The underlying data structure of the system outputs become the foundation for the actual program design.

Data structured design essentially involves a series of transformations or "mappings" between output/input data structure and program structure. These mappings represent the method by which the structure of the data is overlaid upon the structure of the actual program. The basic mapping steps are illustrated in Feature figure 1. Once the actual physical outputs are precisely defined (prototyping greatly enhances this technique), the logical output data structure is gleaned or mapped. From this map of the structure of the output, the logical input necessary to produce this output is defined and mapped into its most efficient form. Given the logical input and logical output structures, a series of steps is developed capable of transforming the logical input into the logical output. This series of steps is the logical process structure that forms the foun-

Feature figure 1. Mappings and structures in data driven design methodology.

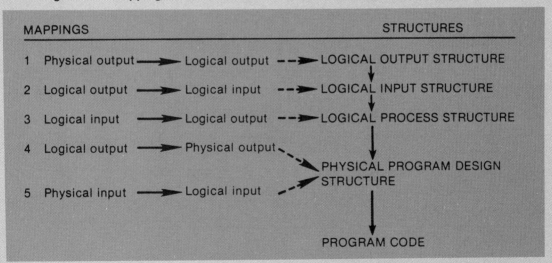

dation for actual program design. The final mappings involve building into the logical process structure the transformations of the logical output into the physical output and the physical input into the logical input.

Each mapping step adds more detail onto the design structure. The structure maps eventually become the overall physical program design structure. As more processing-level details are added, the program design structure takes on the characteristics of psuedocode, which is easily converted into actual program code. Thus the program code is developed directly from the structure of the data, hence the name "data structured design."

The Warnier-Orr diagram, Feature figure 2, is one tool used to model data structure and program design in the data structured design methodology.

Feature figure 2. **Example of Warnier-Orr diagram for program design.**

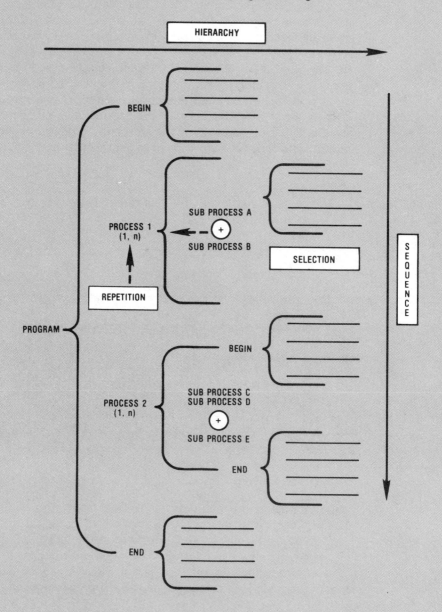

Warnier-Orr diagrams are derived from math set theory and, like structure charts, they model four basic design constructs: hierarchy, sequence, repetition, and selection.

THE DESIGN PROCESS

It should be obvious from the preceding discussion that there is no best method for software design. There are alternative strategies that can be followed, each of which has particular advantages and disadvantages and through which different designs will be produced. Naturally, the designer is looking for a logical process for arriving at the best possible solution. Although there really is no magic formula, the following steps may help guide design efforts:

- To develop "first cut" program divisions, package the data flow diagram from the system specification into its primary processing units based upon stage-one packaging criteria (Chapter 13). (A system flow chart will be developed.)
- Examine the partial data flow diagram associated with each program on the system flow chart.
- For largely sequential data flows, apply transform analysis for first-cut factoring of the programs into major processing routines.
- For largely parallel data flows, apply transaction analysis for first-cut factoring of the programs into major processing routines.
- For programs that do not seem to partition well with either transform or transaction analysis, begin with functional decomposition.
- Further factor the programs on the basis of functional, transform, or transactional analysis where appropriate. Consider, for each processing routine, specific computer techniques for implementing the function and the logic of sequences, repetitions, and selections that must be employed to overlay an execution structure on the functional structure of the system.
- Once a design has been developed, apply evaluation criteria (Chapter 16) to the entire structure. Pay particular attention to input and output interfaces. These interfaces offer possibilities to buffer the program from changes in the external environment.
- Finally, use second-stage packaging criteria (Chapter 13) to restructure the overall system design as necessary.

Application software design, in summary, can be viewed as a skill, or craft, that is still under intensive development. The goal of study in the area is eventually to replace intuitive, creative, and individualistic skill with standardized, predictable, and mechanical methods for developing software. Ultimately, these results will be achieved. However, today, in most shops, mental effort is the primary tool of the software designer. The best available mechanisms for guiding the development process guide the thinking of the designer rather than prescribing results.

REUSABILITY DESIGN

System designers have long been interested in the concept of reusable code. The idea is to write general purpose modules that can be used in many programs, thereby reducing the overall programming and testing effort during development and simplifying the on-going maintenance effort. The large majority of program code involves routine processes such as data entry and verification, file maintenance, and report writing. It should be possible to create a standard set of modules supporting these operations that could constitute 70 to 80 percent or more of the code for a new system.

Despite this apparently good idea, few organizations have made any substantial progress along these lines. Although the routine functions mentioned above are similar in different situations, they are not exactly the same.

A generalized data entry module might have been designed for one system. But when the next system was being designed, it was usually found that the original module and its calling parameters were not quite flexible enough for the new situation. As a result, rather than creating truly reusable modules, developers tended to create new modules using the original as a design pattern.

The creation of new modules from existing design patterns has very little payoff. The set of *similar* modules is in fact a collection of *different* modules that must be separately maintained. A module designed in this fashion is often worse (less maintainable) than it would have been if it were simply designed from scratch for the precise job it needed to do.

Reusability design should focus on *similarity* of function rather than *sameness* of function. Designers should attempt to identify a set of generalized functions that will be similar across all applications. Then, rather than implementing a module that contains the code for one version of a given function, the focus could be placed on implementing a basic system building block—a module that contains multiple versions, with a calling module or other building block selecting the appropriate version for the given situation. These building blocks could be run-time modules or they could be input to a preprocessor that selects appropriate versions and creates the source code for a given application.

SUMMARY

A software design is a representation of programs to be written which specifies program modules, structures of modules, detailed processing within modules, control interfaces among modules, and data interfaces among modules.

Software design is the process of taking the specifications for a job, job step, or on-line procedure and translating those specifications into a hierarchical organization of modules. The basis for the specifications is documentation in the form of system flow charts, data flow diagrams, and supporting data dictionary entries.

In applying software design principles, a large program is broken down into smaller and smaller modules. At succeeding levels within this hierarchy of modules, functions and interconnections are defined. Further, design proceeds downward from a relatively broad definition of processing requirements to exacting operational details at the lower levels.

Statements and modules are the two primitives from which applications programs are built.

Statements are executable programming commands contained within program modules. Attributes of modules include function, logic, and interfaces.

The function of a module is the data transformation it performs. The logic of a module is a description of the actual processing that takes place within the module. Interfaces are connections between modules. These connections cause transfer of both control and data from one module to another.

Program control structures that determine the order of execution include sequence, repetition, and selection.

The hierarchical relationship among modules in a top-down design may be documented in a structure chart, for which there are several graphic conventions.

Design strategies may include functional decomposition, transform analysis, and transaction analysis.

Functional decomposition focuses on the identification of processing functions through a process of top-down partitioning. Abstract functions are decomposed into more detailed functions, proceeding successively down the program hierarchy. Transform and transaction analysis identify functional components by focusing on data as they flow through the system.

In functional decomposition, program modules represent processing tasks defined at several levels of abstraction. At the top levels, decomposition is carried out in light of the business functions that are to be performed. At lower levels, these business functions must be translated into computer processing techniques. Moving from high- to low-level modules, there is a transformation of the design from basically a problem-related structure to a machine-related structure.

Transform analysis is an adjunct to functional decomposition for determining just how to decompose a problem structure and derive a parallel program structure. The flow of data through a system and the transformations applied to those data are used in determining the overall relationships among problem functions. Data flow diagrams are used to model the problem. Design activity translates the business model into a hierarchical organization of software modules that preserve the model of the original problem.

Design based on transform analysis begins with defining a top-level module. Then, first-level factoring identifies the major processing functions. Further analysis involves identification of afferent branches (program inputs), efferent branches (data flows to physical outputs), and central transform branches (remaining portions of the diagram).

Design based on transaction analysis, like transform analysis, focuses on data flow. Parallel data flows often indicate a selection between transaction types. Transaction analysis is a method of design that will take advantage of similarities in processing among transaction types but allows for ongoing system changes to transactions.

The use of data flow diagrams is limited to determining the overall logical structure of a program rather than determining its execution structure. Beyond establishing this logical structure, the designer must apply other techniques such as functional decomposition to factor the design to the lower levels.

A coordinated design approach would be to (1) package the system data flow diagram into a system flow chart; (2) partition data flow diagrams associated with system black boxes on the basis of transform analysis for sequential-like processing, transaction analysis for parallel-like processing, and functional decomposition for all other situations; (3) apply evaluation criteria to the entire structure as specified in Chapter 16; and (4) refine the partitioning using second stage packaging criteria.

KEY TERMS

1. statement
2. module
3. black box
4. module function
5. module logic
6. module interfaces
7. program control structures
8. sequence
9. repetition
10. selection
11. structure chart

12. subordinate module
13. superordinate module
14. module hierarchy
15. functional decomposition
16. transform analysis
17. afferent
18. efferent
19. central transform
20. transaction analysis
21. transaction center

REVIEW/DISCUSSION QUESTIONS

1. Define the term module and state several characteristics of a module.
2. Describe the three basic attributes of modules.
3. Briefly define the concept of *black box* as it applies to software design.
4. Explain the use of the program control structures for sequence, repetition, and selection in the design process.
5. What is a structure chart and what are some of the basic symbols used in structure charts?
6. Briefly describe each of the three software design strategies discussed in this chapter.
7. What are the steps followed for transform analysis?
8. State several situations in which transaction analysis might be an appropriate design strategy.
9. Describe the relative strengths and weaknesses of the three software design strategies presented in this chapter.
10. What is the starting point for software design?
11. In general, what steps could be followed to help guide design efforts during the design process?

PRACTICE ASSIGNMENTS

1. Draw a portion of a structure chart consistent with the following information:

   ■ module A calls modules B, C and D.
   ■ module A passes a data element X and a flag Y to module B.
   ■ module B returns a data element W to module A.
   ■ module A passes a data element L to module C.
   ■ module C returns a data element F to module A.
   ■ module D returns a data element G to module A.

2. Use transform analysis to produce a structure chart from the data flow diagram shown in Figure 15-19 on the next page. Assume the central transform consists of P1 and P4. G is composed of the fields A, B, and C.

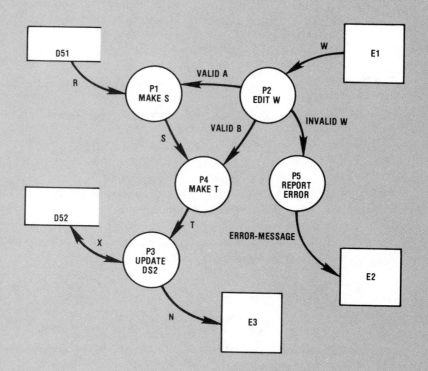

Figure 15.19.   Data flow diagram for use with practice assignment 2.

16

Software Design Objectives and Evaluation

Learning Objectives

On completing reading and other learning assignments for this chapter, you should be able to:

■ Describe the need for and the characteristics of quality software.

■ Explain the criteria of coupling and cohesion in the evaluation of software design decisions relating to the partitioning of modules within a program.

■ Describe how transfers of data and transfers of control between modules may be implemented.

■ Explain how cohesion and coupling are interrelated and what impact this relationship has on design of software modules.

■ Give the levels of coupling and the levels of cohesion and explain how these criteria may be applied.

■ Explain what heuristics may be applied in making software design decisions.

THE NEED FOR EVALUATION CRITERIA

In Chapter 13, it was pointed out that applications software in general is becoming more complex. Complications arise because of several factors, including higher expectations of users, the increased capabilities of hardware and systems software, and the integration of multiple processing routines within on-line systems. For these and other reasons, today's systems of software demand greater skill in their construction and increased attention to quality.

Possibly the most important of the quality dimensions of software is maintainability. Applications systems will be around for a long time. It is not unusual to find, even today, production systems written fifteen years ago. Thus, systems must be developed with an eye on their future impacts. These systems must be designed so that changing business requirements can be integrated easily within the ongoing software products, and the systems must be adaptable to changing hardware-software environments.

Quality software, therefore, exhibits two main characteristics: It is easy to implement and test, and it is easy to maintain and modify. These are qualities that must be built into the software from its inception. Thus, criteria for assuring quality in software must be applied early in the development process, during initial logical design of the system. At this point, and regardless of the design strategy used, the criteria are applied to the various iterations on the design to improve its implementation and maintenance impacts. As a result, considerable time and effort must be applied at the front end of the development process. It is especially important that the designer resist pressures to produce a design quickly and proceed with implementation. Granted, an abbreviated design process may lead to earlier products; but such products will seldom be the easiest to implement, test, and maintain. Over the life of the system, the time saved on design will be absorbed quickly in the time it will take to revise the system to meet changing requirements.

In Chapter 15, various strategies for elaborating a first-cut program structure chart were discussed. During and after such development, the issue of quality of design must be considered. The evaluation of quality of software design usually focuses upon both the external and the internal characteristics of modules embodied in two main criteria, coupling and cohesion.

Coupling is a measure of the degree to which the modules of a computer program are interrelated. For ease of implementation and maintenance, this interrelatedness between modules should be minimized; thus the degree of coupling should be low.

Cohesion is a measure of the interrelatedness of the processing components, or statements, *within* a module. Implementation and maintenance are facilitated to the extent that the statements all relate to a single, well-defined function. The strength of the internal interrelatedness should be high — the degree of cohesion should be high. Cohesion is often referred to as a measure of internal strength.

The criteria of coupling and cohesion are applied to each design decision as the hierarchy of modules is expanded from top to bottom. As each module is factored into its subordinates, consideration is given to the components of the modules and to the interconnections among them. The objective is to develop a software product that has a high degree of cohesion among the elements within the modules and a low degree of coupling among the modules. Software with these two qualities generally will be easier to implement and test and will be easier to modify and maintain over the operational life of the system. When modules are highly independent, that is, loosely coupled and tightly cohesive, a change in one module will have a minimal effect on other modules.

In addition to coupling and cohesion, other factors can be applied in evaluating a design. These include the distribution of decision making within modules of the system, the span of control (fan-out) exhibited by superordinate modules, the general usefulness of detailed processing modules within different portions of the system (fan-in), and the physical sizes of modules.

These criteria can be best classified as heuristics, or rules of thumb derived from experience. There is still a need for considerable judgment to be applied in evaluating a design on the basis of these criteria.

COUPLING

Again, coupling is a measure of the degree of connections between modules in a system. The degree of coupling, high or low, is viewed as the probability that, in designing, implementing, or modifying one module, the characteristics or contents of another module will have to be taken into account. Coupling is an external measure of module quality. Thus, the more free-standing a module, the lower, or looser, the degree of coupling with other modules; the greater the interdependence between modules, the higher, or tighter, the degree of coupling. Modules with high coupling are more susceptible to residual effects of errors or changes from other modules. Modules that are minimally coupled require the least knowledge about their internal features. In effect, such modules function as black boxes. Consequently, the modules can be implemented, tested, and maintained more easily and can be integrated within new applications with the minimum of trouble.

The existence and extent of coupling within a software system is influenced by four factors, type of connection between modules, complexity of the interface between modules, type of information flow across the interface, and binding time of connections.

Type of Connection between Modules

A connection within a program is a reference by an element within one module to the name, or identifier, of another module. Connections occur, for example, with execution of program instructions that CALL or PERFORM a subprogram or subroutine. In these instances, control is transferred from the module containing the branching statement, or selection, to the module named or identified in the instruction. In general, connections between modules serve two purposes — transferring control and passing data.

Upon execution of the branching instruction, program control is sent to the module named in the instruction, and any data required by the receiving module is made available for processing. When a subroutine CALL is issued, the data are passed explicitly as arguments within the CALL command. (Arguments are data elements sent by a particular module.) They are received as parameters by the called module and become available for processing. (Parameters are data elements received by a particular module.) In the case of a COBOL PERFORM the data are available within a global data structure accessible by all the program's internal modules.

Transfers of Control. Typically, control between modules in a structured design would be routinely transferred to and returned from the subordinate module as in the example of the PERFORMed paragraph in COBOL illustrated in Figure 16-1. The statement, PERFORM MOD-B, transfers program control to the module named MOD-B. Statements within this module are executed; and when the end of the called module is encountered, control returns automatically to the statement following the original PERFORM.

The same situation exists with called, independent subprogramming. When the CALL instruction is executed, control branches immediately to the named module. Upon encountering an actual or implied RETURN instruction within the subprogram, the system returns control directly to the calling module, continuing on with the statement following the CALL.

A single connection between modules serves a dual purpose: It serves as the path across which control is sent from one module to another, and it becomes the path through which control is returned. Figure 16-1(A) shows graphically these control paths for modules involved in a subprogram CALL; Figure 16-1(B) illustrates the control characteristics for a PERFORMed paragraph in COBOL. Obviously, the greater the number of connections to subordinate modules from a superordinate, the greater the coupling.

Transfers of Data. In addition to providing paths for the transfer of control between modules, connections serve as data paths, or interfaces. Data can be provided to a receiving module in one of two ways: In one case, data are passed explicitly through argument lists, as is common with subprogram calls. Alternately, data are made available implicitly, without specific reference, by being a part of a global data structure. The DATA DIVISION in a COBOL program is an example of global data.

Within subprogram calls, as illustrated in Figure 16-2, the receiving module has access only to the data elements passed to it. For example, in the following COBOL statement, a subprogram named SUBPGM is called and is provided access to two data fields named DATA-1 and DATA-2 within the calling program:

CALL 'SUBPGM' USING DATA-1, DATA-2.

Control is transferred to the named subprogram, which receives the data through parameters listed in the statement:

PROCEDURE DIVISION USING DATA-A, DATA-B

Although the names in the argument list do not have to match those in the parameter list, as in Figure 16-2, there still must be correspondence in the number of data items and their formats. The important point is that the subprogram has access only to those data items specifically named in the argument list and passed to it.

Such transfers of data are said to be fully **parameterized**, that is, all data items are explicitly defined.

Figure 16.1. *Typical transfers of control in structured design define a single interface across which control is transferred to and returned automatically from a module.*

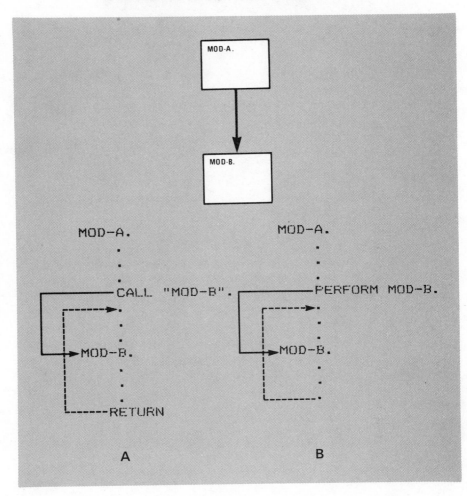

In **nonparameterized** transfers of data, such as those provided with PER-FORM statements in COBOL, data are not passed specifically through argument lists but extracted by the receiving module from a global data pool.

The use of global data by program modules raises some complications, however. Although minimal connection between modules may exist for transfers of control, coupling problems can arise because global data are common to all modules. Any module in the program may change the value of any data element in the global data pool. Further, such changes may occur regardless of whether

Figure 16.2. *A subprogram CALL serves as a parameterized transfer of control and defines a path between modules across which data are passed and received.*

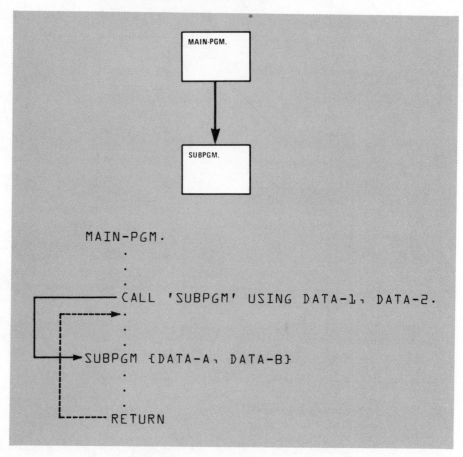

the module, logically, should have access to the data item. As a result, there is not sufficient protection given to data elements to ensure that they will not be changed inadvertently. Thus, strictly speaking, all modules with access to the global data structure are coupled, since a change produced by any one module has potential impact on all other modules that share the data item. Thus the use of global data greatly increases a program's degree of coupling.

In general, the designer should elect fully parametrized transfers of control. Of course, this rule may not be practical for all possible cases of coupling. Within a COBOL program, for instance, the design and coding overhead involved in implementing subprograms for every paragraph would be particularly bothersome. In such cases, careful definition and restrictive use of the global data structure should help keep coupling problems at a minimum. However, the safest policy would be to avoid global data as much as possible.

Complexity of the Interface

The second dimension of coupling is the complexity of the interface. For this purpose, complexity refers to the characteristics of the data being passed from one module to another. From an operational standpoint, complexity relates to the amount of data being passed from one module to another and to the structure of those data.

In general, the number of data elements contained within an argument list in a subroutine call provides evidence of complexity. The larger the number of data items, the more complex the interface. Thus, a subroutine call that contains 25 arguments is generally more complex than one with 10 arguments. Further, such increased complexity contributes an increased degree of coupling between modules. Where data are passed implicitly from one module to another, the degree of complexity and coupling can be inferred by the number of data elements referenced within the receiving module.

This type of coupling cannot be evaluated simply by counting the number of data items passed. The evaluation of complexity should consider the structure of the data as well. For example, an argument list that contains 25 table elements passed as a group to a subprogram would not be a particularly complex interface. Similarly, passing a single record that contains 25 data fields would not be considered complex, as long as the argument list made reference only to the entire record and not to its fields individually.

However, the temptation to pass an entire record when many, but not all, data elements in the record are required by the called module should be avoided. The resulting unused or **tramp data** will have negative implications for the program design similar to those of global data. A system maintainer cannot be certain which modules actually utilize a particular "tramp" element. Another problem may occur when a system designer or programmer is tempted to package unrelated data elements into one structure in order to reduce the number of items passed and thus ease the complexity of the module interface. While it is true that the complexity of the interface will have been reduced, the design will now contain a group of unrelated items all requiring maintenance (of the structure) in the event of a change to any one of them.

In summary, the designer must be aware of the potential for increased coupling when modules are designed. It is likely that excessive numbers of independent data elements being passed between modules are evidence of improper partitioning. Recall that a goal of design is to produce functionally independent modules. Complex interfaces can point out situations in which modules are performing more than one function or in which partitioning has not been carried out fully.

Two types of control relate to the connections between modules. Active control refers to those situations in which modules are connected through transfers and only the data involved in actual processing are transferred across the interface. A second type of control is referred to as coordination. Coordination occurs when one module also passes information to direct the processing that takes place in another module.

To illustrate, consider a payroll program in which a single module performs all payroll calculations. Different sets of calculations are required for salaried and hourly workers. When this module is called, it must both be informed of the type of calculation to perform and receive the record that will be involved in the processing. Thus, the module requires both data and a flag, or software switch, to indicate whether the record is for a salaried or for an hourly employee. This flag represents control information, or coordination. The calling module is involving itself in the internal processing details of the called module by directing the type of calculation to be performed. Thus, coordination couples the modules strongly because neither is functionally independent of the other. Figure 16-3(A) shows this form of coordination between the two modules in the payroll example.

This type of coordination is unnecessary. For example, in the payroll illustration, the calling module evaluates the record type and sets the flag to indicate whether a salaried or an hourly record is being passed. Then, in the called module, this flag is tested again, and one of the two processing routines is executed. Thus, the same test is applied in both modules. If, on the other hand, a separate module were defined for each of the salary and hourly calculations, there would be no need for a flag. The calling module would make the test and send the record to the appropriate subordinate module. Figure 16-3(B) illustrates the design of the modules to eliminate the use of the flag.

The determination of whether a program flag represents either data or control information depends upon the intent of the module passing the flag. Usually, if a flag is passed from a superordinate to a subordinate module, it is a form of coordination. Information is being passed to tell the receiving module what kind of processing to perform. A return flag from a subordinate module, however, is usually not coordination but simply an indication of the results of processing. For instance, an end-of-file flag passed from an input module to its superordinate module represents data, not control. The superordinate is being told what took place; and it can then perform whatever subsequent processing is necessary.

In most cases, the need for coordination arises because the designer has not done an adequate job of partitioning. Lower-level modules have not been broken down into functionally independent subordinate modules. Thus, modules with more than one function must receive information about which of the processing activities to perform. Usually, coordination can be avoided by making sure that lower-level modules implement a single function.

Figure 16.3.   Coordination versus active control.

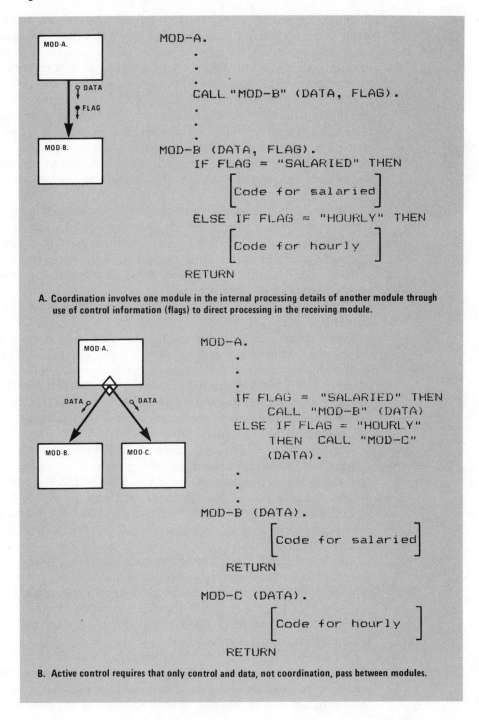

```
MOD-A.
          •
          •
          •
       CALL "MOD-B" (DATA, FLAG).
          •
          •
          •
    MOD-B (DATA, FLAG).
       IF FLAG = "SALARIED" THEN
          ⎡Code for salaried⎤
          ⎣                 ⎦
       ELSE IF FLAG = "HOURLY" THEN
          ⎡Code for hourly  ⎤
          ⎣                 ⎦
    RETURN
```

A. Coordination involves one module in the internal processing details of another module through use of control information (flags) to direct processing in the receiving module.

```
MOD-A.
          •
          •
       IF FLAG = "SALARIED" THEN
              CALL "MOD-B" (DATA)
       ELSE IF FLAG = "HOURLY"
              THEN  CALL "MOD-C"
              (DATA).
          •
          •
    MOD-B (DATA).
          ⎡Code for salaried⎤
          ⎣                 ⎦
    RETURN

    MOD-C (DATA).
          ⎡Code for hourly  ⎤
          ⎣                 ⎦
    RETURN
```

B.   Active control requires that only control and data, not coordination, pass between modules.

Binding Time of Connections

Binding is the process for resolving, or fixing, values of data items in a program. Binding takes place, for example, when a program data item is initialized with some constant value during the data definition of the item or through execution of a program statement. When a program table is dimensioned to a specified number of elements, this value is bound to the program and becomes an integral part of it. Another instance of binding occurs when a program loop is defined and the upper limit of the controlling subscript is specified as a constant. In all these cases, a constant value is embedded within the code. Thus, if changes in processing requirements dictate changes in these constants, the program must be altered and recompiled. In general, the appearance of constants within the source code impairs the flexibility of a program and causes maintenance problems.

When binding takes place early in the implementation phase (for example, when the program is coded), there is an increase in coupling. All modules that make reference to the common constant value are related, or coupled, through that value, and thus cannot function independently. For example, if one module defines a table length of a specified value, all modules that process the table must be aware of and adapt processing to that value. If, for some reason, the table length changes, all modules that process the table likewise must be changed.

For example, consider the need to establish a program table of federal withholding amounts that will be used in a payroll system. The table will be built within the program that calculates weekly payroll. The programming requirement, then, is to establish the table length and to assign withholding values to the table elements. Binding for these values can take place at any of four points in the development of a program, at coding time, at compilation time, at linkage editing time, and at execution time.

At Coding Time. The table-length value and the table values can be coded as constants in the initial definition of the table. In this case, the table length and values become part of the program. Thus, when the next tax year rolls around, the program will have to be updated with the new withholding values. Also, if different withholding categories are established, all modules that make reference to the table will require recoding, since processing is tied to the specified table length.

At Compilation Time. The source code containing table specifications can be placed in a source statement library and added to the program during compilation. In this case, changes can be made to the library code and inserted into the program when the library is compiled. Possibly, all modules that perform table processing can be grouped within this library so that they are readily available when changes are required.

At Linkage Editing Time. Table definitions and values can also be isolated within separately compiled subprograms retained in object code form. The binding of values then would take place when the subprogram is linked with the main program during program linkage. Changes to the program would require only that the subprogram be changed. Other modules could remain in object versions without the need for recoding or recompilation.

At Execution Time. The previous three options require that all or part of the program be rewritten at the source code level when changes occur. This last option requires no recoding, recompilation, or relinkage. In this case the table is initially defined with a range of values for the table size, the upper limit being a value that is not likely to require changing. Table dimensions are then defined as variables within the subsequent modules of the program. Table values would be maintained in a separate data file. When the program is executed, the table is downloaded from the file, with a record counter serving to tally the number of records and establish the dimensions of the table. From a maintenance stand-point, the program would not require modification to adapt to a changing number of records in the file. The dimensions of the table and the upper limits of all loop subscripts used to reference it would vary automatically according to the number or records in the file. Of course, the data file itself would require maintenance, but it is nearly always better to opt for file maintenance over program maintenance.

In general, binding should take place as late as possible. The earlier that values are bound into a program, the less flexible the program will be and the greater the likelihood that revision and recompilation will be needed. Of course, in some cases, a constant may never be expected to change. For example, a module may distribute yearly sales records into a table representing the twelve months of a year. In this case the table dimensions may never change. Therefore, judgments must be made in considering the tradeoffs between program mainte-nance requirements and the consequences of maintaining constant values exter-nal to the program.

Levels of Coupling

The various forms of coupling described above can be summarized within four distinct categories. This classification scheme provides a mechanism for evaluat-ing design techniques on the basis of their effects on coupling. The four levels of coupling, ranked from best to worst are data coupling, stamp coupling, control coupling, and common coupling.

Data coupling should be the goal of design. Data coupling exists in modules connected through active control that transfer only needed data items. Ideally, fully parametrized transfers of control and data should be used as illustrated in Figure 16-4. These types of connections offer the least amount of coupling between modules. (The only possible lower value of coupling is the rare situa-tion in which a called module receives and returns no data to the calling module.)

Stamp coupling relates to situations in which data elements are packaged together into a "stamp" or structure and passed in the interface between mod-ules. If all the data elements are logically related and all are required by the called module, as in Figure 16-5(A), then no problem exists. However, if a calling module passes an entire data record to a subordinate module but only

Figure 16.4. Module interface characterized by data coupling.

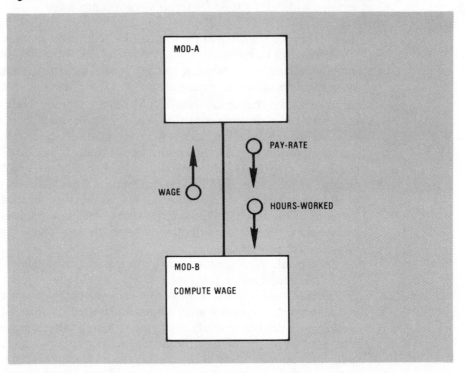

selected fields are required, as illustrated in Figure 16-5(B), then a problem arises. Passing unneeded or "tramp" data elements reduces the integrity of the unneeded data for the rest of the program and needlessly increases coupling. If the record size in the calling module changes, the subordinate module also will need to be changed, even though all the data elements actually used by the called module may be unaffected. The independence of the modules is decreased since they are tied to the same data structure. The subordinate module cannot be easily reused in other programs because of its dependence upon the specific structure.

Control coupling occurs when processing coordination—for example, the passing of a control flag—appears between two modules. This type of control requires that one module be aware of the internal processing details of the other module. Thus, a change made in one of the modules propagates corresponding changes in the other module. Again, the modules cannot function independently. Figure 16-6 depicts two modules exhibiting control coupling. For MOD-B to formulate an appropriate error message, it must receive coordination instructions (ERROR-TYPE) from MOD-A.

Common coupling occurs when two or more modules share access to the same data items from a common pool. Modules lack independence because they are, in effect, linked by the data structure they share. In COBOL, exclusive use of the PERFORM statement rather than the subprogram CALL statement to

Figure 16.5. *Module interface characterized by coupling.*

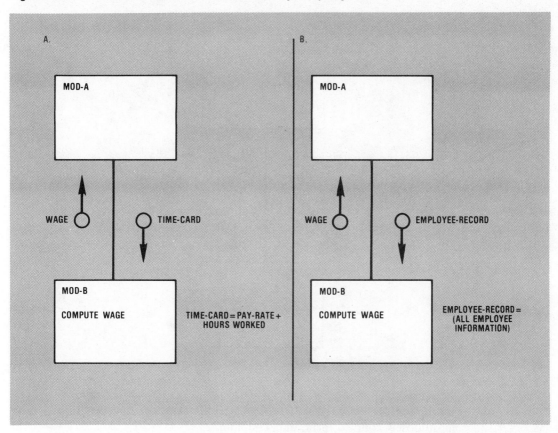

transfer control implies common coupling. All modules share the same data pool as described in the DATA DIVISION. Common coupling also results from early binding of data values. This makes for ineffective design because any change in a constant value requires revision and recompilation of all modules that reference the value. Thus, all such modules cannot function independently. Common coupling is rated as the most severe form of coupling because even minor changes in data values can necessitate extensive changes in the software.

Modules that exhibit more than one type of coupling have the most undesirable degree of coupling. For example if two modules like those in Figure 16-6 were linked by both stamp and control coupling, the interface would be characterized by control coupling. The objective would thus be to redesign the interface to move its characterization to a more desirable coupling type. Figure 16-7 shows how this design might be altered to improve its coupling characterization to stamp coupling. MOD-A now sends the actual ERROR-MESSAGE to MOD-B eliminating the coordination of MOD-B's activities through ERROR-TYPE. Figure 16-8 shows how this interface can be further improved to a data coupling characterization. By sending only the TRANSACTION-CODE#, not

Figure 16.6.   Module interface characterized by control coupling.

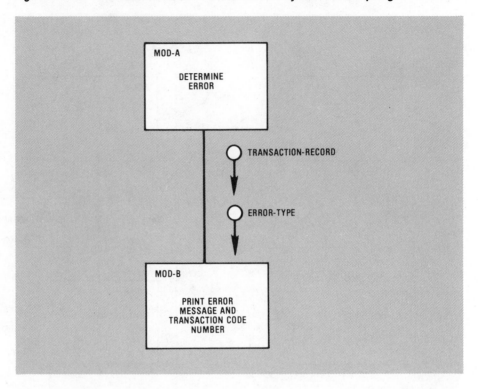

the entire TRANSACTION-RECORD, to MOD-B, the interface now is in its most loosely coupled form, data coupling.

These criteria are not offered as exacting standards. Rather, this discussion surveys coupling consequences of design alternatives. It is not assumed that data coupling will be the best alternative in all cases or that techniques that lead to common, control, or stamp coupling are to be avoided totally. It is possible that in some circumstances design techniques that produce more tightly coupled modules will be the best alternative, given the practical constraints within which the designer works. As designs are being developed, tradeoffs among the coupling consequences of various techniques should be explored.

COHESION

Cohesion is a measure of the degree to which processing elements, or statements, within a module are interrelated. It refers to the degree to which statements contribute toward carrying out a single problem-oriented function. Every statement contributes to the function of the module. Whereas coupling focuses on the external connections between modules, cohesion centers on the connections between elements within modules, and thus is an internal measure of

Figure 16.7. *Module interface from Figure 16.6 improved to exhibit stamp coupling.*

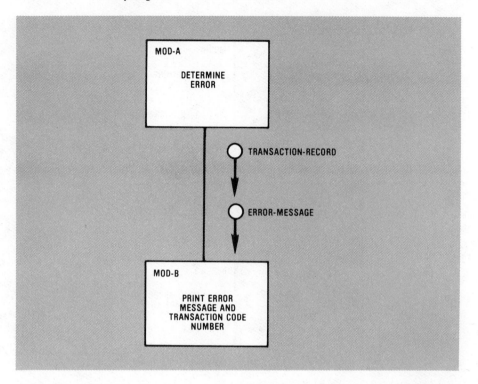

module design quality. Ideally, a module should have maximum cohesion, or interrelatedness, among its statements and internal functions.

Seven levels of cohesion can be identified. In order from best (high) to worst (low), these levels include functional, sequential, communicational, procedural, temporal, logical, and coincidental.

At the high end would be a module in which all statements pertain only to a single problem-oriented function; at the low end would be a module in which none of the statements pertain to a single, clearly identifiable function. In practice, it is unlikely that the degree of cohesion will be this clear-cut. Instead, modules will exhibit varying degrees of cohesion, and the designer should look for opportunities to increase or enhance the relationships among module elements.

Functional Cohesion

A module with **functional cohesion** applies a single transformation to a single item of data. Functional cohesion is rated as the highest level of cohesion because each element within the module contributes only to a specific transformation. Modules with functional strength are preferred because they behave as

Figure 16.8. Module interface from Figure 16.7 improved to exhibit data coupling.

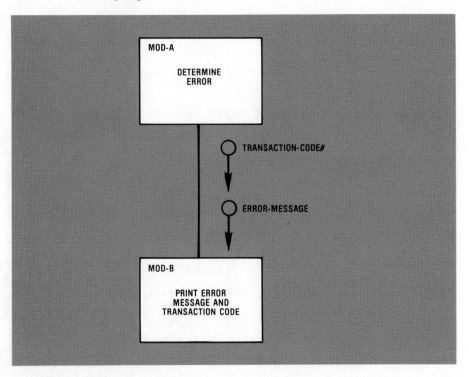

classical black boxes. That is, each item of input is clearly identified, and there is known and predictable output. Further, the module can be used without knowledge of its internal workings. None of the maintenance problems associated with other levels of cohesion are evident in functionally cohesive modules.

A straightforward test of whether a module has functional cohesion often can be made by assigning a name to the module. If the module can be described as performing a single transformation on a single data structure, it probably has functional strength. For example, the following module names suggest functional cohesion:

COMPUTE GRADE POINT AVERAGE
INPUT TRANSACTION RECORD
SEARCH TAX TABLE
PRODUCE PAYROLL REPORT

At first glance, the last module name in the above list — PRODUCE PAYROLL REPORT — might not appear to suggest functional cohesion. To produce such a report, a complete program would be required. Thus, it might be implied that the module must contain all the input, processing, and output instructions required to carry out the function. However, if proper design techniques were applied, this module would be a top-level control module that contains only control statements and calls to lower-level modules that perform the processing. Recall that the name of a module implies the functions of all subordinate modules. Therefore, as a control module, PRODUCE PAYROLL REPORT has functional strength.

Sequential Cohesion

When a module performs multiple processing functions on the same data item and those functions represent successive transformations on the data, **sequential cohesion** results. In effect, the output from one function becomes the input for the next function. Figure 16-9 illustrates a module with sequential strength in which student lists of courses and grades are used to calculate a grade point, the grade point is used to determine class rank, and the class rank is used to

Figure 16.9. *Internal module representation displaying sequential cohesion.*

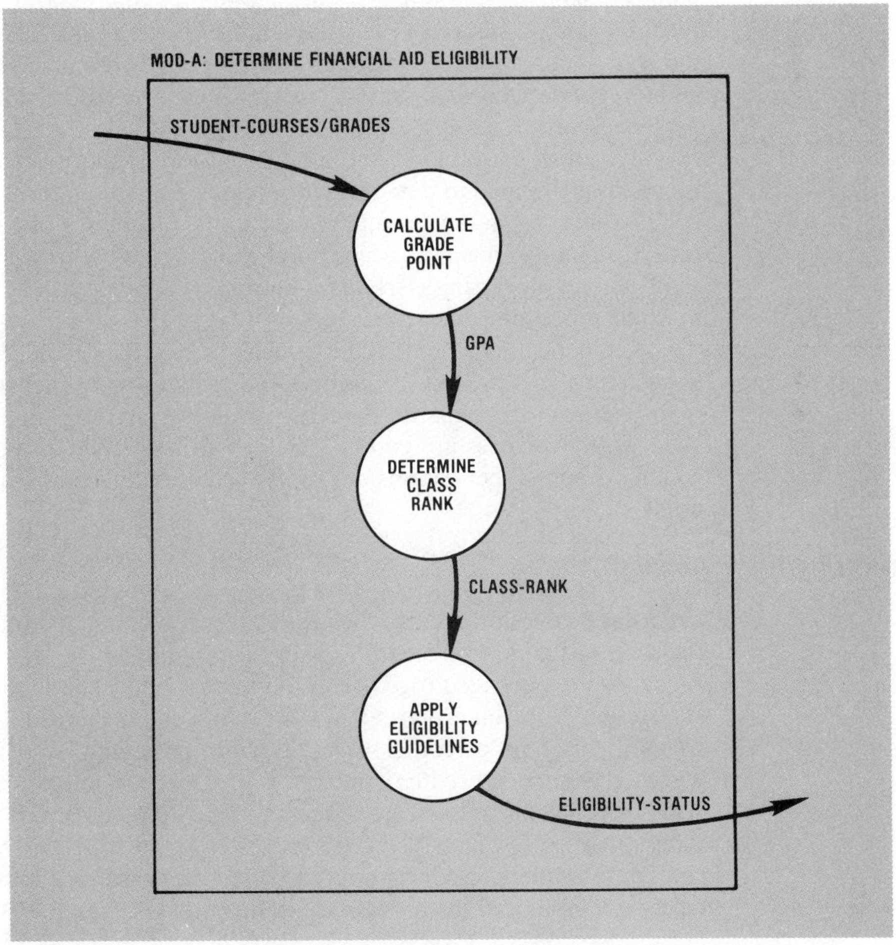

determine financial aid eligibility. Sequential cohesion usually results from packaging related problem structures represented in a sequential fashion on a data flow diagram. It thus reflects the flow of data through the system rather than the flow of control.

The only real problem with modules having sequential strength is that more than one function appears within them. Attendant problems can be resolved easily by further partitioning of the module into two or more subordinate modules.

Communicational Cohesion

Communicational cohesion is found in a module that performs multiple processing functions involving the same set of input or output data. This type of cohesion results from considering everything that can be done with a given item of data and assigning all activities to the same module, usually represented as simultaneous processing functions on a data flow diagram. Usually the order of execution of these items is unimportant. For instance, as in Figure 16-10, communicational cohesion would occur in a module that interrogates a transaction for missing data, displays the transaction on a terminal, and writes a copy of the transaction to a file. Another example might be a module that uses an employee time card to update a working unit's record, update the employee's personnel record, and print a time card report.

In each of these cases, the module performs multiple functions; yet, the functions are related to data transformations that are, in turn, problem related. All elements within the module pertain to the processing of a single data structure. Communicational cohesion represents the lowest level at which relationships among processing elements are problem related rather that associated by machine processing characteristics.

Communicational cohesion is problematic to the extent that multiple functions are included within the module. Normally, however, all such functions are to be performed when the data are available, therefore if that data stream changes, the chances are good a change will be needed in all functions. Thus communicational cohesion is not overly problematic from a maintenance viewpoint.

Procedural Cohesion

Procedural cohesion occurs when the elements within a module are grouped on the basis of the flow of control within the program. That is, possibly unrelated functions are packaged together in the same module simply because control is transferred from one internal module function to another in some fashion. Usually, this type of cohesion results from packaging functions that appear within the same procedural unit of a program. A procedural unit refers to functions that are related by sequence, repetition, or selection control structures.

For example, consider an update program in which addition, change, and deletion transactions are processed, as illustrated in Figure 16-11. Depending on

Figure 16.10. *Internal module representation displaying communicational cohesion.*

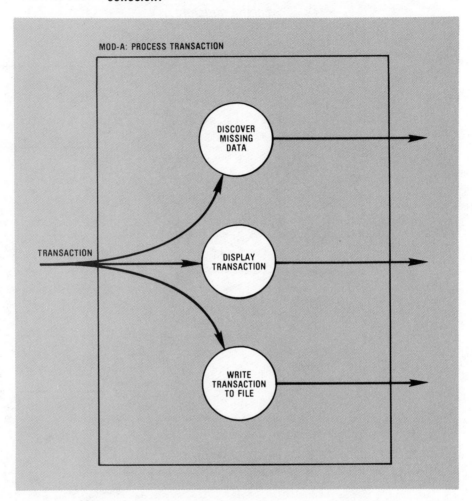

the transaction code, the program will dispatch control to one of three processing modules. If all processing relating to each of the transactions is packaged within a single module, that module has procedural cohesion; its elements are related because they occur within the same decision structure of the program. Another example would be the consolidation of all processing functions that take place in a prescribed sequence within a program loop. In Figure 16-12, input, processing, and output statements are grouped under the rationale that they all are performed in a sequence within the repeat control structure.

Typically, modules with procedural cohesion result from a direct translation of a program flowchart into a modular structure. Because a flowchart documents the procedural aspects of a program, processing functions are tied directly to the control structures within which they appear. An almost unavoid-

Figure 16.11. *Internal module representation displaying procedural cohesion resulting from packaging of functions within a decision control structure.*

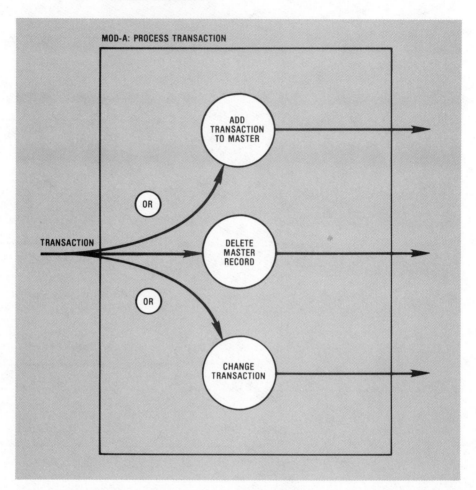

able consequence of modularizing a flowchart, therefore, is a structure of activities related by this flow of control. As with other methods that result in low module cohesion, partitioning on the basis of control procedures can lead to implementation and maintenance difficulties. Modules contain more than one function; the specific order of execution of statements within modules becomes critically important; and data passed from one function to another are related more to the execution sequence of the program than to problem-related structure. Thus they are not necessarily tied to any ordering on a data flow diagram.

Temporal Cohesion

In a module with **temporal cohesion,** the elements are related in time. Statements appear within the module because they all represent functions that must

Figure 16.12. *Internal module representation displaying procedures cohesion resulting from packaging of functions within a repeat control structure.*

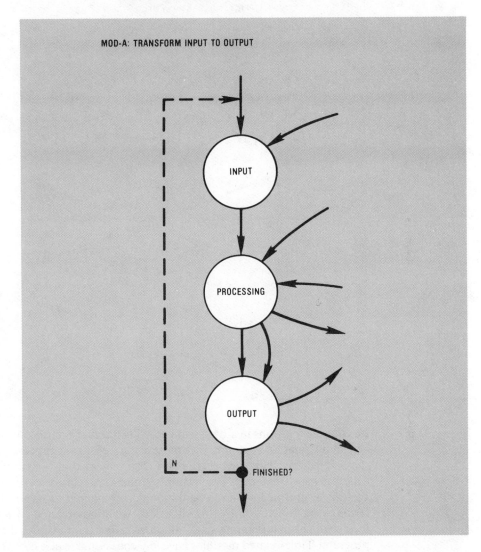

take place within the same time frame during program execution. Examples occur in initialization and termination modules, as illustrated in Figure 16-13. At the beginning of the program, files are opened, counters are initialized, flags are set, and the first input record is read. Since all these functions take place chronologically prior to the main processing function, these temporally related functions may be included within a single module called to perform the housekeeping tasks at the beginning of execution.

Of course, an ordered, time-related presentation of program functions is necessary for computer processing. A computer is a sequential machine that

Figure 16.13. Internal module representation displaying temporal cohesion.

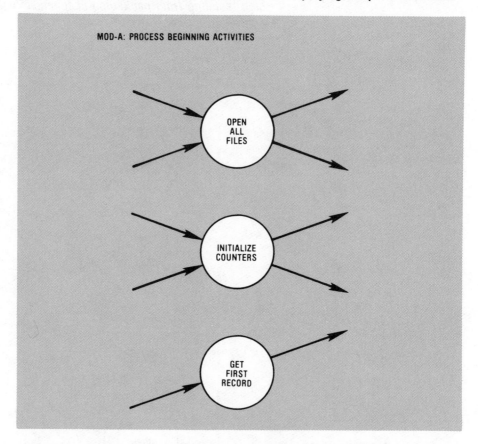

executes instructions in a time sequence. Therefore, functions such as initializing constant values and opening files must occur before any processing that involves those functions. However, there is no requirement that the functions be physically packaged together. For example, functions related to processing a given file can be grouped so that a read module can handle its own initialization and termination functions. In this situation, functions related to a given file are localized within a separate set of modules rather than disbursed throughout the program. Time-related modules have low cohesion because components of more than one function are included, and they are not related by flow of data or control.

Logical Cohesion

The elements of a **logically cohesive** module are related by their inclusion in a general category, i.e., I-O, error handling, or editing routines. Logical cohesion can result from an incomplete partitioning of a program. For example, the system is decomposed to the level at which an editing function is identified.

Since, on the surface, record editing appears to be a single cohesive function, no further analysis of requirements takes place to identify possible subfunctions, and the various editing routines are grouped together in one EDIT module, as illustrated in Figure 16-14.

Logical cohesion may result from attempts to avoid coding redundancy. Using the editing situation as an example, the designer may find that there are several instances in which code can be shared among modules. For two or more fields to be validated, the identical numeric test may be applied. Therefore, the designer might decide to combine edits that happen to involve a numeric check within the same module. The numeric check is coded only once; however, as a result, otherwise unrelated edits are packaged together. A preferable approach would be to create a single numeric-check edit module that could be called by the individual edit modules as necessary using a transaction analysis design strategy as explained in Chapter 15.

Several consequences of logical cohesion are evident. First, the modules cannot function as pure black boxes. Because more than one function is repre-

Figure 16.14. *Internal module representation displaying logical cohesion.*

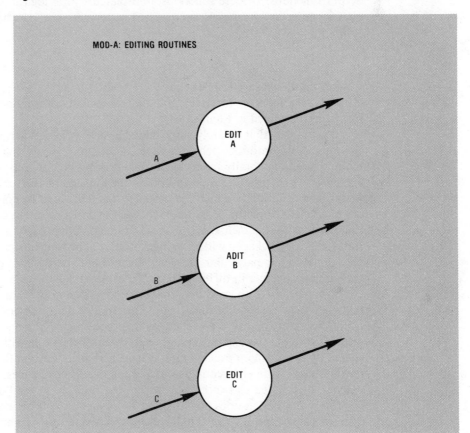

MOD-A: EDITING ROUTINES

EDIT
A

ADIT
B

EDIT
C

sented, the calling module must be aware of the internal logic of the called module. Often, control flags have to be passed to the module to select which of the multiple functions apply at a particular time within the execution sequence. Therefore, modules with logical cohesion require coordination control that increases their coupling. Another problem with logically cohesive modules relates to maintenance requirements. If code is shared by the functions within the module, changes in the code for one function may impact another function inadvertently.

Logical cohesion can easily be avoided through complete partitioning of the program. At each level of design, the designer looks for identifiable subfunctions in which a single, specific processing activity is applied to a single, specific element of data. Even so, there still may be occasions when the designer will opt for logical cohesion in a module to avoid other design problems.

For example, in some cases, it might be beneficial to include all input or output functions that pertain to a single file within a single module to isolate program functions that interface directly with the external hardware-software environment. If different file organization techniques are employed or different hardware devices are used, the greatest impact usually will be upon input-output functions. If these functions are isolated within logically cohesive modules, locating and changing the affected statements becomes a relatively easy task.

Coincidental Cohesion

Coincidental cohesion implies that there is little or no relationship among the elements of a module. In effect, the module consists of a random set of statements, as illustrated in Figure 16-15.

It is unlikely that a purely coincidental level of cohesion actually would exist by design. To produce such a module, a designer would have to designate module functions totally by accident. Yet, it is possible to design modules that exhibit levels of cohesion that approach this low end of the scale. An example would be a situation in which the designer was motivated by concern for memory efficiency. After the program is coded, the designer might recognize recurring patterns of statements. So, to avoid this coding redundancy, these groups of statements are packaged within a single module. The elements of the module are not related to any particular problem function but simply through the fact that they appear together in different portions of the code.

The problem with modules that have coincidental cohesion, of course, is that they have no relationship to the structure of the problem to which they apply. Therefore, if there are changes in processing requirements, it becomes difficult to trace the corresponding code. Also, if the code within a module is shared by two or more processing routines, a change that applies to one of the routines may cause erroneous processing for the other routines, thus requiring patches, or isolated software fixes, within the code. In general, a module with coincidental cohesion does not function as a black box; the designer must have detailed knowledge of its internal workings to design other components.

Figure 16.15. Internal module representation displaying coincidental cohesion.

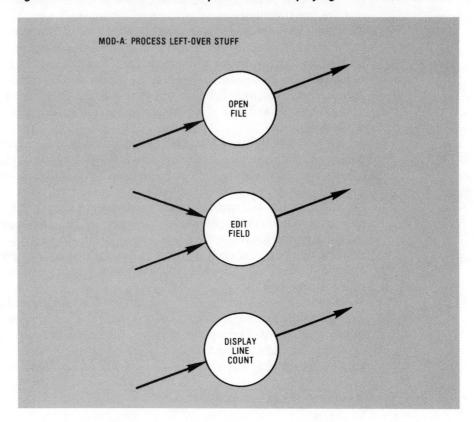

Information Hiding and Informational-Strength Modules

Software design normally will be motivated by the objective of defining hierarchical structures of functionally cohesive modules. In most cases, such a design will contribute to ease of program implementation and maintenance.

In other cases, however, this type of design will not be the best in terms of module independence. Consider a program in which the following three functional-strength modules appear:

BUILD TAX TABLE
SEARCH TAX TABLE ON GROSS AMOUNT
EXTRACT WITHHOLDING AMOUNT FROM TABLE

These three functions may be scattered throughout the program, depending on the sequence in which they are activated. Although the modules are functionally independent from the standpoint of the problem structure, they are all dependent on the structure of the table. If the format of the table changes, all three modules probably would have to be changed.

A solution to the potential maintenance problems associated with modules that are functionally cohesive but interrelated through some information structures lies in the concept of **information hiding**. That is, functions that depend on an information structure or other system resource that is not problem related are isolated, or hidden, within a single module. The structure or resource is made transparent to the designer or user of the software. Changes in the processing environment, therefore, produce software changes only in the informational-strength module and do not require changes in the structure or processing logic of the program.

Figure 16-16 illustrates the use of an informational-strength module for the table-processing situation described above. Here, a single module, coded as a subprogram, contains all processing related to building, searching, and extracting information from a tax table. The table itself is defined within the subprogram. The subprogram contains a separate entry point for each of the processing functions. Superordinate modules call the subprogram and specify the entry points for the desired functions. Within the subprogram, there is no overlapping code, and each function includes a distinct exit point. If changes occur in the structure of the tax table, the processing changes are isolated within this single module.

A module with informational cohesion results from the packaging of two or more functional-strength modules. Of course, this solution lessens functional cohesion and increases coupling. However, the system is maintained more easily to cope with changes in the processing environment. A general design strategy might be to develop a system based on the use of functional-strength modules and then to look for occasions to reduce environmental dependencies by defining informational-strength modules.

RELATIONSHIP BETWEEN COUPLING AND COHESION

As a design objective, coupling should be minimized and cohesion maximized. Coupling and cohesion are closely interrelated. At one extreme, a program might be composed of one module. There would be no coupling since there would be no interfaces between modules; however, the program would also have very low cohesion since all program functions would be contained within the same module. At the other extreme, each module in a program might consist of a single statement. This program would rank not only high in cohesion, because it is likely that each module would have a very specific function, but also high in coupling, because a large number of module interfaces would be required. Of course, neither of these designs is a good solution.

The designer should be guided by the goal of establishing a proper balance between coupling and cohesion. Just what is the proper balance and how to achieve it are questions for which no definitive answer can be given.

Generally, except for the extreme examples just cited, there is no tradeoff between coupling and cohesion. Improvements in coupling will improve cohe-

Figure 16.16. *An information-strength module has multiple entry points and no overlapping code for the multiple function performed.*

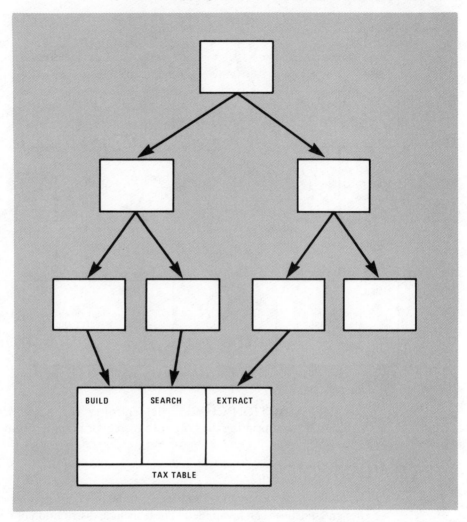

BUILD   SEARCH   EXTRACT

TAX TABLE

sion and vice versa. Therefore design enhancements that decrease coupling will usually increase cohesion. Likewise those that increase cohesion will decrease coupling. Consider the example in Figure 16-17. As shown earlier, Figure 16-17(B) is an improvement to Figure 16-17(A) in that its coupling strength has been reduced from control to data coupling. Notice also that the changes made to improve coupling have also improved the cohesion of MOD-B. It no longer receives the entire TRANSACTION-RECORD structure. In the improved version, MOD-B receives only the data it requires, namely the TRANSACTION-CODE#. MOD-B also now receives only an ERROR-MESSAGE and not an ERROR-TYPE. Thus the function of MOD-B has been changed from extracting

Figure 16.17. *Internal cohesion of MOD-B is increased by decreasing coupling of module interface.*

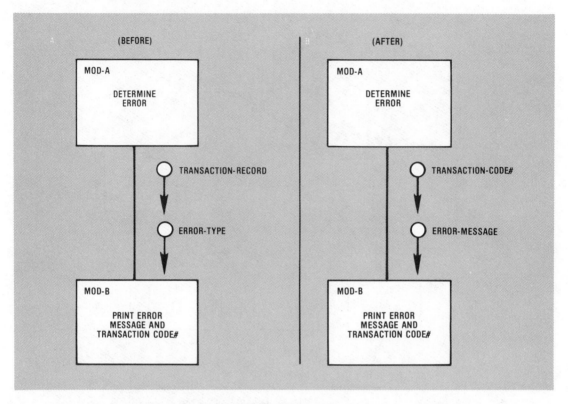

the TRANSACTION-CODE#, determining the appropriate ERROR-MESSAGE, and printing the output to merely printing the output.

OTHER EVALUATIVE CRITERIA

In addition to the main evaluation criteria of coupling and cohesion, other design guidelines can be applied. These include distribution of decision making, fan-out (span of control), fan-in, and module size.

Distribution of Decision Making

The modules that make up the structure chart of any program will fall into two broad categories: *control* or *detail processing*. If the program is well-designed, decision making, or control processing, that is, program management, will be applied by modules at the top levels of the hierarchy. Lower-level modules then will carry out detailed processing or specialized labor. Generally, management activities should be separated as much as possible from the specialized labor. This **distribution of decision making** is shown in Figure 16-18. In this example, the shading in the modules represents the proportion of elements that provide program control functions. As indicated, the incidence of control should decline at lower levels of the structure. A distribution of decision making toward the bottom of a hierarchy or detailed processing toward the top, which would indicate an "inversion of authority," should be reconsidered.

Fan-out (Span of Control)

Fan-out, also called **span of control**, refers to the number of modules immediately subordinate to a module. A high span of control can indicate improper partitioning of a system into upper-, intermediate-, and lower-level modules. Figure 16-19(A) shows a high span of control with wide fan-out, indicating that probably too many modules are subordinate to and under direct control of the higher-level module. Usually three to seven modules subordinate to one superordinate would constitute a workable span of control. A larger configuration might indicate that partitioning of a function has not proceeded hierarchically through intermediate-level abstractions. A possible problem with this design is

Figure 16.18. *Distribution of decision making within modular systems.*

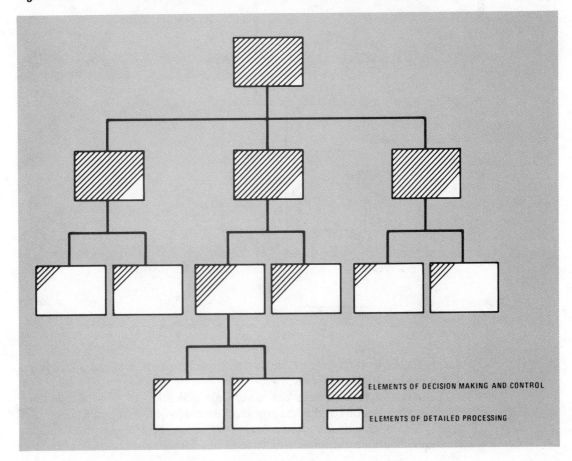

ELEMENTS OF DECISION MAKING AND CONTROL

ELEMENTS OF DETAILED PROCESSING

Figure 16.19. *Span of control in a system indicates the effectiveness of top-down partitioning across multiple levels of abstraction.*

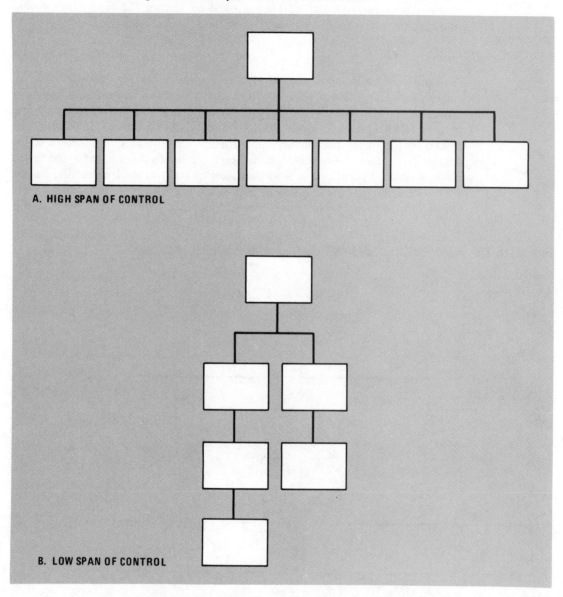

A. HIGH SPAN OF CONTROL

B. LOW SPAN OF CONTROL

that the higher-level module has too many functions to oversee, making the logic of that module highly complex.

However, high fan-out is not always an indication of poor design. For example, a transaction center control module implementing a main menu of a large system might require a great deal of subordinates. However, high fan-out situations should be examined closely for potential areas of repartitioning.

By comparison, Figure 16-19(B) illustrates the opposite extreme. The span of control is possibly too low, indicating that partitioning has gone forward with too much vigor. The excessive control built into this structure means that intermediate-level modules are likely to contain trivial processing functions that can be absorbed into higher-level modules, leaving a simplified configuration.

Fan-In

Fan-in is a measure of the number of higher-level modules that call upon a lower-level module. High fan-in is desirable. It indicates that the called module is highly functional and can be used without modification in several parts of the system. Figure 16-20 shows a segment of a structure chart in which the shaded module has high fan-in.

Figure 16.20. **High fan-in refers to the use of a single, lower-level module by two or more higher-level modules.**

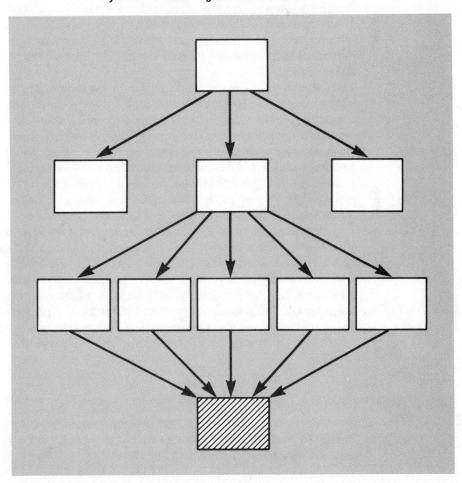

As a general rule, it is desirable to have a lower-level module called by two or more higher-level modules. However, fan-in should not be achieved at any cost. For example, fan-in can be achieved by packaging several related functions within the same module. Various higher-level modules, then, would call this routine and select a particular processing function through use of a control flag. Thus, a module of low cohesion (perhaps logical cohesion) is created and coupled tightly to the modules that call it. Fan-in should not be used if this method results in the use of control flag.

Module Size

As a general rule, large modules often result from an incomplete breakdown of a problem into appropriate subproblems. Thus, one of the measures of effectiveness of design lies in the size of individual modules. Several rules of thumb have been suggested for evaluating module size. One of these holds that no module should be longer than 50 lines of source code. This length corresponds with the number of lines that can be printed on a single page of computer printout. Another suggested size limitation is that no module should contain more than 30 statements. This limit is suggested by studies indicating that a programmer's comprehension of a module drops sharply if it contains more than 30 lines. Individual CIS organizations are known to enforce module sizes ranging up to 500 lines.

The number of lines appropriate within any module, for any programmer, is highly judgmental. However, the principle is that as the number of statements in a module grows, the more it is likely to contain multiple and/or unrelated functions. Excessively large (or small) modules may point out problems affecting coupling and cohesion. Excessive numbers of small modules (i.e., less than 30 lines) will result in increased coupling and will require more system overhead than larger, but fewer, modules performing the same functions. Thus, large modules may require further decomposition; and, as is demonstrated in Chapter 18, they will be extremely difficult to test.

The evaluation criteria reviewed above may be applied in judging the quality of software designs. Such criteria can be applied after a design has been completed; they also can serve as guidelines during the development process. As yet, these criteria do not have the formality of quantitative approaches to quality assessment. It is not possible to apply them as software metrics to rate coupling and cohesion with precision. However, the criteria can promote an awareness of design trade-offs and the consequences of design decisions. Also, this approach can result in software designs that are highly cohesive and that exhibit low coupling.

SUMMARY

Quality software exhibits two main characteristics: It is easy to implement and test, and it is easy to maintain and modify.

To implement quality, the criteria of coupling and cohesion are applied to each design decision as the hierarchy of modules is expanded from top to bottom.

Coupling, or the connection between modules, is influenced by the type of connection between modules, the complexity of the interface between modules, the type of information flow across the interface, and the binding time of connections. Coupling is largely an external measure of module quality.

Cohesion refers to the strength of interrelatedness between statements or functions within a module and is largely an internal measure of module quality.

A good objective of design is to minimize coupling and maximize cohesion.

Connections between modules serve to pass control or to transfer data. Transfers of data may be fully parametrized (passed explicitly as arguments) or may be nonparametrized (shared within a global data pool). The use of non-parametrized data greatly increases coupling.

The number of connections and the number of data elements in a module interface contribute to its complexity and thus its coupling. Also, the extent to which one module may influence the activities of another through the use of flags will increase interface coupling.

Binding is the process of fixing values of data items within a program. In general binding should occur as late as possible, preferably during program execution to reduce coupling.

Levels of coupling, ranked from best to worst, include data coupling, stamp coupling, control coupling, and common coupling.

Levels of cohesion, ranked from best to worst, include functional, sequential, communicational, procedural, temporal, logical, and coincidental.

There is no necessary tradeoff between coupling and cohesion. Generally, a decrease in coupling will also result in an increase in cohesion and an increase in cohesion will result in a corresponding decrease in coupling.

Information hiding is a method of isolating an information structure within a single module where it may be accessed by other modules requiring the same data structure.

Other evaluation criteria include the distribution of decision making within modules of the system, the fan-out or span of control exhibited by superordinate modules, fan-in, and module size.

KEY TERMS

1. coupling
2. cohesion
3. binding
4. parameterized
5. nonparameterized
6. tramp data
7. data coupling
8. stamp coupling
9. control coupling
10. common coupling
11. functional cohesion
12. sequential cohesion
13. communicational cohesion
14. procedural cohesion
15. temporal cohesion
16. logical cohesion
17. coincidental cohesion
18. information hiding
19. distribution of decision making
20. span of control
21. fan-out
22. fan-in

REVIEW/DISCUSSION QUESTIONS

1. What are two characteristics of quality software?
2. Define the terms coupling and cohesion.
3. What are the four factors that influence the extent of coupling within a software system ? Define each briefly.
4. What is "tramp" data?
5. What is binding and when should it occur?
6. Name the levels of coupling and define each briefly.
7. Name the levels of cohesion and define each briefly.
8. What is meant by information hiding?
9. What is the design objective regarding coupling and cohesion?
10. What other criteria in addition to levels of coupling and cohesion may be applied in evaluating a design?
11. Discuss the guidelines related to fan-out and fan-in.

PRACTICE ASSIGNMENTS

1. Draw a portion of a structure chart consistent with the following information:
   - the fan-out of module B is 3
   - the fan-in of module C is 2

2. What level of coupling exists for each of the following interfaces between the calling and called modules?

   a. CALL MODULE-B USING NAME and SS#
   b. CALL MODULE-C USING ADDRESS structure
   c. CALL MODULE-D USING EMPLOYEE RECORD
   d. CALL MODULE-E USING ERROR FLAG
   e. CALL MODULE-F

3. What level of cohesion most likely exists for each of the following short module descriptions?

   a. STARTUP: open files, initialize counters, print heading
   b. CALCTAX: calculate sales tax
   c. REPORTS: produce desired report based on parameter: either sales-person report, manager report, or division report
   d. BILLING: calculate amount due and print bill
   e. TRANS: print transaction information and copy it to tape
   f. ECT: print address labels, calculate employee discounts, and update customer records

Systems Design:
Assuring Quality

The two chapters in Part VI are designed to present the concepts and techniques of designing and testing reliable software. Systems reliability is designed into the software well before the first line of code is ever written. System controls are an essential component in the process of assuring that the integrity, security, and confidentiality of a system is maintained.

Chapter 17 presents the basics of control and reliability design. The points where controls can be applied during the operation of the system; the types of controls and tests that can be implemented; and the use of audit trails, design audits, proper backup procedures, and operational procedures are all discussed in this chapter.

Chapter 18 presents the concepts and techniques of software testing. Software testing is the process for executing a program with the intent to cause and discover errors. Through attempts to cause a program to work incorrectly and then correcting the resulting errors, the software is made more reliable. Several strategies for software tests are discussed, including white-box testing, black-box testing, and error guessing. Unit, integration, and function testing are also discussed.

On completing your study in this part of the text, you should have a reasonable understanding of the purpose and methods for including controls in software systems. You will also have learned several practical techniques for testing the software prior to placing it into operation. You will have gained an appreciation for this important part of the systems development process.

17

Control and Reliability Design

Learning Objectives
After completing the reading and other learning assignments for this chapter, you should be able to:

■ Describe the role of controls in assuring the accuracy, integrity, security, and confidentiality of a system.

■ Identify the points at which controls must be applied throughout the operation of the system.

■ List the types of controls available and the techniques used to implement these controls.

■ Describe tests that may be applied during processing to assure the accuracy and validity of data.

■ Define *audit trail* and tell how auditability of systems can be enhanced.

■ Describe operational procedures that reinforce controls, including documentation and separation of duties.

■ Describe how a design audit is conducted.

■ Describe the importance of backing up data files and programs.

THE NEED FOR CONTROLS

Controls are functions, applied either by machines or by people, that are designed to build the needed level of quality into a computer information system. Controls provide assurance that standards of completeness and accuracy are enforced for each individual record or group of business transactions. Thus, controls are needed for quality assurance. Specific needs met by controls include accuracy, integrity, and confidentiality.

- **Accuracy** means that data entered into the system are exactly as they should be. A commonly used expression describing the need for accuracy is "Garbage in, garbage out." This means simply that the accuracy of input data controls the quality of the entire system. Thus, accuracy control must be established at input and must be applied as needed to assure the quality of results delivered. In this sense, accuracy means that data entered into the system are exactly the same as those presented in source transactions or on source documents.

- The term **integrity** describes controls to assure that specified processing is applied only to the proper authorized files. In the course of running applications, files are altered or superseded. Integrity controls assure that the data files processed represent the actual, current status or condition of the organization. Integrity controls are also applied to assure that, if any files are inadvertently destroyed, the materials and mechanisms will exist to reconstruct those files and to recover processing capabilities. Integrity also implies the use of **security** measures to assure that only authorized transactions will be admitted into a system for processing.

- **Confidentiality** controls are designed to protect the rights of privacy of persons or organizations described by, or represented in, data records. Many computer files contain personal or private data about individuals or groups. For example, data such as medical histories or purchasing and credit information about individuals should be available only to authorized users of application systems.

TYPES OF CONTROLS

If a system is to produce accurate, reliable results, controls must be applied at every stage of system operation including input, processing, output, and file storage. Controls must protect against unauthorized acts and, more frequently, against errors or omissions by persons who operate or use computer information systems. Types of controls that should be considered in the design of computer information systems include these:

- Access controls
- Source document controls
- Data entry controls
- Processing controls
- Output controls
- File controls
- Documentation controls
- Organizational controls

Access Controls

Access controls are designed to limit possession of data resources to authorized persons only. Separate measures are needed to control physical access to computer sites and to limit electronic access to computer systems.

Facilities security is a specialized area about which few systems analysts are consulted. Data access control and security tend to be functions of database management software, communications monitors, and specialized system software. Access control is not normally designed into individual application systems. However, several access controls should be considered during the design of an application system. These include unique transaction codes, nondisplay fields, restricted functions, and separation of duties.

- **Unique transaction codes** permit data access security to be implemented at the individual transaction level. For example, bank supervisors would be able to make adjustments to correct mistakes in a customers' accounts if they attached a special transaction code to the change.

- Use of **nondisplay fields** should be considered when especially sensitive data are being input from a terminal. Although this type of control is effective only for low volumes, fields requiring this degree of confidentiality should be identified.

- **Restricted functions** that allow select individuals, such as supervisors or auditors, to perform control or audit functions should be identified.

- **Separation of duties** should be planned. If application programs are to contain application-specific authentication and/or verification routines, these requirements should be identified so that allowances can be made from a cost, time, and work-assignment standpoint. Sensitive routines should be designed and programmed in pieces by different people and then joined to make up the whole.

Source Document Controls

Before any data can enter a system, an authorization measure should be required. Authorization is usually given in the form of initials or signatures on source documents which would constitute a **source document control**. Operating controls should assume that these authorizations are applied before data are cleared for input.

Use of prenumbered source documents is an additional straightforward control procedure. Prenumbering has the effect of controlling physical access to source documents, since all numbered source documents can be accounted for by reference to some type of master list. Transactions whose document numbers fall out of anticipated ranges may be rejected by the system. This control helps assure that source documents are genuine.

Data Entry Controls

Separate types of **data entry controls** are used in batch processing and on-line systems.

For batch systems, a major control technique lies in establishing control totals to be carried forward into input and processing functions. These **control totals** are designed to assure accuracy of keyboarding and completeness of records. One type of control total is a count of the number of documents or records in a batch. Other types of totals are applied to data fields within all records within a batch. Included are **hash totals** and **monetary** or **quantity totals**.

Each of these types of controls is applied by adding the values in numeric fields of input documents and records. For example, in processing a batch of orders, all the controls described here might be applied. The number of documents in the batch would be counted and recorded on a batch **header record** along with a batch identification number and date. Then, the values of the total amount field for each of the orders would be totaled and recorded as a batch control on the header records.

A hash total is the summation of a numeric field that does not contain quantities or values that are normally added together. For example, the customer numbers on the orders might be totaled. Although this total has no meaning in an information processing sense, it can be used to verify accurate entry of the customer numbers.

When all input data for a batch have been captured, the control totals are checked on an **edit run** before actual processing can take place. During the edit run, the computer develops totals for each control field as it edits the individual records. These totals are then balanced against those entered from the batch header. Unless all controls balance, further processing cannot take place. Failure to balance may indicate that one of the fields was entered incorrectly. (Of course, an out-of-balance condition may also result because an error was made in computing the original control total). It is then necessary to compare source documents and the entered data manually to search for the error. The same control may be applied after each processing run within the system as long as the batch is kept intact.

Clearly defined manual procedures are critical to the effective batch processing of input transactions. Since batches must be checked document by document if totals do not agree, batch size is usually limited to about 50 to 100 documents. After transactions are counted and batch totals are calculated, the results are written on a batch ticket that accompanies the documents.

Before sending the batch to the data entry operation, the batch identification number and date are entered in a **transaction log**. The main purpose of this log is to improve the physical control of the batches themselves. If there are large numbers of batches, it is easy to misplace a batch or even to enter a batch twice. The log provides a method for tracking the physical location and stage of processing for each batch.

For systems using on-line input, the types of controls depend on the design of the processing. Basically, the processing may be either batch or real-time. Under a batch-processing design, some editing may be done as the transactions are entered on-line. The transactions are then placed in a file for later processing. The physical batching techniques and control totals discussed above also apply to this type of data entry.

In real-time processing, each input transaction is released immediately for further processing by the system. This, of course, precludes the use of batch control totals. Rather, any input control must be applied to one document at a time. One technique relies on visual verification by the terminal operator. In the order entry example mentioned earlier, the operator might key the customer number, item numbers, and quantities. The system might then respond by adding the customer name and address and item names. The operator could then verify that the computer-supplied entries correspond to those written on the order form.

In addition to their use of visual verification, analysts and designers usually place an even heavier emphasis on processing controls than they might in a batch environment.

Processing Controls

Processing controls are incorporated within individual application programs. These controls are designed to assure the accuracy and completeness of records each time a file is processed. Two types of processing controls are batch controls and input controls.

Batch Controls. One type of processing control involves the use of **batch controls** for master file processing. A **trailer record** at the end of a file contains entries covering the number of records and totals for numeric fields in all records. Each time the file is processed, totals are taken of these fields and compared with the totals on the trailer record. Alterations of the fields during processing are documented in the control record to keep it up to date. This technique is similar to the use of batch controls to verify data entry. In this case, verification of the actual processing is accomplished.

Input Controls. Some processing controls are designed to assure the accuracy and completeness of input records. These include batch control totals, exception reports, and edit runs. Batch control totals are described in the discussion on data entry controls. During processing, totals are developed to balance back to these data entry batch totals. Unless these totals balance, processing will not go forward. **Exception reports** are special printed outputs that identify either items that cannot be processed or out-of-balance situations.

Edit runs review input transactions for accuracy and completeness. Editing is done at several levels:

- Syntax
- Value tests applied to individual fields
- Cross field
- Cross record

Syntax checks on fields within a record include **numeric, alphabetic, sign,** and **completeness tests**. This last test verifies that a mandatory field is not all blanks.

Value tests applied to individual fields include range tests, reasonableness tests, category tests, and check digits.

A **range test** checks to be sure that the value of entries in a given field fall between high and low levels established by the program. For example, a payroll program might apply a test to be sure that no one is paid for working more than 80 hours per week.

A **reasonableness test** is related to the range test, except that acceptable values are determined individually for each record. Reasonableness is evaluated with respect to master file data and involves matching the content of a field with a given file of alternatives. For example, in a payroll system a reported number of hours of overtime may be judged reasonable by comparing it with an average overtime value stored in the master file.

Category tests are range or reasonableness tests applied to nonnumeric data. These tests often involve **table lookup** techniques under which tables are searched to find entries to match input data. A common example is a state code table that can be searched to verify the accuracy of a state field in an input record.

Check digits provide a validity check. A series of calculations is performed on a numeric key field such as an account number. The results of the calculations upon values in certain positions within the field must equal one of the digits in the field. For example, one simple method is called the alternate digit method. Every other digit beginning with the first digit in a key field is summed and the units position of that total is attached to the key field as the check digit. Suppose the key field is 74329. The alternate digit approach would generate a total of 19 $(7 + 3 + 9)$ and the digit 9 would be added to the key field as a check digit. The resulting key field plus the check digit would be 743299. Whenever this number was used, the same alternate digit method would be employed to verify that 9 is the check digit. If another number came up, that would be evidence that a mistake had been made.

After individual fields have been checked for correct syntax and values, cross-checking may be done among fields in the record. The values in two fields may be valid individually; but, taken together, the combination may be invalid. One example is the state and ZIP code combination. A table matching ZIP code ranges and the corresponding states could be checked to verify that the combination is correct. A similar check would apply in an order entry application, matching item number with item characteristics, such as size, color, and price.

A similar cross-checking principle can be applied across records. Consider again an order entry application in which an order consists of multiple records, one with customer information followed by one for each item ordered. Each of the individual records might be complete, but the total value of goods ordered might exceed the customer's credit limit. A cross-record test could be established to detect this condition.

Communication Controls

A specialized control that helps assure the security and confidentiality of data can be applied during processing through techniques of **encryption**. This means that signals representing data are altered, or encoded, when processing involves transmission over communication lines or networks. When the signals are received, the content is recovered through special decoding devices and the signals are put back in original form. Thus, data are unrecognizable while moving over communication lines or networks. This technique is also known as **signal scrambling**. This type of control will be designed by the technical services staff in the CIS organization. The analyst, however, should be aware of the control and request this service if appropriate.

Audit Trails

Integrity, reliability, and accuracy of data can be assured by building in and applying **audit trail** techniques throughout a system. An audit trail is a series of records that can be used for tracking data through a system from the time a transaction originates to the point when the data are incorporated into master files or summary statistics. Input logs are typically used as key parts of audit trails. In addition, each time data items are altered to a level that causes that data to lose their original identity, backup copies of the files are retained for reference. If processing output is questioned or verification is needed, results can be traced backward to the point of the original input.

Output Controls

Outputs are the end products of a computer information system. Therefore, **output controls** are the final, definitive quality assurance measures that can be applied. It should be considered essential that some measure be incorporated in every system for comparing output report totals with input control totals.

Authorization controls are also critical in the handling of computer outputs. Printed documents or displays should be available only to authorized persons. Output reports with sensitive content should be delivered to authorized persons only. Control systems should require signed receipts.

File Controls

Data files, in effect, are the tools and the means by which a company continues to operate. There have been actual cases in which a loss of data files has led to business failures. Therefore, there should be no compromise in establishing and applying controls over the handling and use of data resources.

Physical controls are the responsibility of the computer operations group. These controls include procedures both for labeling and storing files and for releasing file media for processing. The analyst must be aware of these procedures in planning ways to mesh with the manual procedures of the system being developed.

Two types of **file controls** are of direct concern to the analyst. The first is to include a grand total, generally monetary, as the last record of the master file. As transactions are processed and new record amounts are developed, the totals of transactions are accumulated. The beginning grand total is then added to the accumulated transaction total. This figure is then compared to the new grand total. These must be equal for processing to continue.

The second concern for the analyst is to identify all fields necessary to reconstruct the current versions of critical application files. Critical files are those that are necessary to insure continued operation of the application and the business function served. Included are files necessary to recreate business activity and to satisfy business, legal, and regulatory requirements.

Backup files are used to reconstruct critical application files in case original files are destroyed or damaged.

Processing of sequentially organized files produces backup files automatically. Whenever a sequential master file is updated, for example, a completely new master file is created. The old master file then becomes the backup file. If the new master file is inadvertently destroyed, it can be recreated by reprocessing the transaction file against the old master file. Up to three or four generations of master files are typically maintained. These generations are called the **son, father, grandfather**, and **great-grandfather files**, from the most recent version to the oldest version of the file.

Direct-access files do not automatically produce backup copies because records are updated in place. The old master record is replaced by the new record following updating. In these cases, special backup procedures are required. Periodically, the master file is copied to a backup file. Frequency of backup will depend on the nature of processing and how much effort will be required to recreate the file. In some cases, a backup file is created for each alteration of the file. In some cases, the transaction record and the old master record are logged to a backup file. In other cases, transaction records are logged to a file and the master file is copied periodically. If the master file or any of its records are destroyed, it can be brought forward to current status by rerunning the transactions against the latest backup copy of the file.

Backup files and recovery procedures should be reviewed and checked periodically. If these reviews are not performed, it is possible that laxity has made the procedures unworkable. The company could actually have a false sense of security rather than a backup and recovery plan.

Documentation Controls

All procedures associated with computer information systems should be documented. There are, basically, four major types of documentation—system, program, operation, and user. System and program documentation are maintained within the CIS organization for use in system maintenance. Operations documentation is maintained in the computer operations area to describe all operating procedures. Finally, user documentation guides the users in how to run the system and make use of its results.

All documentation should be updated to reflect current procedures each time changes are made. This text has emphasized many times, that computer information systems are dynamic. Change is a regular occurrence during the useful life of a computer information system. If documentation is not updated to reflect changes, it becomes increasingly likely that erroneous processing will take place. People may follow written instructions that are no longer appropriate. Thus, documentation should be current at all times. Current documentation should be distributed and its use should be enforced as part of the operational procedures that apply to every system.

System development and maintenance projects are designed to provide the basic documentation essential to computer information systems. Thus, it should be part of every project to make sure that documentation is current. As a tool for achieving this, a historic library of documentation in all versions should be maintained. It becomes possible, then, to check copies within the operations center to be sure that current versions are in use.

Organizational Controls

A major technique for protecting the integrity and reliability of computer information systems is the **separation of duties** for CIS personnel. The principle of separation is straightforward: no one individual should have access to, or know enough about, a system to process data in an unauthorized way. This principle applies both during the development and in the ongoing use of a system. System analysis and programming assignments should be divided among a number of individuals. Assignments should be monitored so that combinations of people who have access to major parts of the system do not draw repeated assignments together.

Operationally, no individuals should have full access to an entire system. Thus, it is a common protective measure that programmers are not allowed to run production programs on a computer or to operate the applications they have written. Further, within an operations center, the person who has access to the computer mainframe should, if possible, be restricted from use of the data library or from control over large amounts of assets. An important line of protection lies in separating data resources from the temptations that are basic to human nature.

RESPONSIBILITY FOR DEFINING CONTROLS

Users have a major responsibility for defining the controls required in the system. The user is most familiar with the operation of the system and potential problem areas especially those based on past experience. Since the users will be charged with applying many of the controls after the new system has been implemented, it is all the more important to have strong user input in the definition of those controls.

Despite the desirability of heavy user involvement in the definition of controls, as systems have become more sophisticated the control area has become a speciality in its own right. A good systems analyst must be well versed in basic control techniques. The analyst bears ultimate responsibility for designing controls into the new system, calling on specialists when necessary.

Walkthroughs are discussed in an earlier chapter as a means of assuring the correctness of system products. **Design audit walkthroughs** involving users, analysts, and CIS quality assurance specialists provide an effective means of identifying deficiencies in control design. A series of walkthroughs at multiple levels, from overall system flow to detailed manual or computer processes, should be scheduled to evaluate controls.

CASE ILLUSTRATION

Several of the controls just discussed can be illustrated through a simple case. The following paragraphs describe the APPLY PAYMENT process in a credit card billing system. Figure 17-1 shows the part of Diagram 0 that relates to the APPLY PAYMENT process. The partitioning of this process is shown in Figure 17-2. All cash adjustments for a day are batched (Process 6.2). Payment transactions are grouped into batches of about 50 to 100 (Process 6.1). An adding machine tape is run on the amount field for each transaction in the batch (Process 6.4). The batch ticket contains the date, batch number and type, and batch total. These data are then entered in the DAILY BATCH/DEPOSIT LOG. See Figure 17-3.

After keying all batches for the day, enter the edit-update run (Processes 6.6 and 6.7). The annotated system flowchart corresponding to this run is shown in Figure 17-4. Note that a batch of transactions is considered to be in error if any of the individual transactions contains an invalid field or if the batch

Figure 17.1.   Portion of Diagram 0 covering the APPLY PAYMENT process of a credit card billing system.

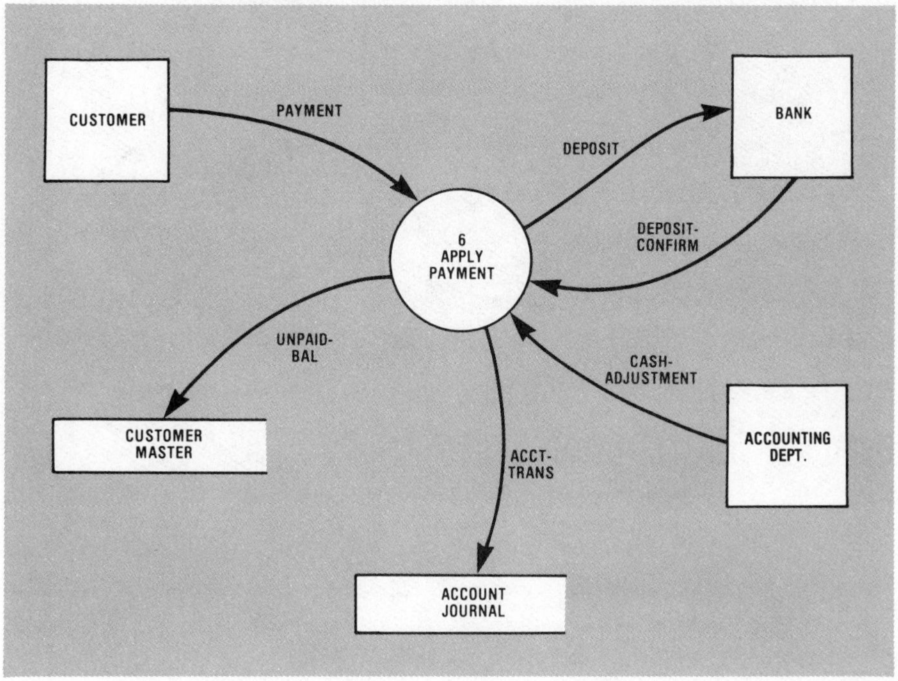

Figure 17.2. *Diagram 6 for the credit card billing system, covering the APPLY PAYMENT processing.*

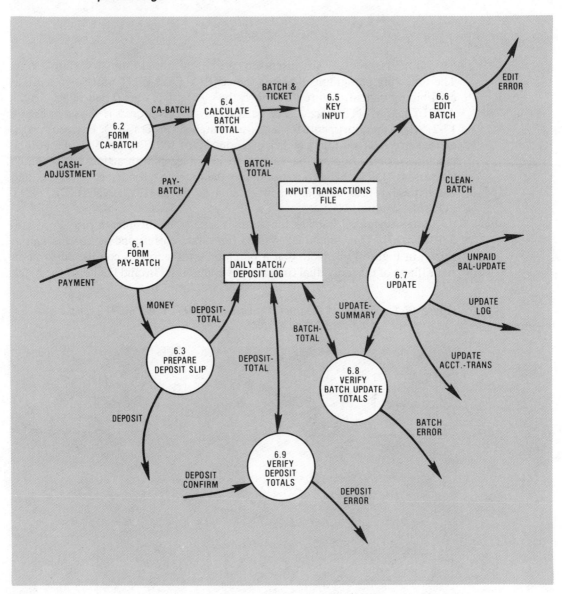

DAILY BATCH/DEPOSIT LOG

DATE	BATCH NUMBER	BATCH TYPE	BATCH TOTAL		VERIFY UPDATE	VERIFY DEPOSIT	COMMENTS
5-5-90	1	P	2816	43	JR		
	2	CA	100	00	JR		
	3	P	3039	08	JR		
	4	P	1887	76	JR		
		TOTAL	7843	27			
		DEPOSIT	7743	27		JR	
5-6-90	1	P	3142	18	JR		
	2	P	2503	25			Batch total error
	3	P	2792	12	JR		
	4	P	2917	63	JR		
	5	P	1131	73	JR		
	6	CA	76	84			Batch total error
		TOTAL	12563	75			
		DEPOSIT	12486	91			

total on the card for the batch ticket does not equal the total computed as each of the error report transactions is edited. If the batch is in error, it is rejected. The billing clerk must then locate the error(s) by referring to the transaction documents, adding machine tape, and input transaction file. The entire batch must then be resubmitted after all errors have been corrected.

Note that when clean batches complete the update, a brief UP-DATE SUMMARY report is produced, showing the total dollars credited, by batch. These totals are verified against the DAILY BATCH/DEPOSIT LOG by the billing clerk (Process 6.8).

Figure 17.4. *System flowchart for APPLY PAYMENT processing under new credit card billing system.*

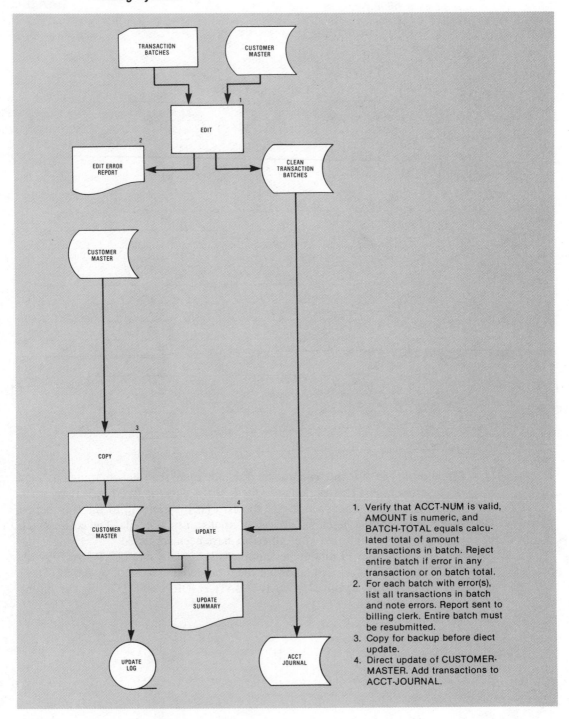

1. Verify that ACCT-NUM is valid, AMOUNT is numeric, and BATCH-TOTAL equals calculated total of amount transactions in batch. Reject entire batch if error in any transaction or on batch total.
2. For each batch with error(s), list all transactions in batch and note errors. Report sent to billing clerk. Entire batch must be resubmitted.
3. Copy for backup before diect update.
4. Direct update of CUSTOMER-MASTER. Add transactions to ACCT-JOURNAL.

SUMMARY

Controls are functions designed to build quality into a computer information system. Controls provide assurance that standards of completeness and accuracy are enforced for each individual record or group of business transactions. Specific needs met by controls include accuracy, integrity, reliability, and confidentiality.

Controls must be applied at every stage of system operation—including input, processing, output, and file storage. Types of controls include access controls, source document controls, data entry controls, processing controls, output controls, file controls, documentation controls, and organizational controls. Each of these types of controls is described and illustrated.

Backup files should be maintained for all critical files within the system. Up to three or four generations of master files are typically maintained. These generations are called the son, father, grandfather, and great-grandfather files.

Backup files and recovery procedures should be reviewed and checked periodically.

All procedures associated with data processing systems should be documented. If documentation is not updated to reflect changes, the likelihood increases continually that erroneous processing will take place.

A major technique for protecting the integrity and reliability of computer information system files is the separation of duties for CIS personnel. No one individual should have access to, or know enough about, a system to process data in an unauthorized way. Operationally, no individuals should have full access to an entire system.

Major responsibility for defining controls should be assumed by the users, who are most familiar with the operation of the system and the potential problems. Also, once a new system is operational, users will have primary responsibility for applying controls. Systems analysts support control definition efforts with expert advice and by leading walkthroughs that help to assure the acceptability of a system's end products.

KEY TERMS

1. controls
2. accuracy
3. integrity
4. security
5. confidentiality
6. access control
7. source document control
8. data entry controls
9. processing controls
10. batch control
11. output control
12. file controls
13. documentation controls
14. organizational controls
15. control totals
16. hash totals
17. monetary totals
18. quantity totals
19. header record
20. edit run
21. unique transaction codes
22. nondisplay fields
23. transaction log
24. trailer record

25. exception reports
26. numeric field test
27. alphabetic field test
28. sign test
29. nondisplay functions
30. range test
31. reasonableness test
32. category test
33. table lookup
34. check digits
35. encryption

36. restricted functions
37. signal scrambling
38. audit trail
39. checkpoints
40. backup files
41. design audit walkthroughs
42. son file
43. father file
44. grandfather file
45. separation of duties

REVIEW/DISCUSSION QUESTIONS

1. Define the term *integrity* and explain why it is important for a CIS data base to have integrity.
2. Access controls protect data resources. List four access controls.
3. Describe the purpose of a transaction log.
4. Define and give examples of the three types of input controls.
5. Define encryption and give an example of a CIS where it would be used.
6. Describe the process and purpose of doing file backup. Is the process different for sequential and direct access files? If yes, how?
7. Who should have the major responsibility for defining system controls? Explain.
8. Explain the check-digit method for error control.
9. Define and explain how an audit trail would be employed in a CIS.
10. What is the difference, if any, between a monetary total and a hash total.

18

Software Testing

Learning Objectives

On completing reading and other learning assignments for this chapter, you should be able to:

- Describe the nature of testing and the rationale for conducting software tests.
- Describe the processes of white-box testing, black-box testing, and error guessing, and explain how each may be applied in testing modules.
- Tell what types of errors are sought, what principles are applied, and what types of data are employed in unit testing.
- Generate appropriate test cases for white- and black-box techniques given a module specification.
- Describe incremental and nonincremental integration testing and describe how incremental integration testing may be conducted in either a top-down or a bottom-up sequence.
- State the criteria applied in function testing.

NATURE OF TESTING

Software testing is a process for executing a program with the intent to cause and discover errors. This purpose contrasts with the common misconception that the goal of testing is to prove that a program works correctly. Just the opposite is true: the goal of testing is (1) to force a program to work incorrectly, (2) to discover the causes of these errors, and (3) to revise the program code to eliminate errors. The objective is failure, not proof that a program works. A program can work perfectly under ideal circumstances and still produce incorrect results under unforeseen conditions.

Putting it another way, testing is a destructive process. A successful test destroys the image of invincibility that people may have had for a program. However, having discovered conditions under which programs can fail, the project team can devise constructive solutions to improve software quality.

At the same time, a rule of reasonableness should prevail. Just as it is impossible to design a piece of software to meet all contingencies, foreseen and unforeseen, so also is it impossible to design tests that can cause all the unforeseen processing problems a program can encounter during its entire useful life. Therefore, part of the challenge of testing design lies in establishing practical limits on the amount of testing to be done and the costs to be borne for this function. Consequently, to make testing as productive as possible, strategies are needed to ensure identification of the errors most likely to occur.

Testing provides a final measure of quality assurance for a software product during the latter phases of the systems development life cycle. As a quality assurance measure, testing, in turn, is a final step in a series of checkpoints applied to assure the quality of software development.

For example, during earlier analysis-related activities in systems development, systems specifications and any programming specifications that evolve from them are reviewed carefully. The purpose of these reviews is to ascertain that the logical and physical requirements placed upon systems components are correct, realistic, and able to be implemented to produce quality products that meet user needs.

During design-related activities of the systems development life cycle, the structured methodologies described earlier in this text are applied as quality assurance techniques. By following structured approaches to software, the designers provide some built-in checking and validation that the designs are sound and will result in quality programs. In addition, design activities should include systematic walkthroughs — step-by-step reviews of documentation end products that ultimately will be used as a basis for software development.

During the implementation phase of a project, there is continued use of structured methodologies and walkthroughs as quality assurance techniques. For example, structured programming adds a new dimension of quality assurance, as does the desk checking of program code. Finally, software testing involves actually running the programs on computers using test data.

In general, testing begins with the development of a high level **test plan**. An overall management-level document is created to delineate the scope of the testing project and identify the components of the system to be tested, by whom, and within what time frame. This high-level test blueprint should be developed as soon as possible after a decision to implement the project is made in the analysis and general design phase of development. Eventually, individual test plans must be created for each of the system components, such as modules or programs. These specific plans can be developed during detailed design development activities. Such test plans include the items to be tested, individual **test cases**, and expected results from the execution of the test cases. Once specific test plans are complete, test data can be created and collected. Ideally, such test data will include the hypothetical data generated by the strategies discussed later, as well as actual production files and situations. Once individual system components are available (i.e., coded), tests may be performed according to the test plans. The results of each test case are then compared to the expected results, and errors can be corrected where necessary. Collecting test data and performing tests occurs during the implementation phase activities.

LEVELS OF TESTING

Testing of application software occurs broadly at five levels, unit testing, integration testing, function testing, system testing, and acceptance testing.

Unit Testing. **Unit testing**, or module testing, is applied to individual program modules. Tests determine whether the modules are logically and functionally sound. Unit testing is done by using the modules to process test data and examining the outputs to determine if expected results are obtained.

Integration Testing. **Integration testing** is applied to interfaces between modules. This type of testing is usually done in parallel with unit testing. That is, as individual units are tested and accepted, the modules then are executed in combinations to determine if the interfaces between them are workable and produce expected results. Integration testing examines the transfer of both data and control among modules in a program.

Function Testing. **Function testing**, or program testing, seeks to identify any variances between the results of program processing and the specifications for the programs as agreed upon and approved by their eventual users. Function testing concentrates upon the results of complete programs.

System Testing. **System testing** deals with the integration of a system, or an integrated group, of application programs with system software, hardware, peripherals, manual procedures, and any other system components. This category extends beyond the computer system to encompass all related procedures and processing. The purpose of system testing is to try out the system as an operational and functional entity. Thus, these tests check to see whether the training and reference manuals are adequate to cover instructions and operational problems that might arise. A system test simulates the actual operation of the entire system before its implementation. In effect, the system test is a preview of how the overall system will work. This testing, which includes throughput, capacity, timing, and backup and recovery procedures, is applied under control of the CIS operations personnel prior to turning the system over to the users.

Acceptance Testing. **Acceptance testing** is performed by the user. Such testing occurs immediately prior to operational status. In effect, an acceptance test is a dress rehearsal to be sure that the users are ready to bring the new system into operation and use it for ongoing production. As implied by its name, acceptance testing is the users' final opportunity before installation to accept or reject the newly developed system as a viable solution to their computing requirements.

The process followed in testing modules, programs, and systems is in the inverse order of the sequence followed in the development of these components. The relationship between the testing and development of system components is represented in Figure 18-1. As shown, the progression of work in systems development moves from systems analysis, to systems design, to software design, to program design, and to module design. The actual testing of the performance of these various system components moves in the other direction—unit testing, then integration testing, then program or function testing, then system testing, and finally acceptance testing.

Prior to actual testing at any given level, a set of test plans, specifications, and data is prepared. A test plan details each condition the system component must be able to process correctly. At the module, integration, and program levels, a test plan documents actual data that must be processed. Thus test files are developed that contain the conditions specified on the test plan for the system component. For each condition to be tested, expected results are listed; and eventually the actual module or program performance will be noted. A test plan for system or acceptance testing must naturally contain more information

Figure 18.1. **Relationships between systems development and testing activities.**

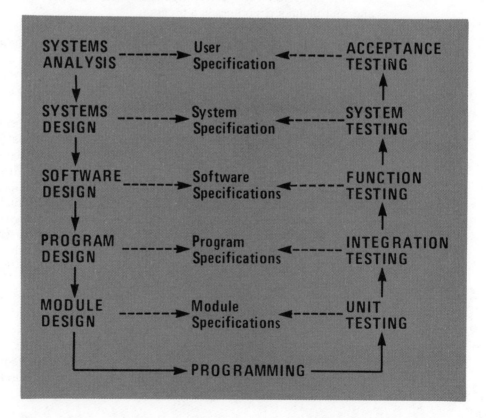

than test conditions contained in a test file. Tests at this level will simulate conditions of actual system operation and thus incorporate procedural aspects of system functioning. The general formats for system and acceptance test plans are similar to those of modules and programs; however, the conditions to be tested will contain procedural as well as data test criteria.

Program Testing Is Expensive and Requires at Least as Much Talent as Program Creation

Several authors have delineated and described the most prominent software design and implementation errors. These are summarized below:

- Typographical errors where the syntax of a programming language statement has been incorrectly written by a programmer.
- Misinterpretation of language constructions by the programmer.
- Errors in developing the detailed logic to solve the problem.
- Algorithm approximations that provide insufficient accuracy or erroneous results for certain input variables.
- Singular or critical input values to a formula that may yield an unexpected result not anticipated in the program code.
- Data structure defects either in the data structure design specification or in the implementation of the specification.
- Misinterpretation of specifications.

Added to these possible errors is the problem that the software requirements may be erroneously, ambiguously, or imprecisely stated, so there is a wide spectrum of opportunity for the software development to go awry. Up to this time, the software development community has generally not been particularly effective in containing, unmasking, and rectifying errors before large-scale software systems are delivered for operational use.

The significance of verification and validation efforts, from a budgetary standpoint, may be seen in statistics on the most visible verification and validation activity—program testing. Fred Gruenberger qualitatively addresses the effort required to test a program, once it has been written, by contending that the intellectual effort required for testing approximates that which created it. This qualitative assessment is in concert with community experience on medium- to large-scale software systems where approximately 50 percent of the software budget goes to testing and integration. The following quotations on percentage of effort devoted to checkout and testing on these actual spaceborne and command-control projects have been reported:

SAGE	47%
NAVAL TACTICAL DATA SYSTEM	50%
GEMINI	47%
SATURN V	44%

Edward Yourdon furnishes an estimate that on the NASA Apollo project nearly 80 percent of the monies expended were devoted to testing. It was predicted that in the early 1980s the present 50 percent figure would increase as the amount of object code generated per line of source code produced by the programmer was amplified. In fact this did happen with the Space Shuttle project, checkout and testing of the software systems required 70 percent of the total effort while the original creation required only 30 percent. These figures illuminate the significance of one aspect of validation and verification in the software development process.

Software quality is approached by two distinct and complementary methodologies. The first is that of assuring that quality is initially built into the product. This involves emphasis on the early generation of a coherent, complete, unambiguous, and nonconflicting set of software requirements. Experience has shown that the most extensive cause of software delivered with inadequate performance, delivered late, or delivered in a cost overrun condition is an incomplete or inadequate requirements analysis. Implementation may then proceed by using organizational approaches that limit software complexity. Once the software has been initially coded, analysis and testing of the product, the second quality tool, are encountered. Testing is a diagnostic exercise that does not introduce quality into the product per se. It provides only a measure of the existing quality level, and it may identify the extent and location of the defects. Some explorations have been made into the use of error statistics derived from testing to predict subsequent software performance reliability. There is a bridge between the two software quality approaches. It concerns the concept that if an initial product can be produced with a high degree of clarity and design simplicity, it is amenable to more effective testing.

Fred Gruenberger, "Program Testing: The Historical Perspective," in *Program Test Methods,* ed. William C. Hetzel (Englewood Cliffs, NJ: Prentice-Hall, 1983).

Edward Yourdon, *Techniques of Program Structure and Design,* (Englewood Cliffs, NJ: Prentice-Hall, 1985).

TESTING STRATEGIES

As stated earlier, complex software, even when developed with rigorously structured design techniques, is difficult to test completely. It is simply impossible to foresee all the potential conditions arising in a dynamic user environment; and even if it were possible to do so, the time and costs of such efforts would be prohibitive. Thus it is not likely that a designer will be able to devise a set of test cases that completely exhaust all possible conditions under which the software might perform. Therefore it is the task of the designer to produce a set of test cases that will include the most likely type of operational conditions and those conditions that have proven to be most troublesome for software in the past. A number of strategies may be employed to systematically determine such test cases.

Depending upon the individual unit of software and the conditions under which that unit will be applied, an individualized testing strategy is devised and carried out. The purpose of such a strategy is systematically to define the test conditions necessary to find any weakness in either the internal structure or the functioning of the model. Remember, tests are performed to find errors, not to prove that the software works. Strategies, in turn, are formed through application of a combination of three approaches, or techniques. The three methods are white-box testing, black-box testing, and error guessing.

White-Box Testing. **White-box testing** considers the logic of modules as if the processor were clear, or transparent. Included are examinations of procedural details, tests covering the execution of all statements in the module, and tracing of all decision paths within the logic of an individual module. Note that white-box testing is carried out only at the module level. It would be virtually impossible to apply white-box testing to an entire program or system at one time. Even in a relatively simple application program, there could be literally millions of potential logic paths open to data being processed. Therefore, it would be impractical to attempt complete, exhaustive program testing at a white-box level. Instead, logic testing at the module level is combined with black-box testing to establish satisfaction with executions of modules and with interfaces among modules.

Black-Box Testing. **Black-box testing** is used to review module or program functions from the outside. As previously discussed, a black-box processor is one in which no knowledge of internal workings is assumed by users and observers. Black-box testing is based upon the external design specifications. For testing purposes, inputs and outputs are monitored, and judgments are reached on the basis of results. There is no concern in black-box testing with the internal logic of a module or program. Rather, the testing is applied to determine whether inputs are accepted as planned and outputs meet expectations.

As a general rule in black-box testing, there is no attempt to uncover all errors. The testing that would have to be applied simply would be too exhaustive because, given no knowledge of the logic of a program, it would be necessary to devise massive inputs to test for all possible logical processing paths. Then, it would be necessary to review massive outputs to compare results with expectations. Instead, it is more effective to combine black-box testing with a review of program logic through white-box techniques.

Error guessing. **Error guessing** simply implies that a list of potential troublesome areas is predictable (guessable), and that test cases may be derived based upon that list. The success of this approach lies largely upon the experience and intuition of the individual tester. Without systematic methods such as white- and black-box strategies, error guessing is the only testing approach. Most often, error guessing alone will result in test cases that are inclusive, but not exhaustive, of those generated by the more systematic techniques.

The typical approach to the design of software testing, then, is to apply white-box testing selectively to evaluate program and module logic. Further black-box tests evaluate program and module functions. In general, white-box testing will supplement black-box testing. The module or program's function, or external purpose, is insured through black-box techniques, whereas white-box techniques insure that the underlying logic used to implement that function is error free. Once these systematic methods are employed, the list of troublesome areas generated by error guessing should be examined to insure a more complete test plan. Because exhaustive testing of all functions and logic paths is not feasible, the designer must decide what subset of all possible tests will uncover the greatest number of errors. As with other areas of systems development, test strategy development becomes largely a cost-benefit tradeoff.

UNIT (MODULE) TESTING

Since the underlying building block of the application software system is the individual module and since its functions and purpose are most precisely defined, the greatest amount of testing rigor should and can be at this level. Unit testing seeks to find errors within the logic and function of individual modules.

Most tests at the module level are applied to check the logic of the design and the logic paths within the coding. Logical checking is accomplished through white-box testing. Thus, most testing of program modules is done through white-box techniques.

However, program modules do not exist as stand-alone software elements. Modules are interdependent; there must be processing interfaces among modules. These interfaces, in turn, are tested most effectively through black-box techniques because emphasis on the interface focuses on inputs and outputs. Thus, at the module testing level, it is a common practice to apply white-box testing supplemented with black-box methods at the entry and exit points of individual modules. Once systematic strategies, such as white- and black-box techniques, have been employed, a more intuitive, less systematic approach is in order, i.e., error guessing. One should examine the test cases generated through the systematic means to insure that the areas of high concern derived through error guessing have been included.

The challenge of unit testing, then, is to derive sets of test data that apply the required tests to individual modules. Not all tests must be applied to every module. Thus, in devising a testing plan, the idea is to determine which types of testing — white-box, black-box, or error guessing — are appropriate for a specific module, then to devise data that apply to these error situations.

Deriving Test Data from White-Box Testing Methods

White-box testing methods are internal module-testing approaches and thus test the internal module design or structure. White-box testing methods include statement coverage, decision-condition coverage, multiple decision–condition coverage, and exhaustive combination decision–condition coverage.

Statement Coverage. The **statement-coverage testing method** is very simple. It involves devising a set of test data that will execute every statement in a module. Figure 18-2 illustrates the decision-control structures and coding segments of MOD-A. A statement-coverage testing method would devise a set of test data to execute every line of code in this module at least once. MOD-A contains four separate decision control structures, two repetitions (DO WHILEs) and two selections (IF THEN ELSEs). These decision control structures are based upon five conditions. A condition is simply a logic test that results in a true or false state of that condition. For example, the second DO WHILE in MOD-A contains two conditions and thus may read DO WHILE (TYPE = R and AMOUNT > 100). Assume for this example that CON-

Figure 18.2.   Control structure and code segments for MOD-A.

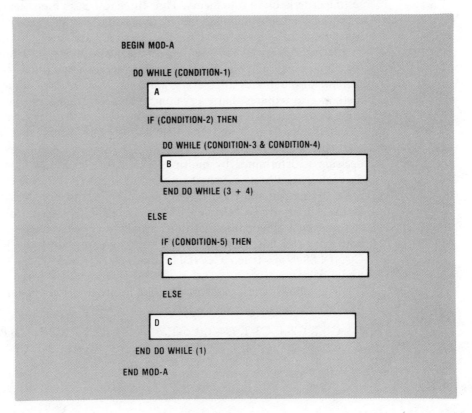

DITION-1 through CONDITION-5 for these control structures are mutually exclusive, that is, they are based upon five different and independent module variables. Sequential code segments (without control structures) are illustrated by code blocks A through D.

Whatever data are necessary to force the desired state of each condition must be provided by each test case. For example, if CONDITION-1 is actually MORE-RECORDS, then in order to execute the true state of CONDITION-1, an input test case must be provided in which MORE-RECORDS is true, that is there are some records supplied. The following test cases would thus insure the execution of all the statements in MOD-A:

1. C1-T (CONDITION-1 = true), C2-T, C3-T, C4-T, C5-T
2. C1-T, C2-F, C3-T, C4-T, C5-T
3. C1-T, C2-F, C3-T, C4-T, C5-F

Test case 1 will force the execution of all the control structures and code segments except the second IF THEN ELSE and code segments C and D. Test case 2 will force the execution of code segment C. Test case 3 will force the execution of code segment D. These test cases account for all lines of code or statements in MOD-A. The logical paths represented by this set of test data are illustrated in Figure 18-3. Three logic paths through this module are required to meet the testing criteria of all statements. Thus three test cases are necessary to force the execution of those required paths. (Note that for all practical purposes and assuming correct logic for MOD-A, C3 and C4 are irrelevant when C2 is false. Similarly, C5 is irrelevant when C2 is true. More about this later.)

Decision-Condition Coverage. The **decision-condition coverage testing method** also requires that every statement be executed at least once. This method also requires that every control structure decision execute its true and false state at least once. For example, in Figure 18-2, test cases that include CONDITION-1 = true and CONDITION-1 = false would insure that the true and false states of the first DO WHILE decision would be executed. If a decision is determined by multiple conditions, each condition within such a decision must also be executed with both its true and its false outcomes at least once. In this example, there is only one multiple condition decision — the second DO WHILE (with CONDITION-3 and CONDITION-4) control structure. Thus to insure that all conditions within this decision be executed at least once with both true and false outcomes, test cases that include CONDITION-3 = true, CONDITION-4 = true, CONDITION-3 = false, and CONDITION-4 = false would be necessary.

The following test cases would thus insure decision-condition coverage for MOD-A:

1. C1-T, C2-T, C3-T, C4-T, C5-T
2. C1-T, C2-F, C3-T, C4-T, C5-T
3. C1-T, C2-F, C3-T, C4-T, C5-F
4. C1-F, C2-F, C3-T, C4-T, C5-F
5. C1-T, C2-T, C3-F, C4-F, C5-T

Figure 18.3. Statement coverage logical test paths for MOD-A.

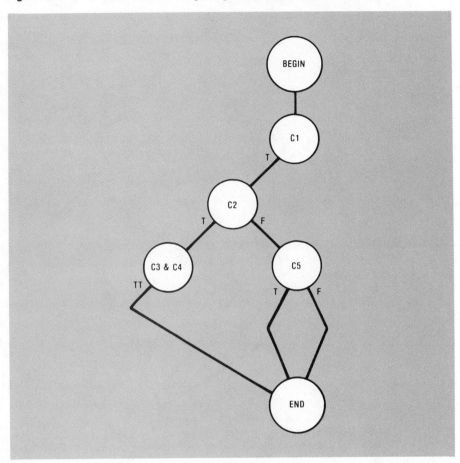

Test cases 1, 2, and 3 insure that all lines of code, the true states of C1, C2, C3, C4, C5 and the false states of C2, C5 are executed. Test case 4 is necessary to execute the false state of C1. Test case 5 is necessary to execute the false states of C3 and C4. Thus all decisions and conditions take on both their true states and their false states at least once. The logical paths represented by these test cases is illustrated in Figure 18-4.

Multiple Decision–Condition Coverage. **Multiple decision–condition coverage testing method** is a still more exhaustive testing technique of module logic. This testing method extends decision-condition coverage to include all combinations of conditions within decisions. For example, MOD-A contains a multiple condition (C3, C4) decision. All true-false combinations of these multiple condition decision must be examined as well as simple decision-condition coverage

Figure 18.4.   Decision-condition coverage logical test paths for MOD-A.

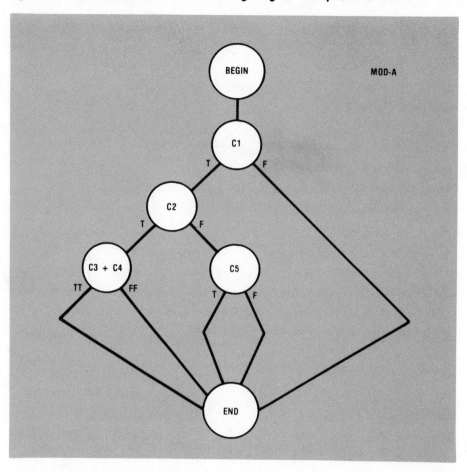

to insure multiple coverage. As illustrated by the logical paths shown in Figure 18-5, the test cases necessary to insure multiple coverage for MOD-A would be

1.   Cl-T, C2-T, C3-T, C4-T, C5-T
2.   Cl-T, C2-F, C3-T, C4-T, C5-T
3.   Cl-T, C2-F, C3-T, C4-T, C5-F
4.   Cl-F, C2-F, C3-T, C4-T, C5-F
5.   Cl-T, C2-T, C3-F, C4-F, C5-T
6.   Cl-T, C2-T, C3-T, C4-F, C5-T
7.   Cl-T, C2-T, C3-F, C4-T, C5-T

All logical paths through the module are plotted, given that each true state and each false state of all conditions and all combinations of multiple conditions are executed. Test cases are then derived to execute each path and multiple-condition combination. Thus test cases 6 and 7 are added to those derived from decision-condition coverage in order to insure the execution of all combinations of the multiple condition (3) C4. (Note, it is assumed that the states of the other conditions are irrelevant for a CONDITION-1 = false.)

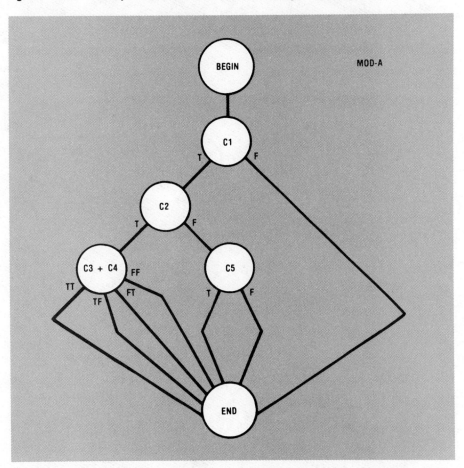

Figure 18.5. Multiple Decision-condition coverage logical paths for MOD-A.

Exhaustive Combination Decision–Condition Coverage. Finally the most exhaustive set of test cases would examine all possible combinations of conditions, whether in single or multiple condition decisions in the **exhaustive combination decision–condition coverage testing** method. For example, MOD-A contains five total conditions, three of which are in single condition decisions (C1, C2, and C5), the other two being in one multiple-condition decision (C3 and C4). To exhaust all potential logical combinations of conditions, all possible combinations of the five conditions must be derived, which, in this example is 2x2x2x2x2 or 32 (five total conditions each with 2 potential outcomes) as illustrated in Figure 18-6. This is the most exhaustive and rigorous examination of module logic or internal structure. The derived test cases for this approach would be

1. C1-T, C2-T, C3-T, C4-T, C5-T
2. C1-T, C2-T, C3-T, C4-T, C5-F
3. C1-T, C2-T, C3-T, C4-F, C5-T
4. C1-T, C2-T, C3-T, C4-F, C5-F

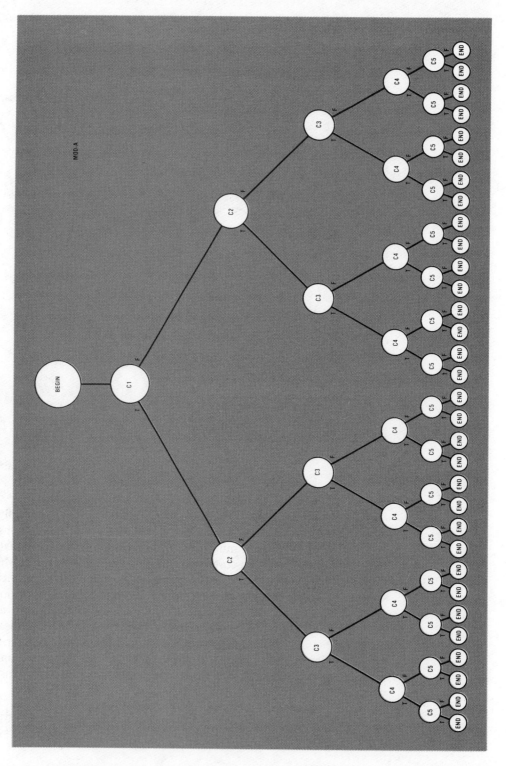

Figure 18.6. All possible combinations of conditions for MOD-A.

Part 6   Systems Design: Assuring Quality

5. C1-T, C2-T, C3-F, C4-T, C5-T	19. C1-F, C2-T, C3-T, C4-F, C5-T
6. C1-T, C2-T, C3-F, C4-T, C5-F	20. C1-F, C2-T, C3-T, C4-F, C5-F
7. C1-T, C2-T, C3-F, C4-F, C5-T	21. C1-F, C2-T, C3-F, C4-T, C5-T
8. C1-T, C2-T, C3-F, C4-F, C5-F	22. C1-F, C2-T, C3-F, C4-T, C5-F
9. C1-T, C2-F, C3-T, C4-T, C5-T	23. C1-F, C2-T, C3-F, C4-F, C5-T
10. C1-T, C2-F, C3-T, C4-T, C5-F	24. C1-F, C2-T, C3-F, C4-F, C5-F
11. C1-T, C2-F, C3-T, C4-F, C5-T	25. C1-F, C2-F, C3-T, C4-T, C5-T
12. C1-T, C2-F, C3-T, C4-F, C5-F	26. C1-F, C2-F, C3-T, C4-T, C5-F
13. C1-T, C2-F, C3-F, C4-T, C5-T	27. C1-F, C2-F, C3-T, C4-F, C5-T
14. C1-T, C2-F, C3-F, C4-T, C5-F	28. C1-F, C2-F, C3-T, C4-F, C5-F
15. C1-T, C2-F, C3-F, C4-F, C5-T	29. C1-F, C2-F, C3-F, C4-T, C5-T
16. C1-T, C2-F, C3-F, C4-F, C5-F	30. C1-F, C2-F, C3-F, C4-T, C5-F
17. C1-F, C2-T, C3-T, C4-T, C5-T	31. C1-F, C2-F, C3-F, C4-F, C5-T
18. C1-F, C2-T, C3-T, C4-T, C5-F	32. C1-F, C2-F, C3-F, C4-F, C5-F

You might ask why it is necessary to test combinations which seem irrelevant. For instance, isn't including test cases 31 and 32 redundant? After all, once CONDITION-1 = false, none of these other multiple combinations are even potential module paths. Also, why be concerned about C5 at all, once the decision with C2 is determined to be true. These combinations are ordered in parallel, not sequence, in the module control structure and thus shouldn't be affected. However, this *shouldn't* is exactly the point! Remember the object is to break the module, not prove that it works. These are the very kinds of errors that creep up as bugs in program after program, that is, situations that "shouldn't" or "couldn't" happen but are none the less possible. Until the module has been tested for these combinations, how can you be certain that these combinations won't have some destructive effect upon its functioning? The logic from which the test cases are derived is merely the module specification. Testing will determine how the module *actually* performs.

As you can see, this type of testing is extremely time consuming. Even the simplest module (only 5 conditions) requires many test cases. Also, keep in mind that this series comprises only the white-box tests of the module logic, not the black-box, external tests. Once module size and complexity reach a point where time and budget will not allow complete possible-condition combinations in white-box testing, careful application of a different level of white-box coverage will have to suffice. This is another reason why module designs should be kept small, with relatively few conditions or decisions.

Deriving Test Data from Black-Box Testing Methods

Black-box testing strategies focus on the module from an external viewpoint. Rather than simulating the internal logical paths or condition combinations, this method is concerned primarily with potential module or program inputs and outputs. There are two common types of black-box testing, boundary analysis and equivalence partitioning.

Boundary Analysis. **Boundary analysis testing** concentrates on data input to or output from a module as either a range or an ordered set of values.

Boundary analysis involves investigating input and output situations at the high and low extremes or boundaries of expected data. Usually, however, data are expected only within a range of feasible data. Feasible data are those that in any way possible may be presented for processing to the system component in question.

Ranges of Values. **Ranges of values** are a consequence of most arithmetic functions applied by programs. For example, if an instruction calls for multiplying two three-digit integers, it can be predicted that the feasible range of values for the derived answer will be anywhere from $-999,999$ through $999,999$. The expected range of values must fall within the feasible range. For such an instruction, the ranges of data values can apply to both multipliers, as well as the answer.

Thus, the procedure in testing the range of values is to look at each data item that may be presented to a module or program and identify whether its values are expected to vary within some range; then to devise data that test the ability of the program to handle these ranges. This selection, which should be done systematically rather than at random, does not require testing for all possible values. Instead, only the boundaries of the ranges that can result should be identified and tested. For any range test, four values can be identified:

- Value at the lower boundary of the range.
- Value at the upper boundary of the range.
- Value that is less than the lower boundary.
- Value that is greater than the upper boundary.

As a simple example, consider a module to calculate GROSS-PAY for an hourly payroll, as illustrated in Figure 18-7. Ranges would be set for expected values of the lowest number of hours that a person could work in any given week and for the highest number of hours. For example, the expected number of hours might be between 8 and 80, with the feasible range for a positive two-integer numeric variable between 0 and 99. Thus boundary analysis test cases for the range of expected values of HOURS-WORKED might be 7, 8, 80, and 81, assuming minimal increments of 1 hour. These are the values at and immediately above and below the range of expected values. Similarly, the expected hourly PAY-RATE might be $4.00 at the low side and $20.00 at the high side. Boundary analysis test cases for hourly PAY-RATE would thus be $3, $4, $20, and $21, assuming minimum increments of $1. The following values would be needed in test cases to provide *input* boundary analysis for MOD-A:

HOURS-WORKED = 7, PAY-RATE = $ 3 → GROSS-PAY = $ 21.
HOURS-WORKED = 8, PAY-RATE = $ 4 → GROSS-PAY = $ 32.
HOURS-WORKED = 80, PAY-RATE = $20 → GROSS-PAY = $1600.
HOURS-WORKED = 81, PAY-RATE = $21 → GROSS-PAY = $1701.

The output value, GROSS-PAY, therefore would have an expected range of values from $32 (8 HOURS-WORKED × $4 PAY-RATE) to $1600 (80 HOURS-WORKED × $20 PAY-RATE). The next feasible low boundary value for

Figure 18.7. Module to calculate gross pay.

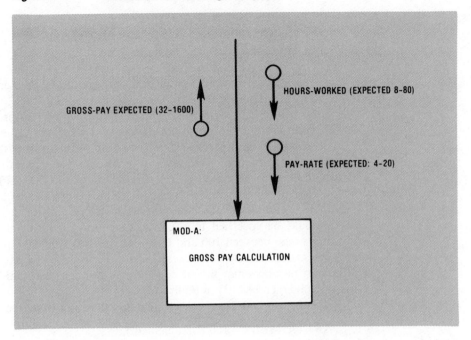

GROSS-PAY under $32 would be $28 (7 HOURS-WORKED × $4 PAY-RATE). The next feasible high boundary value for GROSS-PAY would be $1620 (81 HOURS-WORKED × $20 PAY-RATE). Thus to simulate boundary analysis test coverage for GROSS-PAY, test cases might be required that would attempt to create GROSS-PAY of $28, $32, $1600 and $1620.

These would be the necessary *output* test cases. Meeting the required input-output cases would therefore create a set of input test cases to produce boundary analysis coverage for the input and output for MOD-A:

HOURS-WORKED = 7, PAY-RATE = $ 3 → GROSS-PAY = $ 21.
HOURS-WORKED = 7, PAY-RATE = $ 4 → GROSS-PAY = $ 28.
HOURS-WORKED = 8, PAY-RATE = $ 4 → GROSS-PAY = $ 32.
HOURS-WORKED = 80, PAY-RATE = $20 → GROSS-PAY = $1600.
HOURS-WORKED = 81, PAY-RATE = $20 → GROSS-PAY = $1620.
HOURS-WORKED = 81, PAY-RATE = $21 → GROSS-PAY = $1701.

The test cases include the expected range for both input and output situations.

Ordered Sets of Values. The organization (or lack thereof) of data within files or tables into ordered sets also may be critically important to the execution of a program. For example, in a sequential master file, it is important that records be processed in key order. The same may be true within tables. For modules that include the handling of sequential files or table data, it is necessary to test the ordering of records. Tests are applied to

- Select the first element in an ordered set
- Select the last element in an ordered set
- Select an item known to be missing
- Select excessive cases, both high and low

If a module executes a table search, test data should be devised that cause the instructions to search for the first and last values in that table, to search for an item known to be missing from the table, and to attempt to process subscripts that are both lower and higher than the range of subscript values for that table.

For example, an inventory file may be read into a table within a module in order to expedite numerous searches of the inventory. Assume that the inventory file would contain as many as 500 part numbers and 500 part records. Also assume that part numbers may range in value from 100 to 600. Thus, a table similar to Figure 18-8 might be created to contain these records. The table length would be specified to accommodate up to 500 members and have a subscript range between 100 and 600. Part records would be positioned in the table by part number so that the table could be searched by part number. Some of the part numbers may not be currently active, causing blank table members such as table member 103 in Figure 18-8.

Thus the test cases necessary to test this situation would be

1. PART-NUMBER = 100 (first element).
2. PART-NUMBER = 600 (last element).
3. PART-NUMBER = 103 (item known to be missing).
4. PART-NUMBER = 099 (excessive case — low).
5. PART-NUMBER = 601 (excessive case — high).

Equivalence Partitioning. **Equivalence partitioning testing** focuses primarily on data presented to a module or program either as categories of values or as discrete values. The idea behind equivalence partitioning is to group data values into categorical or discrete types to apply appropriate testing.

Data for testing categories of values are applied within modules that use specific types, or attributes, of values within fields. In such situations, data presented can be either one of the expected types of values or one of the unexpected types.

To illustrate, consider a module in which an on-line user must enter an alphabetic field in response to a request for a customer name. For testing purposes, the actual name entered is not important. Rather, the test is applied to determine whether the module can handle both alphabetic and nonalphabetic data. A representative value would be any combination of valid alphabetic characters within the size parameters of the field. A nonrepresentative value would be any other combination of characters. Thus, in testing a module that incorporates data with certain attributes, it is sufficient to present a single representative test value and a single nonrepresentative value.

Test data also must be generated for data items that will take on selected discrete values. In these cases, it is necessary to supply test values that match

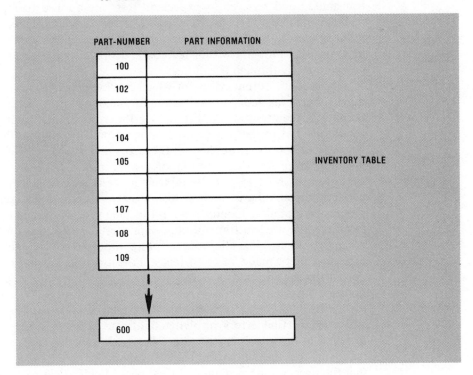

identically all expected execution values and also to provide a test value that is unexpected.

For example, consider an update module that accepts transaction records identified for addition, change, and deletion. In this instance, at least one addition, change, and delete transaction code should be supplied for testing, along with a code value that is invalid. In other words, all valid data values and a single invalid value make up the test data.

Tests for discrete values are applied in checking the branching results in selection control structures. They provide an indication that processing paths exist for all expected values and that the module can handle unexpected values.

Deriving Test Data from Error Guessing

Guessing where errors are likely to occur is often a good strategy. Experience has shown that errors have traditionally tended to cluster around several common troublesome module or program areas. White- and black-box methods are merely a systematic formalization of this realization. Some of these areas of high concern have been input-output errors, data structure errors, arithmetic errors, comparison errors, and control logic errors.

Input-Output Errors. If external files are to be read into or written out of a module, **input-output error testing** is applied to make sure that all records are transmitted and received as expected. Tests are applied to record attributes, including numbers of fields. In addition, errors are sought in record formatting, in the organization of files, and in the use of keys. The idea is to make sure that keys are used properly within records and that files are structured and referenced correctly through use of keys.

Other input-output errors for which checking is done include proper procedures for opening and closing files and for handling errors identified on input or output. Further, tests are applied to look for errors in the flagging of end-of-file conditions and in the proper processing of null, or empty, files. With direct access of files, tests are applied for the errors that would occur if a record with a matching key is found, or not found, as appropriate.

Data Structure Errors. **Data structure tests** seek to discover errors in the handling or building of data elements that are defined and generated within processing modules. Examples would include program-generated tables or interim records used in transforming data. Tests are applied for correctness of table definitions, including subscripting procedures and table sizes. Other checks would be made for consistency in the use of names, for proper initialization in the use accumulators and counters, and for completeness of specifications for data items.

Arithmetic Errors. The results of calculation instructions within modules are tested to find errors involving failure to define properly all data items included in arithmetic instructions. For each data item, tests are applied to make sure that the data are in the proper mode for execution of the instructions, that the sizes of intermediate and final result fields are large enough to accommodate results of computations (eliminating the potential for errors through truncation), that computations are executed in the proper order to produce specified results, and that zero is not used as a divisor. (If division by zero is encountered, the program should have provision for handling this condition).

Comparison Errors. **Comparison error tests** look for errors involving presentation of data items of different modes or data types for comparison functions. The goal is to ensure that a program or module will not permit comparisons of alphabetic fields with numeric fields or among numeric fields of mixed modes. As with other error testing functions, the idea is to present such conditions to the system and to be sure that it can handle them and recover from any consequences. Another comparison test deals with the order of evaluation of relational operators in data comparisons. It can be difficult to be sure that such functions as multiple-nested comparisons are performed in the order intended unless systematically tested.

Control Logic Errors. A computer is a sequential machine. Thus, no special tests are needed for sequential control functions except that these be an appropriate sequence of module components to produce the expected results. However, specific tests should be applied to selections and repetitions, situations in which the natural processing sequence of the computer is altered. Many such **control logic errors** will be encountered using white-box techniques. For example, tests governing selections determine whether valid execution paths are established for all conditions to be tested and for all values of the data elements that are tested. Selection tests also ascertain that all branch points in selection functions are properly labeled and that there are exit points from all open paths.

For repetition control structures, one of the tests applied is to be sure that the loop index or subscript is initialized properly and incremented (and incremented properly) with each iteration of the loop. Tests also ascertain that end-of-loop flags are set, tested, and implemented properly to avoid closed-loop situations in which programs are hung up indefinitely. All subscript values within repetition structures should have subscript values within anticipated ranges.

Testing Checklist. In devising actual test data, it would be a good practice to prepare a checklist of the types of errors that can be made for the data in a given module. This checklist can become a matrix for determining which of the three types of test data described in this chapter can be used to search for the errors that can exist within program modules. Such a checklist may be useful in developing specific unit test plans. Not all items on the checklist are necessarily translated into test cases for a specific module because not all situations may apply to specific modules and some test cases may cover more than one item on the checklist. Table 18-1 may serve as a checklist in determining test cases for unit level testing.

It should also be noted that it is not necessary to perform tests within all modules that process the same data. Usually, edit modules perform many of the testing functions to ensure that only valid data are passed to processing routines. Therefore, unit tests can assume the existence of valid data within reasonable ranges and categories. Edit modules, on the other hand, should receive full tests of both valid and invalid data.

INTEGRATION TESTING

Program integration encompasses the procedures followed for connecting modules to form programs. **Integration testing** encompasses the exercise of these program connections to determine their soundness and workability. Thus, integration testing is applied to the interfaces between modules within any given application program.

Preferably, unit tests have been performed prior to integration testing so that integration testing can focus largely upon interface errors. This type of testing is applied to program segments in which control and data are passed from one module to another. A typical example involves the transfer of processing control from a module to a subroutine or subprogram. One objective of these tests is to determine that the arguments passed to the subroutine correspond with the parameters received. Tests are also applied to be sure of correspondence in the number of data fields, the attributes (type and size) of the data fields, and the order of transmission and receipt. Finally, since unit test data are presumably available, these unit test cases may be used to insure correct functioning of modules appropriately linked.

Table 18.1.   Testing checklist.

_____ White-box techniques
    _____ Statement coverage
        _____ All statements
    _____ Decision-condition coverage
        _____ All statements
        _____ True and false states of each decision
        _____ True and false states of each condition
    _____ Multiple decision-condition coverage
        _____ All statements
        _____ True and false states of each decision
        _____ True and false states of each condition
        _____ All combinations of multiple conditiond decisions
    _____ Exhaustive combination decision-condition coverage
        _____ All statements
        _____ True and false states of each decision
        _____ True and false states of each condition
        _____ All combinations of multiple condition decisions
        _____ All combinations of all conditions

_____ Black-box techniques
Boundary analysis
    _____ Range test
        _____ Value at the lower boundary of the range
        _____ Value at the upper boundary of the range
        _____ Value that is less than the lower boundary
        _____ Value that is greater than the upper boundary.
    _____ Ordering of records
        _____ Select the first element in an ordered set
        _____ Select the last element in an ordered set
        _____ Select an item known to be missing
        _____ Select excessive cases, both high and low
Equivalence partitioning
    _____ Categories of values
        _____ Select an item of the category
        _____ Select an item outside the category
    _____ Discrete values
        _____ Select an item for each discrete valid value
        _____ Select an item that is not one of the valid values

_____ Error guessing
    _____ Input-output
        _____ Proper file opening and closing routines
        _____ Proper definitions of files, records, and fields

Table 18.1. *Testing checklist (continued)*

_____ Proper use for keys for accessing and writing records

_____ Proper handling of end-of-file conditions

_____ Proper handling of input/output errors

_____ Data structures

_____ Proper definitions of table sizes and attributes

_____ Correct definitions and uses of search subscripts and indexes

_____ Consistent use of data names

_____ Proper intitializations of constants

_____ Proper initializations of accumulators and counters

_____ Proper format and attribute definitions of data items

_____ Arithmetic

_____ Proper size, type, precision of intermediate field results

_____ Proper size, type, and editing of final result fields

_____ Proper modes of data items involved in computations

_____ Proper sequencing of arithmetic operations

_____ Ability to handle division by zero

_____ Comparison

_____ Correspondence in attributes of data items to be compared/tested

_____ Proper order of comparisons in multiple AND and/or OR relations

_____ Control logic

_____ Provision for branching paths for all selection results

_____ Provision for common exit point from all selected paths

_____ Proper initialization and incrementation of loop subscripts

_____ Provision for exits from loops

Two approaches can be taken to integration testing:

- Modules can be added to one another for individual testing, possibly as new modules are written. This procedure is called **incremental testing**.
- All modules within a program can be developed first, then joined and tested as an entity. That is, all interfaces between modules are tested at one time for the entire program. This procedure is known as **nonincremental testing**.

Because nonincremental testing can be difficult, it is not recommended. If an interface problem does arise and multiple interfaces are tested in a single operation, it can be extremely tedious to pinpoint the exact location of the problem. By contrast, incremental testing has the effect of building quality into a program as it goes together. If any problems do develop, they can be identified and pinpointed specifically to known sets or groups of modules. To illustrate, if a new module is added to a group of modules that already have been tested and found to work satisfactorily, any execution problems must be either in the new module or in the interfaces between the new module and the previously tested modules.

Thus, incremental testing is the only method recommended and described in the presentations that follow. Two general methods can be used in applying incremental testing, top-down and bottom-up.

Top-Down Testing

Top-down testing is applied to modules from higher-level modules down through detailed modules. A top-down strategy is advisable when the greatest program complexity resides in the control and coordinating or central-transform modules. With this method, these modules will be tested first and most often.

Interface tests thus proceed between modules from top to bottom, following paths derived from the structure chart for the program. To illustrate top-down integration testing, consider the structure chart in Figure 18-9. This structure chart will be used as a model to demonstrate the course of top-down methods and the strategy involved.

Figure 18-10, based on the same program structure, shows how the top-down approach progresses. Figure 18-10(A) indicates that testing begins with the topmost module (A). Connections move from this module to modules at lower levels that have not yet been implemented. Therefore, the portions of the modules that will handle the interfaces are prepared and used in executing test data applied to the connections between Module A and its subordinate modules.

Figure 18.9.   Structure chart for program to be tested incrementally.

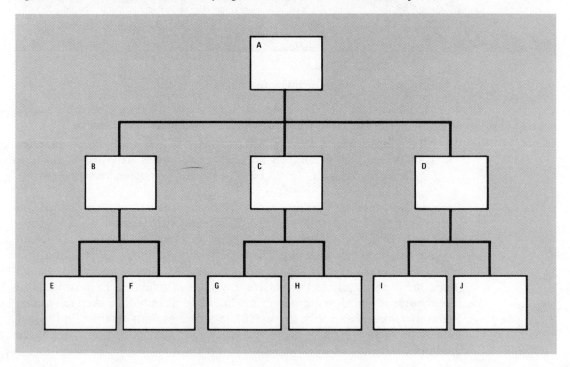

Part 6   Systems Design: Assuring Quality

Figure 18.10.   Possible testing pattern for top-down incremental testing.

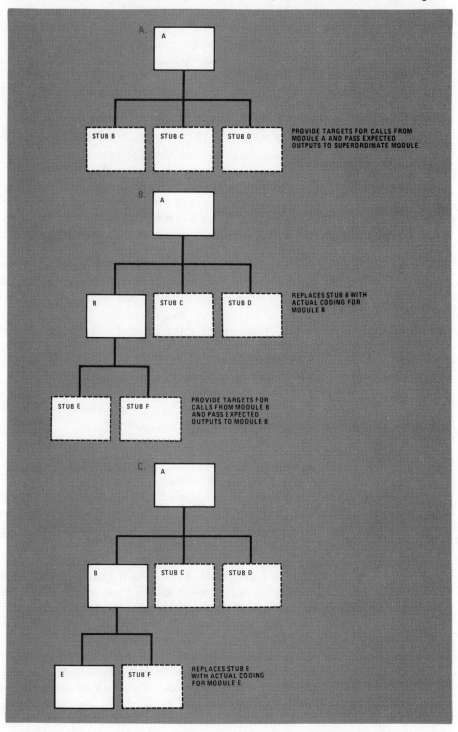

These testing routines are called program **stubs**. Such routines simulate the processing that will take place when the modules actually are coded. During testing, stubs provide targets for subprogram calls so that superordinate modules can exercise their control functions. Stubs also may pass data to superordinates to test interfaces. Usually, the data passed are generated as literal values within the stubs since the stubs have not yet been coded as complete modules. Use of stubs is a common practice in program testing. Testing progresses as stubs at succeedingly lower levels are replaced with the actual modules until eventually the entire program is tested.

Figures 18-10(B) and 18-10(C) show how testing progresses to succeeding lower levels through use of stubs to process data that cross the interfaces to be tested.

Testing with a top-down approach provides early verification both of the major module interfaces and of the overall control logic, which must emanate from the top of the program's structure. Also, by starting at the top and working down, it becomes possible to demonstrate the program functions for the complete program at an early point in the testing procedure. These overall functions cannot be demonstrated if modules at lower levels are tested independently. When combined with a phased implementation strategy, such usable portions of the system can be completed and tested while other detailed pieces remain incomplete.

However, the top-down approach also presents an inconvenience. It can be difficult to provide test cases when testing begins at the highest level. The lower-level input and output modules have not yet been completed and tested. Thus, it becomes necessary to develop stubs to represent the lower-level modules in test situations. Eventually, these stubs will be replaced by complete modules. At this point, however, testing may require multiple versions of the same stub, providing multiple test data to the higher-level modules.

Bottom-Up Testing

The strategy of **bottom-up testing** is to begin at the lowest level in a program structure and move progressively higher as modules are tested and integrated. Bottom-up incremental testing is advisable when the user interface and input-output is of greatest concern. In this method the afferent and efferent program branches are tested first and most often.

The progress of bottom-up testing for the program shown in Figure 18-9 is diagrammed in Figure 18-11. Figure 18-11(A) indicates that testing begins at the module appearing at the lowest and leftmost position in a structure chart. It is desirable, though not absolutely essential, to begin with the input branch, then go to the output branch, as the overall testing strategy. However, depending on individual situations, variations can exist.

Figure 18-11(A) shows that a driver has been developed for the tests of a low-level module. A **driver** plays a role similar to that of a stub, from an inverse position. That is, a driver is a test module, or program routine, that generates calls to lower-level modules and passes data across an interface. A driver simu-

Figure 18.11. *Possible testing pattern for bottom-up incremental testing.*

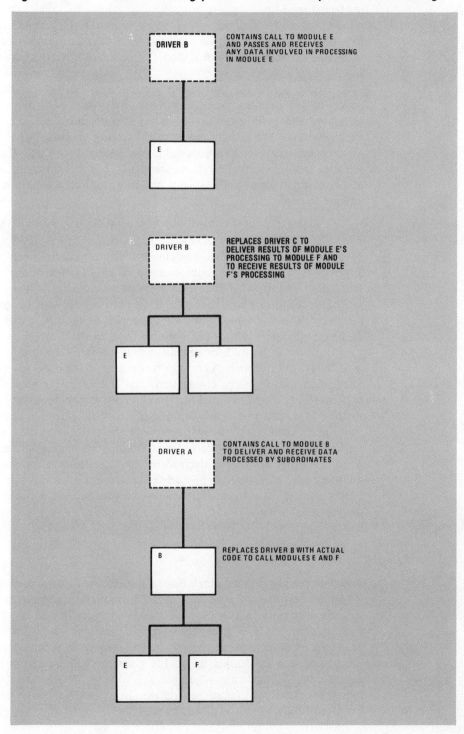

lates the actions of the group of yet-to-be-developed modules superordinate to the tested module.

In Figure 18-11(B), the same driver is used to test a second low-level module. Eventually the driver will be replaced by a finished module and a new driver used at the succeeding higher level. This situation is illustrated in Figure 18-11(C).

Advantages of the bottom-up approach to testing include early identification of any detailed processing flaws that might exist across low-level user interfaces and early exercising of input and output test cases. Thus the users may view these components early in the testing process. For the project team, this approach can serve as a useful public relations tool with the user, who can see some tangible results early. A disadvantage is that this approach puts off the ability to form an overall, skeletal program until all modules have been tested and are in place.

Combined Testing Methods

There are no hard-and-fast guidelines about when top-down and bottom-up approaches to testing are combined most effectively. Sometimes individual work schedules or needs of individual programs may create situations in which it is profitable to start at both the top and the bottom and work toward the middle — a "sandwich" approach. Conversely, in specific situations, it may be best to start in the middle and work toward both the top and the bottom.

All that can be said for certain is that the same methodologies apply on a module-by-module basis. That is, it is necessary to devise a plan for incremental integration testing of the connections and interfaces between all modules in a system. (It should be pointed out that it is not always necessary to add just one module at a time. For example, modules with no intended impact on one another or in completely different parts of the structure may be combined in a testing step, provided that care is exercised.) Also, integration test planning and method may be somewhat defined by the scheduling of personnel to produce module code. Modules can be added to integration testing only after they have been coded. Thus test scheduling must be coordinated with the overall project management scheme.

FUNCTION TESTING

Function testing applies black-box techniques in looking for errors or failures within a complete software program. Chronologically, function testing follows module testing and integration testing. It is impossible to test a complete program until all modules have been tested and necessary adjustments made. Then, the modules need to be integrated individually or in small groups. Ultimately, the testing process builds up to the point at which a complete program is operational. By this time, white-box methods for detailed examination of individual functions or procedures are no longer practical. The amount of detail involved simply would be unmanageable.

The special role of function testing is to exercise the entire program to be sure that external user specifications for inputs and outputs are met. Test cases applied are those developed during systems analysis and general design—activities in which the users participate actively. Criteria applied in function testing include measures of compliance with

- Input formats.
- Output formats.
- File organization.
- File access.
- Human-machine interfaces.

Function testing does just what the name implies. Program functions are exercised to be sure that the software is operating as designed. However, function testing still falls short of performance or systems tests. At this point, there is no attempt to combine operational and procedural relationships between programs at full production volumes; neither is there any attempt to overload the programs with work to see how it reacts to unforeseen strains. The intent is to look at and evaluate the soundness of the individual software programs. Thus, function testing is still within the domain of CIS professionals rather than users.

Systematic preparation of test data at the module level also applies at the function level. Input and output parameters are examined, and both valid and invalid data elements are presented as a means of determining the ability of the program to handle such data. Input records would include situations in which alphanumeric data were too long for the fields designated to hold them, in which the data within fields were positioned incorrectly, in which numeric data were entered into alphanumeric fields, and so on.

Particular attention should be paid to the points at which people and machines interact. In these instances, function tests deal with the documentation and with the reactions of the programs to stimuli from users. Ideally, for example, a person with no existing knowledge of the system would be asked to read the manual and perform input functions. Separately, a more experienced person would input erroneous or invalid data. In each case, part of the testing lies in evaluating the clarity of messages to the user generated by the system. These messages would include both error descriptions and prompts about what should be done next.

At all levels of testing—module, integration, and function—the underlying purpose is to cause the system to fail, to generate and deal with errors.

ERROR CORRECTION

Correcting program errors involves tradeoffs between immediacy or expediency and long-term effectiveness.

The expedient way is to locate the problem and patch the program or module so that its internal logic essentially bypasses the problem upon encountering the error situation. In effect, the result is to program around the error rather than to deal with any logical or functional problems. Patching can get the job done; however, the patch may not necessarily fix the problem. The problem may be avoided but cause other problems downstream. Also, patching almost always impairs the overall design quality. Thus, patching may be justifiable as a temporary measure or in an extreme emergency, but it should not be a standard practice. In addition to degrading the quality of a program, a patch usually will not be well documented. Consequently, when a program requires modification or maintenance at a future time, there may be no adequate documentation with which to work.

The far more preferable approach is to reexamine the program and redevelop a structured solution. Some redesign may be required, as well as the writing of new code and additional testing. In the long run, increased maintainability is worth the effort.

If these procedures are carried out properly, the results of testing should be far more valuable than the sum of the individual parts of the testing plan. That is, there are identified types and levels of tests that can be applied. Cumulatively, the results should produce more than a series of checks on somebody's list. The idea of testing is to produce quality software. Thus, elements of concern and pride should go into the testing. After all, testing is the procedure by which CIS professionals get their product ready to present to users, to the customers who have demonstrated a need for a quality product. So, in a sense, the philosophy that goes into the testing of a program is as important as the series of events that constitutes the test plan.

SUMMARY

Software testing is a process for executing a program with the intent of causing and discovering errors. The rationale behind testing is that it is virtually impossible to design a set of test cases will fully simulate all potential situations that can arise. The key to testing is to systematically design test cases that maximize the potential to detect errors in software.

Testing of software occurs broadly at five levels. These are unit, integration, function or program, system, and acceptance testing.

Testing includes white-box testing, black-box testing, and error-guessing testing strategies. White-box testing examines the internal logic of modules. Black-box testing looks at modules in terms of the inputs applied and the outputs produced. Error guessing is largely intuitive, based upon experience.

The levels of coverage in white-box testing include statement, decision–condition, multiple decision–condition, and exhaustive combination decision–condition.

Black-box testing includes boundary analysis and equivalence partitioning.

Error guessing concentrates on input-output, data structure, arithmetic, comparison, and control logic.

Test cases are derived for unit testing using all three methods wherever appropriate based upon specific module requirements.

Integration testing encompasses the exercise of program connections to determine their soundness and workability. Integration testing may be incremental or nonincremental. Incremental testing may be conducted with either a top-down or a bottom-up approach.

Integration testing with the top-down approach provides early verification of the major module interfaces and of the overall control logic, which must emanate from the top of the program's structure. However, it can be difficult to provide test cases when testing begins at the highest level.

Integration testing with the bottom-up approach provides early identification of any detailed processing flaws across low-level interfaces and early exercising of input and output test cases. A disadvantage is that this approach puts off the ability to form an overall skeletal program until all modules have been tested and are in place.

Criteria applied in function testing include measures of compliance with input formats, output formats, file organization, file access, and human-machine interfaces.

Correcting program errors involves tradeoffs between immediacy or expediency and long-term effectiveness.

KEY TERMS

1. software testing
2. test plan
3. test case
4. unit testing
5. integration testing
6. function testing
7. program testing
8. system testing
9. acceptance testing
10. white-box testing
11. black-box testing
12. error guessing
13. statement coverage testing method
14. decision-condition coverage testing method
15. multiple decision–condition coverage testing method
16. exhaustive combination decision–condition coverage testing method

17. boundary analysis testing
18. range of values
19. equivalence partitioning testing
20. categories of values
21. discrete values
22. input-output error testing
23. data structure tests
24. arithmetic error testing
25. comparison error tests
26. control logic errors
27. integration testing
28. incremental testing
29. nonincremental testing
30. top-down testing
31. bottom-up testing
32. driver
33. stub
34. function testing

REVIEW/DISCUSSION QUESTIONS

1. What is the nature of testing and the rationale for conducting software tests?
2. Briefly describe each of the five levels of testing application software.
3. Describe the testing strategies of white-box testing, black-box testing, and error guessing.
4. What are the methods of deriving test data for unit white-box testing?
5. What are the methods of deriving test data for unit black-box testing?
6. What are several troublesome module errors often identified by error guessing?
7. What is the main advantage of incremental integration testing over non-incremental integration testing?
8. Explain each of the incremental integration testing strategies.
9. Discuss the pros and cons of top-down incremental integration testing versus bottom-up incremental integration testing.
10. Define function testing and list the criteria applied in its use.
11. Discuss the methods of error correction and the tradeoffs involved.
12. Provide examples of a stub module and a driver module.

PRACTICE ASSIGNMENTS

Refer to the psuedocode for MOD-A shown in Figure 18-12 to complete the practice assignments.

1. How may white-box test cases would there be considering all possible combinations of conditions?
2. Provide white-box test cases (through multiple decision–condition coverage) using a form similar to the following:

TEST CASES (each case would include a value for AMOUNT, COLOR)	EXPECTED RESULTS (value of COUNTER at end of module)

3. Provide black box test cases (consider boundary analysis ad equivalence partitioning where appropriate) using a form similar to the following:

TEST CASES (each case would include a value for AMOUNT, COLOR)	EXPECTED RESULTS (value of COUNTER at end of module)

Figure 18.12. **Pseudocode for MOD-A.**

```
BEGIN MOD-A
    COUNTER = 0
    GET (AMOUNT, COLOR)
    DO WHILE (MORE DATA EXIST)
        IF COLOR = RED
            COUNTER = COUNTER + 1
        ELSE
            COUNTER = COUNTER - 1
        IF AMOUNT < 8 AND AMOUNT > 5
            COUNTER = COUNTER + 2
        ELSE NOTHING
        GET (AMOUNT, COLOR)
    END DO WHILE
END MOD-A
Color can be Red, Blue or Green. Amount can be one digit, from 1 to 9.
```

PART 7

The System Development Life Cycle: Applying the Tools and Techniques

An overview of the system development process was presented in Part I. The general flow of development activities was explained in the context of a system development life cycle. The following sections dealt with the basic skills needed to do development work.

But systems development work is complex. The skills applied are many and varied. Gaining proficiency in the use of each individual skill is challenging enough. Understanding when and how to apply these skills so that thousands of separate tasks all come together to create a new system requires a higher level of sophistication.

This section attempts to provide this increased level of sophistication. The systems development life cycle, introduced in Chapter 2, is described here in greater detail. A case study is used to illustrate not only the products produced but how they unfold within the development process.

Building a system is a beautiful and exciting process. There is a heady flow of activity and energies. This excitement needs to be experienced, not just read about. Actually doing your own project, or a case from the appendix, while studying this material will make the life cycle come alive.

19

The Investigation Phase

Learning Objectives

On completing this and other learning assignments for this chapter, you should be able to:

- Describe the purpose of a system development methodology.

- Describe the purpose and structure of a system development life cycle.

- Describe the purpose, objectives, and content of the investigation phase of an SDLC and its two activities, initial investigation and feasibility study.

- Discuss the contents and purpose of an initial investigation report.

- Explain the importance of and techniques for problem and scope definition during the investigation phase.

- Define the term *feasibility*.

- Define and describe the considerations associated with financial, schedule, technical, operational, and human factors feasibility.

- Describe the feasibility report, its contents, and the decisions that will be based on it.

- Discuss the importance of tradeoffs in the development of information systems and identify some of the potential tradeoffs to be considered.

- Explain the concept and importance of layering of work in succeeding activities and phases of the system development life cycle.

- Describe the principle of cumulative project documentation and explain its value.

CONTEXT: A SYSTEM DEVELOPMENT METHODOLOGY

A system development project can involve literally thousands of tasks requiring a broad range of sophisticated skills and performed by a group of people representing a number of different areas of specialization.

How is a two-year effort managed if specialists come and go and if twenty-five or more people are active at any given time (or even a one-year effort involving ten people)? Clearly, multiple groups will work on different subsystems or different parts of the problem. Will they all follow the same approach? Will their products have similar formats? Will one group of specialists communicate clearly with another? Will all necessary work be completed? Will it occur in the right order? When the inevitable problems, delays, errors, changes in direction, and incomplete work, arise, will there be a way to recover? Will there be a base to return to?

These appear to be questions on project management. Indeed, they are! But project management is not magic. Project management must be supported by a framework in which people work. That is a system development methodology.

A **system development methodology** is a context for project management. It typically contains

- a system development life cycle (SDLC).
- a generic set of tasks or base workplan.
- guidelines and standards for various deliverables.
- standard procedures.
- computer-based tools that support various parts of the development process.

All these items help direct the work of skilled professionals, people with knowledge and experience in the areas covered in this text. More is said about the computer-based tools in Chapter 23. Workplans, guidelines, and procedures—usually tailored to each organization—are often quite lengthy. They are not appropriate for this text. An SDLC is the part of a system development methodology that brings direction and order to the development process. It is the context in which all the skills developed in this text take on meaning.

A SYSTEM DEVELOPMENT LIFE CYCLE

The basic structure of a system development life cycle (SDLC) is explained in Chapter 2. The key concepts are reviewed below.

An SDLC organizes the work done in a development project at several levels, here called phases, activities, and tasks. Phases are composed of activities, and activities in turn are composed of tasks.

A phase is a set of activities that brings a project to a critical milestone. In most cases the milestone is accompanied by a management review and decision about whether to proceed with the project. Phases exist to assure that, at critical points in the course of the development effort, the project has the necessary management support in terms of personnel, budgets, and business issues that must be resolved in order to proceed.

An activity is a group of logically related tasks that, when completed, lead to accomplishment of a specific objective. Activities are defined by their specific end-products. Quality control is applied formally and carefully at the activity level.

Figure 19-1 lists the activities that make up the systems development life cycle used in this text. Note that each activity falls within a specific phase of the systems development process. Activities do not overlap phase boundaries. They all begin and end within the phase of which they are a part. However, the activities themselves can be carried out in parallel. For example, in phase 2

Figure 19.1. **Phases and activities of the systems development life cycle.**

INVESTIGATION PHASE

    1. Initial Investigation
    2. Feasibility Study

ANALYSIS AND GENERAL DESIGN PHASE

    3. Existing System Review
    4. New System Requirements
    5. New System Design
    6. Implementation and Installation Planning

DETAILED DESIGN AND IMPLEMENTATION PHASE

    7. Technical Design
    8. Test Specifications and Planning
    9. Programming and Testing
    10. User Training
    11. Acceptance Test

INSTALLATION PHASE

    12. File Conversion
    13. System Installation

REVIEW PHASE

    14. Development Recap
    15. Post-Implementation Review

(analysis and general design) tasks that involve modeling the existing system could be going on in parallel with tasks designed to document requirements for the new system. In fact, work could be progressing on activities 3 through 5 concurrently.

A task is the basic unit used by a project leader to assign work to team members and to track progress. Typically, tasks are basic work steps that can be completed in 10 to 40 hours. The division is somewhat arbitrary. A project leader who defines many small tasks has a greater degree of control but more administrative overhead. Very large tasks, on the other hand, create less overhead but may provide little sense of current status while they are in process.

The key level for understanding an SDLC is the activity level. The project leader and team members should have a clear idea of the purpose or objective of each activity and the deliverable or end-product it is intended to produce. In other words: Why is this being done? What is supposed to be accomplished? What is to be produced? This understanding—objective and end-product—is the base to which the project team returns when problems arise, when conditions change, and when the schedule begins to slip. It is a means of drawing back from the details and reexamining the purpose and direction being taken. Figure 19-2 is a data flow diagram that illustrates the relationship between the five phases of the SDLC, showing the end-products of each phase. This and later chapters examine the objectives, end-products, and procedures followed in each activity.

An SDLC is necessarily a generic organization of work to be done. It must be tailored to fit each development project. Depending on the project, the end-user, and even the politics of the situation, a given activity might be highly critical and time consuming or straightforward and fairly brief. An understanding of the objective is the key to tailoring the activity to the project.

THE INVESTIGATION PHASE

The investigation phase is best understood by having a clear understanding of the objective to be achieved, the end product to be produced, and the decision that management must make as a result of this work.

Objective

The main objective of this first phase of the SDLC is to evaluate a request for systems development as to its scope and feasibility. At the conclusion of the work, one of four courses of action is recommended:

- Continue the development work with the next phase of the SDLC.
- Enhance the existing system through a maintenance project rather than developing a new system.
- Direct the end-user to the information center facility where the request can be satisfied with minimal assistance using established databases and easy-to-learn reporting or small-application building software.
- Do nothing, tabling or rejecting the request.

Figure 19.2.   The systems development life cycle—a process view.

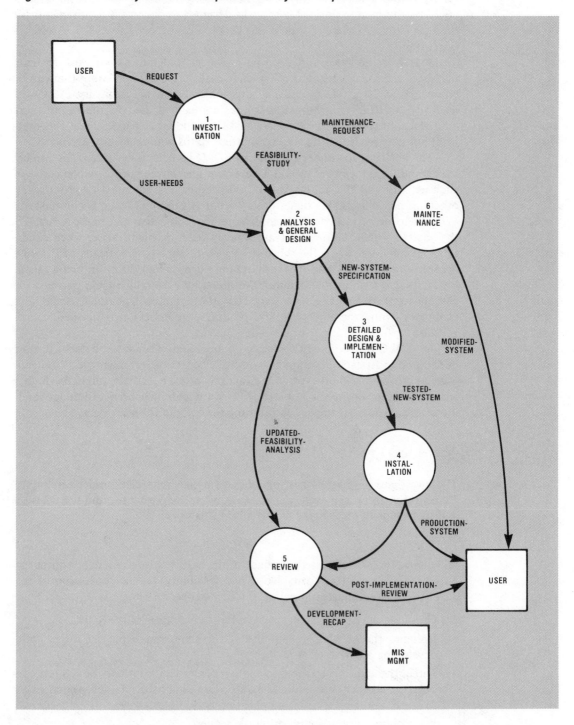

End-Product

The end-product of the first phase of the systems development life cycle is a feasibility report. This contains a recommendation whether the system can be developed and implemented profitably. Included is a review of benefits and costs.

Decision

Decisions are made at two levels. At the first level, the team performing the investigation makes a recommendation on the handling of the request to the management steering committee. At the second level, the steering committee decides on the disposition of the recommendation. If the recommendation of the investigation team is to develop a new system, the feasibility report would normally suggest completing the next phase in the systems development life cycle. The feasibility report would also include a general nondetailed description of a possible system that will solve the problem identified in the initial service request.

If the initial decision is to maintain the existing system or to refer the request to the information center, there might be no feasibility report. Instead, there might be a joint recommendation on a course of action to which the users and the IS department concur.

The steering committee would then have the choice of accepting or rejecting whatever recommendation is made. Other alternatives might be to table or delay the proposed action or simply to do nothing. The steering committee might also request that further study be done or that consideration be given to an alternative other than the one recommended.

CASE STUDY: BACKGROUND INFORMATION

The case study used in this section is based on a real systems development project, occurring in a small city in the Midwest, Central City. Central City has a population of approximately 75,000.

The city operates its own water utility, the Central City Water Department. The water department is a major user of the city's IS installation. Water bills are mailed every two months to approximately 20,000 customers. Bills are processed on a cycled basis, about 5,000 bills going out every two weeks. This spreads the workload in the computer center. The cycling of bills also spreads the work for the department's meter readers, who walk through the neighborhoods and note current readings of the water meters by hand in logbooks set up according to route.

In the computer center, the logbooks become input documents containing two data elements: customer number and current reading. The input data are processed against customer files. The figures for the current reading are entered into files maintained by the computer for each customer. In a separate billing run, the computer processes these files. During this operation, the figure for the previous reading is deducted from the current reading to establish water usage. The resulting figure is then multiplied by the appropriate billing rate, which is combined with other charges to produce a customer bill.

Figure 19-3 shows some of the features of this water billing system, which has been in place for a few years. There have been some complaints from the finance department about difficulties in answering customer question about bills. Also, the external auditors have expressed some dissatisfaction about the auditability of the system. By and large, however, the system appears to be running smoothly.

Assume you are an analyst-programmer in Central City's IS department. Your phone rings one day and a frantic person named Howard Rogers introduces himself. He explains that he is the operations manager for the Midstate Sanitary District, which serves most of the residents in your city, as well as many customers from surrounding suburbs and rural areas. Howard is friendly as well as excited. He puts your relationship on a first-name basis immediately, explaining that he was referred to you by the city manager, Susan Garcia.

As you interpret the conversation, Howard has a problem. As he describes it, you have an opportunity. Until now, the revenue requirements of the sanitary district have been taken care of automatically. District operations have been supported by property taxes. The commissioners of the district could simply get together once a year and decide what tax rate to apply against the property in their area. The city and county agencies then collected the money and passed it along to the sanitary district.

Now, things have changed. An agency of the federal government has ruled that property taxes are not an equitable way of raising money because they penalize one class of people at the expense of others. There has been a ruling that, as a qualification for receiving federal subsidies and grants, districts operating sewage treatment plants must charge their customers on the basis of services received. A number of sewage districts have gotten together and asked for clarification of this new policy. Rather than trying to put meters into the sewage lines to measure usage, it has been decided that, since most water consumed in homes or businesses eventually finds its way into the sewers, billing can be based on water consumption.

Howard, is really glad he met you. All you have to do now is take a rate that he is ready to plug into your system and, as long as you are issuing bills anyway, collect money for the sanitary district.

You make an appointment to visit Howard at the sanitary district offices the following afternoon. You explain that you will have to understand his organization's needs a little better before you can help devise a solution to his problem.

Right after you hang up from this call, your phone rings again. It is Susan Garcia, the city manager. She explains that she has offered the sanitary district full cooperation by all city agencies. Susan explains that she really believes in efficiency in government through this type of cooperation. Then she adds that this looks like a good opportunity to gain some revenue by charging the sanitary district for the service, thus recovering some of the costs of running your computer center.

Figure 19.3. Simplified data flow diagram of the existing water billing system.

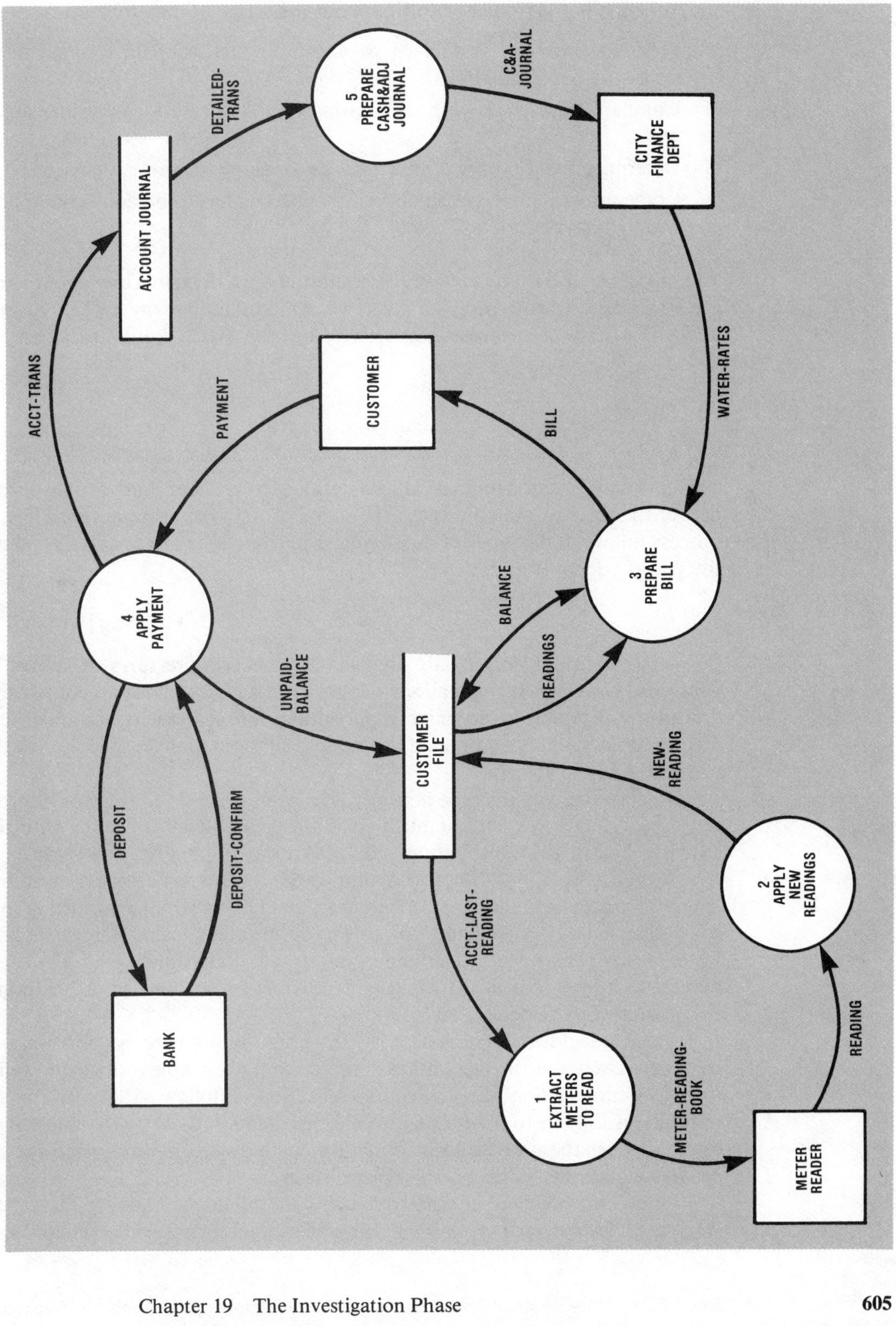

Your job is, very quickly, to figure out the scope of the problem:

- Find out about the customer base and billing needs of the sanitary district under the new regulations.
- Compare these needs with the existing billing system for the water department.
- Determine just how big a job it will be to merge the two systems.
- Come up with a recommendation about what has to be done and approximately how much it will cost.

You recognize also that you have to get all this work done in a day or two. Yours is a small department. Your job is service. But you have many services to worry about. You have been thrust into Activity 1 of the SDLC, initial investigation.

ACTIVITY 1: THE INITIAL INVESTIGATION

This and subsequent activities will be defined in terms of an overview description of the activity, the objectives, the scope of the work, the end-products, the process followed, the types of development personnel involved, and the cumulative project documentation.

Activity Description

Business conditions continually change. Competitive pressures drive new approaches. Government regulations dictate new services or new record-keeping procedures. Employees recognize opportunities for increased operation efficiencies. In today's highly automated businesses, all these changes quickly find their way to the IS department.

Because there tends to be a steady stream of requests for new or improved services, it makes sense to establish standard procedures for dealing with these requests. The initial investigation activity is a way of handling this service.

Suggestions or ideas for new or improved systems are received, examined, and evaluated at a preliminary, exploratory level. The work performed is somewhat superficial, just enough to be able to define and come to agreement about what is being requested. The end result is an understanding of the service request to a level that at least makes it possible to evaluate, on a preliminary basis, what is to be done next.

At the conclusion of this activity, the initial request for systems work has been processed and the person handling the request is able to make a preliminary recommendation about a course of action to follow. Alternative recommendations may be to do nothing, to refer the request to a system maintenance team, to refer the user to an information center, or to move on into the next activity within the systems development life cycle.

Three of these four alternatives, doing nothing, maintaining the existing system, or developing a new system, are self-explanatory. An **information center** is a specialized entity within the IS department that assists users in developing certain applications through the use of sophisticated software tools and necessary databases. For some development requests, it is possible to bypass the extensive analysis and design steps and allow the user to fill the request directly. Information center personnel may, for example, write simple query or report applications to run against mainframe files, or they may write personal computer-based applications for which data can be uploaded to or downloaded from mainframe applications.

Objectives

The objectives of the initial investigation activity are, first, to arrive at a preliminary understanding of the business problem and the scope of the effort and, then, to arrive at one of the following recommendations:

- It is best to do nothing at this time.
- The user could handle the request by applying the tools and services of the information center.
- The request can be satisfied through a relatively small maintenance effort on the existing system.
- The request may entail the development of a new system or a major enhancement to the existing system.

The last recommendation, in essence, authorizes the initiation of the feasibility study activity. If this recommendation is made, an underlying objective is to provide a project plan and a statement of resource requirements for the feasibility study.

Scope

The initial investigation may involve anywhere from two or three days' work by a single analyst up to several weeks' effort by a team of users and analysts. For small changes in an existing system, one person can often conduct an initial investigation in a few days. But for the development of a new information system of considerable scope, it might take several weeks of team effort, all dedicated to studying the impact of requested changes upon the operations of the business.

A systems service request may be motivated by a wide variety of considerations. Many of these are external to the organization. For example, if there is a change in social security or other tax deduction rates, payroll systems must be modified to conform to the law. The post office may reassign ZIP code numbers, requiring extensive changes to name-and-address files. A government agency may require an entirely new kind of report for a specific type of business. The deductibility changes for IRAs generated the need for massive changes in record keeping and reporting for investment companies administering IRA plans.

Often, requests for systems development or improvement respond to forces in the marketplace. An organization can use information systems to increase market penetrations, to lower production costs, or to achieve other purposes. Flexible, responsive information systems are key ingredients in an organization's ability to increase revenues and profits.

Business decisions can also trigger systems development requests. A company may decide to bring out an entirely new product line or to go into an entirely new field. IS support may be needed for the new venture.

Another business consideration would be that existing systems are simply outmoded, for either technological or transaction volume reasons. There is a rule of thumb in the IS field: If a system has been in place for more than five to seven years, some type of major system change is probably indicated. The reason for the change may lie either in electronic technology or in the dynamics of the business itself. For example, as users become more experienced and sophisticated, new opportunities will come to mind. These new opportunities might be associated with better use of information to run the business or with better ways of delivering current information to system users. For whatever reason, most business systems need major revision or replacement in the course of time.

End-Products

Each activity within the systems development life cycle has defined end-products that result from the specific tasks performed. These end-products, in turn, are added to the cumulative documentation for the project. At the end of a phase, the end-products of all the activities are used to produce a consolidated document that serves as a basis for decision making and direction setting.

The initial investigation activity has two end-products. One is an initial investigation report that documents the work done, the findings, and the recommendations. The second is an oral report by the systems analyst that explains and, in effect, lobbies for the recommended action.

Although the extent of documentation in response to a particular request will vary, certain basic elements should be included in an initial investigation report:

- There should be a preliminary statement of the business problem that is to be addressed.
- A context diagram should be used to document an initial understanding of scope and of major system inputs and outputs.
- Any major business functions to be added or changed should be described. (It may also be good to note functions that will not be included in the scope, avoiding any possible confusion.)
- Any operational problems or policy questions that have surfaced during the initial investigation should be identified and explained.
- There should be a very rough, preliminary estimate of cost and of projected benefits that could be anticipated if the request for service is approved and the proposed changes are implemented.

- A recommendation should be stated concerning the request. Again, the options are systems development, system maintenance, referral to an information center, or rejection of the request.
- If the recommendation is for development of a new system, the initial investigation report should contain an estimate of the amount of time and money that would be involved in performing the feasibility study.
- If the recommendation is for maintenance of existing systems, a brief document should be prepared describing what is to be done and the amount of time and money involved.

The Process

A system development life cycle is a guide for project management, not a cookbook. Thus, this section will not list mandated or rigid sets of tasks to be performed within each activity. Rather, the work content or process followed during the activity will be discussed at a general level. With an understanding of the objective of the activity, the end-products, general process, and list of specific tasks required for a given project are fairly easy to derive.

The process followed during the initial investigation activity is very much like the process for the feasibility study activity. It is simply done at a more general, less detailed level. The feasibility study process is very much like that of the entire analysis and general design phase, feasibility being at an intermediate level of detail. This is a key to understanding the entire first half of the system development life cycle. The process is iterative and layered. The same basic process is followed over and over at increasingly greater levels of detail.

Problem Definition. One of the most important tasks in an initial investigation is to define the problem or business opportunity that led to the request. This definition should be stated in such a way that it is clearly understood and agreed to by both the user and the systems analyst doing the initial investigation. Sometimes, the definition arrived at will differ from the initial description provided by the user. It is not uncommon for users, who are very close to the situation, to confuse symptoms with the underlying problems.

The definition of the problem should be placed in the context of the business objectives of the user area for which the systems request has been made, the responsibilities of the area, and the decisions that must be made by its managers. Ultimately, all system modifications and improvements recommended will need to be justified on the basis of these business objectives.

Scope. It is also important to reach early agreement about the scope of the study. A tightly defined scope will avoid misunderstandings and wasted effort as the project progresses. At this level, a context diagram, by highlighting the major outputs and inputs to the area under study, essentially defines the scope. If there is any chance for doubt, it is good to specifically list the major business functions to be included in the scope as well as these that are not included.

Review Existing Procedures. At a relatively high level, the initial investigation report should describe briefly the function of the existing system. A listing of major outputs and input sources would normally be included. The major manual and computerized functions that are a part of the current system would also be reviewed.

Determine New System Requirements. The major requirements driving the request for a new system are documented during the initial investigation activity. At this point the list will normally be short and focus on the business results to be achieved. Later, additional subsidiary requirements will be documented as input to the design activity. That detail, however, is inappropriate here. Recall that the objective of this activity is to determine whether to spend the money on a formal feasibility study. That decision is usually based on just the business requirements that have major impact on the organization.

Case Illustration. The water billing–sanitary district case illustrates both the importance of high level requirements and an exception to the rule. Clearly, the key driving factor in the case is that the sanitary district has a major problem. They must now bill for service using a method for which they have no base. They absolutely must use water consumption as a base. They either build their own system or piggyback on the water billing system. They have one key driving business requirement.

The issue during the initial investigation is whether this requirement can be accomplished through a modification to the existing system or whether it will be necessary to build a new system. Now a certain detail comes into play. Although most people in your area receive both water and sanitary services, some are water customers only and some are sanitary district customers only. From your own experience, you know that homes in some parts of the city are equipped with septic tanks and are not connected to the sewers. You also know that some rural housing developments on the outskirts have their own wells and do not subscribe to water services, even though they are connected to sewers. Thus, although the customer bases for the two systems overlap, they are not identical. This is enough to cast doubt on the modification option. Largely on this basis you will recommend that a more complete feasibility study be conducted.

Generate Possible Solutions. After briefly reviewing the existing system and documenting new system requirements, the third step is to consider major options — still at a very high level. If a feasibility study is to be recommended, one or two general approaches to solving the problem should be described here for further review during the feasibility study activity. The description of each approach should indicate the business functions or processes to be reviewed, especially the additions to or modifications of the existing system, as well as initial suggestions for physical or automated solutions.

Evaluate Feasibility. After one or more possible solutions have been identified, a preliminary determination of feasibility must be made. This decision should be based upon business considerations. That is, a determination should be made about the urgency of the need or the economies to be realized through the proposed system. It is usually not necessary to get into computer hardware or software considerations at this point.

Case Illustration. Feasibility of the sanitary district request is easily determined on a business basis. At the moment, the sanitary district has no billing or collection costs. However, these costs are unavoidable in the future. All you have to do in a case of this type is look at the alternatives to the proposed system. Suppose the water department and the sanitary district each had separate billing operations. Each entity has about 20,000 customers. Suppose you estimate that about 17,500 customers use both water and sanitary services, By combining the systems, a single bill can do the work of two. In other words, the sanitary district can eliminate the prospective cost of issuing 17,500 bills every two months. In the course of a year, the cost of issuing 105,000 bills is avoided. Between the postage and the billing forms alone, savings through elimination of duplication will come to more than $30,000 annually. You don't have to go any further than this to determine that development of a combined system is very probably feasible.

Personnel Involved

From the outset, a systems development project is a team effort. Even at the initial investigation stage, the systems analyst cannot do the job alone but must work closely with at least one user. Often, the systems analyst, together with the person initiating the request, can do most of the work involved in this initial activity. Sometimes, however, the analyst will need to interview several user personnel to build even an initial understanding of existing procedures.

Some form of teamwork must be present right from the start, even though the formal formation of a project team will not come until later in the systems development life cycle.

Cumulative Project File

At the conclusion of the initial investigation activity, the major documentation within the project file will be the initial investigation report. Other accumulated documents may include

- Interview schedules.
- Written notes gathered during interviews.
- An organization chart for the user function.
- The beginnings of a glossary of terms central to understanding the user's business activities.

ACTIVITY 2: THE FEASIBILITY STUDY

Techniques for feasibility analysis are presented in Chapter 10. Those techniques are appropriate at any point during analysis, but they are most formally used during the feasibility study.

Activity Description

Something that is feasible can be done. There is also an implication of suitability or practicality associated with feasibility. This suggests that feasibility is not a binary condition. Normally a proposed design for a new system would not be viewed as either feasible or not feasible. Rather, an attempt would be made to measure its degree of feasibility, or the relative feasibility of two different design proposals would be compared.

By the time activity 2 is complete, the original business problem or need should be well understood, the scope of the effort clearly defined, and alternative solutions considered. It is assumed that a feasibility study will encompass at least two, perhaps more, prospective solutions to the problem. This does not mean that two or more separate systems are designed, them the best one is selected. Rather, it means that several alternatives will be considered before a project focuses on the one that appears best for the situation under study.

A feasibility study should conclude with a clearcut recommendation. That is, a definite course of action should be proposed. At a minimum, this recommendation will indicate whether the project should be continued or abandoned. Feasibility-study recommendations also establish dollar values for systems development projects. One of the results of the feasibility study will be a projected budget indicating the cost of developing the new system. Thus, the recommendations imply that a project is feasible and also indicate the associated cost and potential payback of proceeding with the development project.

A feasibility evaluation involves more than just cost and payback, however. As discussed in Chapter 10, five separate dimensions of feasibility must be evaluated. These are financial, schedule, technical, operational, and human factors.

Case Scenario

The following uses the Central City Water Billing System case to illustrate these five types of feasibility.

Financial Feasibility. Financial feasibility usually results in a cost-benefit analysis. Briefly, the idea is to determine savings and other benefits that would result from implementation of a new system. These benefits are then compared with costs. The extent to which the benefits outweigh the costs is a measure of the degree of financial feasibility.

During the initial investigation activity, the cost savings was estimated to be $30,000 annually. During this activity, as possible solution ideas are being formed, boundary limits for development cost can be developed and benefits can be more carefully idenfitied. Clearly, the system will be worth more than $30,000 (the cost of mailing bills) to the sanitary district. The city may also gain additional benefits through a system rewrite. Finally, federal fuding may be available to sponsor intragovernment efforts such as these.

Schedule Feasibility. Recall that schedule feasibility addresses the question: Can the proposed system solution be implemented in the time available?

For example, the sanitary district billing application may be perfectly feasible on all counts — until you learn that the system has to be in operation within 90 days. Looking around, you find that you just don't have the people or the skills within the city's staff to handle this job in the time available. Under these circumstances, you might contact independent software development companies to see if you can find an outside supplier to do the work in the time available, even though costs might be greater.

Technical Feasibility. Technical feasibility focuses on the question of whether the equipment, software, and technical support that an organization has, or can justify financially, are capable of processing the proposed application. Suppose, for example, that Central City finds it would need a much bigger computer to handle the combined water and sanitary billing application. The larger computer may be more than the city can afford or more sophisticated than its personnel are capable of operating. If this is the case, any proposed solution could be considered unfeasible on technical grounds.

Operational Feasibility. Operational feasibility evaluates whether the organization can gear up to handle the manual processing efficiently and whether the system will work from a people-processing (rather than from a computer-processing) point of view.

For example, the proposed solution for Central City involves adding the sanitary district billing to the water department system. One of the operational considerations is that substantially more money will be handled if a combined system is undertaken. Further, the flow of money will follow closely behind the billing cycles established for the system. Itemizing and accounting for all of these receipts and responding to the increased level of customer questions and complaints could become a major undertaking. Further, while the checks or other payments are being tallied, the money is not earning interest.

Rather than add a major cashiering operation within the city's water department, it might be best simply to have all payments for both water and sanitation mailed directly to a bank. Bank personnel would open all the envelopes and deposit the money to an account that would begin paying interest on the funds the day they are received. The bank would then provide enough detailing about receipts so that the data could be processed routinely, after the fact, within the city's computer system.

Under one approach, one aspect of a proposed system could be operationally difficult. Under another approach, the potential problem is turned into an advantage. Operational feasibility evaluations often lead to better design proposals.

Human Factors Feasibility. The final area of feasibility analysis, human factors feasibility, evaluates whether the reactions of people to a new system might impede or obstruct its development or implementation.

It happens, for example, that Central City's head water billing clerk, Victor Perry, is nearing retirement. Vic is a dedicated, knowledgeable worker who has the respect of the other clerks. Unfortunately, Vic has never overcome a basic dislike for technology. The initial computerization of his department ten years ago was traumatic. The installation now of an on-line system with increased functionality will be very threatening for Vic. He will feel that he has lost his whole basis for value and respect in the department. He may be simply incapable of adjusting. His role will need to be carefully considered, both during development and after installation of the new system.

Objectives

The objectives of the feasibility study activity are

- Clearly define the business problem to be addressed and the scope of the effort.
- Establish approximate costs and resource commitments for the proposed project.
- Recommend a decision and a course of action to the steering committee.
- If a "go" decision is recommended, include project schedule and priority suggestions in the report to the committee.

Scope

The feasibility study activity begins with a review of the initial investigation report and other documentation produced during the first activity. In a global sense, this activity is a preview of the activities and tasks of the next phase in the project, analysis and general design. This activity should cover essentially the same ground as the analysis and general design phase, but in far less depth. Setting the scope for this activity is a good exercise in establishing the layering approach to project management. As the work is done, team members will recognize the need to go deeper and probe further; but they will be constrained by the budgets and schedules to which they have agreed.

End-Products

The principal end products of the feasibility study activity are

- A feasibility report to the steering committee.
- A project plan to be implemented if the steering committee authorizes continuation of the project.
- A preliminary set of working papers for the next phase of the project.

Feasibility Report. The feasibility report contains:

- A concise statement of the business problem to be addressed and the scope of the study. This is usually expressed using a context diagram and a brief narrative.
- A brief description of the existing system, supported by a high level DFD model.
- A high-level statement of requirements for the new system.
- A general high-level description of one or more proposed new system solutions. The level of detail would be only enough to describe the general capabilities of the proposed system and to support the feasibility analysis to follow.
- Five sections addressing each of the dimensions of feasibility for the proposed system(s).

- A proposed schedule indicating both time and people to be involved in the project — comparatively detailed for the second phase of the project, less detailed for succeeding phases.
- A list of policy-level decisions that cannot be made by the project team and must be resolved by management.

Note the last item above. Any systems study is bound to uncover situations that cannot be resolved by the project team — that require management to establish business policies. In the sanitary district study, for example, one such question might involve how partial payments from customers are to be allocated. Suppose a customer owes $62 and pays only $50. Should the water bill be paid in full first and the remainder allocated to the sanitary district? Should the money be divided equally between the two collecting authorities? Should the money be divided proportionally according to the amount owed to each authority? Systems analysis can only pose such questions, not answer them.

A temptation to be resisted during the feasibility study activity is to gather enough information so that costs of installing and operating a new system can be pinpointed with great accuracy. Such accuracy takes time and costs money. It is acceptable during this first phase of a project to present rough estimates only, as long as the quality of the estimates and reservations about their accuracy are made clear to the steering committee. Many organizations, for examples are willing to accept estimates that may be off by 75 to 100 percent — as long as the evidence indicates a good potential for success. Feasibility is evaluated again at the end of the analysis and general design phase, providing an opportunity for more accurate estimates.

Case Scenario. The awareness of this need to limit the feasibility study activity hits you hard as you, Howard Rogers, the chief accountant of the sanitary district, together with the city clerk, and the head of your own department's data entry section, review possible methods for capturing data for the proposed combined system. Since the water billing system is to be expanded, the data entry supervisor, Shizu Matsumoto, suggests that advanced data-capturing methods may now be affordable.

She explains that, rather than keying all meter-reading entries, as is now done, it may be possible to input data directly from meter-reading tickets prepared in the field by using optical character recognition equipment. Shizu also points out that there are automatic meter-reading systems now available. If customer meters are equipped with small radio transmitters, meter-reading personnel can simply drive through the neighborhood slowly, activating the meter transmitters with small transponders they carry with them. This triggers the recording of data on tapes within the transponders. The tapes can then be read directly into the computer.

As an experienced systems analyst, you are prepared for this type of suggestion. You explain that this kind of consideration belongs in the next phase, where you will take a deeper look at the proposed new system. During the feasibility study, the project team does not yet need to get into this level of detail because it isn't necessary to consider such possibilities to determine general feasibility. You ask Shizu to give you information on current data entry costs. Your reasoning is: If it looks feasible to implement the new system with existing key entry techniques, enhanced methods can only improve the picture.

Project Plan. The **project plan** prepared in connection with a feasibility study lays out detailed scheduling and staffing to the task level for the second phase of the project. This plan should list the people involved, at least in terms of skill requirements, along with work hour estimates for each task. For later phases of the project, the plan is more general and more approximate.

Working Papers. In keeping with the layering principle, **working papers** provide start-up guidance for work in the next phase of the project. These documents include the following:

A preliminary review of new system requirements takes an overview look at the requirements for the proposed new system. Included are statements of minimum business objectives to be achieved, descriptions of both required and desired outputs, identification of input data sources, and special processing requirements. This set of documentation will be enlarged and detailed further in activity 4, new system requirements.

A preliminary review of the existing system is documentation that includes relevant organizational charts (showing both formal and informal relationships), a glossary of terms used within the existing system, and overview-level data flow diagrams (both physical and logical) for manual and computerized portions of existing systems. Also provided are estimates of current operating costs, transaction volumes, and operating schedules. These documents will be expanded during activity 3, existing system review.

Possible system solutions are the documentation that includes descriptions of techniques and equipment that could be used to implement the new system. If appropriate, data flow diagrams are included, as are hardware and software specifications. Further study will be given to this topic during activity 5, new system design.

The Process

The feasibility study activity is a classic, though miniature, systems analysis study. To the extent needed for an evaluation of feasibility, all the methods and procedures used in the analysis and general design phase of the systems development life cycle are undertaken. Since these activities are discussed in the next chapter, they are only previewed here.

This activity begins with a review of the initial investigation report. This input serves as a basis for establishing a plan that includes a list of tasks, personnel assignments, time allocations, and a calendar for completing the assignments.

The primary study method involves interviews with users and managers associated with the current system. For the most part, the feasibility study interviews will be conducted with upper- and middle-level managers who can explain the system to the necessary level of understanding. It would be an exception for team members to interview personnel at operating levels during this activity.

It becomes important during this activity for all members of the project team to begin to differentiate between the logical and physical aspects of the system. The logical aspects stress the business objectives of the system, what the system is to do with what data. The physical aspects stress the mechanics of how data are provided and processed. Separate logical and physical documentation should be established during this activity.

From interviews and other data-gathering activities, a preliminary picture of potential benefits and possible cost savings is developed. in the course of these studies, situations requiring policy decisions are identified and listed.

Proposed solutions or approaches to new systems are reviewed with managers of user and IS departments. Persons who would be involved in recommending implementation of the new system must agree to its feasibility and desirability.

Once this base of knowledge has been built, work can proceed on preparation of a cost-benefit analysis, a project plan, and a feasibility report for presentation to the steering committee.

Five special considerations deserve to be highlighted here, scope control, tradeoff decisions, layering, packaged application software, and project management tools.

Scope Control. One result of the initial investigation activity is a clear definition of the problem or opportunity that prompted the request. This definition establishes the scope of the project. Most development projects have a tendency to grow in scope. As project team members and users reach deeper levels of understanding, they see new opportunities to add features to the system or to move into related areas not covered in the original request. This tendency toward project expansion must be controlled. Any significant change in project scope should require formal approval.

A long-standing guideline for systems development is known as the **80-20 rule**. This suggests that 80 percent of the benefits of a system can be achieved for 20 percent of the cost. The remaining 80 percent of the cost goes into providing the last, possibly unnecessary, 20 percent of the benefits. As a result of the feasibility study, the scope of the project should be firmly established in terms of the business objectives to be met, the major outputs to be produced, and the main processing functions to be included. These objectives, outputs, and processing functions encompass the requirements, the 80 percent of benefits. Once this clear understanding of scope is established, it is possible to resist the temptation to enlarge the scope by adding nonessential "bells and whistles" that can increase complexity and costs disproportionately.

Tradeoff Decisions. Throughout the systems development process, the systems analyst is called upon to make difficult decisions, difficult because there is no single right or wrong answer but rather several possible options. Each option may offer certain advantages and certain disadvantages in competition with those presented by other choices.

The process of evaluating two or more possible responses to a given situation and selecting the best solution is referred to as making a **tradeoff decision**. The decision process involves identifying possible responses or options and then selecting the one that maximizes the advantages and minimizes the disadvantages for that specific situation.

Tradeoff decisions are particularly evident during the feasibility study activity. As options to enhance the technical feasibility of a system are considered, costs often increase and hence decrease the financial feasibility. Or, as the level of automation is increased to improve operational feasibility, current manual procedures are further impacted thereby decreasing political feasibility. Which options are better? There are usually no clear-cut answers. The difficult process of making a seemingly endless collection of interrelated decisions can at least be structured if the decisions are approached formally as tradeoff decisions.

Layering. Systems analysis activities during the early stages of a project cover the same general concerns and areas several times, moving to increasing depths of knowledge and understanding with each iteration. This concept of adding to the depth of knowledge through successive iterations is known as **layering**.

It can be tempting to begin designing a new system based on past experience or on a cursory understanding of what currently exists and what is wanted. The danger lies in the possibility that a systems analyst may begin to design a new system before he or she fully understands what is needed or what actually exists at present.

The layering approach avoids this type of pitfall. Phases and activities in the systems development life cycle are structured so that the necessary base of knowledge is built, step by step, before extensive commitments are made to changes that might not work. For example, in the analysis and general design phases, emphasis is on user needs and overall technical solutions rather than on detailed technical design considerations. A complete understanding between systems analysts and users should be a prerequisite before the project moves into detailed technical design and program development.

The analysis and general design phase is actually at the third level in project layering. Because this phase represents a major commitment of time and money, the initial investigation and feasibility study serve as the first two layers. A general understanding of project needs and possible new system solutions is achieved during these activities. This provides a firm base of understanding upon which the systems analyst can build during the analysis and general design phase. See Figure 19-4.

In reality, there may be many layers of understanding. Coming to understand this layering structure has been likened to peeling an onion. The new system is at the center of the onion. Each layer of the onion represents an increasingly detailed understanding of the organization's needs and of the new system possibilities. The center is revealed by peeling the outer layers away one at a time.

Packaged Application Software. High quality **application software packages** are available for a wide range of applications. This option should be considered in any systems-development effort. A package may exist that meets all or a substantial portion of the users' needs.

Figure 19.4. *Systems analysis steps are iterated with increasing layers or levels of detail during the first two phases of the system development life cycle.*

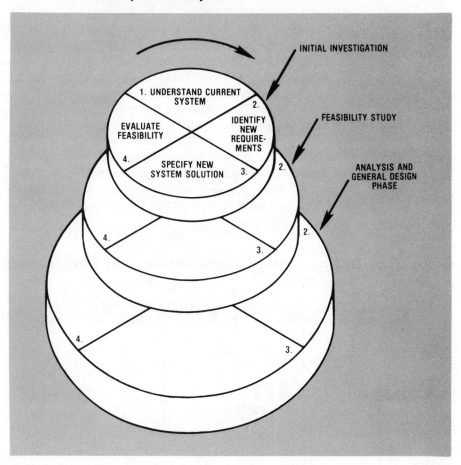

It is often too early, during the feasibility study, to make a software purchase decision. Needs are not yet fully understood. However, potential packages should be identified and solutions should be defined that integrate these packages. A closer evaluation of potential packages and integration problems can be made during the analysis and general design phase.

Project Management Tools. The main purpose of a systems development life cycle is to provide a framework for project management. Specific **project management tools** are described and analyzed in Chapter 3. At this point, it is important to be aware of the need for these tools and the functions they perform:

■ A **project plan** includes lists of tasks and schedules for their performance.

- A **staffing plan** encompasses personnel assignments for the project and includes estimates of days or hours to be worked.
- A **time reporting** system keeps track of work completed and scheduled to be done, with controls applied at the task level.
- Scheduled **status reporting** must be carried out periodically throughout the project. Status reports should include information on tasks completed (including both estimated and actual hours), tasks in process (including estimated hours, actual hours to date, and estimated remaining hours), future tasks (reported in terms of estimated work to be done), and overall project status. Overall project status should be reported on the basis of both budgeted hours and a calendar schedule.

One tool that is commonly used to control schedules as a part of project management is the **Gantt chart**. The purpose of the Gantt chart, as illustrated in Figure 19-5, is to show the start, elapsed time, and completion relationships of work units that make up a project or a part of a project. A Gantt chart does not

Figure 19.5. Gantt chart showing interrelationships among activities of the systems development life cycle.

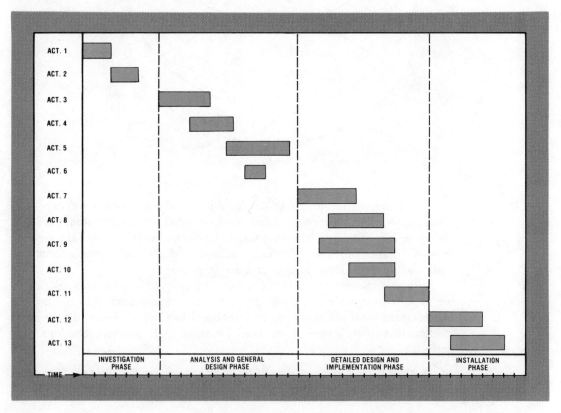

show the intensity of work or level of effort being applied to a work unit at any given time.

Another key tool for project management is some type of **project planning sheet,** such as the one shown in Figure 19-6. This simple worksheet is often automated as part of a project management system. It is used to identify work units or tasks; to assign persons to handle them; and to keep track of planned hours for each assignment, actual hours worked, and planned and actual dates for the beginning and conclusion of work on each assignment.

Personnel Involved

The feasibility study activity marks the formation of a **systems development project team**. Thus, one of the challenges of this activity lies in building teamwork as quickly and effectively as possible. Team members may be strangers at the outset. Very quickly, a sense of purpose and a spirit of cooperation must be established.

Team members need each other. Except in rare instances, users cannot develop systems by themselves. Systems people cannot develop systems unless users want them and will apply them. Thus, a mutual dependence must be recognized at the outset of a project.

The project team leader is usually an experienced systems analyst from the IS department. Other team members at this stage of the project will be middle managers from the user groups and additional systems analysts. Over the life of the project, the composition of the project team will change. The size of the team will depend on the complexity of the project.

Cumulative Project File

At the conclusion of this activity, the cumulative project file will include these items:

- The project plan, which will be revised continually throughout the systems development life cycle.
- The initial investigation report.
- The feasibility report.
- A list of policy decisions that must be addressed before design of the new system can be completed.
- A schedule of interviews conducted and summaries of findings.
- A glossary of terms, which will be updated continually.
- Preliminary documentation for the existing system to serve as a basis for activity 3, existing system review, and preliminary documentation of new system requirements, to be enlarged during activity 4, new system requirements.
- Descriptions of possible system solutions, to be considered and expanded during activity 5, new system design.

Figure 19.6. Project planning sheet.

PROJECT PLANNING SHEET

Project _____

Leader _____

Date Prepared _____

Prepared By _____

☐ Activity List
☐ Task List

Task/Act.	Task/Activity Description	Individual Assigned	Planned Hours	Actual Hours	Planned Date Begin	Planned Date End	Actual Date Begin	Actual Date End

Cumulative Documentation

Closely related to the layering concept for building knowledge is the idea of **cumulative documentation**. This technique calls for the building of systems documentation gradually, keeping pace with the accumulation of information and ideas. A systems development project produces two separate, equally important types of documentation—final and interim.

Final documentation describes the system after the development project is completed. Included are all the required types of documentation of programs, processing, procedures, forms, and files that are critical working tools for an operational system.

All too often, these end-products are regarded as the only documentation required. There is a temptation to wait until the system is developed completely before documentation begins. This end-of-project approach to documentation can be costly because a crash program is usually required to meet all the documentation needs. Further, procrastination can lead to oversight; important items are left out simply because they are forgotten during the last-minute rush.

A better approach is the use of **interim documentation**, building a working base for systems development as the project goes forward. Each activity and phase within the systems development life cycle has well-defined document outputs. These are identified in the end products section for each activity. These documentation requirements have been built into the systems development life cycle for some very important reasons. Documentation is also an essential means of communication. The makeup and nature of a project team change as the development life cycle progresses. If systems are to meet user needs, system specifications must be clear about what is wanted. You can't design and implement systems first and prepare specifications later. Thus, documentation provides an orderly, cumulative dimension to the systems development process.

Documentation is prepared on a dynamic basis. The documentation created in one activity or phase is analyzed, revised, torn apart, and augmented in the course of creating the documentation for successive activities or phases. The documentation evolves as understanding increases. In this way, cumulative documentation promotes creative thinking and supports the layering process.

Finally, when the project is concluded, the required end-product documentation has already been assembled, ready for final editing and production. Last-minute crises are rare in projects that have been documented cumulatively.

SUMMARY

A system development methodology is a framework for project management. One key component of a system development methodology is a system development life cycle (SDLC). An SDLC organizes the work to be done in a development project into phases, activities, and tasks.

The SDLC presented in this text consists of four phases. The first is the investigation phase. Its purpose is to evaluate a request for system development by establishing its scope, determining a possible solution approach, and evaluating its feasibility. The investigation phase consist of two activities, initial investigation and feasibility study.

The initial investigation activity is an established, standardized way of handling requests for new or improved CIS services. The result of this activity is an understanding of the request at a level sufficient to make a preliminary recommendation about a course of action to be followed.

Recommendations that may result from the initial investigation are to do nothing, to handle the request through maintenance of existing systems, to refer the request to an information center, or to proceed to the next activity in the systems development life cycle.

The findings and recommendations of the initial investigation activity are documented in an initial investigation report. This report should include a brief statement of objectives, needs, and projected achievements; a description of major desired outputs from the new system; a list of transaction or data sources for key system inputs; an outline of the relationships among new and existing systems; a discussion of any operational problems or policy questions that may have surfaced during the initial investigation; a very rough, preliminary estimate of costs and benefits anticipated for the new system; and a recommendation for dealing with the request.

If the report recommends development of a new system, one or two general approaches to solving the problem should be described, along with an estimate of the amount of time and money required for a feasibility study. If the report recommends maintenance of existing systems, a brief document should be prepared describing what is to be done and the amount of time and money involved.

The first step in any initial investigation is to define the problem that led to the request. This definition should include statements of underlying business objectives and of systems objectives at a nontechnical, business-oriented level. The problem should be defined clearly and the description should be understood and agreed to by both the user making the request and the systems analyst doing the initial investigation.

Feasibility means that a project is possible, practical, and realistic. Factors to be considered in evaluating feasibility are financial, operational, technical, scheduling, and human.

Completion of a feasibility study means that the original problem or need has been understood, alternative solutions have been considered, and the best one has been recommended for evaluation. A feasibility study should conclude with a clear-cut recommendation as to whether the new system should be developed, along with a projected budget for the systems development project.

The principal end products of this activity are a feasibility report to the steering committee, a project plan to be implemented if the steering committee authorizes continuation of the project, and a preliminary set of working papers for the next phase of the project.

The feasibility report should contain a narrative explanation of the purpose and scope of the project; a description of the problem and proposed solution, including evaluations of technical and operational feasibility; a statement of anticipated benefits, including dollar values wherever possible; preliminary cost estimates for development and ongoing operation of the system; a return on investment (ROI) analysis of the project; an impact statement describing any changes in equipment or facilities that will be needed; a proposed schedule for succeeding phases of the project; and a list of policy-level decisions that need to be resolved by management.

The project plan prepared in connection with a feasibility study lays out detailed scheduling and staffing for each activity and task in the second phase of the project. For succeeding phases, the plan is more general.

The working papers prepared in the course of a feasibility study provide start-up guidance for work in the next phase of the project. These documents include a preliminary review of new system requirements, a preliminary review of the existing system, and suggestions for possible system solutions.

Information gathering for the feasibility study is generally limited to interviews with upper- and middle-level managers associated with the existing system. Available application software packages should be identified so that proposed solutions can incorporate them wherever possible.

Throughout the systems development process, the systems analyst is called upon to make choices among various options, each of which has advantages and disadvantages. These tradeoff decisions can be made only in light of the particular situation, by identifying all viable options, identifying the advantages and disadvantages of each, evaluating them with respect to the situation at hand, and selecting the option that maximizes the advantages and minimizes the disadvantages.

The layering approach to systems development means, in part, that each activity and phase of the project has its own specific objectives. Work should not proceed beyond these objectives until the appropriate decisions and commitments have been made. This ensures that commitments are made on the basis of adequate information while minimizing wasted effort.

Project management tools help keep the systems development project on course and on schedule. The project plan lists tasks and schedules for their performance. A staffing plan lists personnel assignments and estimates of time involved. A time reporting system keeps track of work completed and scheduled work still to be done. Status reports, issued periodically throughout the project, summarize tasks completed, tasks in process, future tasks, and overall project status.

Gantt charts can be used to show start date, elapsed time, and completion date relationships among the various work units that make up an activity, a phase, or an entire project. Project planning sheets keep track of individual tasks, the persons assigned to handle them, and planned and actual start and completion dates.

At the conclusion of this activity, the cumulative project file should contain the project plan, the initial investigation report, the feasibility report, a list of policy decisions to be made, a schedule of interviews conducted and summaries of findings, a glossary of terms (continuously updated), preliminary documentation for the existing system, preliminary documentation of new system requirements, and descriptions of possible system solutions.

Each activity and phase has defined document outputs. The documentation created in one activity or phase is analyzed, revised, torn apart, and augmented in the course of creating the documentation for successive activities. This process of cumulative documentation is a reflection of the layering approach to systems development, helping to organize thinking and ensure effective communication. At the conclusion of the project, a new system documentation is ready immediately, preventing last-minute crises and omissions.

KEY TERMS

1. system development methodology
2. information center
3. cumulative documentation
4. layering
5. application software packages
6. project plan
7. working papers
8. staffing plan
9. time reporting
10. status reporting
11. scope control
12. 80-20 rule
13. tradeoff decision
14. project management tools
15. Gantt chart
16. project planning sheet
17. systems development project team
18. interim documentation
19. final documentation

REVIEW/DISCUSSION QUESTIONS

1. Explain the way a system development life cycle supports the job of project management.
2. Describe the three building blocks of a system development methodology.
3. Describe the general purpose of the entire investigation phase.
4. Describe the purpose and end results of the initial investigation activity.
5. What are the four basic types of recommendations that may result from an initial investigation?
6. What kinds of circumstances might give rise to a systems service request? Give several examples.
7. List at least five items that should be included in an initial investigation report.
8. Explain the importance of a good problem definition and a clearly documented scope. How do these evolve during the investigation phase?
9. Describe how the basic four-step analysis process explained in Chapter 6 is followed in both activities of the investigation phase.
10. What is meant by *feasibility* at the initial investigation stage? What kinds of considerations are involved?
11. Describe the basic methodology, or series of steps, involved in making tradeoff decisions.
12. What is the purpose of a feasibility study?

13. Name the five types of feasibility considerations that should be taken into account and give a brief explanation of each.
14. Name the three end-products of the feasibility study activity and explain why each is important.
15. How does the feasibility study relate to the initial investigation activity? How does it relate to the analysis and general design phase?
16. What is the 80-20 rule, and what is its importance in systems development?
17. What is the purpose of a status report, and what information should it contain?
18. What is a Gantt chart, and how can it help in project management?
19. What is meant by cumulative documentation, and why is it important?
20. What are the contents of the project file at the end of the investigation phase, and what purpose will they serve later?

PRACTICE ASSIGNMENTS

1. You are conducting an initial investigation for the Central City water billing-sewage system. You need to identify options or alternatives for providing customer status information to be used in responding to inquiries. Two identified options are the printing of status reports periodically and on-line inquiry. What are the tradeoffs between these options? Can you identify other options?

2. You are working on a system for billing guests on checkout from a motel. You are interested in determining the best and most cost-effective way of making sure that all charges are included. These can involve charges for telephone calls or purchases at the restaurant, bar, or gift shop. Options already identified are on-line entry of charges from the points at which they are incurred or a plan under which desk clerks call the charge points at the time of checkouts. What are the tradeoffs between these options? Can you identify other options?

20

Analysis and
General Design Phase – Part 1

Objectives
On completing this and other learning objectives for this and the following chapters, you should be able to:

■ Explain the overall flow of activity in the analysis and general design phase and the relationships among the four activities that comprise the phase.

■ State the principal objectives of each activity in the analysis and general design phase.

■ Describe the major end products of each activity in the analysis and general design phase.

■ Describe how the structured analysis modeling process is implemented within the phase.

■ Understand the transition from the results of analysis to a general design for a new system.

■ Understand how the various analysis and design techniques presented in this text are used together on an actual system development project.

THE ANALYSIS AND GENERAL
DESIGN PHASE

Analysis and general design is the second phase of the SDLC. It consists of four activities. The phase begins with the results of the investigation phase and ends with a general architecture or design for a new system to meet the business needs expressed during investigation.

The work of this phase lies at the heart of the material covered in this text. In order to provide deeper coverage of the SDLC at this point, the material has been split into two chapters. This chapter covers the first two activities of the analysis and general design phase, and Chapter 21 covers the remaining two. Before the discussion of the first two activities, the overall phase overview is presented.

Objectives

The key objectives of this phase are to

- determine the requirements for the new system.
- develop a general design or architecture of the new system.
- establish user acceptance of and concurrence in the design.
- obtain a commitment from the CIS department that the design of the new system can be implemented within the established time and dollar limits.
- develop a project plan for performing the work of the next phase.
- present sufficient information that the steering committee can determine whether to continue, revise the scope or approach, or abort the project.

Process

The process followed during this phase is similar in scope to that followed in the preceding investigation phase. Initial findings and proposed design ideas are pursued in substantially more depth.

This phase is perhaps the most critical in the entire system development life cycle. There are two major concerns. First, an attempt is made to fully understand and model the user's requirements for the new system. The ultimate success of the completed system will be directly related to the quality of these requirements. If the analyst finally understands the nature of the user's business, comprehends the operations that must be supported and the type of information that is required, and models them correctly, the resulting system should be more than a mirror of the organization. It should complement and enhance the business.

Second, from an understanding of user requirements, the analyst creates a general design for the new system. This presents a view of the new system as the user will see it and a high-level technical design. This design will be the base on which detailed design work is done. Its quality will determine the long-term stability and maintainability of the system.

Thus, the analysis and general design phase first determines the extent to which the resulting system will enhance the business it serves and second determines the extent to which it can grow with that business.

In Chapter 6, a very natural four-step process for doing systems analysis was discussed (see Figure 20-1). The analyst

Figure 20.1. Four-step process.

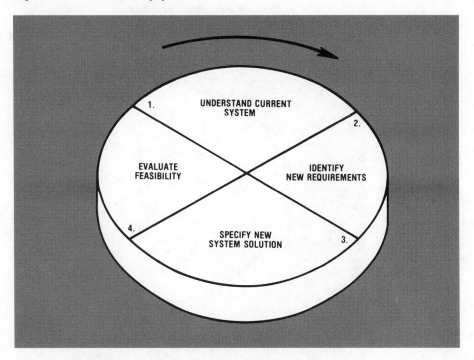

- gains an understanding of the existing system.
- captures requirements for the new system.
- conceives possible approaches or general designs for a new system.
- evaluates the feasibility of these proposed general designs.

This process was completed twice during the investigation phase: first at a very superficial level during the initial investigation and then in somewhat more detail during the feasibility study. These same four basic steps constitute the essence of the process followed during the analysis and general design phase. In this phase considerably more time is spent delving into a much greater level of detail.

The modeling process of structured analysis allows enhancment of the four-step process illustrated in Figure 20-1, as shown in Figure 20-2.

- An understanding of the existing system is gained by creating a physical, then a logical, model.
- As requirements for the new system are determined, they are classified as logical (business) or physical (operational-technical) requirements.
- Possible general designs for a new system are derived by constructing logical, then physical, models for the new system.
- Feasibility is evaluated on the basis of the proposed new system physical model(s).

Figure 20.2. Structured analysis modeling process enhances the basic four-step analysis process.

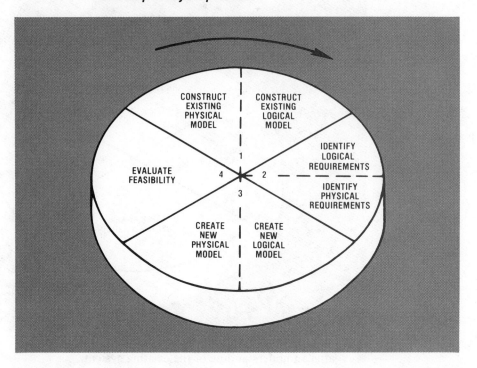

The analysis and general design phase consists of four activities that track closely with the process described above:

- Activity 3: existing system review corresponds to the first step.
- Activity 4: new system requirements includes the second and third steps.
- Activity 5: new system design extends the physical model of Step 3 and completes Step 4. (Design is actually a series of individual design decisions coupled with individual feasibility evaluations.)
- Activity 6: implementation and installation planning is a brief activity to prepare for, and determine the cost of, the next phase of the system development life cycle.

Figure 20-3 presents a process view of the analysis and general design phase. The processes are numbered to reflect the corresponding activities. (Processes 3a, 3b correspond to activity 3 and so on.) While this process tends to have an overall linear flow, as will become clear when the activities are studied in greater detail, there is significant overlapping. While the phase begins with existing system review tasks, work begins very soon on new system requirements and

Figure 20.3. A process view of the analysis and general design phase.

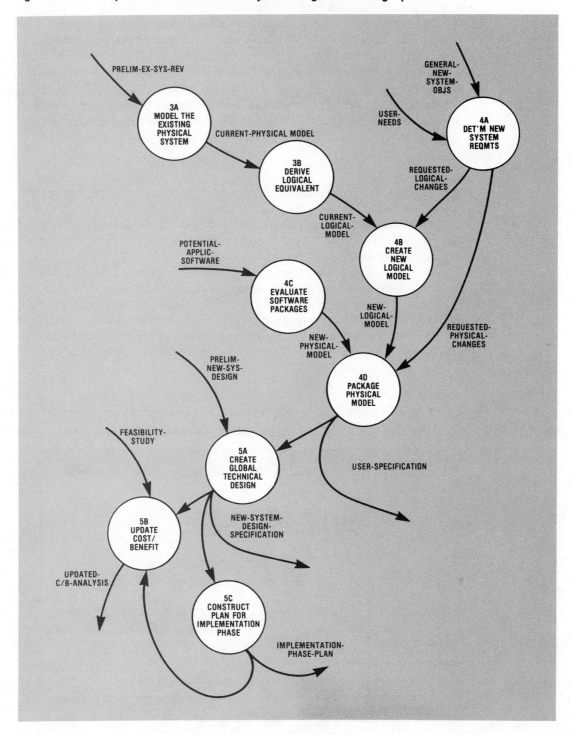

even the initial steps of new system design. This overlapping of activities is illustrated in the Gantt Chart in Figure 20-4.

These activities overlap because the modeling process that drives them is an *iterative* and *layered* process. The basic steps are executed over and over (iteratively) as the analyst works at increasingly greater levels (or layers) of detail within the system. An appreciation for how this iteration and layering occurs within the context of the activities of this phase is the key for doing effective and efficient analysis work. Concentration is on this understanding as the activities are reviewed in greater depth in the following sections of this chapter.

End-product

The analysis and general design phase has two major end products, user specifications and new systems design specification.

The **user specification** presents a physical model of the new system from the user's point of view. Included is a commitment by the user to accept and support implementation of the new system.

The **new system design specification** introduces technical design considerations for the new system, building upon the content of the user specification. This general design permits the feasibility evaluation performed in the first phase to be updated and serves as a basis for the detailed design activities of the next phase. Included here is a commitment from the design staff within the CIS area to implement the system within the budget and time schedule specified.

Figure 20.4.   Gantt chart for the analysis and general design phase illustrates the heavy overlap among analysis activities.

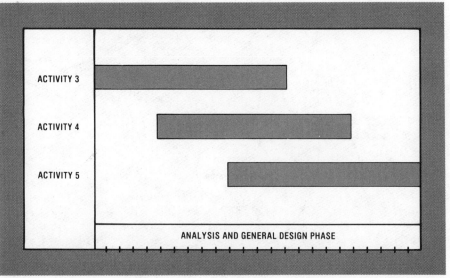

Decision

At the conclusion of this phase, the steering committee is asked to decide whether the new system should be implemented. A favorable decision authorizes the project to go forward into the detailed design and implementation phase.

This is perhaps the most critical decision point for the steering committee. By the end of this phase, a major amount of time has been committed to the project—perhaps up to half the total development time. But a major amount of work remains to be done—as much as two thirds. This is the last point when the steering committee can direct its investment. Near the end of this phase it is natural for the development team to work with the steering committee to identify several implementation options of varying cost and risk.

ACTIVITY 3: EXISTING SYSTEM REVIEW

The existing system review activity establishes the base point for understanding requirements and for designing a new system to meet those requirements.

Activity Description

The existing systems review activity builds an understanding of the business problem being studied and documents the existing systems that relate to this problem. In an effort to save time and expense on a large project, the question is often asked: "Why waste time looking at the existing system?" As long as the existing system is to be replaced, there seems to be little or no value in documenting present forms, reports, procedures, and so on. There is some appeal to the argument. There certainly is no need to waste time on throwaway activity. But there is also a danger in this argument. If the study of the existing system is shortchanged, the development efforts may start with insufficient or inadequate information concerning the business problem that is being attacked and solved. The key to achieving the proper balance is to understand what insights the existing system has to offer.

The reason for studying and documenting the existing system, plainly stated, is that this is how an understanding of business problems and needs is built. Without this understanding, it would be difficult, perhaps impossible, to build an adequate replacement system.

The project team creates first a physical model of the existing system, then a logical model. Their objective is to get to the logical model as quickly as possible. This activity is not concerned with precise documentation of current procedures, files, programs, and so on. The point is to understand the business objectives and business functions of the existing system. This can be a difficult job because these basic business considerations are probably not well documented. But the payoff in terms of understanding is great. For even though the physical system may change drastically as a result of the development project, the underlying business objectives and the logical functions of the system generally will not change by much. It is this logical understanding that carries forward and serves as an important underpinning for the design of the new system.

As a further value, the understanding that leads to a working rapport among members of the project team begins with a sensitivity to things as they are. From this basis, users can better articulate their own needs, and systems professionals can better understand the business needs that the new system should be meeting.

Objectives

The primary objective of the existing system review activity is to build an understanding of the business goals, objectives, and functions involved in the application areas encompassed by the project.

The actual study of the existing system and its results form the secondary objective. That is, as a working tool, the project team should develop documentation at a general level for the existing system. This documentation is not usually important for its own sake. Rather, it provides a basis for understanding key business objectives and functions and for identifying improvements in the new system.

Scope

The feasibility report launches the existing system review activity with documentation that provides an overview of what happens within the existing system The project team has a rough idea of the major functions of the system and, particularly, of its key deficiencies in terms of current business needs. Also known at the outset is the extent to which computers are used, as well as the approaches taken in computer processing, such as batch, on-line, centralized, distributed, or other options.

At the conclusion of this activity, the project team should know all that it needs to know (and probably all that it will ever know) about the existing, in-place system and procedures. The study of the existing system should go to great depth in building an understanding of the logical aspects of the system. In most cases, less depth and detailing are needed in reviewing physical processing, particularly in documenting physical procedures that will be abandoned. However, physical review of the existing systems should contain enough detail to support the updating of the cost-benefit analysis at the end of this phase. Results should include an understanding of any procedures that could profitably be carried forward into the new system.

For example, in the Central City water billing system, at a logical level it is necessary to recognize that preparation of customer bills based on water consumption is a key business function. It is necessary to understand the nature of the water rates, the fact that the cost per unit varies by customer type and level of usage. Also relevant is the business policy about applying penalties to past-due accounts: A 10 percent surcharge is assessed on any balance unpaid at the time the next bill is processed, even though the bill itself states that the penalty will be assessed after 10 days. It is necessary to document the basic design of the current computer system. However, it is probably not necessary to document the individual programs that make up this system.

A heavy overlap exists between this activity and activities 4 and 5. As data on the current system are gathered, they form the base for understanding what must be included in the new system in activity 4: new system requirements and the specification of new procedures in activity 5: new system design. The continuity lies in the modeling that takes place. The logical model of the existing system feeds the logical model of the new system, which in turn feeds the physical model of the new system. Thus, there is a sequence as well as an overlapping. Activity 3 begins first. The next two activities have some concurrent overlapping. But activity 5 concludes last.

End-products

The end-products of the existing system review activity are documents that build cumulatively upon portions of the feasibility report.

Functional (Logical) Model. The model constructed for the existing system should stress the business objectives that the system supports, the main functions that the system performs, and the management decisions that are based on information provided by the system and the affected decision makers. This is the **functional (logical) model**.

This particular end-product emphasizes logical aspects of the existing system rather than physical details. For example, in reviewing the water billing system, the writing of customer bills would be recognized as an important business function and included as logical system content. By contrast, the editing of inputs to be sure that all keyed meter readings were numeric and reasonable would be part of the physical model and would be of no interest at this point.

The focus here is on the key business features of the system, the data and the policies or organizational rules by which they are transformed. These rules for operating the business will need to be included, perhaps in revised form, in the new system. Therefore, these policies or processing rules should be documented carefully and in some detail. Failure to do so at this point may result in the omission of required data elements and data relationships among functions, causing rework and delays later in the project.

Physical Documentation. One reason for avoiding extensive depth in documenting the physical details of the existing system is that there are likely to be so many details that the project could lose its perspective. In practice, a relatively small percentage of all the documents and procedures control most of the services within any given system. The 80–20 rule is a handy guideline. In other words, perhaps 20 percent of the documents represent 80 percent of the value in any given system — including transaction documents, management reports, and decision support outputs.

Thus, systems analysts must develop judgment about what is really important. This judgmental skill can be difficult to achieve. Among the 80 percent of the less critical documents may be reports that are no longer used, processing controls that no longer apply, and even source input forms that are no longer necessary. But beware: a portion of this 80 percent may deal with how to handle certain processing exceptions. An example in the water billing system would be the special documents and processing that send a landlord a composite bill covering all rental properties, rather than directing individual bills to each of the tenants. While the documents themselves are low volume and of relatively little interest as part of the physical documentation, their existence discloses an important business policy, the willingness of the city to provide this special service to landlords. Such a policy must be reflected in the logical model of the system.

Documentation of the existing system is usually guided by some sort of checklist of the kinds of forms or records to be collected. A typical checklist of this type is shown in Figure 20-5. Here are some guidelines for using this type of checklist in gathering information on the existing system:

Figure 20.5.   Checklist of categories of physical documentation to be collected during Existing System Review activity.

VALUABLE FOR USE IN ANALYSIS PROCESS

A. ORGANIZATION

Organization charts
Objective/purpose of each functional unit
    Why is it necessary?
    How does it overlap other units?
    Are there conflicting purposes within the unit or among units?

B. POLICIES AND PROCEDURES

Copies of existing policies and procedures
Current use
    Followed?
    Maintained?
    Method of distribution?
    Used by?
    When used?
Inconsistencies and current problems

C. CURRENT SYSTEM OUTPUTS

Typical copies
    Manual
    Computerized
Purpose/use
Problems with accuracy and use

Figure 20.5. **Checklist of categories.** *(continued)*

D. CURRENT SYSTEM INPUTS

Typical copies (actually filled out)
Purpose/use
Problems with accuracy and use

E. DESCRIPTIONS OF CURRENT PROCESSING

Physical system
    Overall work flows
    Volume and timing considerations
    System performance statistics
    Man/machine boundaries
    Control points and control mechanisms
    Work scheduling and priority handling
    Current bottlenecks and other procedural problems
Logical system
    Flow of data through the system
    Required transformation of data by the system
    Inconsistencies, unnecessary or missing flows

F. DATA FILES (MANUAL OR COMPUTERIZED)

Description of contents
Samples of manual data records
Methods for updating/maintaining files
Problems with currency, accuracy, redundancy

G. PERIPHERAL SYSTEMS

Other systems that must interface with this system
Nature of intersystem dependencies
    Data flows
    Shared files

■ To the extent possible, collect forms or documents that have actually been used for input and output. Do not collect only blank forms or form layouts. Actual examples of entries on the forms hold the key to evaluating the system. From these entries, an analyst can tell what is really happening in the system, as distinct from what was originally meant to happen when the forms were designed. Also, actual entries may show situations in which data are needed that are not called for on the form and might have been missed had a blank form been used. Bear in mind that all this data gathering is of temporary interest only. Forms and other documents do not have to be picture-perfect. Rough entries are sufficient.

- As appropriate, supplementary explanations should be added to input and output forms to document where they are prepared and how they are used.

- All file structures should be documented with file definitions and record layout forms. Any manually maintained files should be described, with all data and information content identified.

- Collect any existing documentation of systems or procedures. These may include manuals, flow charts, or possibly data flow diagrams. However, do not place heavy reliance on existing documentation. There is a high likelihood that the system has been modified and that documentation prepared when the system was developed is obsolete. Thus, any documentation collected should be used primarily as a basis for studying the system further to find out what is actually happening.

- Controls or timing requirements incorporated in the physical system to comply with business processing needs should be noted and described.

- Organizational charts for all departments or groups affected by the existing system should be collected. These should be supplemented with descriptions of the identified jobs.

- Enough data on current operating costs should be collected to support an updating of the cost-benefit analysis.

- Review the documentation about the maintenance history of the existing system. Maintenance efforts can tell a lot about a system. For example, if one portion of the system has been modified frequently, this could point either to volatile business conditions or to an inadequacy in the original design. Conversely, stability in a portion of the system could indicate satisfaction. Or, it could indicate that these procedures are of little importance and may actually have fallen into disuse.

- Informal or "off-the-books" records kept by system users should be noted and described. These could point to deficiencies in the existing system.

Current System Deficiencies. Throughout the review of the existing system, members of the project team should work actively to identify system deficiencies. This goes beyond the routine guidelines for a systems study. If the study is confined to actual documented procedures, deficiencies may never be uncovered. Instead, if a systems analyst pays attention to user complaints about things that aren't happening or services that are unsatisfactory, this information could lead to substantial improvements in the design of the new system.

Some deficiencies in the existing system will be readily apparent to users. These will tend to be physical problems. For example, because of increased business activity, the existing system may be unable to process the current volume of transactions. Or, if users are compiling operating statistics by hand, this could be a sign that an additional report should be added to the new system.

Logical deficiencies might be less apparent to users. For example, if overlapping responsibilities existed in two or more departments, none of the users involved might know about it. This is the type of deficiency that should show up in effective systems analysis. Also, users may be doing things routinely and be unaware that the computer, or improved manual methods, can help them by doing the same work more efficiently. For example, the water department may have people checking through miles of copies of water bills for follow-up on late payments. The person doing this work may be unaware that the computer could do the same thing in a small fraction of the time now being spent on the job.

Interface Points with Other Systems. Most operational systems receive inputs from and deliver outputs to other systems. This is true for both manual and computer-based systems. Information on all such interfacing relationships should be gathered during this activity. The critical information includes the timing, volume or amount, and timeliness requirements for data and information passed among these systems.

Management Policy Decisions. As the project team digs deeper into the procedures of the existing system, additional situations requiring policy guidance may be uncovered. These situations may result from a lack of existing policies, from existing policies that conflict with one another, or from failure to adhere to established policies. These situations should be noted and documented carefully. Management decisions may be needed before work can proceed on design of the new system.

The Process

The existing system review activity builds on the preliminary existing system review produced during the feasibility study. Through extensive use of interviews and other data-gathering techniques, information is collected for the documentation end-product defined earlier. Techniques for this type of information gathering are covered in Chapter 8.

Concurrent with these data collection tasks, the system modeling process begins. This process is covered in Chapter 4. Early in this activity, construction may begin on a model consisting of a set of (physical) data flow diagrams that show how data flow through and are transformed by the system. Such a physical model can tie together and give meaning to the physical documentation elements.

There is no lasting interest in the physical model itself. The desired end-product is a logical model of the existing system. The physical model is, however, a natural starting point. It emphasizes *how* processing is currently done, modeling the system from the user's point of view. This enables the user to verify the accuracy of the model being created. Since the desired end-product is a logical model, however, care should be taken from the very beginning to base even the physical model on the major business activities of the organization rather than on particular people or departments.

As understanding of the existing system improves, analysts begin to develop a logical model. This process is described in Chapter 6 and is illustrated in the water billing system case later on. The key point to understand here is that physical aspects of the system such as editing, backup, auditing, and processing security are downplayed. Emphasis is placed on the essential business functions that are important to the system no matter how it is physically implemented. For the water billing system, this would include such items as preparing bills, processing payments, and responding to customer queries.

The analyst should continually ask "why?" An understanding is needed of why each step in the process is performed, why each data element is necessary, why each output is produced, and even why certain things are not of interest.

The answers to these questions should be consistent with the objectives of the organization and the system under study. This type of questioning may well turn up current practices that are unnecessary or that are not supportable in terms of organizational objectives. In any case, it will ensure an intimate knowledge and understanding of the existing system.

Two standard systems analysis techniques are used heavily during this activity, interviews and walkthroughs. These methods are described in Chapters 8 and 9. The important points to understand here are the areas of emphasis and the projected results anticipated from the use of these methods.

Interviews. During the existing system review activity, interviews are conducted at every level of the organization. However, the sessions should be oriented toward the acquisition of knowledge about business considerations, business decisions, and business objectives. This kind of information, by its very nature, comes primarily from top and middle managers. Thus, while interviews with clerical-level personnel are important for understanding how the system works, special emphasis should be placed on management interviews.

Recognize also that, while the main purpose for the interviews is to gather information to use in modeling the current system, users will be far more interested in discussing complaints and frustrations they have with the current system. Exposure to user complaints or problems is an opportunity that should be exploited. Turn the complaints into positive statements of what the user would like. Then, as interview notes are carried forward into the requirements and design activities that follow, these suggestions can be studied and, if appropriate, incorporated. Such a show of responsiveness can build enthusiasm and support for a systems development project. This illustrates how the several activities of the analysis and general design phase overlap. While attempting to model the current system, the analyst is beginning to identify requirements for the new system and probably forming preliminary ideas for potential solutions to meet these requirements.

Walkthroughs. A walkthrough is, by nature, a troubleshooting technique. It is designed to identify errors in a product. Many CIS professionals are sold on the value of program design and code walkthroughs. But the products of analysis benefit just as much from the walkthrough process as do programming products.

Particular attention should be given to walkthroughs of sets of data flow diagrams and process descriptions on which the model of the existing system is based. Emphasis should be on the completeness as well as on the accuracy of these model components. Obviously, knowledgeable users are key participants in these walkthroughs.

Caution. In studying the existing system, many users, and some systems analysts, find themselves using the terms "system" and "department" interchangeably. These are not the same. A given department may use several data processing systems. A given individual may have several responsibilities and may perform tasks connected with several systems. In working through this activity, and particularly in conducting interviews, care should be taken to focus on the system under study. Extreme confusion can result from describing overall jobs or responsibilities of department personnel rather than describing the processing steps or the way the system under study is used.

Personnel Involved

Members of the project team during the existing system review activity will include

- the project leader.
- systems analysts.
- user managers.
- user operating personnel.

Cumulative Project File

At the conclusion of the existing system review activity the project file will consist of

- an updated project plan.
- the initial investigation report.
- the feasibility report.
- a list of management policy decisions that must be made to enable the project to continue.
- an interview schedule and interview summaries, updated to reflect interviews conducted during this activity.
- an updated glossary of terms.
- a logical model of the existing system.
- additional physical documentation of the existing system.
- a preliminary overview of new system requirements, prepared during the feasibility study activity.
- a description of possible new system solutions, also prepared during the feasibility study activity.

The water billing system case study will be used to illustrate some critical products and key processes of the existing system review activity. If you are working on your own case or miniproject, this would be a good point to finalize your logical model of the existing system and organize the supporting documentation.

The context diagram for the Central City water billing system is shown in Figure 20-6. The next step in modeling the current system is to create Diagram 0, a high level view of the current data and processing. A five-step process for doing this was discussed in Chapter 4.

The first step is to note and list the major data stores currently in use. In the water billing system there are three important existing data stores:

- The customer master file.
- The account journal, which lists payments received from customers and any adjustments made.
- The billing transaction file, which contains records of all bills issued.

The second step is to list the major business occurrences or events within the system. Recall that three important indicators are used to identify these.

- *Acceptance of a major input to the system* (for example, a customer payment).
- *Production of a major output by the system* (for example, a customer bill).
- *Any function triggered by timing* (for example in the water billing system, one of the requirements is an annual report of water consumption by customer type to be used in the calculation of new water rates. Other, admittedly physical, events within the system that are triggered by time are the annual purging of old records from the account journal and the billing transaction file.)

In the water billing application, 10 major business occurrences have been identified. These are listed in Figure 20-7. This list then becomes the basis for the process steps to be included in Diagram 0.

The third step is to draw a segment, or fragment, of a data flow diagram for each of the identified events. Each segment will usually contain a single process bubble covering that event. As the data flow diagram is developed, this bubble will become a high-level parent with relatively large numbers of inputs and outputs. A series of fragments corresponding with the list in Figure 20-7 is shown in Figure 20-8.

Recall that in developing the diagram fragments, both the outputs produced and the events, or necessary inputs, that cause the processing to take place are identified, noting the source and destination of each. These sources and destinations may be external entities, data stores, or other processes. Specifying inputs

Figure 20.6. *Context diagram for current Central City water billing system.*

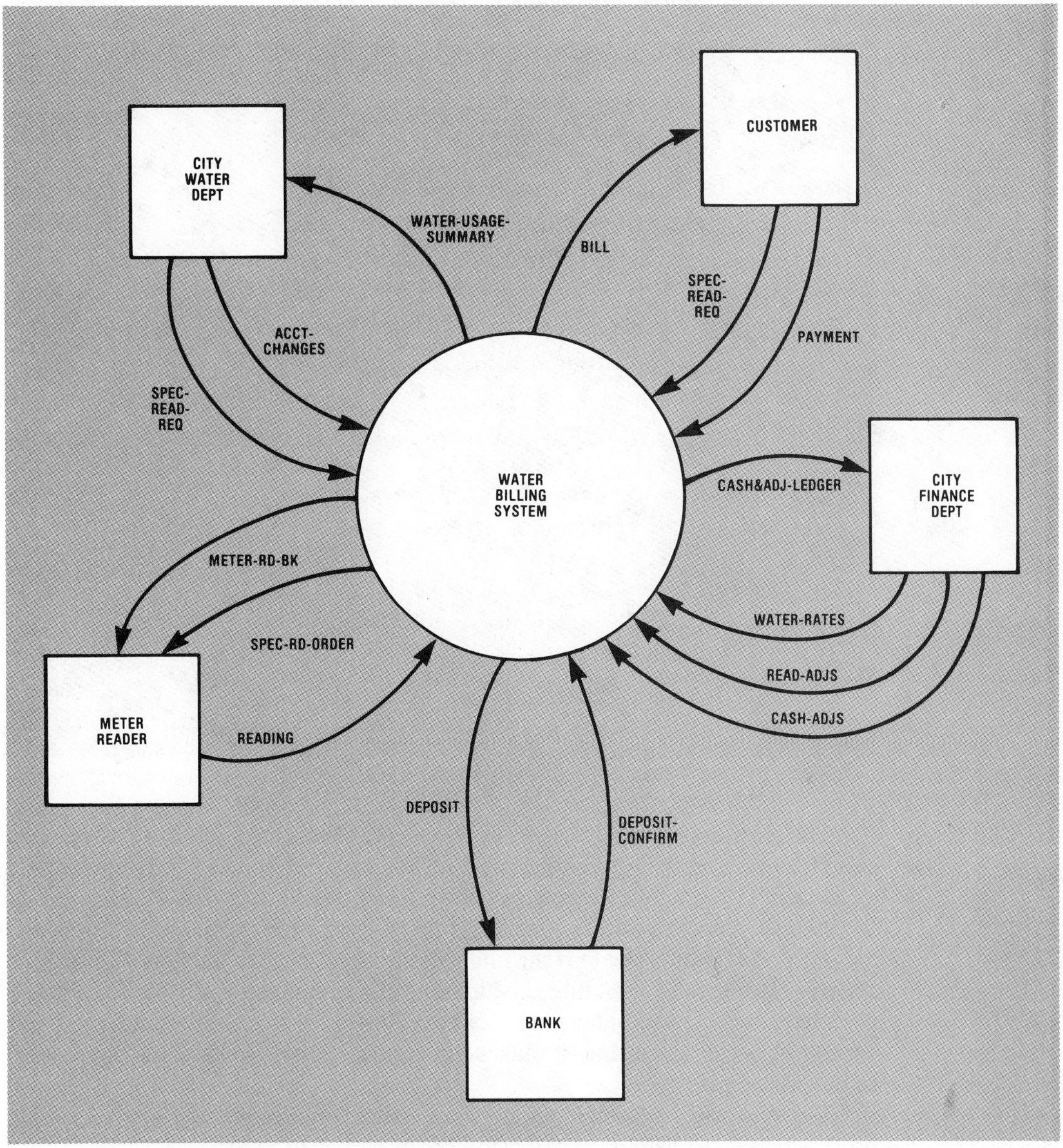

and outputs in this way establishes the scope of the process, in effect, producing a clear definition of what the process does.

The fourth step in the preparation of a Diagram 0 is to assemble the fragments into a single data flow diagram. The first attempt is usually rough. (Try it.)

Figure 20.7. *These are the key business events in the existing Central City water billing system.*

Events tied to production of major outputs
　　1. Prepare customer bill
　　2. Extract meters to read

Events tied to application of major inputs
　　3. Apply customer payments
　　4. Apply new readings

Additional events—tied to minor outputs
　　5. Prepare cash and adjustment journal
　　6. Prepare special reading orders

Additional event—tied to minor inputs
　　7. Modify customer account information

Events triggered by timing
　　8. Prepare annual water usage summary
　　9. Perform annual archiving of account journal transactions
　　10. Perform annual archiving of billing transactions

The fifth and final step is to evaluate this rough model for accuracy and completeness and then to reorganize it for understandability. A refined Diagram 0, the result of several attempts, is shown in Figure 20-9.

At this point, in addition to Diagram 0, there are fragments of lower-level diagrams that model the current understanding of various parts of the existing system. Rather than spending time to carefully organize these fragments into a complete, leveled, and balanced set of data flow diagrams that accurately depict current physical processing, it makes more sense to drive toward a logical model as quickly as possible.

The creation of logical models is described in Chapter 6. The eight-step process presented here is an extension of the earlier process:

■ Replace upper-level parent bubbles with child diagrams, creating one or more large, expanded diagrams.

■ Remove purely physical (nonlogical) processes (e.g., edits, audits, etc.).

■ Remove intermediate or holding files (nonlogical data stores).

■ Connect resulting system fragments.

■ Replace linear sequences of processes with parallel processes when possible.

Figure 20.8. *These data flow diagram fragments correspond with the key business events of the Central City water billing system.*

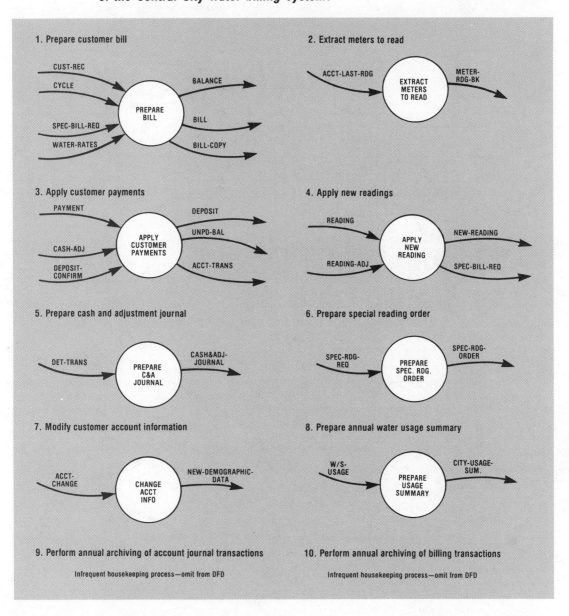

■ Remove excess data from data flows.

■ Replace current files with a set of normalized data stores based on an E-R model for the organization.

■ Regroup the result into a hierarchical set of data flow diagrams.

Figure 20.9. This is a Diagram 0 for the current Central City water billing system.

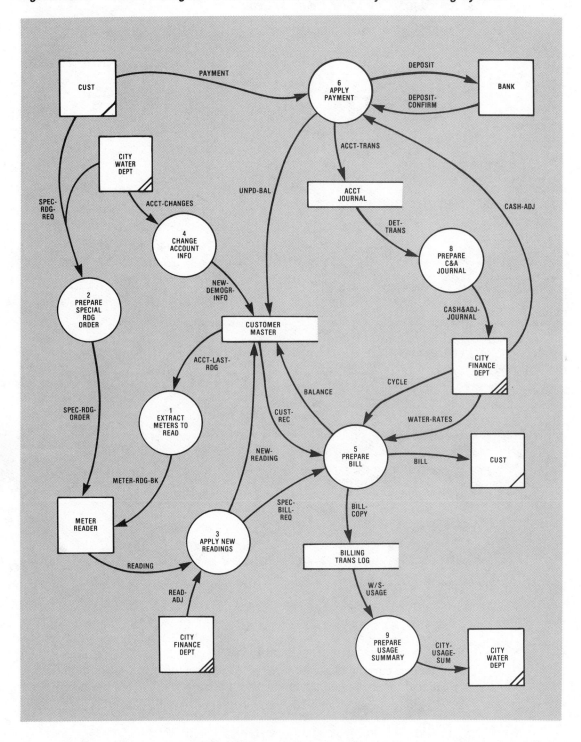

As an illustration of the process of deriving a logical model from a physical model, consider Figures 20-10 and 20-11. Figure 20-10 shows the portion of the expanded data flow diagram for the water billing system that processes new readings and produces incycle bills. This diagram is almost painfully physical. In creating the corresponding logical model, the nonlogical processes (processes 1, 2, and 3) and the update logs can be dropped. Figure 20-11 is the result. Fragments have been connected, parallel processes have been inserted where appropriate, and processes have been starved.

The data flow diagram models are supported by data dictionary entries documenting the key data elements, structures, and stores and by process specifications that capture the key, lower level operating policies of the organization. Illustrations of typical content are presented in Figures 20-12 to 20-16.

ACTIVITY 4: NEW SYSTEM REQUIREMENTS

The new system requirements activity refines the requirements expressed in the investigation phase and creates the standard against which the new system will be evaluated.

Activity Description

The new system requirements activity marks a transition from the study of the existing system to the building of the new one. The purpose is to develop a description and statement of requirements for the new system in sufficient depth so that the user can evaluate and approve the new system from his or her own perspective.

The work in this activity includes further analysis, together with a synthesis process. The probing and information gathering undertaken to determine new system requirements resembles the work performed during the existing system review and occurs at about the same time. As systems analysts study the existing system, they should identify the business functions and needs that must be met by the new system. In part, this involves investigating user descriptions of the inadequacies or problems of the existing system.

The main data-gathering technique used at this point in the analysis process is the interview. Interviews are conducted with both user management and operating personnel. These interviews are aimed at identifying logical and physical requirements.

Modeling techniques are used to begin a transition from the analysis of the existing system toward the design of the new one. Using both the logical model of the existing system and the logical requirements for the new one, analysts develop a logical model for the new system. Next, a physical model of the new system is prepared as a basis for user acceptance. *Alternative* physical models representing varying levels of automated support and cost may be proposed.

Always remember that a computer information system consists of much more than a set of computer programs and processes. The system also involves

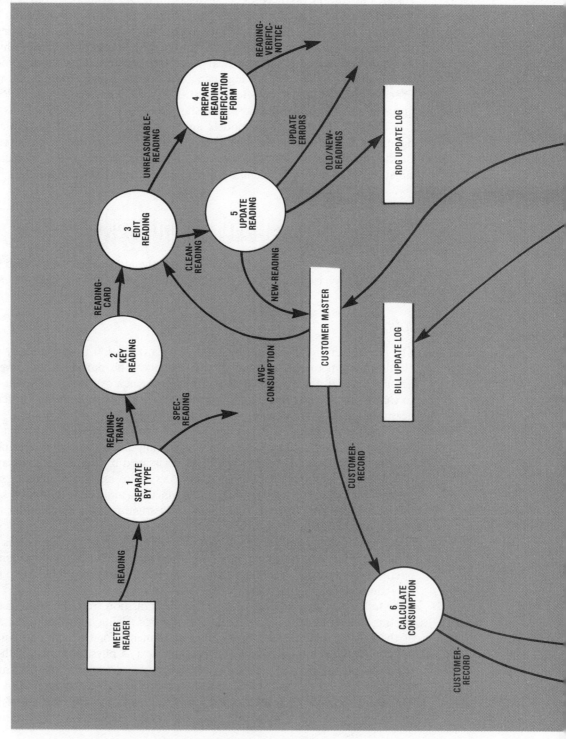

Figure 20.10. Portion of an expanded physical model of water billing system. These procedures process readings and prepare incycle bills.

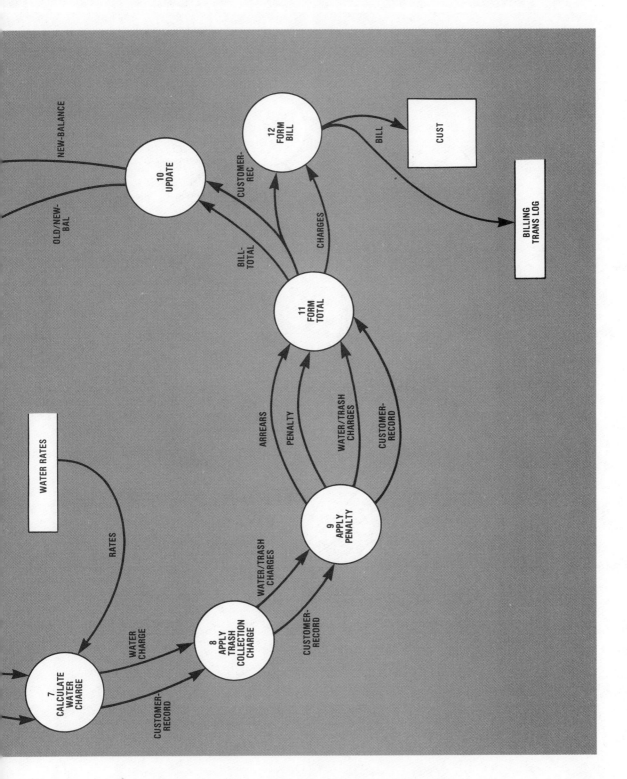

Figure 20.11. *Portion of an expanded logical model of water billing system. These procedures process reading and prepare incycle bills.*

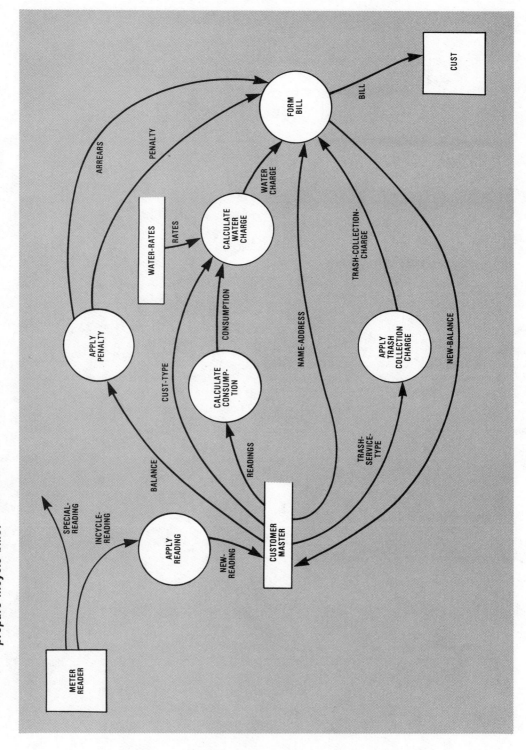

Figure 20.12.   Form used for defining values of data elements.

DATA ELEMENT SPECIFICATION

ELEMENT NAME: READING-DATE

SYSTEM:	Water Billing	**DATE:** 10-20
ELEMENT NO.:		**PREPARER:** KJP
ALIASES:		

DESCRIPTION: Date reading was taken, MM-DD-YY in 6 digits

SOURCE: Meter Reader

USED IN: Prepare Billing, Prepare Usage Summary

STRUCTURES(S)   **DATA STORE(S)**

CUSTOMER MASTER

TOTAL BYTES: **DATA TYPE:**

EDITING:

VALID VALUES/CODES	MEANINGS
MM 01-12	Standard Date Interpretation
DD 01-31	Check numeric Range check Cross check day with month in
YY 00-99	range check

Figure 20.13.   Form used for defining data structures.

DATA STRUCTURE SPECIFICATION

STRUCTURE NAME: INCYCLE-BILL

SYSTEM NAME: Water Billing   **DATE:**   10-27

STRUCTURE NO.:   **PREPARER:**   KJP

ALIASES: RESIDENTIAL-BILL

DESCRIPTION: Contains all data associated with the bill produced
                   for an individual residential customer account

DATA STORE(S):

USED IN:

TOTAL BYTES:

DATA COMPOSITION:

FIELD NAME	ELEMENT NAME	TYPE	BYTES

ACCT #
+ CUST-NAME
+ BILL-ADDR
+ PREV-READING
+ DATE-PREV-READING
+ CURRENT-READING
+ DATE-CURR-READING
+ {CHARGE}_{EACH SERVICE}
+ UNPAID-BALANCE
+ (PENALTY-AMT)
+ TOTAL-AMT-DUE
+ PAYMENT-DUE-DATE

Figure 20.14.   Form used to specify content of a data store.

DATA STORE/FILE SPECIFICATION

FILE NAME: CUSTOMER MASTER

SYSTEM NAME: Water Billing   **DATE:**   12-7

FILE NO.:   **PREPARER:**   TAP

ALIASES:

STRUCTURES:

DESCRIPTION: Used for preparing bills
Also to prepare meter reading book and accept new
readings

DEVICE TYPE: **ORGANIZATION:**   INDEXED

RECORD SIZE: 200 (BYTES)   **AVERAGE VOLUME:**   20 K

                                                                (RECORDS)

PEAK VOLUME: **GROWTH RATE:**   500/yr

KEY(S):

PRIMARY   **SECONDARY**

ACCT #

RETENTION:

Figure 20.14. *Form used to specify content of a data store.* (continued)

ACCESSED BY:

PROCESS(ES)	UPDATE ACCESS METHOD

BACKUP:

INSTRUCTIONS:

RECORD COMPOSITION	APPROX. LENGTH
ACCT #	6
+ CUST-NAME	25
+ SERVICE-ADDR	40
+ BILLING-ADDR	40
+ USER-CLASS	1
+ READING-SEQUENCE	4
+ METER-TYPE	2
+ (METER-READER-MSG)	30
+ CURR-BAL*	35
+ $_6${READING}*	90

*These are data structures

Figure 20.15. *Process forms can use graphic notations or narrative for processing definitions. This example uses a decision tree.*

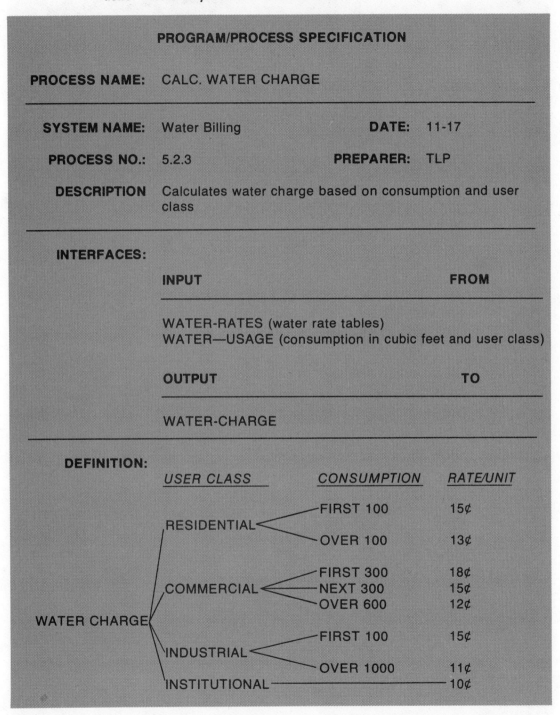

PROGRAM/PROCESS SPECIFICATION

PROCESS NAME: CALC. WATER CHARGE

SYSTEM NAME: Water Billing   **DATE:** 11-17

PROCESS NO.: 5.2.3   **PREPARER:** TLP

DESCRIPTION Calculates water charge based on consumption and user class

INTERFACES:

INPUT	FROM

WATER-RATES (water rate tables)
WATER—USAGE (consumption in cubic feet and user class)

OUTPUT	TO

WATER-CHARGE

DEFINITION:

USER CLASS	CONSUMPTION	RATE/UNIT
RESIDENTIAL	FIRST 100	15¢
	OVER 100	13¢
COMMERCIAL	FIRST 300	18¢
	NEXT 300	15¢
	OVER 600	12¢
INDUSTRIAL	FIRST 100	15¢
	OVER 1000	11¢
INSTITUTIONAL		10¢

WATER CHARGE

Figure 20.16. *This process form uses a narrative for a process definition.*

PROGRAM/PROCESS SPECIFICATION

PROCESS NAME: PREP. IN-CYCLE BILL

SYSTEM NAME: Water Billing   **DATE:** 11-15

PROCESS NO.: 5.2   **PREPARER:** TLP

DESCRIPTION: Batch run to prepare all water bills for specified cycle

INTERFACES:

INPUT	FROM
WATER-RATES (water rate tables)	
CUST-REC	
CYCLE (cycle to be billed class)	

OUTPUT	TO
IN-CYCLE BILL and COPY	
BALANCE (new balance updates CUST-MAST)	

DEFINITION:

There are four residential cycles which are billed bimonthly according to the following schedule:

Cycle   1-2nd week (Jan,Mar,May,July,Sept,Nov)
           2-4th week
           3-2nd week (Feb,Apr,June,Aug,Oct,Dec)
           4-4th week

There is a 5th cycle consisting of all commercial, industrial, and institutional accounts. They are billed using the same process as for residential—except that they are billed the 1st week of each month.

people who accept input, process data themselves, turn some data over to computers for processing, prepare output, and the like. In a sense, the computer processing represents a subsystem within a larger system. The logical model of the current system concentrates on the flow and processing of data, no matter how it is accomplished, by computer or by manual processing. After modifying this logical model to accommodate the functional requirements for the new system, a new computer system within the overall information system is defined as part of the physical model for the new system.

At this point, for purposes of user presentations, the computer system is treated as a black box within the overall information system. That is, the user needs to know what goes into the subsystem and what comes out, but need not be concerned with how things happen inside the black box, the computer processing.

The result of this analysis activity is a specification for the new system from the user's perspective. This user specification defines the entire information system, both computerized and manual processing, from the user's point of view. The user specification covers the key processing functions, the degree of computerization required, the relative use of on-line and batch techniques, the business cycles and functions involved, and other user-oriented factors.

Objectives

The new system requirements activity has two main objectives:

- Develop a complete definition of the necessary capabilities of the new system from the user's point of view. This definition should include descriptions of changes in processing capabilities (logical changes), and also descriptions of new methods of delivery (physical changes).
- Establish user concurrence that the capabilities described in the end-product documents of this activity contain a full and complete statement of user needs and that the solution is feasible, from both an operational and a human factors standpoint.

Scope

This activity, the determination of new system requirements, overlaps extensively with activity 3: existing system review, and activity 5: new system design. Although schedules will vary for individual projects, the extent of overlap can be pictured as illustrated in the Gantt chart shown in Figure 20-4. As indicated on this chart, work on new system requirements begins shortly after the initiation of activity 3. In effect, reports of deficiencies or shortcomings in the existing system feed directly into the identification of requirements for the new system. However, systems analysts will generally stop short of trying to specify new system requirements until there is a satisfactory overall understanding of current processing methods. That is, the systems analysts will want to develop a comprehensive understanding of the existing system as a whole before serious consideration of new system requirements is begun.

The same type of overlap exists during the concluding tasks of this activity and those of activity 5. That is, as analysts begin to build a solid understanding of user requirements, possible design alternatives for the new system are worked out and may be reviewed with the users.

As discussed earlier, the layering concept is fundamental to the systems development life cycle in general and to the analysis process in particular. During analysis, layering is implemented by the iterative modeling technique, increasingly more detailed models of the existing system and the potential new system are constructed. Then, as understanding increases within activity 4, analysts begin to look more closely at the feasibility of the new system. At this point, some doubts may arise about feasibility that were not present in earlier activities. If these doubts become serious, analysts may choose to develop several physical models for the new system. These models would represent varying levels of computerization and degrees of service to users. These variations would then be further described in the design tasks within activity 5.

In some situations, the overlap between activities 3, 4, and 5 may seem so extensive that it is tempting simply to fold them together. The problem with doing this is that a certain level of control over the project is lost. The key importance of the tasks that make up activity 4 may be lost as concentration shifts to the design-oriented tasks necessary for implementing the new system. Bear in mind that the purpose of activity 4 is primarily to build user understanding to a degree that permits acceptance, or signoff, on the specifications for the new system. It is important to secure a signoff before too much actual design takes place. The principle is straightforward: The later changes are permitted and made within the systems development life cycle, the more expensive they will be. Costs of changes actually increase rapidly as a project passes the new system requirements activity. Thus, there are important values, in both organizational relationships and in project development costs, to be gained by retaining an activity dedicated to securing user signoff.

It should be understood, of course, that user signoff is a gradual process of commitment more than it is a single act at the close of an activity. There may be a formal statement of acceptance signed by the responsible user manager; and this acceptance may follow a formal overview presentation of the capabilities of the new system, but genuine user acceptance is built gradually throughout the process of activity 4. Smaller groups of products will be developed with, and accepted by, appropriate users on the way toward building the user specification that is the formal end-product of this activity.

As a general rule, it is desirable to have users become serious about, and extensively involved in, a development project as early as possible. No matter how early user requirements are firmed up and no matter how committed a user may be, there will still be changes in the course of a systems development project. Changes are more easily handled if a mutual commitment between users and computer professionals is established early in the project. Remember that all systems ultimately belong to their users. The earlier this sense of possession can be established, the better a systems development project will proceed.

End-product

The end-product of activity 4 is an extensive document known as a *user specification* for the new system. (In some CIS organizations, the same document may be called a *requirements specification*, or perhaps a *structured specification*.)

The user specification describes and documents all logical processing functions for the new system. Also included are one or more physical models that represent the user's view of the new system. These models will encompass the human-machine boundaries, batch and on-line processing, run cycles for batch processes, and user expectations for performance of the system.

The complete user specification document contains the following parts:

- *Overview narrative.* This document overviews the goals and objectives of the organization as they relate to this project, presenting them as yardsticks against which new system requirements will be evaluated. Any background information that would help guide system designers should be included. There should also be a statement, at a general overview level, describing changes to be made between the existing system and the new one.

- *System function.* This is a brief, concise description of what the system will accomplish for the user. It is free of any description of physical processing functions and is written in user terminology, giving a black-box description of the computer portion of the system.

- *Processing.* The processing to be completed under the new system should be modeled using a context diagram and a hierarchical set of data flow diagrams. A Diagram 0 should identify the major subsystems. Lower-level diagrams should indicate the physical packaging to be achieved from the user's perspective. This physical packaging will identify manual and computer processing, batch and on-line functions, timing cycles, and performance requirements.

- *Data dictionary.* This document defines the components of the data flow diagrams.

- *Process descriptions.* These include narratives, decision trees, decision tables, and structured English descriptions of the lowest-level and selected mid-level processes within data flow diagrams.

- *Entity-relationship and data access diagrams.* These diagrams document the normalized data structures and data access paths from the user's perspective.

- *Interactive dialogues.* For each interactive session a script or flow diagram is prepared documenting the screen flow and options available to the user from any given screen in that session. (See Figure 20-17.) Each script may be accompanied by a set of rough screen layouts for the screens involved in that session.

- *Outputs for users.* An index is prepared listing all outputs to be delivered to users. This index is supported by a series of output documentation sheets like the one shown in Figure 20-18. Each output sheet is normally accompanied by a rough form layout.

Figure 20.17. Interactive dialogue for on-line Central City customer account maintenance processing.

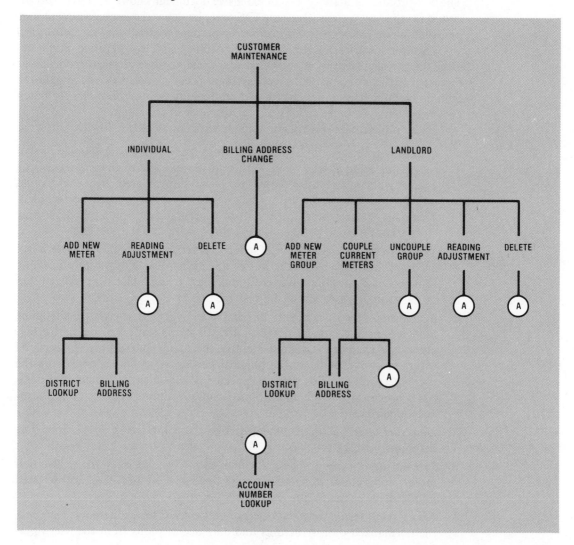

- *Inputs to the system.* An index lists all proposed input forms or source documents. For each input, this index is accompanied by an input document specification form like the one shown in Figure 20-19. With each document sheet, there may be a rough format drawing for the proposed input form.

- *User-specified physical requirements.* For this specification, there should be descriptions of performance needs, such as response time, transaction volumes, and timing. Security and control considerations, as specified by the user, should also be listed, as should any new hardware or application

Figure 20.18.   *Sample output specification form.*

PROGRAM OUTPUT SPECIFICATION

FILE NAME: CUSTOMER MASTER

SYSTEM NAME: Water Billing   DATE: 12-6

OUTPUT NO.:   PREPARER: TAP

ALIASES: OUTPUT FROM:

DESCRIPTION: Listing of all customer accounts not billed in the
"in-cycle" billing run. Used as a control by:

1) Water Billing Clerk—verify reason not billed
2) External Auditor

MEDIUM: Printed Report   FREQUENCY: Bi-weekly with
each "in-cycle"
billing

SIZE: Usually one page   NO. OF COPIES:

DISTRIBUTION: One copy to Finance office (use and file for auditor)

INSTRUCTIONS: Acct # order. Total number not billed.

DATA CONTENT: DATE
+ CYCLE-BILLED
+ ACCT #   MESSAGE:
+ NAME
+ ADDR   "ALL CUSTOMER
+ (VACATION-INDIC)   ACCOUNTS BILLED
+ DATE-LAST-BILL   ALL ACCTS THIS CYCLE"
NOT BILLED

LAYOUT:

Figure 20.19. Sample input specification form.

PROGRAM INPUT SPECIFICATION

INPUT NAME: SPECIAL-READING

SYSTEM NAME: Water Billing   **DATE:** 12-13

INPUT NO.:   **PREPARER:** KJP

ALIASES: **INPUT TO:**

DESCRIPTION: To handle all special readings.
A special reading is any reading that is not an "in-cycle" reading.
(In-cycle readings are entered in Meter-Reading-Book.)
Type: Final Reading (eg—customer moving)
       Initial Reading (eg—new construction; new owner)
       Problem with in-cycle reading

MEDIUM: **FREQUENCY:**

AVE. VOLUME: very low   **VOLUME RANGE:**

SORT FACTORS:

SOURCE:

INSTRUCTIONS: Input completed by: Meter Reader (usually)
     Water Department Inspector (occasionally)
     Customer (rarely)
Final reading must be initaled by Meter Reader
Need rapid turnaround for special billing if moving.
One copy to Water Billing Clerk

Figure 20.19. *Sample input specification form.* (continued)

DATA CONTENT:

```
+ ACCT #                   Note:  ┌─────────────┐
+ NAME                            │ CUSTOMER    │
+ ADDR          REQUESTER =       │ WATER-DEPT  │
+ READING-DATE                    │ FINANCE-DEPT│
+ READING                         └─────────────┘
+ REQUESTOR                       ┌─────────────┐
+ REASON        REASON =          │ FINAL-READING   │
                                  │ INITIAL-READING │
                                  │ CORRECT-ERROR   │
                                  └─────────────┘
```

software preferences or requirements. (These will be refined and extended in the next activity as design begins.)

■ *Unresolved policy considerations.* Any policy considerations that will have to be resolved should be reported.

The user specification is a key product in the systems development process. The value of the user specification lies in these facts:

■ The user can understand and verify its contents.

■ Its content and format provide a natural starting point for system design, as well as a standard for comparison during the implementation phase.

■ The setting of user expectations at this point serves to establish the basis for measuring the ultimate success of the project.

The Process

During the new systems requirements activity, the systems analyst follows a sequence of tasks that is critical to the preparation of the user specification. Involved are:

■ Extensive interaction with and interviewing of users.

■ Extensive use of modeling.

■ Consideration of application software packages, if appropriate.

The Role of the Systems Analyst. Among the services rendered as part of the systems analyst's role during this activity are these:

■ *Analysis.* The analyst identifies, partitions, and studies the structure and anatomy of the existing system.

■ *Criticism.* Constructive challenges are one of the mainsprings of effective analysis. The analyst must question why situations are the way they are found and why changes have been requested or are needed. The analyst evaluates all such findings against organizational objectives.

- *Innovation.* The analyst is a change agent, or catalyst. The systems analyst is expected to identify and suggest fresh approaches for dealing with problem situations.

- *Synthesis.* The analyst draws system elements together, creating solutions to replace problems.

- *Diplomacy.* The analyst must deal creatively with user uncertainties. It is necessary to guide persons who may be unsophisticated technically into a state of understanding and commitment. Analysts may also have to deal with, possibly to defuse, differences or conflicts among users or between users and others within an organization. Such activities may be needed to handle or overcome opposition to change or lack of needed cooperation.

Activities 4 and 5 are the points in the systems development life cycle at which systems analysis plays its most critical role.

Process Overview. Figure 20-3 at the beginning of this chapter gives an overview of the analysis and general design process. Processes numbered 4a through 4d in that diagram are the heart of activity 4:

- Determine new system requirements by analyzing requests for change.
- Modify the current model to incorporate these requests.
- Evaluate possible packaged application software.
- Create from all this a user specification document.

Analyzing Requests for Change. Most systems development projects are initiated as responses to requests from management or from user organizations. The request may result from a change in requirements or may represent an attempt to improve an existing system.

For whatever reason, initiators of change requests are often disappointed in, or frustrated with, things as they are. Requests for systems development almost invariably seek some sort of improvement. Given these motivations, change requests represent opportunities for all parties.

An initial evaluation of the request is made in an earlier activity, during the feasibility study. Now in activity 4, probing and evaluation begin in earnest. In asking questions and reviewing existing practices, the analyst should be on the lookout specifically for

- *New business opportunities.* If the organization or one of its departments has expanded rapidly in size or broadened its business scope, different or greater CIS support may be needed. On the other hand, a new development in computer technology may suggest improvement or enhancement of existing systems.

- *Forced business changes.* These are mandated reasons for systems development. Situations could include either regulatory requirements or decisions at the top level of the organization to meet competitive moves or to enhance market share.

■ *Current system deficiencies.* The analyst should review existing systems with the users and with the CIS staff. In addition to these reviews, it is a good practice to attempt to develop a maintenance history for the existing system. If a system has required frequent updating or maintenance, this could be a sign of problems. The updates may be the result of frequent changes in business needs or policies. On the other hand, if one portion of the system has had to be modified frequently, this could point to a basic design deficiency.

Part of the process of identifying and understanding requests for change includes categorizing each request as a logical request, impacting the new logical model, or a physical request, dictating the nature of the new physical model. Since logical requests relate to the processing that must occur, regardless of who does it or how, this new logical model may include new data elements used by the system, new processing or changed rules governing current processing, and new output information produced by the system. Physical requests involve the method of delivery as well as timing and processing-volume constraints. For example, the users may request greater on-line processing capabilities or, perhaps, greater control over or responsibility for the processing.

In addition to the logical-physical categorization, another classification of requests is necessary. Since, in the final analysis, development costs may make it impossible to implement every request, some prioritization of requests is necessary. Possible priority categories might be

■ Changes that must be made because of government or management mandates. In these situations, system revision is a must.

■ Changes that are urgent but not mandatory. Reasons for such changes could include important competitive advantages, great cost savings, and the like.

■ Changes that can be described as highly desirable but possibly not urgent. Such changes would have to be clearly cost-effective. But the success of the business would not be as closely tied to their implementation as it is in the higher priority categories.

■ Features or system refinements that would be useful as time and funding permit.

If a change is mandated, as in the first category, a deadline for implementation should be included in the evaluation. If not, a range of acceptable dates should be established for other categories.

Responsibilities of the Analyst. It is not enough for the analyst simply to process a request for change. Some user requests may be in the form of proposed solutions rather than functional business requirements. In these cases, the analyst must be sure the proposed solution represents a true statement of the problem.

In all cases, the analyst must understand the situation behind the request. Two approaches help in gaining this understanding: The analyst must put himself or herself in the user's place and must challenge each request. Rather than simply asking the user what he or she would like to have, the analyst must both anticipate requests that may not be expressed and determine why each requested change is needed.

It can be a tremendous challenge for the analyst to "get inside" the mind of the user. When dealing with a user manager, the analyst must think: "Given the objectives of my organization and things for which I am responsible, the following information will be critical for me to be able to do my job." When dealing with user operating personnel, the analyst must be aware of what motivates the staff and what support is required for an efficient and accurate job. This emphasis on viewing the system from the user's perspective will not only give rise to requests that the user may have overlooked, but also make it easier to evaluate actual user requests.

The basic goals and objectives of the organization, as they relate to the system under development, will have been identified during the existing system review. These goals and objectives are then used as a basis for evaluating the requests that have been made. The systems analyst is responsible for working with the user to relate each request to stated organization objectives or, if necessary, to point out that there is no basis for the request. The business need and business use of each requested output and process must be clear. This level of understanding also will be necessary to support the tradeoff decisions that arise in trying to create a feasible design for the new system.

In building an understanding of the business situation behind the request for change, the analyst will frequently enlarge or enhance the definition of needs. The request may have been triggered by what amounts to a symptom rather than by the root problem itself. "Fixes" that deal with symptoms rarely solve problems. To isolate problems, the analyst must examine the situation from the user's point of view. For example, an order entry supervisor may cause an inexperienced analyst to focus on the design of the order form and the on-line editing capabilities of the system in order to increase the throughput of the order entry department. But the awkward form design and the lack of editing capabilities are not the real problem. The real problem is that it simply takes too long to process an order. If the analyst views this problem in the broad perspective and from the point of view of the user, very different solutions may be possible. It may be possible, for example, to eliminate the need for written order forms in 80 percent of the cases by substituting a telephone system that is computer controlled and uses simple digital key input. The point is that focusing on the real problem permits a more creative and effective solution.

Part of the analyst's contribution in evaluating requests may lie in the different perspective he or she brings to the scene. The analyst's expertise in information processing may lead to changes in the systems development request that enhance the value of the project.

The Modeling Process. During the previous activity a logical model for current system was created. In this activity

- a logical model for the new system is created.
- the new logical model is evaluated and modified as necessary.
- one or more physical models are created for the new system.

The physical models highlight the user view of the proposed system. They specify which portions of the system will be automated, which processes will be on-line, which batch, and so on. They do not specify how the automated processing will be designed. This is part of activity 5. The modeling process is described in detail in Chapter 6.

Application Software Packages. Packaged software is an important factor in the computer information system marketplace. The principle is straightforward: If a specialized organization can develop packages that meet the needs of many users, each user can acquire software at far less than the cost involved in developing the application programs from scratch. Further, the lead time in adapting such packages may be significantly shorter.

If application packages are to be considered seriously, this is the point in the systems development life cycle at which they should be studied objectively and carefully. The tool to use in studying application packages is the physical model for the new system. This new system model reflects careful consideration and agreement between users and systems analysts about what is needed. It is logical to use the model as a measure of how well a packaged software application meets the needs of the organization.

This is not to say that there must be a perfect fit between a potential packaged application and the physical model. A decision to accept and use a packaged application may include a commitment to compromise. In a comparison of the model with the software package, it becomes relatively easy to see what changes or adjustments will need to be made in the system or to the software package as part of this compromise. Then the model can be used as a basis for evaluating the impact of the software package and the implications for its effective use. In effect, the physical model of a proposed new system can be an excellent shopping guide for consideration of application packages.

Personnel Involved

The makeup of the project team during this activity remains virtually the same as the team for activity 3. In particular, team membership continues to have a strong user orientation.

Cumulative Project File

At the conclusion of this activity, the project file will encompass these items:

- An updated project plan.
- The initial investigation report (which is of historical interest only at this point).
- The feasibility report.
- A list of management policy decisions that remain unresolved.

- An interview schedule and interview summaries — updated to reflect interviews conducted during this activity.

- A logical model of the existing system, including support documentation (of historical interest only).

- A user specification (defined earlier) that includes a complete physical model for the new system and all required, supporting documentation.

- A description of possible new system solutions, prepared during the feasibility study activity for use in activity 5: new system design.

CASE STUDY: NEW SYSTEM REQUIREMENTS

The user specification for the proposed water billing system for Central City is a rather lengthy document. Some excerpts from it are presented here to provide a glimpse of the final result.

A portion of the data flow diagrams making up the physical model of the new system appear here, as do selected data dictionary entries supporting these diagrams. Figures 20-20 through 20-25 present selected data flow diagrams. For reference purposes, Figures 20-26 and 20-27 show the composition of the key data stores and selected data structures.

Figure 20-20 is the context diagram of the new system. Diagram 0 is presented in Figure 20-21. Processes 1, 3, and 5 are partitioned here. A discussion of Process 6, which requires tighter control procedures, is presented at the end of this chapter.

Note that the sanitary district has been added as a new external entity in the context diagram. They will need to supply sewer rates to the system. They will receive a monthly financial statement and an annual usage summary report.

Diagram 1, shown in Figure 20-22, is straightforward. It does, however, illustrate two points. First, note the data flow — CYCLE — entering bubble 1.1. There is no corresponding flow entering the parent bubble 1 in Diagram 0 — an apparent violation of the balancing rule. Recall that CYCLE is simply a number, in this case between 1 and 4, that denotes a subset of the accounts located in one quadrant of Central City. Meter readings and billings are normally done by cycle. Thus CYCLE is merely a parameter input to process 1.1. To avoid cluttering data flow diagrams, parameter inputs are often shown only with the processes that use them and not with their parent processes. The second point to note about Diagram 1 is that it is "very physical." Processes 1.1 and 1.2, which extract and sort, don't really transform the data; they simply transport it. These processes would not have been included in a logical model for the new system; Process 1 on Diagram 0 would not have been partitioned at all.

The explosion of Process 3: apply new readings is presented in Diagram 3, Figure 20-23. As indicated, the majority of readings, the incycle readings, are keyed and submitted to a batch updating process. Special transactions are entered interactively. A reading value is simply a six-digit number with no inherent meaning. As part of the edit process, the new and previous readings are

Figure 20.20.   Context diagram for a new Central City water billing system.

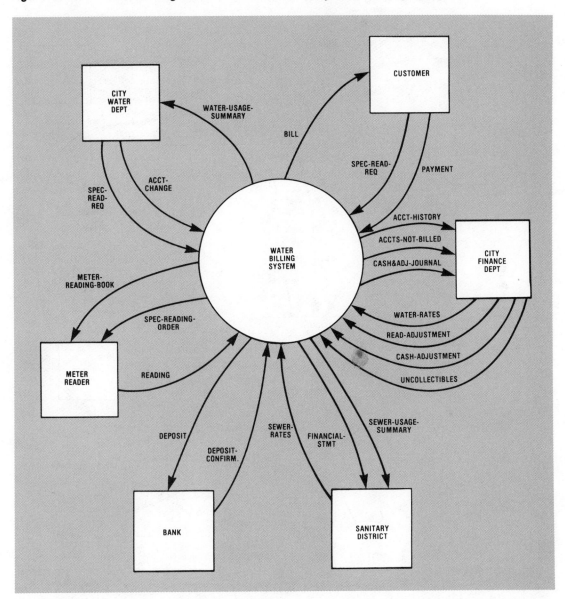

used to compute a trial consumption. This is compared with a rolling average consumption for that account maintained in the CUSTOMER-MASTER data store. If the trial consumption varies from the average by more than the parameter REASONABLE-PERCENTAGE, the reading is rejected as unreasonable. Processes 3.5 through 3.7 are manual procedures to investigate these unreasonable readings.

Figure 20.21. Diagram 0 for a new Central City water system.

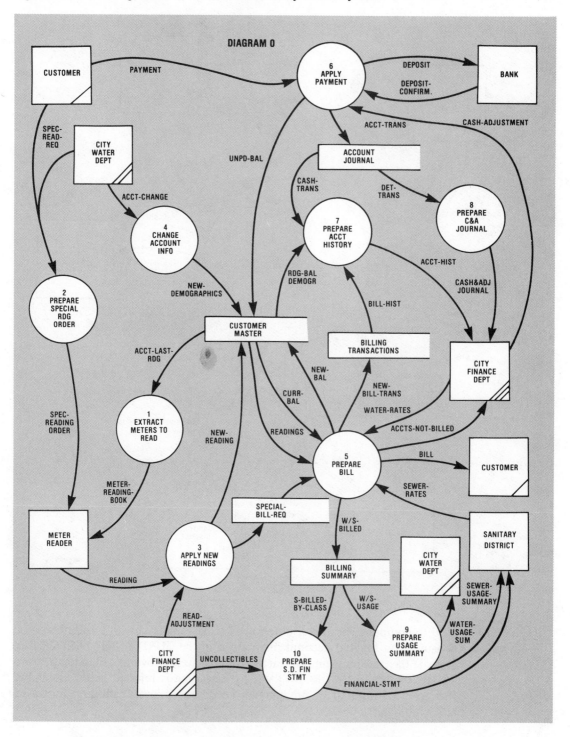

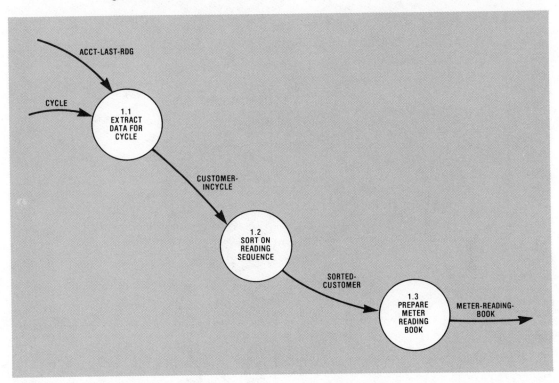

The prepare bill process is partitioned in Diagram 5 of Figure 20-24. As is evident from the diagram, there is a high degree of similarity between the production of incycle and special bills. The production of incycle bills is shown in Figure 20-25. Even though this is part of a physical model, the parallel nature of the lowest-level processing to perform the actual computations is retained here, leaving more flexibility to the program designers during the detailed design and implementation phase that follows.

Figure 20-25 indicates that the INCYCLE-BILL may be one of several formats. Most are RESIDENTIAL-BILLs that are printed and sent as post-cards, with a stub to be returned with the payment. Nonresidential customers (that is, commercial, industrial, and institutional customers) and residences billed to a landlord rather than the actual occupant all have bills prepared as invoices and enclosed in envelopes.

The ACCTS-NOT-BILLED report in Figure 20-25 is a control report requested by the user, specifically by the auditor. This report is produced automatically with each incycle billing run. It lists those accounts in the cycle for which there was no balance due and, hence, no bill produced.

Figure 20.23. Diagram 3—Apply New Readings—corresponding with the Diagram 0 in Figure 20.21.

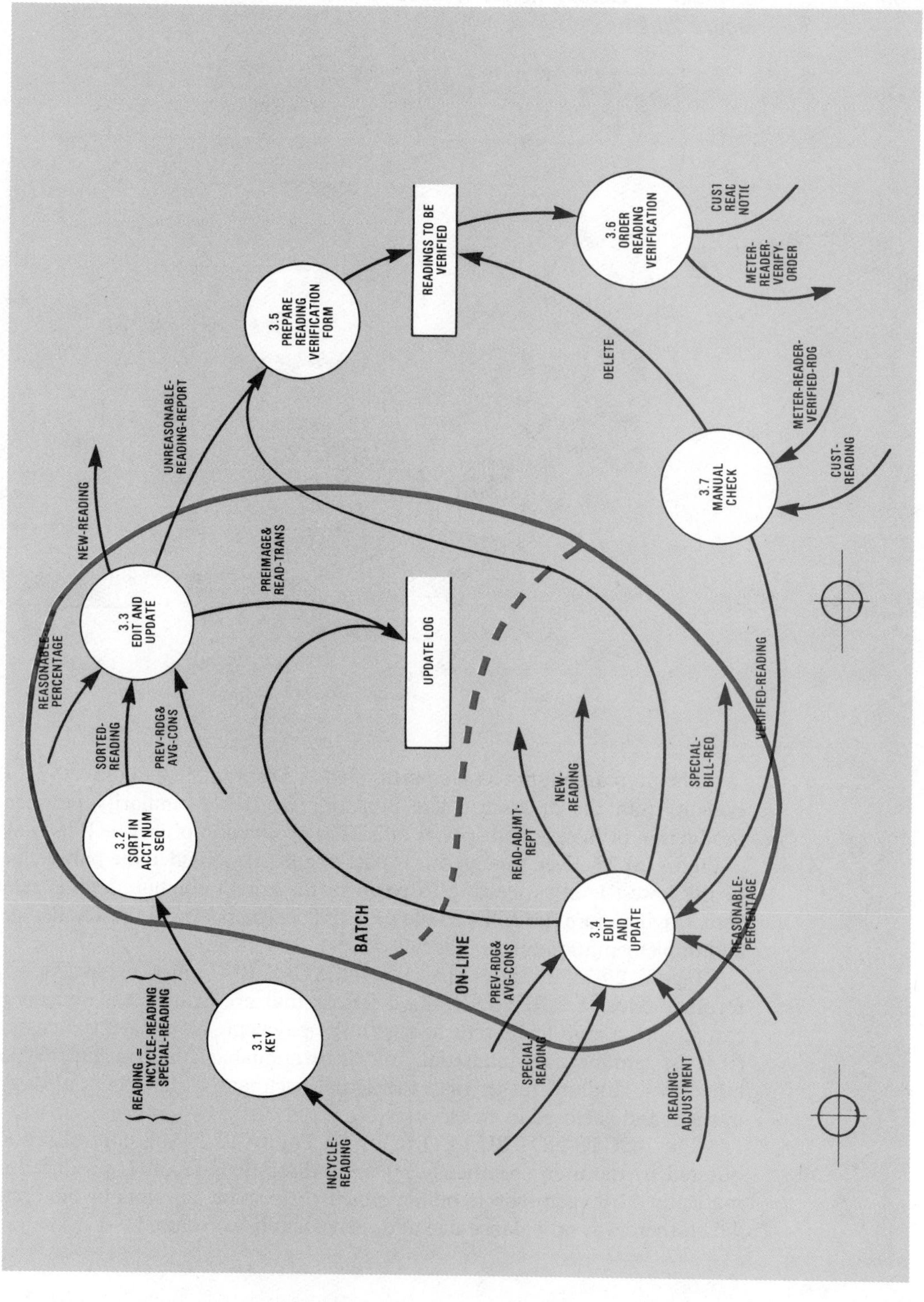

Figure 20.24. Diagram 5—Prepare Bill—corresponding with the Diagram 0 in Figure 20.21.

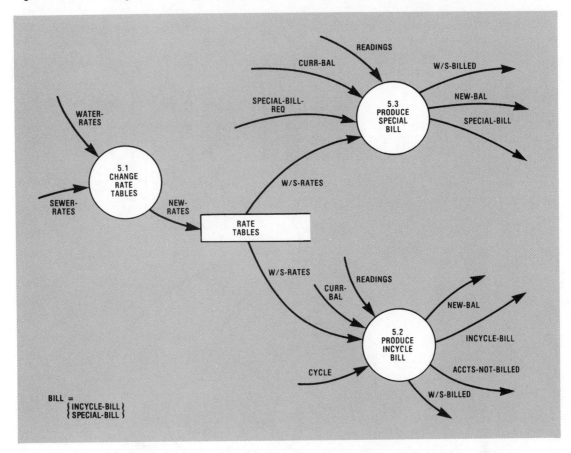

As stated earlier, lowest-level process bubbles must each have a corresponding process description. A process description expressing the rules for calculating the water charge in process 5.2.3 is presented in Figure 20-15.

High-level output and input design are also important elements of the user specification. An example of the type of output and input specification forms that can be used were presented in Figures 20-18 and 20-19.

The discussion that follows illustrates some of the options that might be selected in the water billing system.

The basic document output from a water billing system, obviously, is the customer bill. In the existing system at Central City, water bills are printed on continuous-form postcards. That is, preprinted forms are used. These are printed on a heavy card stock that makes it possible for cards to be sent directly through the mail without having to be inserted in envelopes. This output solution saves both postage and forms-handling costs.

Figure 20.25. Diagram 5-2—Produce Incycle Bill—corresponding with the Diagram 5 in Figure 20.24.

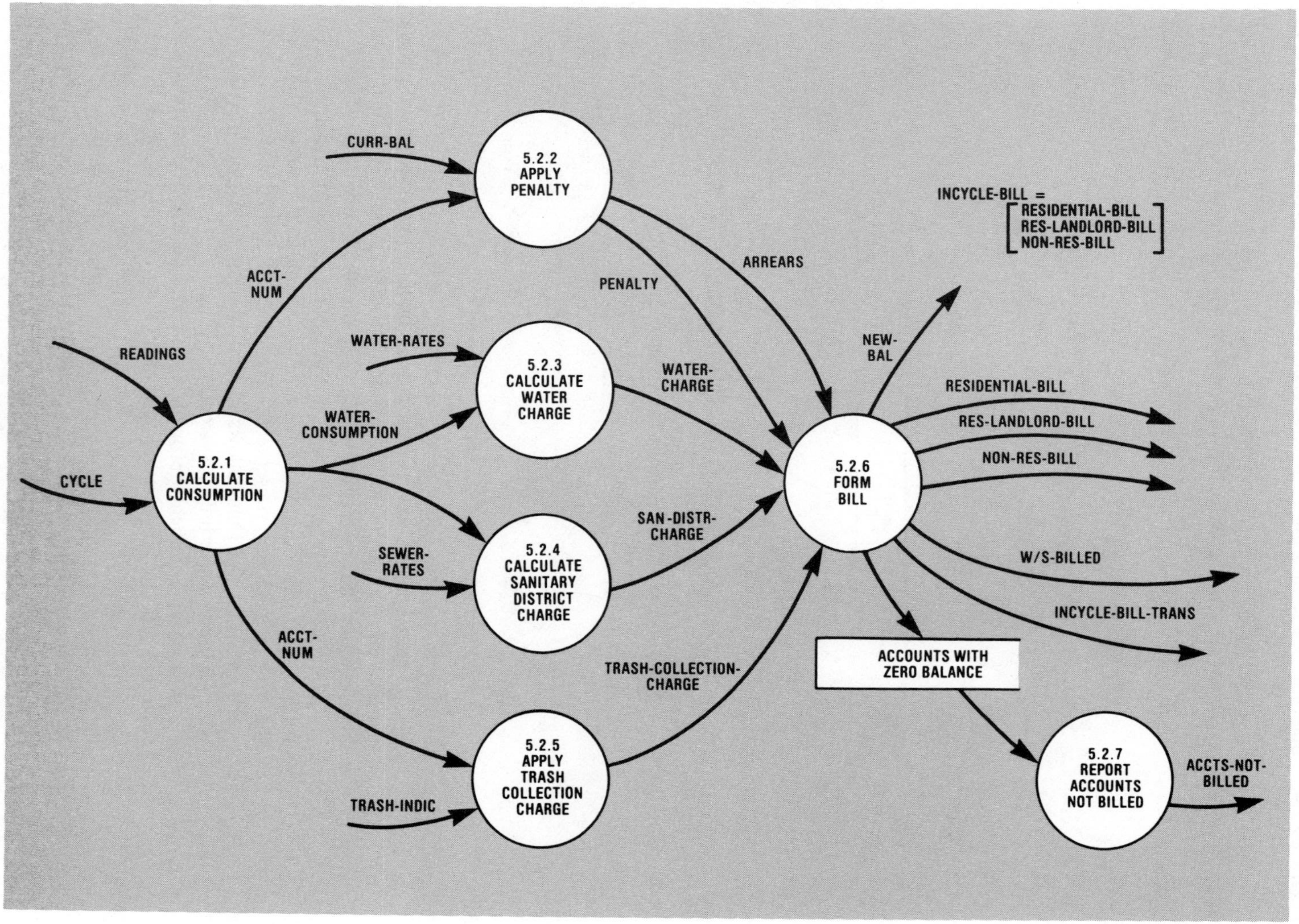

Figure 20.26. *Notations for the content of the four main data stores of the new Central City water billing system.*

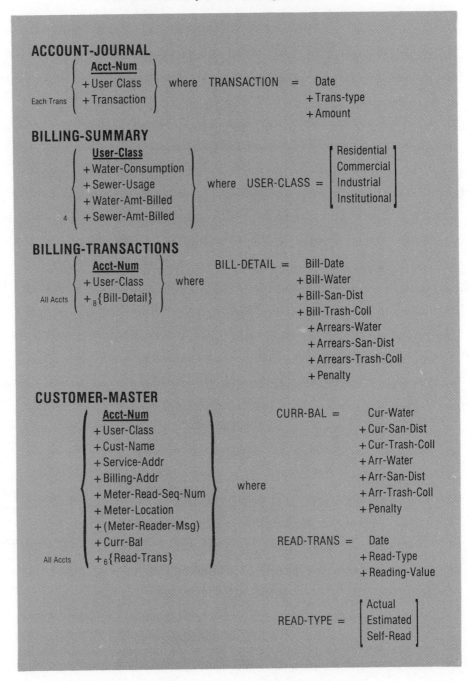

ACCOUNT-JOURNAL

Each Trans $\left\{ \begin{array}{l} \underline{\text{Acct-Num}} \\ + \text{User Class} \\ + \text{Transaction} \end{array} \right\}$ where TRANSACTION = Date
+ Trans-type
+ Amount

BILLING-SUMMARY

$_4\left\{ \begin{array}{l} \underline{\text{User-Class}} \\ + \text{Water-Consumption} \\ + \text{Sewer-Usage} \\ + \text{Water-Amt-Billed} \\ + \text{Sewer-Amt-Billed} \end{array} \right\}$ where USER-CLASS = $\left[\begin{array}{l} \text{Residential} \\ \text{Commercial} \\ \text{Industrial} \\ \text{Institutional} \end{array} \right]$

BILLING-TRANSACTIONS

All Accts $\left\{ \begin{array}{l} \underline{\text{Acct-Num}} \\ + \text{User-Class} \\ + {}_8\{\text{Bill-Detail}\} \end{array} \right\}$ where BILL-DETAIL = Bill-Date
+ Bill-Water
+ Bill-San-Dist
+ Bill-Trash-Coll
+ Arrears-Water
+ Arrears-San-Dist
+ Arrears-Trash-Coll
+ Penalty

CUSTOMER-MASTER

All Accts $\left\{ \begin{array}{l} \underline{\text{Acct-Num}} \\ + \text{User-Class} \\ + \text{Cust-Name} \\ + \text{Service-Addr} \\ + \text{Billing-Addr} \\ + \text{Meter-Read-Seq-Num} \\ + \text{Meter-Location} \\ + (\text{Meter-Reader-Msg}) \\ + \text{Curr-Bal} \\ + {}_6\{\text{Read-Trans}\} \end{array} \right\}$ where

CURR-BAL = Cur-Water
+ Cur-San-Dist
+ Cur-Trash-Coll
+ Arr-Water
+ Arr-San-Dist
+ Arr-Trash-Coll
+ Penalty

READ-TRANS = Date
+ Read-Type
+ Reading-Value

READ-TYPE = $\left[\begin{array}{l} \text{Actual} \\ \text{Estimated} \\ \text{Self-Read} \end{array} \right]$

Figure 20.27. *Notations for the content of selected data flows of the new Central City water billing system.*

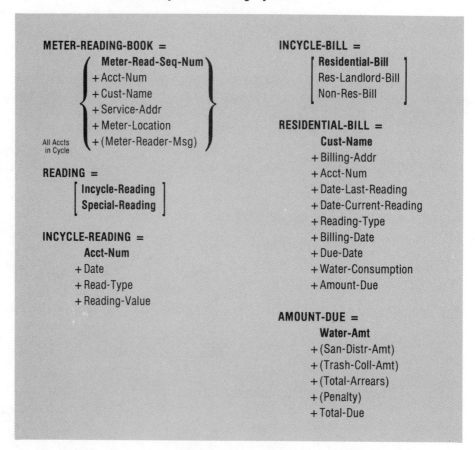

One clear option for the new system is to retain this output form and format, simply modifying it to accommodate the sanitary district billing as shown in Figure 20-28. This approach would meet the objective of minimizing expenses for the new system while optimizing the advantages of scale that come from being able to charge the sanitary district a prorated share of the total system cost.

Another option in the design of the billing for the new system is the use of a turnaround document. That is, the document returned by the customer along with the payment could be machine readable, making it possible to enter customer payment data to the system directly from the bill. In the existing system, the water department does manual keying to input payment information.

Each card, in turn, is perforated so that it can be separated in the middle. The customer returns a stub with each payment. The payment stub includes customer identification and the amount of the bill.

Figure 20.28 Rough format for residential bill.

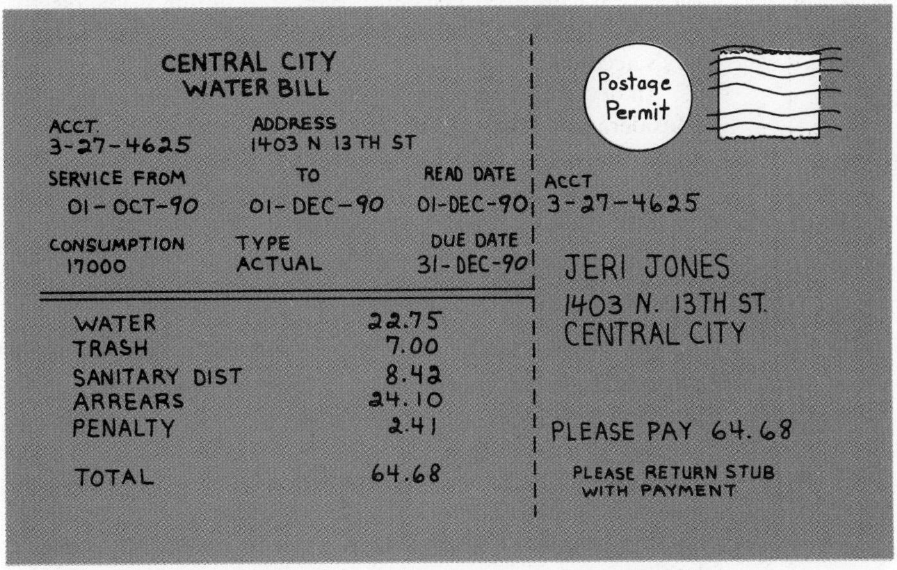

One approach using a turnaround document would be to print the data on the bill in special character formats, or *fonts*, that could be read directly through *Optical Character Reading (OCR)* equipment. Input from OCR bills could either be on machines that read batches of documents at high speeds, entering data directly into the computer, or through the use of *fiber optics wands* that are operated manually to read data from one imprint at a time. With the wand approach, the reading devices could be attached to point-of-sale registers in the finance department.

In order to select among the possible options, it is necessary to consider the input side, how customers pay their bills, as well as the output side. The water billing application, for example, must be able to accommodate three clearcut options.

As one option, the customer can simply walk into City Hall and pay the bill to a finance department cashier. Under the existing system, these items are rung up on cash registers. The finance department then provides a batch total with the billing stubs or substitute receipts prepared by the cashier. When the finance department handles collections, its personnel separate checks from billing stubs and take care of the bank deposits themselves.

As a second option, customers mail payment checks to the city. These receipts are also handled in the finance department, though not by the cashier. Again, payment data are recorded on the customer billing stubs or receipt forms and forwarded to data processing, with checks separated and deposited by the finance department.

Using a third option, customers can pay water bills and other utility bills at any local bank. Payment can be made either through checks against customer accounts or through authorized transfer of funds from customer accounts to those of the utilities. The banks then send billing stubs, receipts, and transaction listings to the city finance department along with a record of a deposit to the city's account.

In deciding between a keyed and an OCR output-input combination, a new consideration arises: If there are many exceptions — partial payments or payments not accompanied by preprinted or punched billing stubs — the advantage of automatic input could disappear rapidly because payment data will have to be input manually. The analyst needs to find out what percentage of bills produce partial payments, what percentage are paid without having the stubs turned in, and what percentage result in return of the stubs with payments in full.

The meter-reading activity presents another opportunity for a turnaround document. In the existing system, the water department uses a computer produced detail report as its meter book. This is a detailed listing of all customers, organized according to the address location where the meter reader walks a route. Name and address information are included on the report, as are previous readings for each account. Space is provided for the reader to enter the current reading from each meter. The report is formatted to fit into a metal binder used by the meter reader.

Again, both the input side (how new readings will be collected) and the output side need to be considered. Traditionally, meter reading has been one of the high cost, labor-intensive data-gathering jobs that has defied mechanization. It is expensive to have someone go to and look at every meter, every month. As the cost of reading meters has increased, the potential for automating this job has become more feasible. Devices and systems have been introduced that make it possible to collect data from meters automatically. Meters themselves are built with miniature, low-power radio transmitters that can be activated by radio signals. A data collector with a specially equipped vehicle can simply drive through a neighborhood using an automatic transponder (transmitter and responder), which activates the radios on the meters and records the transmitted data on magnetic cassettes. These cassettes can then be used for direct computer input.

The tradeoffs in this situation are obvious. Installing the automatic system would involve changing all meters in the service area. This would represent a major capital expense. There would also be some cost, minor by comparison, associated with installing equipment to handle the recorded tapes in the computer center. The new system, however, could continue to use meter books with no additional capital investment. Continuing the present system would involve a continuing expense for the salaries of meter readers as well as a potential penalty in quality of service associated with the errors of manual meter reading and manual input of data.

An example of an exception report for this system would be a listing of all unbilled accounts. This report would be produced at the conclusion of processing for each cycle. This example provides a classic illustration of the value of exception reports in managing a business. Managers don't need to be concerned about accounts that are billed routinely, on their regular cycle dates. They are more concerned with the situation in which billing of amounts due to the water department may have been skipped or overlooked, either purposely or accidentally.

A certain number of customers for any utility operation will not receive bills during any given billing period. Service may have been discontinued because a building has been sold or homeowners are on extended vacations. These types of situations can be encoded so that they are immediately apparent to managers. Such exception situations require little attention.

However, there is always the possibility that a meter reader overlooked or was unable to collect current meter data. It is also possible that an account had a credit balance, resulting in nothing due after charges were computed. Finally, there is the possibility of fraud—a city employee tampering with the system in some way so as to leave the account with zero consumption or zero balance due.

An exception listing of all accounts not billed, automatically produced with each billing cycle, provides a tool for the city financial managers and auditors to monitor potential errors or fraud. Each line on this report should indicate account status and provide some kind of code giving the reason the account was not billed.

Finally, as an example of an on-line output, consider the customer account history records to be compiled under the new system. The situation, briefly: The existing system does not have an adequate way of dealing with customer inquiries or complaints about bills. The solution is to establish an on-line display reference to show the account status for each customer as shown in Figure 20-29. Data on each customer would include current account status and an account history of readings, billings, and payments for at least six months. For reliable support in processing inquiries about a customer's account status, information would be needed that reflects updates from billings, payments received, adjustments applied, and other service transactions that affect status.

SUMMARY

During activity 3 the existing system is studied and documented to build an understanding of its underlying business goals, objectives, and functions. A logical model of the existing system is created as a basis for this study. Physical processing need not be emphasized.

In gathering documentation about the existing system, systems analysts should include forms or records related to organization, policies and procedures, current system outputs, current system inputs, descriptions of current processing, data files, and peripheral systems. Interviews with top and middle managers should be emphasized.

Throughout the review of the existing system, members of the project team should work actively to identify system deficiencies. User complaints aired during this activity can lead to substantial improvements in the design of the new system.

Figure 20.29. Rough format for account history output screen.

INDIVIDUAL ACCOUNT HISTORY

ACCT: 3-27-4625   ADDR: 1403 N 13TH ST

NAME: JERI JONES   CENTRAL CITY

CURRENT DUE: $64.68

READINGS

DATE	TYPE	VALUE	DATE	TYPE	VALUE
01-APR-84	ACT	8044573	01-JUN-84	EST	8044597
01-AUG-84	ACT	8044650	15-SEP-84	ADJ	-33
01-OCT-84	EST	8044712	01-DEC-84	ACT	8044729

BILLINGS

DATE	WATER	SANITARY	TRASH	ARREARS	PEN.	TOTAL
10-FEB-84	10.26	2.44	7.00	0	0	19.70
11-APR-84	14.50	3.20	12.00	0	2.50	32.20
10-JUN-84	35.42	12.85	7.00	0	0	55.27
9-AUG-84	42.25	15.60	7.00	0	0	64.85
10-OCT-84	14.05	3.05	7.00	0	0	24.10
10-DEC-84	22.75	8.42	7.00	24.10	2.41	64.68

PAYMENTS

DATE	TYPE	AMT	DATE	TYPE	AMT
31-DEC-83	P	24.83	1-MAR-84	P	19.70
27-APR-84	P	29.70	17-MAY-84	ADJ	+ 2.50
25-JUN-84	P	55.27	30-AUG-84	P	64.85

The information gathered about the existing system is used to construct a physical model of the system. From this physical model, the systems analyst builds a logical model of the existing system, which in turn will become a basis for designing the new system.

At the conclusion of the existing system review activity, the project file should contain an updated project plan, the initial investigation report, the feasibility report, a list of policy decisions that must be made by management, an interview schedule and interview summaries, an updated glossary of terms, a logical model of the existing system, and additional physical documentation regarding the existing system.

Activity 4 marks a transition from the study of the existing system to the building of the new one. Interviews are used to gather data, including user descriptions of inadequacies of the existing system. Requirements are classified as logical or physical.

The logical model of the existing system and new logical requirements are used to develop a logical model for the new system. Using new physical requirements, a physical model of the new system is prepared. Alternative physical models may be proposed.

The user specification document will include an overview narrative, a description of system function, a model of system processing, a data dictionary, process specifications, entity-relationship and data access diagrams, an index of outputs for users, an index of inputs, description of user interfaces, user specified physical requirements, and any unresolved policy considerations.

The user specification provides a means for user verification and approval. It is a starting point for system design and a standard for the implementation phase. It sets user expectations and can be used to measure success.

The logical model of the new system is then evaluated. Tests of mechanical correctness are made. The model is checked to be sure it is an accurate and complete representation of the business.

A physical model then describes how the logical model will be implemented. Financial, scheduling, technical, operational and human factors tradeoffs are considered. The logical model is marked up to show human-machine boundaries, batch or on-line processes, and timing cycles for batches. Control points for editing and auditing are identified. Performance requirements are specified.

Application software packages are evaluated at this point as a way of reducing costs and lead time. Such packages involve inevitable compromises. These should be evaluated by referring to the model.

The resulting project file will include an updated project plan, the initial investigation report, the feasibility report, a list of management decision requirements, interview schedules and summaries, the user specification, and a description of possible new system solutions.

KEY TERMS

1. functional (logical) model
2. user specification
3. new system design specification

1. Why is it important to study the existing system? What is the principal objective of the existing system review?
2. What are the two major end-products of the existing system review?
3. How does the 80-20 rule apply to documentation of the existing system?
4. Why can't the systems analyst simply build a model of the existing system based on existing documentation? What is the advantage of studying actual input and output entries, rather than blank forms?
5. What can be learned from these entries? What can be learned by reviewing the maintenance history of the existing system?
6. Why do systems analysts first build a physical model of the existing system before constructing a logical model?
7. What is the sequence in the development of system models used during this phase?
8. What is the concept of a black box and how does this relate to the user specification?
9. What are the main objectives of developing the user specification?
10. What documents are included in the user specification, and what is the function of each?
11. What are the objectives of evaluating application software packages and when is it appropriate to do so?

21

Analysis and General Design Phase — Part 2

Objectives

On completing this and other learning objectives for this and the previous chapters, you should be able to:

- ■ Explain the overall flow of activity in the analysis and general design phase and the relationships among the four activities that make up the phase.

- ■ State the principal objectives of each activity in the analysis and general design phase.

- ■ Describe the major end-products of each activity in the analysis and general design phase.

- ■ Describe how the structured analysis modeling process is implemented within the phase.

- ■ Understand the transition from the results of analysis to a general design for a new system.

- ■ Understand how the various analysis and design techniques presented in this text are used together on an actual system development project.

THE ANALYSIS AND GENERAL DESIGN PHASE

This is the second of two chapters dealing with the analysis and general design phase of the SDLC.

Objectives

The key objectives of this phase are to

- determine the requirements for the new system.
- develop a general design or architecture for the new system.
- establish user acceptance of and concurrence in the design.
- obtain a commitment from the CIS department that the design of the new system can be implemented within the established time and dollar limits.
- develop a project plan for performing the work of the next phase.
- present sufficient information that the steering committee can determine whether to continue, revise the scope or approach, or abort the project.

The phase consists of four activities. The first two, existing system review and new system requirements, are covered in Chapter 20. The final two, new system design and implementation and installation planning, are covered in this chapter.

ACTIVITY 5: NEW SYSTEM DESIGN

The new system design activity creates a physical design for the new system that is sufficiently detailed to accurately estimate the cost of constructing the new system.

Activity Description

The new system design activity continues the transition from analysis to design. That is, the analysis of the existing system has been completed and has served, during activity 4: new system requirements, as a basis for development of a user specification, a statement of what the new system should look like. This user specification, based on a physical model for the new system, represents a design of the system from the user's perspective. This design is not sufficiently detailed, however, to meet the objectives of the analysis and general design phase. The key objective of this phase is to provide enough information to allow the steering committee to decide whether to continue, abort, or modify the approach being taken on the project. The decision of the steering committee will be based on three factors:

- An updated feasibility analysis.
- A user commitment that the proposed system will satisfy the specified objectives and that the claimed benefits can be achieved.
- A commitment from the CIS designers that the proposed system can be delivered within the schedule and budget specified.

The user specification is clearly not detailed enough to support these important commitments. All computer processing has been treated as a black box, and options such as batch, on-line, and interactive have been specified in generic terms. Activity 5, then, carries the design to a sufficiently detailed level so that the necessary user and designer commitments can be obtained.

At this point, one of the most significant additions to the design of the new system is building controls into the proposed system model. Also incorporated are provisions for security, backup, and recovery procedures.

Proper controls are critical to the success of any system. Such controls require careful, detailed thought and planning. To some degree, controls may have been discussed, or even specified, during activity 4. However, the level of detailing for controls during activity 4 was left entirely up to the user's discretion. If the user offered no suggestions about controls, none were included. In activity 5, however, careful specification of controls and verification that these controls are workable is critically important.

Building on the data modeling done during activity 4 and expressed in the resulting data access diagrams, basic file design decisions are also made in activity 5.

If application program packages are to be used within the new system, this is the point at which final, detailed evaluation occurs and the decision must be made.

If the new system will require enhancement or addition of computer hardware or system software, specification of these requirements must be made during activity 5.

These tasks culminate in the ability to update the feasibility evaluation for the proposed system. Both the computerized and manual processes must be designed in sufficient detail so that technical and operational feasibility are assured. It must also be verified that there will be no difficulties in the areas of human factors or scheduling. Finally, the financial analysis, the weighing of costs and benefits, must now be fine tuned. The goal is to produce a cost-benefit analysis that will be within 10 percent of the final costs and benefits realized by the system. That is, the actual costs should total either 10 percent above or below the estimate, making for a 20 percent range of accuracy. The accuracy of this cost-benefit analysis is achieved by specifying a design that is sufficiently detailed to enable users to commit to operating the system within this range of the costs and benefits and to enable designers to commit to delivering the system within the same parameters.

Objectives

The general objective of the new system design activity is to provide sufficient information to serve as a basis for a steering committee decision about whether to proceed with implementation of the system.

This general objective is achieved by meeting the following specific objectives:

- Propose a general design for the new system. This design should implement the user specification.
- Obtain a user signoff on this general design. By this signoff, the user is verifying that the predicted operational costs and benefits can be achieved.

■ Obtain a CIS signoff on the general design. The developers are committing, by this signoff, to produce the system within the specified schedule and development cost budget.

Scope

The Gantt chart in Figure 20-4 shows the relationship of this new system design activity with the other activities in the analysis and general design phase. It is worth stressing, once again, the iterative nature of this phase. The iterations inherent in the modeling tasks of activities 3 and 4 have been mentioned several times, but even the design tasks of activity 5 must overlap these modeling efforts.

The physical model for the new system, developed during activity 4, must reflect the design considerations that are part of activity 5. This correspondence is necessary because the model developed in activity 4 represents, in effect, a promise to the user about capabilities of the new system. Without concern for design constraints, it could be possible for the systems analyst to promise capabilities that cannot be delivered. Recall that the layering concept plays a prominent role in the iterations that occur during analysis. As successively more detailed understandings of the new system model are achieved, more and more detailed evaluations of technical design options are also being made. In other words, at each level of development of the new system model, design implications are being considered. This is one reason for the overlap of activities 4 and 5.

There is a special relationship between activities 5 and 6. Activity 5 actually begins before, and runs longer than, activity 6: implementation and installation planning. The purpose of activity 6 is to develop a basic plan and schedule for the next phase. This information is fed into activity 5 and used to help compute development costs for the new system. By the time activity 5 is over, a new system design specification is developed and ready for implementation pending approval by the steering committee.

It is necessary to apply some constraints to the scope of activity 5. There is a strong natural tendency among technical personnel to plunge ahead with detailed design immediately upon beginning design considerations. Full technical design should not be done during this activity, partly because this level of commitment has been neither made nor funded. Moreover, full technical design is not necessary to meet the objective of this activity and phase. For example, document and screen display designs for input and output should simply be in the form of rough sketches; content and access methods should be specified for files; and job streams, with major programs identified, should document the computer processing.

This level of detail will be sufficient for the objectives of activity 5. Detailed spacing charts, precise file descriptions and record layouts, and internal program design are usually not necessary for accurate estimates of implementation costs. These more detailed tasks can, and should, be held to the next phase.

End-products

The new system design activity produces four principal end-products:

- A new system design specification.
- A packaged application software recommendation (optional).
- A technical support specification (if new hardware and system software requirements are identified).
- An executive summary (for user management and the steering committee).

New System Design Specification. The new system design specification is an extension of the user specification. Some of the elements of the user specification are included intact in this later document; others are updated. To illustrate the relationship between these two documents, the portions of the following descriptions appearing in italics indicate content revisions or substantial additions. The blending of existing documents with new content highlights the cumulative documentation techniques used in systems development projects.

- Overview narrative. This document has three parts. The first covers the goals and objectives of the organization and provides a basis against which system requests are evaluated. The second describes the system's purpose, goals, and objectives, as well as the basic logical functions that the system must provide. The third is an overview statement of changes to be made between the existing system and the new one.
- System function. For the user's benefit, a concise but processing-free description of what the system will accomplish is prepared. Written in user terminology, it presents a black-box description of the computer portion of the system.
- Processing. Processing descriptions include a context diagram and a hierarchical set of data flow diagrams. Diagram 0 should identify the major subsystems. Lower-level diagrams should indicate the physical packaging from the user's perspective. Differentiation should be made between manual and computer processing, batch and on-line processing, timing cycles, and performance requirements. *Computer processing should be defined to the job-stream level and should be documented using annotated system flowcharts.*
- Data dictionary. This document supports the data-flow diagrams. It is carried forward intact.
- Process descriptions. These document the rules that govern the lowest level as well as selected mid-level processes in the data flow diagram models.
- Interactive dialogues. Documentation of the user's interface with on-line portions of the system.
- Outputs to the user. This section consists of an index sheet listing all outputs. The index sheet is followed by an output documentation sheet and a

rough format for each output. *Additional outputs related to control and security concerns may be added in this activity.*

- Inputs to the system. This section consists of an index sheet listing all inputs. The index sheet is followed by an input documentation sheet and a rough format for each input. *As with outputs, security and control-related inputs may be added.*

- User organization and procedures. High-level specification of how user personnel will work within the context of the new system. Also included are departmental reorganization recommendations, staffing requirements, and impact on job descriptions. *Specific user responsibilities as they relate to security and control processing are also covered.*

- Entity-relationship or data access diagrams. Documentation of the normalized data structures and required data access paths from the user's perspective.

- *Data files. These documents describe the requirements in terms of files rather than data stores, highlighting the transition from analysis to general design. File access methods and storage media are specified, along with approximate quantity of stored data and anticipated growth.* (Detailed file layouts or database design will occur in the next phase of the life cycle.)

- *Performance criteria. These descriptions of expectations from the new system are critical for both computer and manual processing. Included are required response times, anticipated volumes of transactions, and other performance data.*

- *Security and control. Measures for security and control are discussed as they apply to hardware, computer processing, and manual processing.*

- Policy considerations. This section lists any relevant policy decisions that have not yet been made.

- *Computer operations interface with the new system. These specifications are still at a general level, not detailed operating instructions. However, descriptions should include hardware, data communication requirements, timing, projected volumes, impact on existing operations, backup and record retention requirements, and recovery procedures.*

Packaged Application Software Recommendation. If application software packages are considered, recommendations in this report should include

- an overview description of each package.
- a summary evaluation of each package.
- a summary of modifications that would have to be made, either to the package or to existing software.
- recommendations regarding the value of each package, including lease or purchase considerations.

Technical Support Specification. If the proposed system involves significant hardware or systems software changes, technical specifications should be prepared. These should include

- a detailed description of requirements for new hardware and software capabilities.
- data communication requirements, if appropriate.
- proposals from vendors and analyses of these proposals.
- lease or purchase recommendations.

Executive Summary. The executive summary is a covering document that summarizes the content of the new system design specification at a level meaningful to users and to members of the steering committee. Emphasis is on the impact of the proposed changes upon the conduct of the business. Specific contents will vary with each project, but the following sections would normally be included:

- Overview narrative. This is taken directly from the new system design specification.
- System function. This is taken directly from the new system design specification.
- Recommendations. A management-level summary of recommendations is prepared that centers, principally, on three areas: application software (recommended packages and in-house development), major recommended hardware and system software acquisitions, and a recommended development schedule (a calendar for the next two phases at the activity level).
- Updated feasibility evaluation. A brief summary is presented evaluating the proposed solution in the technical, operational, human factors, and scheduling dimensions of feasibility. In addition, the cost-benefit analysis is updated by summarizing the budgeted and actual development costs to date, revising the cost and time estimates to complete the project and the predicted operating costs and benefits.
- Personnel requirements. The key to success in any development project is to have the right people when they are needed. This section should summarize the person-hour requirements by week or month for the remainder of the project. Requirements should be listed by job category (programmer, analyst, user clerical people, etc.) or by name, for key people. Just as a continuing development budget is implicit in steering committee approval of the project, so is the availability of personnel as specified in this section.
- Critical policy considerations. These are the policy decisions that the steering committee must deal with for development to continue.
- User acceptance statement. This statement is a formal signoff by the user that the proposed system will meet the stated needs, that it can be run within the specified cost limits, and that its use will deliver the projected benefits.
- CIS acceptance statement. This statement is a formal signoff by CIS management that the proposed system can be developed within the established cost and time budgets.

The Process

The primary goal of the new system design activity is to carry the design of the new system to a point where an updated feasibility evaluation can be prepared. This includes preparation of accurate estimates for all five dimensions of system feasibility, financial, technical, operational, scheduling, and human factors.

A related goal is to build a clear understanding of the complexity and effort that will be involved in carrying the system forward into the next two phases — implementation and installation. Personnel requirements from both the user and CIS departments must be clearly specified for these later phases. The key to success in any development project is to have the right people at the right time.

A further goal is to improve the chances of the project's success through close study of any unusually complex or advanced design areas of the new system and by identifying and addressing specifically those areas that might represent high risks.

The process steps within this activity are not strictly sequential. Rather there are broad categories of interrelated and overlapping tasks that must be completed during the course of the activity:

- Adding controls.
- Designing the database.
- Completing the general design of computer processing.
- Evaluating possible application software packages.
- Preparing for additional hardware and software acquisition.
- Updating the feasibility analysis.
- Evaluating the overall design quality.
- Obtaining user management and CIS signoff.

Key concerns associated with each of these major groups of tasks are discussed below.

Adding Controls. Prior to the new system design activity the emphasis has been on specifying the user's view of the new system. While the more obvious controls will have been included in the physical model produced in activity 4, there has been no separate and concentrated effort to be certain the controls are complete.

In a systems sense, controls are the steps inserted in the processing sequence specifically to assure accuracy, completeness, reliability, and quality of results produced. In any endeavor as extensive as a modern computer information system, it is assumed that the system will be exposed to numerous incidents of human error, software error, machine failure, or even attempted fraud.

Controls must start, therefore, before processing even begins. Controls are established at input. At critical points within the system where data are transformed or handled, new controls must also be applied to verify that results are still valid and reliable. Considerations for designing control and reliability functions into a system are covered in Chapter 17.

One of the key responsibilities of the systems analyst is to be sure that adequate controls are designed into the system. During this activity, the proposed system must be evaluated rigorously with respect to the adequacy of its control processing.

Designing the Database. The term database, as used here, refers to all data resources needed to support a system. During this activity, initial database design, which falls far short of detailed technical design, is completed.

The modeling steps of activity 4 resulted in a complete identification of required data elements and a set of data stores, all documented in the data dictionary. This identification was refined to some degree through the data analysis and modeling techniques, covered in Chapter 5 that resulted in an entity-relationship model and a set of data access diagrams. The objective in activity 5 is to carry the database design far enough to support the updating of the feasibility evaluation at least far enough to support the high-level design of the computer processing. It is not necessary, at this point, to complete final technical specifications such as record layouts, storage formats, and the like. Such specifications can wait until the detailed design and implementation phase.

The actual tasks to be performed in managing system data resources depend on the software support available. In particular, these tasks depend on whether traditional file processing will be done or database management system (DBMS) software will be used. In this context, traditional file processing refers to the use of sequential, indexed, and direct file organization methods.

If a DBMS is to be used, a database specialist will begin to work with the development team. It will be the responsibility of the database administration group to complete the design of the physical database.

If traditional file processing is used, master files will be identified, usually by modifying the data stores contained in the physical model of the new system. These data stores resulted from the normalization process. Modifications to data stores are based for the most part on considerations of processing efficiency and newly identified control processing requirements. The modifications are also based on the methods chosen for implementing the required access paths. The choices include use of alternate keys (if supported by the system software), implementation of correlative files as direct files, and extraction of necessary records from the master file for further processing.

For each new proposed master file, the set of data elements to be included, the access keys, and the file organization method will be specified. Backup and recovery procedures for file protection must also be developed. The process of designing the database (given the data access diagrams and E-R models for the new system) is discussed further in Chapter 12.

Database performance requirements for database management are also specified during this activity. These include statistics on the type and amount of database access activity, anticipated growth rates for the database, and required access or response times. Finally, any constraints upon use of the database to meet security or control requirements, or due to limitations in resources, must be spelled out.

Completing the General Design of Computer Processing. General design of computer processing refers to the identification of basic processing jobs or job steps, not to the technical design of computer programs. As with all major tasks in activity 5, the goal is simply to define things specifically enough to support the updating of the feasibility evaluation of the new system.

The physical model of the new system, produced as part of activity 4 and possibly modified on the basis of database design decisions, identifies

- those processes that are computerized (the human-machine boundary).
- those computer processes that are batch and those that are on-line.
- the cycle and timing requirements for the batch processes.

The design is extended in activity 5 by first specifying which data and which processes are maintained centrally and which are distributed, either to user areas at the main location or to totally remote sites. Consider, for example, the motel reservation system introduced in Chapter 2. That system was developed by the CIS department at the home office of the motel chain. Portions of the data and some of the processes, such as those involving profitability analysis, were handled there. On the other hand, some data and processing were distributed to the individual motels, for example, those involving specific room assignments and individual billing.

After decisions are made about the portions of the system that are to be distributed, basic computer job streams are defined. In this way, the major computer programs are identified but not internally designed. Also, the required communication between programs, or job steps, is defined. The decisions are documented using annotated system flow charts. To illustrate, consider the abstract physical model, Figure 21-1, that might have resulted from the new system requirements documentation of activity 4. This physical model is a design of the system from the user's point of view. In Figure 21-2, the model has been modified to show that a portion of the processing and one data store are distributed. In addition, a more detailed look has been taken at the weekly batch processing. Three major programs or job steps have been identified: The first contains process P1; the second contains processes P2 and P3; the third contains process P4.

These basic design decisions may be documented using a system flow chart. To illustrate, Figure 21-3 contains the portion of the data flow diagram corresponding to the weekly processing on the left and the resulting system flow chart on the right. Note that the manual input, I1, to process P1 is depicted as keyed input to STEP #1 and that the outputs, 01 and 02, leaving the computerized portion of the system from the processes P3 and P4, are depicted as printed reports. Note also that temporary files, TF #1 and TF #2, must be created to communicate the results from STEP #1 to STEP #2 and from STEP #2 to STEP #3.

Clearly, a number of high-level design decisions are being made here. The data flow diagrams will probably represent some middle level of detail, certainly more detail than a Diagram 0, but usually not the lowest-level diagram. In some cases, a single bubble on the data flow diagram will become a single program to carry out a batch job or interactive application. In some cases, a process may be implemented as two or more related programs; or several processes may be integrated into a single program. Such tentative design decisions point out the need for the analyst to have both sufficient technical skill to design the high-level program architecture of the system and an astute business sense.

The analyst will be guided in these decisions by an understanding of software capabilities, design methodologies, and availability of packages. In general, there are three ways of acquiring or developing software:

- Application software packages that can provide many of the processing requirements without modification.

- Data management, inquiry, and report-writing systems that can be interfaced with the systems data files and employed by the end-user to handle many of the system output requirements.

- Custom programs written to extend application package capabilities, to interface with other systems, and to provide specialized processing not otherwise available.

The relative mix of these three components will vary by system, but a fundamental rule of good design is to keep them separate. For example, avoid modifying programs by inserting custom code in an application package. If necessary, write a separate program and interface it with the package instead. In general, design the overall program architecture in such a way that the three types of software stand alone and can be separately maintained.

Evaluating Possible Application Software Packages. The evaluation of packaged application software was begun in activity 4. At the time the logical and physical models of the new system were created, it was possible to evaluate potential software packages in terms of functions provided, completeness of data elements, ease of use, and so on. This evaluation is extended in activity 5 to the point at which necessary modifications, interface modules, and other requirements can be identified. These items are needed to update the feasibility analysis. The possible use of application software packages is covered in greater depth in Chapter 23.

Preparing for Additional Hardware and Software Acquisition. If new computer hardware or software is needed to implement the proposed system, these requirements are identified as part of the general design of the computer processing in activity 5. The actual acquisition tasks, preparing requests for proposal, dealing with vendors, purchasing, and testing, are normally handled by specialists in the technical support area of the CIS department. A representative from this group would begin to work with the project team during activity 5, using the performance requirements provided. It is necessary for technical services to become involved now, rather than to wait until the next phase, because of the lead time required to purchase and test new hardware and software.

Updating the Feasibility Analysis. The feasibility analysis is the ultimate basis for deciding whether the new system will be implemented. During the new

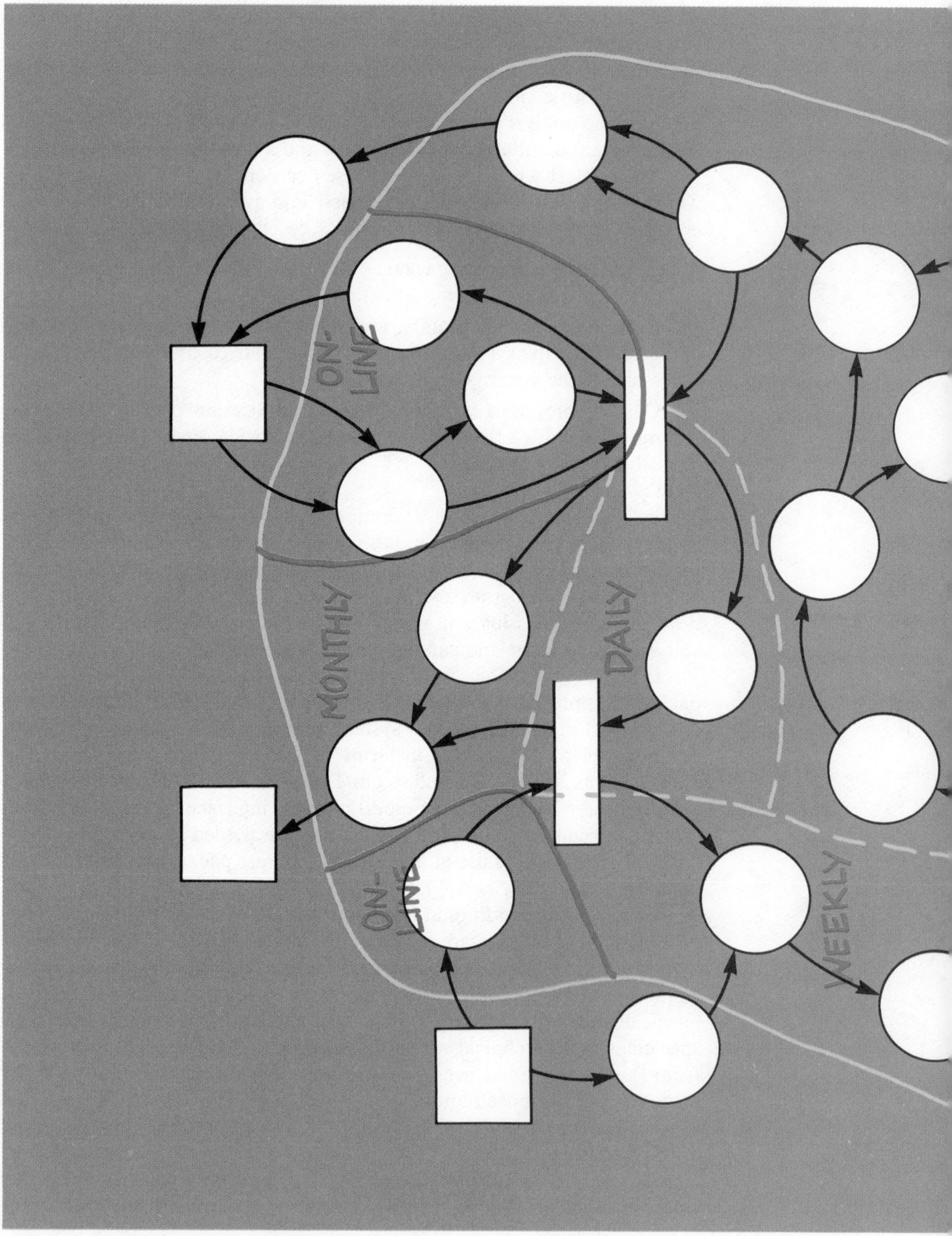

Figure 21.1. Physical model of new system.

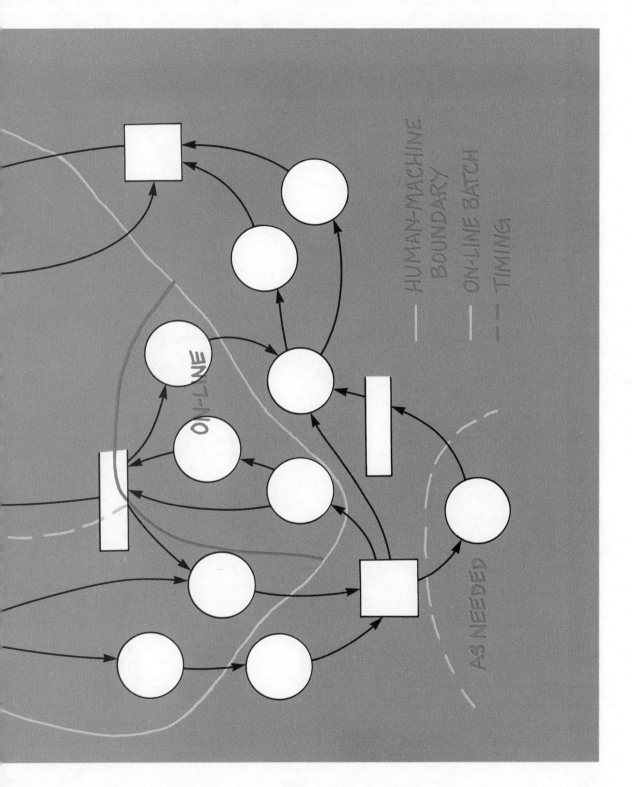

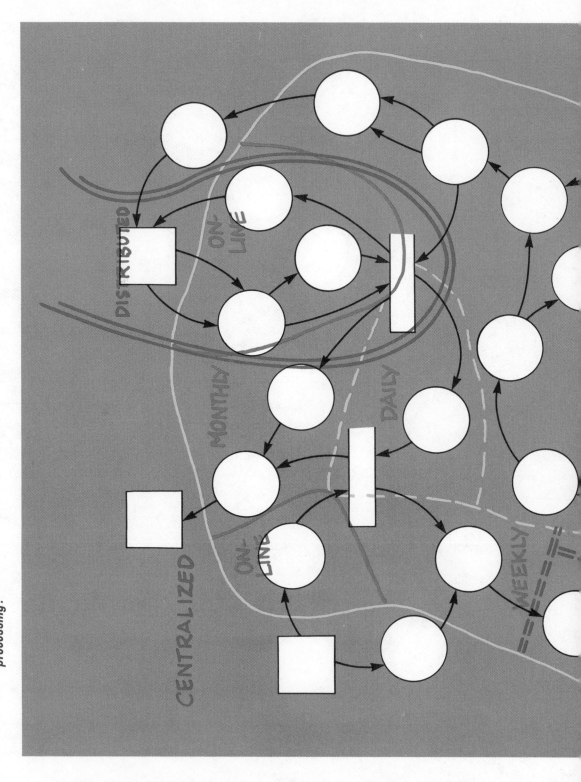

Figure 21.2. Physical model of new system with distributed processing identified and job stream defined for weekly processing.

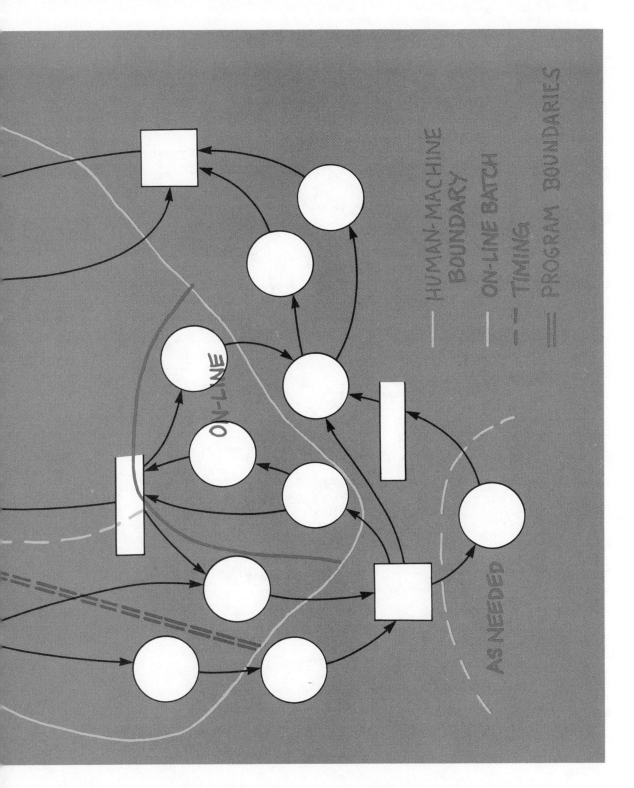

ON-LINE

HUMAN-MACHINE BOUNDARY

ON-LINE BATCH

TIMING

PROGRAM BOUNDARIES

AS NEEDED

Figure 21.3. *Transition from physical model to system flowchart.*

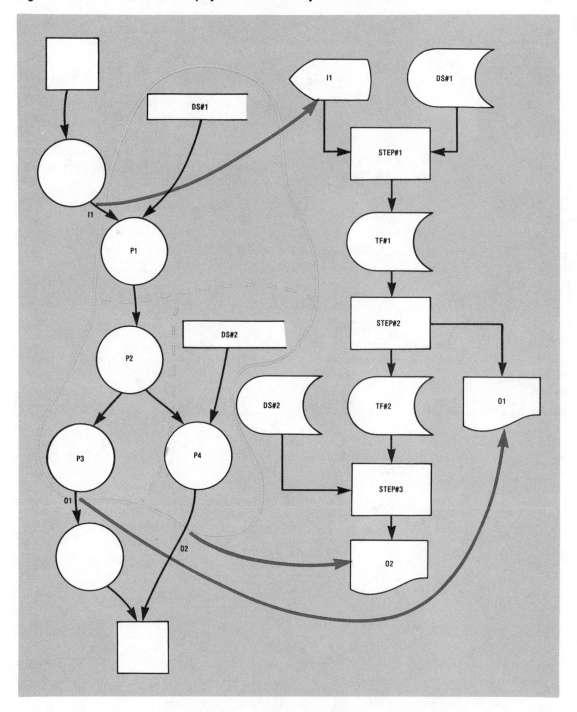

system design activity, the management steering committee will expect the feasibility analysis to be refined to a level that will make it possible to rely on it as a basis for committing the extensive funds needed to complete development of the system.

Thus, during this activity, all five dimensions of feasibility must be revised. In particular, for financial feasibility, it is necessary to bring the project status up to date by comparing budgeted figures with actual time and dollars. Also required to determine financial feasibility are developmental costs to complete the project, projected operating costs and benefits for the new system, and the opportunity cost that will be lost if the system is not developed.

Evaluating the Overall Design Quality. The design specifications for the new system will become the basis for its development and implementation. Therefore, this activity provides a last chance to make sure that the desired level of quality has been designed into the system. If quality is not designed into a computer information system, building it in later can be expensive and frustrating.

Quality analysis is done by a series of walkthroughs using the design documents for the new system. Evaluations are made for such items as accuracy, completeness, adequate controls, adherence to standards, and design principles such as coupling and cohesion.

Obtaining User Management and CIS Signoff. The importance of this step cannot be overemphasized. There are dual concerns: Make good estimates and make the estimates good. The analyst can put great time and effort into making good estimates, but the system will not succeed without a commitment on the part of the developers and the users to make the estimates good.

The role of the analyst is not unlike that of a real estate broker, in this case acting as a broker between developers and users. The developers must examine the contract, the new system design specification, to understand exactly what is required. Developers must also come to a conviction that it is possible to develop the system specified within the stated time and dollar limits. Similarly, users must understand what is required of them and come to a conviction that it will be possible for the system to achieve the specified benefits.

While the formal signoff represents the culmination of the entire analysis and general design phase, true signoff is really a matter of creeping commitment. Throughout this activity, numerous design decisions are being made. Various members of the user community participate in these decisions, thereby incrementally committing themselves to the final product. The formal signoff is critically important because it represents user and CIS management commitment to the system specified in the new system design specification, but the document itself should be something of an anticlimax.

Personnel Involved

The makeup of the project team begins to shift somewhat during activity 5. Normally, additional analysts or designers will be added to the team as emphasis shifts toward design. If appropriate, a database analyst will join the team. If significant changes in hardware or software are contemplated, members of the organization's technical services staff will also be called upon.

As the work in this activity moves forward, emphasis shifts away from user orientation increasingly toward the technical. The makeup of the project team shifts accordingly. The role of the user is to keep the project on a correct business course, to confirm appropriateness of products, and to supply necessary input for control processing and manual procedures.

Cumulative Project File

The project file assembled at the close of this activity includes some documents produced during activity 6. The cumulative content encompasses these items:

- A complete project plan at a task level for the implementation phase of the life cycle that is to follow.
- The initial investigation report (of historic interest only).
- The feasibility report, updated to provide a current appraisal. This report will be used in the review phase of the project.
- Documentation of the existing systems (to be discarded after the new system has been implemented).
- New system design specification (to be carried forward to activity 7: technical design).
- Data dictionary.
- Interview schedules and summaries (to be discarded after implementation of the new system).
- Preliminary test plan (from activity 6).
- Preliminary installation plan (from activity 6).
- User training outline (from activity 6).

CASE STUDY: NEW SYSTEM DESIGN

The new system design specification for Central City's water billing system cannot be presented in its entirety here. However, three significant components of that document and the thinking surrounding them are to be considered:

- The data base design for the new system.
- The transition from physical model to overall program architecture, expressed in system flowcharts, for key processes.
- An example of system controls added during activity 5.

Database Design

The Central City water billing system is a fairly straightforward operation, and the files to support it are not very complex. The file structure was developed in a somewhat intuitive manner, grouping those data elements that most often tend to be processed together. An analysis of the volume and frequency of the system inputs and outputs suggests an overall file structure. This analysis is contained in Figure 21-4.

It is clear from the frequency and volume analysis that there are three key outputs (METER-READING-BOOK, BILL, ACCT-HIST) and two key inputs (READING, PAYMENT) that should influence most heavily the definition of the master files for the system.

The resulting master files, together with the file organization method selected, are shown in Figure 21-5. Other approaches to designing the database are certainly possible. Some of the questions relating to this particular arrangement are discussed below.

Should the data in the BILLING-TRANSACTION file be included in the CUSTOMER-MASTER file? Note that each bill contains 8 fields. Saving 8 bills for each customer amounts to 64 fields, or about 250 extra bytes. If these data were added to the CUSTOMER-MASTER file, each record would be lengthened

Figure 21.4. *Analysis of outputs and inputs of Central City water billing system.*

OUTPUT	MEDIUM	VOLUME	FREQUENCY
1. METER-READING-BOOK	PRINTED	HIGH	BIWEEKLY
2. BILL	PRINTED	HIGH	BIWEEKLY
3. ACCT-HIST	ON-LINE QUERY	MED	30 PER DAY AVG
4. SPEC-READING-ORDER	MANUAL	LOW	2 PER DAY AVG
5. ACCTS-NOT-BILLED	PRINTED	LOW	BIWEEKLY
6. CASH&ADJ-JOURNAL	PRINTED	MED	WEEKLY
7. WATER-USAGE-SUMMARY	PRINTED	LOW	ON DEMAND
8. SEWER-USAGE-SUMMARY	PRINTED	LOW	ON DEMAND
9. FINANCIAL-STMT	PRINTED	LOW	MONTHLY
10. DEPOSIT	MANUAL	LOW	DAILY

INPUT	INPUT METHOD	VOLUME	FREQUENCY
1. READING	KEYPUNCH and ON-LINE	HIGH	BIWEEKLY
2. PAYMENT	KEYPUNCH and ON-LINE	HIGH	DAILY
3. SPEC-READ-REQ	MANUAL	LOW	2 PER DAY AVG
4. ACCT-CHANGE	ON-LINE	LOW	3 PER WEEK AVG
5. READ-ADJUSTMENT	ON-LINE	LOW	5 PER MONTH AVG
6. CASH-ADJUSTMENT	ON-LINE	LOW	5 PER MONTH AVG
7. WATER-RATES	ON-LINE	LOW	VERY INFREQUENT
8. SEWER-RATES	ON-LINE	LOW	VERY INFREQUENT
9. UNCOLLECTABLES	MANUAL	LOW	VERY INFREQUENT
10. DEPOSIT-CONFIRM	MANUAL	LOW	DAILY

Figure 21.5. *Definitions for the master files and access methods for master files and access methods for the new Central City water billing system.*

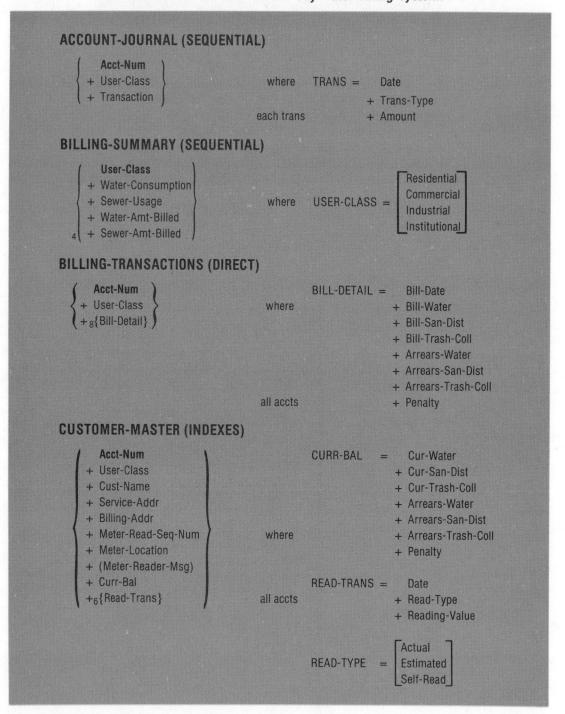

ACCOUNT-JOURNAL (SEQUENTIAL)

$$\left\{ \begin{array}{l} \textbf{Acct-Num} \\ + \text{User-Class} \\ + \text{Transaction} \end{array} \right\}$$

where   TRANS =   Date

each trans   + Trans-Type

                    + Amount

BILLING-SUMMARY (SEQUENTIAL)

$$_4\left\{ \begin{array}{l} \textbf{User-Class} \\ + \text{Water-Consumption} \\ + \text{Sewer-Usage} \\ + \text{Water-Amt-Billed} \\ + \text{Sewer-Amt-Billed} \end{array} \right\}$$

where   USER-CLASS = $\begin{bmatrix} \text{Residential} \\ \text{Commercial} \\ \text{Industrial} \\ \text{Institutional} \end{bmatrix}$

BILLING-TRANSACTIONS (DIRECT)

$$\left\{ \begin{array}{l} \textbf{Acct-Num} \\ + \text{User-Class} \\ + {}_8\{\text{Bill-Detail}\} \end{array} \right\}$$

where   BILL-DETAIL =   Bill-Date

                        + Bill-Water

                        + Bill-San-Dist

                        + Bill-Trash-Coll

                        + Arrears-Water

                        + Arrears-San-Dist

                        + Arrears-Trash-Coll

all accts   + Penalty

CUSTOMER-MASTER (INDEXES)

$$\left\{ \begin{array}{l} \textbf{Acct-Num} \\ + \text{User-Class} \\ + \text{Cust-Name} \\ + \text{Service-Addr} \\ + \text{Billing-Addr} \\ + \text{Meter-Read-Seq-Num} \\ + \text{Meter-Location} \\ + \text{(Meter-Reader-Msg)} \\ + \text{Curr-Bal} \\ + {}_6\{\text{Read-Trans}\} \end{array} \right\}$$

where   CURR-BAL   =   Cur-Water

                       + Cur-San-Dist

                       + Cur-Trash-Coll

                       + Arrears-Water

                       + Arrears-San-Dist

                       + Arrears-Trash-Coll

                       + Penalty

all accts   READ-TRANS =   Date

                           + Read-Type

                           + Reading-Value

READ-TYPE = $\begin{bmatrix} \text{Actual} \\ \text{Estimated} \\ \text{Self-Read} \end{bmatrix}$

significantly. The BILLING-TRANSACTION data are used only for the account history query, while the CUSTOMER-MASTER data are used by 3 other major processes that do not require billing information. Including billing data in CUSTOMER-MASTER might significantly degrade the performance of these 3 processes.

A similar question could be raised concerning the data on meter readings. Why are the reading transactions included in CUSTOMER-MASTER? Should the readings be split off in a separate file?

Note that the BILLING-SUMMARY file contains only four records—each holding the water and sanitary district totals by user class. This file is used to prepare the periodic usage summaries. Is it necessary? No. All necessary data are in the BILLING-TRANSACTIONS file. On the other hand, by summarizing total usage and amount billed by user class each time bills are produced and by using these subtotals to update the BILLING-SUMMARY file, year-to-date summary reports can be produced quickly and easily.

The final question to be considered here concerns the organization of the BILLING-TRANSACTIONS file. Should there be one long record for each individual account, as specified? Or should there be a separate record for each bill to each account, perhaps with the key ACCTNUM + BILL-DATE. The main advantage of the first option is faster access of billing information for the account history on-line query, the application for which the file was created. The update of the file probably performs better under the first option also. In this case, the overhead consists of rolling the bill occurrences forward each time a new bill is added, a time-consuming process. Under the second option, each new billing record would have to be inserted in the file, maintaining the logical order required for the query process. This latter option is probably even more time consuming.

Overall Program Architecture

Selected data flow diagrams from the physical model of Central City's water billing system were presented earlier in the case study section following activity 4 (see Figures 20-21 through 20-25). They cover processes for preparing the meter-reading book, applying new readings, and preparing bills. The system flowcharts corresponding to these portions of the physical model are presented here.

Figure 21-6 presents the annotated system flowchart for the job stream that prepares the meter-reading book. This corresponds to diagram 1 in Figure 20-22.

The system flowcharts for the batch and on-line processes that apply new meter readings are given in Figures 21-7 and 21-8. They correspond to diagram 3 in Figure 20-23.

The system flowchart for the batch processing of in-cycle bills is given in Figure 21-9. Refer to diagrams 5 and 5.2 in Figures 20-24 and 20-25.

Figure 21.6. *System flowchart for EXTRACT METERS TO READ job stream that prepared meter reading books.*

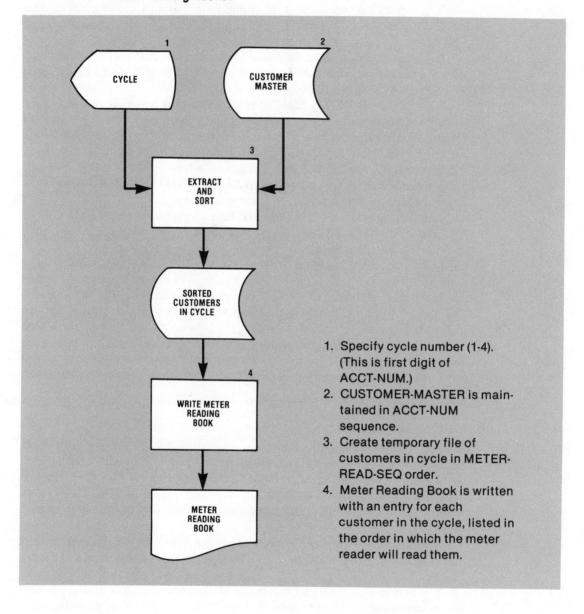

1. Specify cycle number (1-4). (This is first digit of ACCT-NUM.)
2. CUSTOMER-MASTER is maintained in ACCT-NUM sequence.
3. Create temporary file of customers in cycle in METER-READ-SEQ order.
4. Meter Reading Book is written with an entry for each customer in the cycle, listed in the order in which the meter reader will read them.

Figure 21.7. System flowchart for APPLY INCYCLE READINGS job stream.

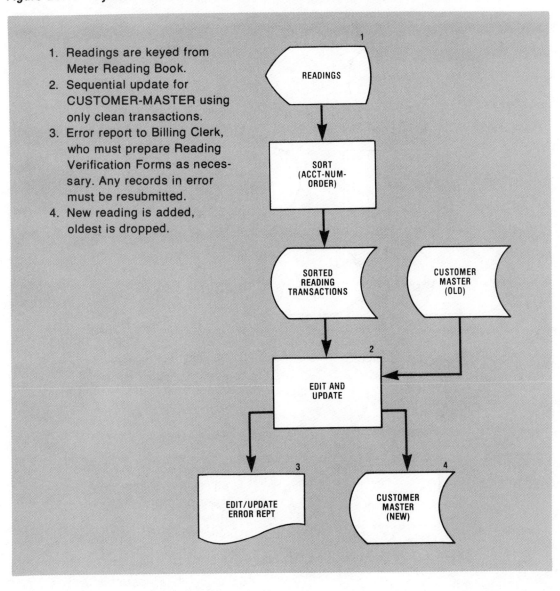

1. Readings are keyed from Meter Reading Book.
2. Sequential update for CUSTOMER-MASTER using only clean transactions.
3. Error report to Billing Clerk, who must prepare Reading Verification Forms as necessary. Any records in error must be resubmitted.
4. New reading is added, oldest is dropped.

Figure 21.8.   System flowcharts for APPLY SPECIAL READING jobs.

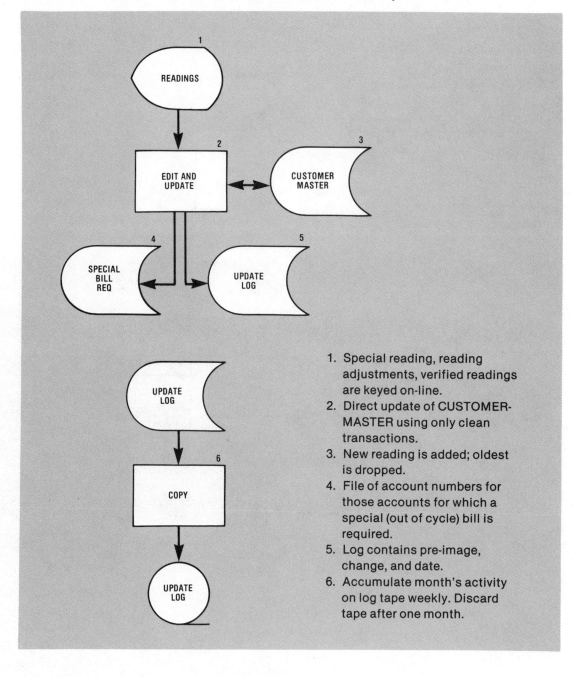

1. Special reading, reading adjustments, verified readings are keyed on-line.
2. Direct update of CUSTOMER-MASTER using only clean transactions.
3. New reading is added; oldest is dropped.
4. File of account numbers for those accounts for which a special (out of cycle) bill is required.
5. Log contains pre-image, change, and date.
6. Accumulate month's activity on log tape weekly. Discard tape after one month.

Figure 21.9. System flowchart for PRODUCE INCYCLE BILL job system.

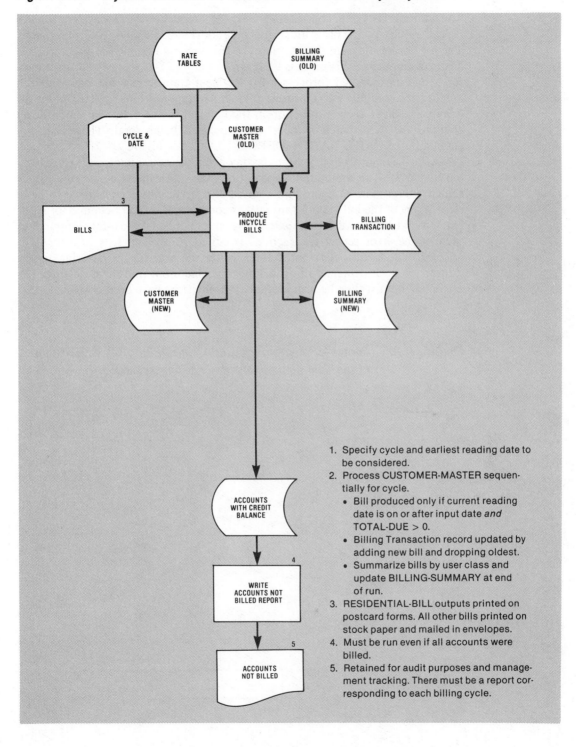

1. Specify cycle and earliest reading date to be considered.
2. Process CUSTOMER-MASTER sequentially for cycle.
   - Bill produced only if current reading date is on or after input date *and* TOTAL-DUE > 0.
   - Billing Transaction record updated by adding new bill and dropping oldest.
   - Summarize bills by user class and update BILLING-SUMMARY at end of run.
3. RESIDENTIAL-BILL outputs printed on postcard forms. All other bills printed on stock paper and mailed in envelopes.
4. Must be run even if all accounts were billed.
5. Retained for audit purposes and management tracking. There must be a report corresponding to each billing cycle.

System Controls

The addition of system controls to the physical model of the new system is a key aspect of activity 5. This is illustrated here for the APPLY PAYMENT process. The portion of diagram 0 that relates to this process is shown in Figure 21-10. The partitioning of this process is shown in Figure 21-11. All cash adjustments for a day are batched (process 6.2). Payment transactions are grouped into batches of about 50 to 100 (process 6.1). An adding machine tape is run on the amount field for each transaction in the batch (process 6.4). The batch ticket contains the date, batch number and type, and batch total. These data are entered in the DAILY BATCH/DEPOSIT LOG. See Figure 21-12.

After keying, all batches for the day enter the edit–update run (processes 6.6 and 6.7). The annotated system flowchart corresponding to this run is shown in Figure 21-13. Note that a batch of transactions is considered to be in error if any of the individual transactions contains an invalid field and/or if the batch total on the card for the batch ticket does not equal the total computed as each of the error report transactions is edited. If the batch is in error, it is rejected. The billing clerk must then locate the error(s) by referring to the transaction documents, adding machine tape, and input transaction listing. The entire batch must then be resubmitted after all errors have been corrected.

Figure 21.10. *Portion of diagram 0 covering the APPLY PAYMENT process of the new Central City water billing system.*

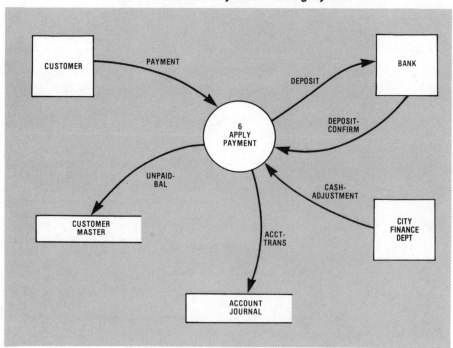

Figure 21.11. Diagram 6 for the new Central City water billing system, covering *APPLY PAYMENT* processing.

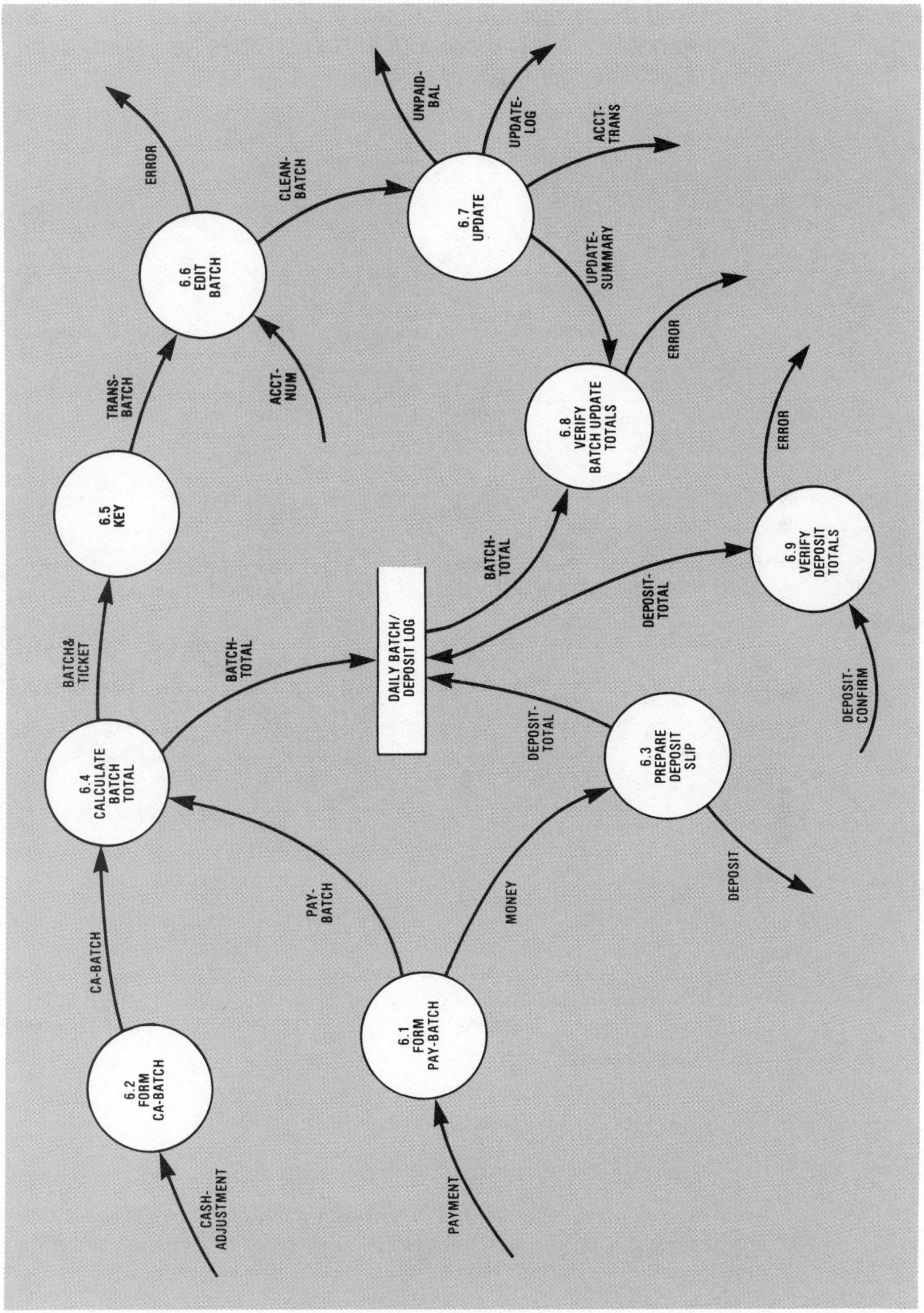

Figure 21.12. *Sample of the document used for control of processed batches and deposits on a daily basis in connection with APPLY PAYMENT processing under the new Central City water billing system.*

DAILY BATCH/DEPOSIT LOG

DATE	BATCH NUMBER	BATCH TYPE	BATCH TOTAL		VERIFY UPDATE	VERIFY DEPOSIT	COMMENTS
5-5-90	1	P	2816	43	JR		
	2	CA	100	00	JR		
	3	P	3039	08	JR		
	4	P	1887	76	JR		
		TOTAL	7843	27			
		DEPOSIT	7743	27		JR	
5-6-90	1	P	3142	18	JR		
	2	P	2503	25			Batch total error
	3	P	2792	12	JR		
	4	P	2917	63	JR		
	5	P	1131	73	JR		
	6	CA	76	84			Batch total error
		TOTAL	12563	75			
		DEPOSIT	12486	91			

Note that when clean batches complete the update, a brief UPDATE SUMMARY report is produced, showing the total dollars credited by batch. These totals are verified against the DAILY BATCH/DEPOSIT LOG by the billing clerk (process 6.8).

ACTIVITY 6: IMPLEMENTATION AND INSTALLATION PLANNING

Activity 6, implementation and installation planning, looks ahead to the work to be done during the next two phases. It provides information to help update the feasibility analysis at the end of activity 5, new system design.

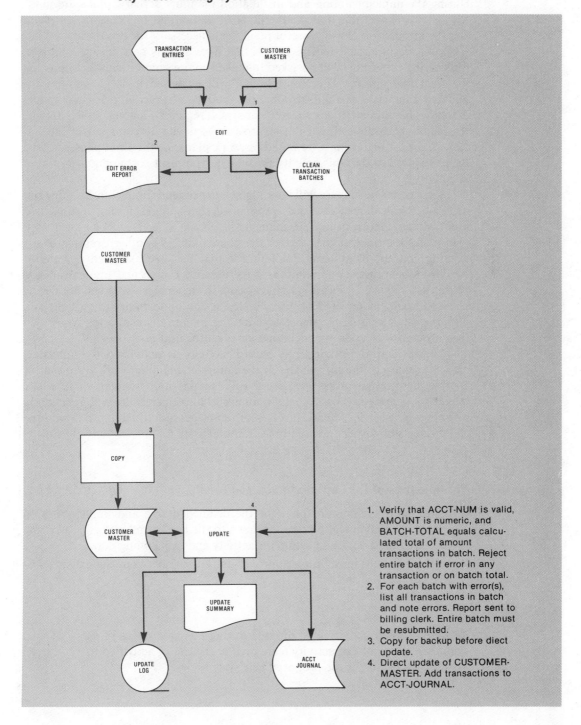

1. Verify that ACCT-NUM is valid, AMOUNT is numeric, and BATCH-TOTAL equals calculated total of amount transactions in batch. Reject entire batch if error in any transaction or on batch total.
2. For each batch with error(s), list all transactions in batch and note errors. Report sent to billing clerk. Entire batch must be resubmitted.
3. Copy for backup before diect update.
4. Direct update of CUSTOMER-MASTER. Add transactions to ACCT-JOURNAL.

Activity Description

During the implementation and installation planning activity, plans are made for the two phases that follow: the detailed design and implementation phase and the installation phase. Careful planning is necessary for two reasons.

First, despite the extensive efforts that have already gone into the project, the steering committee will be asked to make a major commitment in approving the final two phases. This commitment will be based in large part on the updated financial feasibility evaluation produced by activity 5: new system design. This updated cost-benefit analysis requires, among other things, reasonably accurate estimates of the cost to complete development of the system. These estimates must be based on work plans for the final phases. Thus, the plans produced in this activity feed the development cost updates produced in activity 5.

Second, the next phase will have many independent, parallel tasks going on: detailed technical specifications, program design, programming, testing, and user training, among others. To manage these tasks effectively, a detailed work plan is needed right at the start of the phase. This is another example of the layering concept of systems development that has been stressed repeatedly. Activity 6 bears the same relation to the detailed design and implementation phase that activity 2: feasibility study bears to the analysis and general design phase just being completed. Activity 6 presents an opportunity to estimate and plan the remaining development activities at a more detailed level. Work will then proceed with greater understanding when the next phase begins.

Rather than being buried as part of activity 5, activity 6 is established mainly because of the differences in the nature of planning work from that of analysis and design tasks. Activity 5 still remains user oriented, with heavy interaction among users and systems analysts. Implementation and installation planning, on the other hand, involves different people. In reality, however, the end products of activity 6 actually feed into activity 5.

Objectives

The objectives of the implementation and installation planning activity are to

- establish a preliminary plan for the detailed design and implementation phase. This plan will be defined down to the level of major tasks, working days required, and a schedule for activity and task completions.
- recommend an installation approach for conversion from the existing system to the new one.

Scope

As stated earlier, activity 6 is initiated during the later stages of the activity 5 work; and the results of activity 6 are used at the end of activity 5 to update the feasibility analysis for the proposed new system.

End-products

The principal end products of this activity are

- preliminary detailed design and implementation plan.
- preliminary system test plan.
- user training outline.
- preliminary installation plan.
- hardware and software plan.

Preliminary Detailed Design and Implementation Plan. The preliminary detailed design and implementation plan contains

- a list of major tasks to be performed. Note the word *major*. This is not a detailed plan, but a preliminary working document.
- at the task level, a listing of working day requirements.
- at the task level, also, a proposed staffing plan.
- a proposed timetable at the activity level (not at the task level). This timetable uses an elapsed-time basis, rather than specific calendar dates. The timetable is simply a planning document.

This preliminary plan will be used, early in the next phase, as a basis for more detailed planning and to update estimates of development costs before activity 5 is completed.

Preliminary System Test Plan. The preliminary system test plan contains

- criteria for acceptance of the new system. These criteria establish expectations of the results to be delivered in the areas of new hardware to be installed, any additional system software to be utilized, application software, user procedures, and operations instructions. All of these are implementation requirements for the new system.
- an initial list to identify the portions of the system to be tested. This identification is done at the subsystem and program level (without getting into the modules that make up individual programs). This listing covers the major products or functions to be tested and the interrelationships among those products or functions.
- in addition to system and program test identification, the same type of list for testing the workability of user procedures.

User Training Outline. The user training outline contains

- content outlines for the manuals to be used for user training.
- outlines of separate manuals to cover user procedures.
- a list of proposed assignments covering the activities of users and analysts who will be involved in the writing of the manuals for user training and user procedures.

Preliminary Installation Plan. The preliminary installation plan contains

- a description of the file conversion and system installation approaches to be taken at a preliminary level.
- a preliminary list of major files to be created or converted. This list includes any necessary forms that will be used to collect new data.
- identification of any computerized file conversion programs that will be needed.
- a preliminary list covering the installation tasks for the new system. This list includes any special considerations for coordination that may be needed between such areas as file conversion tasks and the overall application programming effort.

Hardware and Software Plan. If the design for the new system calls for installation of new computer hardware or acquisition of new system software, an installation plan to meet these requirements is developed at this time. This work, usually done by the technical support staff, is outside the working area of the members of the project team. Typically, the project leader and the head of the technical support team coordinate this activity to produce the needed plan.

The Process

At this point, it is not yet possible to review all process implications of the implementation and installation planning activity. The process is devoted to the planning of future phases, which have not yet been described. Thus, within the context established so far, it is possible to make only a few general observations about the process followed during this activity.

The general design completed during activity 5 identifies only the major application programs within the new system. Although an individual program identified at this stage may later be broken down into as many as fifteen or twenty individual program modules, the general design is sufficiently detailed to support workable estimates of program development and testing requirements for the next phase.

At this time, it is also desirable to identify alternatives that can be used in converting from the existing system to the new one and to select one of those alternatives. Conversion alternatives are discussed further in Chapter 22.

The tasks needed to prepare a preliminary installation plan are completed. Note that during this activity, program development plans for installation are closely integrated with plans from activity 5. Specifically, any programs required for file conversion are every bit as important as the application programs specified in activity 5. Even though these programs will have only temporary use, they should not be treated lightly or casually. Failure to prepare quality conversion programs can result in errors in the new system master files.

The preparation of user training and procedures manuals can be particularly critical. When all technical activities have been completed, these manuals *are* the system, at least as far as the users are concerned. Therefore, careful consideration should be given to the appointment of user personnel to document procedures and actually write drafts of manuals. Without effective and strong user involvement, the training and procedures manuals may lack the credibility essential for acceptance and effective use.

Test specifications and the test data yet to be developed represent the final criteria to be applied by users in accepting the new system. Therefore, it is important to be sure, during this activity, that users understand what the acceptance criteria are. Users should be asked to sign off on the descriptions of test procedures prepared during this activity.

Agreement must also be reached with computer operations personnel about the testing and acceptance criteria that will determine when the computerized portions of the new system will be considered operational. In this context, computer operations personnel become users who must sign off and "buy into" the new system before it is considered fully operational. After a new system has been implemented, computer operations personnel will be primarily responsible for service to users. Therefore, it is important that operations personnel understand, at this point, the jobs to be undertaken and the expectations that will be placed upon their staff.

Personnel Involved

In the portions of the implementation and installation planning activity that deal with planning for user training, systems analysts coordinate closely with carefully selected supervisory and mid-level management personnel from the user areas. Some of the users who join the project team at this point may be entirely new to the systems development effort. Thus, special indoctrination sessions and special amounts of patience may be necessary.

The other planning aspects of this activity will be the primary responsibility of the project team leader, since the activity is devoted largely to project management planning.

Cumulative Project File

The results of the implementation and installation planning activity are incorporated into the final report for activity 5. Outputs from this activity were included in the description of the cumulative project file for activity 5.

SUMMARY

Activity 5, new system design, marks the beginning of a transition from analysis to design. The user specification developed in activity 4 is not sufficiently detailed to meet the objectives of the analysis and general design phase. One of the most significant additions to the design of the new system at this point is the building of controls into the proposed system model. Also incorporated are provisions for security, backup, and recovery procedures.

An updated feasibility evaluation helps to verify that there will be no difficulties in the areas of human factors or scheduling. The financial analysis is updated to produce a cost-benefit analysis that will be within plus or minus 10 percent (or a range of 20 percent) of the final cost and benefits realized by the system.

This activity produces four principal end-products: the new system design specification, a specific recommendation about packaged application programs, a technical support specification (if appropriate), and a high-level summary for user management and the steering committee.

The primary goal of this activity is to carry the design of the new system to a point where an updated feasibility evaluation can be prepared. This includes preparation of accurate estimates for all five dimensions of system feasibility: financial, scheduling, technical, operational, and human factors.

A related goal is to build a clear understanding of the complexity and effort involved in implementation and installation.

The physical model of the new system prepared in activity 4 identifies which processes are computerized, which computer processes are batch and which are on-line, and the timing of batch processes.

The design is extended in activity 5 by first specifying which data and which processes are maintained centrally and which are distributed. Basic computer job streams are then defined. Major computer programs are identified but not internally designed. The required communication between programs, or job steps, is defined. The decisions are documented using annotated system flowcharts.

Quality analysis is assured by a series of walkthroughs using the design documents for the new system. Evaluations are made for accuracy, completeness, adequate controls, adherence to standards, and the design principles of coupling and cohesion.

As the work in this activity moves forward, emphasis shifts away from user orientation and becomes increasingly technical. The makeup of the project team shifts accordingly.

The project file assembled at the close of this activity includes a complete project plan at a task level for the implementation phase of the life cycle, the initial investigation report, the updated feasibility report, documentation of existing systems, the new system design specification, the data dictionary, interview schedules and summaries, a preliminary test plan, a preliminary installation plan, and an outline for the training of user personnel.

During activity 6, plans are set for the two phases that follow: the detailed design and implementation phase and the installation phase. The next phase will have many independent, parallel tasks going on. To manage these tasks effectively, a detailed work plan is needed from the start of the phase.

The objectives of this activity are to establish a complete project plan for the detailed design and implementation phase and to recommend an installation approach for conversion from the existing system to the new one.

The principal end-products of this activity are a preliminary detailed design and implementation plan, a preliminary system test plan, a user training outline, and a preliminary installation plan.

If the design for the new system calls for installation of new computer hardware or acquisition of new software, an installation plan to meet these requirements is developed by the technical support staff.

Careful consideration should be given to the selection of user personnel to document procedures and actually write drafts of manuals.

It is important during this activity to be sure that users understand what the acceptance criteria are. Agreement must be reached on testing and acceptance criteria.

REVIEW/DISCUSSION QUESTIONS

1. What is the purpose of updating the feasibility evaluation in activity 5? What is the target accuracy of the cost-benefit analysis, and how is this accuracy achieved?
2. How are additional controls incorporated into the system design during activity 5?
3. How is the design of the physical model extended in activity 5?
4. How are system flowcharts used in this phase?
5. What are the ingredients of an effective detailed design and implementation plan, an effective system test plan, an effective user training plan, and an effective training program for implementation of a new system?
6. For each activity in the analysis and general design phase,
   a. What is the key objective?
   b. What are the principal end products?
   c. What is the relation to the other activities?

22

Detailed Design and Implementation Phase

Learning Objectives
On completing the reading and other learning assignments for this chapter you should be able to:

- Explain the overall flow of activity in the detailed design and implementation phase and the relationships among the five activities that make up the phase.

- State the principal objectives of each activity in the detailed design and implementation phase.

- Describe the major end-products of each activity in the detailed design and implementation phase.

- Differentiate the three levels of design that occur during systems development.

- Discuss the major concerns addressed during detailed technical design.

- Describe the five levels of testing that occur during the detailed design and implementation phase.

- Describe the preparation and use of procedures manuals and training manuals and the role of the user in training for the new system.

- Explain the difference between system and acceptance testing.

THE DETAILED DESIGN AND IMPLEMENTATION PHASE

What is design? This easily stated question is incredibly difficult to answer. Basically, design is a series of tradeoff decisions. By definition, a tradeoff decision has no right or wrong answer. It involves the selection of one from among many options, each option having a set of inherent advantages and disadvantages. The goal is to select the option that maximizes the advantages *in the given situation*. For example, should a given function be automated or remain manual. If automated, should it be batch or on-line? If batch, what is the timing? If on-line, are real-time updates required? What is the necessary response time? Will it involve a single screen or an interactive conversation?

The difficulty is that there are hundreds, often thousands, of these decisions to be made. And they are interrelated. A decision to implement a business function as an on-line conversation consisting of an initial query with subsecond response time and a subsequent real-time file update completed in less than three seconds severely limits the options for physical data base design. Design decisions cannot be made "in order." However, design activities can be grouped.

The life cycle attempts to reduce the complexity of the design activity by dividing it into three logical groupings. The first group consists of the more general, architectural design decisions addressed in activity 5: general system design. The other two groups both reside in the detailed design and implementation phase. A second level of design activity, including software design, data base design, network design, takes place early in the phase. Then a third level, emphasizing detailed program module design occurs later in the phase.

The detailed design and implementation phase, then, marks a transition in the development project. It is not so much a transition from analysis to design (for, as noted earlier, design work began in the previous phase) as a transition in the nature of the work, the mindset of the people involved, and often the people themselves.

The emphasis during the first two phases has been on understanding the business problem, effective communication with and responsiveness to users, and establishing a high-level architecture or general design for the proposed system. During this phase the emphasis begins to shift to more detailed and more technical design considerations. More technical CIS specialists may join the team. Even the user involvement is more detailed and technical with an emphasis on the definition of rigorous user procedures, training, and testing.

There is no abrupt division between the second phase, analysis and general design, and this one. In practice it is a gradual transition. The activities and processes of this third phase must be understood in order to truly understand those of the second phase. The detailed design work in this phase builds on the general architecture already established. During phase 2, the experienced analyst-designer is continually influenced by an understanding of how the products being produced will be used in phase 3.

Objectives

The objectives of the detailed design and implementation phase are to

■ Produce a completely documented and fully tested new system (or incremental unit, or version of a system) that encompasses computer processing, manual procedures, and all necessary interfaces between computerized and manual processes and among multiple computerized processes.

■ Secure approval to proceed with system installation from users, from the CIS operations group, and from the management steering committee.

Process

The detailed design and implementation phase consists of five activities. The relationship among these activities is depicted in Figure 22-1.

Work begins with the new system design specification prepared at the conclusion of phase 2. Recall that this document emphasizes the general design of the proposed system from the user's point of view. It includes just enough design of computer processing to support an updated feasibility evaluation and permit a fairly accurate time and cost projection for the remainder of the development effort. This document serves as a basis for the detailed technical design work of activity 7, including detailed design of programs, specific design of files, input record designs, and output document or display designs. Next, after test specifications have been prepared, individual program modules are written and tested. (activities 8 and 9).

During this same period, user training begins (activity 10). Once trained, users become involved almost immediately in acceptance testing activities. This testing encompasses both computerized and manual procedures. During the acceptance test (activity 11), the new system is operated under conditions that are as close as possible to normal production conditions, with the project team observing the procedures and results. Any final, fine tuning of the new system takes place during this comprehensive testing activity.

Two key design decisions can have a great impact on the work that occurs during this phase: the decision to purchase an application software package and the decision about how to install the new system.

For many systems, 50 percent or more of the development resources are expended in this phase. However, the time and resources required for this phase may be reduced significantly if a decision is made to use an application software package rather than developing all the programs internally. This option, in fact, dominates many application areas as large numbers of software houses have brought comprehensive and flexible application systems to market. If purchased application software is used, the nature of the programming activity within this phase changes. The emphasis is on programs for converting master files, providing special interface functions to meet special needs of specific users, and, as a last resort, modifying portions of standard programs for specific needs.

In some cases, this programming activity can be enormous, especially for data conversion of very old files. In others, the use of application software greatly reduces the programming effort. No matter where application software originates, however, the user training and acceptance test activities associated with this phase will remain relatively unchanged.

The installation approach can also have a major impact on how this phase progresses. The traditional approach is to design and implement the entire

Figure 22.1. *Relationship among activities of the detailed design and implementation phase.*

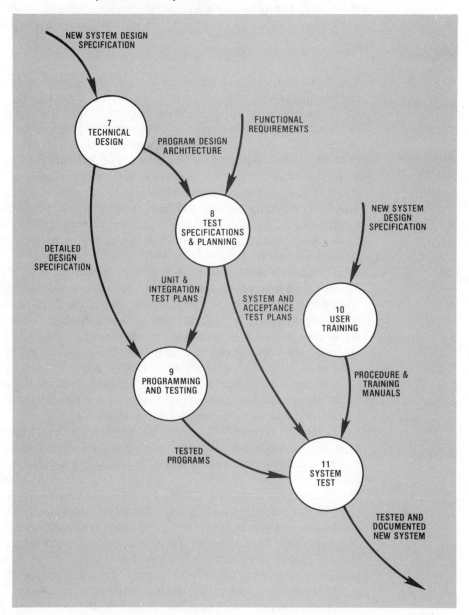

system completely, then to do a massive acceptance test, and finally, to install the system following one of several possible methods. However, in larger systems with reasonably independent components, a far more effective approach can be to implement and install the system in incremental steps, or versions. In this way, users can learn to use the system effectively, a step at a time; and developers can produce the system with good control over schedules and budgets.

The delineation of the appropriate increments or versions is a complex process that may begin early in this phase or even toward the end of the previous phase. This approach parallels the natural evolution inherent in any business operation: There are short- and long-range plans, the short-range plans designed to realize certain objectives that fit into a long-range pattern. Similarly, the incremental pieces or versions of a system should realize short-term objectives within a long-range system plan. The net result is an iteration of the detailed design and implementation and the installation phases for each version. Additional remarks concerning version implementation are presented in Chapter 23 as part of the discussion of rapid development techniques.

End-product

The end-product of the detailed design and implementation phase is a fully tested and documented system (or version of a system), including

- A complete set of tested application and data conversion programs.
- Training and procedures manuals.
- Fully tested manual procedures.
- A complete test log and generations of test files for unit, integration, and systems tests.

This product is developed in stages through several activities. Since these activities overlap one another, they must be coordinated closely. For example, while technical design is still proceeding, work has begun on preparation of test data for modules already designed and programming and unit testing has begun on still others. While all this is happening, user training may begin. The need for close coordination is clear. Major end-products are described in later sections according to the activities in which the products are produced.

Decision

Phase boundaries represent major go–no-go decision points. At the end of each of the first two phases, project cancellation was a possibility. While still possible, cancellation is far less likely at the end of this phase. The issue is more whether the system is ready to be placed in full production or additional testing and fine-tuning is required. The main drivers for this decision are the users and the CIS operations and technical support groups.

ACTIVITY 7: TECHNICAL DESIGN

The work done during the technical design activity determines the ultimate technical quality of the new system.

Activity Description

Technical design is a pivotal activity. The framework for the remainder of the project and for the structure of the system itself is formed at this point. As described earlier, a transition from analysis to design takes place between the second and third phases. This transition is implemented during activity 7. Members of the project team work from the new system design specification (prepared in activity 5). The major output of technical design, a detailed design specification, serves as a blueprint for the system to be implemented and installed as a production system.

During activity 5, certain general design decisions had to be made as input for the technical design work of this activity. For example:

- Processing volumes must be defined and quantified before hardware specifications can be set.
- Decisions must be made about the mix of on-line and batch processing within a system before application software can be designed and programs written.
- The processing cycles for portions of the system (daily, weekly, monthly, for example) also are necessary inputs for application software design.
- Policy decisions about centralization or distribution of both processing and data will shape all aspects of the system, particularly to establish whether and what data communication capabilities must be implemented.

These general design decisions are all open for review at the start of activity 7. There are sound reasons for this. The emphasis has shifted. The product of systems analysis, in effect, documents user desires. As systems design activities progress, these desires must be modified in keeping with such realities as requirements of other systems used within the same organization, physical constraints of hardware, budgets, changes in the economy, and many other factors.

Technical design is a two-part activity. Initially, an overall systems design and a general data base design are devised as part of a series of events that review and challenge the new system design specification. This effort produces a set of technical specifications and guidelines which in turn drive a series of tasks dedicated to detailed design of specific portions of the new system. Specific tasks and products of detailed design are covered further in the process section later in this chapter.

Objectives

Two major objectives should be met during the technical design activity:

- The transition from analysis to design as a preparation for implementation of the new system should be bridged successfully.
- A detailed technical design for the new system should be produced and carried forward as a basis for program design and implementation activities that follow.

These objectives are critical because the technical design activity is the point within the life cycle at which quality is built into the new system. It is well understood that quality cannot be added after the fact, nor can quality be inspected into a product. Rather, quality must be an integral, organic part of the process from which a new system is derived.

One measure of the quality of a system is the length of its useful life. The determination of useful life, in turn, depends upon the maintainability of the system.

All computer information systems, no matter what the application, exist in a dynamic business environment. Any new system, no matter how sound its initial design, will be modified throughout its life. The degrees of urgency and necessity for these modifications may vary, but they will occur. Therefore, a major measure of quality (and a major objective of the technical design activity) lies in the extent to which future systems maintenance requirements can be anticipated and long-term flexibility can be assured by the overall design.

Another measure of the quality of the work done in this activity is the precision and rigor of the documentation generated, particularly the detailed design specification. In any sizable CIS project, a number of people who have not previously been associated with the project will be brought in at this point. This is particularly true for programmers. A number of programmers may be assigned to work on a variety of subsystems. Precise and complete definitions are essential: The work of many contributors must fit together so that the individual work products can function eventually as an integrated system. The following are especially critical:

- A precisely defined data base (down to the level of storage formats, field sizes, access methods, and other specifications) must be specified.
- Inputs and outputs must be defined down to levels that include exact spacing, the content of standard labels and messages, and the precise terminal displays that occur for on-line portions of the system.
- Program definitions must encompass both the processing within individual modules and the passing of control and data between modules.

Scope

The scope of the work of activity 7 is illustrated in the Gantt chart in Figure 22-2. Clearly, this activity leads the detailed design and implementation phase; none of the other activities is launched until technical design is well along. All other activities either continue or do not start until activity 7 is concluded.

The working scope of this activity involves a reconfirmation and possible modification of the new system design specification produced during analysis and general design and a transition from the new system design specification to a detailed design specification.

Overlapping and interdependency are particularly strong between the technical design activity and activities 8 and 9, involving the preparation of test specifications and the writing of programs. The first parts of the system to be

Figure 22.2. Gantt chart illustrating the parallel nature of the activities of the Detailed Design and Implementation phase.

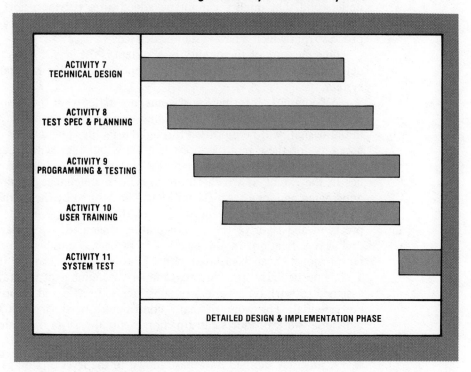

designed can move forward to the latter two activities even while design continues on other portions of the system.

Activity 10, relating to user training, is largely independent of the others in this phase. User training will, of course, depend in part on the results produced during the programming activity and on the terminal dialogs established during the technical design activity.

Activity 11, involving the testing of the complete system by users and operations personnel, cannot begin until all other activities have been completed.

End-products

Three end-products result from the technical design activity:

■ The detailed design specification.
■ Computer operations documentation.
■ Specifications for special programs to be used for file conversion.

Detailed Design Specification. The **detailed design specification** includes and also extends the new system design specification developed at the close of the analysis and general design phase. The list below shows those products that are newly added, or heavily modified, in *italics*. Note that the system documentation and program documentation for the new system are essentially complete, although in rough form, at the end of this activity. Contents of the detailed design specification can include

- An overview narrative that describes the system's purpose, goals, and objectives, as well as the basic logical functions that must be performed.

- Processing descriptions that include a context diagram and a hierarchical set of data flow diagrams. Diagram O should identify the major subsystems within the system being developed. Lower-level diagrams should indicate the physical packaging decisions that have been made for the new system.

- *Precise specifications for data base or file definitions. These specification include access methods or paths, record layouts, storage formats, edit criteria, and other details.*

- *Documentation for hardware, systems software, and network design requirements. These may simply confirm that existing resources are sufficient, or they may be specifications for additional resource.*

- *Annotated systems flowcharts for each job stream. In the process, program identifications are established and all necessary procedure language or job control language (JCL) statements are written.*

- *Designs for individual programs and specifications through the use of structure charts. Structure charts are created for all major job steps in the computerized portion of the system.*

- *A program inventory to cover all programs in the system. This inventory is organized according to program identification and name, the job stream or streams in which each program occurs, and the external programs (if any) that call each particular program.*

- *Program specifications. These specifications include detailed descriptions of modules, of interfaces among modules as specified on the structure charts, and of inputs and outputs. In addition, processing descriptions for these modules and program components are prepared.*

- Specifications for backup requirements and recovery procedures for all files in the system.

- A description of the audit trail and logging requirements to be incorporated into the new system.

- Updated data dictionary definitions as necessary to support the processing specifications.

- Development of a catalog to show all outputs to be delivered to the user, either printed or displayed. Usage descriptions and *precise layouts are prepared for all outputs. If preprinted forms are to be used, final designs are prepared.*

- A catalog that lists all inputs, including descriptions and *layouts. If necessary, preprinted forms are prepared.*

- Reviews of user interfaces with the system and validation or modification as necessary. *Precise terminal dialogues for all on-line functions are created.*

- Documentation for performance criteria that are critical to either computer or manual processing. These performance criteria can include response times, volumes, or other quantifiable specifications.
- Documentation for security and control measures aimed at limiting access to either equipment or files. (Security and control measures that deal with processing are included within processing specifications.)
- Review of policy considerations associated with the new system. Any unresolved decisions are presented for resolution.

Computer Operations Documentation. **Computer operations documentation** comprises instructions about the setting up and execution of programs for each application. These instructions can include brief narratives describing the processing of systems and subsystems for the benefit of computer operators.

Operations manuals should include estimates of processing volumes and run times. For each job stream, a descriptive sheet should be prepared that covers the name of the job stream, input file requirements, set-up instructions, outputs, data control provisions, backup procedures, recovery and restart instructions, and any special requirements.

Conversion Programs. **Conversion programs** are necessary to create the initial files for the new system. Very often, it is necessary to prepare special programs, used one time only, to accept existing files as inputs, restructure those files, and create the files to support the new system. One of the end-products of this activity is a set of technical specifications for any such conversion programs.

The Process

At the start of this chapter is a discussion of the complexity of the design process and the fact the SDLC divides it into three logical groupings. The technical design activity represents the second level. Human-machine interface design, data base design, network design, and application software design are considered at this level.

Detailed program module design occurs in activity 9: programing and testing.

Detailed design issues are covered in greater detail in other chapters. However, to make clear the scope and focus of the technical design activity, the following sections review some of the key concepts associated with each of the areas that make up detailed technical design.

Human-Machine Interface Design. Some fairly straightforward procedures can be followed in analyzing and designing interfaces between people and automated processes. It is important to understand which procedures take place during this activity. Rough sketches of all input documents, output reports, and on-line screens, which were produced during analysis, are input to this activity. The job here is to turn the rough sketches into precise formats. Design includes specific content of standard messages and labels, as well as detailed specifications for format and spacing.

On-line interfaces present a special concern. In this activity, the designer takes the basic input and output screens identified earlier and builds on-line conversations based on them.

Although the emphasis usually is placed on these on-line conversations, it is important to remember that the human-machine interface also may involve submission of batch inputs and production of printed reports. It is also important to specify all the detailed procedures the user must follow within the scope of the system. Specifications for on-line conversations feed the detailed software design and programming and testing activity. The following represent important human-machine design considerations:

- Readability of reports or screen formats should be evaluated for each delivered item. Spacing should enhance user recognition and understanding. Data elements should be presented in logical groups corresponding to the way the receiver actually will use the information. As a general rule, the normal reading sequence, top-to-bottom and left-to-right, should be followed. To the extent possible, the overall design of reports and displays should be kept uniform throughout a system. This uniformity can enhance their readability and understandability, especially for the occasional user.

- The amount of data presented to a user at any given time should be considered. On displays, for example, data content should not be overloaded to a level that inhibits recognition or reaction time. In both reports and displays, emphasis should be placed on delivering what is needed, not all that is known. The key to determining content is the purpose or intended use of the output.

- Terminology should match the words, phrases, or terms natural to a user and should be standardized throughout the system. Avoid use of codes or abbreviations when designing outputs for occasional users.

- Messages displayed on terminals should have common or similar formats for easy recognition. Diagnostic messages should be stated clearly and be meaningful to the user.

- Don't assume that a user will be familiar with rules or procedures after using them once. As user procedures are defined, outlines are prepared for user manuals and training materials that will be developed later during the user training activity. For on-line portions of systems, much of this material can be provided in the form of *help* screens that can be called up at the user's request. These help screens should be self-contained and easily accessible to the inexperienced user and should be capable of being bypassed by the knowledgeable user.

- The level of sophistication of users should drive the content and design of interactive conversations and guide the selection of instructional aids or other options that are made available.

Database Design. A logical data model to support the system was created during the analysis and general design phase. This model served as input to the general data base design tasks of that phase. If the system is to be supplied by traditional computer files, the result was a specification of the data content, file organization, and access keys for each of the files specified. If the database management software is to be used, the database administration group will have specified various user views of the data, the views that will be used by the programmer and supported by the particular database software package to be used. This group also will have specified the necessary changes to the physical database in order to support the estimation of implementation costs. The results from that phase now are reviewed and refined in light of the system design decisions reached at the start of this activity. In general, major changes should not be required.

After completion of the general data base design tasks, the detailed file design is fairly straightforward. Precise record definitions are specified for each file. These definitions include exact record layouts, storage formats and lengths, primary and secondary keys, and the like.

Both general data base and detailed file design considerations are covered in greater depth in Chapter 12.

Network Design. Basic decisions in the area of network design increasingly concern the degree of centralization or distribution of processing functions and data resources. Flexibility and creativity can pay big dividends both in terms of the cost of equipment and communications facilities and in terms of system responsiveness and business services provided.

Most of the detailed network design tasks will be performed by communications software and hardware specialists working in parallel with the project team during this activity. It is the responsibility of the project team to provide the necessary input to these support people concerning business requirements as they affect network design. This input includes

- An outline of the geographic distribution of sites and the system functions to be supported at each site. Many of these sites may be local. Some may be remote.

- Specifications regarding the type of processing by function and site. Which functions will be batch and which on-line.

- For each function and site, specifications regarding the response time required. The time will depend on the nature of the business. For example, pricing routines used with a bar-code reader in a grocery checkout application require subsecond responses. An airline reservation system can tolerate responses within several seconds, while response to queries in a nationwide medical diagnosis system could take several minutes or longer. Response time measured in days may be adequate for some other applications.

- When remote sites are involved, analysis of where the different data elements are used in addition to the required response times. This analysis is particularly important because it will affect decisions about which data elements to keep at a central location and which to distribute to remote locations. Clearly, these decisions have an impact on the network design.

- Normally, some communication network capability is already in place. Communication needs for the system under development should be tied into the larger picture of existing communications among local and remote sites. Comparing the communication needs of this system with those of other existing systems will help communications specialists determine the adequacy of current equipment and network support.

System designers on the project team must work closely with communications support personnel to develop an understanding of communications requirements and impacts. Network design decisions will impact directly both data base and software design decisions and, hence, the ultimate cost to implement and run the system. Tradeoff decisions involving cost and level of service certainly will be necessary.

Application Software Design. It is highly significant that the architectural design of application programs and the detailed design coding and testing of program modules are separate activities within the systems development life cycle. This separation stresses the importance of assuring thoroughness and quality in executing and evaluating designs before detailed module design and coding even begin. The design tasks done during this activity concentrate on creating overall designs for each of the application programs at the structure chart level. The emphasis is on creating tight, functional modules and clearly defining the data relationships among them. Algorithm design to implement individual modules is normally part of the later programming and testing activity.

In the design of application software, extensive sets of tools are available for identifying modules that are related closely to business functions, for determining the data relationships that should exist among those modules, and for evaluating the correctness and maintainability of the program designs as documented in the resulting structure charts. These program development principles and techniques are covered in Chapters 15 and 16.

A number of concerns should be addressed through out the process of application software design. Four of these concerns follow:

■ Always remember that a program is an implementation of a plan to solve a business problem. It can be tempting, as the work becomes detailed and technical, to concentrate on program efficiencies and refinements that may be implemented only at the expense of the business objectives to be met. Supposedly elegant program designs are useless if they are not ready in time or, worse, if they do not solve the specified business problem. Software designers should resist all impulses to deal with technical challenges for their own sake, even though the technical aspects of a system may seem more intriguing. In short, never lose sight of the business objectives for any given application.

■ Almost invariably during application software design, some opportunities for system enhancement will be uncovered. It can be tempting to modify existing designs in the belief that these changes will make the system significantly better. However, such decisions should not be made at this stage. The job of an application software designer is to meet existing specifications. If additional opportunities are uncovered, those opportunities should be carried forward into the list of enhancements to be considered in the review phase.

■ Each application software program should be designed to accomplish as much as possible within defined specifications. Many options are available in the structuring and execution of program designs. That is, there always will be two or more ways to implement any given set of specifications. It is the designer's responsibility to select the option that presents the best long-range value for the system and its users. Thus, it would be best to choose an option that is most compatible with the perceived future needs and directions of the system. The designer should avoid options that would work equally well at present but might present greater difficulties when the system is modified or expanded in the future.

■ Any temptation to rush or shortchange the program design step should be put down. Many programmers are far more comfortable writing code than they are designing programs. As a result, there can be a temptation to rush to coding. Almost invariably, a design derived hurriedly will demonstrate low quality and produce more problems at higher costs.

Personnel Involved

The makeup of the project team shifts dramatically during the technical design activity. Up to this point in the project, there has been a mixture of users and CIS professionals. At this point, the active membership of the team is largely technical. Depending upon the size of the project, a number of designers and programmers should be added to the project team. Some systems analysts may be reassigned to other projects.

Even though users may not be involved actively in day-to-day design tasks, it is important to keep lines of communication and consultation open. One method for doing this is to hold regular formal status meetings conducted by the project leader and attended by key user managers and supervisors of technical activities that are currently in process.

The purpose of such meetings is not to solve problems but to keep the various user areas informed of activity and progress. Typically, topics would include

■ Review of the major tasks completed since the last meeting.

■ Review of the major tasks currently in process.

■ Outline of the work scheduled to be completed before the next meeting.

■ Discussion of any scheduling problems.

A 30- to 60-minute meeting held weekly or biweekly usually is sufficient to meet the objectives.

Bear in mind that users have been involved actively in project development for perhaps six or nine months. Bear in mind also that this will be their system, and they are likely to anticipate its benefits, perhaps with some impatience, as they become more aware of the shortcomings of methods they are using presently. It would be counterproductive to cut them off entirely during the technical phases and activities of a project. Although the project team is mainly technical, users are still on call and should be consulted during the technical design activity.

Technical Support Considerations. Certain projects may require technical support from outside the project team. Two common situations are database considerations and hardware and system software concerns. These situations are significant because of the coordination that must occur between the project team and technical support capabilities these specialists can provide.

Assuming the new application will run on a computer system that utilizes database management software, there will be special concerns and considerations connected with integrating the data requirements and outputs of the new system with existing databases. In such a situation, a database analyst often will begin to work with the project team during the last portions of the analysis and general design phase.

The database administration group may be responsible for the physical database design. Later, this group will handle the creation of the physical database during the conversion and installation activities. The database group also will be involved during testing to oversee program efficiency in terms of database accesses and access paths.

Special technical consideration will arise if the system under development requires new computer equipment or new systems software capabilities. To put this requirement in perspective, there probably will be no special concern unless significant new hardware or systems software purchases are required. However, if the computer installation is being altered to accommodate the new application, a technical specialist would begin work with the team late in the analysis and general design phase. This person would become a key member of the team during technical design. The technical services group would be responsible for the acquisition, testing, and acceptance of new hardware and systems software.

Cumulative Project File

The principle of cumulative documentation is particularly apparent during technical design. The detailed design specification document is added to the project file at the end of this activity. The degree to which it is merely an extension of the new system design specification was illustrated in the discussion of endproducts. Also, as mentioned then, the rough form of the final system documentation and program documentation are essentially complete.

CASE STUDY: TECHNICAL DESIGN

In the previous chapter, several aspects of the general design specification for Central City's new water billing system were presented, including the design of the new data base and the addition of system controls. Part of the high-level application software design as represented in several system flow charts was discussed.

Here is an illustration of how the software design ideas might be modified as more detailed technical design is added.

Batch Processes

A closer look at the bill preparation function will be used for the illustration. The user's timing requirements have been added to diagram 5: prepare bill, shown in Figure 22-3. Initially, the special billing process will be considered as a semimonthly process. Later, the effect of alternative timings on the design will be discussed. Figure 22-4 reflects the job step packaging of diagram 5.2 for this batch job. A similar packaging would exist for diagram 5.3.

The resulting systems flowchart appears in Figure 22-5. Several considerations have gone into this design. Although the calculation processes for incycle and special bills have many similarities, the processes have been packaged into different job steps because different data drive each. An incycle bill is generated for each account with a billing cycle that matches the input cycle. Calculations are based upon the current reading stored, if the reading date is on or after the input billing date. The readings for these accounts are updated by a separate file maintenance job stream that is run as meter readings are received, batched, and input. This processing requires sequential processing of the CUSTOMER-MASTER file (or a subset of it if an alternate index access path by cycle is available and feasible).

The creation of special bills, by contrast, depends upon the account numbers in SPECIAL-BILL-REQ. This file is processed sequentially, and the matching CUSTOMER-MASTER is accessed directly. To retrieve the date of bill preparation within a single job step would add unneeded complexity. The concern over the apparent duplication of program code that ultimately will be written can be addressed through the structured design of the software in each job step. The commonly needed functions, such as CALCULATE WATER CHARGE, can be provided by a single well-defined routine that is invoked in each job step. The strategies and design evaluations that govern this approach are discussed further in Chapters 15 and 16.

The preparation of the actual bills has been packaged into a separate job step because both step 1, INCYCLE BILLING, and step 2, SPECIAL BILLING, will generate bills. An additional basis for this design decision is that a financial savings on postage can be realized if the bills are presorted by ZIP code. This step is followed by a report-writer job step that actually prints the bills for mailing.

In producing the ACCOUNTS NOT BILLED report, an intermediate file containing accounts with zero balances is created. The report then can be produced through a relatively straightforward report-writer step.

Of course, different timing considerations for producing SPECIAL-BILLs would change the design. The primary effect would be to create two systems flowcharts and job streams that differ only in the first step, one with INCYCLE

Figure 22.3. Diagram 5—PREPARE BILL—with timing considerations added.

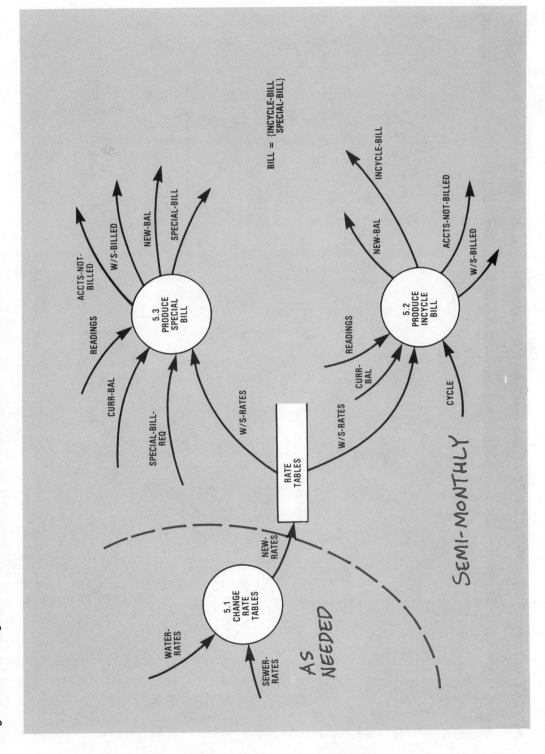

Figure 22.4. Diagram 5.2—PRODUCE INCYCLE BILL—with job step packaging.

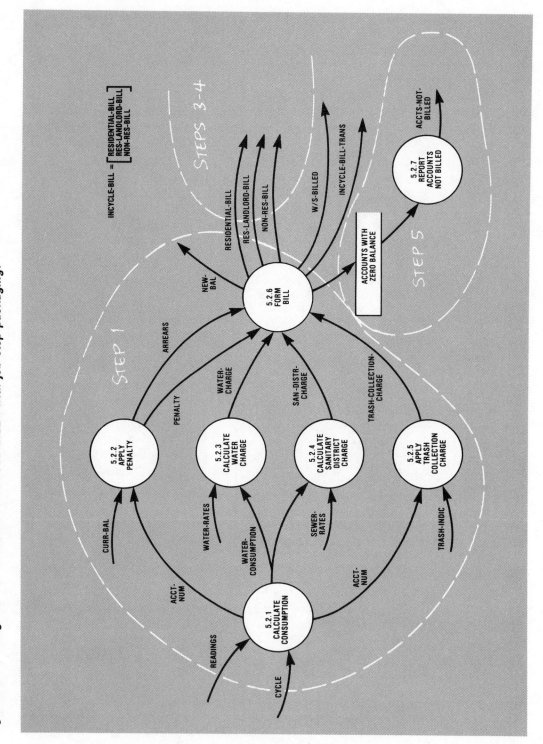

Figure 22.5. Billing job stream systems flowchart.

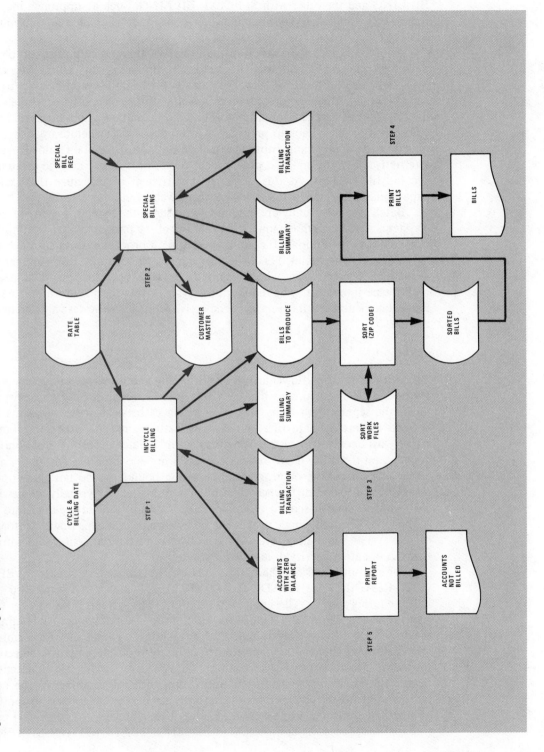

BILLING and the other with SPECIAL BILLING. Such an approach may be more likely because the special requests may need servicing on a more frequent basis.

An additional consideration in the design of this job is the backup of the data currently on the computer files before the update is run. All the files have been shown as on-line disk files. One means for backup would be to copy all such files to another portion of reserved on-line storage or to off-line media such as tape. This design decision usually is based on equipment limitations and off-site security needs. Backup procedures often occur either before updating begins or at its completion. Input transaction data must also be retained. As an alternative, a log of pre- and post-update copies of a record may be created to provide file backup. At this point, it is sufficient to recognize the backup capabilities must be added to the systems flowchart in Figure 22-5.

Batch systems usually are initiated by a user in the form of a job request to a systems scheduler who manages the running of the particular job. A computer operator may then initiate the job by executing a procedure through an operator's console or terminal. For a specific request, the operator also supplies the needed parameter values where required. Because operator intervention and multiple peripherals may be required, the systems flowchart is useful for operations documentation. Its overview perspective of the job provides valuable information.

On-line Considerations

The value of systems flowcharts is less dramatic and apparent in documenting the design of on-line processing. In batch systems, separate programs exist for all of the separate job steps. Usually, interfaces between these programs are defined by intermediate files. As described above, natural processing boundaries exist between processing functions within a batch system. Within on-line systems, on the other hand, several processes are encompassed within a single processing procedure, or program. Processing boundaries do not show up as transitional files or differences in timing requirements. Typically, somewhat independent, smaller-scoped groups of processes are brought together into an on-line job. Thus, the single processing box shown in a systems flowchart for an on-line system may imply several processing steps from data entry and editing through updating, retrieval, and display.

For example, consider the EDIT AND UPDATE process 3.4 used for SPECIAL-READINGS or READING-ADJUSTMENT shown in Figure 22-6. As indicated, this process is designated to be online. The systems flowchart for this job is shown in Figure 22-7. Unlike the batch processing of the incycle readings, the on-line job handles only a single reading and does so at the time the terminal operator inputs the reading. Immediate editing of input data occurs; detection of error is displayed for operator action; and records are updated with accepted data. The results of a single such transaction then are available to the next person accessing the updated record. In this example, the job appears to contain only a single processing transaction. A more detailed review of process 3.4 may find that the processing of SPECIAL-READING, READING-ADJUSTMENT,

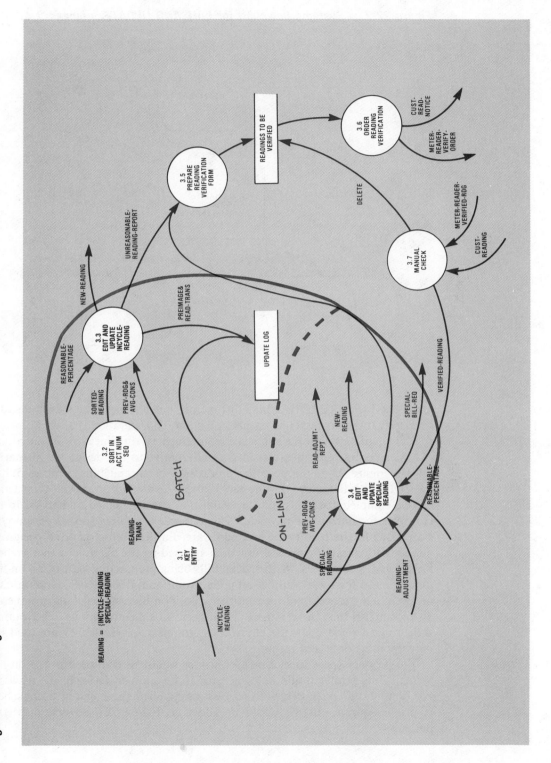

Figure 22.6. **Diagram 3—APPLY NEW READINGS.**

READING = {INCYCLE-READING
          {SPECIAL-READING

READINGS TO BE VERIFIED

3.5 PREPARE READING VERIFICATION FORM

3.6 ORDER READING VERIFICATION

CUST-READ-NOTICE

METER-READER-VERIFY-ORDER

3.7 MANUAL CHECK

METER-READER-VERIFIED-RDG

CUST-READING

DELETE

UNREASONABLE-READING-REPORT

NEW-READING

REASONABLE-PERCENTAGE

SORTED-READING

PREV-RDG& AVG-CONS

PREIMAGE& READ-TRANS

UPDATE LOG

VERIFIED-READING

3.3 EDIT AND UPDATE INCYCLE-READING

3.2 SORT IN ACCT NUM SEQ

BATCH

ON-LINE

READ-ADJMT-REPT

NEW-READING

SPECIAL-BILL-REQ

REASONABLE-PERCENTAGE

PREV-RDG& AVG-CONS

3.4 EDIT AND UPDATE SPECIAL-READING

READING-TRANS

3.1 KEY ENTRY

SPECIAL-READING

READING-ADJUSTMENT

INCYCLE-READING

Figure 22.7. Systems flowchart for EDIT AND UPDATE, process 3.4.

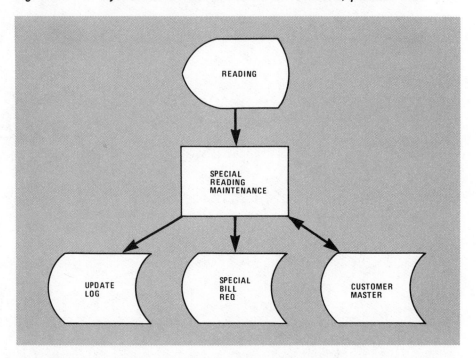

and VERIFIED-READING may differ from one another. The users's decision to specify these processes as on-line takes into consideration that each involves special handling by people and has a requirement of timeliness for its execution.

As a second example, consider an alternative to the design for preparing bills in Figure 22-5. Suppose the production of special bills, process 5.3, is packaged with the above on-line capabilities. As a result, a special transaction can be completed which produces a bill that can be mailed or handed to the customer for immediate payment. This approach requires special design considerations for both software and hardware. Earlier, well-structured design required that commonly needed functions be used by the batch jobs that prepare incycle and special bills. With special bills being prepared as part of an on-line job, the need for these routines remains. Additional design consideration must be given to the usability of the routines in both on-line and batch environments. To accomplish this, these routines must perform single functions. The routines should not depend upon the physical environment in which they are used but only upon the data they receive.

To produce these special bills, a printer would be dedicated to the on-line system. This printer would be considered to be another device in the network. For flowcharting purposes, both processes would be represented by a single box. A printed output, BILL, would be added to Figure 22-7 to document this design.

The typical approach in designing the on-line component of a CIS system is to group several transactions or business tasks together under an "umbrella." Each transaction is based upon some event in the business: a customer closes an account; an adjustment is made to an incorrect reading; the rate per unit for water for commercial users is changed. The transactions are not related to one another except for a possible tie to a common data base of information. The umbrella often is implemented through a menu program. That is, the on-line system displays a list of processing options from which the terminal operator can choose. Figure 22-8 is an example of a menu for the water billing system. Each option reflects a transaction or business function. Through the keyboard, the user selects the processing function that is needed. After this entry, control is passed to a program that manages or controls the processing associated with the selection: requesting additional input data, editing data, acting upon data, manipulating retrieved data, or displaying a response.

Several menus may appear in an on-line system, each corresponding to a particular grouping of functions. These groups usually reflect security con-

Figure 22.8. **Water billing system service menu.**

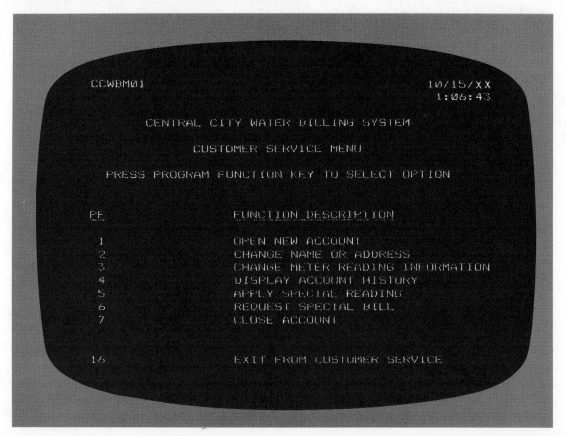

siderations about who is allowed access to what functions. For example, a water billing service clerk would have access to a menu such as that shown in Figure 22-8 but not to one that contained the function from process 5.1, CHANGE RATE TABLES.

Backup and recovery of data in an on-line system requires more sophisticated approaches than these functions in batch processing. Because the system is needed continuously for sending and receiving timely information, special concern must be given to such problems as program failure, interruption of power, and loss of communications.

When documenting on-line systems, all these considerations are condensed into a single box on a systems flowchart. Additional documentation of these design decisions is necessary. To document the user's interaction with the system, rough screen formats such as the one shown in Figure 22-8 can be used to describe a "conversation" with the on-line system.

In addition, attention must be given to the internal structure of the on-line job. The scope and organization of batch processing are documented with a system flow chart. For on-line systems, delineation of functions often occurs with the preparation of structure charts rather than systems flowcharts. If a flowchart shows the entire system as a single processing symbol, a structure chart details the separate procedures. A structure chart, or hierarchy chart, is used to illustrate the processing functions within a system and to describe the relationships among those functions. The structure chart presents a top-down view of the organization of software components of the system, in succeeding levels of detail. The topmost level of the structure chart, corresponding with the systems flowchart process symbol, indicates the overall function of the system to be developed. Additional levels present the different processing functions that must be performed. Only the major processing functions and the data interfaces between those functions are indicated. Later, during program design, these structure charts are expanded to lower levels to include program module design. Structure charts are used throughout software design but are especially useful at this stage with on-line systems.

ACTIVITY 8: TEST SPECIFICATIONS AND PLANNING

This activity, while brief, sets the stage for all testing to be done prior to system installation.

Activity Description

At the start of this activity, technical, or implementation-oriented, design work has begun for the new system. Before programming can begin, standards must be set for acceptability of the processing that will implement the user specification. It should be stressed that the specifications and plans developed during this activity go beyond program tests. All manual procedures, the forms, and the verification of value for the results produced are encompassed in the specifications and the test procedures that are evolved. The specifications and procedures for tests that are developed in this activity are applied at several levels.

- **Unit testing**, or **module testing**, is applied to individual program modules. Tests determine whether the modules are logically and functionally sound. Unit testing is done by using the modules to process test data and examining the outputs to determine that results are as expected.

- **Integration testing** is applied to interfaces between modules. This type of testing is done in parallel with unit testing. Integration testing tests the transfer of both data and control between modules for a program.

- **Function testing** seeks to identify any variances between the results of program processing and the specifications for the programs agreed to and approved by users. Function testing concentrates upon the results produced by complete programs to be sure that results meet user expectations and requirements.

- **System testing** deals with the integration of a system, or integrated group, of application programs with system software, hardware, peripherals, manual procedures, and any other system components. This category of testing extends beyond the computer system to encompass all related procedures and processing. The idea is to try out the system as an operational and functional entity. Thus, the tests check to see whether the training and procedures manuals are adequate to cover instructions and operational problems that might arise. A system test simulates actual operation of the entire system prior to its conversion and continuing use. In effect, the system test is a preview of how the overall system will work. This testing also applies to throughput, capacity, timing, and backup and recovery procedures.

- **Acceptance testing** focuses on the user. In effect, an acceptance test is a dress rehearsal to be sure that the users find the new system acceptable for use in an ongoing production mode.

The first three tests deal with application software. The first of the tests, unit testing, deals with the lowest level of program entity, the module. To carry out tests at this level, data are selected to test the correctness of the programming logic for the instructions within each module. The second level of testing, then, deals with the capabilities for pairs and groups of modules to interact with one another. The dimensions tested deal with the passing of data and control between modules. Function testing deals with the level of programs at which identifiable end-products are produced. A function, in this sense, is a program that accepts input and produces usable output. The programs involved can be complete systems or parts of larger systems of programs. The standards applied in measuring the results of tests are user expectations.

The last two levels of testing, system testing and acceptance testing, deal with multiple programs that make up complete processing systems. The philosophy represented by the system test is that CIS professionals should satisfy themselves that the systems of programs are performing to expectations before the systems are turned over to users for acceptance tests under conditions that simulate actual use. Even through system tests are performed by CIS professionals, the criteria for evaluating the results come from user-approved documentation and specifications.

Objectives

Three important objectives should be met during the test specifications and planning activity:

- Define all conditions that must be tested at the program, subsystem, and system levels.
- Prepare all necessary test data and create test files to be applied during activity 9: programming and testing.
- Prepare a system test plan for coordinating the tasks of activity 11: system test.

Scope

Technical design feeds the test specifications and planning activity, and this activity in turn feeds programming and testing. All three may overlap one another heavily.

As technical specifications are produced during activity 7, they are reviewed here. The individual programs and program modules are identified as work units for which test specifications and test data must be assembled.

The activity then encompasses the identification of all products to be tested during activity 9 and the preparation of data for the testing of each.

At the conclusion of this activity, a set of documentation should exist that includes specification and test data. As appropriate, the test data may be incorporated in input files that can be used in actual test processing. These tests should cover the complete application system from the lowest module level through complete implementation of computerized and associated procedures.

End-products

Separate sets of end-products are produced to incorporate specifications and plans. The specification products include the following.

- **Acceptance test specifications** include detailed lists of all user requirements (from activity 4) that must be tested. Broad test case matrices are formed to ensure that all specified requirements are tested.
- **Program test specifications** include extensive and detailed lists of all conditions that must be tested. For each specification, there is a related reference to the test files to be used.
- **Test data files** are prepared for each program. Emphasis is upon the quality of data in terms of the specific properties of each module or program to be tested.

- **Job stream test specifications** list the conditions under which each job stream is tested. These specifications assume successful completion of tests for individual modules and programs. Again, corresponding test files are referenced in these specifications.
- **System and subsystem test specifications**, as well as any other required testing procedures, are documented, with accompanying cross references to test files.

In a separate set of documents, a **test plan** outlines the steps to be followed in testing an application. Components of a test plan include the following:

- The steps, or phases, of a test plan are spelled out and objectives are stated for each phase.
- Completion criteria, or acceptance criteria, are established for each testing task.
- Complete schedules are developed for testing tasks.
- Responsibilities for performance of testing tasks and completion of tests and their covering documentation are prepared.
- Provision is made for the computer resources needed to perform the tests. This usually includes substantial storage requirements for several generations of test systems and test data as well as considerable machine time.
- An overview document encompasses plans for integrating all of the tasks associated with program and system testing.

The Process

In effect, the process followed in testing programs and systems is in the inverse order of the sequence of work performed as part of the systems development life cycle. These relationships are represented graphically in Figure 22-9. As shown, the progression of work in systems development moves from systems analysis, to systems design, to software design, and to the design of individual modules. The preparation of specifications and the performance of program tests, by contrast, moves in the other direction. That is, the first testing activity is unit testing. Unit testing is applied to the results of module design, the last of the systems development procedures. This inverse relationship follows through to the final testing activity, the acceptance test, which is applied to the product of systems analysis.

This relationship stems from the nature of systems development itself. That is, as each product is developed during the systems development life cycle, the criteria for evaluating and testing that product also are prepared. This correspondence between development and quality assurance is inherent in the process of systems analysis, systems design, and the overall development cycle.

In applying tests to systems and their components, it is inevitable that errors will be encountered. Programs and procedures do not anticipate all logical paths or occurrences. It would be impossible to predefine all conditions that may be faced by a complex system of programs. Thus testing becomes a matter

Figure 22.9. *Relationships between systems development and testing activities.*

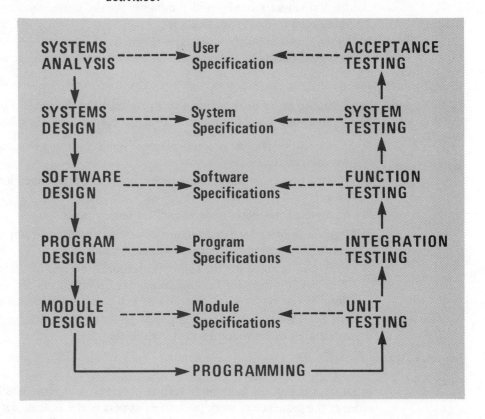

of identifying and correcting errors as they occur. Following correction, retesting takes place.

As a test program moves through its cycle of finding and correcting errors, each correction, in turn, can cause situations that create new errors. Thus, for some period of time, the incidence of errors encountered usually will increase. There is no way to say, for any given program or module, how long this process will continue. However, it is a typical pattern that the incidence of errors grows as a testing program is launched. Then, at some point that seems to vary for different programs, the incidence of errors begins to decrease. An important part of testing philosophy and policy lies in knowing when the incidence of errors has decreased to a level where a system or component of a system becomes acceptable. Theoretically, it might be possible to keep testing until no more errors occurred. However, to follow a test program through to this level would be impractical and exorbitantly costly. Rather, some time after the incidence of errors begins to decrease significantly, a decision must be made about the existing level of confidence. When the level of confidence in the system reaches a point of acceptability, testing can be terminated. This level of confidence may be reached a relatively short time after the decrease in error incidences is noted.

Thus, the level of errors and the pattern of errors should dictate the cycle for testing of any given program component or system. This is the only measure that should be followed. Attempts are sometimes made to set time limits on testing. For example, it may be arbitrarily decided that testing for a given program can be completed in two weeks. At the end of this time, the plan would call for discontinuing the testing. It is not practical to predict or commit to the establishment of quality on a time basis only.

When a testing program reaches the point where the entire system is to be exercised as a single coherent entity, system test (a special objective viewpoint) should be brought to bear. Although the system is not ready at this point to be put into user hands, some outside objectivity is desired. A sound, often-adopted practice is to have system test procedures performed by key users and CIS professionals who were not part of the project team. Occasionally, outside consulting organizations are asked to perform system test functions.

From a process standpoint, the acceptance test can be a critical juncture in the activities within a systems development life cycle. This testing activity involves broad, active user participation, with the users beginning to assume control over the system. Thus, in planning for acceptance testing, provision should be made for full briefings and preliminary training of user personnel who will be involved.

A more detailed discussion of testing and testing strategies is given in Chapter 18.

Personnel Involved

Ideally, an independent group should perform most of the test specifications and planning. Persons who do the design and programming work approach these tasks with the expectation that their final products will work correctly. There may be reluctance to test vigorously in an attempt to verify the incorrectness of the system. Independent testers would be less hesitant about proving problems with the system. Members of the user group should be involved in establishing the specifications and data to be used in acceptance testing.

Cumulative Project File

Existing documentation already in place in the cumulative project file is not affected directly by this activity. However, parts of the cumulative documentation file, specifically those statements that spell out requirements and performance criteria for the new system, become the guidelines for development of test specifications and plans. Thus, the documentation created during this activity, specific test specifications, a testing plan, and files of test data enhance and build upon the cumulative project file.

ACTIVITY 9: PROGRAMMING AND TESTING

The programming and testing activity includes programs that will be part of the new system as well as temporary programs to be used for data conversion.

Activity Description

High-level program design was done during activity 7: technical design. Typically, that activity specifies the precise format of inputs and outputs and identifies major program modules and the data and control interfaces between them.

This activity consists of detailed module design, coding, and testing at the unit, integration, and function levels.

One of the most important, misunderstood, and maligned aspects of programming is documentation. Accurate documentation is essential for the ongoing maintainability of the system. However, the key word is *accurate*. Comment-level documentation as part of a program listing, while sometimes necessary, is notoriously inaccurate in older systems. It simply is not updated as programs are changed.

A proper understanding of documentation focuses on design standards. If an organization has a good set of design standards and if they are rigorously applied by the project team during the technical design and the programming and testing activities, the resulting application software will be predictable, straightforward, and readable. This is the essence of proper documentation.

Objective

The objective of the programming and testing activity is to produce a complete, documented, and tested system of programs ready for testing with manual and other external functions as a complete system. The testing within this activity is limited to unit, integration, and function testing. All the programs should function to specification and on their own. However, the testing portion of this activity does not encompass complete system or acceptance testing.

Scope

As stated above, this activity is fed by, but can heavily overlap, the prior two activities, technical design and test specifications and planning. Once programs are specified and the interrelationships of modules are understood, test specifications can be written and the actual design, coding, and testing of program units or modules can begin. Because of the structured, modular approach, entire programs can be developed and tested in top-down fashion one module at a time.

If modular design has been executed effectively, it is possible to overlap program development. That is, lower-level modules can still be in the design phase while middle-level modules undergo test planning and higher-level modules are coded and tested, all within the same time period. Because of the structured approach, overall coordination and management of program development can continue on a module-by-module basis without loss of management control over development of the program as a whole. This overlapping of development tasks makes clear the need for extremely careful and precise definitions of module functions and intermodule linkages during technical design.

End-products

End-products are function-tested programs that are documented fully, tested, cataloged in the program library, and supported with operating instructions for personnel in the computer operations center.

The Process

The nature of the programming and testing process should be well understood. It does vary depending on whether third or fourth generation languages or more powerful lower-CASE tools are used.

No matter what the tool, there is always a tendency to drive straight to coding. More powerful generators intensify that tendency. Thus it may be good to recall the basic steps that still apply in a wide range of environments.

1. Problem analysis. The programmer should first review technical specifications and build an understanding of the nature of the problem to be solved. In some instances, complete structure charts for the programs will exist. In other instances, the programmer will have to develop structure charts. This first step may involve meetings with other programmers to assure an understanding of the boundaries of modules to be developed by different people. Also discussed will be the intermodule communication interfaces for passing data. Programmers may work individually on modules or be part of teams assigned to groups of modules. The team approach prevails on larger systems, and in situations in which programmers are receiving on-the-job instruction from more senior professionals.

2. Program design. This design step focuses on the control logic of the program or module. It involves elaboration of existing structure charts to a level of detail needed to support the writing of pseudocode.

3. Program specification. In this step, the programmer prepares pseudocode for each assigned module. This pseudocode defines the processing logic for the module. Pseudocode for higher-level modules will tend to focus on overall control logic. That for lower-level modules, which tends to emphasize data transformation, may be available directly from the processing specifications prepared earlier. Pseudocode should be reviewed thoroughly in walkthrough sessions. This review serves both to check the individual module and to oversee the needed module-to-module compatibility.

4. Program coding. If the process has been followed effectively, this step is a relatively straightforward translation of specifications into instructions written in a selected programming language. Bear in mind that writing code should not be the major part of program development. Rather, if planning and design are handled effectively, programming becomes a routine procedure.

5. Program testing and debugging. The keyword here is precision. As logic errors are uncovered, there is pressure to get them fixed as rapidly as possible. By now it is likely that the entire project is behind schedule and that additional testing is being delayed because of a problem in one program. Unless work is done calmly and precisely, changes made at this point can easily (1) introduce additional errors and (2) violate the overall design that was so carefully conceived.

Documentation should be prepared for all responsibilities and activities required of computer center personnel. For on-line programs, emphasis will be on maintenance or troubleshooting activities. For batch programs, documentation will be more extensive, involving complete setup, run, and follow-up procedures. Setup procedures deal with program loading and peripheral-device preparation. Run procedures detail the console messages that can be expected and the reactions that should be taken while the program actually is being executed. Follow-up would include instructions for handling backup, logging, or new generation files that would be created, as well as disposition for the existing media. In addition, instructions must be provided for handling outputs and returning program media to the library.

Personnel Involved

Personnel who complete this activity are entirely within the programming group of the CIS function. In large shops and for large jobs, programmers may work in teams. If so, there will be team leaders responsible for blocks of programs associated with the application under development.

Cumulative Project File

A program file is prepared for each separate program. Files also are prepared for each special program required during data conversion. These special programs may be required to convert files from existing formats to those required by the new system. Use of such programs will be one-time only. However, full documentation support still is needed. Each program file contains

- The latest source code listing or reference to the listing in the source code library.
- The specifications for the program.
- The test log for each program, including notations on each test run, the date, the test file version used, the results, and notations on any modifications made.

This documentation, of course, is added to the existing documentation for earlier activities in the project. Personnel who will perform succeeding activities for training users and testing complete systems, may require access both to earlier documentation and to these end products.

ACTIVITY 10: USER TRAINING

A system consists of both computer and manual processes. The user-training activity attempts to bring the same rigor and precision to the manual part of the system that programming brings to the computer part.

Activity Description

While the intensively technical activities for program design and development are being carried out, users and systems analysts with heavy user involvement work concurrently on a series of user training and testing tasks. These involve writing procedures manuals, preparing training materials, and conducting training programs. In addition, all manual procedures are tested thoroughly within the user organization. The training of users and the testing of manual procedures are principally user functions, with systems analysts observing and advising rather than directing. The underlying idea is that the first group of users trained on a new system then proceeds to train the other users who will be involved.

User training will be a mix of instructional sessions and hands-on practice to provide simulated experience in the use of the new system. The objectives should be to build an understanding of the needs being met by the new system, of the philosophies followed in meeting those needs, and also of the specific techniques to be used. In these training sessions, one of the elements being tested is the adequacy and appropriateness of the user documentation. There should be two categories of documentation ready by the time training of users begins. One includes the manuals used for ongoing operation of the system. This form of documentation typically comprises **procedures manuals**, or procedure manuals. The second includes separate **training manuals**. Training manuals provide cross-reference for and guide to the use of procedures manuals. Procedures manuals, in turn, are structured so that people who need guidance on the job can look up and be directed specifically to the areas that will help.

Objectives

The objectives of the user training activity include the following:

- On completion of the tasks in this activity, user managers should have a clear understanding of how the new system will operate.
- The user operating staff should be trained fully in the tasks they will perform and the responsibilities they will assume under the new system.
- All user personnel should acquire sufficient documentation to guide them in day-to-day operations and problem solving.
- A supervisor or manager within the user group should be designated as coordinator or liaison person for the resolution of future training needs or the securing of answers to questions that might arise.

Scope

User training can overlap many other activities in the detailed design and implementation phase. The activity begins with the design and documentation of manual procedures. It then follows with the design and creation of training programs and materials. This work can begin as soon as the technical design is sufficiently stable.

Actual training sessions will tend to occur later in the phase. A core group of users is first trained to be trainers. Then sufficient additional users are trained to support the system test activity. Training for the remainder of the users may be held until the installation phase that follows.

Timing is everything. Training must begin early enough that there is time for new procedures to be fully understood. On the other hand, training must be done as late as possible so that the new procedures can be quickly put to use.

End-products

The end-products of the user training activity include procedures or reference manuals and training manuals. These documents are described in Chapter 9. Following conversion to the new system, the procedures manual will be the ongoing documentation needed by user operating personnel. However, because it may be necessary to train new groups of user personnel periodically, the user's manual, or training manual, should be kept up to date, and additional training sessions should be planned as required.

A final end-product of this activity should be designation of personnel within the user group who will be specialists in training new employees or solving the problems for the existing staff.

The Process

Training users in the implementation of a new system can present an extremely delicate challenge. People earning a living at specific jobs, who are therefore professionals in their respective fields, are being asked, in effect, to change. This very requirement may pose a psychological threat to some people. Thus, one of the challenges in structuring a training program lies in putting people at ease and establishing a feeling of mutual growth for all persons involved. To do this, the presentation techniques should be structured for credibility. Credibility can be established by pretraining persons who can address the future trainees within the user group as peers. These trainers can then say, convincingly, that the new procedures are not difficult. The trainers also can say that they have found the new procedures helpful in job performance and capable of enhancing the smoothness and efficiency of operation in the department. An IS professional could not credibly make such statements. Therefore, IS professionals should work closely with and indoctrinate selected users. These users, in turn, should train their peers.

In actual training, there should be a careful mix between building background understanding and establishing confidence in the actual procedures. Terminals should be available at the training site. Trainees should perform enough functional cycles of their respective activities so that they feel comfortable, have confidence in their ability to remember the procedures, and know they can perform efficiently.

One other topic deserves special consideration at this point, how to handle change requests from users at this stage of the development process.

Change Requests from Users. As user personnel undergo final preparation, testing, and training, they will inevitably begin to identify new opportunities. Frequently, these opportunities will require modification of the system to encompass new functions or outputs. Basically, the idea that users are discovering increasing potential for the system is healthy and should be encouraged. At the same time, however, it is important that user training programs establish the need to implement the system first, then change it.

Introducing changes into a system while it is in final development and testing can be dangerous. It is not always possible to tell how a seemingly minor change in input, processing, output, or files will affect the system as a whole. It is a safe bet, however, that any change, however minor, will result in an interrelated impact elsewhere in the system.

Therefore, a policy should be established about the kinds and extent of changes permitted during this phase. For example, reversing the positions of two columns on an output report or display might be minor enough to handle, but the production of a complex new report should probably be delayed.

Because suggested enhancements to the system will almost surely develop at this point, it is a good policy to establish a postimplementation maintenance list that describes all these opportunities. Right after the system has been implemented, consideration can begin for the introduction of these new ideas as part of a system maintenance.

Of course, mandatory change requirements can come up any time. If such requirements do arise, they must be dealt with during this phase as during any other. For example, suppose a new law or government regulation is introduced while the system is still under development. It may be necessary to incorporate a change to reflect this before implementation. Judgments must be applied continuously. Necessities must be incorporated in the system; enhancements can be deferred for later consideration.

Personnel Involved

Except for standby resource personnel from the CIS group, training is entirely a user activity. Personnel involved include the users appointed as trainers, user management, supervisors within the user group, and all operating personnel affected by the new system. Any CIS personnel involved should maintain as low a profile as possible and should be available for consultation with user trainers. As they begin to take control of the system, users must be encouraged in every way possible.

Cumulative Project File

Procedures and training manuals are added to the cumulative project file. No additional documentation is required to support this activity. Content of the procedures and training manuals will vary according to methods followed in individual organizations and according to the needs of the systems. However, the following is a general outline of the elements of the procedures manual.

- Table of contents.
- Narrative overview describing what the system does and where it fits within the user organization.
- Individual job descriptions and procedures.
- Input and source data forms, including any necessary explanations, preparation instructions, and manual processing-procedure descriptions.
- Data entry instructions, including procedures, controls, error correction instructions, and procedures for handling exceptions.
- File maintenance descriptions, including explanations of any updating responsibilities of users, error correction, and backup procedures (Such descriptions are provided for both master files and for any tables that need updating).
- Output documents or reports, accompanied by explanations of content, lists of distribution, and objectives for intended use.
- Any needed policy statements.
- Procedures for updating the manual.

The training manual includes

- Copies of any special handouts needed for training sessions. An example would be completed forms.
- Copies of the operating procedures. Operating procedures should be placed in chronological sequence rather than in reference order. Thus, users should be able to follow the training manual from beginning to end. By contrast, the procedures manual is segmented according to function, facilitating on-the-job reference.

ACTIVITY 11: SYSTEM TEST

The system test activity is the culmination of the detailed design and implementation phase. It verifies that the full system, both manual and computer processing, is ready to run in a production environment.

Activity Description

The system test activity encompasses both technical system test and user acceptance test functions. That is, at the beginning of the activity, CIS professionals perform all the procedures and use all the equipment associated with the new system and test all programs, manual procedures, off-line equipment, and the like. When the CIS group is satisfied, users are phased into the activity and perform all testing for ensuring that the system functionality meets their requirements and that the personnel who ultimately will be responsible for operating the system are competent and proficient.

Within this framework, two types of tests are performed. The first is a **functional test**. Procedures are designed to make sure that all operations covered in the specifications actually can be performed and that expectations for results actually can be met.

The second type of test is **performance testing**. These procedures test the quality of performance rather than straightforward functions. For example, one of the performance tests that should be applied is gradually to overload the system with volumes of transactions to the point where it cannot handle the processing volume. The purpose is to make sure that the system can respond to such exceptional situations. Other performance tests deal with response times, delivery time, the usability of outputs, security (from an access standpoint), backup procedures that assume temporary system failure, and recovery from system failure.

These test procedures should be complete before installation of the new system begins.

Objectives

Prior to the system test activity, individual programs have already been tested. The objective of this activity, then, is to test the system as an entity. Testing includes evaluating the ability of the system to function in coordination integrating manual, off-line, machine, and computer processing to be sure that all procedures are compatible and can be integrated.

Scope

This activity has little or no overlap with other activities in this phase. Programming and individual program testing should be complete. User training, if not complete, will have been started and its activity put on hold until closer to the time of final system installation.

The activity encompasses an initial set of tests applied by CIS professionals. Then, the professionals back away, retaining only minimal, advisory involvement as a previously trained group of users takes over and operates the system under conditions that are as realistic as possible.

At the conclusion of this activity, the detailed design and implementation phase comes to a close. The system is ready for file conversion and installation for ongoing use.

End-products

End-products of the system test activity include:

■ A proven system ready to be put into operation.

- Procedures manuals that have been tested under lifelike conditions and proven adequate.
- Run books and any other needed manuals for the computer operations staff.

Another result of this activity is that there will be a group of people who have used the system and built both the competence and the confidence necessary to put it into operation.

The Process

The process followed during the system test activity is straightforward. It is driven by the plan established earlier during the test specifications and planning activity.

The emphasis should go beyond simply ensuring that all parts can run as an integrated whole. The ability of the system to withstand unusual circumstances must also be ensured.

At some point during the system test, the system should be loaded with transaction and processing volumes that far exceed its specified limitations. The object is to find out whether and how well the system can deal with overloads. A concerted attempt should be made to force the system to a level at which it cannot handle the work load that has been presented. Recall that the purpose of testing is to expose the conditions under which the system will fail. Accordingly, the system test is, in effect, a stress test. In forcing failure, the idea is to determine whether recovery can be implemented as planned.

Another system capability to be tested is response or delivery time. There should be specifications about the response time required for various on-line transactions and the turnaround time required for various batch processes. These requirements of system operation should be tested to discover the point at which timing standards cannot be met.

Although they are outside the realm of routine operation, procedures for backup and recovery should be considered as important portions of the system to be tested. A system that cannot provide backup service or recover from disruption is effectively worthless. Therefore, all backup and recovery procedures should be used. One of the important results of this phase of testing is that users build the confidence to know that they can stay in business if the system goes down.

Security measures should also be tested. System tests need not be concerned with physical measures within a computer installation itself because these measures are part of the overall operations function. However, strenuous attempts should be made to access system files and procedures illicitly. If the system itself is sufficiently sensitive, a consultant who specializes in breaking hardware and software access codes should be engaged to find out just how secure the system is and how well it will protect the privacy of the files it processes.

It is worth repeating and stressing that, when users are going through acceptance testing, the CIS staff should stay as far away from the system as possible. Project team members should be designated to field questions and provide assistance when requested to do so. This support should be provided as realistically as possible, simulating conditions that will exist when problems come up after the system is in regular use.

Problems will be discovered during system tests. For each problem, an evaluation should be made of its importance and potential impact on actual operations. Only corrections necessary for reliable use of the new system should be made prior to file conversion and installation. Other required changes should be scheduled as maintenance projects.

Personnel Involved

During system tests, the project team leader and members of the technical design staff monitor results. However, it is better if other experienced CIS professionals, either from the same shop or from an outside organization, perform the actual test procedures.

During acceptance testing, users should perform all functions, interacting only with designated CIS resource persons.

Cumulative Project File

During the system test activity, procedures manuals to be used in conversion and operation of the new system should be updated as necessary, reproduced, and distributed to authorized users. The same should apply to operations manuals, which should become part of the operations center library.

Any required changes in programs or system documentation should be incorporated in library copies as well. Procedures should be followed for identifying and dating all changes to existing documents.

The accumulated documentation from the earlier phases and activities should be assembled and prepared for examination during the review phase.

SUMMARY

The detailed design and implementation phase marks a transition in the development process from a user view to a detailed technical view. As a result of this phase, a completely documented and fully tested new system is produced. The phase consists of five activities. Design work, begun in the previous phase, is completed during two of these activities.

Design work represents a long series of interrelated tradeoff decisions. The life cycle attempts to reduce the complexity of the design process by dividing it into three logical groupings. First, the general architectural design is done in activity 5: general system design. Next, high-level software design and detailed database and network design are completed in activity 7: technical design. Finally, detailed program module design is done in activity 9: programming and testing.

Activity 7: technical design begins with the new system design specification produced in the previous phase and derives a detailed design specification. This includes precise and rigorous specifications for the database; all inputs, outputs, and on-line conversations; and program designs down to the program module level. Special concern is also given to network design and the design of the human-machine interface.

Activity 8: test specifications and planning sets the stage for later testing activities at five levels: unit, integration, function, system, and acceptance. As a result of this activity, all conditions to be tested are defined, test data and test files are created, and a system test plan is prepared. Ideally, this activity as well as the actual testing work in the other activities should be performed by an independent testing group.

Activity 9: programming and testing consists of detailed module design, coding, and testing at the unit, integration, and function levels. This work is based on the results of activity 7, during which major program modules were identified along with precise inputs, outputs, and intermodule data and control interfaces.

Activity 10: user training results in the preparation of procedures manuals, training materials, and a core group of trained users. This core group will then train other users during the installation phase, closer to when the system will "go live."

Activity 11: system test encompasses both the technical system test and the user acceptance test functions. The system test, conducted by CIS personnel, should include stress testing, testing the ability of the system to function under very heavy processing loads and to provide specified response and delivery times. The acceptance test, conducted by the users and CIS operations personnel, forms the basis for authorization to install the new system in a live production mode.

KEY TERMS

1. detailed design specification
2. computer operations documentation
3. conversion program
4. unit testing
5. integration testing
6. function testing
7. system testing
8. acceptance testing
9. acceptance test specifications
10. program test specifications
11. test data files
12. job stream test specifications
13. system and subsystem test specifications
14. test plan
15. procedures manuals
16. training manuals
17. functional test
18. performance test
19. structure chart

1. For each activity in the detailed design and implementation phase answer the following.

   a. What is the key objective?
   b. What are the principal end-products?
   c. What is the relation to the other activities?

2. Explain the three levels of design that occur during the system development process and where each occurs in the SDLC.

3. Describe the contents of the detailed design specification and their relation to the new system design specification prepared during the analysis and general design phase.

4. Discuss the four key detailed design areas that must be addressed during technical design.

5. List and describe the five levels of testing and where they occur in the SDLC.

6. Why are test plans critical? How do test plans relate to the work of the analysis and general design phase?

7. Explain the inverse relationship between the testing process and the development process.

8. What are the basic steps that need to be followed during the programming and testing activity?

9. What are the key differences between technical manuals and training manuals? How should each be written and used?

10. What is the role of the user during the user training activity?

11. How can requests for systems changes be controlled or managed during this phase? Are changes ever justified? How?

12. Explain the difference between function and performance testing and between system and acceptance testing.

23

Installation Phase and Review Phase

Learning Objectives

On completing the reading and other learning assignments for this chapter you should be able to:

■ Explain the overall flow of activity during the installation phase and the relationships between the two activities that make up this phase.

■ State the principal objective of each activity in the installation and review phases.

■ Describe the major end-products of each activity in the installation and review phases.

■ Describe the four basic methods of system installation and explain the advantages and disadvantages of each.

■ Identify the steps involved in data conversion.

■ Discuss the transitions to user ownership and system maintenance that must occur during the installation phase.

■ Identify the scope and objective of the system development recaps and postimplementation reviews that follow a systems development effort.

THE FINAL PHASES

The final two phases of the system development life cycle presented here include four activities as shown in Figure 23-1.

The installation phase begins with a system of both computer programs and manual procedures that has been fully tested, a set of data conversion programs, and a core group of trained users. During activity 12: data conversion, the data conversion programs are used to create the new production database

Figure 23.1. *The final two phases of the SDLC include four activities.*

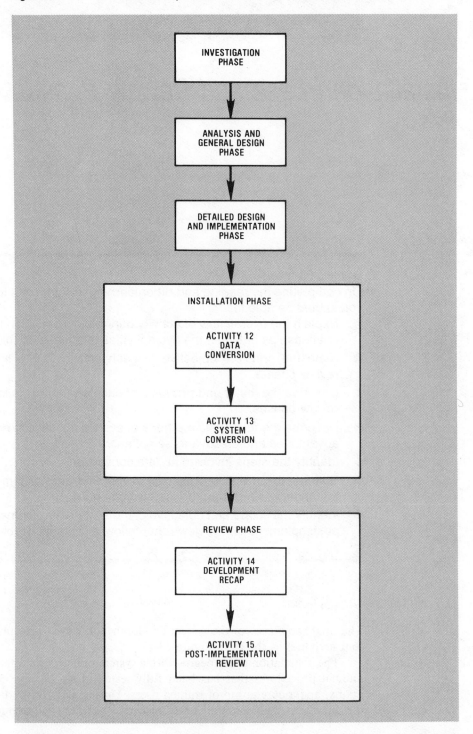

from existing computer files, manual files, or both. The actual installation of the new system in production mode and the phaseout of the existing system occur in activity 13: system conversion. The objectives and work of these two activities are so interrelated that they are discussed together in the following section.

The final phase, review, has two separate emphases. During activity 14: development recap, the just completed system development process is critiqued by team members with an eye toward improving the process and the quality of future projects. Then, about three to six months after system installation, activity 15: postimplementation review is performed to measure the extent to which the new system is achieving its anticipated benefits and to make recommendations for modifications or enhancements.

The actual skills applied in each of these phases go beyond what can typically be practiced in a classroom-oriented course. Thus, the general principles involved are emphasized here.

THE INSTALLATION PHASE

The installation phase is critically important for two reasons. First, it marks the culmination of development efforts and the realization of the proposed new system. Second, it is a critical transition time for the users. Actual, realized (as opposed to projected) benefits will depend on how the user group learns to adapt to the system during the installation phase.

During this phase, users actually take over ownership of the new system. Development is complete. The new system is operational. The new database is in day-to-day use. A relationship has begun between users and CIS operations, with systems analysts fading gradually from the picture.

The actual method of installation for the new system will depend upon its design, upon the needs and preferences of user managers, and upon the risks that can be tolerated. Options include:

- Cutover can be abrupt, with the old system simply discontinued and the new one begun at the same instant.

- The old and new systems can be operated in parallel for some time while results of the two systems are compared.

- There can be a parallel conversion in which the old system is gradually phased out while the new one takes over.

- *Version installation* techniques can be used. Under this approach, the system is divided into a series of functional areas, or incremental steps, called *versions*. These versions can be installed in any of the three ways described above. However, the entire system will not be fully implemented until all versions are in place.

These options, and the tradeoffs involved, are discussed later in this chapter.

Objectives

The installation phase has two principal objectives.

- First, the existing system is replaced with the new, tested, documented system. This replacement assumes user acceptance and ongoing user responsibility for the system. The project team is disbanded, and analysts and programmers are removed from routine involvement with system operation. In connection with system implementation, all files utilized by the old system are converted to the new system database, and use of the old system is discontinued.

- Second, to maximize the potential benefits of the new system, the user must be taken beyond simple how-to training to a deeper understanding of the full power of the system that has been installed.

Scope

The Installation phase begins with the existence of a complete system (or, if appropriate, a version) that has been completely tested under realistic conditions and is ready for installation. In addition, any needed data conversion programs have been written and tested.

The phase ends with a new system, or version, implemented and in day-to-day operation, with no further intervention or supervision by members of the project team. The conclusion of this phase is also marked by discontinuance of the old system. The result is **system conversion** or system installation.

End-Products

No major new end-products are produced during the installation phase. Rather, previously designed and developed products are installed. A new data base is created or converted from existing files and put into regular use in support of the new system.

In addition, all previously prepared documentation is updated and placed in maintenance status. Processing schedules or calendars to be followed by both users and the CIS operations group are established and put into regular use.

The Process

The installation phase comprises two activities:

- Activity 12: data conversion.
- Activity 13: system installation.

In some cases, data conversion tasks are straightforward and quickly completed. More often, data conversion represents a considerable challenge. Data from the current system are fragmented, incomplete, and frequently inaccurate. A small "throw-away" system must be developed just for the data conversion activity in order to take current data, purify and extend them, and create the new database. Whether straightforward or complex, the data conversion activity must be carefully coordinated with the approach selected for system installation.

This overview of the installation process focuses on three concerns, strategies for **data conversion**, basic system installation alternatives, and personnel transitions that must occur as the responsibility for the system moves from the development team to the user organization.

Data Conversion. Some data conversion complexities may be due simply to the sheer size and age of the existing database. Consider the case of a life insurance company operating a twenty-year-old system that supports over a million policies (some of them more than forty years old) representing over a billion dollars in assets. The system uses an antiquated master file structure in which each policy master record consists of a variable number of variable-length physical records. Many data are missing; some are inaccurate. Over the years, the same field has been given different meanings for different types of policies; and the documentation for this is suspect. The data are vitally important. Among other things, they contain past cash values and the parameters needed to feed the complex formulae that update these values each year.

During the prior phase, an entire system of data conversion programs has been written and tested. These programs must assemble and interpret data associated with a given policy, edit it, automatically correct errors if possible, create new master file data, and report problems requiring manual intervention. Obviously, for over one million policies, the number requiring manual intervention must be minimized. The actual conversion process could require a run time of four to seven days, essentially preventing the company from processing business for a week. When processing does resume, user efficiency will be impaired by inexperience with the new system and dealing with data that were not successfully converted. (Even if 99.5 percent of the policies are successfully converted, there are still more than five thousand that will require manual intervention.)

In addition to problems associated with the size and age of the database, other data conversion complexities result from the need to support both systems or parts of both systems concurrently. There is likely to be some delay, or lag time, during which the old system still needs its files while the new one also requires access to files that have already been converted. Thus, one system or the other may be operating with files that are not completely current.

Such problems can be avoided if the nature of the system lends itself to an abrupt conversion. For example, changes in general ledger accounting systems are typically made at year end just to avoid this type of problem. At the end of the fiscal year, the old system begins its closeout routines. The new system then starts up with all current balances at zero. If payments or bills are received that should be accounted for in the prior year, these can be processed under the old system. Transactions dated after the first of the year are run through the new system. Historical values can be updated later. There are minimal processing conflicts or file conversion problems because a clean break has been made.

However, this kind of transition is not always possible. For example, suppose a conversion is being made in an accounts receivable system. The existing files represent all unpaid bills owed to the organization. As the new system is implemented, all data from the existing files must be captured into the new database. In the interim, while the old system is still in operation, there could be trouble in finding such information as current customer account balances for the purposes of credit authorization. To avoid such problems, arrangements are usually made to maintain and access both databases during some interim period.

In general, file conversion involves the following basic procedures:

- Existing computer files are prepared for conversion. This means that all master files are brought up to date. Accuracy should be verified. Errors should be identified and corrected.

- Existing manual files are prepared for conversion, and data entry of manual data is done.

- New files or data bases are built and validated as they are created.

- Maintenance on the new database is begun. Input data continue to update old files until after implementation, but the converted files must also be updated. The basic procedure is first to establish a cutoff date for each file to be converted. Then, any input documents that represent transactions after the conversion are batched and used for periodic updating of the new database until installation of the new system.

- A final check of accuracy, or balancing, between the new files and the old ones is made.

Installation Alternatives. The methods used in converting files will depend at least in part upon the alternative selected for installation of the new system. The installation technique selected depends chiefly upon the nature of the new system and the tradeoffs involved in the various installation alternatives. The basic alternatives are

- Abrupt cutover.
- Parallel operation with a single cutover point.
- Parallel operation with a gradual shift from the old system to the new.
- Version installation.

Figure 23-2 illustrates the relationship between data conversion and system conversion as the installation alternative varies.

Abrupt Cutover. An **abrupt cutover** involves a simultaneous dismantling of the old system and startup of the new one. At a predetermined time, the old system no longer exists. The new one handles all transactions.

One advantage of this approach in situations where it can be used is that costs are minimized. There are no transition costs because there is no transition.

In some cases, an abrupt cutover may be the most natural, if not the only, way to solve a problem. In addition to the year-end conversion of accounting systems, abrupt cutover is also common in situations when a new system changes the way a company does business. This would be true for the life

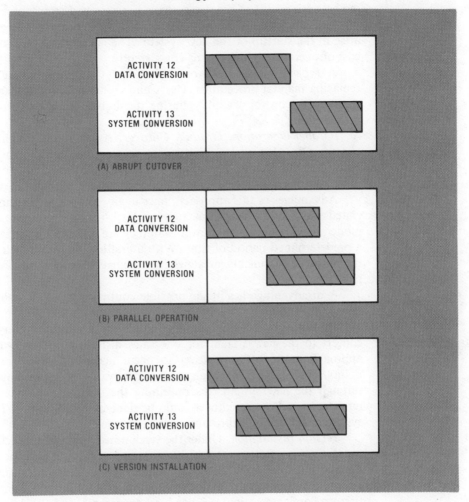

insurance company in the example cited earlier. The new policy processing system, since it changes the entire accounting and work flow, demands an abrupt cutover.

The major disadvantage of this approach is that it can carry a high risk. In an abrupt cutover, the old system is stopped. If a major problem develops with the new system, it may be very difficult, perhaps impossible, to return to the old system. Depending on the system and its role in the organization, the ability to carry on the business could be curtailed.

Parallel Operation, Single Cutover. Under the **parallel operation** approach, both systems are operated concurrently for some period of time. Often this parallel operation period coincides with business processing cycles, such as weeks or months. During this interim period, all input transactions are used to update the databases that support both the old and the new systems. A balancing between results of the two systems is performed regularly.

An advantage of this approach is that risks are relatively low if problems arise in the startup of the new system. The corresponding disadvantage is the cost of operating both systems concurrently.

A typical use of this approach occurs when a computerized system is replacing manual procedures. Users already trained in the manual procedures simply carry on for a while, phasing themselves out after the new system has proved itself.

Parallel Operation, Gradual Cutover. Again, both systems are operated concurrently. However, rather than having a single cutover point between systems, the old system is discontinued gradually. Discontinuance of the old system can be made according to geographic location, line of business, or other criteria.

Advantages of this approach, once again, include minimizing the risk associated with any problems that may arise with the new system. Costs are more moderate with a gradual cutover than they are if the old system is continued for a predetermined period of time. With a gradual cutover, the old system can be discontinued as quickly or slowly as management feels comfortable with the new one.

A disadvantage lies in the possible confusion that can result if people are unsure about which system to use.

To illustrate how this approach might work, an order entry system might convert to the new system for one sales district at a time. Another possible approach would be for cutover to occur according to the order processing points. For example, on a given day, one warehouse would put all its orders through the new system, discontinuing the old. In the water billing system introduced earlier, the cutover could be done by billing cycles. That is, the new system could be applied to one cycle of customers at a time.

Version Installation. Under the **version installation** approach, a basic set of capabilities is implemented within the first version of the system, then additional capabilities are added in subsequent versions. Each version goes through a complete implementation and installation cycle of its own. Some time after the first version is operational, procedures, programs, and the database are implemented for the second version, which then goes through the installation process. This procedure is repeated for each version. In effect, version installation involves breaking the proposed system into a series of incremental steps, or versions, at the end of the analysis and general design phase and then implementing and installing the system one step at a time. This option is discussed more fully in the following chapter on rapid development techniques.

Personnel Transitions. Up to this point in the project, users and systems analysts have literally formed a team. Close relationships and understandings may have evolved, and friendships may have been built.

Whatever personal relationships may exist at this point, installation marks a transition. Once the system is installed and in regular operation, it belongs to the users. Users are the owners of operational systems. Systems analysts have completed their mission; it is time for them to move on to other projects. At this point, it is part of their job to disengage as expeditiously as they can.

Another systems analysis responsibility associated with installation is to avoid making any system changes that are not absolutely necessary at this point. A list of maintenance changes to be made following implementation is initiated in the previous phase and continued through installation. What must be avoided is a situation in which a new system remains incomplete or is permitted to overrun costs exorbitantly because of a flurry of last-minute modifications and changes. A management nightmare in the systems development field is the system that is 99 percent complete—indefinitely.

One way to be sure that the old system is discontinued is to terminate use of its documentation and programs. The documentation and programs for the old system should be relegated to the archives as part of the installation procedure.

Two special concerns are worthy of additional notice at this point, one, assuring that the user has the understanding to make the best possible use of the system and, two, establishing a procedure for moving into the maintenance phase of the system life cycle.

Building User Understanding. Despite the user-training activity during the detailed design and implementation phase, the installation of a new system is seldom routine. The problems usually involve the user. System analysts can predict ahead of time what the computerized portion of the system will do, but it is difficult to predict what the user will do. Often users have a much bigger problem adapting to the new system than the developers had building it.

A good user-training program is only the first step in building user understanding of the new system. Also, training programs tend to be most effective at the clerical or operational level. The initial training program should be followed, during and after installation, by a series of discussions with users at all levels. At the start, these discussions can center around perceived problems with the system.

Later, for situations in which several users interact with the system in much the same way, these sessions can emphasize insights gained by individual users in making full use of the system. The point is to encourage the user to go beyond a merely mechanical use of the system to a deeper understanding of its capabilities. The user should learn to exploit the system. It is not at all uncommon for a user who understands how a system works to successfully apply parts of it in ways that would not have occurred to the original project team.

There are two main requirements for developing user understanding of the new system. The first is that the system work effectively, that it be reliable and easy to use. A system that is straightforward, with clean input requirements and clearly understandable outputs, is far superior to a system with numerous functions, some of which may not always perform reliably, and more complex, unnatural rules for describing inputs and outputs. The second requirement is an alert user management, one that provides the motivation and education required to make effective use of the system.

Preparation for Maintenance. Ongoing maintenance of a new system is considered to begin from the time the installation phase ends. To the extent possible, maintenance projects should be held for consideration until after the postimplementation review activity, when it becomes more feasible to consider the impact of the new system and to put the need for and role of maintenance in perspective.

However, there may be requirements for maintenance that just can't wait until formal reviews have been performed. When maintenance is needed, it should be done following in-place maintenance procedures, rather than as an extension of the development project.

Within each CIS operation, there will usually be one or more staff analysts with maintenance responsibility. Maintenance requests should be routed through these regular channels. Normally, early maintenance requests will involve either correction of errors considered to be important or minor procedural changes that are easy and quick to make. Major enhancements of the system, unless they are mandated by regulatory agencies or changes in corporate policy, should wait until after the review phase is completed.

Personnel Involved

Data conversion work during this phase is handled by data entry personnel, programmers, and analysts. Installation responsibilities are coordinated among analysts, key users, and CIS operations personnel.

Cumulative Project File

At the end of the installation phase, the project file should contain

- *The complete project plan.* This plan now shows both planned and actual hours spent on all activities. It will serve as the main basis for the review phase, after which it may be discarded.
- *The initial investigation report.* At this point, it is of historic interest only.
- *The feasibility report.* This report will be carried into the review phase, after which it is of historic interest only.
- *The new system specification.* This will also be used as a review phase document then saved for its historic value.
- *A postimplementation maintenance list.* This document will form the basis for ongoing maintenance projects.

The following documents will become permanent support files for the new system:

- Data dictionary.
- System documentation.
- System test folder.
- Program documentation and test logs.
- User procedures manuals.
- Computer operations manuals.

THE REVIEW PHASE

This phase is devoted to intensive study and analysis of project results. The phase begins with activity 14: development recap. This activity is devoted to an in-depth study of the development activities that have just been completed. The purpose of the recap is to prepare specific suggestions aimed at

- Helping individual team members to perform more effectively on future project assignments.
- Sharpening management skills for the organization as a whole and for the project team leader in particular.
- Finding approaches that might enhance or improve the organization's skills and methods in systems development.

Activity 15: Postimplementation review is conducted after the new system has been in operation for some time. This time lapse permits the new system to become a regular part of day-to-day operations and the people involved to gain a measure of detachment. The purpose of this review is to

- Evaluate how well the system has performed in meeting original expectations and projections for cost-benefit improvements.
- Identify any maintenance projects that should be undertaken to enhance or improve the implemented, ongoing system.

The second activity within the phase is particularly useful as a review of projects for which personnel or other cost savings were projected. This activity provides an opportunity to compare actual results with earlier projections.

Objectives

Objectives for the review phase are to determine

- The effectiveness of the life cycle and the management techniques applied during system development.
- Whether projected benefits have actually been realized from the new system.
- Whether modifications or enhancements to the new system are desirable and justifiable.

Scope

The development recap should begin immediately after the system is operating routinely. Even if some lingering tasks or details associated with installation remain to be completed, the recap should take place when the project is still fresh in the minds of the team members.

The postimplementation review is usually performed some three to six months after final completion of the installation phase, when the system is running smoothly.

End-products

The review phase produces two end-products, the system development recap report and the postimplementation review report.

Systems Development Recap Report. The systems development recap report is prepared for CIS management. Its contents, of course, reflect the nature of the individual project. But, certain basic items should be included:

- Development costs should be analyzed. The presentation should compare the projected budget with actual costs, breaking the figures down by cost category within each activity. Any significant variances should be analyzed and explained.
- Reported working time on the project should be analyzed. Comparisons should be made between budgeted and actual work hours for each activity. Variances should be analyzed to determine cause, including rework required by user changes; rework required to meet outside mandates, such as rulings from regulatory agencies; rework caused by design errors; rework caused by programming errors; overruns due to failure of development team members to complete work as scheduled; and overruns due to errors in estimation.
- Any design errors identified during the review should be described and classified according to their nature and related to any required rework.
- Programming errors should be similarly reported and classified.
- Suggested revisions in the systems development methodology should be described and evaluated.

Postimplementation Review Report. The **post implementation review report** is prepared for review by CIS and user departments. It may also be delivered to the steering committee. The following elements should be covered:

- The original requirements and objectives that led to the systems development project should be listed. Accompanying this list should be an evaluation of the extent to which the original requirements and objectives are being met by the installed system.
- The costs of developing and operating the new system should be reviewed and compared with original cost estimates.
- The originally projected benefits should be compared with the benefits actually realized.
- The new system should be reviewed as a functional entity to determine, first, whether any steps can be taken to realize more of the original or additional benefits and, second, whether any modifications are needed in the near future.

The Process

The process approach for each of the activities in the review phase is fairly straightforward.

Development Recap. Systems development is difficult to structure and do well largely because it is so people-oriented. A great deal of interest and effort is devoted to developing new techniques and methodologies that can make the development process more effective. But for an organization to incorporate these new ideas and approaches into its own systems development methodology, it is necessary periodically to pause, reflect on past experiences, and suggest modifications based both on these past experiences and on new techniques that have been developed.

The purpose here is to give both the project team and the organization an opportunity to reflect on the project that has just been completed and to draw lessons and recommendations for improvement from the experience. As a starting point for this activity, the project leader prepares statistical reports that recap the development effort. These include comparisons between projected and actual expenditures, in money and in working time, for each activity. Causes should be assigned to any variances reported. Causes of variances should be readily supportable from statistics gathered during the development project. These may include specification changes that resulted in rework, identifiable errors that led to rework or overruns, inaccurate original projections, or performance by team members that was different from what was expected.

Team Participation. The development recap activity offers professional growth opportunities to each member of the project team. To realize these benefits, a series of meetings should be held to deal with each of the activities or phases of the project. Persons who were active during each of the phases or activities covered by a meeting should be present. With this level of participation, persons attending the meeting can understand and participate in the reviews and critiques of the work done. On the basis of their experience, participants can take part in brainstorming sessions aimed at improving project development and administration methods. Active participation in sessions of this type should enhance the professionalism of each of the individual team members.

Skill is needed to keep meetings of this type on track and productive. They must be approached with a positive attitude. The emphasis must be on making positive recommendations for future development work, not on retributions for past mistakes. Otherwise, the activity can degenerate into a forum for finger pointing and excuse making.

Importance of the Development Recap. Many systems development life cycles do not list a development recap as a separately identified activity. This is understandable. First, there is the pressure to "move on." While the recap may be seen as "nice to do," there is normally a backlog of development projects awaiting action; and management sees greater payoff in beginning them with no further delay. Second, without the proper approach and management backing, the recap may be seen as a threat to members of the project team. They may view it only as an exercise in covering past errors and failures.

However, without this recap activity it is very difficult for an organization to break out of its old approaches to problems and take advantage of advances being made in the systems development area. With a separately identified development recap activity, and with positive management support and expectations, the stage is set for growth in the ability of an organization to respond to systems development needs.

Postimplementation Review. The **postimplementation review** is an actual review of the new system after it has been installed and operating for three to six months. Depending on the size of the system, this review may require the efforts of one or more analysts. These analysts may or may not have been members of the original project team.

Standard systems analysis techniques are used, including interviews with users and operations personnel. Data are collected on processing volumes and operating costs as a basis for analysis and comparison with the projections made during the feasibility study and updated at the end of the analysis and general design phase.

The job of the systems analysts completing this work is, in part, to determine whether user objectives are being met. The results of the new system are compared with the stated objectives. These objectives are contained in the user specification and also in the new system design specification documents produced during the analysis and general design phase. In addition, the analysts are charged with determining whether projected benefits for the new system are being realized. A comparison is made between existing costs and benefits and those projected during the analysis and general design phase of the development project.

Any problems noted should be analyzed and described. If appropriate, recommendations for corrective action should be submitted.

TRANSITION INTO MAINTENANCE

Throughout the system development life cycle there is an emphasis on keeping the scope of the project within boundaries approved by the management-level steering committee. If possible, extensive modifications of or additions to a system under development should be kept on hold until after installation, considered during the review phase, and scheduled for **maintenance** projects. Thus, almost from the day a system becomes operational, it becomes a candidate for enhancement, updating, or revision through maintenance projects. Maintenance projects stem from four major sources:

■ Mandates. Government regulations or industry requirements may dictate the inclusion of new or modified features within an existing system.

■ Management policies or strategies. As business changes occur in an organization, new requirements emerge in all the systems that constitute that organization. Information systems, an integral part of these corporate systems, must be changed to support the directions established by management.

■ User perceptions. Users become progressively more sophisticated as systems are developed and used. The more experienced they become, the more opportunities they are apt to discover for enhancing the systems they have. Most systems development requests originate with identification of user needs. The same is true for systems maintenance. An alert group of users will generate a continuing stream of opportunities to enhance existing systems.

■ Technological advances. Computers are at the hub of one of the most dynamic fields of endeavor in the world. Whole new generations of concepts and equipment are brought into use every five to six years. In between, there are many additional, significant improvements in hardware and software. At any given time, new equipment or new methodologies may make it economically feasible or competitively necessary to modify existing systems to accommodate advanced capabilities.

As the IS field itself has matured, maintenance has become an increasingly important segment of the activities of systems analysts, systems designers, and programmers. Current estimates are that in "mature" IS shops maintenance projects now occupy as much as 60 to 80 percent or more of the time of systems and programming personnel. Thus, cumulatively, maintenance projects can be greater factors than systems development projects in terms of working days of systems and programming time consumed.

It makes sense to comment on the close similarities between maintenance and systems development projects. Make no mistake about it; systems maintenance is a project-oriented kind of undertaking. In maintenance, as in new systems development, it is essential to go through a series of steps that involve understanding the problem, analyzing needs and opportunities, then devising solutions and designing them technically before going ahead with implementation. In other words, maintenance is not a patchwork undertaking. If maintenance is treated on a "quick-and-dirty" basis, there is a great danger that the systems being maintained will, in fact, be destroyed by those who want to enhance them. All the principles about sound design and maintainability apply in maintenance projects just as they do in systems development projects. Therefore, it follows that all of the skills acquired in connection with the study of systems development are equally appropriate in maintenance projects. The principles of sound systems maintenance are essentially the same as those for systems development. Only the scale tends to be different. Quality is quality, wherever needs are encountered.

SUMMARY

The installation phase marks the culmination of development efforts and the realization of the proposed new system. It is also a critical transition time for users as they take over ownership of the new system.

The method of installation depends on the type of system, the needs and preferences of user managers, and the risks that can be tolerated. Options include an abrupt cutover, parallel operation with a single cutover, parallel operation with a gradual cutover, and version installation.

The installation phase has two principal objectives. First, the new system must be placed in full day-to-day operation and the old system discontinued. Second, the user must gain an intimate and detailed understanding of the new system.

The general procedure for file conversion involves the following steps.

- Prepare existing computer files for conversion by updating, verifying accuracy, and correcting errors.
- Prepare existing manual files for conversion.
- Build and validate new files as they are created.
- Begin maintenance on the new files.
- Make a final check of accuracy, or balancing, between the new files and the old ones.

After a new system is operational, there should be two reviews of results, a recap shortly after implementation and a postimplementation review four to six months later.

The recap should begin as soon as the system is operating routinely. Its purpose is to help individual team members perform more effectively on future project assignments, sharpen management skills, and find approaches that might enhance or improve the organization's skills and methods in future systems development projects.

The systems development recap report prepared for CIS management should compare projected costs, both in money and in working time, against actual costs. Any design errors or programming errors that may have necessitated reworking should be reported and classified. Any suggested revisions in the systems development methodology should be described and evaluated.

The purpose of the postimplementation review is to evaluate how well the system is meeting original expectations and projections and to identify any maintenance projects that should be implemented to enhance or improve the system.

The postimplementation review report should include a list of the original requirements and objectives and an evaluation of the extent to which these have been met. Developmental and operational costs of the new system should be reviewed and compared with original cost estimates, and the originally projected benefits should be compared with the benefits actually realized. Finally, the new system should be reviewed as a functional entity to determine, first, whether any steps can be taken to realize more of the original or additional benefits and, second, whether any modifications are needed in the near future.

Ongoing maintenance of a new system is considered to begin from the time that the installation phase ends. To the extent possible, maintenance projects should wait until after the postimplementation review phase has been completed. If maintenance is required, however, it should be handled through normal maintenance channels. The basic process and skills applied to the development of a new system can also be applied to systems maintenance.

KEY TERMS

1. data conversion
2. system conversion
3. abrupt cutover
4. parallel operation
5. version installation
6. postimplementation review report
7. postimplementation review
8. maintenance

REVIEW/DISCUSSION QUESTIONS

1. What are the four basic alternative approaches to system installation?
2. Under what circumstances are file conversion problems most likely to arise? Why?
3. What are the basic steps involved in file conversion?
4. What are the principal tradeoffs between abrupt cutover and parallel operation with a single cutover? Under what circumstances would you be likely to choose one approach over the other?
5. Describe a situation in which parallel operation with a gradual cutover might be the most appropriate installation method. Why?
6. Explain how a version installation might be combined with each of the other three installation methods.
7. What reviews should be conducted following the implementation of a new system and what should they contain.
8. What are the advantages from review activities for

    a. users of the new system?
    b. project team members?
    c. CIS management?
    d. top company management?

9. How can procedures for systems development be employed for systems maintenance?

24

Rapid Development Techniques

Learning Objectives

On completing reading and other learning assignments for this chapter, you should be able to:

- Explain the need for rapid development techniques.
- Describe the type of environment that must be established in an IS organization in order to achieve rapid development.
- Discuss when and how to apply a variety of rapid development techniques within the context of the system development life cycle.
- Describe alternatives to the system development life cycle that may help speed the development process.

THE NEED FOR RAPID DEVELOPMENT APPROACHES

This chapter is about large, complex system development projects — projects that may require one to three or more years to complete and involve 20 to 50 or more development people at any time. These are not the kinds of projects that can be simulated in a classroom setting, but they are common in the commercial IS world. The very size of these projects adds elements of risk far beyond the complexity of the system itself. These projects simply take too long! Some never finish. Benefits are realized late. New products that rely on the system cannot be brought to market. Needs change before the system can be delivered.

Long system development projects spell problems for an organization: lost revenue, lower service, increased cost, and missed strategic opportunities. Rapid development approaches have become mandatory.

Case: Manmouth Manufacturing Company

Consider the case of Manmouth Manufacturing (M^2), an international firm that manufactures and distributes lawn care products. These products range from rakes to lawn mowers to small tractors and from seeds to organic fertilizers to chemicals. Manufacturing sites are located in the US (10), Europe (4), and Southeast Asia (2). In addition, there are thirty distribution sites world wide.

M^2 products are sold by hardware and lawn stores under the M^2 brand name, Big-One. M^2 also manufactures for several large retail chains under each chain's name. M^2 has recently experimented with two company-owned retail stores, Weekend Warrior Supplies, to sell the Big-One product line.

Historically, M^2 has been a manufacturing driven company. It has been organized around three divisions:

- Tractor division.
- Small tool division.
- Seed and fertilizer division.

The divisions were fairly autonomous, each with its own accounting, sales, and IS divisions. Accounting, sales, and IS divisions also existed at the corporate level. Corporate accounting and IS helped to provide divisional support and summary reporting. Corporate sales concentrated on the large retail-chain contracts.

In response to intense competition, M^2 determined six months ago that it needed to focus more heavily on marketing and on the integration of its product line. This precipitated a company-wide reorganization around three new divisions:

- Big-One products division.
- External products division (serving the retail chains).
- Weekend Warrior Supplies division.

The manufacturing sites were allocated between the first two divisions.

The new divisions were strongly marketing oriented. The general managers for the new divisions came from the tractor division, the seed and fertilizer division, and the corporate office, respectively. All three were strongly driven by a need to know weekly sales results, monthly inventory and order backlogs, and detailed quarterly profit and loss analyses.

The information needs of the three general managers were certainly straightforward, yet they were impossible to meet without huge manual effort. Because of the autonomy of the three former divisions, all accounting systems were largely unrelated—only very highly summarized results were reported to corporate management. Charts of accounts differed, level of detail varied, and even inventory valuation formulas had been different in the three original divisions. The IS departments were also separate. Each division had its own computer hardware and communication networks. Some application systems were related (i.e., the same at one time, but maintained separately), others were completely different.

M² had recognized that it would need to gradually realign the accounting and IS divisions to support the new divisional structure. Management had hoped this would be relatively painless. However, because of the urgent need for profitability information and the virtual impossibility to provide it on a timely basis — even with unlimited manual work — M² determined that it must centralize its basic accounting operations, standardize its accounting rules, and establish a common IS system — all within 6 months! (The initial estimate from their corporate IS group was a minimum of 18 to 24 months.)

Does M² have any chance to meet this deadline? As a start, it must first analyze where delays are likely to occur.

Some Barriers to Rapid Development

The M² case illustrates a number of barriers to rapid development.

First, M² is starting without any shared vision of the key enterprise-wide framework in which the new system must operate. There is no common information architecture, no enterprise-wide E-R models and data models. There is no overall application architecture, no definition of the key functionality of this new system and how it must relate to other major systems. There is no common technical architecture; hardware platforms and communication networks — which go beyond the needs of this system — must be established. And finally, management upheaval has occurred. Roles, responsibilities, and reporting relationships are only partially defined. There is no management architecture.

Second, the analysis and requirements definition process is likely to be very difficult. The supervisors and middle-level managers — who will need to make decisions about the new accounting procedures, how the new system should operate, and what functions should be automated — come from very different backgrounds. It could easily take six months just to generate consensus within this group.

Third, once consensus is reached and requirements are set, the resulting design might not be very stable. When financial people have been accustomed to a manufacturing-driven organization and the financial reporting that supports it, it is difficult to fully comprehend requirements for financial reporting in a marketing-driven organization. Some requirements will be obvious, but it may take actual use of a base system to understand what is really necessary. As the understanding of requirements evolves, the design of the system could be dramatically affected.

Finally, the corporate IS group is unprepared for the challenge. The original group had been quite small and did very little new development work. With the reorganization, it picked up people from the original divisional IS groups. The numbers and raw talent are in place. But there is no common development approach and no commonly understood automated tools.

Approaches for achieving rapid development can be thought of in three categories. Each category represents a broad spectrum of opportunities, from the application of sound project and department management principles to the effective use of today's technology to techniques that are still leading edge and require more powerful tool support.

The first category has to do with establishing the proper **framework for rapid development**. The second category involves a set of techniques and tools that can be used to compress the time required for various blocks of work within the system development life cycle. The final category addresses techniques outside the framework of the traditional life cycle (see Figure 24-1).

The three categories are discussed in the remaining sections of this chapter to provide basic awareness of the various opportunities and approaches not to build skill in performing them.

Figure 24.1.   There are three general approaches to achieving rapid development.

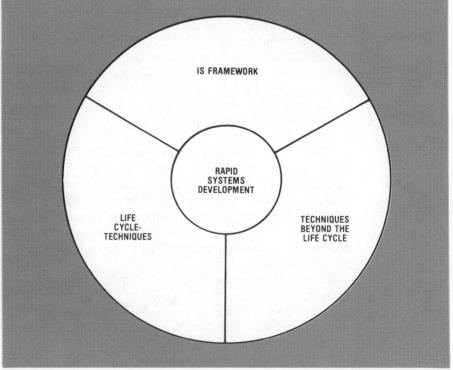

A FRAMEWORK FOR RAPID DEVELOPMENT

The most dramatic way for an IS organization to improve its ability to deliver systems rapidly is to establish the proper framework in which to do the development work. Two aspects of this framework are particularly important (Figure 24-2).

- An enterprise-wide IS architecture.
- An effective development infrastructure.

Enterprise-wide IS Architecture

Manmouth Manufacturing faces a problem common to many IS organizations. Each new system is built in a vacuum. There is no sense of how this system fits in the overall application portfolio of the organization.

It is very likely that a new database is established for each system. Time is spent modeling and designing it and attempting to rationalize and interface it

Figure 24.2. A framework for rapid development.

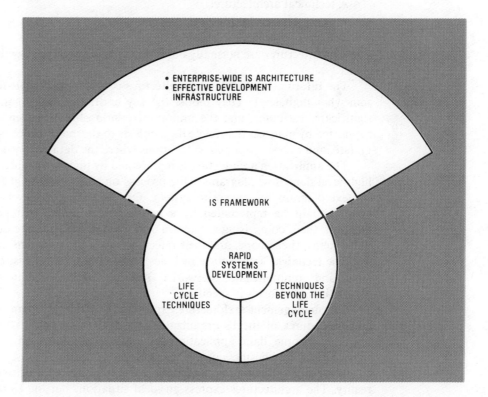

with overlapping databases for other systems. Time is wasted and the resulting design is suboptimized.

The precise relationship of the new system to already existing systems is not clear in terms of functionality or data. Time is wasted in discussions of scope. Related issues are these: What functionality belongs in the new system? If a given process does not seem to belong in this new system, is it performed in some other system, and are the results accessible?

Even questions of technology may slow the development effort. For example, if the organization has processing and data distributed across multiple platforms, perhaps in different locations, should the new system be distributed as well? If so, how should this be done? If additional processing capacity is required, what should it be? How should it be integrated with the hardware already in place.

Finally, pure management issues may delay the project. For example, is it clear how the project should be staffed? Are qualified professionals available? Are standards and quality assurance processes in place?

An **enterprise-wide IS architecture** addresses these problems. It actually consists of four distinct architectures:

- An information (or data) architecture.
- An application architecture.
- A technical architecture.
- A management architecture.

These architectures are normally built as part of an enterprise-wide IS planning effort.

The **information (or data) architecture** is represented by E-R models at a somewhat high level. They model the key entities of the organization, their significant attributes, and the important relationships between them. This is supported by matrices that relate data objects to the major processes that create, update, and access them and to locations where the data are used and stored.

The **application architecture** is represented by high-level function charts and high-level data flow diagrams. One process on this model might represent the context diagram for an entire system. Or, depending on level of detail, the system might be represented by a group of processes — that portion of the diagram, then, comprising a diagram 0 for the system. In any case, the individual systems, their scope, and their interfaces with other systems are clear.

The **technical architecture** includes all hardware platforms, operating systems, and communication networks. The distribution of data and processes across these platforms is specified.

The **management architecture** expresses the strategies, standards, policies, and procedures of the IS organization. It deals with how to manage the IS resources (people, data, application systems, and technology) in order to effectively support the business objectives of the organization.

With each of the four architectures, there is a difference between theory and reality. The architectures express an ideal situation, but the IS resources have been developed over time and do not necessarily match the ideal situation. The architectures do, however, provide a framework for making decisions as new systems are being built. This framework greatly speeds the decision process — and hence the overall development process. Moreover, the decisions made are of higher quality since they are consistent with the long-range direction of the IS organization.

It is a time-consuming process to bring reality closer to the ideal in the case of the first three architectures. Usually, progress can be made only as very large development efforts are undertaken. The management architecture is different. It can, and should, be addressed independently from development efforts. An approach for doing this is discussed next.

An Effective Development Infrastructure

An IS development organization is complex. It normally operates under a great deal of pressure. It faces far more work than it can handle, constantly shifting priorities, and unreasonable deadlines. Creating an **infrastructure for effective systems development** in this type of environment requires a clear understanding of the individual infrastructure components and the relations among these components. It is not usually possible to address only one component at a time because of the interrelationships. Improvement programs must be gradual, addressing multiple components in a coordinated fashion.

An infrastructure for effective development begins with a base system development methodology, perhaps like the SDLC presented in this book. This methodology provides a framework for project management. It exists to help the IS function support the business objectives of the organization, as shown in Figure 24-3(a). This methodology is in turn supported by various techniques (like those presented in this book) and by people who have mastered the individual skill sets necessary to perform these techniques. These, as shown in Figure 24-3(b), are supported by automated tools. Finally, all these elements must exist within a set of project and departmental management disciplines, as illustrated in Figure 24-3(c).

These five key infrastructure components of an effective development group are all focused on supporting the business objectives of the organization. They can each be gradually improved, but only in concert with the others. The extent to which this infrastructure exists has a major impact on the speed of individual system development efforts.

LIFE CYCLE TECHNIQUES FOR RAPID DEVELOPMENT

A second general approach to speeding the development process is to analyze the system development life cycle, identify labor intensive activities or places where the process is likely to slow down, and develop techniques to address them. These are eight **techniques** or categories **for rapid development** (see Figure 24-4):

Figure 24.3. The components of an effective development infrastructure.

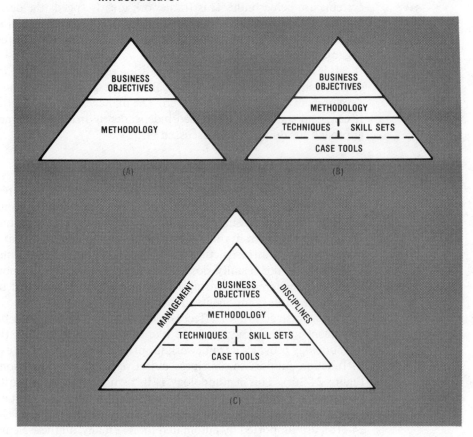

- Scope control.
- Joint application design (JAD).
- Prototyping.
- Version development.
- Application software packages.
- Application generator tools.
- I-CASE.
- Life cycle tailoring.

While this list is not exhaustive, these are important techniques with very broad applicability.

Figure 24.4.   Life cycle techniques for rapid development.

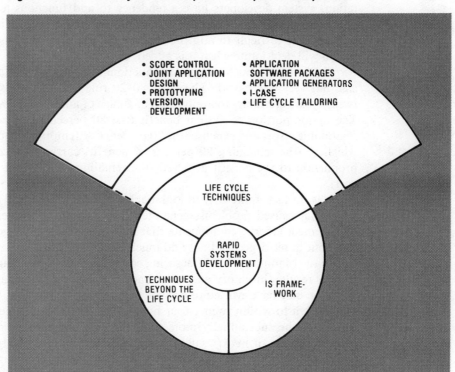

Scope Control

Scope control is so obvious it is easily overlooked. Yet many projects drag on far longer than necessary because scope control is addressed only at the start of the project and only at a very high level. This is probably the most common cause of unnecessarily long development efforts.

Typically, a statement of project scope is made very early in the investigation phase. It includes a high-level statement of objectives and a description of the major functions or capabilities to be included. This is not unreasonable. In fact, it is all that is possible early in the project. Not enough is known to be more explicit.

The problems typically begin during analysis and general design. As more detail is understood, questions arise as to whether specific items are within the project scope, or at least within the scope of the new automated system. There is an understandable tendency on the part of end-users to push for all they can get. Development backlog is so large in most organizations that users see a major development effort as their one opportunity for the next several years to get the automated support they want.

As the project moves from general design to detailed design and implementation, system developers have a tendency to add functions to the automated portion of the system in order to "do it right the first time." There is a fear that it will be more difficult to add the functionality later or that the overall system design will deteriorate when it is added.

Nevertheless, much automated functionality added during analysis and design has very low payoff. The basic 80–20 rule that has worked well for over twenty years continues to apply, even in an age of automated development tools. The major portion of system benefit (the 80 percent) can be achieved with reasonable effort and expense (the 20 percent). Attempting to add the "bells and whistles" (the remaining 20 percent of benefit) carries a price tag far out of proportion to the benefit achieved (the remaining 80 percent of development cost).

It is, in fact, quite easy to look back on most projects and identify components that caused problems, generated heavy costs, and generally slowed the development effort—components that may have seemed like good ideas at the time, but in retrospect did not add much value.

In the Manmouth Manufacturing case, driven by top management's interest in sales results, inventory and order backlogs, and profit-loss analysis, a determination may have evolved to provide this information on line, fully integrated, and current to within twenty-four hours. The cost and time needed to provide this would be substantially more than the cost and time needed to meet the original request of *weekly* sales results, *monthly* inventory and order backlogs, and *quarterly* profit-loss analysis with some on-line decision-support capability.

But an 80–20 rule applied after the project is over is of little value in speeding a development effort. How can the bells and whistles, the features that will add major cost and development time without adding significant value, be identified during the development effort. The timing is subtle. Bells and whistles are usually not purely frivolous—they do add value. The extent to which they will individually contribute to the cost is not clear when they are proposed. Later, during design, when costs and time begin to escalate these bells and whistles have become simply part of the entire requirements statement. It would be nearly impossible to track their individual impact.

The solution lies in the rigorous application of a very simple three-step decision process:

1. Eliminate.
2. Simplify.
3. Automate.

Repeatedly, throughout the development effort, on large issues as well as small, first attempt to *eliminate* the functionality. Is it really necessary to have it to run the business? If it cannot be eliminated, examine it carefully and *simplify* it. Most functions or processes, as they evolve, become far more complex than necessary. Rethinking at a purely business or logical level, normally presents opportunity for tremendous simplification. Finally, consider *automation* only for simplified functions that are critical to conducting the business.

Applied throughout the development process, this approach to rigorous scope control works very well when the enterprise-wide IS architecture is in place. It permits a base system of absolutely critical functionality to be installed first. Then, as experience is gained, additional functionality can be judged on its own merit — benefit versus cost. If the original system was built in the context of the overall IS architecture, the cost of adding the new functionality will at least be minimized.

Joint Application Design (JAD)

Joint Application Design (JAD) is a technique that can greatly reduce the elapsed calendar time spent on analysis and general design. It may not reduce total person hours spent on the project, but it can cut the elapsed time for analysis by a factor of four or more.

Consider the type of activity that occurs during analysis and general design. Multiple interviews and other information gathering activities are conducted to understand the current situation and to gather requirements for the new system. This information is frequently reviewed and cross-checked for consensus and accuracy. As new system design ideas are formulated, these are reviewed repeatedly with the same audience.

This process can be extremely slow when no one person has a good grasp of the entire business area. Multiple interviews reveal only parts of the puzzle, and it is time consuming to reconcile differences. This was certainly the situation in the M^2 case following the reorganization.

The M^2 case illustrates another cause for delay. There is no uniform understanding of how the new system should operate. Tremendous time could be lost going from user to user continually modifying processing rules, requirements statements, and preliminary design ideas.

In many cases — not all — large amounts of time can elapse in scheduling (and rescheduling) appointments and revisiting the same issue in an attempt to get concurrence. The JAD technique applies particularly well to this type of situation.

The term *joint application design* is used here in a somewhat broad and generic sense. Various organizations have developed their own versions of the process — and given it a unique name. There is no standard. The term *facilitated session* is often used, but that is too broad. The technique should be more structured than that.

A JAD session is an intense working session lasting about four days, run by a leader (facilitator), and attended by 6 to 10 key people who have (a) knowledge about the area under study and (b) the authority to make decisions for that area. The session normally has one of two purposes: to determine requirements for the new system or to develop a general new system design. (In the context of the SDLC presented in this book, JAD sessions might be run to support activity 4: new system requirements and activity 5: new system design.)

There are certainly many variations on this main theme, and many techniques and guidelines have been developed to enhance the success of the session. However, the key components are those outlined here.

A JAD session may be run to quickly generate the critical requirements for the new system. This may need to begin with a verification and evaluation of the current system. Models of the current system and the new will probably be generated. In fact, the goal should be to produce as much of the new system requirements document — in rough draft from — as possible.

When viewed in this way, a number of guidelines become apparent. A significant amount of preparation must be done in advance of the session. Multiple sessions may be required. Different sessions may address different aspects of the system. (Typically, participants cannot maintain the required energy level for more than three or four days.) Participants must be carefully chosen — high enough in the organization to speak with authority about the area under study, yet low enough to possess the required amount of detailed knowledge about how things work. The leader, or facilitator, must be highly skilled in order to ensure that the desired deliverables are produced in the end. CASE tool support, provided by an assistant to the leader, with daily or twice-daily updates is probably essential.

When a JAD session is run to develop the general design for a new system, the participants may change to some extent, but the general guidelines remain much the same.

JAD sessions have the potential to accomplish in four days what might take a month or more. But there are costs. First, a major time commitment is required — up to four ten-hour days from ten key people in the organization. The session must be beneficial. Thus, second, the leader must be well prepared and highly skilled — the amount of skill and experience directly related to the difficulty of the audience.

Prototyping

Prototyping was introduced in Chapter 2 as a technique for better understanding user requirements. It is included again here to evaluate its ability to speed up the analysis process.

Recall that a prototype is a working model of a system, or portion of a system. A prototype usually focuses on the on-line or interactive portions of the system. It is not difficult for a user to understand how batch inputs and reports will work in the system. But an interactive conversation is less clear. It may change the very nature of the work the user does.

Chapter 2 contains a description of the prototyping process, a process in which working models are developed and repeatedly refined as the user works with the prototype. (It would be appropriate to reread the last section of Chapter 2 at this point.)

The use of prototyping on large, complex systems has had mixed results. There is the potential for large savings of time and effort, especially when the interactive prototyping tool set is more robust. Yet, the process often takes longer and produces an inferior system in the end. Why does prototyping fail? How can it be appropriately applied?

There are two main ways in which prototyping efforts fail. First, the process simply gets out of control. The prototypes are so easy to build and revise that proper management controls are ignored. It is very easy to lose control of the *scope* of the new system. Application of the eliminate-simplify-automate process for controlling scope that was discussed earlier in this chapter is difficult when prototyping is used too early in the analysis process. In addition to losing control of scope, it is also easy to lose control of the work process. Revision iterations continue without any easily defined stopping mechanisms. Prototyping is not bad, but by its very nature it is inconsistent with traditional project management controls.

The second potential problem with prototyping is more subtle. It can affect the quality of the final product. Prototyping tends to stress only the physical aspects of a system. The entire emphasis is on user input concerning *physical* requirements and the rapid realization of a *physical* system that supports those requirements. The prototyping process does not support the *logical* modeling of requirements and proposed solutions. Thus, system specifications based only on prototypes are likely to carry forward inefficiencies, and even errors, that were part of the original system.

How can prototyping be appropriately applied? It helps first to understand what benefit is expected. Normally, people have two benefits in mind when prototyping is introduced. First, there is an expectation that prototyping will shorten the analysis and general design process. If the user can more easily understand how the system will work, a stable set of requirements should emerge more rapidly. Second, there is at least a hope that portions of the automated prototype can carry forward, thereby reducing the final programming effort.

Combining the prototyping risks discussed above with these desired benefits, the best way to use prototyping—on large, complex systems—becomes more clear.

The best time to use prototyping is later in the analysis process—during the creation of the physical model for the new system. At this time, major groups of business functions can be identified and prototyped separately. It is true that the prototyping effort may uncover data elements and some processes that were overlooked and need to be incorporated back into the logical model, but usually these are refinements of what already exists. They do not normally affect the basic data and system architecture.

If the prototyping tools are sufficiently strong, prototypes built during the creation of the new physical model have a better chance of being carried forward into the new system. They can be built consistent with the data and processing architectures to be used in the new system.

While this discussion has assumed that prototyping is used within the context of the SDLC, some organizations have used prototyping to change the nature of the SDLC. Prototyping used in that way, rapid iterative prototyping, is discussed later in this chapter.

Version Development

Version development follows a very simple principle: develop a large, complex system by breaking it into a series of parts, versions, that can be separately designed and implemented. Typically, a basic version is implemented first.

Then, other versions are added to provide additional functionality that enhances the previous version.

Consider, for example, a project to develop a comprehensive student information system at a college or university. This would be a major undertaking, but one which could break apart quite naturally into a series of versions. The initial version could support the basic functions of course registration and grade reporting. After this version was installed and running smoothly, a second version could be developed that would contain the first version and add the capability to perform degree audits—to verify that students had met degree requirements. Automatic prerequisite checking at the time of course registration could then be added to version two in order to create a version three. Finally, a fourth version might add an individualized course planning feature that could be used for student advising and could be summarized for course demand analysis and schedule planning. Successive versions add new capabilities rather than changing those provided by earlier versions.

Version development does not necessarily shorten the entire development effort, but it can certainly speed the process of installing a base version of the system. This partial completion can be particularly attractive if tight deadlines are involved. For example, it may be possible to quickly implement the version that provides critical capability (e.g., base processing for a new product or regulatory compliance processing), leaving enhancements to the system for later implementation.

The key decision in the effective use of version development is when to identify the various versions. Certainly, the sooner this can be done the better. Some cases, like the student record system, are fairly obvious from the start. In this case it might be appropriate to identify versions at the end of the investigation phase—taking a little extra care to ensure that the data model and high-level process model were fairly well understood and stable. More often, however, it is better to wait until the end of the analysis and general design phase to identify versions.

Some definite advantages accrue from the practice of analyzing and designing a system in its entirety even though it may be implemented and installed in different versions. One of these is that the database can be designed with the total system needs in mind. Thus, because the interrelationships among versions are understood from the outset, the complete system will be supported as each version is implemented and installed. Similarly, some of the application programs in the total system may be shared by different versions. If the entire system has been designed in advance, the finished programs will be more appropriate for the final jobs they are expected to do.

If version development is used, there will be some modification in the structure of the systems development life cycle. Steering-committee decisions at the conclusion of the second and third phases of the project will be limited to one version at a time. This means that the resources allocated in individual decisions will be smaller. On the other hand, financial feasibility may be difficult to justify for the first version because costs may be relatively high and benefits limited. Moreover, changes in cost could result in decisions not to implement successive versions after the first one has been installed.

Application Software Packages

An **application software package** refers to a complete computerized system that can be bought off the shelf. It is normally self-contained in the sense of using its own data files and programs. Some degree of customization is usually necessary so that the programs can run on a particular hardware platform. And some customization of screens and reports is usually permitted to allow the purchaser at least to use its own terminology.

Application software packages can be either generic or industry-specific. For example, a general ledger accounting package may be appropriate for the financial reporting needs of virtually any business. On the other hand, specialized applications may have limited general applicability. Application software packages appropriate in a specific industry can have great value. Often these applications support highly complex or regulated portions of an industry. To develop and maintain such applications in house becomes prohibitive in cost. Further, the knowledgeable professionals and other resources for maintaining such systems are scarce. As an example, packages have been developed for use by common carrier trucks required to report mileage in specific states. Between these two extremes, there are generalized applications, such as job cost analysis, order fulfillment, or inventory, that have some industry features but are fairly general in their applicability.

Some industries make heavy use of packages to support basic day-to-day processing. This is particularly true in fields such as health care, insurance, and banking. They may then attempt to differentiate themselves by building their own custom systems to interface with these basic packages and offer additional services to their customers.

The possibility of finding and using application software packages is mentioned prominently in earlier chapters of this book, particularly in connection with activities in the analysis and general design phase. This is the point within a project at which a decision should be made about whether application packages are to be used and, if so, which packages should be selected.

The most obvious potential advantage of application packages is that if they fit they can save substantial time and money. There is also a degree of assurance, since other users have applied and found success with the package, that the programs are workable and of relatively high quality.

The main disadvantage is that if the package does not represent an exact fit with identified needs it may be necessary to modify the procedures of the user organization. To use the package, the company may have to forego some system features that would have been desirable or change some of its procedures. If the misfit is great enough, it may be necessary to revise or rewrite portions of programs to tailor them to the specific needs of the company. This is usually a dangerous practice.

Evaluation of software packages — especially large packages that must interface with other systems in the organization—can be very complex. It goes far beyond simply verifying that the package will run in a given hardware environment. Evaluation should focus on at least four areas in addition to hardware—functionality, data, integration, and maintainability.

The first and most obvious matter to evaluate is the **functionality** of the package. Does the package implement the functions required by the user, and does it apply processing rules that are at least acceptable to the user? While an important evaluation criterion, functionality is unfortunately difficult to verify. Vendor literature is usually too general, and the source code of the package—if available—is too detailed to use in order to verify functionality. The usual approach is to prepare test data files, run them against the package, and note the results in terms of outputs or file updates. This is essentially equivalent to acceptance testing of a custom built system. The effort can be substantial.

Because of the difficulty in testing package functionality, it is usually best to evaluate the **data** inherent in the package. The master files or database are much more accessible than the application code. The data elements involved in the package can be mapped against the data model for the new system derived during analysis. There is the difficulty of translating data names used in the package, but differences between the package and the new system data model can be found rather quickly. This mapping can help focus the functionality evaluation. If data are missing from the package, processing or functions that should use those data are probably missing as well. If the package has additional data elements beyond the new system model, it probably also has functionality that was not originally specified.

The third area of evaluation is **integration.** If the package is to operate in a stand-alone fashion, this will not be a major issue. Most packages, however, do not run alone. Order entry systems integrate with inventory systems. Insurance policy processing systems integrate with claims systems. Hospital admission systems integrate with patient care systems. And nearly all systems integrate with accounting systems. Two basic aspects must be considered: data conversion and file interfaces. Do the data currently exist to initially populate the package files? If they do not, will that cause problems in operating the new system? In view of all this, what will the data conversion effort be? And, second, can the necessary integration with other systems be accomplished by writing interface code that may access and even update data in the package system.

The fourth area of evaluation is **maintainability.** In most cases the package code should not be touched. Maintenance of the internal package should be the responsibility of the vendor. This maintenance would be impossible for the vendor if the individual organization has modified the package in any way. Yet, if an organization has entrusted a major part of its operation to a software package, it must be assured that the vendor can and will maintain it. To this end, it may help to evaluate the internal design and code of the package. This would, at least, indicate the inherent maintainability of the package. Equally important is an evaluation of the software vendor itself—its financial position and its professional staff.

The nature of these evaluations highlights the advantages of holding off on decisions concerning application packages until the analysis and general design phase is nearly complete. At this point in the life cycle, the needs of the new system are understood with considerable clarity. The new system has been specified at both logical and physical levels with such aids as E-R models, data flow diagrams, and supporting documents. Thus, it becomes possible to compare individual data elements, key business processing functions, and even specific process descriptions of software packages with those specified for the new system. At the end of the analysis and general design phase, the tools exist to evaluate with considerable precision whether an available package fits the system and, if the fit is not exact, just what needs to be done to adapt it.

Application Generator Tools

The techniques for speeding the development process that have been discussed up to this point have centered on the front half of the SDLC, the investigation phase and the analysis and general design phase. Indeed, these phases are most often the cause for projects running longer than necessary, but many **application generator tools** have been developed that speed the program design and testing activity during the detailed design and implementation phase as well. Some of these tools are central to the prototyping process, and most have been introduced at various points in this book.

Among the types of application generator tools currently available are the following:

- *Relational database systems* with SQL (structured query language) interfaces that make the data access portions of programs easy to produce and maintain.
- *Screen painters* that allow on-line screens to be quickly designed and the associated control logic automatically produced.
- *Report generators* that allow batch reports to be designed and the code automatically generated, given the structure of the data to be accessed.
- *Conversation generators* that have the ability to produce logic that strings multiple screen transactions into a full session conversation.
- *Non-procedural* or *fourth generation languages (4GLs)* that produce program control logic from nonprocedural statements of desired results.
- *Code generators* that can produce application code from specifications, such as action diagrams, created during analysis.
- Automated *testing tools* that simulate interactive sessions and compare results with specified outcomes.

One of the challenges in applying these tools is their lack of integration. They overlap; they often do not interface with one another; they may apply only to restricted technical environments; and they may produce object code rather than COBOL code that could be separately maintained. As a general rule, the more powerful the tool, the more narrow its applicability—either in terms of the technical (hardware, communications, database) environment or the type of application (report generation, computational logic, control logic) for which it is suited.

Typically, each IS organization will specify an approved set of application generator tools and provide guidelines for their use. Then, as part of the structuring of each individual development project, the specific tool set for that effort will be selected. This selection must be completed early in the analysis and general design phase, for the tools to be used will impact the design of the system.

I-CASE

Computer-Assisted Software Engineering (CASE) tools are discussed in Chapter 7. The topic is mentioned again here for the sake of completeness in this discussion.

I-CASE refers to *integrated* CASE tools. These individual modeling tools are typically based on a common underlying encyclopedia or repository. This common repository is what makes the integration possible. Each individual tool can access and update the repository, and the change to the repository impacts all the tools. For example, a change in a data element name in a data model is automatically made in any DFD model that uses that data element.

As CASE tools are enhanced they typically begin to pick up prototyping capabilities, then code generation features, and so on. The distinction between application generation tools and I-CASE is blurring.

Life Cycle Tailoring

Life cycle tailoring is the step that brings all the previous discussion together. No SDLC is expected to be used in the same way on every project. It is necessary to use the SDLC as a base and then tailor it to a given situation.

Tailoring is essentially a project planning activity in which the objectives and end-products or deliverables of each phase and activity are examined and modified or tailored to meet the challenges unique to the project. At this time strategies are set to speed up the development process. Each of the techniques discussed in this section is considered. The work plan is then created to incorporate the use of the selected techniques.

TECHNIQUES FOR RAPID DEVELOPMENT BEYOND THE SDLC

The third general approach to speeding the development process involves techniques that fall outside the framework of the traditional system development life cycle. These three techniques are rapid iterative prototyping, reengineering, and object-oriented development (see Figure 24-5). All these techniques are being made feasible by the emergence of powerful automated development tools.

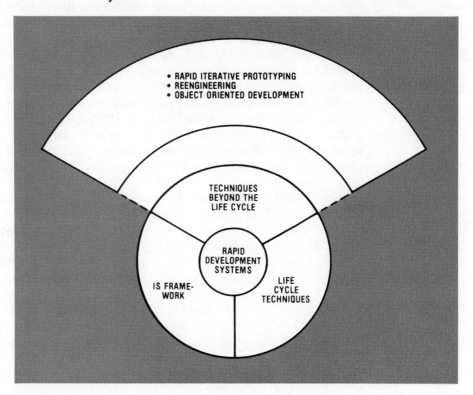

Rapid Iterative Prototyping

Prototyping is included in the prior section as a technique to be used within the context of the SDLC. How does rapid iterative prototyping differ? The difference is not in the underlying motivation (*why* prototyping is done) or in the basic prototyping process (*what* is done). The difference lies in the use of very powerful tools (*how* prototyping is done) and the extent to which these tools allow the prototyping process to be carried.

Recall why prototyping is of interest. Prototyping is of special interest when users are unable to specify a stable set of requirements, when the ability to work with a model of the system would stimulate the users' thinking and generate a more complete, consistent set of requirements.

The traditional view of prototyping is to build a prototype or model of the system based on a preliminary understanding of requirements, allow users to work with the prototype and suggest changes in requirements, modify the model, and repeat the process.

Rapid iterative prototyping, based on very powerful development tools, changes the traditional view in two ways. The first is speed. Prototyping is of course an iterative process, but powerful tools allow the prototype to be changed quickly and easily. Rapid iterative prototyping, then, refers to an environment in which many iterations are possible in a short period of time — where the prototype can evolve rather quickly in response to user input.

The second way in which rapid iterative prototyping goes beyond the traditional view is based on the modes in which the prototyping tools run. The more powerful tools may come in two versions, simulation and code generation. The simulation version typically runs on a PC in interpretive mode, interpreting the specifications and omitting coding and compile steps. This is what makes rapid changes to the prototype possible. The specifications are stored in an encyclopedia that can be uploaded to a mainframe and used by the code generation version of the tool to produce the production system. More powerful tools permit more of the application to be simulated on the PC, thus producing a more robust prototype.

Some tools support data prototyping as well as process prototyping, presenting the user with a prototype model that is a much more realistic representation of the intended system. If the tool set supports prototyping of on-line conversations, inputs and reports, key logic, and the data model, much of the system can be modeled and used in prototype form. This might leave only mainframe communications and database access procedures to be completed and performance tuning to be done.

Impact on the SDLC. What is the impact of rapid iterative prototyping on the system development life cycle? Two things are readily apparent. First, with the ability to make rapid changes in the prototype, there is a chance that the iterative process can get out of control. Controls imposed by a traditional life cycle have little impact. Second, with the more powerful prototyping tools, work normally completed during the detailed design and implementation phase is being done before the analysis and general design phase is complete. The two phases, in fact, overlap — perhaps to a considerable degree (see Figure 24-6). This means that most work developing the system could be done without any major management review — another loss of control.

For these reasons, when rapid iterative prototyping is used, the traditional SDLC may require modification. To understand how this modification might occur, consider what impact the tools have on the timing of the *design freeze*. In the traditional SDLC, the requirements and general system design ideally are frozen before the start of detailed design and implementation. Prototyping tools permit the design freeze to be moved later in the process — the more powerful the tool, the later the freeze point (see Figure 24-7).

This suggests that a more appropriate life cycle might be like the one pictured in Figure 24-8, where the iterative prototyping phase actually consists of five activities as shown in Figure 24-9. The phase would begin by using the preliminary requirements from the investigation phase to do an initial prototype design. Management control could then be reestablished by formalizing the prototyping iterations, with appropriate management decisions to continue each successive iteration and, finally, to proceed with the environment construc-

Figure 24.6. *(a) The traditional SDLC treats phase boundaries as go–no-go decision points. Hence, phases do not normally overlap. (b) with rapid iterative prototyping, the work done in the two main phases can overlap substantially.*

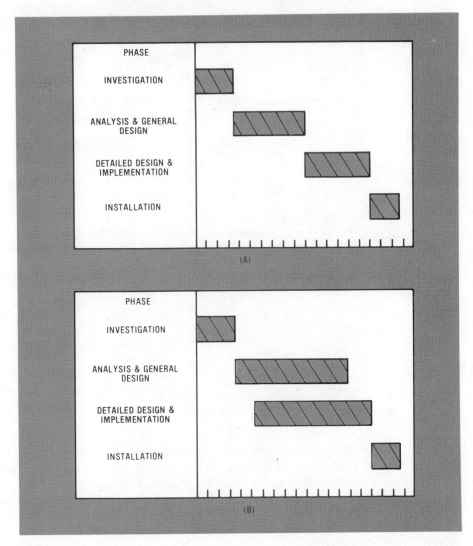

tion phase. This phase would consist of code generation in the production environment, completion of database and communications coding, performance tuning, and final stress and acceptance testing.

Future of the SDLC. With rapid iterative prototyping, is the system development life cycle dead? Not at all. First, tools do not yet exist in all target production environments to do all levels of prototyping and code generation

Figure 24.7. *Prototyping tools permit the design freeze point to be moved later in the development process. The more powerful the tool, the later the design freeze point.*

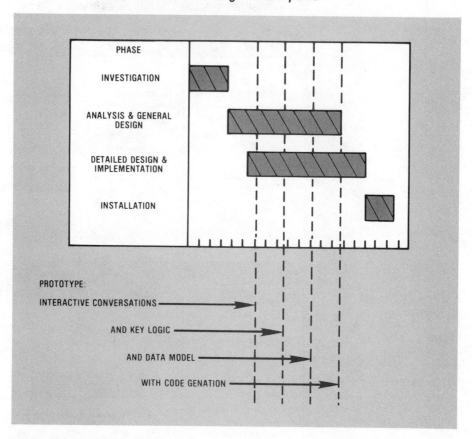

suggested above. Second, even where tools do exist, the motivation for prototyping—the inability to get a stable set of user requirements—may not exist. If requirements can be obtained without extensive prototyping, the more traditional approach—using techniques of the previous section to speed the process—will probably produce a better system design and do it more quickly.

System Reengineering

The motivation for system reengineering comes from a recognition that most organizations have a tremendous investment in their existing systems. In many cases, existing systems, consisting of millions of lines of code, embody a large percentage of the necessary functionality but have become technically obsolete.

When a new system development effort involves replacing an existing computerized system where much of the data and many of the processing rules will carry forward with only slight modification, the development process would go

Figure 24.8. *A possible rapid iterative prototyping life cycle at the phase level.*

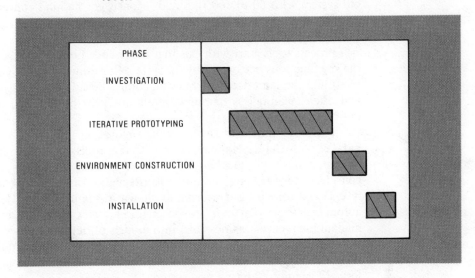

Figure 24.9. *Five activities composing the iterative prototyping phase of the life cycle in Figure 24.8.*

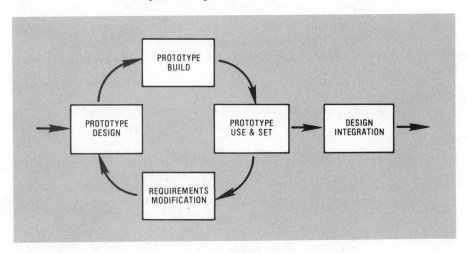

faster if much of the current functionality could be automatically captured and "reengineered" into the new system.

A great deal of tool-building activity has focused on identifying the functionality of an existing system, modeling it at a physical (or design) level, and then modeling it at a logical (or analysis) level. The process is referred to as **reverse engineering**. Separate tools have addressed the reverse engineering of data and processes.

Data tools start with existing file or database definitions and attempt to create, first, physical data models, then normalized logical data models. In an old system with 50 to 100 files and inconsistent naming conventions, this is a difficult job, one that inevitably requires a certain amount of manual intervention.

Process tools start with existing source code libraries and attempt to model the key functions performed by the system (for example, at a COBOL paragraph level) and the data used by these functions. Because of poor program designs and often meaningless naming conventions, this process too requires manual intervention.

The development of these reverse engineering tools has been occurring in parallel with the development of the CASE tools, including code generators, discussed thus far in this book. The tools discussed in previous sections could be considered **forward engineering** tools. **Reengineering** then attempts to combine reverse and forward engineering as shown in Figure 24-10. The goal is to use automated tools that can reverse engineer an existing system, with as little manual intervention as possible, into models of data and processes that can be stored in a development encyclopedia, then use automated tools to transform these models into models for the new system. Finally, these models would be forward engineered into a new system.

The required tools are not yet fully developed, but a sufficient number currently exist to permit at least parts of the process to be automated at three different levels (see Figure 24-11). Source code restructuring tools exist that read source code, unravel the logical flow of poorly designed programs, and note logical inconsistencies. These tools can also transform the programs into better-constructed new programs, and additional functionality can be added to create a reengineered system at the physical system level. This approach works well

Figure 24.10.   Reengineering consists of three steps: reverse engineering, transformation of the system, and forward engineering.

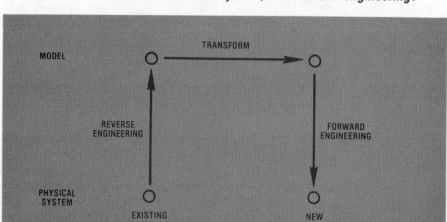

Figure 24.11. *The re-engineering process can be performed at one of three levels.*

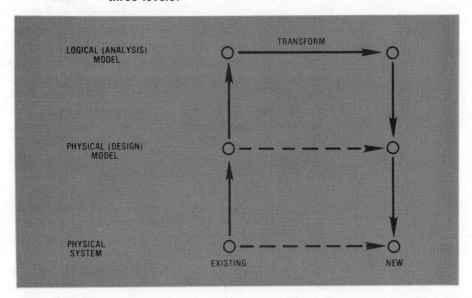

when the basic functionality of the system is complete and the database does not require change.

More powerful tools (and more manual work) can drive the reverse engineering process up to the physical design level. This level would include the current physical data model and a model of the data and processes at the program and paragraph level of detail. This might be an appropriate level for changing hardware or system software platforms, changing some batch processing to on-line, or improving the high-level architecture of the system.

Still more powerful tools (and still more manual work) can drive the reverse engineering process to the logical analysis level, consisting of normalized data models and logical DFD models. This would clearly provide the best base for modifying, designing, and forward engineering the new system.

Object-oriented Development

Object-oriented development is the most future oriented of the techniques discussed here. Based on the theory of abstract data types, object-oriented programming was being discussed in the early 1970s. Only with the development of more powerful tools have the techniques started to enter the general commercial marketplace. Throughout the 1990s, tools will evolve to make greater and greater use of this very powerful concept.

Traditional programming languages separate data from processing code. Programs must be written to access data from a database, apply processing code, and then store the result. Very often, the key sets of processes applied to given data are the same — or very similar — in every program.

Object-oriented techniques are based on *objects* that consist of both data and sets of processes that can act on that data to produce a result. The programmer, then, can focus on sending messages to objects, requesting them to perform some set of procedures on themselves or other objects. An object-oriented database management system, rather than simply managing different views of data, must manage the data, their structure, and the operations applied to them.

For example, data-validation processing rules could be associated with the data themselves in a single object. Then, when the programmer needed to apply validation processing to the data, it would only be necessary to call the object with a message to apply the data validation processing. Later, the object could be called with a message to apply a given reporting process.

A detailed description of object-oriented development techniques is beyond the scope of this book. It is important to understand, however, that in building systems the focus is moved away from identifying key data entities and attributes, designing normalized data models and physical databases, and then designing and writing processing code to manipulate these data. The focus, instead, is on identifying key objects that consist of both data groups and the standard processes that can act on them. These objects become the building blocks for the new system.

Object-oriented approaches will have a major impact on future system development techniques. The techniques that evolve will depend on the object-oriented tools: the object-oriented programming languages that manipulate the objects, the object-oriented database management systems that maintain the objects, and the object-oriented operating systems that provide the environment in which to build and run the systems.

The potential payoff from the use of object-oriented development techniques will be a very high degree of reusability through the standard sets of procedures that are part of each object and the ability to build systems much more rapidly using objects as basic building blocks.

SUMMARY

Large, complex systems development projects can create special problems for organizations because of the length of development time required. Operating problems occur, strategic opportunities are missed, and service suffers. Rapid development approaches are mandatory.

Approaches for achieving rapid development are discussed in three areas: establishing the proper IS framework, using techniques that can be applied within the traditional SDLC, and exploring techniques that extend beyond the SDLC.

An effective IS framework for rapid development has two major components. The first is an enterprise-wide IS architecture. This consists of an information architecture represented by E-R models; an application architecture represented by high-level function charts and DFD's; a technical architecture including all hardware platforms and communications networks; and a management architecture expressing the strategies, standards, policies, and procedures of the IS organization.

The framework also includes an internal IS infrastructure to support effective systems development. This infrastructure must include a development methodology, rigorous techniques, people with the necessary skill sets, automated tools, and a set of departmental and project-management disciplines.

Within the traditional SDLC, eight techniques are described for speeding the development process. The most obvious is scope control, a rigorous process of trying to eliminate functionality, simplify what cannot be eliminated, and only then to use automating as an effective means of scope control.

Joint application design is a technique using facilitated sessions that can greatly reduce the elapsed calendar time spent during analysis and general design.

Prototyping has the potential to reduce analysis time when user requirements are difficult to pin down. This may be the case, for example, when an online system is replacing a batch system and the resulting changes in user operations are difficult to visualize. Scope control is more difficult in a prototyping situation, and final system design might not be as solid.

Version development is a technique of breaking a large system into a series of parts or versions that can be separately designed and implemented. It does not necessarily shorten the entire development effort, but it can permit key parts of the system to be implemented earlier.

Application software packages have the potential to save considerable time and money, but they must be carefully evaluated. In addition to verifying hardware requirements, package evaluation should also address functionality, the data used in the package, the ability to integrate the package with other systems, and the maintainability of the package.

A complete set of application generator tools can speed the detailed design and implementation activities.

Ideally, all tools — from those that support data and process models, to code generation and testing tools — will be integrated around a common encyclopedia. This is known as an I-CASE environment.

Finally, life-cycle tailoring is used during project planning to establish the appropriate strategies for speeding the development process on a specific project.

Three techniques are discussed for speeding the development process that lie outside the traditional SDLC. All rely on the continuing emergence of powerful automated development tools.

Rapid iterative prototyping refers to a prototyping environment where the tools are so powerful that very rapid evolution of the prototype model is possible and where very significant portions of the system can be built in interpretive mode on a PC then uploaded to a code generator on the mainframe. This causes a substantial overlap of the detailed design and implementation phase with the analysis and general design phase, eliminating many of the controls built into the traditional SDLC. For this reason, a modified rapid prototyping life cycle is often required.

System reengineering applies the use of automated tools and manual procedures to reverse engineer an existing physical system back to a physical design model, then a logical analysis model. Transformations can be applied at the model level to change the system in order to accommodate new requirements, then to forward engineer the system using CASE development tools.

Object-oriented development is based on the concept of objects that contain both data and sets of standard processes that can act on those data to produce a result. These objects become the basic building blocks for new systems. The potential for speeding the development process is based on the high degree of reusability that can be captured in the sets of procedures and in the ability to work with higher-level building blocks—objects instead of detailed program code.

KEY TERMS

1. framework for rapid development
2. enterprise-wide IS architecture
3. information (or data) architecture
4. application architecture
5. technical architecture
6. management architecture
7. infrastructure for effective systems development
8. techniques for rapid development
9. scope control
10. joint application design (JAD)
11. prototyping
12. version development
13. application software package
14. functionality
15. data
16. integration
17. maintainability
18. application generator tools
19. I-CASE
20. life cycle tailoring
21. rapid iterative prototyping
22. reengineering
23. reverse engineering
24. forward engineering
25. object-oriented development

REVIEW/DISCUSSION QUESTIONS

1. Discuss typical barriers to the rapid development of large information systems. What conditions studied in this part of the text might have slowed the development of the Central City Water Billing System?
2. Describe the components of an enterprise-wide IS architecture. Why is each component important?
3. Describe the interrelationships among the five components of an infrastructure for IS development.
4. In what way are scope control issues likely to slow development in the M^2 case?
5. Explain the joint application development process. How might it be applied in the M^2 case?

6. Contrast prototyping (within the SDLC) with rapid iterative prototyping. What are the potential advantages and problems with each?
7. How could version development be applied in the M^2 case?
8. Are application packages likely to play a role in the M^2 case? Why? How should they be evaluated?
9. What types of tools should be included in a comprehensive set of application-generation tools?
10. What is meant by integrated CASE tools? What benefit do they achieve?
11. Apply the concept of life-cycle tailoring to the first two phases of the SDLC in the M^2 case.
12. Explain the concept of reengineering. Would it make sense in the M^2 case? Explain.

Appendix: Case Studies

CASE STUDY 1: STUDENT RECORDS SYSTEM

Situation

Place yourself as project team leader in the CIS department of a large state university. You are to develop designs that will serve to implement a new student records system. At present, virtually all processing is done on a batch basis, although the university does have some on-line capabilities. The plan is to revise the existing system for greater responsiveness in tracking student academic progress.

One of the main reasons for wanting to develop this system is to achieve greater student registration efficiency. The current procedure involves a centralized, walk-in registration center where students wait in long lines as clerical workers process their registration requests over on-line terminals. This procedure has been plagued with difficulties. Adding extra staff during the actual registration is expensive and problematic. Also, registration must be carried out in the computer-service building where large banks of computer terminals are available. This building becomes virtually unusable for its normal operation during registration period as long lines of students weave around the halls and stairwells.

Before registration, students must clear any outstanding financial delinquencies (i.e., parking or library fines) through the university cashier's office. Coordination, or lack thereof, between the cashier and the registration office has resulted in students waiting in long lines only to discover that they may not register because of financial delinquencies, which they may or may not have already paid. Students also find courses for which they have been approved closed by the time they reach the front of the line. These problems often result in excessive numbers of drop-add requests at the close of registration.

There is a strong demand for some form of student phone-in system to provide increased currency in reporting class offerings and for an expanded registration session that occurs over several weeks rather than being compressed within one or two hectic days.

At the same time, a new computerized system could assist advisers in performing services that are inconvenient to provide under present methods. Currently, advisers are responsible for determining student registration qualifications in terms of declared majors and completion of prerequisites. It is hoped that the new system will be able to automate registration checks of this type, leaving advisers more time for the substantive parts of their jobs.

Another target for the new system is to improve recording and record-keeping procedures. Grade reporting and transcript preparation could be integrated into the system. The availability of transcript files could mean that fewer advisers would be needed to monitor student registrations to assure completion of prerequisites. Students, in effect, would gain more responsibility in determining their own courses of study.

Context Diagram

Over the past several months, the project team has analyzed the current system and developed documentation for the new logical system. This documentation will serve as the starting point for new system design. The scope of the system you are developing is defined by the context diagram shown in Figure A-1. As indicated, the student records system interacts with four external entities:

■ The student will use the new system for phone-in registration for classes. The ability to support phone-in registration capabilities was one of the prime motivations for authorizing development of the new system. The processing of registration requests and requests for changes in classes results in the preparation of student course schedules. Also, the system will support processing of student declarations of major. This process assigns students to academic advisers and ties each student to a particular degree program. A final interaction between the system and the student lies in grade reporting. At the end of each term, the student will receive a report of the grades earned in each class and a summary of credits earned to date.

■ The faculty constitutes another key external entity that interacts with the system. Faculty members receive class rosters from the system at the beginning of each term. They submit class grade reports used in producing the student grade reports at the close of the term. In addition, grade change requests are submitted for changing grades that were submitted on the class grade reports. The ability to process this information on-line and as free from paper as possible is highly desirable.

■ Academic advisers are responsible for overall tracking of student progress. The adviser receives copies of declarations of majors for students that have chosen a major in the academic area. At the end of each term, advisers receive copies of student grade reports; and as necessary, they can request copies of student transcripts to verify academic progress toward degree requirements.

Figure A.1. Context diagram: STUDENT RECORDS SYSTEM.

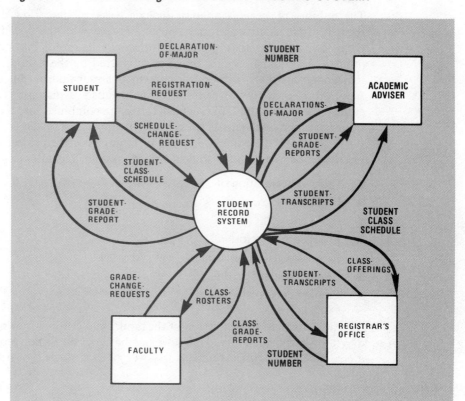

■ The registrar's office is responsible for maintaining student academic records. This office, in response to a graduation request, receives a copy of the student's transcript and makes a final check on the meeting of degree requirements. The office also submits class offerings for the upcoming term. Offerings originate in the academic departments and are compiled in the office and released to the student record system.

Of course, as currently conceived, the system does not provide all possible services to the identified entities or to other potential users. This project represents an initial attempt at devising a system that can be expanded later with additional features. For example, future plans call for interfaces with the cashier's office and the office of student financial aid along with facilities for providing automatic degree evaluation and checkout. At this time, the interest is an establishing a foundation of procedures and data files that can expand and grow into a totally integrated system.

Processing Events

The outputs of systems analysis include a set of data flow diagram (DFD) segments that identify the major processing events in the system and show the data flows and files that interact to transform the inputs into outputs for each process. The data flow diagrams are supported by the data dictionary entries that document the structure and content of input and output data flows and files. Also, process narratives provide detailed explanations of processing events. The individual DFD segments then are combined into a diagram 0 data flow diagram that describes the completely integrated system.

In studying the context diagram in Figure A-1, the project team identified several major events in the student records system, including

- Process declaration of major.
- Process grades.
- Build class file.
- Produce transcript.
- Process registration request.
- Change student grade.
- Prepare class rosters.

This list is derived from a review of the inputs and outputs shown on the context diagram. Although every data flow on the diagram is not represented as an event, the list does identify events to cover all data flows shown.

System Documentation

In the documentation for the new system, each event is described by its own data flow diagram segment. The segment is supported by data structure layout entries for the identified input and output documents, screens, and files and by process specifications detailing the processing activities that make up each processing event. These process specifications are still at a rather high level, describing the business-related activities that are performed to a greater degree than the computer processing steps necessary to implement them.

The diagram 0 for the system is illustrated in Figure A-2. The DFD segments for each process are shown in Figures A-3 through A-9. At this point, the documentation presents a high-level overview of the proposed system. In effect, each bubble represents a suggested subsystem that would be developed to implement the event. As needed, however, lower-level diagrams will have to be developed to partition the processes for further clarification; and diagrams could be combined into integrated software products.

First-cut process specifications are included for all bubbles on diagram 0. These specifications are shown in Figures A-10 through A-16. They describe the processing activities that make up the system processing events, along with the data files and data elements that are affected.

Figure A-17 contains the data required on the system's inputs and outputs. The inputs and outputs are described logically in terms of data components and

Figure A.2. Diagram 0: STUDENT RECORDS SYSTEM.

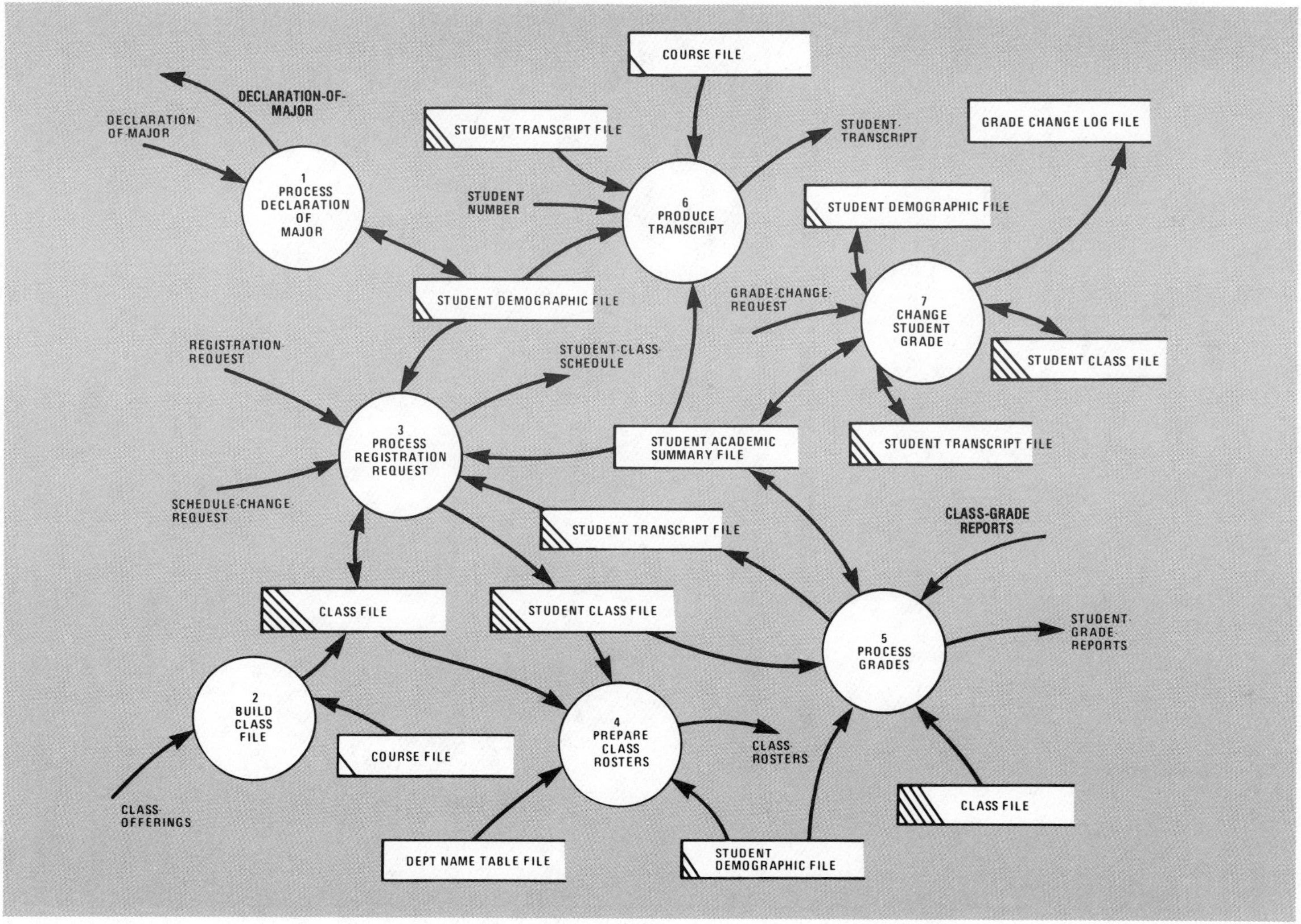

Figure A.3. Data flow diagram. Process 1: PROCESS DECLARATION OF MAJOR.

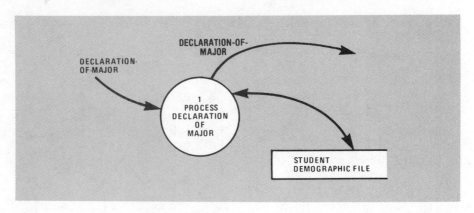

Figure A.4. Data flow diagram. Process 2: BUILD CLASS FILE.

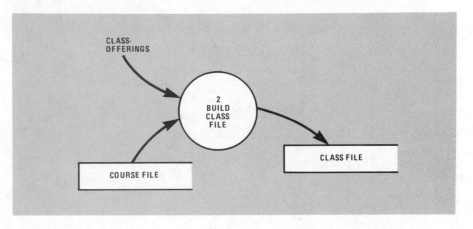

Figure A.5. *Data flow diagram. Process 3: PROCESS REGISTRATION REQUEST.*

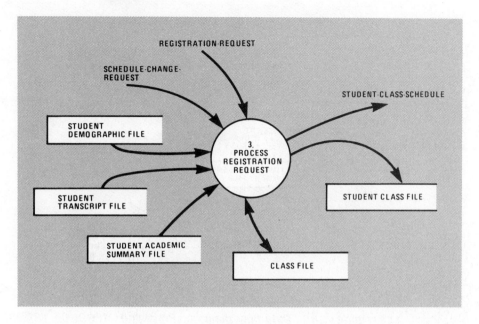

Figure A.6. *Data flow diagram. Process 4: PREPARE CLASS ROSTERS.*

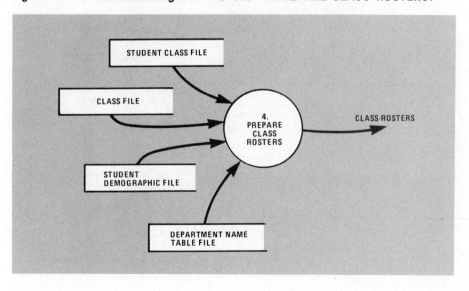

Figure A.7. Data flow diagram. Process 5: PROCESS GRADES.

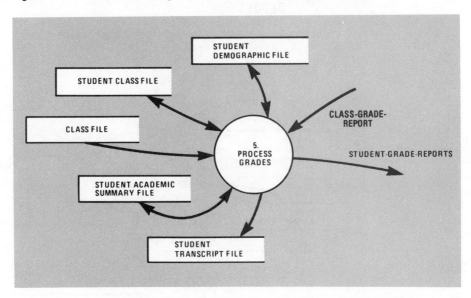

Figure A.8. Data flow diagram. Process 6: PRODUCE TRANSCRIPT.

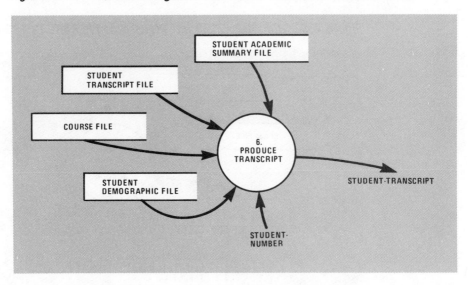

Figure A.9.   Data flow diagram. Process 7: CHANGE STUDENT GRADE.

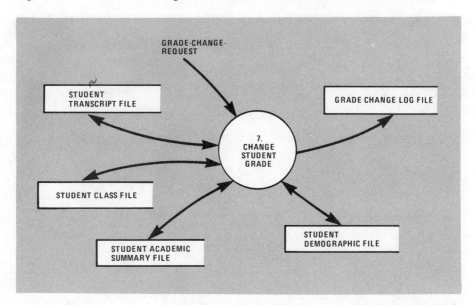

Figure A.10.   Process declaration of major.

PROGRAM/PROCESS SPECIFICATION

PROCESS NAME: Process Declaration of Major

SYSTEM NAME: SRS   **DATE:**   --/--/--

PROCESS NO.:   P1   **PREPARER:**

INTERFACES:

INPUT	FROM
DECLARATION-OF-MAJOR	STUDENT
DEMOGRAPHIC-RECORD	STUDENT DEMO-GRAPHIC FILE

OUTPUT	TO
DEMOGRAPHIC-RECORD	STUDENT DEMO-GRAPHIC FILE
DECLARATION-OF-MAJOR	ACADEMIC ADVISER

DEFINITION: The student returns the original copy of the DECLARATION OF MAJOR form to the Registrar's Office after it has been completed and signed by the student and the academic adviser.

Within the Registrar's Office, the new or changed-to major and/or minor are entered into the STUDENT DEMOGRAPHIC FILE. The student's record is accessed on STUDENT-NUMBER, and the new major and/or minor codes are added. MAJOR-CODES are the same as those used for course prefixes in the major academic areas. Each is a three-character alphabetic code. Also, the ADVISER-NUMBER for the new academic adviser is added to the student record replacing the number for the previous adviser.

After the file is updated, the DECLARATION-OF MAJOR form is filed within the Academic Adviser in sequence by STUDENT-NAME.

PROGRAM/PROCESS SPECIFICATION

PROCESS NAME: Build Class File

SYSTEM NAME: SRS   **DATE:** --/--/--

PROCESS NO.:   P2   **PREPARER:**

DESCRIPTION: Class file is built

INTERFACES:

INPUT	FROM
CLASS-OFFERINGS	REGISTRAR'S OFFICE
COURSE-RECORD	COURSE FILE

OUTPUT	TO
CLASS-RECORD	CLASS FILE

DEFINITION: CLASS-OFFERINGS are submitted by academic departments through the REGISTRAR'S OFFICE for the current term. These are checked by the Registrar's Office for conformance with style and completeness before being released for data entry.

CLASS FILE is built with information from the CLASS-OFFERINGS and from the COURSE FILE. The CLASS-NUMBER appearing on the CLASS-OFFERINGS form is used to access the class information from the COURSE FILE. These data are displayed for verification of the offerings, and are used in building the CLASS FILE.

Figure A.12.   Registration request.

PROGRAM/PROCESS SPECIFICATION

PROCESS NAME: Process Registration Request

SYSTEM NAME:	SRS	**DATE:** --/--/--
PROCESS NO.:	P3	**PREPARER:**
DESCRIPTION:	Student submits registration request	

INTERFACES:

INPUT	FROM
SCHEDULE-CHANGE-REQUEST	STUDENT
REGISTRAITON-REQUEST	STUDENT
CLASS-RECORD	CLASS FILE
DEMOGRAPHIC-RECORD	STUDENT DEMOGRAPHIC FILE
TRANSCRIPT-RECORD	STUDENT TRANSCRIPT FILE
ACADEMIC-SUMMARY-RECORD	STUDENT ACADEMIC SUMMARY FILE

OUTPUT	TO
SEATS-AVAILABLE	CLASS FILE
STUDENT-CLASS-RECORD	STUDENT CLASS FILE
STUDENT-CLASS-SCHEDULE	STUDENT
STUDENT-CLASS-SCHEDULE	REGISTRAR

DEFINITION: Student completes REGISTRATION-REQUEST form at home.

Registration is carried out by phone. Course requests are entered interactively into the computer. CLASS FILE is accessed to determine if seats are available, and to check on prerequisites. If there are prerequisite for enrolling in a course, the STUDENT DEMOGRAPHIC FILE, STUDENT TRANSCRIPT

FILE, and/or STUDENT ACADEMIC SUMMARY FILE are checked to make sure that there are no conflicts within the requested schedule. For classes that are filled, alternate sections may be offered for selection. Students are led through the process via a series of prerecorded messages. Students re spond to voice instructions by entering data through touch tone telephone. Students experiencing difficulties may request a live operator who will then conduct registrtion in the same manner as previous on-line system.

After final schedule is verified, the CLASS FILE is updated by subtracting 1 from the SEATS-AVAILABLE. A record is written to the STUDENT CLASS FILE for each class in which the student enrolls. A CLASS-GRADE field is appended to the record for later use in recording the grade earned in the class.

A STUDENT-CLASS-SCHEDULE is printed and mailed to the student for verification. Information from the STUDENT DEMOGRAPHIC FILE and CLASS FILE is combined on the form. A copy of the schedule is retained in the Registrar's Office, filed sequentially by STUDENT-NAME.

Changes to student schedules are also carried out via telephone. Requests for added courses are verified for availability and prerequisites as is done in original registration request.

Following verification of new schedule, CLASS FILE is updated by adding to the SEATS-AVAILABLE field. Records are added to or deleted from the STUDENT CLASS FILE as necessary.

A STUDENT-CLASS-SCHEDULE is printed and mailed to the student. A copy of the revised schedule is retained in the Registrar's Office under the STUDENT-NAME.

Figure A.13. Prepare class rosters.

PROGRAM/PROCESS SPECIFICATION

PROCESS NAME: Prepare Class Rosters

SYSTEM NAME: SRS   **DATE:**   --/--/--

PROCESS NO.:   P4   **PREPARER:**

DESCRIPTION: Prepare rosters of students in each class

INTERFACES:

INPUT	FROM
CLASS-RECORD	CLASS FILE
STUDENT-CLASS-RECORD	STUDENT CLASS FILE
DEMOGRPHIC-RECORD	STUDENT DEMO-GRAPHIC FILE
DEPT-NAME	DEPT NAME TABLE FILE

OUTPUT	TO
CLASS ROSTERS	FACULTY

DEFINITION: CLASS FILE is accessed in sequence by DEPT-ID, CLASS-NUMBER, and SECTION-NUMBER.

For each class, STUDENT CLASS FILE is accessed on CLASS-NUMBER + SECTION-NUMBER to identify all students within the class. Using the STUDENT-NUMBER recorded in the STUDENT CLASS FILE, the STUDENT DEMOGRAPHIC FILE is accessed to get student information for printing on the rosters. This student information is sorted by STUDENT-NAME.

Rosters are printed in DEPT-ID/CLASS-NUMBER/SECTION-NUMBER order using information from the CLASS FILE and sorted information from the STU-DENT DEMOGRAPHIC FILE. A total of the number of students in each class is tallied and printed on the rosters. DEPT-NAME is pulled from a table of department IDs and corresponding names built from the DEPT NAME TABLE FILE.

Figure A.14.   Process grades.

PROGRAM/PROCESS SPECIFICATION

PROCESS NAME: Process Grades

SYSTEM NAME: SRS   **DATE:** --/--/--

PROCESS NO.:   P5   **PREPARER:**

DESCRIPTION: Process grades submitted by each department

INTERFACES:

INPUT	FROM
CLASS-GRADE-REPORT	FACULTY
STUDENT-CLASS-RECORD	STUDENT CLASS FILE
CLASS-RECORD	CLASS FILE
DEMOGRAPHIC-RECORD	STUDENT DEMO-GRAPHIC FILE
ACADEMIC-SUMMARY-RECORD	STUDENT ACADEMIC SUMMARY FILE

OUTPUT	TO
CLASS-GRADE	STUDENT CLASS FILE
ACADEMIC-SUMMARY-RECORD	STUDENT ACADEMIC SUMMARY FILE
TRANSCRIPT-RECORD	STUDENT TRANSCRIPT FILE
DEMOGRAPHIC-RECORD	STUDENT DEMO-GRAPHIC FILE
STUDENT-GRADE-REPORT	ACADEMIC ADVISOR, STUDENT

DEFINITION: CLASS-GRADE-REPORTS are submitted by each faculty member on-line. These data are then sorted on CLASS-NUMBER within STUDENT-NUMBER, and the sorted file is used to update the STUDENT CLASS FILE by adding the appropriate letter grade within the CLASS-GRADE field.

The STUDENT CLASS FILE is primary input to this routine. For all class records for a particular student, the CLASS FILE is accessed on CLASS-NUMBER and SECTION-NUMBER, and the corresponding CLASS-NAME and CREDIT-HOURS are input.

HOURS-ATTEMPTED is calculated by totaling the number of CREDIT-HOURS taken for which a grade was earned.

HOURS-COMPLETED is calculated by totaling the number of CREDIT-HOURS for all classes for which a passing grade was earned.

CREDITS-EARNED is calculated by multiplying CREDIT-HOURS by the numeric grade equivalent (A=4, B=3, C=2, D=1, F=0) for each class, and then totaling the products of the calculations.

TERM-GPA Is calculated by dividing CREDITS-EARNED by HOURS-ATTEMPTED.

The STUDENT ACADEMIC SUMMARY FILE is accessed on STUDENT-NUMBER and TERM-ID for the previous term, if available. The cumulative hours, credits, and GPA values are used to calculate the cumulative values for the current term. A new summary record for the current term is added to the file.

The STUDENT TRANSCRIPT FILE i supdated by adding a record for each course taken in the current term.

The STUDENT DEMOGAPHIC FILE is accessed on STUDENT-NUMBER. The CUMULATIVE-HOURS-COMPLETED through the current term is used in assigning the new ACADEMIC-LEVEL value in the record (0–30 hours = FR, 31–60 hours = SO, 61–90 hours = JR, Over 90 hours = SR). The name and address fields from this file are combined with the information that was calculated and with that from the other files in order to print a STUDENT-GRADE-REPORT.

Appendix: Case Studies

Figure A.15. Produce transcript.

PROGRAM/PROCESS SPECIFICATION

PROCESS NAME: Produce Transcript

SYSTEM NAME: SRS   **DATE:** --/--/--

PROCESS NO.: P6   **PREPARER:**

DESCRIPTION: Creates student transcript

INTERFACES:

INPUT	FROM
DEMOGRAPHIC-RECORD	STUDENT DEMO-GRAPHIC FILE
ACADEMIC-SUMMARY-RECORD	STUDENT ACADEMIC SUMMARY FILE
TRANSCRIPT-RECORD	STUDENT TRANS-CRIPT FILE
COURSE-RECORD	COURSE FILE
STUDENT-NUMBER	ADVISER, REGISTRAR

OUTPUT	TO
STUDENT-TRANSCRIPT	ADVISER, REGISTRAR

DEFINITION: The student transcript is produced for either the academic adviser or the registrar by request of the student. DEMOGRAPHIC FILE Is accessed on STUDENT-NUMBER to input student name and address information.

STUDENT—NUMBER is used to access ACADEMIC SUMMARY FILE. Each record in this file contains summary information for the term identified by the TERM-ID along with the accumulated hours, credits, and GPA up through that term. All records for the particular student for multiple terms are input.

Using the STUDENT—NUMBER and TERM-ID from the ACADEMIC SUMMARY FILE, the TRANSCRIPT FILE is accessed. CLASS-NUMBERs and CLASS-GRADEs for each of the classes taken during each of the terms is input.

The CLASS-NUMBERs from the TRANSCRIPT FILE are used as partial keys for accessing the COURSE-FILE. CREDIT-HOURS and CLASS-NAMEs for the corresponding classes taken are input from this file.

Information from the four files is combined on the STUDENT-TRANSCRIPT, which lists the classes taken and grades earned for each term along with the term and cumulative academic summary. The transcript is printed in order by term.

Figure A.16. *Change student grade.*

PROGRAM/PROCESS SPECIFICATION

PROCESS NAME: Change Student Grade

SYSTEM NAME: SRS   **DATE:** --/--/--

PROCESS NO.: P7   **PREPARER:**

DESCRIPTION: Update and change the student's grade

INTERFACES:

INPUT	FROM
GRADE-CHANGE-REQUEST	FACULTY
TRANSCRIPT-RECORD	STUDENT TRANSCRIPT FILE
STUDENT-CLASS-RECORD	STUDENT CLASS FILE
ACADEMIC-SUMMARY-RECORD	STUDENT ACADEMIC SUMMARY FILE
DEMOGRAPHIC-RECORD	STUDENT DEMOGRAPHIC FILE

OUTPUT	TO
TRANSCRIPT-RECORD	STUDENT TRANSCRIPT FILE
STUDENT-CLASS-RECORD	STUDENT CLASS FILE
ACADEMIC-SUMMARY-RECORD	STUDENT ACADEMIC SUMMARY FILE
DEMOGRAPHIC-RECORD	STUDENT DEMOGRAPHIC FILE
GRADE-CHANGE-LOG-RECORD	GRADE CHANGED LOG FILE

DEFINITION: The STUDENT-NUMBER & TERM-ID & CLASS-NUMBER from the GRADE-CHANGE-REQUEST is used to access the STUDENT TRANSCRIPT FILE to input the reported CLASS-GRADE.

Information from the STUDENT TRANSCRIPT FILE is displayed for verification and the CLASS—GRADE is changed interactively through the computer terminal.

The STUDENT CLASS FILE for the corresponding term is accessed and displayed, and the change is reflected in this file as well.

The STUDENT ACADMIC SUMMARY FILE is updated. Recalculations are made for the hours, credits, and GPA values both for the current term and cumulatively.

If the grade change causes the HOURS-COMPLETED to change the academic level of the student, the STUDENT DEMOGRAPHIC FILE will require updating to effect the changed level.

A record is written to the GRADE CHANGE LOG FILE. This file journalizes changes. The record contains the original CLASS—GRADE, and the CHANGE-DATE.

relationships. At this point, little concern has been given to the physical layout of the actual documents or screen layouts. Figure A-18 contains the data structure layouts for the expected system files. Again, physical design has not yet taken place. File content represents the major entities about which the system maintains information and the keys through which access takes place. Yet to be determined are the file organization techniques and data field arrangements. Reorganization of record keys may be necessary to comply with programming language requirements.

The documentation here is a first-cut at the proposed registration system. Much more work needs to be done in order to complete a fully detailed design effort.

Figure A.17.   Data components and relationships.

INPUT/OUTPUT DOCUMENTS

```
CLASS-GRADE-REPORT = DEPT-ID +              CLASS-ROSTER       = DEPT-ID +
                     TERM-ID +                                   TERM-ID +
                     REPORT-DATE +                               ROSTER-DATE +
                     DEPT-NAME +                                 DEPT-NAME +
                     INSTRUCTOR-NAME +                           INSTRUCTOR-NAME +
                     CLASS-NUMBER +                              CLASS-NUMBER +
                     SECTION-NUMBER +                            SECTION-NUMBER +
                     CREDIT-HOURS +                              CREDIT-HOURS +
                     CLASS-NAME +                                CLASS-NAME +
                     LOCATION +                                  LOCATION +
                     DAYS-OFFERED +                              DAYS-OFFERED +
                     TIME-OFFERED +                              TIME-OFFERED +
                    ⎧ STUDENT-NUMBER + ⎫                        ⎧ STUDENT-NUMBER + ⎫
                    ⎨ STUDENT-NAME +   ⎬                        ⎨ STUDENT-NAME +   ⎬
                    ⎩ STUDENT-GRADE +  ⎭                        ⎨ MAJOR-CODE +     ⎬
                     TOTAL-STUDENTS +                           ⎩ ACADEMIC-LEVEL + ⎭
                     INSTRUCTOR-SIGNATURE                        TOTAL-STUDENTS


CLASS-OFFERINGS    = DEPT-ID +               DECLARATION-OF-MAJOR = STUDENT-NUMBER +
                     DEPT-NAME +                                    STUDENT-NAME +
                     CURRENT-DATE +                                 STREET-ADDRESS +
                     TERM-ID +                                      CITY +
                    ⎧ CLASS-NUMBER +   ⎫                            STATE +
                    ⎪ SECTION-NUMBER + ⎪                            ZIP +
                    ⎪ CREDIT-HOURS +   ⎪                            PHONE-NUMBER +
                    ⎪ CLASS-NAME +     ⎪                            MAJOR-NAME +
                    ⎨ LOCATION +       ⎬                            MAJOR-CODE +
                    ⎪ DAYS-OFFERED +   ⎪                            (PREVIOUS-MAJOR-NAME) +
                    ⎪ TIME-OFFERED +   ⎪                            (PREVIOUS-MAJOR-CODE) +
                    ⎪ INSTRUCTOR-NAME +⎪                            (MINOR-NAME) +
                    ⎩ SEATS-MAXIMUM    ⎭                            (MINOR-CODE) +
                                                                    DECLARATION-DATE +
                                                                    STUDENT-SIGNATURE +
                                                                    ADVISOR-SIGNATURE +
                                                                    ADVISOR-NUMBER
```

```
REGISTRATION-REQUEST     = STUDENT-NUMBER +          STUDENT-CLASS-SCHEDULE = STUDENT-NUMBER +
                           STUDENT-NAME +                                     STUDENT-NAME +
                           STREET-ADDRESS +                                   STREET-ADDRESS +
                           CITY +                                             CITY +
                           STATE +                                            STATE +
                           ZIP +                                              ZIP +
                           PHONE-NUMBER +                                    ⌈REGISTRATION-DATE +  ⌉
                           REGISTRATION-DATE +                               ⌊SCHEDULE-CHANGE-DATE +⌋
                           TERM-ID +                                          ⎧CLASS-NUMBER +
                          ⎧CLASS-NUMBER +                                     ⎪SECTION-NUMBER +
                          ⎪SECTION-NUMBER +                                   ⎪CLASS-NAME +
                          ⎪CLASS-NAME +                                       ⎨CREDIT-HOURS +
                          ⎨CREDIT-HOURS +                                     ⎪LOCATION +
                          ⎪LOCATION +                                         ⎪DAYS-OFFERED +
                          ⎪DAYS-OFFERED +                                     ⎪TIME-OFFERED +
                          ⎪TIME-OFFERED +                                     ⎩INSTRUCTOR-NAME +
                          ⎩INSTRUCTOR-NAME +                                  TOTAL-HOURS
                           TOTAL-HOURS +
                          (ADVISOR-SIGNATURE) +
                          (ADVISOR-NUMBER)            STUDENT-GRADE-REPORT  = STUDENT-NUMBER +
                                                                             STUDENT-NAME +
                                                                             STREET-ADDRESS +
                                                                             CITY +
SCHEDULE-CHANGE-REQUEST = STUDENT-NUMBER +                                   STATE +
                          STUDENT-NAME +                                     ZIP +
                          STREET-ADDRESS +                                   ⎧CLASS-NUMBER +
                          CITY +                                             ⎪CLASS-NAME +
                          STATE +                                            ⎨CREDIT-HOURS +
                          ZIP +                                              ⎩STUDENT-GRADE +
                          PHONE-NUMBER +                                     HOURS-ATTEMPTED +
                          SCHEDULE-CHANGE-DATE +                             HOURS-COMPLETED +
                          TERM-ID +                                          CREDITS-EARNED +
                         ⎧ADD-COURSE-NUMBER +                                TERM-GPA +
                         ⎪ADD-COURSE-SECTION +                               CUMULATIVE-HOURS-ATTEMPTED +
                         ⎪ADD-COURSE-NAME +                                  CUMULATIVE-HOURS-COMPLETED +
                         ⎨ADD-CREDIT-HOURS +                                 CUMULATIVE-CREDITS-EARNED +
                         ⎪ADD-LOCATION +                                     CUMULATIVE-GPA
                         ⎪ADD-DAYS-OFFERED +
                         ⎩ADD-INSTRUCTOR-NAME +
                         ⎧DROP-COURSE-NUMBER +
                         ⎨DROP-COURSE-SECTION +
                         ⎩DROP-COURSE-NAME +
                          (ADVISOR-SIGNATURE) +
                          (ADVISOR-NUMBER)
```

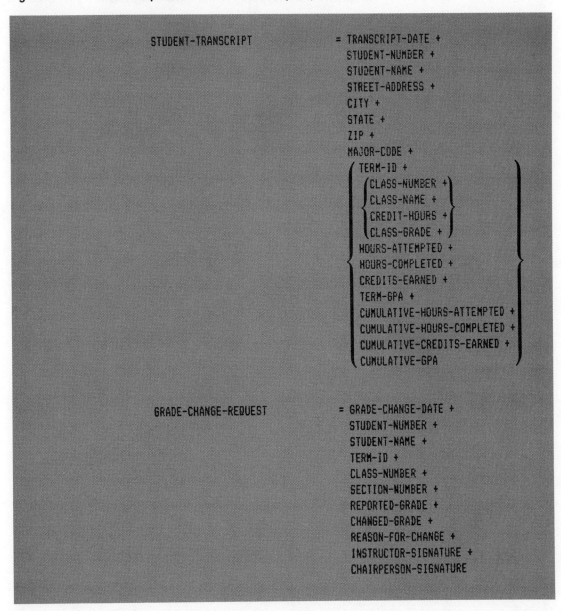

```
STUDENT-TRANSCRIPT          = TRANSCRIPT-DATE +
                              STUDENT-NUMBER +
                              STUDENT-NAME +
                              STREET-ADDRESS +
                              CITY +
                              STATE +
                              ZIP +
                              MAJOR-CODE +
                              ┌ TERM-ID +                        ┐
                              │  ┌ CLASS-NUMBER + ┐              │
                              │  │ CLASS-NAME +   │              │
                              │  │ CREDIT-HOURS + │              │
                              │  └ CLASS-GRADE +  ┘              │
                              │ HOURS-ATTEMPTED +                │
                              │ HOURS-COMPLETED +                │
                              │ CREDITS-EARNED +                 │
                              │ TERM-GPA +                       │
                              │ CUMULATIVE-HOURS-ATTEMPTED +     │
                              │ CUMULATIVE-HOURS-COMPLETED +     │
                              │ CUMULATIVE-CREDITS-EARNED +      │
                              └ CUMULATIVE-GPA                   ┘


GRADE-CHANGE-REQUEST        = GRADE-CHANGE-DATE +
                              STUDENT-NUMBER +
                              STUDENT-NAME +
                              TERM-ID +
                              CLASS-NUMBER +
                              SECTION-NUMBER +
                              REPORTED-GRADE +
                              CHANGED-GRADE +
                              REASON-FOR-CHANGE +
                              INSTRUCTOR-SIGNATURE +
                              CHAIRPERSON-SIGNATURE
```

Figure A.18. *Data structure layouts for the expected system files.*

```
                              FILES

    CLASS-FILE                     = {CLASS-RECORD}
    CLASS-RECORD                   = DEPT-ID +
                                     CLASS-NUMBER +
                                     SECTION-NUMBER +
                                     CREDIT-HOURS +
                                     CLASS-NAME +
                                     LOCATION +
                                     DAYS-OFFERED +
                                     TIME-OFFERED +
                                     INSTRUCTOR-NAME +
                                     SEATS-MAXIMUM +
                                     SEATS-AVAILABLE +
                                     (PREREQUISITE-MAJORS) +
                                     (PREREQUISITE-HOURS) +
                                     (PREREQUISITE-COURSE-GRADE)


    COURSE-DESCRIPTION-FILE        = {COURSE-DESCRIPTION-RECORD}
    COURSE-DESCRIPTION-RECORD      = ⎡ CLASS-NUMBER +             ⎤
                                     ⎣ {CLASS-DESCRIPTION-TEXT}   ⎦


    COURSE-FILE                    = {COURSE-RECORD}
    COURSE-RECORD                  = DEPT-ID +
                                     CLASS-NUMBER +
                                     CREDIT-HOURS +
                                     CLASS-NAME +
                                     (PREREQUISITE-MAJORS) +
                                     (PREREQUISITE-HOURS) +
                                     (PREREQUISITE-COURSE-GRADE)


    DEPT-NAME-TABLE-FILE           = {DEPT-NAME-TABLE-RECORD}
    DEPT-NAME-TABLE-RECORD         = DEPT-ID +
                                     DEPT-NAME


    GRADE-CHANGE-LOG-FILE          = {GRADE-CHANGE-LOG-RECORD}
    GRADE-CHANGE-LOG-RECORD        = TERM-ID +
                                     STUDENT-NUMBER +
                                     CLASS-NUMBER +
```

```
                                        CLASS-GRADE +
                                        CHANGED-GRADE +
                                        GRADE-CHANGE-DATE

STUDENT-ACADEMIC-SUMMARY-FILE     = {STUDENT-ACADEMIC-SUMMARY-RECORD}
STUDENT-ACADEMIC-SUMMARY-RECORD   = STUDENT-NUMBER +
                                    TERM-ID +
                                    HOURS-ATTEMPTED +
                                    HOURS-COMPLETED +
                                    CREDITS-EARNED +
                                    TERM-GPA +
                                    CUMULATIVE-HOURS-ATTEMPTED +
                                    CUMULATIVE-HOURS-COMPLETED +
                                    CUMULATIVE-CREDITS-EARNED +
                                    CUMULATIVE-GPA


STUDENT-CLASS-FILE                = {STUDENT-CLASS-RECORD}
STUDENT-CLASS-RECORD              = STUDENT-NUMBER +
                                    CLASS-NUMBER +
                                    SECTION-NUMBER +
                                    CLASS-GRADE


STUDENT-DEMOGRAPHIC-FILE          = {STUDENT-DEMOGRAPHIC-RECORD}
STUDENT-DEMOGRAPHIC-RECORD        = STUDENT-NUMBER +
                                    STUDENT-NAME +
                                    STREET-ADDRESS +
                                    CITY +
                                    STATE +
                                    ZIP +
                                    PHONE-NUMBER +
                                    MAJOR-CODE +
                                    (MINOR-CODE) +
                                    ACADEMIC-LEVEL +
                                    ADVISOR-NUMBER


STUDENT-TRANSCRIPT-FILE           = {STUDENT-TRANSCRIPT-RECORD}
STUDENT-TRANSCRIPT-RECORD         = STUDENT-NUMBER +
                                    TERM-ID +
                                    CLASS-NUMBER +
                                    CLASS-GRADE
```

CASE STUDY 2: ORDER PROCESSING SYSTEM

Situation

You have been appointed project team leader in the CIS department of a large mail-order merchandising company. The company specializes in computer products and supplies, which it sells through catalog orders to both individuals and businesses. Merchandise is maintained in an inventory from which all orders are filled. Your task is to produce a new system design for an automated order processing system. This system will permit the acceptance of customer orders, the preparation of shipping orders, and the preparation of customer invoices and statements. The analysis phase of the project has begun. Preliminary data flow diagrams, process narratives, and input-output and file data structure layouts have been developed for the new system. This documentation is to be used to further design the procedures and processing activities that will implement this as a computer-based system.

Context Diagram

The scope of the system you are to develop is defined by the context diagram shown in Figure A-19. As noted, the order processing system interacts with four external entities:

■ Customers will use the new system for placing orders with the company. Orders originate either by mail or by phone. In either case, the order is entered into the system in a standard form, denoting the bill-to and ship-to addresses of the customer and one or more order items identifying the products and quantities ordered. During this data entry process, the customer's credit standing is checked, along with the availability of the products ordered. It is assumed that all ordering is done on account. That is, the customer must have established an account with the company before ordering merchandise. After credit is approved, the customer is added to the list of approved customers. Items not in stock will be back-ordered. When the merchandise is shipped to the customer, a packing slip is included. This form lists the products that were shipped and provides a count of the number of items shipped and backordered. After the shipment, an invoice is prepared and sent to the customer. The invoice shows the pricing for each item ordered and the total amount of the order. Later, during the company's regular billing cycle, the customer receives a statement. This document provides the total amount due the company for all invoices for each customer. Backorders can be canceled before shipment. Also, customers may return merchandise and receive either credit on their accounts or cash refunds.

■ The order-processing system provides picking orders and packing slips to the warehouse. The picking orders are used by merchandise pickers who assemble orders from the stocks in the warehouse. The picking orders indicate the products and quantities, printed in order by warehouse location to

Figure A.19. *Context diagram: ORDER PROCESSING SYSTEM.*

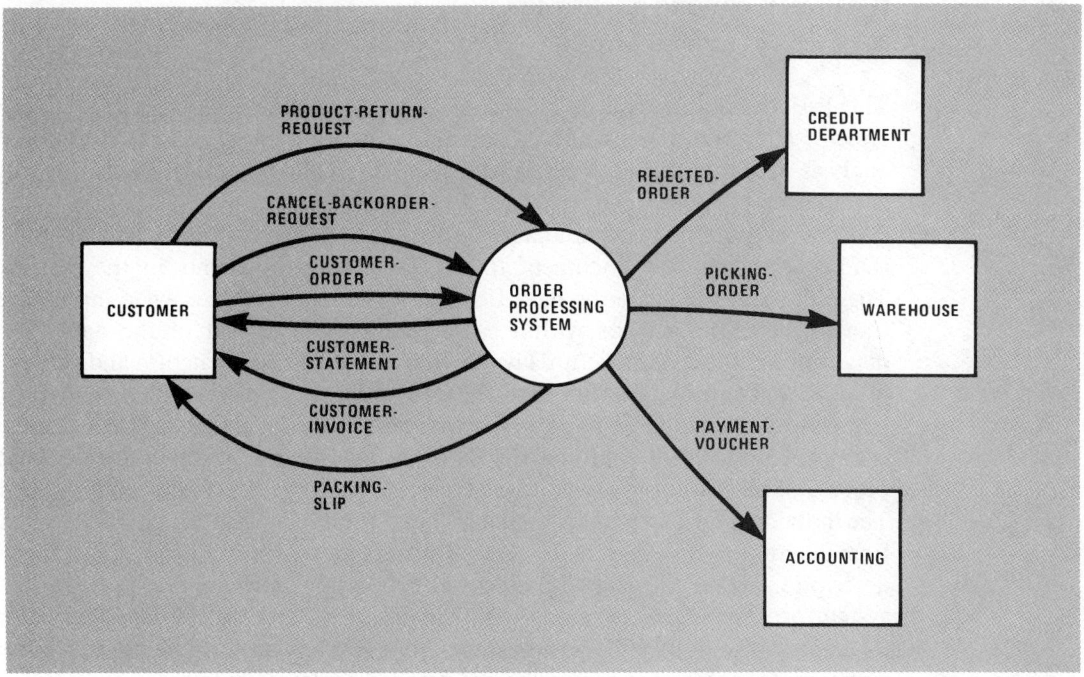

facilitate assembly of orders. The packing slips also are sent to the warehouse so that they can be included in the order that is sent to the customer.

■ If the customer does not have an account with the company, or if the value of the merchandise ordered is over the approved credit limit, the order is rejected and forwarded to the credit department. This department contacts the customer to establish an account or to adjust the order for possible resubmission.

■ When items are returned, the customer can elect to apply the value of the merchandise against the account balance. Alternatively, the customer may choose a cash refund, in which case a payment voucher is sent to the accounting office as a request for payment.

Processing Events

In studying the context diagram in Figure A-19 and other collected documents, the project team identified several major events in the order-processing system. In particular, the following events were identified:

■ Write customer order.
■ Prepare customer statement.
■ Prepare backorders.
■ Cancel customer back-order.

- Prepare shipping order.
- Process returned merchandise.
- Prepare customer invoice.

This list does not necessarily include all possible or necessary procedures in the system. However, it represents a starting point for general design. Additional analysis probably will be necessary to understand and document further details within each process.

The outputs of systems analysis also included a set of data flow diagram (DFD) segments that document the major processing events in the system. These diagrams indicate the data flows and files that interact when inputs are transformed into outputs within each process. In support of the data flow diagrams are the data structure layouts that document the structure and content of input and output data flows and files. In addition, first-cut process specifications have been prepared to provide explanations of the activities that make up each processing event. In total, the DFD segments, data structure layouts, and process specifications provide logical descriptions of the system under study. The individual DFD segments then have been combined within a diagram 0 data flow diagram to describe the integrated system as shown in Figure A-20. These descriptions cover the general patterns of processing activities that make up the system processing events, along with the data files and logical data structures that are involved. It will be necessary, however, to develop leveled data flow diagrams for selected processes before detailed design is begun.

System Documentation

The set of data flow diagram segments for the major processing activities of the order processing system is given in Figures A-21 through A-27. At this point, the documentation presents a high-level overview of the proposed system. As needed, lower-level diagrams will be prepared to partition processes for further description and clarification of activities.

First-cut process specifications are included for all the bubbles on diagram 0. These specifications are shown in Figures A-28 through A-34. They describe the processing activities that make up the system processing events, along with the data files and data elements affected.

Figure A-35 contains the data structure layouts for the input and output documents of the system. These documents are described logically, in terms of data components and relationships. At this point, little concern has been given to the physical layout and format of the source, input, output, and transaction documents.

Figure A-36 contains the data structure layouts for the files. Physical design has not yet taken place. File content represents the major entities about which the system maintains information, as well as the access keys. File organization techniques and record layouts are still to be determined.

Figure A.20. Diagram 0: ORDER PROCESSING SYSTEM.

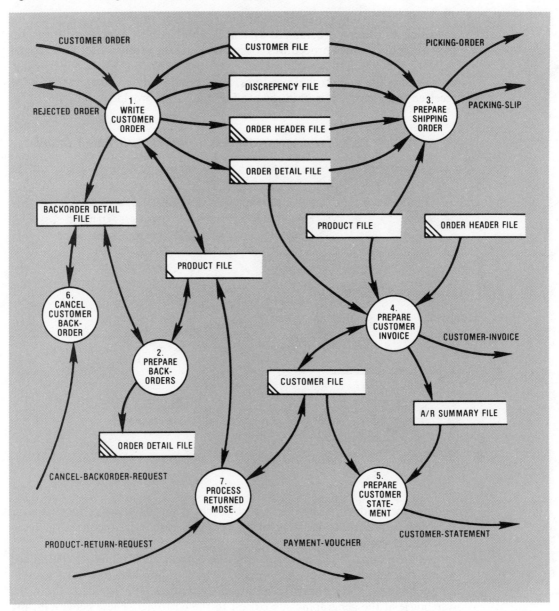

Supplementary Project

The order processing system described in this section provides basic services for accepting and filling orders. The system has not yet been expanded to encompass inventory control procedures for maintaining the product file. As a supplementary project, add these necessary features to the system. In particular, provide inventory control procedures for recording data about merchandise received from suppliers within the product file. Also, provide the capability for

Figure A.21.   Data flow diagram. Process 1: WRITE CUSTOMER ORDER.

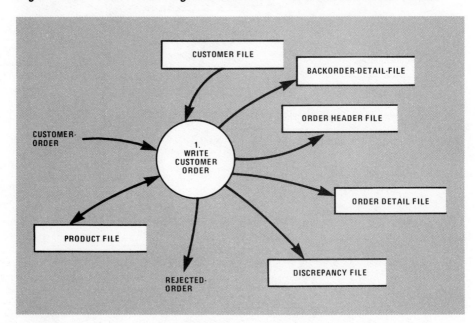

adding new products to inventory and for changing the prices of merchandise. Establish a procedure for reordering products when the quantity on hand reaches the reorder point.

As an optional supplement, assume that ordering and billing are centralized within the main offices of the company. Order filling and inventory maintenance, however, will be distributed activities. Orders will be filled within the warehouse at the geographic site closest to the customer. These geographically dispersed locations will establish and manage their own inventories.

Figure A.22.   Data flow diagram. Process 2: PREPARE BACKORDERS.

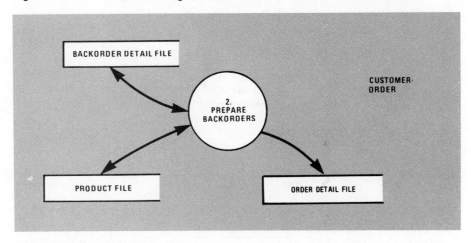

Figure A.23.   Data flow diagram. Process 3: PREPARE SHIPPING ORDER.

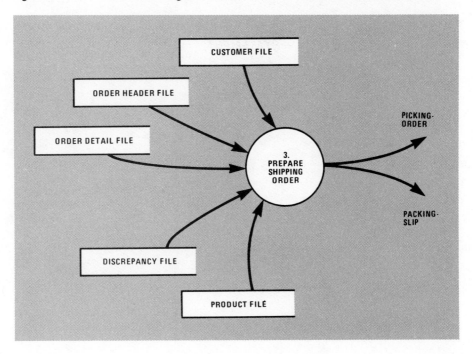

Figure A.24.   Data flow diagram. Process 4: PREPARE CUSTOMER INVOICE.

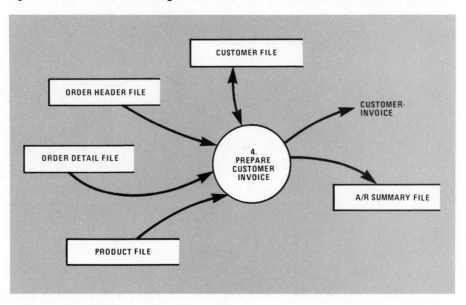

Figure A.25.   Data flow diagram. Process 5: PREPARE CUSTOMER STATEMENT.

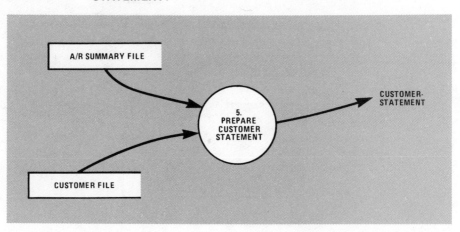

Figure A.26. *Data flow diagram. Process 6: CANCEL CUSTOMER BACKORDER.*

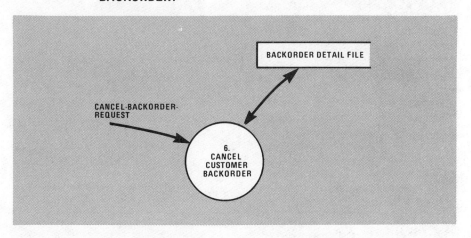

Figure A.27. *Data flow diagram. Process 7: PROCESS RETURNED MERCHANDISE.*

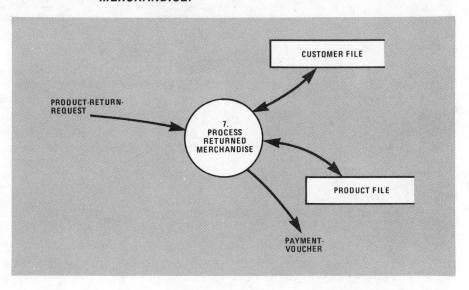

Figure A.28. Write customer order.

PROGRAM/PROCESS SPECIFICATION

PROCESS NAME: Write Customer Order

SYSTEM NAME: OPS   **DATE:**   --/--/--

PROCESS NO.:   P1   **PREPARER:**

DESCRIPTION: Process either mail or telephone orders

INTERFACES:

INPUT	FROM
CUSTOMER-ORDER	CUSTOMER
PRODUCT-RECORD	PRODUCT FILE
CUSTOMER-RECORD	CUSTOMER FILE

OUTPUT	TO
PRODUCT-RECORD	PRODUCT FILE
REJECTED-ORDERS	CREDIT DEPARTMENT
DISCRPEANCY-RECORD	DISCREPANCY FILE
ORDER-DETAIL-RECORD	ORDER DETAIL FILE
ORDER-HEADER-RECORD	ORDER HEADER FILE
BACKORDER-RECORD	BACKORDER DETAIL FILE

DEFINITION: Customer orders either by mail or over the telephone. In either case, the order is captured in a standard format. A computer terminal is to be used for entering the order into the system.

The account number submitted with the order which is verified against the ACCOUNT-NUMBER in the CUSTOMER FILE. If the account number is valid, the order is processed. If the customer does not have an account, the order is forwarded to the credit department and no further processing takes place within the order processing system.

The total amount of the order is verified against the CREDIT-LINE reported in the CUSTOMER FILE. The limit on the amount of the order is given by subtracting the ACCOUNT-BALANCE from the CREDIT-LIMIT. If the ORDER-TOTAL Is equal to or less than the order limit, the order is processed. Otherwise, the order is forwarded to the credit department.

An ORDER-NUMBER is assigned to the order. If there is no ship-to information on the CUSTOMER-ORDER, the customer name and address (the bill-to address) are used as the ship-to infomration. A record is written to the ORDER HEADER FILE keyed to the ORDER-NUMBER.

Order details are written to the ORDER DETAIL FILE. For each PRODUCT-NUMBER on the CUSTOMER-ORDER,

    a. The product record is accessed form the PRODUCT FILE using the PRODUCT-NUMBER.

    b. If the PRODUCT-NUMBER is valid and if there is sufficient QUANTITY-ON-HAND to fill the order, the QUANTITY-SHIPPED Is equal to the QUANTITY-ORDERED. If there is not sufficient merchandise in stock to fill the order, the QUANTITY-SHIPPED becomes the QUANTITY-ON-HAND and the QUANTITY-BACKORDERED is the difference between the QUANTITY-ORDERED and the QUANTITY-SHIPPED.

    c. The PRODUCT FILE is updated to show the reduction in merchandise for quantities shipped. The QUANTITY-ON-HAND Is reduced by the QUANTITY-SHIPPED.

    d. A record is written to the ORDER DETAIL FILE.

If the PRODUCT-NUMBER reported on the CUSTOMER-ORDER is invalid, a record is written to the DISCREPANCY FILE. When shipping orders are prepared, these numbers will be listed on the PACKING-SLIP.

Figure A.29. Prepare backorders.

PROGRAM/PROCESS SPECIFICATION

PROCESS NAME: Prepare Backorders

SYSTEM NAME: OPS   **DATE:** --/--/--

PROCESS NO.: P2   **PREPARER:**

DESCRIPTION: The BACKORDER DETAIL FILE is used to fill orders

once product quantities become available.

INTERFACES:

INPUT	FROM
BACKORDER-RECORD	BACKORDER DETAIL FILE
PRODUCT-RECORD	PRODUCT FILE

OUTPUT	TO
BACKORDER-RECORD	BACKORDER DETAIL FILE
PRODUCT-RECORD	PRODUCT FILE
ORDER-DETAIL-RECORD	ORDER DETAIL FILE

DEFINITION: Periodically the BACKORDER DETAIL FILE is accessed to locate orders for which backordered quantities exist.

The PRODUCT FILE is accessed to determine if there is sufficient merchandise in stock to fill the backorder. If so, the BACKORDER DETAIL FILE and PRODUCT FILE are updated to indicate filling of the order.

A back-order is written as an ORDER-DETAIL-RECORD and is processed like a customer order.

PROGRAM/PROCESS SPECIFICATION

PROCESS NAME: Prepare Shipping Order

SYSTEM NAME: OPS   **DATE:** --/--/--

PROCESS NO.: P3   **PREPARER:**

DESCRIPTION: A PICKING ORDER and a PACKING SLIP are created

INTERFACES:

INPUT	FROM
ORDER-DETAIL-RECORD	ORDER DETAIL FILE
ORDER-HEADER-RECORD	PRODUCT FILE
CUSTOMER-RECORD	CUSTOMER FILE
PRODUCT-RECORD	PRODUCT FILE
DISCREPANCY-RECORD	DISCREPANCY FILE

OUTPUT	TO
PICKING-ORDER	WAREHOUSE
PACKING-SLIP	CUSTOMER

DEFINITION: The same procedure is used for preparing shipping orders for both regular orders and back-orders.

The ORDER-HEADER-RECORD is accessed on ORDER-NUMBER and the corresponding record from the CUSTOMER FILE is accessed on the ACCOUNT-NUMBER in the header record.

For all matching ORDER-NUMBERs in the ORDER DETAIL FILE, the ORDER-DETAIL-RECORDS are accessed.

The PRODUCT-RECORD is accessed on PRODUCT-NUMBER for each product ordered. The products are sorted on LOCATION-CODE prior to printing of PICKING-ORDERs and PACKING-SLIPs.

Figure A.30. *Prepare shipping order.* (continued)

Information from the ORDER-HEADER-RECORD, ORDER-DETAIL-RECORDs, and PRODUCT-RECORDs is combined in printing the PICKING-ORDER and PACKING-SLIP. For the PACKING-SLIP, the DISCREPANCY FILE is accessd on ORDER-NUMBER to identify invalid PRODUCT-NUMBERs. These numbers are printed on the PACKING-SLIP, which is included in the delivered order. The invalid numbers are not included, however, if the shipped order is a backorder.

Figure A.31. *Prepare customer invoice.*

PROGRAM/PROCESS SPECIFICATION

PROCESS NAME:	Prepare Customer Invoice	

SYSTEM NAME:	OPS	DATE:	--/--/--
PROCESS NO.:	P4	PREPARER:	
DESCRIPTION:	The customer's invoice is prepared		

INTERFACES:

INPUT	FROM
ORDER-HEADER-RECORD	ORDER HEADER FILE
CUSTOMER-RECORD	CUSTOMER FILE
ORDER-DETAIL-RECORD	ORDER DETAIL FILE
PRODUCT-RECORD	PRODUCT FILE

OUTPUT	TO
CUSTOMER-INVOICE	CUSTOMER
CUSTOMER-RECORD	CUSTOMER FILE
A/R-SUMMARY-RECORD	A/R SUMMARY FILE

DEFINITION: The ORDER-HEADER-RECORD is accessed using the ORDER-NUMBER.

Using the ACCOUNT-NUMBER from the ORDER-HEADER-RECORD, the customer record is accessed from the CUSTMER FILE.

For each order item, the ORDER-DETAIL-RECORD is accessed on ORDER-NUMBER and the corresponding PRODUCT-RECORD is accessed on PRODUCT-NUMBER.

Individual PRODUCT-AMOUNTs are calculated by multiplying the QUANTITY-ORDERED by the UNIT-PRICE. The INVOICE-SUBTOTAL is an accumulation of all the PRODUCT-AMOUNTs for a particular order. SALES-TAX is calculated at 5% of the INVOICE-SUBTOTAL. INVOICE-TOTAL Is then derived by adding the SALES-TAX amount to the INVOICE-SUBTOTAL.

CUSTOMER-INVOICE is printed by combining information from the ORDER HEADER FILE, CUSTOMER FILE, ORDER DETAIL FILE, and PRODUCT FILE.

The CUSTOMER FILE is upadated by adding the INVOICE-TOTAL to the ACCOUNT-BALANCE. A summary record is written to the A/R SUMMARY FILE.

Figure A.32.   Prepare customer statement.

PROGRAM/PROCESS SPECIFICATION

PROCESS NAME: Prepare Customer Statement

SYSTEM NAME: OPS   **DATE:**   --/--/--

PROCESS NO.:   P5   **PREPARER:**

DESCRIPTION: Prepare the customer's statement

INTERFACES:

INPUT	FROM
A/R—SUMMARY- RECORD	A/R SUMMARY FILE
CUSTOMER-RECORD	CUSTOMER FILE

OUTPUT	TO
CUSTOMER-STATEMENT	CUSTOMER

DEFINITION: All summary records for a particular customer are accessed from the the A/R SUMMARY FILE.

The INVOICE-TOTALs are accumulated.

The customer's record is accessed from the CUSTOMER FILE using the ACCOUNT-NUMBER from the summary file.

The statement is written by combining information in the CUSTOMER FILE and A/R SUMMARY FILE. The INVOICE-TOTALS are presented in order by ORDER-DATE.

PROGRAM/PROCESS SPECIFICATION

PROCESS NAME: Cancel Customer Backorder

SYSTEM NAME: OPS   **DATE:**   --/--/--

PROCESS NO.:   P6   **PREPARER:**

DESCRIPTION: Process canceled backorders

INTERFACES:

INPUT	FROM
BACKORDER-RECORD	BACKORDER DETAIL FILE
CANCEL-BACKORDER-REQUEST	CUSTOMER

OUTPUT	TO
BACKORDER-RECORD (delete)	BACKORDER DETAIL FILE

DEFINITION: For each backorder product that is canceled, the BACK-ORDER DETAIL FILE is accessed on ORDER-NUMBER + PRODUCT-NUMBER. The record is deleted from the file.

Figure A.34.   Process returned merchandise.

PROGRAM/PROCESS SPECIFICATION

PROCESS NAME: Process Returend Merchandise

SYSTEM NAME:	OPS	**DATE:**	--/--/--
PROCESS NO.:	P7	**PREPARER:**	

DESCRIPTION: Prepare merchandise returned by customer.

INTERFACES:

INPUT	FROM
PRODUCT-RETURN-REQUEST	CUSTOMER
CUSTOMER-RECORD	CUSTOMER FILE
PRODUCT-RECORD	PRODUCT FILE

OUTPUT	TO
CUSTOMER-RECORD	CUSTOMER FILE
PAYMENT-VOUCHER	ACCOUNTING DEPARMTENT
PRODUCT-RECORD	PRODUCT FILE

DEFINITION: If the request is for a credit to the customer's account, the CUSTOMER-RECORD is accessed and the amount for the product is applied against the ACCOUNT-BALANCE. If the request is for a cash refund, a PAYMENT-VOUCHER is prepared and forwarded to the accounting department.

The PRODUCT FILE Is updated by adding the returned items back into the QUANTITY-ON-HAND.

Appendix: Case Studies

Figure A.35. **Data structure layouts for the input and output documents of the system.**

```
                        INPUT/OUTPUT DOCUMENTS


CANCEL-BACKORDER-REQUEST = ACCOUNT-NUMBER +         CUSTOMER-ORDER  = ORDER-DATE +
                          ORDER-NUMBER +                             ACCOUNT-NUMBER +
                          CANCEL-DATE +                              CUSTOMER-NAME +
                          CUSTOMER-NAME +                            STREET-ADDRESS +
                          STREET-ADDRESS +                           CITY-STATE-ZIP +
                          CITY-STATE-ZIP +                          / SHIP-TO-CUSTOMER-NAME + \
                         { PRODUCT-NUMBER-CANCEL + }               (  SHIP-TO-STREET-ADDRESS + )
                         { QUANTITY-ORDERED-CANCEL }               \ SHIP-TO-CITY-STATE-ZIP + /
                                                                    / PRODUCT-NUMBER +         \
                                                                   (  QUANTITY-ORDERED +        )
CUSTOMER-INVOICE        = INVOICE-DATE +                           {  UNIT-OF-MEASURE +         }
                          ORDER-DATE +                             {  PRODUCT-DESCRIPTION +     }
                          ORDER-NUMBER +                           (  UNIT-PRICE +              )
                          ACCOUNT-NUMBER +                          \ PRODUCT-AMOUNT +         /
                          CUSTOMER-NAME +                            ORDER-SUBTOTAL +
                          STREET-ADDRESS +                           SALES-TAX +
                          CITY-STATE-ZIP +                           ORDER-TOTAL
                         / PRODUCT-NUMBER +      \
                        {  QUANTITY-ORDERED +     }
                        {  UNIT-OF-MEASURE +      }
                        {  PRODUCT-DESCRIPTION +  }  PRODUCT-RETURN- = RETURN-DATE +
                        {  QUANTITY-SHIPPED +     }  REQUEST           ACCOUNT-NUMBER +
                        {  QUANTITY-BACKORDERED + }                    CUSTOMER-NAME +
                        {  UNIT-PRICE +           }                    STREET-ADDRESS +
                         \ PRODUCT-AMOUNT +      /                     CITY-STATE-ZIP +
                          INVOICE-SUBTOTAL +                            ORDER-DATE +
                          SALES-TAX +                                   ORDER-NUMBER +
                          INVOICE-TOTAL                                 PRODUCT-NUMBER +
                                                                        UNIT-PRICE-PAID +
                                                                     [ CASH-REFUND-REQUEST   ]
CUSTOMER-STATEMENT      = BILLING-DATE +                             [ ACCOUNT-CREDIT-REQUEST ]
                          ACCOUNT-NUMBER +
                          CUSTOMER-NAME +
                          STREET-ADDRESS +
                          CITY-STATE-ZIP +
                         / ORDER-DATE +    \
                        {  ORDER-NUMBER +   }
                         \ INVOICE-TOTAL + /
                          AMOUNT-DUE
```

```
PACKING-SLIP  = ORDER-DATE +              PAYMENT-VOUCHER = VOUCHER-DATE +
                ORDER-NUMBER +                              ACCOUNT-NUMBER +
                ACCOUNT-NUMBER +                            CUSTOMER-NAME +
                CUSTOMER-NAME +                             STREET-ADDRESS +
                STREET-ADDRESS +                            CITY-STATE-ZIP +
                CITY-STATE-ZIP +                            PAYMENT-AMOUNT
                SHIP-TO-CUSTOMER-NAME +
                SHIP-TO-STREET-ADDRESS +
                SHIP-TO-CITY-STATE-ZIP +  REJECTED-ORDER  = * A CUSTOMER-ORDER for
              ⎧ PRODUCT-NUMBER +       ⎫                    which the customer has
              ⎪ UNIT-OF-MEASURE +      ⎪                    not established an account
              ⎨ QUANTITY-ORDERED +     ⎬                    or for which the order
              ⎪ QUANTITY-SHIPPED +     ⎪                    total exceeds the
              ⎪ QUANTITY-BACKORDERED + ⎪                    credit limit *
              ⎩ PRODUCT-DESCRIPTION +  ⎭
                (INVALID-PRODUCT-NUMBER)


PICKING-ORDER = ORDER-DATE +
                ORDER-NUMBER +
                ACCOUNT-NUMBER +
                CUSTOMER-NAME +
                STREET-ADDRESS +
                CITY-STATE-ZIP +
                SHIP-TO-CUSTOMER-NAME +
                SHIP-TO-STREET-ADDRESS +
                SHIP-TO-CITY-STATE-ZIP +
              ⎧ LOCATION-CODE +        ⎫
              ⎪ PRODUCT-NUMBER +       ⎪
              ⎪ UNIT-OF-MEASURE +      ⎪
              ⎨ QUANTITY-ORDERED +     ⎬
              ⎪ QUANTITY-SHIPPED +     ⎪
              ⎪ QUANTITY-BACKORDERED + ⎪
              ⎩ PRODUCT-DESCRIPTION    ⎭
```

Figure A.36. *Data structure layouts for the system files.*

```
                                    FILES


A/R-SUMMARY-FILE       = {A/R-SUMMARY-RECORD}   ORDER-HEADER-FILE    = {ORDER-HEADER-RECORD}
A/R-SUMMARY-RECORD     = ACCOUNT-NUMBER +       ORDER-HEADER-RECORD  = ORDER-NUMBER +
                         ORDER-NUMBER +                                ORDER-DATE +
                         ORDER-DATE +                                  ACCOUNT-NUMBER +
                         INVOICE-TOTAL                                 SHIP-TO-CUSTOMER-NAME +
                                                                       SHIP-TO-STREET-ADDRESS +
                                                                       SHIP-TO-CITY-STATE-ZIP

BACKORDER-DETAIL-FILE   = {BACKORDER-DETAIL-RECORD}
BACKORDER-DETAIL-RECORD = ORDER-NUMBER +
                          PRODUCT-NUMBER +       PRODUCT-FILE         = {PRODUCT-RECORD}
                          BACKORDER-QUANTITY     PRODUCT-RECORD       = PRODUCT-NUMBER +
                                                                        LOCATION-CODE +
                                                                        PRODUCT-DESCRIPTION +
DISCREPANCY-FILE        = {DISCREPANCY-RECORD}                         UNIT-OF-MEASURE +
DISCREPANCY-RECORD      = ORDER-NUMBER +                               UNIT-PRICE +
                          INVALID-PRODUCT-NUMBER                       QUANTITY-ON-HAND +
                                                                       REORDER-POINT +
                                                                       REORDER-QUANTITY +


CUSTOMER-FILE           = {CUSTOMER-RECORD}
CUSTOMER-RECORD         = ACCOUNT-NUMBER +
                          CUSTOMER-NAME +
                          STREET-ADDRESS +
                          CITY-STATE-ZIP +
                          CREDIT-LIMIT +
                          ACCOUNT-BALANCE



ORDER-DETAIL-FILE       = {ORDER-DETAIL-RECORD}
ORDER-DETAIL-RECORD     = ORDER-NUMBER +
                          PRODUCT-NUMBER +
                          QUANTITY-ORDERED +
                          QUANTITY-SHIPPED +
                          QUANTITY-BACKORDERED
```

Glossary

Abrupt cutover. Simultaneous discontinuation of an old system and start up of a new system without a transition period.

Absolute position. Specific physical point on a disk surface where a record is located. *See also* relative position.

Acceptance review. Session at which project team presents information to a management group on an activity or phase for which approval is necessary.

Acceptance testing. A final procedural review to demonstrate a system and secure user approval before a system becomes operational.

Access controls. Controls that limit physical access to computer sites, and that limit electronic access to computer systems only to authorized persons.

Access diagram. *See* data access diagram.

Access path. The correlations or relationships between record keys that establish connections among data items imbedded in file records.

Access time. The time necessary to locate a data record on disk and read it into memory. Design consideration when choosing access method.

Accuracy. Conformity to a standard, or true value. Consideration when establishing controls throughout a system, especially where input data are entered.

Action diagramming. A technique for process definition similar to structured English but characterized by fairly rigorous construction rules. *See also* Structured English.

Active control. A connection between program modules through conditional or unconditional transfers or processing responsibility, allowing only data to cross the interface.

Activity. Within the systems development life cycle, a group of logically related tasks that lead to, and are defined by, the accomplishment of a specific objective.

Activity rate. Frequency of record access by an application. Design consideration when choosing access method.

Adjustment. Correction or modification generated by feedback within a control process to bring system input or processing back into line with expectations.

Administrator (walkthrough). Experienced system analyst who provides organizational or administrative support for a walkthrough.

Afferent. The branches of data flow in which physical inputs are transposed into logical inputs to prepare data for processing.

Algorithm. A formula, or series of steps, for defining a problem and describing its solution.

Algorithmic approach. A fixed, procedural methodology that provides relatively little flexibility in program design.

Alias. An alternate name that can be used to represent an identified data structure within a data dictionary notation.

Alphabetic field test. Test to verify that specific data fields contain only alphabetic characters and blank spaces. Used for specific processing control within a computer program.

Amplitude modulation (AM). A method for imparting volume and tone to radio transmissions through variations in signal volume.

Analysis. The process of breaking situations or problems down into successively smaller elements for individual study and solution. *See also* systems analysis.

Analysis and general design phase. A major segment (phase) of the systems development life cycle. Includes: establishing definitions and descriptions of existing systems, defining requirements for and designing features of a proposed replacement system, and doing a cost/benefit analysis. The report to management at the conclusion of this phase provides the basis for a go/no go decision on implementation of a new system.

Application architecture. High-level view of individual systems, their scope, and their interface with other systems.

Analysis enhancement. A component of CASE systems that permits verification of consistency and removal of errors and inconsistencies.

Application generator. Software that submits prepared program formats to a programmer via a series of menus and prompts. The programmer selects appropriate formats and adds parameter specifications to fit the application requirements. Coding is generated automatically.

Application software package. Predesigned software for a specific application, available for purchase and ready for use (possibly with minor modification) in an appropriate CIS; used in place of custom-designed software to reduce overall system costs or shorten development time.

Architectural design. The logical structure of processing functions within a software product.

Archival file. File that has been processed and retained for special research or historic reference.

Archival record. Permanent record of business activity made for legal requirements, historic perspective, and backup security.

Archival storage. Storage of archival records in a form that can be easily protected and will not degenerate over time, yet will be accessible when needed.

Argument. Data passed to a called module. In a table, a data item.

Attribute. Data item that characterizes an object. A consideration in choosing which data structures should be assembled into a composite data structure in the process of normalization.

Attribute file. A file that contains data describing or characterizing an entity about which information is maintained in a CIS.

Audio output. Data output that is audible and usable—in human language or sound.

Audio response. Audio computer output that delivers data as spoken messages generated from digitized voice storage or voice synthesis.

Auditability. Degree to which a system is capable of having a successful and complete audit made to evaluate the integrity of data that rely on a system.

Audit trail. Printed documents and computer-maintained records that can be used by auditors in tracing transactions through a system—from input source, to master file update, to output reports—for purposes of verification.

Author. Initiator or developer of a specific CIS product. Leader of the walkthrough of that product.

Background. Work that is initiated by programs separate from but complementary to the main processing program.

Backup file. Separately retained duplicate physical copy of a transaction file or historic master file, used for reconstruction and recovery of damaged or destroyed files.

Balance. Correspondence of amounts between an entered control figure and a computer-developed total. Used as a processing control. Also, correlation between parent and child elements of data flow diagrams in terms of flows in and out and functions accomplished.

Balancing. *See* Balance.

Bar code. Data expressed as a series of bars and spaces printed in a small field on a tag or product label, for capture by optical code reading equipment.

Batch control. Technique for verifying accuracy in master file processing through the use of trailer records.

Batch processing. The handling of records or transactions in groups or batches.

Baud rate. A unit of measurement of data transmission indicating the binary units of information transmitted per second.

Benefit. Favorable tangible or intangible result that offsets cost; savings or improvements that can be assigned values (either tangible or intangible) that can be balanced against costs as a basis for decision making. *See also* cost.

Bi-directional. Capability of a serial printer to print lines of data from left to right, or right to left, in both directions, to eliminate time needed to return to the left side of the paper.

Binding. The process of resolving or fixing data values in a program.

Bits per inch (bpi). *See* Bytes per inch.

Bits per second (bps). A measurement of the rate of data transmission.

Black box. Processing entity that produces a predictable output for a given input and whose general function is known, but whose internal processing rules are not known.

Black box testing. Monitoring the inputs and outputs of a module in terms of expectations and acceptability, without regard for internal processing logic.

Blaming. A communication style based on the assumption that someone is always at fault for any problem. Evokes negative feelings and hurts morale.

Block. A discrete segment of a physical record, determined by the characteristics of a storage device.

Bottom-up. Testing technique that begins at the lowest level in a program structure and moves progressively higher as modules are tested and integrated.

Boundary analysis testing. Testing technique that uses input and output situations at the extreme high and low ends of the ranges.

Branch. A statement that alters the normal sequential execution of a series of program statements.

Break-even point. The point at which the costs of an existing system and those of a proposed system intersect and the proposed system becomes profitable.

Bubble. Circular graphic representation within a data flow diagram of a point within a system at which incoming data flows are processed, or transformed, into outgoing data flows.

Buffer. The primary storage area of a CPU into which physical records are brought one block at a time before processing.

Bytes per inch (bpi). The number of data bytes that can be recorded in an inch of storage space on magnetic media. Also referred to as bits per inch.

Capital investment. Financial resources committed by a business for the purchase of equipment or facilities.

Case construct. A program module with a selection control structure that executes alternate processing functions chosen on the basis of data content.

Category test. Range or reasonableness test applied to non-numeric data that may include table lookup techniques. A processing control.

Cathode ray tube (CRT). *See* CRT terminal.

Central transform. The processing branches that lie after the afferent branches and before the efferent branches. These comprise the main processing functions of the application.

Channels. Recording patterns on magnetic tape, consisting of bytes recorded next to each other that form rows of aligned bit positions.

Check digit. Data bit used for a validity check in which a series of calculations is performed on a numeric value in a certain position within a field. The result must equal one of the digits in the field. A processing control.

Check point. A verification step, usually applied through use of periodic output reports of sampled transactions to verify that processing is proceeding to acceptable standards. A processing control.

Child diagram. Exploded version of a parent bubble, showing processing or transformation in greater detail. *See also* Parent.

Cohesion. Degree to which a process has a singular business purpose.

Coincidental cohesion. The random existence of relationships between the elements of a module.

Collector. Symbol for a point within an information system where separate streams of data are merged, repackaged, and forwarded. Indicated on data flow diagram by a half circle.

Common coupling. Shared access to data in a common pool by two or more modules.

Communication. The act of imparting information that is understood by its intended receiver.

Communicational cohesion. The lowest level at which processes are related within a module through the sharing of inputs or a data pool.

Completeness. Control requiring that all appropriate data to be gathered appear on the source transaction. Also, condition of possessing adequate and appropriate data for the processing at hand.

Complexity. A measure of the processing complications or amount of data to be passed from one module to another.

Computer-aided design (CAD). Software system that supplies automated assistance in industrial design.

Computer-aided-instruction (CAI). Educational and instructional methods using a computer to guide a learner through an instructional program.

Computer-aided manufacturing (CAM). Software system that supplies automated assistance in industrial manufacturing.

Computer-aided software engineering (CASE). A software system that uses a computer to supply automated assistance in applying the tools, techniques, and methodologies of systems development such as data flow diagrams and data dictionaries.

Computer information system (CIS). A total, coordinated information system that includes computers, people, procedures, and all the resources necessary to handle input, processing, output, and storage of data useful to an aspect of the organization.

Computer operations documentation. Written instructions for the setting up and execution of computer programs including—but not limited to—data control, back-up procedures, outputs, and any special functions.

Computer output to microfilm (COM). The recording of system outputs on microfilm, usually for archival storage.

Concatenate. To link two or more keys together to form a new, combination key. Used to allow unique identification of records and, at the same time, to permit access to related records in a file.

Concatenated key. A series of linked keys used for record identification and access.

Concentrator. A computer processor that monitors and logs the transmission traffic of several peripheral processors or other user devices, forming a coherent data stream for delivery of messages to their destinations.

Conditional. An exchange of control to and from a subordinate module during the execution of a program on the basis of the results of condition tests.

Confidentiality controls. Controls designed to protect rights of privacy of persons or organizations described by, or represented in, data records.

Connection. A reference by an element within one module to the identifier of another module.

Context diagram. Graphic model of an information system that shows a flow of data and information between the system and external entities with which it interacts, to establish the context, or setting, of the system.

Continuous value. Data element whose value can vary over a range of optional values. *See also* Discrete value.

Control. Any method or function that monitors input, checks processing, or evaluates feedback to determine if system performance meets expectations.

Control break. A sensed change in record content that triggers the writing of summary data and the resetting of accumulators in the generation of summary reports.

Control coupling. The interface that occurs if a subordinate module is passed information that directs its processing.

Control (systems development). The organizational activities that govern the systems development process to monitor functions, budgets, schedules, and quality.

Control totals. Numeric totals used for comparison to assure keyboarding accuracy and completeness of records. Includes count of number of documents or records in a batch, hash totals, and monetary or quantity totals.

Conversion program. Special program that reformats files of one system for use with a different system.

Coordination. Information passed by a module to direct the processing of another module.

Corporate culture. The totality of the beliefs, philosophies, and goals of an organization.

Correlation. Special identifying relationship between objects and composite data structures.

Correlative file. A special file of relationships between record keys appearing in two separate files. Used to establish access paths among physically separate files.

Cost. Tangible or intangible expense associated with any system function; encompasses any out-of-book expense associated with any function within a system, as well as human-related intangible costs. *See also* Benefit.

Cost-benefit analysis. Study and evaluation of a course of action, or proposed solution to a problem or need, that compares projected savings and other benefits to projected costs.

Cost-effective. Course of action that produces maximum relative benefit at minimum relative cost.

Coupling. Interface on data flow diagram between two higher-level processes, represented by the number of data flows connecting them. Processes with minimum coupling are more independent and more easily maintained. *See also* Cohesion.

Critical activities. Necessary and essential activities that must be performed individually and that, together, account for the total elapsed time of a systems development project. *See also* Critical path, Critical path method.

Critical path. Sequence representing minimum amount of time necessary for project completion; represented on a critical path method (CPM) visual representation by the longest path through the activities.

Critical path algorithm. Mathematical formula used to help identify the longest sequence of activities that will lead to a completed project. *See also* Critical path, Critical path method.

Critical path method (CPM). Planning and scheduling method for predicting and measuring trade-off relationships between relative costs and alternative completion dates for a project; presented visually on a project graph. *See also* Critical activities, Critical path.

CRT terminal. Unit that contains a video (cathode ray tube) display screen and a keyboard for entry of data. The data may go into a recording device, or directly into a computer.

Cumulative documentation. Relevant documentation generated during CIS project analysis and design phases to support later developmental stages.

Custom programming. The creation of new programs for specific business applications. *See also* Application software package.

"Cut and paste." The kind of time-consuming rearrangement of graphic elements eliminated by graphics generators. *See also* Graphics generator.

Data access diagram. Graphic representation of data files showing formats of files and corresponding relationships, or access paths, between files.

Database. Data organized so that multiple files can be accessed through a single reference, based upon relationships among records on the various files rather than through key values or physical position. Also, all data resources needed to support a system.

Database management. Direction or control of a database through special software that identifies relational values for records, then executes access commands through sequential, direct, or indexed sequential reference methods, whichever is appropriate to define the relationship specified by the user.

Data capture. Procedures for recording and putting data into a system through keyboarding or other methods.

Data coupling. The interface of modules connected only through active control and passing only essential data items.

Data dictionary. Listing of terms and their definitions for all data items and data stores within an information system.

Data driven. Focusing on the data objects of a system rather than its functions.

Data element. Basic unit of data that has a specific meaning for the system in which it is used.

Data entry. Converting or transcribing source data into a form acceptable for computer processing.

Data flow. Movement of data through a system, from an identified point of origin to a specific destination; indicated on a data flow diagram by an arrow.

Data flow diagram (DFD). Graphic representation and analysis of data movement, processing functions (transformations), and the files (data stores) that are used to support processing in an information system. Used to improve present utilization or to plan future changes in the system.

Data independence. In a database management system, insulation of data from specific applications programs or user needs.

Data input. Transmission of data into a computer, especially by machine. *See also* Data capture, Data entry.

Data integrity. The preservation of a high degree of consistency and quality of data.

Data item. A unit of data as defined in a data dictionary. *See also* Data dictionary.

Data management. The hardware and software technology needed for data organization, storage, retrieval, and presentation for processing.

Data management system. A collection of generalized file-management software designed to take over many of the processing functions traditionally implemented through applications packages.

Data processing system (DPS). Collection of methods, procedures, and resources designed to accept inputs, process data, deliver information, and maintain files. Provides direct support for an organization's basic transactions and operations.

Data security. Limits to data access, permitting it only to authorized users.

Data store. Storage area for collections of data input or generated during processing; indicated on data flow diagram by open rectangle.

Data structure. Packet of logically related data that can be decomposed into subordinate data components or data elements.

Data structure diagram. Graphic representation of relationships among attribute data structures. Indicates: access keys, access paths, access through correlative structures, and relationships among attribute structures sharing the same key.

Debugging. Finding and correcting improperly written statements or logic errors in a program.

Decision-condition coverage testing. Testing technique in which every statement in a module is executed at least once and every control structure executes both its true state and its false state.

Decision support system (DSS). Type of computer information system that assists management in formulating policies and plans by projecting the likely consequences of decisions.

Decision table. Representation of decision-making process showing a multidimensional array of conditions and outcomes with points of correspondence at the intersections of these vertical and horizontal elements. Used for description and/or analysis of processing alternatives.

Decision tree. Graphic representation of conditions or processing alternatives and outcomes that resembles the branches of a tree.

Decompose. *See* Partitioning.

Decomposition. The process of partitioning a system into increasingly detailed functions that can be studied separately in relative isolation.

Dedicated lines. *See* Leased lines.

Demodulation. The conversion of information structured in ASCII binary analog code into a digital signal for use by a computer communications system.

Density. Average number of data bits per unit of storage space.

Design. A representation of an object to be constructed.

Desk checking. *See* Walkthrough.

Detailed design and implementation phase. The portion (phase) during the systems development life cycle that refines hardware and software specifications, establishes programming plans, trains users, and implements extensive testing procedures, to evaluate design and operating specifications and/or provide the basis for further modification.

Detail report. Report of data content of file records.

Detailed design specification. The output of technical design that serves as the framework for the implementation and operation of a computer system.

Developmental benefit. One-time benefit resulting from undertaking a systems development project; includes economic benefits, as well as increased experience and competence for systems developers.

Developmental costs. Costs of establishing a new system and bringing it into use. Depreciable as a capital investment over the anticipated useful life of the system.

Development recap. Review of a project immediately after completion to find successes and potential problems in future work.

Diagram 0 (zero). Graphic system documentation and specification model that uses a symbol vocabulary to identify main processing functions, data flows, external entities, and data storage points.

Dial-up service. A simple telephone service that can be adapted to point-to-point computer communications.

Differentiation. The process of identifying a company's unique characteristics in order to design an information system oriented toward fulfilling specific needs.

Digitizer. Pen-like device moved along a graphic shape whose movements are assigned digital values by a computer. Used for entering drawings and graphics as data.

Direct cost. Cost of installation that is completely attributable to the introduction of a new system.

Direct file. A file organized directly, by location key, and also relatively, by position of a record within the entire field. Data can be accessed randomly from a direct file. Serial or sequential access is also possible.

Direct manipulation. An interaction style that provides a visual representation which permits the user directly to manipulate the objects of interest.

Discrete value. Noncontinuous, distinct value. Refers to data element that has only specific options, rather than a range of options, for its value. *See also* Continuous value.

Diskette. A small, flexible, circular magnetic recording medium on a plastic base, enclosed in a paper envelope. Most often used as a storage medium with microcomputers. Also called a floppy disk.

Disk pack. Multi-surface recording device that consists of a set of magnetic disks on which data can be written and read at random, or directly.

Documentation assistance. The production of standard systems documentation with the help of computer software such as CASE. *See also* Computer-aided software engineering.

Documentation controls. Control procedures used to assure that correct, updated copies of current processing procedures are available to users and that all previous versions of documentation are maintained.

Down time. Unexpected interruptions in service in a data processing system.

Download. The periodic transfer of information files from a central maintenance facility to distributed computer locations.

Driver. A test program routine used in bottom-up program design to call subprograms, pass information, and serve as a temporary superordinate program.

Dump. A procedure in which the contents of memory are recorded onto an output medium.

Early finish (EF). Earliest time at which a project activity can be finished, determined by adding estimated completion time to early start time. Used in critical path method (CPM).

Early start (ES). Earliest possible time (date) at which project activity can begin. Used in critical path method (CPM).

Edit run. In batch processing, a program that checks control totals.

Efferent. Branches of data flow that convert logical outputs into usable physical outputs.

80/20 rule. Guideline for systems development costs stating that 80 percent of the benefits of a system can be achieved for 20 percent of the cost of the total system; the remaining 80 percent of the cost provides only an additional 20 percent of benefits. Used as guideline in evaluating system features and capabilities.

Electrostatic (laser) printer. Highest speed nonimpact printing device. Forms images on a copier drum, then transfers outputs to paper.

Encryption. Alteration or encoding of signals representing data. Used when processing involves transmission over communication lines or networks. Also known as signal scrambling.

Entification. Decomposition of a many-to-many relationship so that it becomes a one-to-one relationship or a one-to-many relationship.

Entity. An object within a business (e.g., customers or parts) about which information is accumulated.

Entity pairing. In building an E-R diagram, the potential combination between individual entities.

Entity-relationship (E-R) diagram. A model that defines system data entities and their corresponding relationships.

Equivalence partitioning. Testing technique that groups data values into categorical or discrete types.

Ergonomics. Study of human factors related to job performance and use of equipment.

Error guessing. Testing technique based on the prediction (guessing) of likely trouble areas.

Error message. Message from a system to a user, should be specific, positive, and clear in its instructions.

Evolutionary approach. An approach to systems development whereby the overall scope of a system is defined through hierarchical decomposition.

Exception. Condition outside of the range defined as normal.

Exception report. Specially produced report indicating exceptions. Used to identify conditions that require human decision, items that cannot be processed, or out-of-balance situations.

Execution structure. The specific processing statements and sequences needed to implement an application on a computer.

Execution trace. Routine used in troubleshooting programs. Causes a computer to document a sequential log of processing events.

Existing system review. The beginning of the analysis and general design phase, intended to elicit an understanding of the scope of a project.

Expert system (ES). Type of computer information system that supports tasks requiring specialized knowledge.

Explode. To expand a unit of a diagram 0 (zero) representation to a more detailed level for further scrutiny.

External entity. Person, organization, or system that supplies data to or receives output from a system being modeled. Indicated on data flow diagram by a rectangle.

External output. Documents or reports produced expressly for use outside an organization; includes reports to governmental agencies, documents sent to customers, communications with stockholders, paychecks, etc. *See also* Internal output.

Face validity. Appearance of underlying authenticity and purposefulness in an information-gathering questionnaire.

Fan-in. A measure of the number of higher-level modules that call upon a lower-level module. The higher the value, the greater the overall usefulness of the lower-level function.

Fan-out. The number of modules that are immediately subordinate to a given module, indicating the degree to which hierarchical partitioning has occurred within a system.

Father file. *See* Generation.

Feasibility report. End result of a feasibility study. Includes recommendation for a specific course of action, description of the existing problem and anticipated changes, preliminary estimate of costs and benefits, impact statement detailing needed changes in equipment and facilities, proposed schedule for completion, and a list of policy level decisions to be resolved by management.

Feasibility study. Study that, when completed, will have evaluated initially the relevant factors involved in a problem or need, considered preliminary alternative solutions, recommended a definite course of action, and projected estimated costs and benefits to be derived from the recommended solution.

Feedback. A specially designed output used for verification, quality control, and evaluation of the results of data processing.

Fiber optics wand. Hand-held device used with optical character reading equipment to "read," capture, and input data recorded in bar code or a special character set from a printed document or label.

Fiche. Flat multi-image film sheet. Used with computer output to microfilm (COM) device.

File. A collection of records relevant to an application under development.

File controls. Procedures and methods used to assure proper and authorized handling, storage, use, and backup duplication of files.

File conversion. Process of changing master and transaction files to meet specifications of new system processing requirements.

File organization. The physical patterns in which data are recorded on storage devices.

Fill-in-the-blank. Questionnaire item that seeks specific, finite, factual answers not restricted to a given set of choices.

Final documentation. Detailed report of systems development project after completion. Included are documentation of programs, processing, procedures, forms, and files to assist in solving day-to-day system operational problems or questions when the system is in operation.

Financial feasibility. Evaluation that results from consideration of the economics of a proposed course of action, to determine potential profitability.

Finish time (T). Time at which a project will be completed. Identified on project graph by the symbol T. *See also* Critical path method, Project graph.

Finite. Having a definite or definable beginning and a specific ending point.

First-level factoring. The process of identifying the major processing functions that must be performed to accomplish a specified program function.

First normal form. Preliminary partitioning of data structures containing repeating groups into two or more relations without repeating groups that accomplish the same purpose. *See also* hierarchical partitioning.

Fixed costs. Continuing costs involved in assuring the ongoing existence of a business enterprise that must be considered in any proposed systems development plan. *See also* Variable costs.

Fixed-length record. Record within a file so designed that all records are the same length and contain the same fields. *See also* Variable-length record.

Fixed-type printer. Impact printer device that uses a rotating circular printing element in front of a striking device to imprint characters.

Flag. In programming, a data item used to signal the occurrence of an expected event or special condition that arises during processing.

Flexibility of access. Feature of database management systems that permits access to data through multiple references.

Floppy disk. *See* Diskette.

Font. Format that gives a printed character set its particular "look."

Form fill-in. Interaction technique most applicable to data entry techniques.

Forward engineering. The traditional practice of specifying first a logical model and deriving a physical model from it.

Fourth-generation language (4GL). A nonprocedural programming language such as those used in application generators.

Frequency modulation (FM). A method for imparting volume and tone to a radio transmission through variations in the signal frequency.

Function. The transformation that takes place when a program module is executed. A specific computer processing operation.

Function testing. A procedure used to identify discrepancies between the results of module execution and the expectations established in specifications.

Functional cohesion. Performance capability of a module to apply a single function to a given data item, producing a predictable output.

Functional decomposition. A method of system and software design that breaks a complex problem into a set of individual, solvable subproblems.

Functionally dependent. Describes the relation between nonkey data elements and the primary key in the second normal form. Uniquely identified only by a complete concatenated key, rather than by just a partial key.

Functional model. Model of an existing system that stresses the business objectives the system supports.

Gantt chart. Graphic representation of a work project showing start, elapsed time, and completion relations of work units in a project. Used to control schedules as part of project management. *See also* Critical path method, Project graph, Project planning sheet.

General design specification. Derived from the user specification, the basis of detailed design activity. *See also* Detailed design specification, User specification.

Generation. Version of master file produced by processing a transaction file against a master file; the previous master file becomes a backup file. Three generations, known as the son file (most current), father file (previous master file), and grandfather file (predecessor of father file), are typically maintained.

Global. Encompassing all aspects of a system.

Global understanding. Understanding of the functioning of a CIS as a complete system by a systems analyst. Represented and documented by high-level physical and logical models.

Goal. Long-term objective of an organization.

Grandfather file. *See* Generation.

Graphics generator. A component of computer-aided software engineering used to model system representations.

Hard copy. Output in the form of permanent records such as paper documents or microfilm.

Hardwire. To interconnect computer devices through directly attached cables.

Hash function. A formula applied to a record key to determine the storage location for the record in a direct file organization.

Hash total. Summation of a numeric field that does not contain quantities or values normally added together. Used only to verify data entry.

Header record. Record indicating number of documents in a batch, batch identification number, and date of processing. Input control.

Heuristic. Method providing aid or direction in the solution of a problem; a "rule of thumb."

Hierarchical. An ordering and division of problems or functions into successively smaller increments, according to logical and/or functional sequence.

Hierarchical decomposition. *See* Hierarchical partitioning.

Hierarchical partitioning. Breaking down a large problem or project into a series of structured, related, manageable parts through iteration, for the purpose of understanding clearly the functions and requirements of individual system parts.

Hit rate. *See* Activity rate.

Holistic data modeling. A data-driven approach to systems development that views organizations at various levels largely from a data perspective rather than a process perspective.

Human engineering. *See* Ergonomics.

Human factors feasibility. Evaluation that results from consideration of human reactions to a proposed course of action, to determine whether such reactions might impede or obstruct systems development or implementation.

Hypothesis testing. Program troubleshooting technique that attempts to isolate a processing error by devising specific test data that will retrigger the mistake.

I-CASE. Integrated CASE tools based on a common underlying encyclopedia. *See also* Computer-aided software engineering.

Identifier. An assigned name. Applied to each module within a program.

Impact printer. Printing device that creates impressions by striking a ribbon that transfers images to paper. *See also* Line printer and Serial printer.

Implode (to a higher level). To combine the detail of several lower-level diagrams on a single higher-level diagram.

Incremental. Step by step.

Incremental step. Implementation and installation of a larger new system with reasonably independent components in increasingly complete stages. Allows users to learn to use the final system effectively, in stages. Makes it possible to develop the final system with good control over schedules and budgets.

Incremental testing. Technique of adding modules one at a time for testing.

Indexed sequential file. File arranged in sequential order, according to key, and also containing an index, or table, to identify the physical location of each key within the file. File can be searched in ascending order according to key, or a single record can be randomly accessed by reference to a physical location in the index.

Indirect cost. Cost of installation that cannot be directly linked to the introduction of a new system.

Information. Meaningful data transformed through processing, or knowledge that has resulted from the processing of data.

Information architecture. The key entities of an organization, their significant attributes, and the important relationships between them, as represented in an E-R model.

Information center. A specialized computer facility that uses sophisticated software tools to generate functional computer applications in direct response to user service requests.

Information hiding. Isolating functions not directly related to the problem within a module so that changes in the processing environment will not require changes in the structure or logic of the program.

Information system. The methods, procedures, and resources for developing and delivering information.

Initial investigation. Activity to handle and evaluate requests for new or improved CIS services. End result is an understanding of the request at a level sufficient to make a preliminary recommendation as to the course of action to be followed.

Initial investigation report. Report documenting the initial investigation activity, findings, and recommendations.

Ink jet printer. Nonimpact printing device that sprays microscopic ink particles onto paper to form characters.

Input. Data that serve as the raw material for system processing or that trigger processing steps. Also, to access data and place them into a computer system. Input tasks include data capture, data entry, and input processing.

Input controls. Controls used to assure that only correct, complete input data are entered into the system. Encompasses control totals for batch processing, video display, and maintenance of a transaction log to produce control totals for on-line systems.

Input-output error testing. Technique to make sure that all records are transmitted and received as expected.

Installation phase. Portion (phase) in the systems development life cycle during which the new CIS is installed, the conversion to new procedures is fully implemented, and the potential of the new system is explored.

Instrumental input. Data recorded directly by a machine, without human interpretation; examples are supermarket bar code reading devices and optical character recognition devices.

Intangible. Real, but not easily assessable. Describes business costs or benefits not easily quantifiable in monetary terms. *See also* Tangible.

Intangible benefit. Delivered, identifiable improvement that must be identified, and for which a value that is not easily quantified must be ascribed.

Intangible cost. Cost, in most cases readily identified, but not easily quantified, usually attributable to human reactions to changes in the work environment.

Integration. *See* System integration.

Integration testing. Procedures that examine the interfaces between system components or modules, certifying that information and control are passed correctly and that output is as expected.

Integrity. Completeness and unimpairedness. Integrity controls assure that: data files processed represent the actual, current status or condition; materials and mechanisms will exist to reconstruct destroyed files and recover processing capabilities in the event of loss; only authorized transactions will be admitted to a system.

Intelligence. Built-in electronic processing capability within a CRT terminal. May include microprocessors, memory units, printing and document originating capabilities.

Interactive software development tools. The elements needed to create a prototype in a form both flexible and easy to use.

Interblock gap (IBG). The space between blocks on a storage medium.

Interface. A connection between modules. The hardware or software that must be used to interconnect systems or devices within a system.

Interim documentation. Documents generated during the analysis and development phase of the systems development life cycle to provide orderly, cumulative records of the development process. *See also* Cumulative documentation.

Internal output. Documents or reports produced for use within an organization, as distinct from documents for use outside the organization. Includes reports to management, job tickets or production schedules, employee time cards, etc. *See also* External output.

Interrecord gap (IRG). The space between records on a storage medium.

Interview. Planned interactive meeting between a data gatherer and one or more subjects for the purpose of identifying information sources and collecting information.

Investigation phase. Portion (phase) at the inception of the systems development life cycle to determine whether a full systems development effort or another course of action is appropriate.

Iteration. Repetition; indicated on data flow diagram by braces {. . .}. Also, partitioning a problem repeatedly to reach increasing levels of understanding. *See also* Hierarchical partitioning and partitioning.

Job. A grouping, or packaging, of processes into a single processing unit.

Job control language (JCL). The operating system software tool used to identify programs being submitted and the necessary software and equipment support requirements for the processing of application programs.

Job step. Within a batch processing environment, an independent segment of a job that has been subdivided into separate processing units, or steps.

Job step boundary. The limits of an independent segment of a job stream containing inputs, processing steps, and outputs.

Job stream. A sequence of programs or steps that make up a single processing job.

Job stream test specification. An extensive, detailed list of all conditions to be tested and the test files to be used.

Joint application design (JAD). Technique that assembles key personnel for an intensive session to determine requirements for a new system and develop a general new design.

Journal. A log or record kept on a daily or regular basis. *See* Transaction log file.

Key. Access control field that uniquely identifies a record or classifies it as a member of a category of records within a file.

Key attribute. Primary key to other data structures and the attributes of those other data structures.

Key-to-disk machine. Keyboard entry device that usually includes a CRT terminal and a recording system that processes entries and places them on disk packs.

Key-to-diskette machine. Keyboarding device, with or without a CRT, that enters machine-readable data directly onto a diskette.

Laser. A high-powered coherent beam of light. *See also* Electrostatic (laser) printer.

Late finish (LF). Latest completion of an activity. Determined by adding the activity duration to the late start time. Used in critical path method (CPM).

Late start (LS). Latest time at which an activity can begin without extending the total project completion time. Determined by deducting elapsed time from late finish time for an activity. Used in critical path method (CPM).

Layering. Iteration of systems analysis studies to produce additional knowledge and/or understanding of problems and system operations.

Leased line service. A fixed, dedicated communications link.

Level of abstraction. One of a series of isolated units, or levels, within a top-down process of breaking a problem into increasingly detailed subproblems.

Library routine. Software modules that preserve programs for later use in different applications.

Life cycle tailoring. Planning activity in the SDLC that examines objectives and end-products of each phase and modifies them to meet the challenges unique to the project.

Light pen input. Input device, resembling a pen, that allows users to manipulate data on the face of CRT screens. Used chiefly for engineering and design applications.

Line item. Data represented on a single line of a report or document, such as a single item in an extensive order.

Line printer. Printing device that prints documents a full line at a time.

Local area network (LAN). A series of computer processors that share files and peripherals.

Logical cohesion. The degree of correspondence of module elements when a single module performs more than one type of logically related function or class of functions.

Logical data structure. A model indicating the content of files.

Logical model. Model of a CIS showing only logically necessary data content and handling to aid in documenting and/or analyzing a system. *See also* Physical model.

Logical record. The combination of data fields presented to a program for processing in a single READ operation.

Log in. A procedure under which a user establishes interaction with a computer system, including entry of codes that authorize access for that individual.

Logistics systems. Collectively, the people, equipment, materials, and procedures that procure the materials and services used in conducting business activities such as manufacturing, marketing, transportation, or human resources.

Longest path. Minimum time required for project completion, as indicated on a project graph network. *See also* Critical path.

Lookup table. Program table searched to find entries to match input data. May be used in a category test for processing control.

Lower CASE. The CASE tools most useful in preparing actual programs and systems, usually having to do with application generation.

Magnetic ink character recognition (MICR). Input method developed and used by banking industry to identify checks, deposit slips, and other documents preprinted with a special magnetic ink.

Mainframe. A large central processing unit (CPU) that operates on short cycle times and may be responsible for organization-wide processing, having many satellites.

Maintenance. Altering or replacing software or hardware of a CIS to meet new or changing processing requirements.

Management architecture. Collectively, the strategies, standards, policies, and procedures of an IS organization within an enterprise.

Management information system (MIS). Type of computer information system that provides meaningful summarization of data to support organizational management control functions and highlights exception conditions requiring attention or corrective action.

Management summary. Summary report prepared for management. Recommends a course of action to solve a problem.

Many-to-many relationship. The relationship of two associated entities in which both entities may have many different values.

Mark sensing. Optical or electrical document reading method that uses the position of marks to indicate the meaning of data.

Master file. File containing permanent or semipermanent basic information to be maintained over an extended lifespan. Contains one record for each entity covered.

Master-to-slave. A computer configuration system that includes a master, or central, processor and one or more peripheral "slave" processors.

Materiality. A measure of the relative importance (significance) of a data item within an application.

Matrix printing element. Impact printing device containing a series of points that are projected forward to cause printing impressions, thus forming characters.

Memory dump. Printouts showing the status of a memory at a given moment. Often used in program troubleshooting.

Menu selection. An interaction approach in which users read a list of items and select the one most appropriate to their task.

Metric. A formal unit of measurement that can be applied to a software design as opposed to heuristics, simple rules of thumb.

Microcomputer. Computer designed for a single user.

Minicomputer. Computer designed to accommodate the requirements of a department or business area, usually designed for use in an interactive environment.

Minimodel. Individual changes in a proposed CIS, modeled separately.

Mnemonic. An assigned name or value that serves as a memory aid.

Model. Mathematical or logical representation of a system that can be manipulated intellectually to assess hypothetical changes. Also, to make graphic or written representations of an information system and its functions, to help people understand the system.

Modem. From MODulator-DEModulator, a device that translates analog code into digital code, and digital to analog, allowing computers to utilize telephone lines for direct communication.

Modulate. To vary the amplitude, frequency, or phase of a transmitted signal.

Module. In programming, a solution component representing a processing function that will be carried out by a computer.

Module hierarchy. Arrangement of modules in order of activation.

Module testing. Procedure used to determine the soundness of logic and functions within a processing step.

Monetary total. *See* Quantity total.

Monolithic. Programs that behave as single, interrelated blocks of code. These programs are generally large and difficult to implement, maintain, and modify.

Most probable time estimate. "Best guess" of the time that will be required to complete an activity, assuming a normal number of problems or delays. Used in project evaluation and review technique (PERT).

Multiple-choice. Questionnaire item that provides the respondent with a series of finite, specific choices.

Mutually independent. State when it is verified that each nonkey data element is independent of every other nonkey element in the relation; test for third normal form.

Narrative description. Prose presentation (of anything that can be described), unworkable alternative to modeling.

Net present value (NPV). Present value of benefits, minus present value of investments; can be positive, zero, or negative. Used to compare alternative investment opportunities with a stated benchmark, or standard. *See also* Present value.

Network. Graphic flow diagram relating the sequence of activities to the sequence of occurrence. Used in project evaluation and review technique (PERT) and critical path method (CPM). *See also* Project graph.

Networking. Linking of multiple devices through communications lines for distribution of processing and/or the transmission of data.

New system design specification. Comprehensive proposal for a new CIS, encompassing both user specification and all updated and/or additional detailing of hardware, software, procedures, and documentation needed for actual implementation. Presented to both users and CIS design group for signoff.

New system requirements. A definition of the necessary capabilities of a new system from the user's perspective. *See also* User specification.

Network data model. Similar to hierarchical models, in that the major data structure is called a record and the overall schema expresses the relationships between records of different types.

Node. Beginning or ending point of an activity, represented on a project graph by a circle. A control point processor within a network that monitors and logs data transmission traffic. *See also* Network.

Noise. Electronic interference on a transmission channel that degrades or distorts the signal.

Nondisplay field. An access control technique that permits invisible entries.

Nonimpact printer. Printing device that causes images to be imprinted without actual contact between print mechanism and paper. *See also* Electrostatic (laser) printer, Ink jet printer, and Thermal printer.

Nonincremental. A program design technique that creates all modules before testing them simultaneously as a program.

Nonparameterized. Conditional transfers of control that gather information from a global data pool rather than from passed argument lists.

Nonredundancy. Criterion for logical data design, characterized by avoiding inclusion of the same data component within two or more data stores, and/or avoiding inclusion of the same data in different forms within the same data store.

Nonredundant. Components of data files that appear only once or in only a single form in the entirety of those files that model the data structure of an organization.

Nonrepetitive. Performed only once, characteristic of most projects.

Normalization. Process of replacing existing files with their logical equivalents, thereby deriving a set of simple files containing no redundant elements.

Numeric field test. Test to verify that a given field contains only numeric characters. Used for processing control.

Object. Entity, or thing, described by or represented in a data structure. *See also* Attribute.

Objective. The overall scope and purpose of any systems development activity.

Object-oriented development. Technique based on objects that consist of both data and sets of processes that can act on those data to produce a result.

Observation. Method of gathering information utilizing a highly trained, qualified person who watches firsthand the actual processing associated with a system and records information and impressions of the process.

One-to-many relationship. The relationship of two associated entities in which a value of the first entity has many corresponding values in the other.

One-to-one relationship. The relationship of two associated entities in which a value of the first entity has only one corresponding value in the other.

On-line processing. Handling transactions or records one at a time until complete.

On-line tutorial. Technique of making technical manuals available on computer.

Open-ended question. Questionnaire item offering no response directions or specified options. Used to allow a wide variety of potential responses.

Operational benefit. Recurring benefit that results from the day-to-day use of a system, such as reduced operational costs.

Operational control. Procedures within computer information systems that deal with access, authorization, and verification.

Operational costs. Variable costs that are associated with the use and maintenance of a system.

Operational feasibility. Evaluation that results from consideration of manual processing needs and overhead costs of a given systems operation by an organization.

Optical character recognition (OCR). Data input technique that uses reflected light to "recognize" printed patterns.

Optimistic time estimate. "Best guess" estimate of minimum time required to complete a project, assuming all conditions will be ideal. Used in project evaluation and review technique (PERT).

Optimum. Most favorable in terms of cost-benefit analysis. Describes business option that produces greatest benefit for the least relative cost.

Organizational chart. A graphic representation identifying the subsystems of a business and showing their relationship.

Organizational controls. Methods and techniques for protecting the integrity and reliability of data within a system through patterns of job responsibility. *See also* Separation of duties.

Organizational structure. A formal recognition by the management of a business of the subsystems that make up the business organization. Reflects fundamental strategy for achievement of the organization's goals. Often represented on an organization chart.

Output. A product, or result, of data processing.

Owner (system). Upper-level personnel who manage lower-level users of a CIS. *See also* User.

Packet. A block of data, identified by length and destination prefixes, that moves along a network until it reaches its designated user.

Parallel operation. Concurrent operation of an old system and its replacement for a period of time.

Parameterized. A type of control structure that draws specific information from argument lists.

Parameters. Specifications given to a program generator that define program limits and processes, allowing the generator to create source code.

Parent. Single bubble in high-level data flow diagram that can be exploded to produce a more detailed version. *See also* Child diagram.

Partition. To reduce the complexities of a problem or situation into smaller elements that can be approached as individual, soluble items.

Partitioning. Division of a complex problem or situation into smaller separate elements for ease of understanding, and/or solution. *See also* Hierarchical.

Patch. A program coding subset used to fix or update an application module.

Payback. *See* Payback period.

Payback analysis. Method for determining period necessary for a new system to generate savings great enough to cover developmental costs.

Payback period. Length of time necessary to earn an amount equal to the amount required for acquisition of a capital investment.

Peer-to-peer. A relationship within a distributed computer network in which separate processors function as equals; there is no central or dominant processor.

Percentage of completion. Indication on a Gantt chart of the proportion of a project that has been finished.

Performance testing. Procedures used to verify the quality of system processing before the system becomes operational.

Pessimistic time estimate. Maximum completion time of a project, assuming that everything that can go wrong will go wrong. Used in project evaluation and review technique (PERT).

Phase. Set of activities and tasks that, when completed, delimits a significant portion of a systems development project.

Physical model. Graphic representation of the processing activities in an information system, shown in sequence and reflecting all data transformations, file alterations, and outputs.

Physical record. One or more logical records grouped to conform to the storage and processing requirements of a secondary storage device.

Planning. Study and development of projected courses of action for meeting goals or dealing with anticipated problems.

Plotter. Computer-driven graphic output device that creates images on paper by guiding a pen-like stylus.

Pointer. *See* Key.

Point-of-sale terminal. Electronic cash register that transmits sales entries into a recording device or computer.

Point-to-point. A communications channel, usually a telephone line, that establishes a direct connection between two users.

Policy. Rule or guideline for the conduct of a business.

Poll. A transmission initiation procedure in which the central processor contacts each network point sequentially, allowing each point time to respond.

Population. Total group of persons with a commonality of identification. Information providers identified as potential respondents for a questionnaire.

Post-implementation maintenance list. List of change requests from users, made during system implementation, and noncritical changes to be made after system test procedures, that are to be handled as maintenance after full system implementation.

Post-implementation review report. Report prepared for CIS, user departments and steering committee. Covers review, conducted after a new system has been in operation for some time, to evaluate actual system performance against original expectations and projections for cost-benefit improvements. Also identifies maintenance projects to enhance or improve the system.

Predictability. Characteristic of systems projects because the outputs to be achieved are known.

Preliminary detailed design and implementation plan. Planning document used as a basis for detailed planning, and also to update estimates of development costs before new system design is completed. Encompasses: activities down to major task level, working days required, proposed staffing plan, and dependable planning schedule for activity and task completions.

Preliminary installation plan. Document prepared during implementation and installation planning. Contains: file conversion and system installation approaches; preliminary list of major files to be created or converted and forms to collect new data; identification of necessary computerized file conversion programs; and preliminary list of installation tasks for the new systems, including any special coordination considerations.

Preliminary system test plan. Document prepared during implementation and installation planning that establishes expectations of results to be delivered in each system area. Identifies major system products, or functions and interrelationships, and modules to be tested. Also specifies system, program, and user procedures tests.

Presentation capability. A high-level component of CASE systems that eases the preparation of presentation materials for team members, management, and technicians.

Present value. Current value of money. To determine the value of money in constant dollars, future economic values are discounted backward in time to the present.

Present value factor (pvf). Multiplicand used to determine the present value of a sum of money to be received at a certain time in the future.

Prime data area. In an indexed sequential filing scheme, the disk area that holds data records.

Primitive. A basic, simple function that can be executed routinely by a computer.

Printing device. Output device that produces printed documents.

Private network. A multiple-user data communications system created by an organization for its own use.

Procedural cohesion. The grouping of elements within a module on the basis of the flow of control through that module.

Procedure. The manner in which work is performed—who does what, when, with what equipment, and under what rules.

Procedures manual. Instructional document written to aid people in performing manual procedures within a computer-based system. *See also* Training manual.

Process. To transform input data into useful information through performance of certain functions: record, classify, sort, calculate, summarize, compare, communicate, store, retrieve. Indicated on data flow diagram by a circle, or bubble.

Process description. Set of rules, policies, and procedures specifying the transformation of input data flows into output data flows.

Processing controls. Controls designed to assure accuracy and completeness of records each time a file is processed. *See also* Exception report and Trailer record.

Production systems. Collectively, the people, materials, equipment and procedures that design and produce goods and services.

Program folder. Documentation within the cumulative project file that supports the certification of each program within a system.

Program integration. The procedures used to connect modules to form programs.

Programming and testing. Detailed design and implementation phase activity encompassing actual development, writing, and testing of program units or modules.

Program test log. Document describing problems noticed as system was tested and brought into use. Log is updated to provide current information as changes are made to individual program modules and programs themselves.

Program test specification. Extensive, detailed listing of criteria for testing a program.

Project. Extensive job involving activities that are finite, nonrepetitive, partitionable, complex, and predictable.

Project evaluation and review technique (PERT). Project scheduling and control methodology that provides graphic displays to: identify project activities; order activities in time sequence; estimate and completion time for each activity, relationships among activities, and time required for the entire project; and identify critical activities and noncritical activities. *See also* Critical path method (CPM).

Project graph. Graphic network that represents activities as paths between beginning and ending points. Used in project evaluation and review technique (PERT) and critical path method (CPM). *See also* Network, Node.

Project management. Method or combination of techniques that facilitates planning, scheduling, and control.

Project management review. Meeting at which technical or general reports by members of project team are reviewed by team leaders or project managers.

Project plan. Detailed account of scheduling and staffing—to task level—for the second and succeeding phases of a systems development life cycle.

Project planning sheet. Worksheet used to identify work units, make personnel assignments, and keep track of planned and actual hours worked and dates of completion. Used for project management. *See also* Gantt chart.

Project team. A team brought together to carry out a systems development project, representing all user needs and perspectives, usually headed by a senior systems analyst, and including other information system specialists and representatives from each of the functional areas impacted by the system.

Protocol. An informal set of rules that governs the exchange of data transmission between processing systems.

Protocol emulation. A type of software within data communications systems that interfaces different data formats or binary structures to implement accurate, meaningful data exchange between dissimilar systems.

Prototype. A working system that can be developed quickly and inexpensively, given the necessary software tools, to evaluate processing alternatives and specify desired results.

Prototyping. Specialized systems development technique using powerful application software development tools that make it possible to create all of the files and processing programs needed for a business application in a matter of days or hours for evaluation purposes.

Pseudocode. A technique for process definition similar to but more formal than structured English.

Quality total. *See* Monetary total.

Query. A single inquiry sentence that, with a database reference, would seek out and organize all relevant, related records, and present them in a sequence stipulated in the query.

Questionnaire. A special-purpose document requesting specific information that can be quantitatively tabulated, usually from large populations of source respondents. Used by systems analysts to gather information relating to potential CIS development.

Random access. Disk access technique in which records can be read from, and written directly to, disk media without regard for the order of their record keys.

Randomizing routine. Algorithm applied for assigning record locations for applications in which keys cannot be used directly as locators.

Range test. Test to verify that values of entries in a given field fall between the upper and lower limits established by a program. Used for processing control.

Ranking scales. Questionnaire item that asks the respondent to order a response in terms of preference or importance.

Rapid iterative prototyping. Use of powerful development tools to create many iterations in a short period of time through the use of simulation and code generation.

Rating scales. Questionnaire multiple-choice item that offers a range of responses along a single dimension. Used to assess responses to a given item or situation.

Readability. The output of processed information that is delivered to users in a format that is usable and meaningful in the context of the application.

Reasonableness test. Test applied to determine whether data in a given field fall within a range defined as reasonable, compared with a specified standard. Used for processing control.

Redundancy. Unnecessary repetition or duplication, such as the maintenance of two separate files containing the same data.

Reengineering. Technique that combines reverse and forward engineering.

Reference file. File containing constant data to be used each time an application program is run. Used, in conjunction with data from transaction files, to update master files.

Reference manual. Procedural documentation on use of a system.

Referent. Identifiers or calls that are placed within modules to define paths for sending and returning unconditional transfers of control.

Relational model. A model that expresses data structures and relationships in the form of a table.

Relational value. The comparison, or ordering, of one record relative to another. Used in database management to identify a record to be accessed through sequential, direct, or indexed-sequential reference methods.

Relationship. The association between entities in an E-R diagram (e.g., customers *purchase* parts).

Relative position. Record position on disk media identified relative to the basing point, or first record, in a given file.

Reliability. Description of level of confidence that can be placed on probability of performance as expected for a function or device.

Repetition. *See* iteration.

Report. Data output from a file in a format that is easily readable and understandable.

Report and screen designer. An element of a CASE system that permits rapid presentation of report and screen designs.

Reprographic system. System that forms graphic images for typesetting, printing page makeup, or displays.

Required rate of return. The percentage rate an investment must earn to be financially attractive.

Requirements specification. *See* User specification.

Respondent. Person selected as potential information source, who receives and answers a questionnaire.

Response time. In direct access applications, the amount of time required for response to an inquiry or other input to occur.

Restricted function. Access control technique that permits only selected individuals to perform certain functions.

Return on total assets (ROTA). A measure of profitability derived by dividing net income by total invested assets.

Reverse engineering. Technique of beginning analysis by creating a physical model and deriving the logical model from it.

Reviewer (walkthrough). Member of a team appointed to review quality.

Review phase. Portion (phase) during systems development life cycle that include two activities: the first to evaluate the successes and failures during a systems development project, and the second to measure the results of a new CIS system in terms of benefits and savings projected at the start of the project.

Ring structure. A circular, decentralized distributed-processing system in which messages are passed continuously around the circuit.

Robustness. The ability of software to respond to and deal with unexpected situations encountered by nontechnical users.

Router. Point in an information system where a cumulative flow of data is broken down into a series of individual data streams. Indicated on data flow diagram by reverse-facing half-circle. *See also* Collector.

Run time. The amount of time required to complete a processing function.

Sample. A subset of a population of respondents chosen to represent accurately the population as a whole in an information-gathering process.

Sampling. Method used to gather information about a large population of people, events, or transactions by studying a subset of the total population that accurately represents the population as a whole. Statistical methods are used to infer characteristics of the entire population.

Schedule feasibility. Evaluation that results from consideration of time available to complete a proposed course of action, to determine whether or not it can be implemented in the time available.

Scheduling. Relating project activities that must be completed in a time sequence. *See also* Planning.

Schema. The logical view of an entire database composed of the set of entities, attributes, and relationships that describe the logical organization of data needed to support all users of the database.

Scope of control. The range of effect of a decision on its respective module as well as all modules subordinate to that module.

Scope of effect. The range of effect of a decision on the total group of modules encompassing conditional processing based on that decision.

Second normal form. Second step in normalization, when it is verified that each nonkey data element in a relation is functionally dependent on a primary key.

Secondary storage device. Equipment used to write data to, and read data from, magnetic media.

Secretary (walkthrough). Members of quality review team who produces a technical report listing identified errors or problems noted.

Security controls. Controls applied to protect data resources from physical damage, and from intentional misuse or fraudulent use.

Selection. Group of data structures or data elements out of which one, and only one, item may be selected for use.

Separation of duties. Policy that no one individual should have access to, or know enough about, a system to process data in an unauthorized way, either during development stages or during ongoing use of the system. Major technique of organizational control.

Sequence. Linking together of data elements or data structures; indicated by " + " sign between units.

Sequential access. Access technique to read from and write to records and files in an order determined by a logical identifier, or key, that is generally a data field within the record.

Sequential cohesion. A process in which multiple functions, comprising successive data transformations, are performed on the same data element.

Sequential file. File in which the physical and logical sequences of records match. Records are accessed in an order determined by a key, usually numeric.

Serial access. Access technique to read from and write to records and files in the same chronological order in which the records were initially recorded.

Serial file. File in which records are recorded in chronological order, as transactions are entered into a computer.

Serial printer. Impact printing device that prints one character at a time to produce documents.

Service function. Function or activity that is initiated in response to, guided by, and aimed at satisfying, user need for information.

Signal scrambling. *See* Encryption.

Sign off. To agree formally and commit to a proposed course of action, for the purpose of proceeding with a project.

Sign on. *See* Log in.

Sign test. Test to identify and verify presence of positive or negative values in fields. Used for processing control.

Significance. The relative impact of a data item on its respective application. *See also* Materiality.

Simplicity. A requirement that all components of data stores within logical data structures be fixed-length records accessible only by primary keys.

Simulation. An imitative representation of the functioning of a system or process. *See also* Model.

Skeleton programming. Prerecorded modules, usually from existing applications, that serve as frameworks for additional applications. These range from simple formats to sophisticated, high-level modules.

Slack. Without tight constraints. Used to describe time spent on subsidiary projects not affecting duration of an entire project.

Software design. A model of a program outlining its structural and functional characteristics.

Software engineering. The application of formal procedures and disciplines to the construction of computer programs.

Software package. *See* Application software package.

Software testing. Executing a program under conditions designed to cause and discover errors.

Son file. *See* Generation.

Source document control. Authorization measure that must be applied before data are accepted for input to a system; *See also* Input controls.

Space (blank) test. Test to check whether a given field contains some data value or is totally blank. Used for processing control.

Span of control. *See* Fan-out.

Speech synthesizer. A sound-generating device that can produce sounds understandable by humans as language.

Staffing plan. Detailed account of personnel assignments, and days or hours to be worked, for a systems development project.

Stamp coupling. The passing of superfluous data elements to a module; increasing the complexity of the intermodular interface and reducing the independence of both modules.

Star network. A centralized, distributed data processing system in which the central processor acts as the control point in logging and monitoring information transmission.

Start time. Time at which a project begins, indicated on a project graph by the symbol *S*. *See also* Critical path method (CPM).

Starving the process. Showing, in a logical model, only the logically necessary elements or steps needed. Distinguished from a physical model's representation of an actual processing sequence.

Statement. In programming, a single command that directs a computer to carry out a processing operation.

Statement-coverage testing. Testing technique that uses a set of test data to execute every statement in a module.

Status review. Meeting held to keep user management informed on progress of a project. Participants include project leader, key user manager, and possibly project team members who can make special contributions.

Steering committee. A committee that sets organizational priorities and policies concerning CIS support. Composed of top management personnel representing all user areas.

Stepwise refinement. Top-down abstractions of problems to create workable submodules that can be coded, related, and implemented. *See also* Hierarchical partitioning.

Strategic information system (SIS). Type of computer information system that assists management in strategic planning by projecting the likely consequences of decisions.

Structure chart. Graphic representation of overall organization, and control logic of processing functions (modules) in a program or system.

Structure clash. A noncongruence of input and output data structures that must be resolved before a program structure can be designed.

Structured analysis process. The objective of data flow analysis, leading from a model of an existing system to a model of a new system.

Structured English. Formal English statements using a small, strong, selected vocabulary to communicate processing rules and to represent the structure of a program or system.

Structured specification. *See* User specification.

Stub. A routine applied in top-down program testing that simulates the processing that will take place in modules still to be coded.

Stylus. Electromechanically driven writing device used on a plotter to produce lines.

Subordinate module. A lower-level module activated by its immediate superordinate.

Subschema. User view of a subset of a database. *See also* Schema.

Subsystem. A secondary or subordinate small system within a large system.

Subsystem test specification. *See* Systems test.

Summary report. Report showing accumulated totals for specific groups of detail records. Used by middle-level managers for review of business activity.

Superordinate module. A higher-level module activates its immediate subordinate.

Synergistic. The way that a system's parts function together, producing results with a greater value than would be produced by the system's separate parts working alone.

Synthesis. The process of bringing information system component parts together into a remodeled system in which previously existing problems have been eliminated.

System. A set of interrelated, interacting components that function together as an entity to achieve specific results.

System conversion. *See* System installation.

System flowchart. Graphic representation of a system showing flow of control in computer processing at the job level. Represents transition from a physical model of computer processing to a set of program specifications that will be prepared at the start of the detailed design and implementation phase.

System installation. The process of starting the actual use of a system and training user personnel in its operation.

System integration. The complete concurrence of all elements within a system.

System life cycle. Activities or conditions common to all computer information systems from inception to replacement: recognition of need, systems development, installation, system operation, maintenance and/or enhancement, and obsolescence.

Systemic control. Measures taken to deal with hardware configurations and software updating to establish full compatibility.

Systems analysis. The application of a systems approach to the study and solution of problems, usually involving application of computers.

Systems analyst. A problem-solving specialist who analyzes functions and problems, using a systems approach, to produce a more efficient and functional system, usually involving application of computers.

Systems approach. Way of identifying and viewing component parts and functions as integral elements of a whole system.

Systems design. The technical plans and methods for implementing a computer information system.

Systems development. Process that includes identifying information needs, designing information systems that meet those needs, and putting those systems into practical operation.

Systems development life cycle (SDLC). Organized, structured methodology for developing, implementing, and installing a new or revised CIS. Standard phases presented in this book include investigation, analysis and general design, detailed design and implementation, installation, and review.

Systems development recap report. In-depth review document prepared for CIS management covering completed systems development project. Aimed at enhancing or improving individual members' and the organization's performance on future projects.

Systems test. Extensive test of full system. Conducted chiefly by users after all programs and major subsystems have been tested. Assures that data resources handled by the system will be processed correctly and protected fully. Careful documentation is maintained through program test logs and system test logs.

Systems testing. Test procedures conducted by CIS personnel to view the entire system as an operational, functional entity. Provides an overview of the implemented system and all procedures relevant to user training.

Table. An index that records the physical location of each key within an indexed-sequential file, making possible random access to individual records.

Table look up. A testing technique in which tables are searched to find entries that match input data.

Tangible. Cost or benefit readily quantifiable in monetary terms. *See also* Intangible.

Tangible benefit. Benefit realized when a new system makes or saves money for its organization.

Tangible cost. Cost of equipment or human factors associated with the operation of a system.

Tape drive. Peripheral storage unit that performs input and output of data on magnetic tape. Also called a tape unit.

Task. Smallest unit of work that can be assigned and controlled through normal project management techniques; normally performed by an individual person, usually in a matter of days. *See also* Activity.

Technical architecture. All hardware platforms, operating systems, and communications networks of an enterprise.

Technical design. Activity within detailed design and implementation phase that builds upon specifications produced during new system design, adding detailed technical specifications and documentation.

Technical feasibility. Evaluation that results from technical consideration of available computer hardware and software capability to carry out a proposed course of action.

Technical review. *See* Walkthrough.

Teleprocessing. The utilization of telephone lines for data communication between devices in a computer system.

Temporal cohesion. Also called classical cohesion, this term describes related functions that are specified to occur in the same time frame.

Test data file. High-quality information to be input for module testing. Care must be taken that each file is specific to the function of its respective module.

Test plan. Documents listing the schedules, objectives, criteria, and procedures for system testing. An overview document encompassing all plans for integrating the tasks of program and system testing.

Test specifications and planning. Activity during detailed design and implementation phase to prepare detailed test specifications for individual modules and programs, job streams, subsystems, and for the system as a whole.

Third normal form. Third stage of normalization process, during which duplicate data elements or elements that can be derived from other elements are removed. *See also* Mutually independent.

Timeliness. Quality factor. Meeting needs of users or process for delivering results when needed to meet service requirements.

Time reporting. Accounting procedure for reporting work completed and still to be done. Controls are applied at the task level.

Time scale. Horizontal axis on a Gantt chart reading from left to right, indicating passage of time.

Time value. Changing value of money as time goes by, assuming inflationary devaluation or investment growth. Money invested at a percentage return will have a value equal to principal plus interest; money left uninvested loses purchasing power as inflation occurs.

Top-down. Partitioning of functions into successive levels of detail from the top-level module, representing the general system or program function as a whole, down through to lower-level modules that perform actual processing.

Top-down testing. Procedures applied to test a program from its highest, most general module down through more specific modules.

Topology. Physical pattern of interconnection between nodes.

Total slack. Time difference between the early start and late start dates, or early finish and late finish dates, for a noncritical activity. *See also* Critical path method (CPM).

Touch-screen input. Method of inputting data directly through touch contact with specially sensitized locations on the face of CRT terminal video display screens.

Track. *See* Channels.

Tradeoff. Term referring to decision-making consideration that weighs advantages and disadvantages of alternatives as a basis for selection.

Trailer record. Last record in a file, containing totals for all numeric fields in all records in the file. Compared with field totals each time the file is processed. *See also* Processing controls.

Training manual. Easy-to-use reference manual that teaches operators how to learn to perform procedures within a computer-based information system. *See also* Procedures manual.

Tramp data. Data in a record that are not required for processing and are therefore unnecessary.

Transaction. A basic act of doing business. The exchange of value for goods or services received.

Transaction analysis. A data-flow-oriented design process that organizes system design around the transactions in the higher-level modules and recaptures processing similarities using lower-level modules with high fan-in.

Transaction document. Form upon which data generated by transactions are recorded. Used to capture data at its source to report on results of transactions, control business activity, and for historic purposes.

Transaction file. Collection of records containing specific, timely data pertaining to current business activity. Used to update master files.

Transaction log file. Continuously updated master accounting record that records all transactions of an on-line processing system chronologically. Serves as starting point for an audit trail and can be used for recovery purposes if master or transaction file data are damaged or lost.

Transaction processing systems (TPS). Information processing systems that establish operational controls over the day-to-day activities of business organizations.

Transform. To process data for conversion (transformation) into information.

Transform analysis. Modeling a problem structure by decomposing the problem into data flow and transformation requirements.

Turnaround document. Computer output document that also serves as input document for a follow-up processing activity.

Turnaround time. The amount of time required for a system to accept input, process data, and output meaningful information.

Unconditional. A transfer of control in which the receiving module then determines the next assignment of control rather than routinely returning control to the originating module.

Unique transaction code. An access control technique that provides for access security.

Unit record. A single keypunched card containing an entire data record that may be broken into several fields.

Unit testing. The inspection of individual program modules to determine the soundness of their logic and functions.

Universal product code (UPC). Bar code used extensively in supermarkets and other retail outlets for optical sensing of product identification.

Upper CASE. The CASE tools most useful in the front end of system development, usually having to do with documentation assistance and analysis enhancement.

User. Term referring both to lower-level personnel who use, and upper-level personnel who own, a CIS. *See also* Owner (system).

User concurrence. Agreement by user that capabilities described in the user specification contain a full and complete statement of user needs and that the solution is feasible from operational and human factors standpoints.

User-friendly. A phrase used to indicate a high degree of user convenience.

User procedures manual. *See* Procedures manual, Training manual.

User specification. User-oriented report presenting a complete model of a new CIS for user evaluation and approval. Can include data flow diagrams, description of system inputs and outputs, performance requirements, security and control requirements, design and implementation constraints, and unresolved policy considerations that must be dealt with before the system can be implemented.

User training. Activity during detailed design and implementation phase of the systems development life cycle. Encompasses: writing user procedure manuals, preparation of user training materials, conducting training programs, and testing manual procedures.

User training outline. Specification document prepared during implementation and installation planning that includes: content outlines for user training manuals, details for preparation of manuals to cover user procedures to be installed, and list of proposed activities and assignments for users and analysts who will write these manuals.

Utility. Programs that provide standard functions such as sorting, collating, and report writing.

Validity. Description of transaction or data to indicate they are authorized, that transactions actually took place, and that data really exist.

Variable costs. Costs incurred only when a system is used. *See also* Fixed costs, Operational costs.

Variable-length record. Record in a file that can be of any length, its size established by a field that tells the system its length.

Version. *See* Incremental step.

Version development. Technique of developing large, complex systems by breaking them into a series of parts and developing each separately.

Version installation. Technique of installing a new system as a series of functional areas or incremental steps.

Video display. Visual data display device using a CRT (cathode ray tube).

Voice input. A method of inputting data directly through voice commands.

Volatility. Rate of change and expansion of a file. Factor to be considered in determining file organization.

Walkthrough. Technical quality review of a CIS product that can be identified as a separate unit capable of introducing errors into the system.

White box. The exposure of the logical functions of a module to clarify its functions and operations for systems analysts and designers.

White box testing. Complete tracing of the decision path(s) of data through a module.

Wide area network (WAN). A series of computers and processors that are interconnected despite great geographical distances.

Wide area telephone service (WATS). A contracted communications service that reduces the costs of heavy telephone utility use.

Word processor. Software or hardware that permits the entry, editing, storage, and output of text.

Working model. *See* Prototype.

Working papers. Documents accumulated during work completion that are useful for project review or for guiding the performance of ongoing work.

Work station. The physical area in which people and computers interact.

Index

Business need, 28
Business objective: system 81; system design, 36
Business system, defined, 5

CAD. *See* Computer aided design 220
CAM. *See* Computer aided manufacturing, 220
Captioning, alternatives, 442; need for clear, 441
Case scenario, 615; water billing system, 612
Case study: apply new readings, 741; billing system service menu, 743; Central City Water Department, 603-606; existing system review, 644; incycle bill, job steps, 738; job stream systems flowchart, 739; prepare bill, timing, 737; systems flowchart, edit and update, 742
CASE. *See* Computer Assisted Software Engineering
Category tests, 553
Central transform branch, 488; modules, control, 586
Centralization, advantage, 364
Centralized systems, explained and compared 364-365
Change transaction, 502
Check digits, 553
Child diagram(s), 93; construction, 103
Chronological approach, 377
CIS. *See* Computer information systems
COBOL: code, 797; language, 431; section, 472
Code generator(s), 797; integration, CASE, 236
Cognitive diversity, 452
Cohesion, 202; defined, 526; communicational, 530; component interrelatedness, 514; highest level, 527; procedural, 530
Coincidental cohesion: display, 537; module elements, 536
Combined interaction, 130
Command language, 461
Common coupling, 524
Communication: CIS projects, 294; defined, 79; identifying audiences, 296; line speeds, 354; myths and realities, 295; need, 34; receiving skill, 296; sending skill, 295
Communication style, 310-313; participant involvement, 311; self-assessment 312-313
Communicational cohesion, 530, 531
Comparison error tests, 582
Complete system testing, 728
Complexity characteristics, interface, 519
Computer aided design (CAD)/CAM CASE, analogous, 219; industrial technology, 220
Computer Assisted Software Engineering(CASE), 122; analysis, enhancements, 234; application generators, 237; automated assistance, 219; components, 221, 232; current usage, 243;

data dictionary, 222; development, information engineering, 246; documentation assistance, 233; expanding area, computer technology, 220; future conditions, 245; graphic generator access, 229; incorporating integrated components, 238; product, word processor, 229; project coordinators, 235; reluctance to use, 244; report and screen designers, 230; screen layout, 231; system, 239-242; system development, 221; symbols, 223-225; tools, 408; tools, access encyclopedia, 247; upper and lower, major components, 237-239; word-processing template, 230, 231
Computer digital code to analog link, 353
Computer information systems (CIS), 1, 4, 27; designer commitment, 686; development analysis, 20-21; functions, 126-129; group, 757; group and personnel, 755; operations group, 766; professionals, 757; resource persons, 759; role, large organizations, 125; signoff, 692, 701; staff, 758; synergism, 5; system definition, 5
Computer network architecture, large organization, 360
Computer operations: documentation, 730; interface, 690; manuals, 772
Computer support, modeling tasks, 122
Computer viruses, 358
Computerized file conversion, 716
Computing processor workload, 344
Concatenating, 159
Conceptual enterprise modeling, 137
Conditions, all possible combinations, 576
Confidentiality, need for, 549
Connection types, 515-518
Content outlines, 715
Context diagram, 81-82, 91; water billing system, 645, 671
Control(s), 15; machine or people functions, 548; need, 549; new system design, 692; operational/systemic, 362-363; project management, 60; types, 549
Control coupling, 524
Control design, deficiency identification, 556
Control document, processed batches, 559
Control levels, system design, 39
Control structure: and code segments, 571; modules, 474
Control totals, 550
Conversation generators, 797
Conversion: programs, need, 730; strategy, activity relation, 769
Coordination *vs.* active control, 521
Corporate data, access, 127; changing nature, 125
Correct action techniques, 459

Correlative files, key values, 372
Cost benefit analysis, 323–327; characteristics, 324–327; information, need for, 324; preliminary, 327
Cost elements: development, 325; operating, 326
Cost of money factor, 331
Costs: application design, 432; direct and indirect, 321; fixed or variable, 321; tangible, 322
Coupling, 202; binding time, 522; and cohesion, 538, 540; connection, between modules, 515; control, module interface, 526; defined, 526; heavy, 203; levels, 523; module interface characterized, 525; module measure, 514; reduced, 204; second dimension, 519
CPM. *See* Critical path method
Criteria, preliminary system, 715
Critical and alternative path identification, 67
Critical path, 65; algorithm use, 67
Critical path method (CPM), 62; design tool, 63
Criticism, systems analyst, 665
Cumulative documentation, 623
Cumulative project file, 643; contents, 621, 669–670, 702; final report, 717
Custom programming, CIS, 429

Data: architecture, 176; capture, 342–343; centralization, 359; communication link, 349, 350; confidentiality, 553; conversion, 767; departmental specific, 126; diagram(s), 373, 374, 690; different forms, 462; display guidelines, 454–455; distribution, 359; evaluated, 796; independence, DBMS, 394; integrity, DBMS, 354; modeling, 135, 137, 176; narrative, 38; normalization, 156; objects or entities, 138; optimization, CASE product feature, 233; redundancy, 126; relationships, 135; security, 395, 553; specification, design tool generated, 232; transmission rate measurements, 354; validation processing, 806; value, 125
Data coupling, 523; module interface, 524, 528
Data definition language (DDL), 396
Data dictionaries, 38, 80, 109–111, 190, 661, 689, 772; building and maintaining, 107; CASE, 222; entries, 496; data element entry, 109; data flows and stores, use in, 106; data model need, 138; data store entry, 111; data structure entry, 110; 4GL CASE, 237; partial, 158; revised, 171; types of entries, 109
Data driven design, 130; methodology mappings, 505
Data element(s), 109; defined, 106; or fields, 138; form, values defined, 653
Data entry: controls, 549, 550; general guidelines,

456; screen design, 457, 458; specific principles, 457
Data file, 361, 690
Data flow: approach, 485; content notations, 678; documentation, 417
Data flow diagram (DFD), 1, 131, 139, 147, 379; CASE tool, 226; constructing, 85–89, 106; fragments, 104; logical characteristics, 185; model abstract, 487; as modeling technique, 80; name importance, 85; on-line boundaries, 418; oriented design process, 499; physical boundaries, 418; physical characteristics, 184; preliminary, 147; productivity measure, CASE, 239; readability, 81; sales processing, 422–423; simplification, 91; symbols, 84; transformation of data, 37; water billing system, 605
Data management: defined, 391
Data storage, 343
Data store(s), 154; criteria, 155; data flow diagram, 84, 96; on DFD, 138; form, content specification, 655–656; notations, water billing system, 677
Data structures, 109; defined, 107; form, 654; notation conventions, 108; processing, change adaptable, 375; redundancy elimination, 169; tests 582
Data structured design, 131; defined, 505; software, 505
Database: administrator (DBA), 128; design, 702, 726, 731; models, 396; new system design, 692; performance requirements, 693; system feature, CASE, 233–234;
Database management systems (DBMS), 128, 228, 370, 693; benefits, 394; defined, 392; environment, 394; and 4GLs, 431; information centers, 431; products described, 399; representation, 396
DBA. *See* Data base administrator
DBMS. *See* Database management system
Deadlines, meeting, 433
Decision levels, SDLC, 254, 603
Decision support systems (DSS), 11
Decision table, 116; covering loan policy, 116; general format, 117
Decision tree: bank policy, 115; explained, 114
Decision-condition coverage testing method, 572
Decomposition rules, 490
Dedicated lines, 358
Definitions, master file, water billing system, 704
Delete transaction, 502
Design: audit walkthrough, 556; effort, guide steps, 507; evaluation sequence, 342; quality evaluation, 692, 701 Design specification: contents, 181; new system, 181
Design strategies evaluation, 504

Designer(s): building blocks, 430; CASE, 230
Detailed design and implementation, 49
Detailed design and implementation phase, 717, 721; activity description, 726; activity relationship, 723; cumulative project file, 735, 749, 752, 756; end-products, 725, 728, 746; objectives, 722, 726, 746; personnel, 734, 749, 752; process, 722, 747; program/test activity description, 749; programming and testing process, 751–752; scope, 746, 727; SDLC, 600; software package and installation, 723; system test, 756, 758; technical design, 725; test specifications and planning, 744; user training description, 753
Detailed design: of programs, 723; specification contents, 728–730; specification document, 735
Development life cycle: potential case, 243; traditional system, 242
Development recap, 51; importance, 775
DFD. *See* Data flow diagram
Diagram: breadth, 94; depth, degree of partitioning, 94
Diagram 0 (Zero), 91, 786; analysis process use, 207; apply payment process, 710; in context diagram, 82; correspondence, 205; corresponding, 674; fourth step, 645; initial development, 100–103; portion, 550; new readings, 674; new water system, 672, 673; system, 83; TAB checking account system, 105; water billing system, 648
Dial-up, 350; connections, 358
Digital signal, 357
Diplomacy, systems analyst, 666
Direct access, 377; devices, sequential or random, 377
Direct file organization: convenience, 384; interactive file, 389; key field value, 383; master file, 385; reorganization and rebuilding, 384; speed, 389
Direct manipulation, 461
Display, 412
Distributed data processing, problem, 365
Distributed sites, 365
Distributed systems, 359; explained and compared, 364–5
Distribution of decision making, 540, 541
Document, 412; permanent support file, 772
Documentation: assistance, CASE, 237; CASE needs, 221; CASE tools, 221; controls, 549; existing, 266; existing system review 638–639, 1
Downloaded, 361
DS. *See* Data stores
DSS. *See* Decision support systems

Early finish (EF) formula, 67
Early start (ES), 67, 70
Edit programs, 503
Edit run, 551, 552
Efferent branches, 488; factoring; 492; 80–20 rule, 617, 790
Electronic interference, 358
Electronic mail (E-Mail), 350
Eliminate-simplify-automate, 790, 793
Encryption, 358, 553
Encyclopedia, 247
End products: case study, 608; listed, 715; new system, 689; SDLC, 252, 603, 614; user specification, 661
End-user: computing (EUC), 129; oriented lan-language, 431
Enterprise modeling, 131; architecture, 176
Enterprise-wide architectures, 176; IS, 785–787
Entification, 146
Entify relationships, 145–151
Entity: combination formula, 148; definition pairing, 148; IS specialized, 607
Entity relationships (E-R), 149, 690; and data access diagrams, 661; diagrams, 131, 137, 139, 152, 370, 373; diagram, normalized data stores, 372; diagram pairing, 149; diagram purpose 139; diagram steps to build, 146; graphic symbols, 140; model, billing system, 180; modeling process, iterative nature, 138; models, 80, 137, 140, 178, 179, 786, 797
Equivalence partitioning testing, 580
E-R. *See* Entity-relationship
Ergonomics defined, 452
Error: control, improvement need, 458; correction, 591; guessing, 569, 581; messages, 458, 460 ES. *See* Early start
ES. *See* Expert systems
EUC. *See* End-user computing
Evaluative criteria, 540
Evolutionary approach, 36
Exception reports, 552
Existing system review, 45, 635
Expense form sample, 443
Expert systems (ES), 10, 12, 425, 426; nonexpert performance, 12
Exploded to lower-level, 222
External entity: data flow diagram symbol, 84; inclusion, 96
External sources, 267

Face validity, 281
Facilitated session defined, 791
Facility costs, 323
Fan-in, higher level modules, 543

Time: formula, average or expected for task, 71; reporting, 620
Timeliness, 433
Timing cycles, 415
Top-down: estimating base, 335; incremental test pattern, 587; partitioning, 91, 542; testing, 586
Topologies, 351
Total slack time, 69, 70
TPS. *See* Transaction processing systems
Tradeoff(s): application design, 432; decision, 376, 617; DBMS, 395; error correction, 591
Traditional programming languages, 805
Trailer record, numeric fields, 552
Training: manuals, 306–307, 753; outline, contents, 715
Tramp data, 519; elements, 524
Transaction: analysis, 499; center, 502; in data flow diagram, 503; files, dynamic, 370; log, 551; log, files, accounting journal, 371; processing systems (TPS), 10
Transaction-centered design structure, 501
Transfer, 516
Transform analysis, 485, 497; first-cut structure chart, 493
Transformation: of system, 804; and transaction analysis, advanced, 504
Transmission rate relation, 355
Tree-structured, 396
True power, 72
Turnaround document, 447, 679
Tutorials and help functions, 465

Umbrella grouping, 421
Understanding, communication component, 79
Unique transaction codes, 550
Unit (module) testing, 565, 570, 745
Upper CASE, 237–239; tools, 122, 202
User(s): commitment, 686; manuals, 465, 772; organization and procedures, 690; perceptions, 776–777; understanding, 771; view, 392

User management: new system design, 692; sign-off, 701
User requirements, 200; identification analysis process, 191
User specification, 48, 634; contents, 661; development, 717; physical requirements, 662; value, 665
User training, 723, 728; end-products, 754; objectives, 753; personnel, 755; process, 754; scope, 754
Utility programs, 430

Validity, 281
Value analysis, net present, 331
Value tests, 552–553
Variable-length record, 379
Verification processes, CASE tools, 233
Version: development, 788, 793–794; installation, 50, 770
Visual support, 308
Volatility, master files, 390

Walkthroughs, 556, 642; administration 299; defined, 298; end-products, 300; pitfalls, 301; purpose, 299; recorder, 299; structure, 300
WAN. *See* Wide area networks
Warnier-Orr diagram, program design, 506
WATS. *See* Wide-area telephone service
Waveforms, data communications, 357
White-box testing, 569, 570; methods, 571
Wide area networks (WAN), 350
Wide area telephone service (WATS), 350
Word processor, CASE products, 229
Work areas, 262; flow diagram 265
Work flow and tasks, 269
Workability, 715
Working: model, 792; papers, 616
Written report guidelines, 304

Xerox: Corporation, 462; D machines, 464